Applied **Urban Design**

Applied Urban Design combines 'why' we design and 'who' we design for, with 'ho
the reader with a comprehensive and accessible bespoke framework for both understanding and practicing urban design in a contextually responsive manner from appraisal to design delivery. The framework is presented across four distinct steps, covering analysis at strategic and local scales; the urban design program; design development; and technical design. The authors unpack the functional blueprints, liveable qualities, contextual dynamics, and technical components of quality urban design, identifying the role of urban designers in shaping spaces and places across differing local contexts through a responsive and multiscalar approach. International best practice examples and two original 'live' case studies in Aalborg, Denmark and Manchester, UK demonstrate the application of the framework across differing scales and contexts – each supported by the authors own images and graphics that illustrate the broad range of urban design visualisation techniques and methods.

Visually compelling and insightful, **Applied Urban Design** is for all who seek to understand, demand, and create people-centred, high-quality, contextually responsive places and spaces.

Dr Philip Black is Director of the Manchester Urban Design LAB (MUD-Lab) and Senior Lecturer in Urban Design and Head of Urban Design Programmes at the University of Manchester, UK. He is co-author of *The Urban Design Process* with Dr Taki Sonbli. Philip has an extensive track record of research and publications on applied urban design with a particular focus on design quality, design control/governance, and urban design process and professional practice.

Dr Michael Martin is a Lecturer in Urban Design and Planning and Director of the MA Urban Design and Planning at the University of Sheffield. Previously he was an Assistant Professor in Urban Design at Aalborg University, Denmark. Michael's research and publications in urban design cover a range of themes specialising in child-friendly cities, sustainable mobility, urban regeneration, temporary urbanism, and placemaking processes.

Mr Robert Phillips is a Director at Urban Imprint Ltd, a planning and design consultancy in Macclesfield, UK, and an Honorary Lecturer in Urban Design at University of Manchester. Bob is a chartered town planner and urban designer who has been involved in delivering planning and design projects for a broad range of clients and companies.

Dr Taki Sonbli is Manager of the Manchester Urban Design LAB, and the Technical Lead Specialist for all urban design programmes at University of Manchester. Taki is co-author of *The Urban Design Process* with Dr Philip Black and has also published in the areas of culturally sensitive urban design, and the graphical language of urban space.

Applied Urban Design
A Contextually Responsive Approach

Philip Black,
Michael Martin,
Robert Phillips,
and Taki Sonbli

Routledge
Taylor & Francis Group

LONDON AND NEW YORK

Cover design by Philip Black
Cover and Rear Images: Eixample, Barcelona, Spain
Frontispiece: Promenade Operaen, Oslo, Norway
Contents Image: Kings Cross, London, England
Final Image: Cheonggyecheon, Seoul, South Korea

First published 2025
by Routledge
605 Third Avenue, New York, NY 10158

and by Routledge
4 Park Square, Milton Park, Abingdon, Oxon, OX14 4RN

Routledge is an imprint of the Taylor & Francis Group, an informa business

© 2025 Philip Black, Michael Martin, Robert Phillips, Taki Sonbli

The right of Philip Black, Michael Martin, Robert Philips, and Taki Sonbli to be identified as authors of this work has been asserted in accordance with sections 77 and 78 of the Copyright, Designs and Patents Act 1988.

All rights reserved. No part of this book may be reprinted or reproduced or utilised in any form or by any electronic, mechanical, or other means, now known or hereafter invented, including photocopying and recording, or in any information storage or retrieval system, without permission in writing from the publishers.

Trademark notice: Product or corporate names may be trademarks or registered trademarks, and are used only for identification and explanation without intent to infringe.

Library of Congress Cataloging-in-Publication Data
A catalog record for this title has been requested

ISBN: 9780367903985 (hbk)
ISBN: 9780367897543 (pbk)
ISBN: 9781003024163 (ebk)

DOI: 10.4324/9781003024163

Typeset in Avenir Next and Futura
Designed by Philip Black

Publishers Note:
This book has been prepared from camera-ready copy provided by Philip Black.

Printed and bound in Great Britain by
TJ Books Limited, Padstow, Cornwall

Acknowledgements

This book has been almost 10 years in the making. It would not have been possible without a great number of people and institutions who have helped us shape the AUD Framework that forms the basis of **Applied Urban Design**. Whilst the journey began at the University of Manchester - it has since expanded to take in Aalborg University, University of Sheffield, Urban Imprint Ltd, and a number of professional practices and professional bodies. We owe each of these gratitude for their support and the academic freedom to test new ideas and develop our approach to educating and training urban designers. Special thanks must go to Manchester Urban Design LAB (and staff past and present) – set up to support our research and pedagogy development in urban design - and often the 'testing bed' for much of what has become this book. Ultimately that 'testing' and 'refining' is the result of the hundreds of students that we have taught many iterations of the AUD Framework - in Manchester, Aalborg, and Sheffield. As authors we are eternally grateful to all the students we have had the privilege of teaching – their enthusiasm for urban design, commitment to our applied studio-based approach to education, and fair critiques have been invaluable to us. Our ambition has always been 2-fold - to train the next generation of passionate urban designers who are equipped to make a genuine positive contribution to the world - and to contribute ourselves to the ability of others to deliver more people-centred, contextually responsive, quality urban design. We are convinced that the many hundreds we have graduated in the institutions named above are now making those differences in practice - and we hope this book and the AUD Framework it demonstrates can prove of some benefit to the wider field, in academia and professional practice.

Co-authoring with 4 people across different institutions can be a challenge – yet this book has never been anything less than a joy to develop and deliver. We have held author symposiums over a number of years and cities to work together to ensure **Applied Urban Design** is the best it possibly can be. It never felt like 'work' - just 4 friends enjoying their shared passion for urban design. We would also like to especially thank Routledge for supporting this project – in particular Kate and Selena who have been immensely supportive of our ambition for this book.

Philip would like to thank Emma, Mya, and Cora - there have never been three more understanding, patient, beautiful, and amazing ladies. God blessed me.

Michael would like to thank Eira, Eloïse, and Luca for their wholehearted and continuous support throughout. This project was a family endeavour - starting in Aalborg and finishing in Sheffield, two kiddos later. I'd also like to thank Matthew who continues to inspire resilience.

Robert [Bob] would like to thank the team at UI (past and present) and friend and business partner Jo, for all her support and inspiration. He also thanks his parents and family for their encouragement whilst writing this book.

Taki would like to thank Jouliana, Hassan, and Ryan for all their love and support through this project - thanks for being the most cherished part of my life.

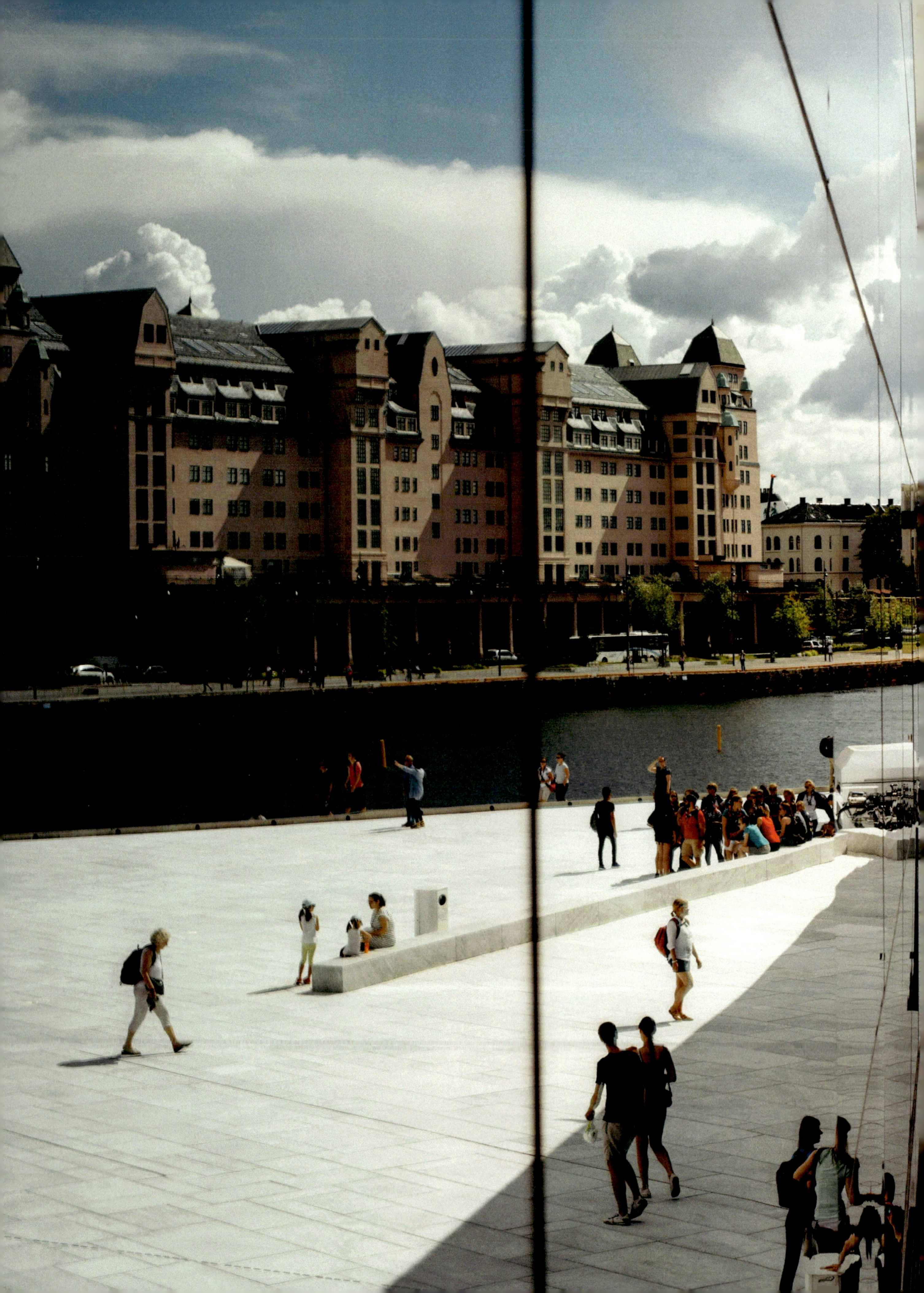

APPLIED URBAN DESIGN

A CONTEXTUALLY RESPONSIVE APPROACH

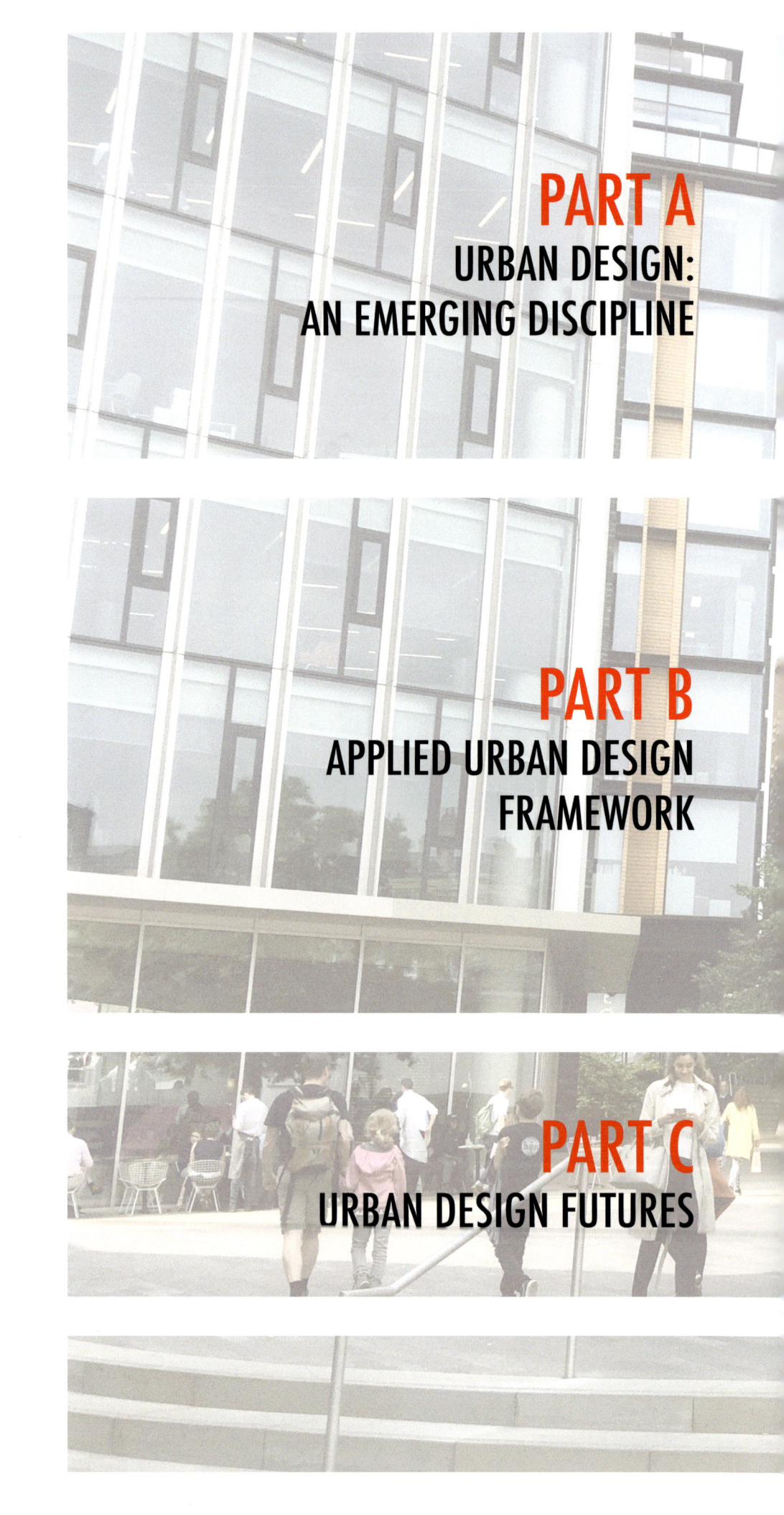

PART A
URBAN DESIGN: AN EMERGING DISCIPLINE

PART B
APPLIED URBAN DESIGN FRAMEWORK

PART C
URBAN DESIGN FUTURES

4	CHAPTER 1	**URBAN DESIGN? THE DISQUISITION**
14	CHAPTER 2	**TOWARDS CONTEXTUALLY RESPONSIVE URBAN DESIGN**
22	CHAPTER 3	**THE APPLIED URBAN DESIGN FRAMEWORK**
34	CHAPTER 4	**MAKING SENSE OF DESIGN**
86	CHAPTER 5	**STRATEGIC ANALYSIS**
114	CHAPTER 6	**LOCAL ANALYSIS**
174	CHAPTER 7	**URBAN DESIGN PROGRAM**
196	CHAPTER 8	**DESIGN DEVELOPMENT**
214	CHAPTER 9	**TECHNICAL DESIGN**
280	CHAPTER 10	**DESIGN DELIVERY**
298	CHAPTER 11	**REFLECTIONS ON THE APPLIED URBAN DESIGN FRAMEWORK**
314	CHAPTER 12	**RE-FRAMING URBAN DESIGN**
329		**INDEX**

MAAT, Lisbon, Portugal

PART A
URBAN DESIGN - AN EMERGING DISCIPLINE

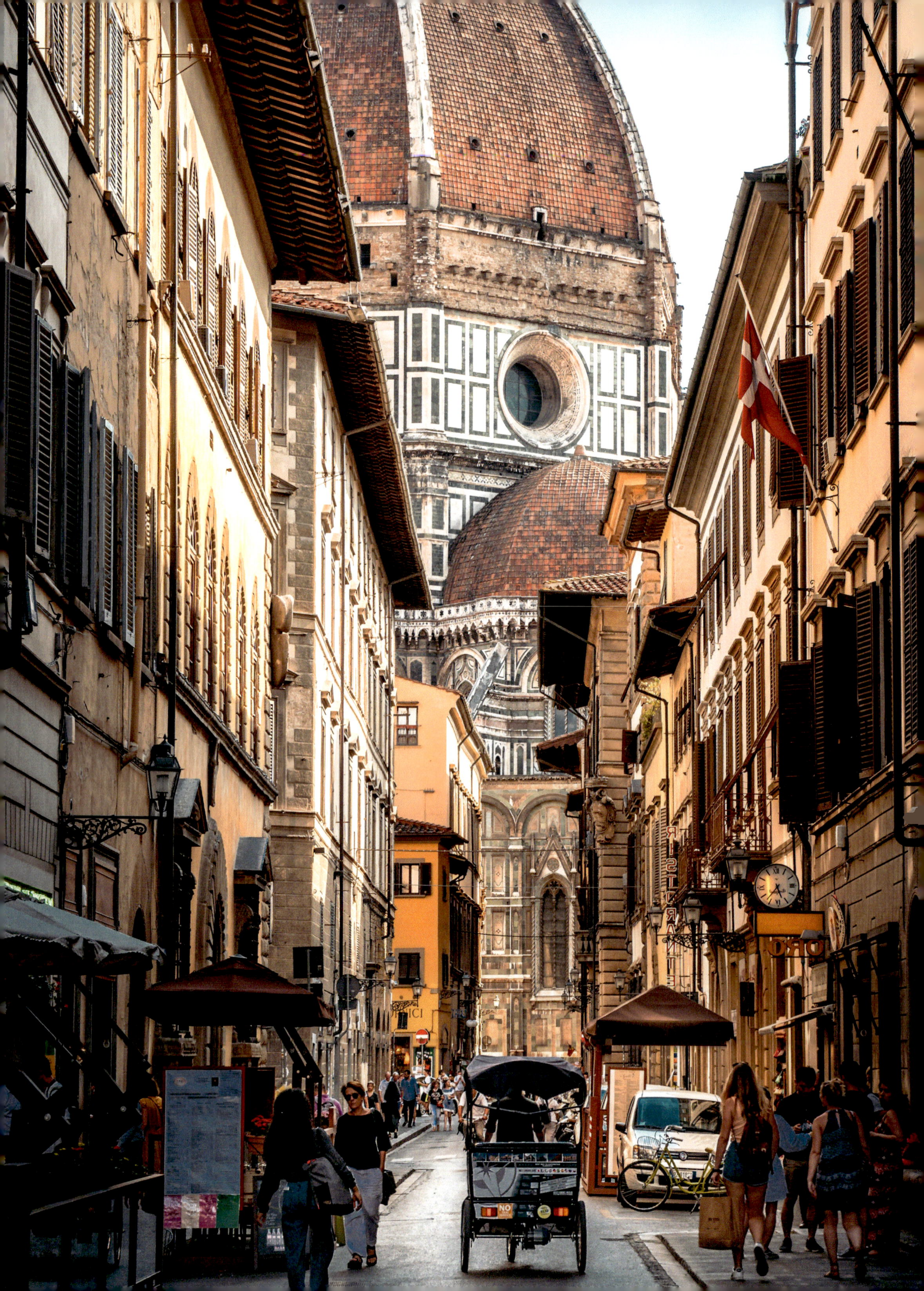

CHAPTER 1: URBAN DESIGN? THE DISQUISITION

CHAPTER 1
Urban Design? The Disquisition

Urban design can be a confusing field - a discipline that can be traced back to the earliest human settlements yet argued as a relatively new addition to the suite of built environment vocations; a field that is equal parts theoretical and yet also practical; an arena with multiple territories it can act within, yet also contested without a clear mandate or domain. The story of **urban design** can be viewed in 3 logical parts.

1. Urban Design Pre-1950's
2. Urban Design Post-1950's
3. The [Emerging] Urban Designer

This chapter will unpack this narrative, from early city development and into the rapid urban growth of the industrial era; to the landmark Harvard Conferences of the 1950's where contemporary urban design was born and subsequently cultivated over recent decades; to what we argue is a new emerging period for the field - the emergence of a more defined vocational role - the urban designer.

1.1 URBAN DESIGN PRE-1950s

Cities are complex, it is not one thing but rather many things in negotiation and they are in a continual state of flux, sometimes slow, oftentimes rapid (Smith, 2023). Cities are also designed – not necessarily in a structured or ordered manner, but they are put together with a form of logic, to deliver connections between people, be that the routes delivered, the structures created, the spaces contrived, or the resultant activity. From the earliest known cities of Mesopotamia and its contemporaries, through the great cities that anchored empires, to the wealthy cities of the Middle Ages and later imperial period, cities have formed part of a wider urban system and delivered their own social hierarchies and distributions of wealth. Without some form of 'urban design' inherent in how they function cities and urban settlements would have failed.

There are crudely 2 types of cities – the planned/created (determined pattern) and the unplanned/grown (organic pattern). Often when considering cities today it is possible to identify both the planned and the organic – or the formal and informal. Organic city forms can have a wide number of drivers that explain layout including topography or the natural landscape setting. A river, harbour, natural hill or slope can define the natural growth of a city, see examples in Gubbio, Italy, Marina Corricella, Procida, or the Nerudova, Prague.

Cities can also display organic traits as settlements grow and merge into one another. Major metropolises such as Athens, Venice and Rome showcase this synoecism (Kostoff, 2001).

ABOVE: Corricella, Procida. Organically developed around the natural harbour and sloping topography.

LEFT: Venice, Italy. 126 islands merged to form the city - A unique model of synoecism.

OPPOSITE: Florence, Italy. Development in the city is restricted to protect views of the Duomo di Firenze

The planned city form is often set out to provide a sense of order, Le Corbusier famously argued that rational order and right angles were the way of humans – moving logically towards a goal in an efficient and pre-destined manner. Perhaps the most common pattern for planned settlements is that of the grid – simultaneously good for defence, surveillance, agriculture, trade, and movement there is evidence that such urban designs were being created as early as 2500 BCE. The city of Mohnejo-Daro in Pakistan, one of the earliest major cities in civilisation, consisted of a clear planned layout with rectilinear buildings forming the grid and a high level of social organisation focused on a central marketplace. The grid was also common across China, with cities such as Chang'an illustrating diagrams based on political symbolism and power, and Greece, where a more pragmatic approach to grid design was utilised for establishing new colonies in places such as Corinth, or Syracuse, Sicily (Kostoff, 2001). Perhaps the most famous grid patterns today can be found in New York and Barcelona. The Manhattan grid, initiated via the Commissioners Plan of 1811, was a response to uncontrolled development and health epidemics associated with cramped irregular streets and a political desire for order and convenience. Barcelona's Eixample extension neighbourhood, by Ildefons Cerda, consists of 520 octagonal blocks and long straight streets – this grid structure considered ease of movement, sunlight, ventilation and even greening.

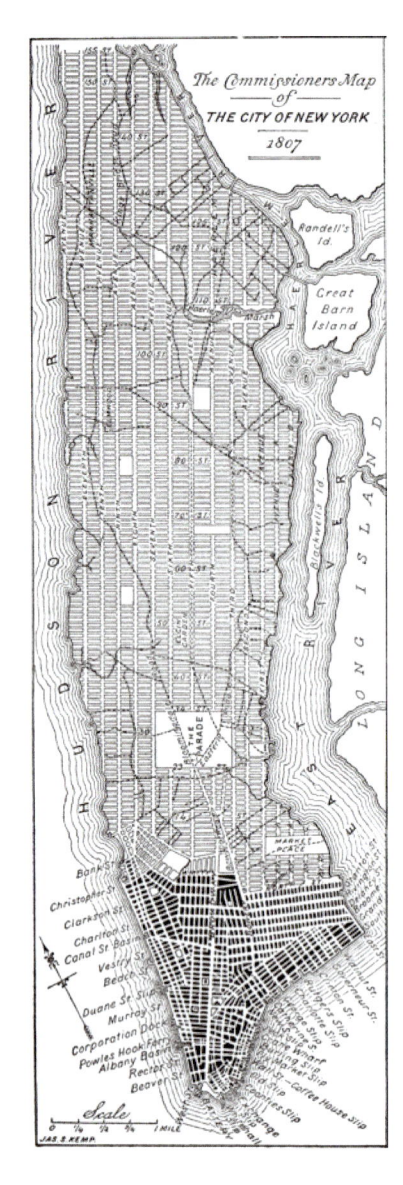

LEFT: The Commissioners Plan of 1811 - Manhattan, New York.

BELOW: The octagonal blocks and grid pattern of Cerda's Eixample Neighbourhood, Barcelona.

CHAPTER 1: URBAN DESIGN? THE DISQUISITION

The industrial revolution was a major driver behind the boom in city development from the mid-18th Century through to the early 20th Century. This period of economic development and growth bore witness to the expansion of cities as they sought to keep pace with industrial needs in regards manufacturing, transport for trade, and residential capacity for large workforces. Given this rapid growth there were natural negative impacts, with industry needs overpowering the needs of citizens. Leading to the destruction of traditional communities and poor quality of life becoming synonymous with developing industrial boom cities such as those in the UK and wider Europe, and North America. To tackle these rapidly emerging urban issues, a series of new approaches to how city design should be delivered started to gain prominence. The first was coined the **City Beautiful** movement. This design approach is best associated with the beautification and monumental grandeur designed into cites such as Chicago, Detroit, Cleveland, and most famously Washington DC (The MacMillan Plan, 1901). Responding to the poor quality of life residents in these cities were suffering as a direct result of rapid growth and poor planning, the aim was to create moral and civic pride through harmonious social order. Critics however saw the approach as overly cosmetic, an *'architectural design cult'* (Jacobs, 1962). Daniel Burnham's Plan for Cleveland is the embodiment of the movement, based on Burnham's own prototype city from the Chicago World's Fair (1893) where balance, symmetry, and splendour took centre stage. Such an approach proved expensive and its focus on civic architecture somewhat neglected the plight of normal citizens living beyond the civic core of the city. The philosophy did little to improve quality of life for people in their day-to-day activities and living, but much of the architecture, public spaces, green infrastructure interventions, and central mall/grand manner ideas remain popular to this day in the cities that adopted this approach.

A competing approach around this period was the **Garden City** (or Social City) movement initiated by Ebenezer Howard in 1898. This design agenda focused more attention on the communities within cities and how to overcome issues that had developed in relation to over-crowding and increasing industrial pollution.

Howard sought to plan for self-contained communities surrounded by greenbelts, creating garden cities that ensured people had easy access to natural and designed landscape and avoided over reliance on core centres. Raymond Unwin's Garden City in Letchworth, UK and Adrian G. Iselin's Residence Park, New York are influential examples of this design thinking. As with City Beautiful, the Garden City agenda had several vocal critics – with arguments that it was anti-industry, a major issue during this time of industrial boom – and that its approach ironically was damaging to nature, given the focus on manicured designed green infrastructure and more low density sprawled neighbourhoods that blended with natural topography and required greater distances of travel across the city scale. Much of the criticism aimed at Garden Cities was fair, yet several of the ideals it proposed remain prominent in urban design thinking today, particularity within the **New Urbanism** movement that promotes environmentally friendly places and walkable neighbourhoods.

TOP: Influenced by the City Beautiful movement - The MacMillan Plan, 1901, Washington D.C.

BOTTOM: Hampstead Garden Suburb, London [1907] was heavily influenced by Raymond Unwin's Letchworth and its garden city ideals.

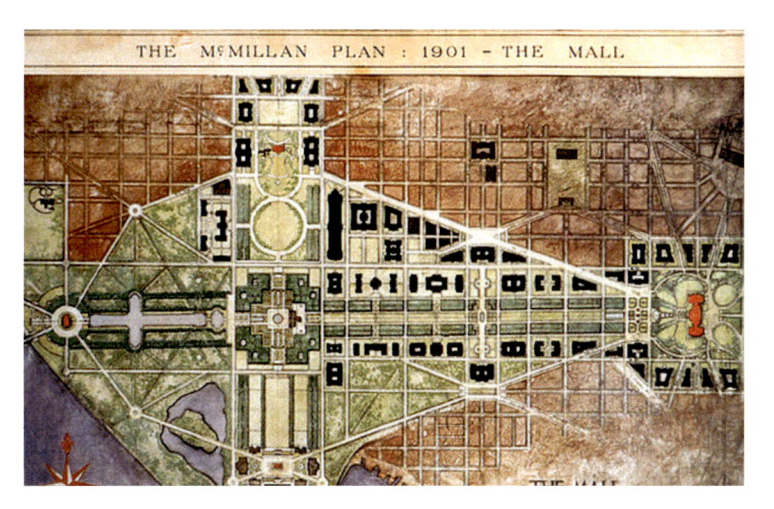

The failure of these two movements to appropriately tackle the, now alarming, issues being presented in cities saw a group of influential European architects, led by Le Corbusier, form **The Congres Internationaux d'Architecture Moderne** (CIAM) in 1928. This assembly sought to spread the principles of modern design into the realm of planning and city design, aiming to provide places with better functionality with people at the core of the design process.

The Athens Charter (1943), named for the location of the group's 4th conference in Athens, Greece, became their de facto manifesto and proposed social problems in cities be sorted through a strict functional segregation plan – with the distribution of the population into tall blocks at widely spaced intervals a central aim. The charter was loosely based on Le Corbusier's *'Ville Radieuse'* (1935) and his ideas that in essence people crave structure and function above all else in design. Many of the ideas presented by CIAM were highly influential after World War II as many of Europe's major cities required re-building, and such rigid rules provided an ideal, and inexpensive, template from which to work from. However, these rigid rules also lacked awareness of issues such as neighbourhoods, and it concealed a narrow view of how to develop place. A lack of attention to community and amenity was detrimental, and the provision of large open spaces without consideration for how people might use them led to criticism and a negative reaction from many of those living in these modernist locations. One of the best examples of the CIAM approach to city design is Brasilia, Brazil, planned by Lucio Costa in the 1950's and significantly influenced by the architectural contributions and modernist principles of Oscar Niemeyer. This city focused on the development of superblocks, functional in nature and aiming to provide spaces that engendered social equality and justice, but also suffered from a lack of usable space for people – such as the 220-foot-wide central government axis – and the major road axis dividing the city into north and south. Schemes such as Alt-Erlaa, Vienna designed by Harry Glück, did showcase how the modernist approach could be successful

LEFT: Alt Erlaa, Vienna. Designed by Harry Glück - a rare success story for the modernist approach to city planning.

BELOW: Plan Piloto, Brasilia. Planned by Lucio Costa according to CIAM principles.

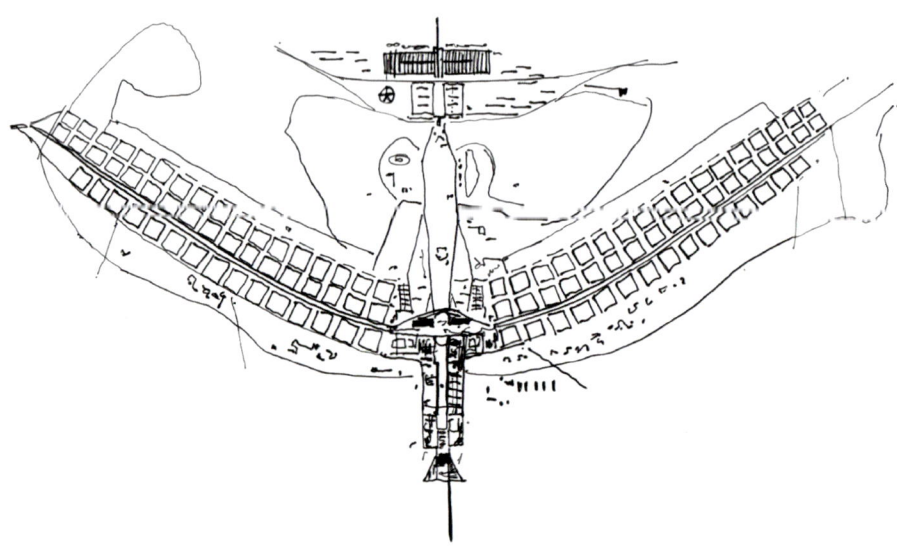

given the right conditions, but in general the approach was accepted as a failure, even by its most prominent supporters – with CIAM disbanding in 1959 recognising new and better ways of thinking about the plight of the city were required. The demolition of the Pruitt-Igoe housing scheme in St Louis, Missouri, in 1972 (designed in accordance with CIAM functional city ideals) was claimed by Charles Jencks to be the death of the modern architecture and city design movement.

1.2 URBAN DESIGN POST-1950s

Whilst past design movements had issues, they did tie together through their shared focus on people, yet under closer examination each philosophy was driven by other priorities with people failing to be central. City Beautiful was ultimately more about architecture and limited in wider spatial impact, notably were people lived; Garden Cities were more interested in the landscape and failed to be fit for growth purposes; and CIAM was fixated on structure and order and forgot context. Perhaps these resultant flaws should have been expected – given the backgrounds of those shaping these approaches – predominantly architects, landscape architects, and planners. These other disciplines did not provide a dedicated space for considering city development, to test, research and theorise on workable and viable solutions. It was this knowledge that directly led to a series of critical Ivy League conferences in the USA – the most prevalent of which was the 1956 Harvard Conference. It was at Harvard that Josep Lluis Sért, Dean of the Graduate School of Design (GSD), and a founding member of CIAM, developed a new vision – aiming to shift thinking about cities to a more holistic perspective. The call for action in the urban realm and desire to move beyond civic design to concerns with the living conditions of people shaped the calls for a new type of urban facilitator, between the disciplines (and scales) of architecture and planning. It was from such thinking that '**urban design**' was born at Harvard and developed into a unique curriculum in the GSD. To develop this emerging discipline Sért organised a series of symposium conferences, to begin to define 'urban design'. Despite some discord urban design quickly established its own territory, however more as a field of activity than as a professional discipline in its own right.

Whilst being viewed by Harvard GSD as a 4th design discipline, alongside the historic vocations of architecture, landscape architecture, and town planning (Black, 2024), beyond Harvard this new field acted more as a suitable arena for theorists and designers to develop and test ideas and research that would shape urban design moving forwards.

Since the birth of the modern field of urban design there have been a number of highly influential individuals whose research and approaches to development and placemaking have significantly impacted the discipline – and who remain critical to our understanding of the design process. What connects these thinkers and designers is a more persistent ambition to place people, often specifically local people, at the very heart of analysing and designing place. The works of Gordon Cullen (1961), Kevin Lynch (1960), Jane Jacobs (1962), Christopher Alexander (1966), to only name a few of the seminal works, pioneered urban design's early evolution and set the tone for a myriad of future studies and design ideas that had aided the discipline's maturation.

Cullen (1961) defined urban design as the '*art of relationships*', placing emphasis on emotional impacts people have when in place – with the resultant goal of the designer to manipulate the physical form of the city to allow for visual drama. That the primary design driver should be considering the point of view of a local person in the environment being created. His work today is still influential in how we think about character and human perspective, with unique techniques such as the sequential or serial, vision acting a s a key analytical and design technique to this day [including the **Applied Urban Design Framework** this book introduces]. Lynch (1960) concurred that people and perceptions should be a central consideration for designers – specifically his work focused on how easily, or otherwise, people understand design at a wider scale, how they mentally process the form of a city through its physical elements that make it. Lynch coined the term 'imageability' and his detailed work on mental mapping and analysing places for legibility have had a profound impact on how designers today perceive and deliver urban environments.

Lynch inspired a generation of works on environmental psychology and behaviour in cities. Jacobs (1962) coined several phrases that shape contemporary urban design approaches through her celebration of the dynamic qualities of cities and urban life. Jacobs argued that successful places must be designed for people to be connected, multi-functional, and varied. She believed cities were organisms and streets the lifeblood – her contributions to the field on how streets should be public spaces, creating social interactions and a sense of belonging for communities (the *'sidewalk ballet'*) has influenced the later works of key contemporary thinkers such as Jan Gehl, William Whyte, and Allan B. Jacobs. Alexander's ideas (1966) began to consider the ways in which a city is organised and designed to ensure life can flourish, arguing we must find answers in successful places of the past, in particular those that have organically developed into places that work for people and how they live.

During this early boom in urban design research there were of course other noteworthy contributors, but these touchstones of the field retain much of their power today and many of the more recent works can be traced back directly to these seminal studies. They played a significant role in the increase of interest and exposure of urban design – leading to a growing call for more consolidated theory or definition of the field. Recent years have seen the knowledge base growing consistently year on year, with discourses such as climate, sustainability, health, wellbeing, and ageing increasing the scope of urban design.

PROFESSIONAL CHALLENGES

Making sense of the substantive knowledge base that has developed is necessary to consolidate the discipline – a challenge for those practicing urban design given the field is both conceptual and spatial. The broad nature of the academic element of urban design remains disjointed from the practical application of urban design in cites - What is the role of urban design in a professional practice setting? Has this new emerging design discipline enhanced our approaches to delivering better quality cities? Urban designs post-1950's evolution has occurred alongside a period of global growth and economic re-structuring of many of the world's largest cities – cities are never in a state of stasis, but recent history has witnessed cities changing at a greater rate than ever before. This rapid global development has directly led to a recognised global vernacular where context-less places have become common (Watson 2013). Cities such as Dubai have become symbols of economic growth and global architecture – and such prosperity and perceived success has encouraged others to follow a similar path where localised design culture is rejected in favour of internationally outward facing design.

The issue with rejecting local context is that places fail to represent local people and communities, disconnecting from the very people who live in them. They lack identity, fail to deliver character, and instead become generic. Backlashes to such generic global approaches are becoming commonplace. Local populations in cities such as Lagos, Nigeria, are fighting back against perceived elimination of vernacular, local traditions, or public participation in the new neighbourhood of Eko-Atlantic (Watson, 2014). Such design is infected by ideology rather than by place, it dumbs down urbanism by displaying a culture of the regular and an intolerance of any form of disorder. Much of this comes from beliefs around progress, development, and growth (Boano et al., 2014). Projects focus on final form over process and often the local population are viewed as homogeneous consensual players. As cities structurally shift their economic base this becomes reflected in social and spatial organisation – much like cities of the past our design today can be shaped by the powerful forces of the era - economic progress and globalisation being dominate in why and how cities today are changing.

LEFT: Eko-Atlantic, Lagos, Nigeria, has witnessed grassroots opposition to the lack of participation in the design process and the perceived focus on more global design language and rejection of local culture and vernacular.

Photograph: Eko Atlantic.

These contemporary drivers run counter to the key focus of urban design – people. This presents a serious examination for the field, urban design must operate within this current context and ensure it can effect appropriate change in how we think about cities and how they work, not only for people but for the dominate forces often at work. It can be argued that urban design is needed now more than ever, to ensure places remain contextual, responsive and empowering for people as they progress – equally though it can be argued that urban design is failing in this task given the proliferation of designs neglecting these core aspects.

THE BLURRED REALITIES
Part of the problem for urban design is as it grows and becomes more prominent as a discipline in its own right, it becomes more blurred due to the tensions between key stakeholders in the built environment. Urban design can contribute to the design of cities by addressing the needs and wants of a range of stakeholders – leading to a natural tension between perspectives. Broadly speaking there are 3 core stakeholder groups:

1. The Investors in the City (developers / landowners etc.)

2. The Regulators of the City (authorities / planners etc.)

3. The Users of the City (individuals / communities etc.)

Each of these groups has a growing appreciation of the role of urban design. The *'investors'* in the city see added value with urban design in social, economic, and environmental terms (Carmona et al., 2010). Urban design and its role in providing clarity of design process and outcome can assist in stabilising market conditions (through masterplanning, design coding etc.), providing greater certainly for private sector investment. Urban design quality impacts are being recognised (MHCLG, 2020) as being marketable, a selling point in an increasingly visual culture - a sophisticated market is interested in better quality products. The *'regulators'* increasingly value the potential for urban design to make a place more competitive internationally, especially in a market where global competition is fierce, but regulators can see value in urban design to deliver more distinctive local places simultaneously – the best of both worlds, enhancing the investment opportunities whilst maintaining local confidence and sense of place. Urban design is also being used more frequently to contribute towards better governance, again processes such as masterplanning and coding can create place-based visons and strategies that often encourage collaborations across sectors. And *'users'* of the city can buy into urban design's focus on functionality of place and promotion of accessible, inclusive, and contextual environments.

ABOVE: Dubai, UAE has become a symbol for many of economic success - with cities across the globe seeking to replicate its more globalised forms of architecture.

The tensions that exist between such perspectives lead us to ask - how can urban design strike the correct balance and whose interests and values does urban design safeguard? There is a clear danger that economic considerations become the main driver of development (investors), or top-down solutions are normalised (regulators), or we generalise the wishes of society and fail to understand the diversity of local populations in design (users). The value of urban design to all groups has led to a blurring of professional boundaries and overlapping agendas on issues of placemaking. It leaves urban design in a crisis of identity as a discipline, in particular as a professional applied vocation. With competing perspectives of the role of urban design, it can be viewed as a *'magpie'* discipline – incorporating lots of ideas and approaches without a singular or consolidated definition. There are several territories that urban designers operate in (both spatial and conceptual) today, these *'spheres of urbanistic action'* (Keriger, 2006) include urban design as public policy (Punter, 2002); as community advocacy, the architecture of the city, as landscape urbanism, as a vehicle for smart growth, and even as a less technical discipline and more a frame of mind for engaging and facilitating discussions around wider urban issues.

1.3 THE [EMERGING] URBAN DESIGNER

With more than half the world's population now living in urban areas (UN, 2018), and growing, cities need to find a new significance in a rapidly developing world. Urban design can be at the forefront of adjusting cities to structural change, but it must begin to move through its current haze of amiable platitudes and find a clarity in how to deliver its commitment to city life through urban enhancement. A new approach is required for city design and placemaking and urban design must act as the standard bearer – and set a high bar. As discussed, cities are constantly evolving, therefore context is constantly adapting, urban design cannot therefore stand still. It is time to move the discipline out of the post-1950's growth era and into a more defined practical period – where the wealth of theory and lessons developed are effectively utilised in shaping the role of the '**urban designer**' and ensuring tangible impact on how places are designed, delivered, and experienced in the real world.

We, the authors, argue that urban design requires a clear vocational consolidation as an applied discipline, in which our territory of action deals directly with the physical forces of the city, translating policy and strategies into actual design interventions and solutions. Such an approach does not dilute the role of urban design as an arena for research on wider urban concerns, this is a critical aspect for any field to remain relevant and innovative (Black, 2024). The practical application for the outputs of such work does however require a distinct technical offshoot that is tailored to seeking out methods and approaches for physically manifesting and testing such ideas. Within the field of architecture the breadth of research and theory is significant, with many contributing to our understanding and moving the field forwards and retaining contemporary relevance, yet the role of the *'architect'* is more narrowly defined, as are the core skills, competencies, and knowledge required to practice this specific role. Similar arguments can be made for landscape architecture and planning and *'landscape architects'* and *'planners'*. Urban design, as the 4th design discipline, is primed to take a similar step – and such a step requires a new bespoke process to provide clear structure for education and professional practice. The **Applied Urban Design Framework** was developed to illustrate how urban design can deliver as an applied technical discipline to provide more contextually responsive interventions in our cities and places.

OPPOSITE: Physical design intervention - new playful public realm Miroir d'eau Bordeaux, France.

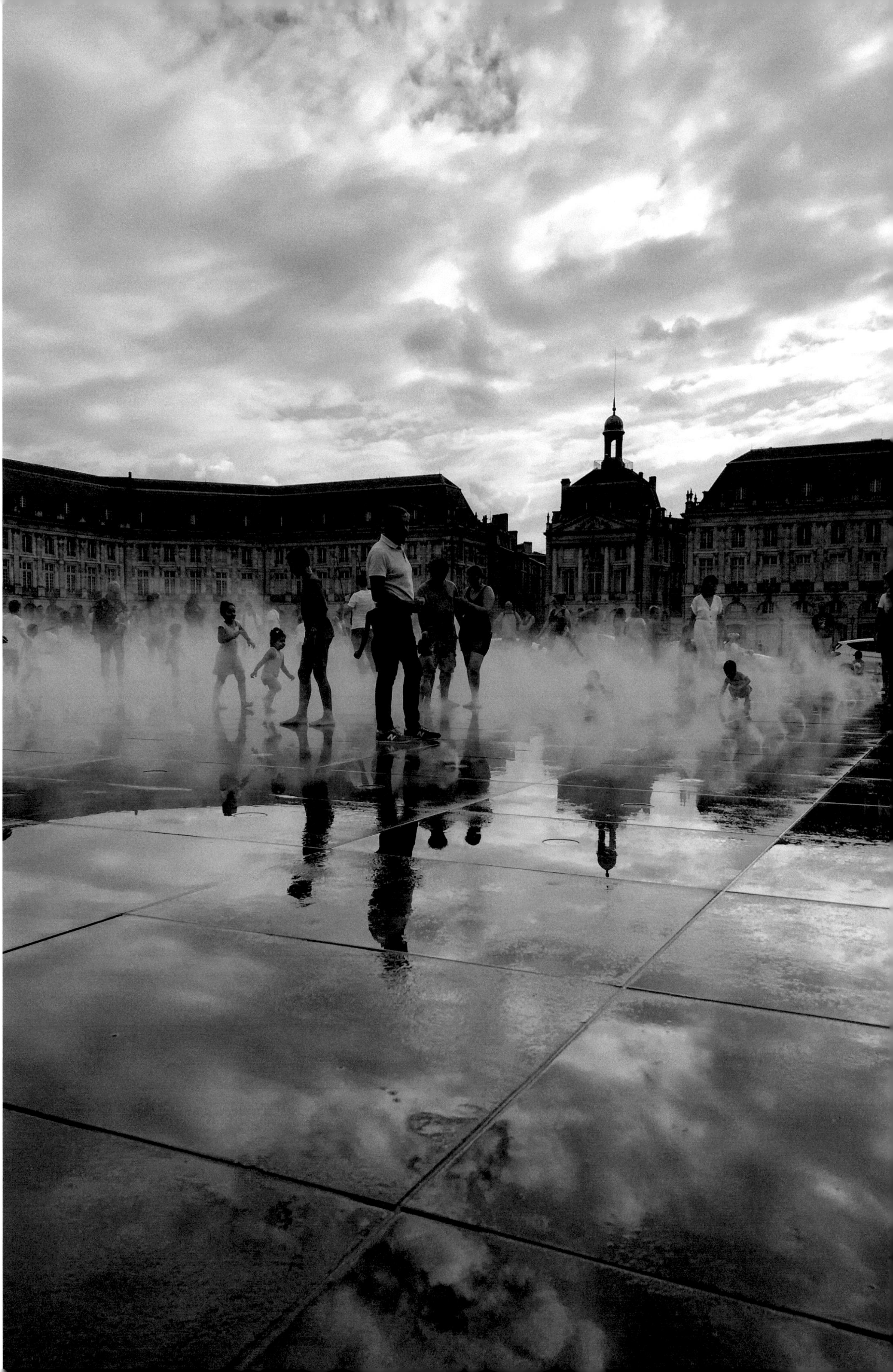

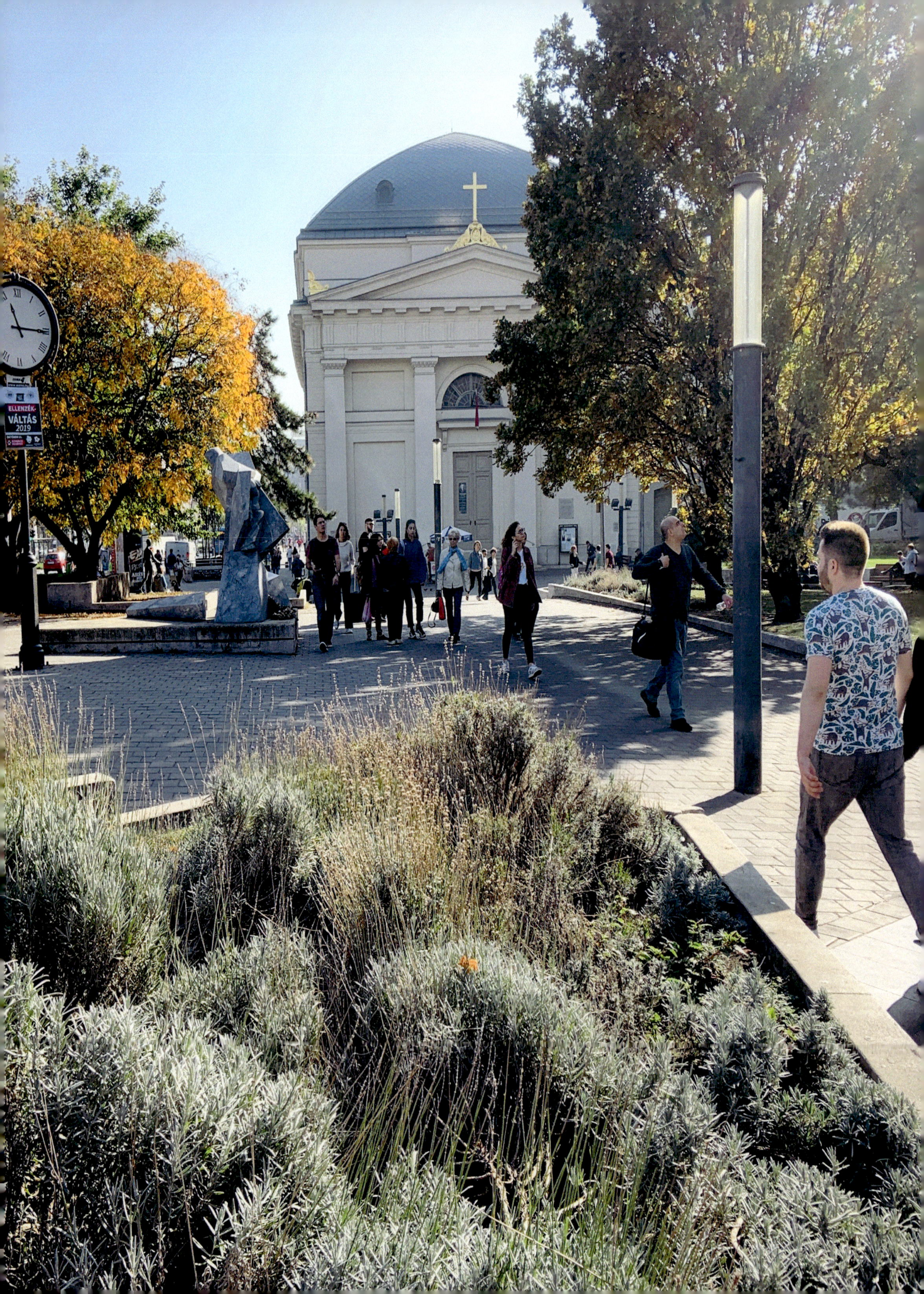
ELLENZÉK-
VÁLTÁS
2019

CHAPTER 2: TOWARDS CONTEXTUALLY RESPONSIVE URBAN DESIGN

CHAPTER 2
Towards Contextually Responsive Urban Design

Good urban design is more than simply knitting together the townscape, urban designers must configure a rich network in which buildings come and go; a framework of transport, built fabric and other features which will create natural locations for things – urban design must structure activity. The benefits of quality urban design are well researched and understood – with evidence demonstrating urban design can have value in not only the physical built form, but also provide gains socially, environmentally, and economically. Urban design is the art of making places for people, of providing conditions for a flourishing economic life, the prudent use of natural resources, and for social progress (DETR and CABE, 2000). A quality urban design scheme must contribute to the environment in which it is located, deliver a range of wider social and economic benefits, and be adaptable to emerging challenges it may face.

OPPOSITE: Deak Square, District V, Budapest.

2.1 BENEFITS OF URBAN DESIGN

PHYSICAL

The most visual of the benefits of urban design given it is a physical medium, is that the physical built environment can be enhanced – upgrading the aesthetic impact of place. The essence of the built environment is in the delivery of physical places and spaces and the routes that connect them together – these are tangible visible features and as such are open to individual judgements regarding the issue of quality. It would, however, be incorrect to distil this into a matter of only aesthetics, beauty, and taste – despite each of these having an important role to play.

Delivering physical quality extends beyond these more 'subjective' matters to include a designs' requisite to be functional, to be sustainable, to afford the appropriate range of activities, amenities, and facilities essential for any local community. Quality urban design should elicit positive emotional responses in people as they take pleasure in the inherent visual appeal, be that through material choices, colour palette, or the relationship between buildings, streets, spaces, and landscape. It should provide sustainable environments that reduce car dependency, waste, and low-quality spaces/structures – augmenting what makes a place visually appealing, attractive, and local.

LAS SETAS DE SEVILLA at La Encarnacion Square, a public space in Seville, Spain designed by Jurgen Mayer is a fine example of the physical benefit of quality urban design. Built on the site of a 19th Century market that had become a dead space between key destinations in the city, this intervention reanimated and reactivated a key public space for locals and tourists alike. The contemporary design integrated into the existing historic fabric – adding movement and interest without losing human-scale. It was a reaction to the physical surroundings and added a new plaza dynamic that compliments nearby traditional plazas. The physical sensuous forms provide associations with nature and energy, whilst the insertion of a new market, archaeological museum, skyview rooftop walkway, and democratised open space add new amenity to the local environment and draw in all types of users.

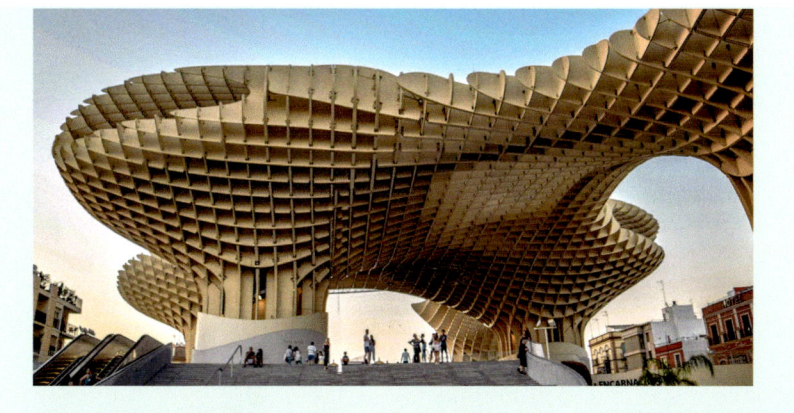

SOCIAL

Good urban design should enhance the quality of life of all those who use the built environment – whether they be working, playing, or simply living. Well-designed places are more likely to enrich wellbeing in those who utilise it – to do this fairly design must be inclusive, it needs to consider the needs and wishes of all those in society, not just the few. By designing in ways that promote and engender accessibility for all and viewing communities as non-homogenous in the delivery of place, urban design can enable equity across the diversity of individuals (McIndoe et al., 2005). It can increase civic pride and social cohesion, shaping sense of place and local identity. Designers need to understand the different ways in which people interact with their surroundings and each other – creating places where people feel comfortable and safe. When designers create human-centric environments they contribute to the wellbeing of all society (Carmona, 2021).

ENVIRONMENTAL

Investment in green and blue infrastructure as an integral component of all urban design has been shown to deliver significant benefits to individual and communal health, controlling conditions such as asthma and obesity, and by providing spaces that aid memory and physical interactions with nature for people who experience mental health issues (Mell, 2019). An essential element of creating liveable, functional, and attractive urban designs is the incorporation of nature. Designing environments that are exciting, interactive, and usable for all users and age-groups will only benefit people and their sense of identity and physical condition (Louv, 2005). How place is designed and delivered can not only be beneficial to the humans who inhabit them, but equally be beneficial to wider sustainability goals and concerns around issues such as climate change. Urban design has the responsibility of ensuring projects are biodiverse – and considerate of energy, water and waste cycles that exist. The impact of design on our planet can be significant and devasting, with 80% of all global emissions estimated to be accounted for by urban environments (Newton, 2014). What is required today is design that seeks to make a genuine contribution to the survival of the planet and provides new forms of climate awareness.

C.S. LEWIS SQUARE. Belfast is a city divided by faith, culture, even language. '*Peace*' walls scar the cityscape, erected to separate communities - yet attempts are being made through urban design delivery to bring about social change and promote cohesion through shared narratives and icons. C.S. Lewis Square was strategically positioned to connect key parts of the city utilising the existing Comber Greenway network - and provide a destination for all people based around a shared cultural icon, the author of the Narnia series of books -C.S. Lewis. This space aims to be for everyone in Belfast and be a place all can identify with.

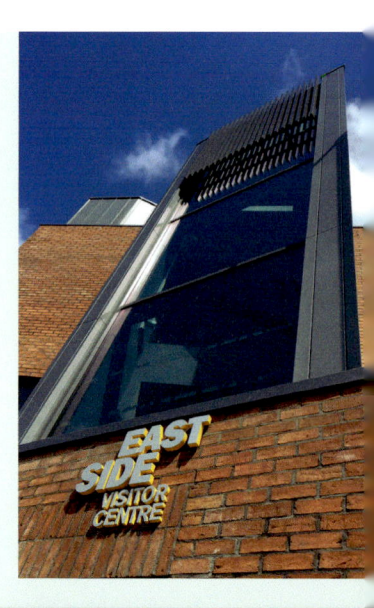

GARDENS BY THE BAY in Singapore is a leading example of the environmental benefits urban design can provide. This ambitious scheme sought to create a city in a garden and was driven by strategies around water management, green infrastructure provision, energy capture, waste systems, and biodiverse spaces for people. It has been instrumental in re-shaping Singapore's identity as a sustainable and environmentally friendly city.

BRINDLEY PLACE, Birmingham, UK masterplanned by Sir Terry Farrell, delivered a 17-hectare mixed-use canal side development. The scheme illustrates the power of quality urban design providing tangible business benefit. Investing in quality of place ensured that the development attracted an array of potential investors and increased the overall economic value of the scheme. Businesses were convinced due to the ability to market such a quality environment to potential clients and employees, understanding the value in being part of a wider urban whole and the connections and benefits this would bring long-term.

ECONOMIC

The economic benefits of good urban design have been well established, not only can quality design impact market perceptions and behaviour in a positive fashion, but it can create markets where none previously existed. Development based on quality design principles have been shown to raise value by up to 25% (Savills, 2016) and increase capital values and letting/sales rates by 20% (NWDA, 2007). CABE (2001) discuss the wealth of research consistently concluding that good urban design adds economic value in the form of better value for money, higher asset exchange value, and better lifecycle value. Developers are beginning to recognise these impacts (MHCLG, 2020), as quality design can make places more competitive against other locations through making them more distinct, it can manage economic shifts and development, and bring certainty and structure to markets through masterplanning and design coding. Quality spaces and places also attract tourism – as people are drawn to visiting those cities that provide positive urban experiences and memories (Robinson et al., 2019).

POOR DESIGN

Whilst we can see the clear benefits of pursuing a high-quality urban design approach or agenda, it is equally valid to consider the negative impacts of poor design on place and people.

Today places are still too often designed without people and their needs at the forefront of the process – these places fail to effectively deliver economically, environmentally, or socially. Such places lack appeal or coherence, design interventions such as gated developments, peripheral commercial strips, and out of town commercial/leisure parks (Carmona et al., 2017). The production of context-less generic housing and office tracts characterised by strict land use segregation, limited physical connectivity, and excessive reliance on the car often lead to social and economic dysfunction and a reduction in value of the surrounding areas (MacMillan et al., 2021). Poor design can not only mitigate any positive economic boon but can actually place financial burdens on both the public and private sectors in the long run (CABE, 2001). Poor quality manifests in the built environment for several reasons - the public sector's lack of commitment to demanding/promoting quality design, the private sector often favouring single-use schemes with little regard to the wider townscape, and an absence of accepted guidelines for procuring high-quality design (Steiner and Butler, 2012). Carmona et al., (2017) argue that the main drivers of poor urban design are a lack of, or ineffective, knowledge on what makes quality urban design and why it should be a prerequisite of all placea and spaces.

WHAT QUALITY DESIGN LOOKS LIKE?

Articulating what quality urban design looks like is not something that can be done with any precision or certainty. Attempts to do so can only be, by the nature of the discipline, somewhat vague and principle led. There is a wealth of publications that aim to bring together key principles to drive quality in urban design practice, such as *By Design* (2000), *The Urban Design Compendium* (2000), and most recently the *National Model Design Code* (2021), and whilst they will differ in terminology, quite often they share key fundamentals that are required in the delivery of a great place. Perhaps the most comprehensive attempt to unpack the attributes that make up quality design is **The Place Diagram** from *Project for Public Spaces*. This tool was developed to assist communities in evaluating places, and proposed interventions, for quality. The inner ring represents a place's key attributes, the middle ring its intangible qualities, and the outer ring measurable data.

The challenge facing designers when using this tool, or similar, is the lack of clarity in regards what these attributes look like in the real-world.

If quality urban design is about delivering contextual places for people, then design that directly responds to unique location settings and the needs and aspirations of diverse and complex local communities is necessary. If design is to be characterful, provide identity, and be distinctive and memorable then it must adapt from place to place. Any attempts to replicate, transfer, or mimic design from one location to another fails to consider the unique setting or context of each. Rather than ask what quality design looks like, we instead solicit how to best provide the conditions for quality urban design to transpire in each location. Shifting the focus in this way requires urban designers to understand the need for the broad attributes, such as those highlighted by *The Place Diagram*, and have an extensive experience of how these have been delivered in other places (best practice). It also requires a clear knowledge for how design works in practice (explored in detail in Chapter 4) - and critically a method for exploring context to ensure it drives design decision making and process (The **Applied Urban Design Framework** introduced in Chapter 3).

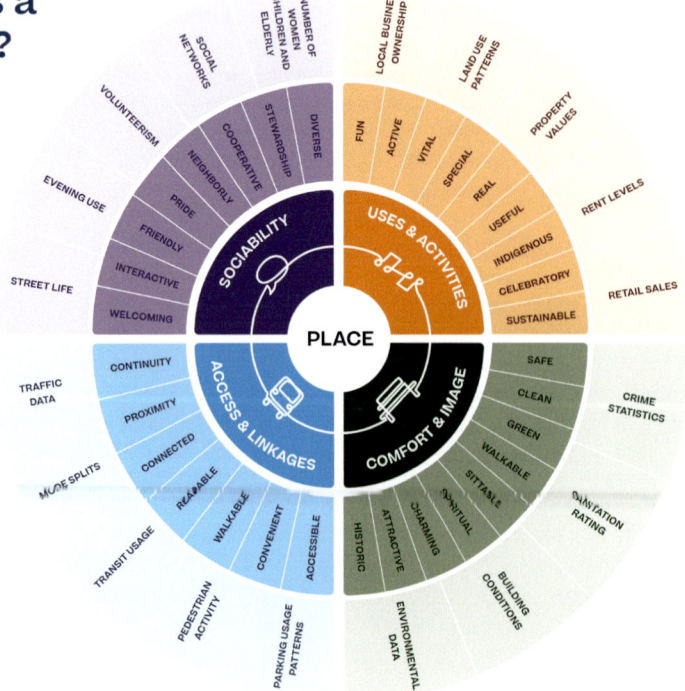

LEFT: The Place Diagram (*Project for Public Spaces*).

CHAPTER 2: TOWARDS CONTEXTUALLY RESPONSIVE URBAN DESIGN

2.2 WHAT IS MEANT BY 'CONTEXT'?

When talking about urban design we habitually use the term context, but it is often not fully understood or appreciated. Context is described in dictionary definitions as being the '*setting*' of an event or idea, and how it can be fully understood. Context, at least to the urban designers, is about the elements of our townscapes and landscapes that make up distinctive places and refers to the way that we understand and respond to these distinctive elements. As noted in the first chapter of this book, the birth of the urban design movement was in response to architects and city planners ignoring, or misunderstanding, the 'context' when proposing design interventions. Landscape architects and urban planners of the late 20th century engaged with context as being an understanding of the physical attributes of a place, responding to them only as part of developing design solutions.

Context, for the urban designer, is much more than just understanding the physical attributes. Context is multifaceted, including those social, economic, and environmental components discussed earlier. Urban or rural, large or small, the places that we live and work in are endlessly diverse, and their appearance and functionality (both good and bad) is the result of many complex interactions between people and places. It is useful to remember that context is as much about how people use a place, not just the attributes of that place itself. People can shape the buildings and spaces of towns, cities, and villages to meet their desires and demands, but thereafter the buildings and spaces shape the way that people go about their daily lives. Context in urban design terms is about the architectural styles, walking and cycling routes, and the location and quality of green spaces, but it is also about so much more.

Whilst as urban designers we are often focused on the environmental and physical elements of the places that we work in; we should not ignore context in its widest view. This includes the political and social trends and preferences, economic objectives and patterns, as well as the aspirations for an area's growth or development. Collectively this is often called the local culture. In this way context is not something that is fixed, its ever changing and ever evolving. This means that we must pay as much attention to what has happened historically, as well as what might happen in the future. It is important that we do not ignore this temporal dimension in our understanding of context. Simply put, no two places will ever be the same.

Whilst many have tied to create typologies or trends to be able to group places and arrive at interventions, these will never be able to fully embrace the dynamic and ever changing (and sometimes messy) townscapes around the globe. To understand context, we must accept that every place is different and needs to be explored as such. For example, whilst Rome and London are both European capital cities, they are very different in their built form and architecture. This is a direct response to their history, their political and governmental organisation, and even the pastimes and foods enjoyed by their residents - the cities context. Understanding context means gaining insight into the people living and working in the areas where we practice. It is a significant challenge and responsibility and is not always easy.

TOP: The Baroque architecture and art of the Piazza Navona, Rome.

BOTTOM: Classic red-brick Victorian architecture of Mayfair, London.

As urban designers we are challenged with making sense of context and devising design interventions that respond to this context. This means working with something that is multifaceted, something that is not just physical, something that is not just about the present day, and importantly something that requires us to understand the people who live and work in an area. This means that we will need to look across a range of different variables and use a variety of different techniques. Understanding context means visiting and immersing yourself in a place, it is not something that can be done exclusively from secondary data, or a desktop analysis, but requires the urban designer to visit a place, experience the smells, sounds, tastes, and visual qualities of our urban areas. Consequently, context is multi-sensory as well as multifaceted.

Therefore, it is vital we have a method that allows us to integrate these ideas into our design process, as well as present these in an efficient and understandable way for other built environment professionals and wider general consumption by the very people that we are designing for – those who live and work in these areas. The role of the urban designer is to package together the multifaceted, multisensory, and temporal materials of context, present them in an easily understandable way, and from them develop interventions that that can respond to the uniquely fluid nature of our townscapes and landscapes. A contextually responsive approach to design seeks to design place of, for, and with local people.

2.3 SHAPING URBAN DESIGN - AS A TECHNICAL VOCATION

Urban Design as a technical vocation requires suitably qualified and experienced professionals to effectively practice in the real-world. It has a professional responsibility that is beyond the traditional remit of the architect, the landscape architect, and the urban planner with a strong focus on understanding and responding to context. In the quest to deliver contextually responsive places, there are four key elements that shape the approach to professional practice. Understanding, and importantly applying, each of these elements clearly defines the role and remit of the urban designer. In short, the urban designer must engage with the complexity of context and undertake a process of balancing the needs of people and the demands of place.

Whilst urban design can be defined as a technical profession, it should not be viewed or practiced in a *'technocratic'* manner. The importance of collaboration, consultation, and communication is inherent to the purpose of urban design. People are at the heart of urban design as a profession, taking upon itself the challenge to champion the quality of the human experience of our towns and cities. This responsibility is often referred to as 'human scale'. Each of the elements is introduced in turn below, and it is evident of how the approach of the urban designer is skewed towards the 'human scale'. These elements are intended to showcase a general perspective of the complexity of the role of the urban designer today – for a more detailed understanding and appreciation of the fundamental building blocks of urban design practice *see* Chapter 4.

Scales - Urban design operates at several broad scales which progressively focus down on the site or project area. Working in scales allows the urban designer to 'nest' ideas within each other allowing progressive levels of detail to be explored. Working at the larger scale offers the opportunities for some of the less physical contextual ideas (politics, projections, aspirations etc.) to be considered most effectively. Each of the remaining elements should be considered at all scales. Importantly this ensures that some of the larger contextual matters – such as politics or growth aspirations – are not lost in a directed site-specific study, but also allows for very detailed, and necessary elements to be understood at a smaller scale. This has the added advantage of ensuring that the urban designer works 'smartly' focusing in on key issues and identifying areas for specific and targeted later study.

BELOW: A full appreciation of Little Italy, Lower Manhattan, New York requires you to visit and experience first-hand the unique sights, sound, tastes, smells, and visual impact.

Structures - Not referring simply to building and other structures, although these are key parts of structure, but rather the recognisable and tangible pieces of an urban area that can be identified, catalogued, and shaped. In short, structure is about how one element is arranged with, or against, another. The urban designer essentially seeks to identify and replicate relationships between different elements understanding and using patterns or trends. For example, the way that buildings relate differently to a small local residential street as opposed to a main high street. These structures are vitally important as they form the foundation for an area's context. This is far beyond the traditional land use planning perspective, embracing ideas of mixed-use, multiple densities, and historical patterns.

Connections - Whether this is understanding the nature and role of the streets and spaces within an area, or a more complicated consideration of the accessibility of key services or facilities by public transport connectivity is a key element of the urban designer's profession. Increasingly the urban designer has a strong remit for prioritising the role of sustainable transport modes (walking, cycling, and public transit) within the city, with a strong focus on the quality and convenience of these connections. Encouraging people to walk for their shorter, local journeys is as much about the street's urban design attributes - including safety, quality, comfort, or activity – as opposed to simply providing pavements as part of highways design. The role of good design is also to connect people, providing the physical platform for life to occur, for people to socialise, to trade, to communicate. Design has the power to connect people to each other, to amenity and facility, to nature, to the past (culture / heritage), and even the future (technology).

Principles - The final of these four elements is principles. Urban design theorists have studied and unpacked cities and towns for over 70 years, many taking the time to unpack the way in which people use and interact with spaces employing observational methods (watching people and recording their actions). Collectively this body of knowledge has resulted in a series of ideas and principles that collectively seek to articulate good urban design. The urban designer needs to have strong working knowledge of how to deliver these principles in the real-world.

There is often a misconception that following these principles slavishly is the remedy for the problems that beset our urban areas, but this is not the case, as there are inherent contradictions between these principles which the urban designer is tasked with addressing. The ability to adapt and prioritise these principles, working across the scales, is the challenge that is set for the urban designer. Replicating past design successes (best practice) can lead to generic context-less design, what works in one place does not necessarily translate as effectively to another – rather best practice should be investigated to understand the core principles that enabled success. Such lessons can then be applied across different settings, shaping but not mimicking design.

Whilst each of these elements are important in their own right, the true ambition must be to arrive at a point whereby these are balanced – against the needs of the clients and companies who will invest, considering the needs of the people who will live, work and play in any place that is designed, and against the need to address some of the big issues that challenge us in the 21st century, (e.g. climate change mitigation/adaptation).

To find the appropriate balance, a process for delivery is required that is universal, iterative, transferable, and repeatable. A process that can be employed by urban designers to best assist in the quest for contextually responsive people centred places. Presently there are a lack of applied processes for practicing urban design. As discussed earlier in this chapter, there are existing frameworks for understanding quality attributes and principles, and for evaluating design, existing or proposed – and whilst these are critical tools, they are geared towards understanding design rather than the process of designing itself in an applied practical way.

The **Applied Urban Design Framework** was conceived to perform this precise function – a bespoke design process that takes a site to a place through a clear step-by-step methodology that consistently demands designers integrate context and people centred thinking across all elements of design. Chapter 3 discusses the development of the AUD Framework, how it provides structure in education and practice for applied technical urban design, and how it can be practically operationalised to stimulate a contextually responsive approach to placemaking internationally.

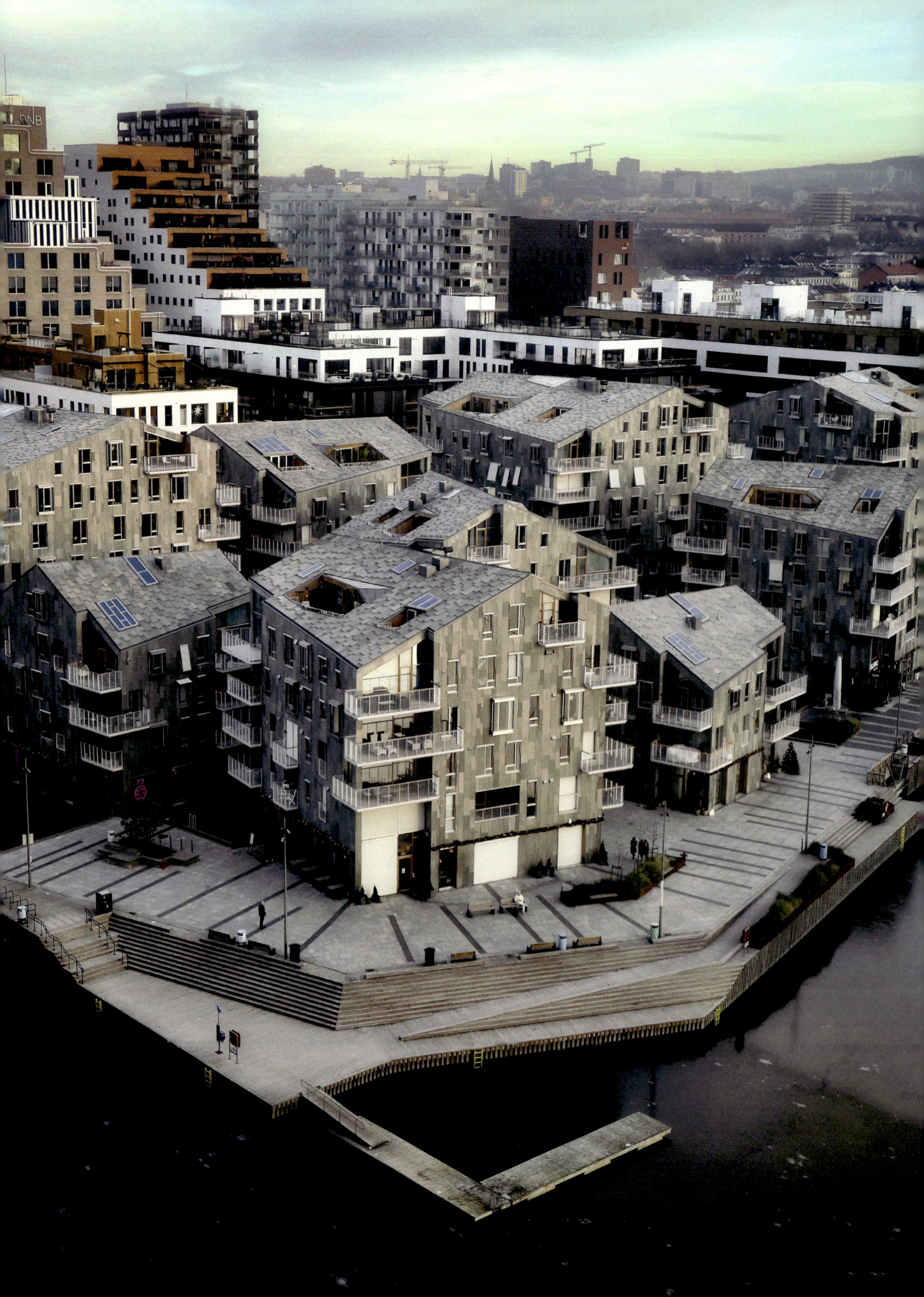
DNB

CHAPTER 3
Applied Urban Design Framework

With the proliferation of context-less designs internationally stemming from beliefs around progress, development, growth, and the notion urban design ideas can travel easily and be replicated, we argue urban design must usefully attend more carefully to the local contexts in which it is practiced. Augmenting traditional proscriptive (critiquing poor practice design) and prescriptive (suggesting best practice design) approaches with new critical thinking on context to deliver contextually responsive design interventions and solutions. In this chapter we outline our bespoke approach, the **Applied Urban Design [AUD] Framework**. The AUD Framework acts as a scaffolding for '*practicing*' urban design – combining both '*why*' we design, with '*how*' we design and critically '*who*' we design for.

URBAN DESIGN SKILLS

The need for a new approach to practicing urban design, one that is not tied to one particular context or setting but is transferable internationally, requires new thinking for urban design educators and programmes. What skills should the next generation of urban design graduates have to enable them to make positive contributions to the future of cities? A significant obstacle in responding to these challenges is the lack of time or dedicated space allocated to the study of the discipline in current higher education pathways. Too often urban design is a specialist pathway within planning or architecture postgraduate degrees (Palazzo, 2014) – relegating the field to a sub-set within more established professions and doing a disservice to the fundamental role it can play in aligning them in a more effective way in practice. There are a limited number of postgraduate programmes that offer a dedicated urban design education, yet these arguably mirror the lack of agreed mandate, with contrasting teaching models.

Elisabete Cidre at UCL, for example, brought together perspectives on emerging pedagogies in urban design in the *Journal of Urban Design* (2016, 21, vol.5) which unpacks some of the variance visible in contemporary education approaches. The journal contributions showcase the array of thinking on what urban design should influence and how this can be taught – with climate change, housing, public space, food production, health, ageing, sustainability, and design quality claimed to be within the remit of urban designs professional scope (Romice et al., 2022). It poses the question of what are the priorities for urban design, the research undertaken to support its development, and its education? It is imperative therefore that urban design education evolves to allow the discipline to facilitate more effective alignment with landscape and indeed other design disciplines (Black and Mell, 2024). To achieve this, four areas must be targeted:

1. Dedicated time/space for the study of urban design.
2. A robust curriculum that clearly articulates the role of urban design in practice and the core competencies and skills required of urban designers.
3. A focus on multi-disciplinary co-production of the built environment employing urban design as a key facilitator.
4. Integration of design-led research to enhance student engagement with real world planning/design scenarios.

3.1 AUD FRAMEWORK DEVELOPMENT

The authors have collectively worked together in research and teaching in direct response to these four targets above - initially at the University of Manchester, UK, and in recent years across other national contexts and professional settings. At the University of Manchester this work was formalised as part of the 2020 established **Manchester Urban Design LAB** (MUD-Lab - www.manchester.ac.uk/mudlab). Directed by Black, the MUD-Lab is made up of colleagues from planning, urban design, architecture, and landscape, and acts as a forum exploring and 'testing' more effective alignment of multi-disciplinary research and teaching of urban design (Black and Mell, 2024). The MUD-Lab/authors approach urban design as a technical product and applied discipline that focuses on people, experience, interaction, and context by

OPPOSITE: The Applied Urban Design Framework provides a structure for the delivery of contextually responsive, people centred, high quality urban design. It combines *why* we design, with *how* we design, and *who* we design for. Residential development in Oslo, Norway that prioritises people, sustainability, and quality of life - yet respects the city context in scale, density, layout, climatic response, and the local resident's dynamic relationship with the outdoors.

building on the seminal work *Responsive Environments* by Bentley et al. (1985) and those theorists discussed prior. Urban design is thus taught as a discipline that works between the scale of the town planner and architect/landscape architect, shaping place through effective engagement with local context and character.

Much of our work is influenced by the thinking on urban design from the turn of the 21st century with guidance such as *By Design* (DETR and CABE, 2000) and *The Urban Design Compendium* (Llewelyn-Davies, 2000). To achieve this, we advocate a studio-based approach using traditional design skills across multiple scales. Our territory is dealing with the physical forces of the city, representing the local and enhancing life and urbanism through comprehensive analysis and logical process. From this premise **The Applied Urban Design Framework** [AUD Framework] was developed based on research and experience in practice. The Framework created is an applied technical process for the production of contextually responsive design, compatible with theoretical approaches to the urban condition, and designed to engender better collaboration across the design process with broader stakeholders and professionals. A contextually responsive approach seeks to design places of, for, and with local people. This process was the author's response to the need for a structured, yet flexible, framework that enables individuals to develop the core skills necessary to practice urban design as a technical product, to develop projects along a logical pathway that still requires creative approaches, thinking, and commitment, and provide a roadmap to engage with other professions. The AUD Framework has been extensively refined and tested through our teaching over a number of years, not only in Manchester (Black; Sonbli) but also in Aalborg University, Denmark and the University of Sheffield (Martin), and in a UK professional practice setting as part of the Royal Town Planning Institute's core development training (Phillips).

The AUD Framework is presented in a linear fashion, from one stage to the next, yet it remains adaptable and flexible, as the context of the site being developed is always unique. There are also several steps that require evaluation back through the framework, ensuring a formative approach rather than a tick-box exercise. The aim is to provide a detailed and useable framework that better equips the designer with the necessary contextual detail to make evidenced decisions and avoid generic or context-less results. Those who undertake this process during their studies develop a broad range of skills: the ability to analyse place across different scales; A deep understanding of the importance of, and how to engage with, people; The ability to identify and interpret relevant policy and guidance; An understanding of design composition and complexity; Skills in collaborating with key stakeholders and other design professions; Developing design ideas and concepts; Evaluating design for quality and contextual awareness; Competence in rationalising design decisions and real-world feasibility; As well as the technical skills to present urban analysis, ideas, designs, and complete project narratives in a clear and comprehensive manner to both design professionals and non-expert audiences.

CHAPTER 3: APPLIED URBAN DESIGN FRAMEWORK 24

The AUD Framework provides clarity on the role of the urban designer – and transparency on the design process and delivery for all stakeholders. It requires urban designers to think beyond a fixation on site scale alone, to consider the wider implications of any intervention, on both place and people. It ensures people have a voice within the process, with participation critical across the relevant professional disciplines as well as local communities, businesses, and users. It provides local authorities and communities with a clear means from which to hold designers and developers accountable, and from which to evaluate proposals and their local impact and broader contextual consideration. It creates a template for educators, professionals, and interested parties, not only within urban design but related fields, to shape curriculum, practices and processes, and identify necessary core skills and competencies. And it affords designers the necessary evidence to support design decision making as they can rationalise choices based on robust analysis and evaluations. The AUD Framework, if employed appropriately, will ensure that all design is driven by local context and needs.

3.2 APPLIED URBAN DESIGN FRAMEWORK

The Applied Urban Design Framework features four clear steps that must be undertaken to progress from initial site through to a final design intervention. Each step has a series of specific outcomes that urban designers should present – illustrating the process undertaken, and rationalising the decisions made in reaching a final design. It is the steps that provide the roadmap and ensure the process remains contextual and robust, and the outcomes provide the transparency and allow design to be evaluated and scrutinised more fairly. Key to the AUD Framework's success is the duality of this approach – a distinct process to undertake and follow with clear outputs required at each stage. The framework does not dilute the skill of the designer as a creative force, it does not design, the designer does. The AUD Framework better informs the designer and promotes consistency of approach across every project. The transparency comes from providing a clear, flexible, and holistic approach where each step informs the next – improving public trust and holding designers and key stakeholders to account across their decision making and the wider design process.

IMAGES: The AUD Framework was developed in Manchester, UK (TOP) before being tested across various international and professional contexts, including Aalborg, Denmark (BOTTOM).

APPLIED URBAN DESIGN

PROCESS

OUTCOMES

SITE & CLIENT

CONTEXT

1. Analysis
   Strategic
   +
   Local

   → Strategic Profile

   → Area Profile
      Site Profile

PIVOT

2. Urban Design Program

   → A: Design Considerations
      B: Design Brief

DESIGN

3. Design Development

   → **Optioneering**
      Immature
      ↓
      Mature

4. Technical Design

   → Functional
      ↓
      Liveable
      ↓
      Contextual
      ↓
      Deliverable

PLACE

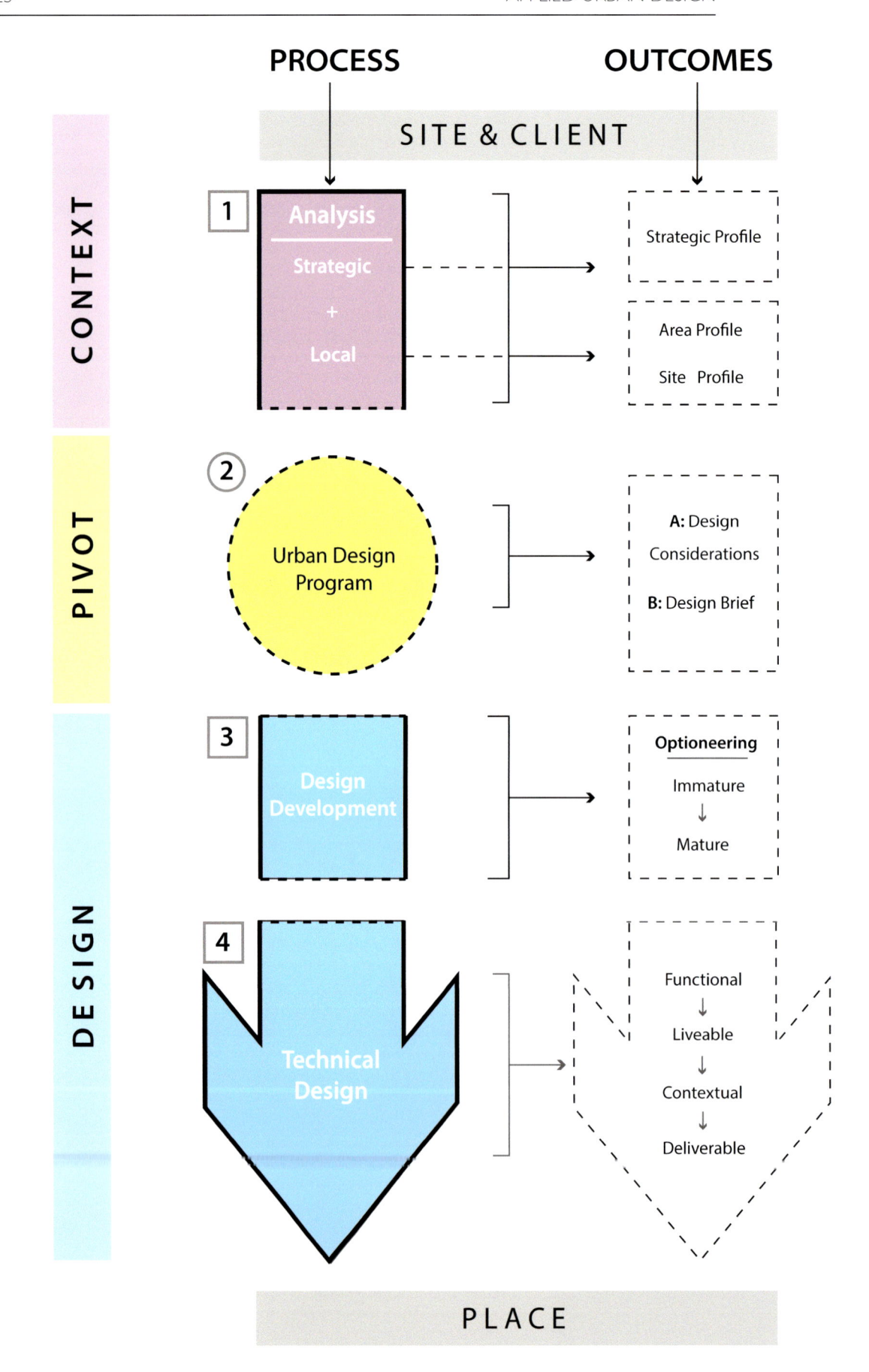

CHAPTER 3: APPLIED URBAN DESIGN FRAMEWORK

What distinguishes the AUD Framework is the foundation of contextual analysis and understanding that then informs each subsequent step – placing analysis at the heart of the design process. Analysing and understanding each project/site's unique context (moving beyond a fixation on the physical environment to also include the social, environmental, economic, and cultural) across a range of scales (strategic and local) provides the necessary knowledge and information that can shape not only the final form of a design, but also the most appropriate type of intervention(s). To utilise this contextual detail prior to designing the AUD Framework introduces *The Urban Design Program* – a bespoke tool for linking analysis to design, acting as a pivot point between information gathering and information application. Finally, to ensure contextual design meets with design quality it is imperative designers understand how to deliver proposals effectively, being armed with the necessary competencies and skills to arrive at final design solutions that have been robustly tested for functionality, quality, contextual responsiveness, and feasibility.

STEP 1: CONTEXTUAL ANALYSIS
Chapters 5 and 6

Habitually designers often begin their analysis at the site level – considering the immediate context within the red-line boundary where they can officially 'design' and construct within, extending out at times only to the proximate surrounding context of adjacent buildings, streets, and spaces. The AUD Framework points designers to begin their analysis at a much wider scale, considering the strategic value of their site as a priority. **Strategic Analysis**, unpacked in Chapter 5, requires the analyst to think firstly about the bigger picture, to ascertain where and how it sits outside its visible limits. Urban design needs to operate beyond the human or architectural scale, considering the greater whole that is made up of the smaller developments that occur across towns and cities. The boundaries of the strategic scale will change from site to site, placing the onus on those analysing to define this explicitly from the outset.

Step 1 also demands that analysis is conducted extensively at the **'Local'** level, explored in further detail in Chapter 6, this is helpfully divided into 2 scales – the area and the site.

The site scale is related to more traditional design analysis techniques, considering the immediate site boundary and adjacent surroundings, to understand the nature of the physical environment and observable visual impacts from neighbouring streets, spaces, and structures. The area scale aims to place this site into a broader local context, understanding the nuances of the proximate neighbourhoods and districts. The area scale must be defined through the analysis conducted but is critical given it is at this scale we can identify the local people who will be most impacted by any future development or design intervention.

Step 1 Outcomes: The production of 3 '**Profiles**' (strategic; area; and site) that outline and illustrate the salient information from the analysis conducted across each scale. These profiles are the culmination of the context building undertaken and are designed to communicate findings to a wide audience of stakeholders. The key feature of these profiles is they are produced before the design stage. Too often analysis is an 'add-on' after the design is presented, to justify particular choices made. Within the AUD Framework the analysis conducted is independent of the design, and the resultant 'Profiles' can be employed by local authorities or communities to better understand their places and spaces and to evaluate and evidence the contextual responsiveness of any future design proposals.

STEP 2: URBAN DESIGN PROGRAM
Chapter 7

Upon completion of the analysis in step 1 there will be a wealth of contextual data that needs to be organised to better assist in developing contextually responsive design approaches. Step 2 introduces the **Urban Design Program** – a bespoke approach for ensuring designers can begin to make sense of the conducted analysis and begin to think about how this will shape and guide potential design solutions. It is therefore a vital 'pivot' point between analysis/context and the design process that follows. The stated outcomes within the Urban Design Program define this pivot. Beginning with *Design Considerations*, here the designer translates key details from Step 1's profiles into how they positively or negatively might impact potential design on the site. Once these design considerations are complete the designer should re-visit the client brief

OPPOSITE: The Applied Urban Design [AUD] Framework.

for the site – testing the demands of the brief against the now identified considerations. From this point the Urban Design Program can deliver the *Design Brief* (made up of 'project objectives' - a series of broader statements of the ambitions for any future design) and 'design actions' (a series of specific guidance for designers to maximise the potential of the site), culminating in a wider *'vision'* for the design that can encapsulate the nature, quality, and ambition of the future development plan. The Urban Design Program has several critical roles to fulfil – shaping contextually responsive design choices of designers following it; providing stakeholders and local communities with clear information on design plans for a site; and acting as a template for the evaluation of design proposals for all interested parties.

STEP 3: DESIGN DEVELOPMENT
Chapter 8

This step moves into the 'design' phase of the AUD Framework, that also includes the final step 4. The design development stage is the exclusive territory of the urban designer and requires a robust understanding of the fundamentals of design (discussed in Chapter 4). The design development stage requires urban designers to translate the Urban Design Program [Step 2] into potential workable design proposals – in essence the process of delivering contextually responsive proposals. To achieve this the AUD Framework provides a definitive **optioneering process**, allowing designers to develop a design from *immature* to *mature* options whilst ensuring function, quality, and context are at the forefront. This optioneering process is critical in allowing designers to 'test' different design outcomes and allow proposals to evolve and be refined.

Shaping design through this optioneering process requires an in-depth and technical understanding of how urban design works in practice – here the AUD Framework provides its user with the design layers that are essential. Twelve layers across 4 'themes' are introduced that provide designers with the design tools to shape function, quality, and context in design terms. These layers act as the blueprint for a proposal, they are the elements that come together to allow the design to operate effectively in practice, and it is in the balance between them that quality place-making occurs.

STEP 4: TECHNICAL DESIGN
Chapters 9 and 10

The final step in the AUD Framework is the Technical Design – this is the final proposed design intervention that is the culmination of steps 1-3. It is the definitive workable and deliverable scheme. A number of key elements are required to be detailed in a design masterplan to ensure it can move towards construction. Chapters 8 and 9 outline the range of details required and how to present these to a wide range of audiences, including planning authorities, clients, local populations, and contactors. The outcomes of Step 4 include technically accurate drawings and plans, essential instructions and guidance, 2D and 3D renderings and illustrations, and a variety of other materials that can effectively communicate core design decisions. This final step also considers how to deliver design, navigating the myriad of challenges and bureaucracy that often complicate urban design projects in the real world.

3.3 HOW THE BOOK WORKS

This book unpacks and articulates the AUD Framework (*see* page 25) across all 4 steps. Supplementing the main body of text are a series of international best practice cases, that bring to life a range of the key concepts and ideas being discussed; and two *'live'* case study projects, that demonstrate the AUD framework in action on 'real-world' sites. These additional elements are provided to illustrate the applied nature of the Framework, moving beyond the theoretical underpinnings to deliver physical interventions in place. The best practice studies are purposefully selected from across a wide range of international settings and design scales to demonstrate the impact of quality urban design, allowing the reader to engage with, and better understand, the nature of urban design as a product. The 'live' cases studies are 2 existing sites, across 2 distinct scales and locations, that have been chosen by the authors to walk-through the AUD Framework process and outcomes – providing the reader with worked-up examples of how the Framework can be operationalised in practice, and critically demonstrate its ability to respond to the unique context of each site it is utilised on.

CHAPTER 3: APPLIED URBAN DESIGN FRAMEWORK

LIVE CASE STUDIES
Two live case studies have been selected by the authors to act as vehicles, and exemplars, for exhibiting the AUD Framework in action internationally. These case studies were carefully chosen to maximise our ability to illustrate the AUD Framework's flexibility, iterative nature, and attest that the process is not a tick-box linear exercise, but rather a contextually driven methodology that will deliver contextually responsive design solutions that are quality focused and people centred. To achieve these goals, we have carefully identified sites that represent very different scales in regards site size; that are within differing geographical, cultural, social, political, and historical settings; and that offer up very different challenges for understanding context and delivering design. By undertaking the AUD Framework on 2 international sites the reader can recognise how the process can be undertaken effectively at a smaller site scale and masterplan scale and learn how outcomes and lessons will differ across heterogenous contexts. It was also vital that the sites be easily accessible to the authors, given both would be worked into complete prototype schemes – for this reason sites in Manchester, UK and Aalborg, Denmark were determined given authors Black, Sonbli, and Phillips are based in Manchester and Martin was, at the time of selection, located in Aalborg.

Each site was treated as a separate urban design project – with the authors acting as a de facto professional urban design practice (Design Lead: Black; Aalborg Analysis Lead: Martin; Manchester Analysis Lead: Phillips; Graphics Lead: Sonbli). Each project undertook the complete AUD Framework process, including the delivery of a final proposed design scheme. Sites visits were carried out at regular stages, by all authors, through the process at both locations.

All visuals, graphics, and details provided within the book for each site project are original work conducted and visualised by the authors. Given the scale of both projects neither is shown as a completed distinct scheme, rather the projects are presented at different times to best represent the AUD Framework in action. Given the book format and the intention of the case studies, it was not possible to always provide all the analysis for both studies. When both are presented simultaneously this is to compare and contrast outcomes to assist the reader in appreciating the unique contexts and how the framework deals with each in different ways. The case studies are not intended to be judged as stand-alone design projects, but rather be understood as aids to assist the reader in developing a clear understanding of the AUD Framework itself. An introduction to the sites follows on pages 29 and 30.

BELOW: Locations of live case study sites - Manchester, UK and Aalborg, Denmark.

APPLIED URBAN DESIGN

AALBORG, Denmark: Sygehus Nord og Gåsepigen [Site Introduction]

Aalborg represents a small-medium sized European city and the fourth city of Denmark with a population of just over 220,000 people. The city is located in the North of the Country and is the capital of the Northern Jutland Region. Situated at the narrowest point of the Limfjord (a body of water spanning the peninsula separating the North Jutlandic Island from the rest of the Jutland Peninsula) the city has an active port, Portland (with trade across the Baltic sea) and cruise liner destination. Since the late 1990s Aalborg has undergone substantial economic restructuring and successive waves of urban regeneration transforming the city from an industrial hub to a knowledge centre and service-led economy. Aalborg is 100km north of Aarhus (Denmark's second city) and with daily connectivity to Copenhagen, Oslo, and Amsterdam via the city's airport (the third airport of the country), it boosts efficient links to the country's capital and wider European cities.

Our site in Aalborg, which is approximately 6ha, is located close to the city centre on the area of land predominately occupied by the city's maternity and children's hospital – known locally as Sygehus Nord-området (Northern Hospital Area) or Sygehus Nord og Gåsepigen (North Hospital and the Goose Girl). A large portion of the site is an important employment area scheduled for closure in 2021 with the health care functions of the site being subsumed by the creation of a new Super Hospital to the south of the city. The site was selected as it sits on the boundary of the historic city centre, the emerging urban quarter of Reberbansgadekvarteret (Reberbans Street Quarter) with it's distinctive *'food street'* as it is known locally and the residential areas of Vestbyen and Hasseris. The Skaagen railway boundary runs along the S/SW of the site creating a distinct edge. The recreational waterfront of the Limfjord and associated regeneration areas are five blocks north (0.5km). Supported by policy and an accompanying development prospectus, the local government (Aalborg Kommune) wish to transform the unique site into a mixed-use hub and capitalise on the opportunity to create a new neighbourhood in the city centre.

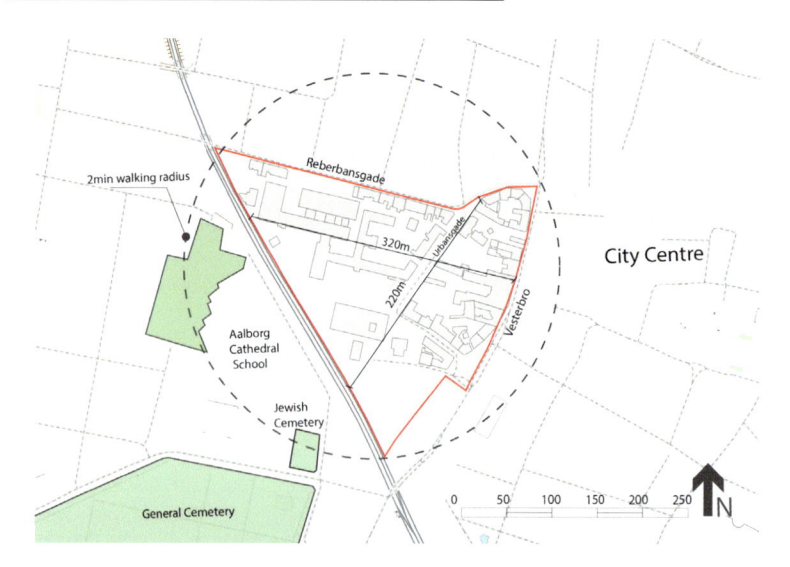

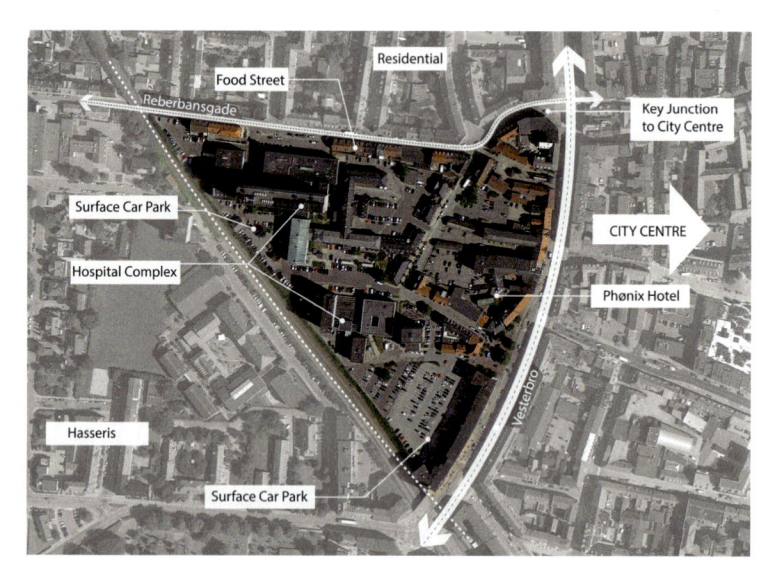

TOP: Aalborg site dimensions.

MIDDLE: Aalborg site top down image and key features.

BOTTOM: Aalborg site - existing hospital.

AALBORG
Site Introduction

CHAPTER 3: APPLIED URBAN DESIGN FRAMEWORK 30

MANCHESTER, United Kingdom:
Ancoats / Miles Platting [Site Introduction]

Manchester was the world first industrial metropolis (Hebbert, 2010), it was a centre for textile manufacturing during the industrial revolution growing rapidly from the middle of the 17th century before, like many of industrial cities in the UK, experiencing equally rapid decline during the post-war period. Manchester city is within the conurbation of Greater Manchester, that hosts a population of 2.8million across an area of 1277 Km2 often being described as England's 'second city'. It is located in the North-West of England, forming part of the Northern Powerhouse, a collection of core cities and regions in the North of England the goal of which is to improve economic output for a series of former industrial cities. Sitting 260Km north of London, Manchester is bordered to the north and east by the Pennines, a chain of upland hills and heathland. Manchester has grown and changed significantly since the mid-1990s, partly triggered by the major regeneration in the city centre in the aftermath of a bombing in 1996 that destroyed much of the historic retail core. The rapid development and international investment in recent years has witnessed Manchester reinvent itself as one of Europe's premier city destinations for both businesses start-ups and tourism.

Our site in Manchester, which is approximately 60ha, is located immediately north-east of the city centre. It is typical of sites in and around Manchester, and northern Europe more generally, where land at the edge of industrial cities, much of it having been a former railways goods depot and latterly the post office, has declined leaving large areas of previously developed – and often contaminated land – within walking distance of successful urban centres. It is indeed only 10–15 minutes walk from the main shopping streets. It comprises of two neighbourhood districts, Ancoats and Miles Platting. The site is in close proximity to two major railway interchanges of Manchester Victoria and Manchester Piccadilly, but also sits between two important arterial routes into the city from the north-east, Oldham Road and Rochdale Road.

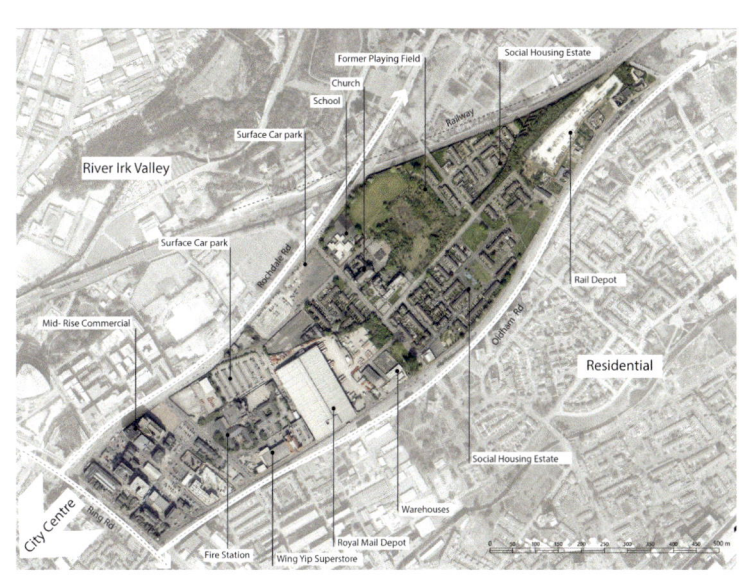

The Ancoats/Miles Platting site is of significance as a part of Manchester City Council's rejuvenated interest and policy initiatives to regenerate the northern fringe of the city with strategic masterplans for adjacent areas to our location including NOMA, and Collyhurst. This is in part driven by a desire to improve the existing neighbourhoods, but ultimately to deliver significant residential growth (in the region of 50,000 new homes) over the next 25 years as part of the city council's 'Neighbourhoods of Choice' initiative.

TOP: Manchester site dimensions.

BOTTOM: Manchester site top down image and key features.

MANCHESTER
Site Introduction

BOOK LAYOUT
Below is a chapter-by-chapter guide to how the book is laid out and structured.

PART A: URBAN DESIGN – AN EMERGING DISCIPLINE

Covering the opening 4 chapters, this section provides readers with a critical overview of the discipline of urban design and introduces them to the core contribution of the book, the Applied Urban Design Framework.

Chapter 1: Urban Design? The Disquisition – A detailed synopsis of the history of urban design, tracing the discipline's roots from early city development, through the 1950's conferences that defined the field as a distinct design vocation, to the present-day complexities and challenges facing the field. This chapter sets out the need for urban design to consolidate its substantive knowledge and move forward in delivering clearer and more appropriate applied approaches for designing and re-developing place.

Chapter 2: Towards Contextually Responsive Urban Design – The chapter considers urban design as an applied and technical vocation, by discussing why design matters and what quality design might look like. Readers are introduced to how urban design can be shaped in this manner through 4 themes: scales; structures; connections; and principles. We introduce the centrality of context in the design process – advocating the need for urban design interventions that are contextually responsive and propose a process for the delivery of such context-led design - The Applied Urban Design Framework.

Chapter 3: The Applied Urban Design Framework – Establishes the approach that forms the basis of this book, showcasing the AUD Framework's development, transferability, and flexibility. This chapter announces the Framework itself, providing a simple guide to the process step-by-step – and how the book aims to articulate and illustrate it effectively across each subsequent chapter, supplemented by International best practice and 2 live case studies in Manchester, UK and Aalborg, Denmark (both of which are introduced).

Chapter 4: Making Sense of Design – This chapter is designed to establish the fundamental knowledge required for effective application of the AUD Framework, presenting the building blocks of how urban design works, the key to delivering quality contextually responsive design in practice, and centralising a people first approach. Functional design layers are examined, as are the liveable aspects that ensure quality for people.

PART B: APPLIED URBAN DESIGN FRAMEWORK

The core of the book and main contribution – Chapters 5-10 cover the main stages of the AUD Framework in detail – from context to pivot to design. This section includes the 2 live case studies that act as worked exemplars of the AUD Framework in practice internationally.

Chapter 5: Strategic Analysis – This chapter unpacks the nature and purpose of strategic analysis – with a clear introduction of the core elements a designer or analyst must consider as part of their process. Critically the chapter also provides the reader with techniques for applying strategic analysis and how they can take lessons from their findings.

Chapter 6: Local Analysis – Continuing with contextual analysis, this chapter articulates the purpose and the main elements of 'local' analysis – proposing 2 scales, the area, and the site, from which to work. The chapter establishes the range of variables that should be considered and how to organise and apply findings. The 'Profile' outcomes are also discussed, illustrating how to present and visualise salient analysis data to a range of audiences.

Chapter 7 – The Urban Design Program – The beating heart of the AUD Framework is the Urban Design Program, a pivot that seeks to effectively link the wealth of contextual analysis conducted into contextually responsive design drivers. This key chapter discusses how to apply the analysis to deliver design considerations, incorporate the client's brief, and develop clear and justified design objectives and actions that will form the basis of a design proposal and any future design evaluations. The Urban Design Program seeks to bring all aspects together to find synergies, overcome tensions, and establish the most appropriate way forward.

OPPOSITE: Local street, Severitgasse, Vienna, Austria.

Chapter 8: Design Development – Covering step 3 of the AUD Framework, this chapter provides a clear understanding of how to move beyond the analysis stage and begin designing. Introducing a bespoke optioneering process driven by the Urban Design Program – and how this can be evaluated to ensure maximum quality and contextual response.

Chapter 9: Technical Design – This chapter tackles the final step of the AUD Framework - providing readers with a detailed understanding of how design works, considering the functional blueprints necessary for structuring contextually responsive urban design - and the human scaled details that elevate a design to be liveable, sustainable, and high-quality. These are discussed utilising three 'super-components' of design - urban blocks, the public realm, and green infrastructure.

Chapter 10: Design Delivery – The final chapter of PART B focuses on how to communicate applied urban design to a diverse range of audiences through a range of professional techniques and visualisations. It ends by thinking through real-world delivery and implementation.

PART C: URBAN DESIGN FUTURES
This final section incorporates 2 short chapters that look to the future, of both the application of the AUD Framework but also the discipline of urban design.

Chapter 11: Reflections on the AUD Framework – Considers how our bespoke approach can shape place under different circumstances and contexts – The chapter critically reflects on the live cases studies and discusses the transferability of the Framework, and its wider considerations. The world is constantly evolving and cities are having to adapt to growing challenges and emerging issues – we argue that urban design must be flexible, equipped, and ready to respond.

Chapter 12: Re-Framing Urban Design
 Tho final chaptor is our, the authors', call for urban design to evolve and take on more responsibility in how our cities and places provide quality for people. We see the role of the urban designer as central to the success of urban environments – and petition for action in education, policy, politics, and in the professional world of urban design.

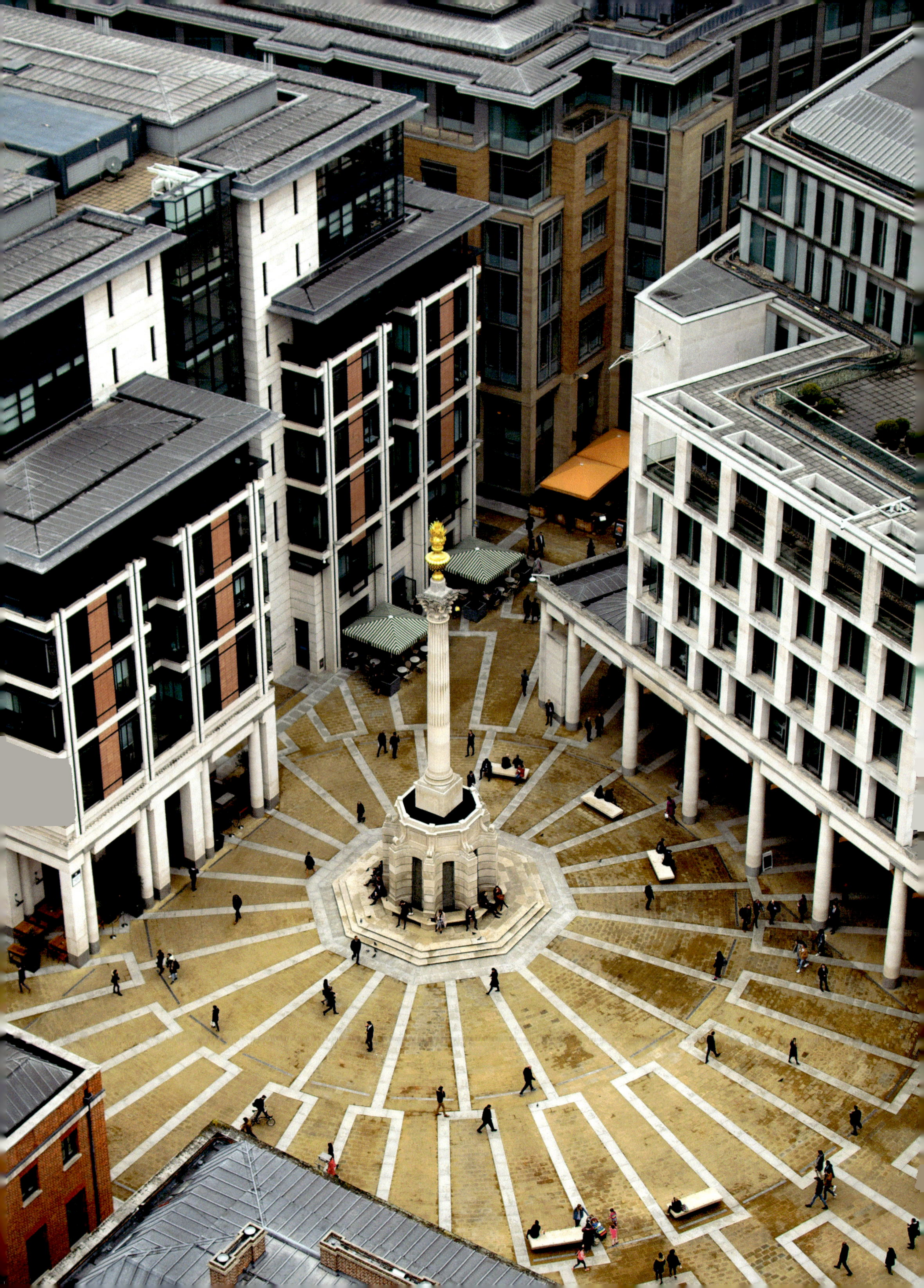

CHAPTER 4
Making Sense of Design

To successfully engage with the Applied Urban Design Framework (introduced in Chapter 3) in practice, it is critical for the user (be that a designer, planner, local community, or other interested party) to have a working knowledge of the fundamental components of urban design, the building blocks of placemaking. The key to delivering quality contextually responsive solutions through applying the AUD Framework, we argue, is a necessary awareness of 3 core considerations.

1. Contextual Dynamics
2. Liveable Qualities
3. Functional Blueprints

Chapter 2 articulates the meaning of 'context' for urban design – and its vital importance in shaping and delivering places for people. For the AUD Framework to work in the way it was intended it is essential that the contextual dynamics at play for each site/location are analysed and understood. Chapters 5 and 6 are dedicated to this pursuit. It is not enough however, to build contextual knowledge – having the working knowledge and competencies to pivot this information into design solutions is imperative. This chapter is therefore dedicated to providing instruction on the core design principles that define *'liveable qualities'* – and the central design layers necessary provide the *'functional blueprints'* for any proposed scheme. It is in the balance of these 3 considerations noted above, **contextual dynamics**; **liveable qualities**; and **functional blueprints** that quality place-making occurs.

4.1 URBAN DESIGN AS PLACEMAKING

The emphasis on designing quality, liveable environments for people is now central to the practice of urban design - much of this work is achieved through placemaking. Over the past 30 years, a place-making/shaping tradition of urban design has focused on the revitalisation of urban cores, the promotion of density and mixed-use, and changes to public spaces and street-level design (Jensen et al., 2021). Place design, public realm design, masterplanning, design policies, guidance, and control, as well as community or participatory urban design have built steadily in that time as the dominating practices of the urban design profession (Carmona, 2021). Contemporary urban design is simultaneously concerned with the physical design of urban places and their aesthetic qualities as well as the behavioural settings of buildings and spaces for people and their activities.

Notable early examples of people-first urban design could be seen in the reprioritisation of pedestrians in cities and public spaces, particularly in European cities, to promote walkable city streets and districts, such as the Dutch concept of a woonerf and the US complete streets (Jensen et al., 2021).

More recently in response to COVID-19, cities internationally radically reprioritised urban infrastructure to promote active movement and sustainable mobility – providing new evidence of the emancipatory potential of people-first placemaking in cities (Deas et al., 2021). A body of global work has appeared on the significance of people-oriented design and planning. Building on the seminal works of Jacobs (1961), Gehl (1987), and Lynch (1990) amongst others, contemporary research and practice has expanded considerations of urban design to a multitude of broader issues, including public health, climate change, social equity, and sustainable mobility. These discourses have helped determine new indicators for designers to embed quality in their practice - expanding the place-making tradition of urban design and the territory of the discipline more broadly (we explore a range of these *'liveable'* qualities in this chapter).

**OPPOSITE:
Paternoster Square, London, England.**

PLACEMAKING FRAMEWORKS

Place-making has been embraced in "'official' definitions of urban design" internationally and is now synonymous with the discipline itself (Carmona 2002: 10). As part of the making-place tradition of urban design, frameworks which seek to identify desirable qualities of successful urban places and/or 'good' urban form have materialised internationally. Underpinning, and in many ways defining, the notion of placemaking are a wide variety of indicators such as vitality (Lynch, 1981), liveability (Jacobs and Appleyard, 1987), permeability (Bentley et al., 1985) and pedestrian freedom (Tibbalds, 1992) to name a few examples. One of the most important versions of this came with the publication of *By Design: Urban Design in the Planning System: Towards Better Practice* (DETR and CABE, 2000) in 2000. *By Design* established a more rounded and complete definition of urban design in England as the *'art of making places for people'* and stipulated seven objectives for successful placemaking: 1. character, 2. continuity and enclosure, 3. quality of the public realm, 4. ease of movement, 5. legibility, 6. adaptability, 7. diversity and sustainability. The seminal publication shaped the practice of urban design and planning toward better practice to great effect, influencing much of the urban regeneration to occur in the UK and beyond since the millennium (Punter, 2009), until its disbandment in 2010.

An important consideration here is how placemaking components change over time, and their susceptibility to change over time, as societal needs evolve. In the two decades since, the seven place-making criteria of By Design were officially replaced with the "*10 Characteristics of Well-Designed Places*" in the *National Model Design Code* 2021 (MHCLG, 2021). Defined as 1. Context, 2. Identity, 3. Built form, 4. Movement, 5. Nature, 6. Public Spaces, 7. Uses, 8. Homes and Buildings, 9. Resources and 10. Lifespan. While some continuity exists between terms from By Design, changes over time are very likely and thus it is important to recognise place-making as an iterative dynamic process heavily influenced by what is 'deemed' desirable at the time. We can see the spread and acceptance of the practice of place-making through the wide range of urban design policy replicated around the world such as the *Street Design Manual for Oslo*, or the *Central Melbourne Design Guide*.

Learning from established placemaking/shaping frameworks, the AUD Framework operationalises and defines specific indicators for the practice of contextually responsive place-making and design. Nonetheless, it is important to publicise a disclaimer here. While theoretical frameworks and the 'qualities of good places' listed across numerous design policies and guidance provide helpful tools to define desirable design principles – urban design cannot be reduced to a linear formula. Rather urban design is a complex, creative, goal-oriented activity, and one that is site/situation specific. Frameworks of design quality stress the outcomes or products of urban design, rather than the process and the iterative, interactive nature of urban design: they indicate the qualities of 'good' or 'best practice' design but not how such places can or should be delivered or achieved (Carmona, 2021).

IMAGES: *Street Design Manual for Oslo and Central Melbourne Design Guide.*

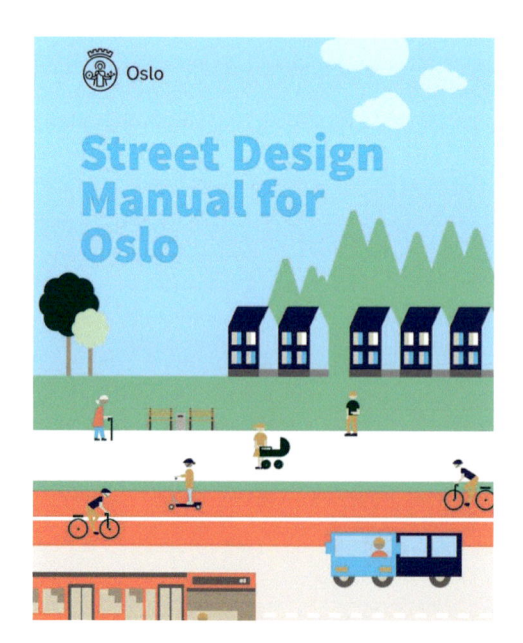

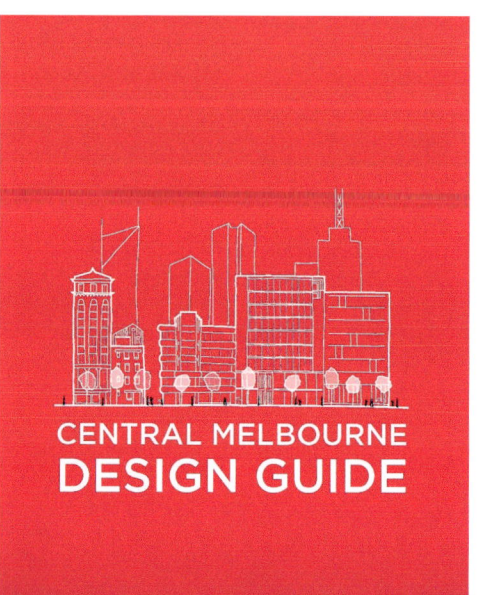

CHAPTER 4: MAKING SENSE OF DESIGN

SERVING HUMAN NEED

In designing quality places, urban design serves human need. Successful urban design and place-making must attend to, and get people on board, promoting the types of activities, uses and interventions that serve the public interest. Ultimately, urban design should express social values and should act in the name of the public interest (Cozzolino et al., 2020). Of particular importance is the role of participatory practices of urban design, collaborative urban design, and co-creative placemaking with communities. New variations of these practices, which seek to incorporate the views and opinions of those individuals/groups who have been side-lined, and even removed, from the design discourse and matters of design historically, show the social progression of the discipline in recent years. A notable example includes the burgeoning expansion of designer-child collaboration and the promotion of children/youth as active agents in the design and planning of contemporary city spaces (Martin et al., 2023).

Urban design and designers thus need to understand the contexts (social, cultural, economic, environmental, and physical) within which they operate, the processes by which places are made and developments realised and how to respond to the changing nature of the urban condition (Black and Sonbli, 2019; Carmona, 2021). The Applied Urban Design Framework outlined in this book, advocates urban design as the process/practice of providing quality contextually responsive places for people. We set out the theory and practice of how urban design can deliver as an applied technical discipline to promote and provide more contextually responsive interventions in our cities and places. In doing so, we feel that specific qualities of design should be prioritised and that ultimately urban design should be people first. To help exemplify our thinking, we unpack **10 Liveable Qualities for Urban Design** to help make sense of quality contextually responsive design. Following these aspects, we provide the critical *'design layers'* that allow designers to create such spaces and places, the *'functional blueprints'* that underpin how design works in the real-world.

IMAGES: Walking neighbourhoods with communities as a form of co-creative placemaking.

TOP: Nordbhanhoff, Vienna, Austria.

BOTTOM: Av. Diagonal, Barcelona, Spain.

4.2 10 LIVEABLE QUALITIES FOR URBAN DESIGN [A-J]

A: PEOPLE FIRST

The heart of quality urban design is to approach all design decisions with people as central to the process and outcome. Urban design must play a central role in creating places that are easy to understand for all in society, mixing compatible developments that work in harmony to create viable places that aim to provide what people want and need. The core principle, and indeed the entire field of practice of urban design, is that all design should be human scaled. Transferrable lessons internationally over a sustained period have shown the importance of urban design solutions which promote, prioritise, and protect design that is optimised for human use. This applies to multiple perspectives from the physical i.e. the ways in which the urban fabric has been designed, constructed and made in terms of the choice of materials, spatial layout, crafted morphology and programming but also the psychological (how we register the world around us and perceive the environment in an embodied and specific way).

Urban design and the articulation of policies, plans and designs for cities must be aware of the ontological dimensions of their projects. The way we perceive and sense the world as we move through it is of fundamental importance to how we understand it. Thus, as urban designers we must consider how we structure the activities of the city to promote positive embodied experiences, healthy urban lifestyles, and liveable, social urban environments. Wayfinding, wayfaring, and nudging (how it feels to move in/through the city) must be designed to maximise human experience and elicit the best response from human users.

Across the world, the arrangements, and networks of cities are too often designed for the prioritisation of cars and highways. To make our cities more liveable, urban design must promote choices and priorities that are consistent with the human-scale city. Walkable, cyclable cities are core to this agenda, promote better air quality and foster a healthier approach to mobility irrespective of ability or age (Jensen et al., 2021).

Sustainable mobility choices go hand in hand with active places and spaces. In responding to the 1970s oil crisis with the promotion of walking and cycling, cities across Denmark, the Netherlands and Sweden were able to promote urban cycling infrastructure as a serious form of transport.

Through safer cycling/walking routes activities remained rooted in the urban context making urban living more sociable and attractive. As emphasised by Sim (2020), recognition and care for the human dimension of urban design was instrumental in creating a renaissance in urban living in Copenhagen through dense low-cost housing, sustainable mobility, sensitive changes to existing city blocks (rather than slum clearance or mass demolition) and the integration of ecology. Dense-low streets and public spaces are those which choose people first. The point is to change attitudes to the design of roads as places, as streets for all – placing the individual, not the car as the priority.

People first urban design is life orientated and should aspire to be socially just, equitable and inclusive, and for the benefit of all citizens. Urban design should be playful, encourage activity and relationships. We are beginning to see this in urban design solutions focused on intergenerational design. In recognition of broader demographic shifts globally, with projections that the global population of individuals over 60 years of age will exceed the number of people under 10 by 2030, designers must navigate the implications of a society that expects to live longer and better in urban environments. New directions in urban design in the form of intergenerational place, space and communities highlight the unique possibilities in urban interventions that transcend older and younger generations.

CHAPTER 4: MAKING SENSE OF DESIGN   38

ABOVE: Cheonggyecheon, Seoul, South Korea. The city removed an elevated vehicle highway to provide a 11km long stream and public space, putting people at the centre of design in the city.

BOTTOM LEFT: Protecting pedestrians with restricted vehicle access in Bratislava, Slovakia.

BOTTOM RIGHT: Seville, Spain transformed its mobility options with over 100km of segregated cycle lanes creating people-friendly neighbourhoods across the city.

B: FOR EVERYONE

Our experiences of the city are dependent on our gender, race, class, age, ability, and sexual orientation (Doucet, et al., 2021). Cities around the world are divided and are becoming increasingly unequal. A critical function of urban design is to pull back the curtain on many of these pre-existing inequalities. Urban design must engage directly with different communities around the world. As professionals, urban designers must give a voice to those who experience poverty, discrimination, and marginalisation in order to put them in the front and centre of design, planning, policy and political debates that make and shape cities (Doucet et al., 2021).

After decades of research in the US, we know that low-income or disadvantaged households – particularly foreign-born people or those whose parents were foreign-born – experience more environmental disadvantages and exposure to pollution (Banzhaf et al., 2019). In Europe, recent research has shown that in Austria, the risk of living near industrial facilities is twice as high for immigrants than for the majority population (Glatter-Götz et al., 2019). Likewise, studies in Germany show that migrants and ethnic groups are exposed to more disadvantages than ethnic Germans including access to better quality neighbourhoods and green spaces (Jünger, 2022).

In designing for more equitable, representative, and just spaces it is worth considering the now 30-year-old gender-sensitive planning and design agenda of Vienna as well as projects such as Superkilen in Nørrebro, Copenhagen which was designed to improve social cohesion in one of the city's most diverse and multi-ethnic neighbourhoods through the development of public spaces that promote and encourage intercultural encounters (Daly, 2020). Superkilen Park includes features that represent public spaces in over 60 countries associated with the diverse residential migrant population of the neighbourhood.

It is important to develop a comprehensive appreciation of the diversity of the local community associated with the city and the site – this should be done in an attempt to understand how representation and inclusivity can come forward in other aspects of the analysis (*see* Chapter 5). Urban design has an ever-increasing role to play towards building social cohesion in multicultural cities, a detailed understanding of the diversity of the community is a critical starting point in this endeavour. We recommend using recent policy and demographic data to build this picture.

VIENNA, AUSTRIA has undertaken a programme of gender-mainstreaming which considers the needs of persons who are often overlooked. Thus, gender, age, and group-specific interests and effects are systematically examined. Through innovative urban governance, including the formation of the *Department for Gender Mainstreaming*, Vienna's gender-mainstreaming initiative has given rise to a wide range of inclusive design interventions including: an outdoor performance space in Reumannplatz, Mädchenbühne (girls' stage) – specifically requested by local schoolgirls, the city's first transgender crosswalk located close to the Vienna General Hospital; determined efforts to make the queer community more visible including illustrations of same-sex couples in traffic lights; and a pavement widening program to provide parents navigating the city with prams or children with more space (Illien, 2021).

LEFT: LGBTQ+ crosswalk installed in efforts to make city spaces feel more inclusive for under-represented minorities.

CHAPTER 4: MAKING SENSE OF DESIGN 40

TOP: Superkilen Park, Copenhagen - designed to represent over 60 countries associated with the local residential population.

MIDDLE: Provision of play-space for teenagers in Elizabeth Ter, Budapest.

BOTTOM: Copenhagen, Denmark delivering a renaissance in urban living through people-first design and sustainable mobility options.

C: EXPERIENCE MATTERS

People want characterful places, places with their own distinct identity and that reflect the local community and history of the space - how we experience a place matters and how we design for experience is core. Mixed densities and typologies can stimulate interest and differentiate spaces. Providing layers of experiences allow residents to work, live, and play all within the same place and foster unique characteristics that contribute to its distinctiveness for people (Black and Sonbli, 2019). Recognising that mixed-use development is key to attract people to live in higher-density areas, it is important to invest strategically in human-scale density and ground-floor spaces for non-residential uses. Buildings with active frontages should be deliberately placed along busy routes. Urban block typologies which prioritise street-life and ground floor experiences are key to successful urban living and revitalisation as demonstrated by the world-famous Superblock model of Barcelona or more recently, Milan's Piazze Aperte (open piazza) initiative. Milan, through tactical urbanism using only paint, planters, benches, and ping-pong tables, brought streets back to life in 38 places across the city, creating 22ha of new pedestrian space. The project redesigned neighbourhood streets as places for social interaction, vitality and gathering with a particular focus on children, the elderly, and disabled people. Through low-cost, high-impact street transformations and working with residents, Milan has successfully activated underused and unequipped space encouraging community spirit, and the promotion of cultural and group activities that can add value and life to the street (City of Milan, 2022).

The cases of Barcelona and Milan emphasise that both designing for street life and retrofitting to (re)create street life are important – prioritising character-led place-making by working with communities. People's engagement with the ground floor is key, and accommodating multiple functions by layering are core to liveable urban design. Spektrumhuset in Gothenburg Sweden is an excellent example of how contemporary design, covering a full urban block, can have active frontages on all four sides (Sim, 2020). The building takes full advantages of layering with bowling in the basement, a restaurant, and shops on the ground floor, two levels of school classrooms, a co-working space and a playground across the top floor and roof terrace. Examples like the Spektrum building show how one building can contain many different uses and, at the same time, activate its edges toward the surrounding streets. Market halls are excellent examples of similar uses internationally, with many entrances creating affordances for street-life on all sides.

Urban design can create street-life through unique ground-floor experiences, it's about more than just shops. Different kinds of active ground floors can include murals/public art, family homes, special needs home, offices, workshops, childcare, healthcare, showrooms/galleries, salons, fitness, concept shops/specialist stores. Personalisation of the edge can take many forms, townhouses with a mini garden of potted plants out front, folding chairs outside of stores, awnings around cafes and display tables outside shops can all spread activities into the street creating a vibrant pedestrian promenade (Sim, 2020). Overall, soft density, human-scale heights, and active streets matter for quality urban design.

BELOW: Piazze Aperte 'Open Squares' is a tactical urbanism program in Milan, Italy, which enhances public spaces turning them into community gathering places. The program extends pedestrian areas and promotes sustainable forms of mobility to improve the quality of life in the city.

LEFT: Venice, Italy. How we feel in a place matters - how we remember it matters. The emotions it evokes in us should be positive and enhance our wellbeing. Urban design has the power to deliver places that uplift people.

D: TRANSPARENCY OF SPACE(S)

The creation of places that are easy to understand for all in society, both in terms of moving around the city, but also in appreciating the different roles of spaces in the city are critical. Urban design carefully configures the fabric of our cities and this has a lasting effect on how we use or inhabit them – as well as who uses and inhabits them (Lara-Hernandez, 2022). The importance of democratic, attractive public space in supporting a sense of safety, public life and social interactions are central to high-quality urban design (Andersen et al., 2016). The transparency of urban spaces is not only about set pieces such as plazas or public squares but also refers to the routes that connect them. As pioneered by Kevin Lynch, thinking about how to produce more legible environments i.e. the qualities which make a place graspable - in terms of recognisable paths (routes), focal places such as nodes and well-considered landmarks - can enable people to develop a clearer sense of the choices and qualities a place offers and the type of place it is, between public, private or semi-private (Bentley et al., 1985).

Public and private spaces are necessary in cities, if everywhere were accessible to everyone, there would be no privacy. The interplay between public and private gives people another major source of richness and choice, but people need to be able to understand the interfaces between them and determine what is private and public space (Bentley et al., 1985). These layers of the city should be easy for users to visually recognise and interpret, making place transparent and ensuring that people feel at ease, avoiding confusion as they move in/through the city. Successful urban design interventions carefully consider the democratic fabric of the city, where common spaces, shared private spaces (or semi-private spaces) and completely private spaces all co-exist. One particularly successful example of this practice is the Barbican area in London – through a combination of signage, boundary treatments, defensible spaces and soft barriers, a clear demarcation between public, semi-private, and fully private spaces has been realised. This is complimented by additional rules on the hours of operation for public space to ensure privacy and comfort for residents.

In our use of cities, we typically only make use of routes and spaces where we feel represented. Urban design can make people less likely to use public spaces if designers do not pay heed to what local people actually think of their city. The rise of privately owned public spaces in cities blurs the boundaries of democratic space stretching the interface between open and accessible public spaces and closed inaccessible private spaces, adding a new category, accessible spaces with rules. These spaces are hotly debated in urban design as deeply problematic (Rosenberger, 2020), or alternatively, a common feature of the urban realm where privately owned but publicly accessible spaces have always existed, with many publicly owned and managed spaces also restricted in how we can use them. What matters is how 'public' they are.

In cities around the globe – from Algiers, Auckland, and Chicago to Hanoi, Mexico City, and Seoul – research shows that transforming urban spaces, particularly public spaces, markedly affects the diversity of what people do in them, and whether they use them (Lara-Hernandez, 2018). The historic Alameda Central Park neighbourhood of Mexico City, after it was transformed in 2013, recorded a notable decline in the diversity of activities people undertook there (Giglia, 2013). Before, family, and religious gatherings, street art, music and informal vendors would temporarily appropriate and use the space. Instead, the law now prioritises touristic activity over local people's everyday needs and allows the authorities to operate a zero-tolerance approach towards anything deemed disruptive – particularly vending. Our rights as citizens within space are key. The Alameda Central Park example highlights the implications of redefining what should be inclusive public spaces for local people as exclusive spaces for specific defined activities.

Placemaking for people aimed at increasing social interaction, heightening safety, and improving accessibility improves transparency. Lighting, signs, benches, bollards, fountains, planters, in addition to surveillance equipment are now the common street furniture in urban places. Simple interventions g can make a significant difference to how spaces are used and enjoyed by stakeholders that may otherwise avoid those locations.

CHAPTER 4: MAKING SENSE OF DESIGN   44

ABOVE: Alameda Central Park, Mexico City - re-designed to enhance '*quality*' but in doing so restricted '*choice*' - opening a debate around how '*public*' the space now is for local users.

LEFT: The Barbican, London - created clear demarcations between private, semi-private, and public.

E: FIRST AND LAST MILE

Integrated mobilities design is central to contemporary placemaking. The promotion of multi-modal transportations hubs and systems of infrastructure are a fundamental requirement of designing for quality in our cities. Modernist design agendas promoted a distinct separation between different modes of transport through physical barriers. However, current design and planning practices are challenging this idea (Jensen, 2014). The prioritisation of everyday mobility as more than just the movement of people from A to B but as a method to promote travel time as a social interaction with other physical and mental health benefits represents a critical shift in policy and practice agendas. Rather than as a synonym for 'cars' or 'transportation', new perspectives within urban design and planning are more closely connecting mobility with liveability (the quality of urban life, standard of living or general well-being in the city).

How urban mobilities systems are designed is key to ensuring that multi-modal networks are supported by successful transportation hubs rooted in the heart of cities, that the first and last mile are integrated and supported by uninterrupted infrastructure and that journeys are pleasant and terminated by destinations that are integrated into/with the principles of the network such as the ability to park a bike at a rail/tram stop or alternatively that these systems support passengers taking their bikes onto the network.

In Salerno, Italy for example they have created an attractive pedestrian link from the main railway station to the city centre - that passes by the city's university and main colleges. The tree-lined walkway provides much needed shade and has a dedicated cycle-lane and ample seating points along the route to allow rest. It is not only now a key journey from a key node to a key destination, but is in fact an attraction in itself and has cut the need for less sustainable transport into the city centre district.

ABOVE: Creating a well-designed and comfortable journey from the main station to the city centre attractions - Salerno, Italy.

CHAPTER 4: MAKING SENSE OF DESIGN   46

THE CITY OF AARHUS, Denmark, is a best practice example of how these principles can be achieved in policy and practice. Since 2008, Aarhus Kommune (municipality or local authority) has prioritised an ambitious target of becoming a carbon neutral city by 2030 (Aarhus Kommune, 2015). To reach this goal, the city has focused strategically on designing a multi-modal mobilities system, constructing a light rail (completed in 2017), improving the conditions for cycling, re-routing traffic, and requiring all urban transformation comply with the Kommune's liveability goals. Supported by high level local policy, including the *Urban Development Vision*, 2015 and the *Municipal Plan* 2017, Aarhus promotes an approach to mobility centred on liveability to "promote integrated solutions between infrastructure and services and social, leisure, psychological and spiritual wellbeing" (Aarhus Kommune, 2016). The City's vision was that *"the car has less priority due to spatial restrictions and environmental challenges. Focusing on growth in public transportation, cycling and walking in the inner city will lead to new possibilities for public space in the city"* (Ibid.).

A wide range of projects for cycling, walking, and public transport have since materialised. The creation of the city's first bicycle highway on Grønnegade, a new integrated route that connects residential areas, the city's business park, and the new University Hospital to Aarhus Central Rail Station. Upgrades to the city's historic bicycle ring (implemented in 1996) which minimises the number of cars in the city centre and enables cyclists to move around the inner city without cutting through the inner pedestrianised core. These included transforming 11 streets into cycling streets all of which are integrated into the city-wide cycle network which connects across Aarhus and into suburban neighbourhoods as well as the creation of 180 new bicycle parking places, the installation of air pumps across the city, information signs around bicycling infrastructure and speed tables for safe crossings. However, the flagship of this approach to liveable and integrated transport is Aarhus' Dokk 1, a cultural transportation hub on the city's waterfront. Opened in 2015 and featuring a culture centre, public library, children's play area, rental offices, and a local government building, Dokk 1, is representative of smart and sustainable urban mobilities design.

The project features a recreational belt through which the light railway and a new cycle network runs with a dedicated station at Dokk 1 and over 450 cycle parking spaces. A larger under-ground car park for private vehicles also serves the building. The transport project has resulted in a new civic hub for the city, connecting the city with the port and water, the wider infrastructure network and showcases best practice in urban mobilities design.

F: GREENING / COMFORT

The local ecology of cities is of critical importance to urban design, delivering quality design at the intersection of ecology and landscape must be at the heart of contemporary urban projects if they are to be considered effective and responsive practice. The critical functions of green/blue infrastructure are social and economic as well as environmental, including bringing benefits for recreation, mental well-being, air quality, micro-climate, water, food, energy, and wildlife (Barton, 2017).

Here, research consistently shows how quality, integrated green infrastructure can impact positively on quality of life. An ecological approach to urban design that takes the natural features of an area as a starting point – to promote access to landscape, water courses, wildlife corridors, and recreational walking and cycling routes as well as multi-functional open spaces as part of a connected network – are imperative for the future-proofing of cities both in their response to broader crises.

While networks are of critical importance, greening is also about recognising the importance of incorporating green features at multiple scales across the built environment. Street trees and green roofs, for example, perform many important functions in cities. Street trees add aesthetic quality to an urban area, making places inviting to stop, stay, and rest by providing shade, reducing urban temperature, mitigating wind-chill and airborne pollution as well as increasing biodiversity. To ensure the comfort and health of the city and its citizens, urban design must bolster green and blue infrastructure provision at a range of scales – from linear features to individual components – and ensure equitable access to green/blue spaces for all people.

TURIA GARDENS, Valencia

transformed the former course and dried riverbed of the Turia river into a 12km long linear park, connecting the neighbouring city of Mislata with the Port of Valencia. Meandering through the historic centre of Valencia and at 160m wide, Turia Gardens is an international best practice example of greening, comfort, and access to high quality urban greenspaces for an entire city. Responding to climate challenges, promoting the urban health agenda, urban habitat, and creating dynamic spaces for a wide range of leisure activities including intergenerational approaches that engage children and the elderly directly. Turia Gardens includes numerous civic services and functions including cafes, cycle paths, sports facilities, ponds, play spaces, fountains, and museums. The project has encouraged and facilitated new forms of active travel and is used as a principal means of commuting from the city centre to adjoining parts of the city as well as the wider metropolitan area. Turia Gardens is representative of a broader trend in urban design and landscape architecture to renew and upgrade disused linear infrastructures for the promotion of urban ecology including the High Line in New York, the Cheonggeyechon River in Seoul, and the Castlefield Viaduct in Manchester

CHAPTER 4: MAKING SENSE OF DESIGN 48

ABOVE: Integrating green infrastructure in innovative ways - underpass in Girona, Spain

LEFT: Vertical greening for climate response and comfort - Bosco Verticale, Milan, Italy.

G: SENSE OF PLACE

Urban designers, through their processes and practices, must develop an understanding of *'sense of place'* (Eisenhauer et al., 2000). Sense of place refers, firstly, to people – the social interactions between family and friends, related activities, and traditions, plus the memories associated with these. Secondly, it refers to the physical environment – the natural, landscape, scenery, climate, geological features, environmental setting, and wildlife. However, and most importantly, it refers to emotions and experience – how a place makes a person feel.

Sense of place is strongly linked with heritage, culture, and character. Places that are distinctive, memorable, and have their own identity are typically more popular with residents, everyday users, and visitors. While all places have distinctive place-based qualities and characteristics, in urban design, the most successful places and spaces build on the past, incorporating heritage and culture, distinctive assets and materiality in the present to ensure they form part of the city's future. Urban design must work directly with local vernacular, the local design features and elements that present the material fabric of the place – local building materials, historic building practices, detail, form, and function.

Collectively, these aspects showcase what makes a place unique, whether that be the historic nature of the architecture, the configuration and design of streets, or the upgrading and renewal of lost or previously covered natural features such as the de-culverting of historic waterways. Sense of place is more than historic areas or a focus on protected features, rather it is about working with a place over time to capture the evolution of multiple eras and imprints on the city – how the distinctive identity changes over time between social, physical, and multisensorial factors. In Puerto Madero in Buenos Aries or the Aalborg Waterfront we see how historic dock areas can be re-galvanised to provide new city experiences building on a place's working industrial past and industrialised watercourses to create places and spaces which celebrate their unique local qualities and provide new opportunities for leisure, work, and play.

TOP: Bo-Kaap area of Cape Town, South Africa with its distinctive pastel coloured houses creating a unique sense of place.

BOTTOM: Aalborg, Denmark waterfront redevelopment builds on the city's rich industrial heritage.

CHAPTER 4: MAKING SENSE OF DESIGN   50

DERRY/LONDONDERRY, Northern Ireland, has worked directly with its history of conflict to create new urban experiences which capture Derry's unique sense of place. The city's historic Guildhall, city walls, and river have been brought together through a series of high-quality upgrades to the public realm (including water features, public art, and green infrastructure), a new visitor centre unpacking the city's historical development and the realisation of the Peace Bridge – connecting, for the first time, the west bank of the River Foyle with the Waterside area of Derry/Londonderry at Ebrington Square (a former military site). Collectively, these projects tackle the city's post-conflict identity, they work with memory, landscape, and emotion to design a shared urban fabric and future. The city's unique sense of place and character saw it recognised, in 2013, as the first UK City of Culture.

TOP: Derry is the only completely intact walled city in Ireland - the walls were constructed in 1613-1619.

MIDDLE: Shipquay Place frames the neogothic ornate Guildhall and sits adjacent the Peace Flame - an enclosed eternal flame representing all cultures coming together.

BOTTOM: Derry light marbles - part of the UK City of Culture celebrations.

H: CONTINUITY

The design of the built environment creates separations between different types of settings. The typical fabric of the city, where common spaces, shared private spaces (or semi-private spaces) and completely private spaces all co-exist and must be carefully distinguished. For the built environment to be intuitive to users, urban design should promote the continuity of street frontages and the enclosure of space through development which clearly defines and distinguishes public and private areas. Working with context is critical to making the urban fabric coherent as development can either contribute to and enhance the urban fabric or undermine it entirely (DETR and CABE, 2000). The perimeter courtyard blocks of Danish and Swedish cities – with common active spaces fronting to the streets, shared private communal green space in the middle of the block, and private gardens, decks or balconies which flow directly off the communal space - provides a clear, understandable, and well-defined pattern of continuity and enclosure, particularly as the pattern is repeated across the district, neighbourhood, or city in these contexts. The most significant aspect of the repeated pattern are the different outdoor spaces created between buildings.

The UNESCO world heritage site of Christiansfeld, Denmark provides a unique example of continuity in a planned settlement. Founded in 1773, its pioneering egalitarian and humanistic urban design created a continuous collection of buildings oriented along two tangential east-west streets surrounding the Church Square. Characterised by one and two-storey buildings in yellow brick and red tiled roofs, with consistent proportions, materials, and craftsmanship. The town's unique atmosphere of harmony is achieved through unity and functional distribution creating high quality enclosure throughout.

Successful urban space (including street space) is defined and enclosed by buildings, structures, and landscape. Enclosure creates comfortable private space and security which is protected physically and visually (Sim, 2020). In working with context, buildings that relate to a common building line reinforce and define the street. Repeating the historic or traditional building line helps to integrate new development in the street scene, maintains the continuous urban fabric, and avoids places of concealment (DETR and CABE, 2000).

To increase robustness, the edge between buildings and public spaces must be designed to be active. Animated edges, such as clearly identifiable building entrances, residential balconies, shopfronts, terraces, cafes and restaurants, and display areas for shops help define streets and public spaces as active (Bentley et al., 1985). Edge treatments which provide purposeful set-backs to accommodate and provide either publicly accessible open space with a high level of amenity or semi-private spaces to buffer public and private functions and add a layer of defensible space to preserve indoor privacy are also key for robustness. Architecture that supports animation and features distinction in the façade either through detailing or other visual cues helps to improve continuity. The central pedestrian street of Florida, Buenos Aries provides a continuous and well-defined street wall, reinforcing the street, while also providing considered and consistent set-backs for activation and safety within the public realm.

BELOW: Well-defined street wall of Florida, Buenos Aires, Argentina.

CHAPTER 4: MAKING SENSE OF DESIGN   52

Clear edge conditions with distinctive historic and contemporary architecture, a consistent ratio of enclosure (between height and width) and strong blocks, coupled with innovations such as parklets, a shared street design with specific traffic calming measures, and links to multiple modes of transport including the city's tram network ensure successful continuity (and enclosure) across the urban fabric. The Buenos Aries example also demonstrates the importance of responding to context, with design approaches that also include the creation of successful arcades and shading through canopies. Florida establishes a clear line of sight, provides active frontages, and connects between existing public streets while also ensuring a form of weather protection during the summer. Its design provides a thoroughfare for cooler air helping to support responsive continuity for people in the city. Continuity of movement for people is key, either through links to multiple modes of transportation, or in the case of Florida, through consistent opportunities for movement in multiple directions – either to smaller pedestrianised streets and public realm or larger arterial routes to access bus and tram services – made possible by the clearly distinguished, repeated, grid pattern of urban blocks.

LEFT: Continuity of the building style, materials, and roof lines create a legible environment in Linz, Austria.

BELOW: Intuitive public space within the pedestrian network in Aalborg, Denmark.

I: SUSTAINABLE

The development and construction of the built environment is one of the most carbon intensive sectors of the any nation. In Europe, for example, the buildings sector represents 40% of the EU's energy demand and 80% of this relies on fossil fuels (UNEP, 2022). This is no longer acceptable or sustainable. Urban design, given its intrinsic links to the buildings sector, is a profession and practice that must take immediate action to promote short and long-term energy security, prioritising sustainable design and development across all urban projects.

Attempts to decarbonise by 2050 are crucial to sustainable development, as well as to achieving a resilient buildings and construction sector. Urban design must take a leadership role in the implementation of zero-carbon strategies for new and existing urban spaces and buildings. Well-designed placed and buildings should conserve natural resources, including buildings, land, water, energy, and materials (MHCLG, 2021). Urban designers must engage with the by-products of development to ensure renewable, resilient, and carbon conscious spaces and places are realised – those that take a systems approach to waste, recycling, energy, air, biodiversity, among other factors.

Significant advances have been made in the incorporation of good or better practice in sustainable design, including through the improvement of energy efficiency of existing and new buildings, the optimisation of passive solar gain (passive energy design), local low carbon networks and heating systems, integration of renewable sources, the promotion of circular construction, and increased recognition and requirements to meet environmental standards such as: embodied energy/carbon, whole life-cycle carbon, modern methods of construction, water usage and ratings such as BREEAM. Established in 1990, *Building Research Establishment Environmental Assessment Method* (BREEAM) is the world's longest established method of assessing, rating, and certifying the sustainability of buildings and masterplanning (*BREEAM Communities*) – considering energy (embodied and operational), water, transport, management, waste, pollution, health and well-being, land use and ecology, materials and robustness. *LEED* (USA/International) and *Green Star* (Australia) perform similar functions.

Designers working with local authorities are well-placed to deliver projects that demonstrate best practice in energy and sustainability.

Our case study city of Aalborg is an excellent example of sustainability leadership in urban design and development. It's compact and walkable neighbourhoods with a mix of uses and facilities reduce demand for energy and support health and wellbeing. The city took early steps to invest and implement city-wide district heating systems, whereby as of 2023, over 90% of all residential properties in the city were supplied with energy with a district heat pump. Likewise, strategic projects to de-culvert and re-open historic waterways have been ongoing since 2018 – creating a city-wide blue/green infrastructure network. By using land efficiently, Aalborg is better placed to adapt to the future – increasing the ability for CO_2 absorption, sustaining natural ecosystems, minimising flood risk and the potential impact of flooding, and reducing overheating and air pollution (NMDC, 2021).

BELOW: Aalborg, Denmark has re-opened historic disused waterways (TOP) and introduced seasonal sustainable urban drainage (BOTTOM) strategically across the public realm as part of a city wide sustainability project.

CHAPTER 4: MAKING SENSE OF DESIGN

MASDAR CITY by Foster and Partners is situated in Abu Dhabi, UAE. It is located within a harsh desert environment, with temperatures exceeding 55 degrees Celsius in summer. Anticipating the future of the oil-rich country, the UAE has notably shifted its policymaking towards diversifying the economy, focusing on investments in tourism, technology, and renewable energy. Sustainability frames these changes, rethinking how future cities should function and appear in the UAE, which is of critical importance. Out of this context, Masdar City emerged.

THE ARABIAN CITY

Masdar City's design is rooted in the ancient Arabian city - a self-cooling, environmentally friendly city enduring even in the harsh Arabian desert climate. The Arabian city features high density, low-rise compact structures primarily made of local materials like mud and stone. A system of buildings design, block courtyards, wind towers, and narrow alleys creates shade and varied wind pressure, aiding in cooling.

CLIMATE ADAPTATION

Masdar adopts these techniques while integrating technology for more efficient results. High-tech wind towers, for instance, regulate wind strength and humidity, channelling wind towards a green infrastructure network (the 'green fingers') irrigated by *Atmospheric Water Generation*, an innovative method of generating water from the air. Buildings are constructed using low-carbon cement and recycled waste materials. Most roofs and canopies are equipped with solar panels, shielding from direct sun, and generating energy supplies.

SUSTAINABLE MOBILITY

Creating walkable cities in the UAE context poses challenges, yet Masdar's urban design prioritises the human-scale experience. Rather than conventional streets, two main layers of automated mobility operate in Masdar: an underground network of electric, self-driving cars for services and mobility, along with compact, solar-powered buses above ground. This design maintains the city's compact structure, providing well-enclosed, safe paths and an underground service for mixed-use development. The city's orientation maximises shading on main paths, encouraging cycling and walkability.

TOP: Masdar's buildings borrowed heavily from the design principles of the traditional Arabian City.

MIDDLE: The bespoke wind tower captures and redirects natural air flow to cool spaces and streets.

BOTTOM: The orientation and enclosure of streets was designed to ensure shading allowing for more comfortable walking and cycling.

J: LONG TERM

Urban design must be future orientated; cities are in a state of constant flux and adaptation is central to ensuring the success of design in the long term. Long-term thinking in design enables projects to respond to changing (and predicted) social structures, market demands and most importantly, the acceleration of the climate crisis (with the impacts of climate change experienced in a larger proportion of urban contexts than ever before). At its most basic, long-term thinking in design quality concerns the upkeep and maintenance of spaces and places, who is responsible for this and what controls are in place to ensure the space is managed successfully. Part of this concerns the policing of spaces, and how safety is prioritised. The policing of spaces through technology is now a common form of 'oversight' but not necessarily the most democratic solution. The presence of CCTV cameras and security companies (particularly in private-public spaces) reflect broader societal issues and extreme events such as terrorism that urban design cannot control but can readily design for, to soften the hardness and harshness of these elements in cities. The most important component is that urban design / revitalisation does not remove comfort or safety.

Places must be adaptable to respond to how we use space now as well as how we may need to use it in the future. Responding to these needs is extremely complex but examples of long term thinking in urban design demonstrate how places can meet a wider spectrum of individual needs and consequently there is a better chance that these places will enjoy longevity and make people's lives easier now and in the future.

Adaptive urban design, focused blue-green infrastructures and nature-based solutions are key strategies to achieve this, these approaches provide wider socio-ecological benefits in the form of amenity spaces, dissemination and education programmes, cooperation and knowledge exchange among urban actors as well as playing a key role in facilitating the active participation of communities.

In recent years, evidence of improved urban design policy, guidance and practice for climate change adaptation have emerged across the globe. Huge potential has been identified to increase urban resilience and climate change adaptation by integrating adaptive capacity into urban design through approaches such as water-resilient or water-sensitive urban design (Palazzo, 2019). Cities such as New Orleans, New York, and Zhejiang – heavily hit by hurricane events – are now leading the way with new *'sponge-city'* design solutions that increase urban resilience and reduce flood vulnerabilities while aiming to design more adaptable but also equitable urban areas (Palazzo, 2019). Sponge-city practices prioritise submersible surfaces in public spaces (Silva and Costa 2016), or 'safe-to-fail' flood approaches (Ahern, 2011) and are representative of the future-proofing solutions urban design must prioritise. For further details on a range of nature-based solutions and adaptive urban design practices from Australia, China, Singapore, the Netherlands, France, the US, Denmark, Germany, India, among others, *please see*: Palazzo, 2018; Mell, 2016; 2019 or Counsell and Stonerman, 2018.

BELOW: Water-sensitive design tackling growing climate issues - Brasilia, Brazil.

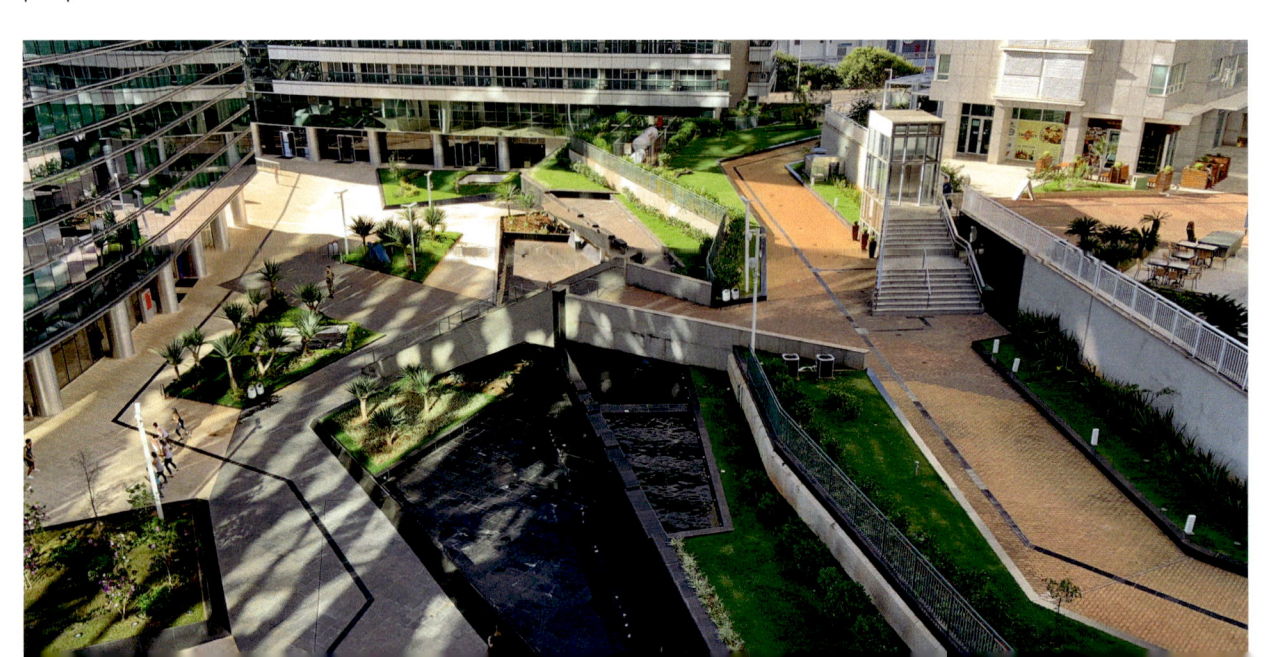

CHAPTER 4: MAKING SENSE OF DESIGN

BELOW: Rotterdam's Central Station and new public realm was designed to assist with the planned growth of economy and tourism. It was an investment in the future as well as the present.

LEFT: Places need to function well to deliver good quality. The layers of design work together to provide the functional blueprints for cities. Msheireb Downtown, Doha, Qatar.

4.3 FUNCTIONAL BLUEPRINTS - 12 DESIGN LAYERS

The practicalities of delivering good urban design means not only understanding wider contextual issues and human scale 'liveability' elements, but also how a place works – its functionality. Urban areas can be split into a series of interconnected layers, which collectively ensure that places are designed to meet the needs of the people working and living in any location. Here, we unpack the functionality of design across four broad categories – *Networks, Arrangements, Features* and *Feel* – and **12 Design Layers.** While these layers are split for ease of communication, responsive urban design should consider these 12 layers holistically. The 12 Design layers are introduced over the subsequent pages, alongside some of the key design challenges.

Where relevant, reference is made within the text to the other layers to help demonstrate the linkages between these considerations. The assessment of the context (that will follow in subsequent chapters) will provide a wealth of data that can be used to ensure that the dimensions used as part of any project can reflect the local context.

For those designing, the 12 layers have been presented in a logical order which should allow designers to consider each in turn, adding levels of detail and complexity to help achieve contextually responsive design solutions. Nonetheless, we recommend that the site and context define how to consider each of the layers presented here - there is no requirement (or indeed overarching positive benefit) to address these in the order presented.

Before considering the final two layers within the *'feel'* category, it is important to understand that the urban designer's approach to these will be inheritably different from those already considered. The 10 layers that precede them include a series of principles or standards that could be applied and followed (on a sliding scale) where they will work in concert with one another, to help deliver good placemaking. These final two, character and maintenance, are different insofar as they are somewhat more ethereal, and don't easily result in a series of clear rules. With the *'feel'* layers urban designers will have to consider much more how people will use and interact and experience the space. Before approaching design through the 12 layers urban designers must recognise that for every design decision made in one layer, this will impact on another, and as a result they cannot be applied with equal importance. As a designer, it is vital that you consider hierarchies; prioritisation; and justify your decision making (Chapters 8 and 9 illustrate these layers in our *'live'* design examples). There are no 'wrong' answers, but it is important that every decision is thoroughly and clearly rationalised.

BELOW: The AUD design layers that provide the functional blueprints of quality urban design.

NETWORKS — ARRANGEMENTS — FEATURES — FEEL

NETWORKS	ARRANGEMENTS	FEATURES	FEEL
1. ROUTES 2. PUBLIC REALM 3. GREEN / BLUE INFRASTRUCTURE	4. URBAN BLOCKS 5. USES 6. FRONTAGE 7. SERVICE / ACCESS	8. BUILDINGS 9. ENCLOSURE 10. CORNERS	11. CHARACTER 12. MAINTENANCE / MANAGEMENT

NETWORKS

Networks are key to how efficiently and effectively a place functions in practice. They consider connections, both physical and social – the ways in which people will move around the city and the options to do so, as well as how people will connect with one another through interaction and activity. Better places allow people to engage with their communities and access all parts of the city inclusively, equitably, and sustainably. There are 3 of the 12 design layers to unpack here.

1. Routes
2. Public Realm
3. Green and Blue Infrastructure

1. ROUTES

Routes are probably the most easily understood of all the design layers and include a range of different types. Routes describe any path or street which allows people to move, from one place to another. At the simplest level, each road, street, or lane is a route, but for designers to make use of these there is a requirement for value judgements to be made on their quality and functionality.

When designing using this layer, designers must balance the competing demands of different users and functional requirements In this respect, designers will have to carefully consider *'movement corridors'* which refers to designing routes so that different modes of movement are arranged in a series of integrated corridors (NACTO, 2013).

Type – The network of routes in any area will feature a mixture of different types or modes – the most common being traffic routes, public transport routes, walking/cycling routes. While each network may have common features (for example a high street at 15-20m wide may feature all three types/modes) they will create different networks, with different patterns and structures. In the design of routes, it is necessary to think carefully about which route networks (or networks) they will contribute to. However, it is important to remember that not all routes will need to be designed for all movement types.

Hierarchy – In any network not all routes are the same and consequently are not used in the same way. There will be routes that are vitally important and others less so. Identifying and establishing a clear hierarchy of routes is important to ensure that places function effectively. For example, a route that receives (or is likely to receive) very few cyclists does not necessarily need to be designed with substantial cycle infrastructure across it. In the same way, not every route will need to be designed to accommodate larger vehicles – many residential areas only needing occasional access for waste collection and other emergency vehicles. Consideration of balance is required.

Connectivity – Any network of routes should think carefully about the way that it connects to where people live, work, and spend their leisure time. Thinking carefully about how the network of routes encourages people to use more sustainable modes (walking, cycling and public transit) to meet their daily needs is important. For example, ensuring that a neighbourhood is provided with a strong network of cycle and pedestrian routes that connect to local schools and public transit interchanges will help encourage daily commuting by sustainable modes across a range of users and ages.

LEFT: A fully pedestrian main street connecting across the city centre in Lisbon, Portugal.

CHAPTER 4: MAKING SENSE OF DESIGN   60

TOP: Multi-modal street with sustainable transport focus - Belfast, Northern Ireland.

MIDDLE: Shared street with trams, cycles, and pedestrians - Bordeaux, France.

BOTTOM LEFT: Use of cloisters to create dry and shaded routes in Santander, Spain.

BOTTOM RIGHT: Local street, low on the route hierarchy of Turin, Italy.

2. PUBLIC REALM

There is often a misconception that routes and public realm are both the same thing, and whilst it is true that they often compete for the same space within a city they are very different in their nature and function. Routes have a strong movement component and consider a range of different modes, whereas public realm is concerned with human comfort and experience (Black and Sonbli, 2019). Public realm refers to pavements/sidewalks and the key public spaces and places within the city, but it is not solely focused on the movement corridors associated with vehicles, rather the network and quality of public realm across the city. Christopher Alexander (1977) describes the nature of public places as being the largest public rooms, built for social interaction. Public realm also has an important role to play in linking *network* layers to the *arrangement* layers.

Human comfort – Public realm should be designed for the human scale, ensuring individual comfort, through the provision of shelter from weather and traffic and making spaces that are safe and secure. Many existing sidewalks on streets are too narrow – less than the required 2-2.5m – for two people to comfortably pass, lack appropriate separation from busy vehicular traffic routes and are not well lit or overlooked by other users. Reallocating space to walking and cycling (see Routes) and introducing additional planting (see Green Infrastructure) can help achieve improvements to the quality of public realm.

Different users – When considering the design of the public realm it is necessary to think about the different spectrum of users of these spaces. User needs will vary depending on a series of demographic characteristics, including but not limited to, age, gender, or mobility. At the outset it is vital to think about who is using - or will use - the spaces that you are designing. Designing spaces that are attractive and engaging for children may include elements of informal play or colour, whilst designing for older people often requires provision of benches and shelter. Alongside this, designing spaces that are inclusive and suitable for a range of mobility types is vital.

Edge conditions - Public realm has a strong relationship with the buildings that surround it (see Enclosure). The design of the public realm will change depending on the functions of the buildings around it – for example, a retail use is likely to have a strong delineation between public and private space with buildings that are set-back from the public realm and building line, typically between a range of 2.5-4m, to provide opportunities for pausing, socialising, and play (DfT, 2007). The public realm in many areas will need to respond to a mixture of uses (both at installation and over time) so building in flexibility is vital. Chapter 9 introduces public realm as one of 3 '*super-components*' of designing place (see 9.3).

BELOW: Integrating informal play - Belfast, Northern Ireland.

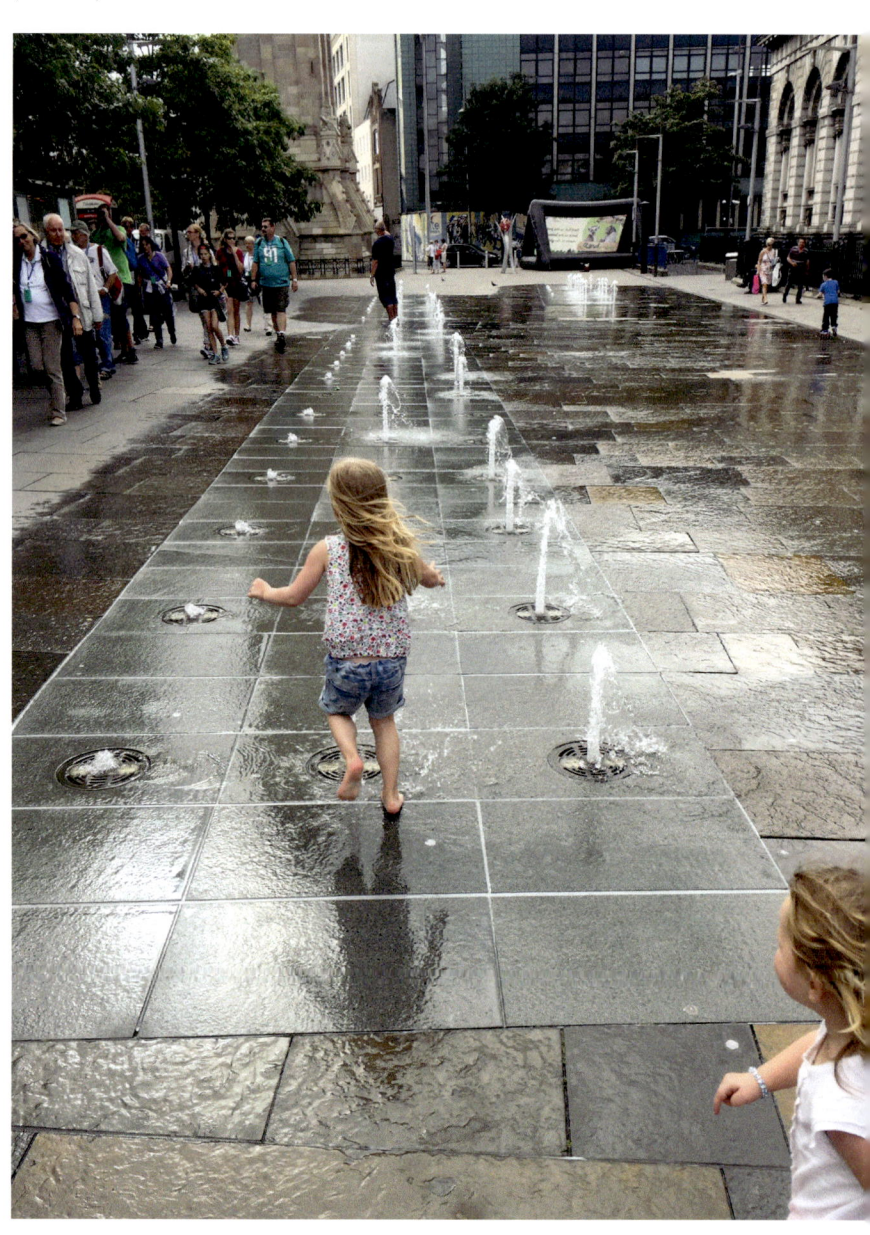

3. GREEN/BLUE INFRASTRUCTURE

Green and blue infrastructure (GI) is a design layer that covers a wide range of different typologies and scales but are strongly linked by the presence and network of green or natural elements (Mell, 2019). Green and blue Infrastructure networks can constitute a range of elements from tree lined streets and private garden areas to public parks and areas of natural planting. There is strong linkage to the other network layers, with GI often forming part of key routes, or functioning as key public spaces. GI also offers a much wider opportunity to respond to the demands of climate change, with planting providing urban cooling and shade in hotter weather and managing rainwater and flood risk during increased rainfall or cloud burst events. When approaching green infrastructure, designers need to think effectively about the role landscape features can play for a variety of users, as well as how it can practically help with adapting to climatic change and enhancing biodiversity.

Variety of users - A successful GI network considers a range of different formats, types, and uses of green space which can be accessed and enjoyed by different ages and abilities. When considering design and development proposals, it is important to think about providing a variety of green and blue spaces. Children require opportunities for play and exploration whilst older people might require places to sit and relax, or even play sports. Thinking carefully about what is provided as part of new designs and how these complement existing variety is a challenge for urban design.

Climate adaptation - The urban heat island effect is well documented, as are the impacts of increased rainfall causing surface water flooding. Green and blue infrastructure offers a strong opportunity to adapt to these impacts. Trees can provide shading and urban cooling and help in reducing surface water flooding but require careful consideration at the design stage to ensure that they can be effectively accommodated in the medium and long term. Small areas of planting, functioning as rain gardens or pocket parks help can deal with peak weather effects – both items can be introduced in streets and neighbourhoods. At the larger scale, areas of woodland, or meadowland assist with urban cooling.

Biodiversity and natural environments - GI has an important role to play in supporting wildlife and biodiversity (Barton, 2017). Whilst urban design is primarily focused on creating places for people, it can also provide a variety of natural and semi-natural habitats. Access to natural green space has been identified as being able to improve human health and wellbeing. When implementing projects, it is important to consider the opportunities that can be generated by including semi-natural and natural green spaces. Even the smallest projects should look for opportunities to introduce native planting, or even informal flower gardens to supports bees and other wildlife. Thinking about how the network of these features links to existing natural environments or protected landscapes at the strategic level is an important city scale consideration (*see* Chapter 5). Chapter 9 provides more design detail for integrating GI (*see* 9.4).

TOP: Green and blue infrastructure informing movement and providing cooling - Kings Cross, London.

BOTTOM: Sustainable urban drainage (SuDS) and planting protecting housing development from winter snow melt flooding in Helsinki, Finland.

DISTRICT V

ZRINYI U. to St. STEPHEN'S
A key east to west pedestrian link that terminates with views of the historic Basilica (east) and Stephen Szechenyi Ter, a landscaped green space (west). Views down the street towards the Basilica can be seen from one of the main arterial bridges connecting to the west of the Danube - the old city of Buda. Populated with a range of cafes and restaurants the street is active throughout the day - the defined enclosure is only transitioned when opening onto the main public space surrounding St. Stephen's.

WATERFRONT WALK
A major north to south pedestrian link that takes in a number of key public and green spaces in the city - including Marcius Sq., Stephen Szechenyi Sq, and further north the Parliament and Olympic Park. Tree lined for shading and to dampen the noise of the adjacent vehicular route. The walk maximises the cities relationship to the River Danube, and provides vistas to the rising hills and historic castle to the west in old Buda. A number of critical public realm nodes are created along the walk that link people into the city centre to the east.

VAROSHAZA PARK
A major arterial route running north to south for all forms of transport, including trams, cycling, and walking. This generous route incorporates a number of key movement nodes, such Deak Sq., Elizabeth Ter, and St. Stephen's Basilica. Varoshaza Park provides informal seating, play-space, and an outdoor gym - creating a more casual space than the more formalised public spaces surrounding. It also provides a visual and welcoming gateway to the city centre for the residential areas directly to the west.

Vörösmarty Square
Zrinyi U.
Stephen Széchenyi Square
József Nádor Square
Vörösmarty Square
DANUBE
Waterfront Walk
Szervita Square
Marcius Square
TO BUDA

Key node ○   Pedestrians network ↙   Pedestrians only route ↙

BUDAPEST

LIBERTY SQUARE
One of the largest green spaces of District V - Liberty Square provides welcome landscaping and a wide range of green and blue features. The park is surrounded by mid-density residential uses and the range of activities it boasts, including playgrounds, seating, bowls, cafes, and picnic spaces ensures it is well used all year round. The park also acts as a critical pedestrian and cycling route connecting the north of the city to the city centre.

ELIZABETH SQUARE
Elizabeth Square is the largest public space in Budapest city centre - It sits at the top of the public realm hierarchy and is designed to provide users with a wealth of activities. The square has a large viewing wheel, cafes, seating areas, formal gardens, play spaces, water-sensitive design, and pop-up opportunities for Christmas markets and other cultural events. Its central location ensures it is easily accessible and its well considered movement corridors allow people to pass through easily or remain to enjoy the high quality environment.

JOZSEF NADOR SQUARE
A more formal piece of public realm and GI provision - this space provides local city centre residents with a quiet environment to enjoy nature. It also provides easy links to the underground stop at Vorosmarty Ter and links to Elizabeth Sq via an arcade housing cafes and bars. The Square sits above an underground car park and servicing area with lifts allowing direct access to the space above. A noticeably less busy space, but of critical importance to how District V functions and ensures separation of people and vehicles.

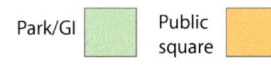

ARRANGEMENTS

Arrangements are how the land is divided up to provide a shift from nature to urban. A city is made up of physical elements, and how these are ordered provides places with unique characteristics and spatial layout. There are 4 of the 12 design layers to unpack here.

4. Urban Blocks
5. Uses
6. Frontage
7. Service and Access

4. URBAN BLOCKS

The urban block is a key principle of creating successful urban design and relates to the way in a buildings can be grouped together, or organised so that they can function effectively. Examples of the use of urban blocks are found around the world, but the most obvious example is the 'Eixample' in Barcelona designed by Cerda. Even in irregular cities, the principles of the urban block are still commonplace. In its simplest form the urban block, typically 50m-70m wide, is an arrangement of perimeter buildings in a rectangular form surrounded by public routes or public realm (NMDC, 2021). Whether fine grain or coarse grain, whether a flat landscape or a on a hillside, the urban block can conform to the patterns of the city – it doesn't always need to be a rectangular form but where this is possible this allows it to function most effectively. We unpack urban blocks in more detail in Chapter 9 - considering how they are designed and their unique benefits for placemaking (*see* 9.5).

Fronts and backs - The urban block principle ensures that every building, regardless of its use has a front – its public face with main entrance interfacing with the public realm – and a back – the private face to the rear. Arranging buildings into a block where all the backs face together on the 'inside' of the block and the fronts face out onto the public realm is crucial to the legibility of the design, allowing the public realm to be animated (see Frontage). The interior of the block in most cases are for servicing the surrounding uses (for parking, bin collection, deliveries etc). Urban blocks ensure that the interior of the block can be secure or private for residents/communities.

Not just one building – One of the biggest misconceptions about urban blocks is that they are one building. Whilst there are occasionally urban blocks that are composed of one building (museums, government buildings etc.) typically an urban block is made up of a number of separate buildings and can have different uses or different scales. Once the format or shape of the urban block has been established – e.g. perimeter blocks, courtyard blocks, or mews blocks - they can be used for whatever building types is desired. An urban block could include a mix of scales or sizes of buildings and a mix of different uses, or it could comprise of buildings of all the same size and use, allowing for flexibility.

Size and shape of the blocks – The overall size of urban blocks will vary depending on a variety of factors, and aside from several practical considerations the size and shape of the urban block can vary considerably (Bentley et al., 1985). As a starting point urban blocks ought not to have an external measurement in excess of 150m in any direction as this would ultimately result in a lack of permeability for pedestrians and cyclists through the city. Blocks in residential use are unlikely to be less than 50m in width as sizes less than this would result in insufficient privacy between the bedroom windows of facing residential properties. However, as a starting point it is recommended that a 120m by 80m urban block should be considered, as this provides flexibility to customise blocks to accommodate a wide range of programming. It must also be noted that blocks can be laid out in numerous configurations together - creating very different networks as a result - from the grid pattern, such as Cerda's Barcelona or Manhattan, New York - to more organic permeable layouts such as in Paris.

BELOW: The compact urban blocks of New York, USA.

CHAPTER 4: MAKING SENSE OF DESIGN   66

ASPERN SEESTADT is a 240 hectare site which seeks the redevelopment of the former Vienna Aspern airport for a mixed use residential use neighbourhood based around a strong masterplan. The masterplan developed by Swedish firm Tovatt Architects & Planners (adopted 2007), makes extensive use of the urban block with a distinct 'Viennese twist'. The masterplan includes a new light rail connection, new train station, and a network of streets and spaces, including a circular boulevard and a large lake – hence the name Seestadt or 'Lake City'.

SHARED INTERNAL COURTYARD
All of the urban blocks have a shared internal courtyard which is for the use of the apartments that surrounding it. These internal courtyards include harder seating areas, children's play facilities and small growing areas. These areas are accessed through small gaps (between 3-10 metres) between buildings that make up the block. Whilst in almost every case these are open to the public, they are rarely accessed by others beyond the residents as the interior feels very private and separate from the public realm.

USE OF THE URBAN BLOCK
The design team sought to provide a modern interpretation of the traditional Viennese urban block which is rectilinear in form and built to a scale of between 5 and 7 storeys. Seestadt replicates this effectively. Blocks are arranged around a clear hierarchy of routes all enclosed by apartment buildings. Away from the main routes some routes provide vehicular access and service to one side of the urban block (the backs). This means that the remaining sides of the blocks and routes need not accommodate servicing.

MIXED USES
At Seestadt the design team were predominantly focused on creating residential blocks, but they were also aware of the need to provide shops and services for the community that lived and worked there. Within the core of the site, and along some of the key routes (the circular boulevard) they have created a series of mixed use urban blocks which have shops, offices and leisure facilities fronting these routes, with residential development on the routes behind. To facilitate these they have used the interior of the block for service, but have covered this providing a courtyard at first floor level (a podium deck).

TOP: Shared internal courtyard of a residential urban block. Semi-private approach allows for local movement.

MIDDLE: Seestadt mimicked density of the typical Vienna block, but added variation in layout and carefully designed servicing to ensure surrounding public realm would be car and clutter free.

BOTTOM: Ground floors provide shops and cafes and other key services - adding activity and amenity for locals - as well as active frontage along main pedestrian streets.

5. USES

One of the key elements of any city is the use of land (or land use). It is important to think about existing uses of land, but also more widely about the use of streets, urban quarters or even neighbourhoods and how they contribute to our understanding of the pattern of our urban areas (Hebbert, 2016). At its most basic level we can break our towns and cities up into areas of residential, commercial, retail, and industrial uses. Nonetheless, there is scope to consider and apply land use in a much more granular level of detail; we can think about mixed uses, upper floors and even how land use effects the activity and experience across a range of scales e.g., street-level or district level.

Dominant uses or locations – It is important that urban designers look for dominant uses or local trends/patterns in use. There are clear areas of our cities that have a dominant use, or one that is important to the areas character, identity, or functionality such as a local retail high street, or a higher education campus. Urban design is concerned with understanding how ground floor uses will increase both the enclosure of streets and spaces but also the use and activity within the public realm.

Activity – Land use is closely linked to activity. Certain land uses will be associated with specific activities within an area. For example, a retail shopping street is likely to have a range of different activities beyond shops. This reflects some of the concepts articulated by Jan Gehl who highlights that land uses that provide necessary activities – such as going to work or to the local shops - will create resultant activities – like meeting friends and neighbours or stopping somewhere for food or drink (Gehl, 1987). Designers should acknowledge that certain land uses will generate more activity than others. Urban design should encourage different uses and activities at different times of the day / night.

Mixed use and upper floors – Designing places that are mixed in use is a key goal for urban design. Mixed use places can ensure activity and vibrancy at different times of the day and night. Mixed use can be provided by placing different land uses side by side or by placing different uses on different floors of a building. It is easier to consider ground floor uses whilst upper floors are a little more complicated as access and service (see Service) may restrict certain uses such as retail or industrial that requires ground floor access. Care needs to be taken to ensure that the uses that are chosen are compatible, for example placing busy bars and clubs adjacent to family housing will cause conflict unless high quality materials are used such as triple glazing and hours of operation are agreed. It is easier to provide mixed use within retail and commercial environments where these daytime uses sit comfortably alongside a range of possible uses. As a general rule, a depth of 10m will provide a suitable floorplate for a mixed-use building with retail or leisure uses on the ground floor and office or apartment uses above.

ABOVE: The mixed uses of the MuseumsQuartier, Vienna - a place designed to encourage multiple activities and social engagement.

CHAPTER 4: MAKING SENSE OF DESIGN 68

6. FRONTAGE

The frontage layer provides a link between the urban block and the public realm. The outward 'face' of the urban block will comprise of its frontage, the public face of a building. The treatment of this frontage will depend on the uses of the buildings and the hierarchy of the street or space with which it interacts.

Active frontage – Urban design stresses the importance of providing active frontage within design projects, however, it is can often be misunderstood. Active frontage, as a type of frontage, has a specific character and nature where the internal use of the building will interact with the external spaces. This could simply be the set-back to a retail shop, or a café that spills out onto the pavement, but it could also be a civic space in front of a town hall. Active frontage cannot be used for every frontage within an urban block and should be used sparingly to help reinforce key routes or key public spaces. That said, even frontages that are not active can play a key role in achieving successful urban areas via the incorporation of public art, murals, or other forms of animation.

Transparency of use – In order to aid the legibility of places it is important that the uses of buildings are clear from the public realm. This is not just a matter of providing complete glazed frontages; it is about providing users with an understanding of the interior uses. On a basic level this is about ensuring that buildings have clear doors and entrances from publicly accessible locations, however, there are a range urban design considerations that can assist with ensuring transparency. Large windows on commercial and retail premises can assist with providing a link between the public realm and the activities that happen inside.

Passive Surveillance – Jane Jacobs (1961) introduced the concept of passive surveillance in urban design. Passive surveillance describes the role frontage, animated with windows and entrances onto a street, will provide *'eyes on the street'*. Residential homes with living areas and kitchens within their frontage allow users to passively survey and overlook their public realm. The same role could be played by the entrances to apartments or office buildings where there is a transient coming and going of users.

It is important that routes are enclosed (see Enclosure) by buildings that provide a strong frontage to ensure they benefit from passive surveillance making urban locations feel safe and secure, even when they are less visibly busy.

ABOVE: Active frontage creates a clear understanding that the buildings are public and accessible. St Annes, Manchester, UK.

LEFT: Passive surveillance can be introduced with balconies overlooking streets and public realm - Vienna, Austria.

7. SERVICE AND ACCESS

Ensuring that buildings and urban blocks have effective services and access is paramount. Retail and industrial uses have the most intensive and often unpredictable service requirements, whereas office and residential uses have much lighter and regular requirements. Rear servicing in a shared courtyard is often the most appropriate design solution for most building functions as it keeps servicing away from the public realm and means that car parking can be provided behind the building line so as not to impact negatively on the wider streetscape. Inner courtyards are typically used for servicing, access, parking, and deliveries. Here, it is important from a servicing and access perspective that sufficient room for manoeuvring of HGVs (Heavy Goods Vehicle) within the block interior is provided (approximately a 25m turning circle) or that a one-way system is implemented. Access to a block interior does not need to be disproportionately wide – a 5-6m break in the frontage can allow a HGV vehicle access.

Deliveries – It is important to consider how the uses that you propose will be effectively serviced, otherwise there is a risk of ill-conceived and ad hoc servicing arrangements. Large retail premises are likely to have regulated servicing by occupiers to a dedicated service bay within the block interior. More complicated are mixed use areas with smaller units where they are typically serviced by a myriad of different suppliers all using the internal courtyard, which requires some consideration. Front servicing of smaller retail shops and parades is historically quite common, nonetheless, this should be seen as the exception to the rule, (perhaps for a sole café or small local shop within a residential neighbourhood) to ensure the quality, access, and safety of the streetscape and public realm are prioritised.

Bin collection - It may seem very mundane, but thinking carefully about how refuge will be collected from a development is an important consideration. This means that the urban designer needs to think about two elements. First, what is the nature of refuse storage – is it for each individual premises or will it be shared? Where will the bins be stored and where will they need to be brought to for collection? Second, how will they be collected – will it be from a large refuge vehicle on each road? Would all bins be brought to a central collection point or is another method to be employed? While designers are not responsible for developing a comprehensive refuge collection strategy, it is important that broad decisions are made during the design process at the layout or masterplan stage.

Emergency access - While it is difficult to define the final detail at the urban design stage, it is worth considering how emergency access could be provided throughout the development (e.g., a minimum road width of 3.7m and gateway width of 3.1m). Car free neighbourhoods, for example, still need to ensure suitable access for ambulance or fire services to each block and building within a development. Similarly, the public realm might need to function in emergencies as an evacuation or fire route. In working with urban design layers you can consider multiple options for detailed design work to take forward and implement in the latter stages of the design process.

BELOW: Whilst servicing buildings via their main entrance is possible for uses (such as residential) with infrequent service needs - for more regular service uses, like retail or leisure, it is advised to design hidden servicing when possible to avoid delivery vehicles having to utilise main routes and public realm. On Mariahilferstrasse, Vienna front servicing is necessary due to historic design decisions - however they limit delivery access to early mornings and evenings to avoid clashes with the main pedestrian footfall periods.

CHAPTER 4: MAKING SENSE OF DESIGN

UNIVERSITY OF MANCHESTER

University campuses require a lot of different service and access considerations. The University of Manchester is a campus full of large buildings, some of which have unique servicing needs - yet the campus must also be welcoming and attractive for students throughout the year. This necessitates a clear service and access plan to provide appropriate segregation with the public realm and heavy pedestrian movement corridors. During the recent campus masterplan the University implemented a variety of service methods.

UNDERGROUND

The Alliance Manchester Business School is housed in the large AMBS building that includes an underground level for large service deliveries. The underground servicing also provides the required service for the range of cafes, bars, restaurants, and shops on the newly delivered *University Green* project. By putting this underground it allows the public realm to remain vehicle free throughout the day and night.

INTERIOR BLOCK

The Engineering and Materials building is one of the largest building footprints in the whole city - and requires some heavy servicing with regular deliveries of HGV trucks. The design of the block was deliberately linear in fashion to allow for a dedicated one-way service route through the centre - with large format doors for access. Pedestrians can use the route, however other more attractive and safer routes run parallel.

SHARED SPACE

Brunswick Place is a key component of the public realm network of the university, with numerous student facing buildings fronting onto it. It was imperative service was kept segregated from the busy pedestrian thoroughfare. This was achieved through the delivery of a shared street/space alongside the Alan Turing Building - this space prioritises pedestrians, but allows for controlled service deliveries and emergency vehicle access at certain times of the day and throughout the night.

CONTROLLED ACCESS

Alan Gilbert Square is a well enclosed quiet public green space on campus, popular with students seeking outdoor study space. The square is bounded by the main library and Learning Commons. It is critical that access be non-vehicular. Yet the need for emergency service access due to the busy nature of the space and its lack of direct street connection. The university provided limited access points into the space - also enabling it to be utilised as an events space.

TOP: University Green and the AMBS Building - fully serviced via underground provision.

TOP MIDDLE: Rumford Street acting as a heavy goods service route through the centre of the Engineering and Materials block.

BOTTOM MIDDLE: Shared service street that prioritises pedestrians but also ensures all university buildings in Brunswick Park are fully accessible and serviceable.

BOTTOM: Controlled access for emergency services and events - into Alan Gilbert Square.

FEATURES

Features refers to the elements of a city that most easily define its experience for users – specifically in urban design we are thinking about the physical elements that we can utilise to enhance this – such as buildings. There are 3 of the 12 design layers to unpack here.

8. Buildings
9. Enclosure
10. Corners

8. BUILDINGS

Buildings are an obvious layer for urban design, and in many ways are one of the most tangible elements for casual observers of the city. As discussed, several buildings make up each urban block, working together to provide the arrangements of the place. However, within the block the buildings themselves can add variation and interest to the places that we design, through their type, size, and architectural detailing. When considering this layer, the role of the urban designer is not to become an architect and '*design*' the final elevations and room layouts of individual buildings but instead set out broad guidelines for how the buildings will look, feel, and work as part of a wider urban ensemble.

Height and mass – Height is typically described as the number of floors any building has/will have. The height of the buildings should work effectively alongside the public realm and routes to ensure that streets and spaces have the correct sense of enclosure. Mass refers solely to the bulk of the buildings in three dimensions rather than in terms of height. For the promotion of human scale, buildings above six storeys often become overbearing and uncomfortable. Taller and denser buildings might be appropriate where they are required to acts as landmarks to aid legibility or where the character of a place demands a different approach to be taken. One of the most effective ways of increasing development density whilst maintaining the 5-6 storey '*gentle density*' is to set storeys above that back away from the front/ building line or to include them within the roof profile (like a Mansard roof in Paris). The extreme case of this is the New York skyscraper with 50 plus storeys above a 6-storey base, but in many cities two to three storeys are provided in this way.

BELOW: Mansard Roof, Paris.

CHAPTER 4: MAKING SENSE OF DESIGN 72

Plot size and density – Density can be determined by the scale or height of the building (how many floors) or by the plot size (the individual ownership boundaries of any given building) and the intensity of the built form within a plot. Consider exploring whether all the buildings have the same density or will the block transition between different densities? When determining the correct approach each case will depend on how the buildings relate to the surrounding routes, spaces, and land uses.

Responding to the vernacular – Whilst it is not the role of the urban designer to specify the final architectural style, it is common to consider how the development ought to respond to the local built language or vernacular. In certain cases, such as in historical environments or adjacent to heritage assets, the most appropriate course of action may be to focus on the design of buildings that reflect local details and features. Of course, it may also be valid to explore the possibility of engaging with a more contemporary design approach to the arrive at a new architectural fabric.

LEFT: Vernacular can include materials, colour palettes, architectural style, detailing, even scale and continuity. Amsterdam, the Netherlands.

BELOW: Yaletown, Vancouver, Canada. The buildings are a range of heights and densities that work together in perimeter blocks and provide frontage onto the surrounding public realm.

9. ENCLOSURE

Earlier in this chapter we discussed the importance of enclosure in relation to the layers of Public Realm and Frontage. Enclosure describes the way buildings line the edges of routes, spaces, and green infrastructure. Gordon Cullen (1961) considered that the pedestrian moving through the city, understood their journey as a movement between a series of 'views' of the city created via the enclosure of each space by buildings, what he termed as the *serial vision* of the townscape. By varying the elements of enclosure, through different street ratios and rhythms designers can create changes in the way that humans experience the townscape.

Street ratio – Enclosure is typically defined as the relationship between the height of the buildings measured against the space or route that they enclose. This is known as the height to width ratio or street ratio. Reflecting the human scale, the ratio usually sets out that the width of the street is wider than the height of the buildings at a ratio of 2:1 but there are no specific targets or requirements for this. The use of larger or wider ratios often would indicate that a route was more important or has a greater number of public uses along it. Residential streets would likely have a ratio smaller than 2:1 to suggest a sense of intimacy and privacy. Designers can use street ratios and enclosure to help define how people experience the city at human scale. Cullen (1961) emphasised that movement from enclosed streets into more open spaces, through a series of visual portals (or entrances) is an important consideration of how users navigate the townscape.

Portals or entrances – White (1999) introduced the concept that a journey through the city can be determined by a series of enclosed paths (routes), a series of portals (entrances/transitions between spaces and routes) and places (key destinations or public spaces). In varying the enclosure ratio, to create wider or narrower routes, the designers are able to form an engaging urban journey, creating arrival or entrance spaces from a series of well enclosed routes into key public spaces or parks. It is important that the transition zone between routes and spaces (the portal) is well defined through enclosure; that is either opened out or pinched. When used effectively alongside a hierarchy of routes and spaces, enclosure can create a dynamic townscape (Kostof, 2001).

Rhythm – Rhythm is often overlooked in considerations of enclosure but, in many contexts, can enhance the legibility and identity of a place. Rhythm refers to the repetition of similar architectural forms at regular intervals within the building's enclosure. This could be ensuring that plot and building width are even or regular, or more subtly, the regular positioning of windows and doors. Typically, rhythm can be seen as a response to the local building language or vernacular.

TOP: Poor enclosure in Brasilia, Brazil. Creates illegible space and lacks human scale - making the environment too 'open'.

BOTTOM: Well defined enclosure in Verona, Italy. Clear routes enter the space and provide smooth transitions.

CHAPTER 4: MAKING SENSE OF DESIGN

10. CORNERS
Corners are an important part of understanding and articulating the design of our towns and cities but in urban design are frequently overlooked as considerations for the final architectural design of the buildings. Urban blocks, if implemented effectively will create a series of corners all of which can/should work to enhance the townscape, by providing landmarks and features within a street scene that help to draw people along and through the neighbourhood (Black and Sonbli, 2019). As a general guide, the adage of 'less is more' applies to corners perhaps more than any other layers. There are countless real-world projects that have sought to make every corner unique and stand out from the wider townscape resulting in a discordant and confusing townscape. In this respect, not all corners need to be emphasised, some are *'just a corner'*, unless you can argue that a different approach might be appropriate.

Legibility – Making corners which stand out are important to aid the broader legibility of the townscape. Corners can act as landmarks at a variety of scales, helping people to navigate the urban fabric. Corners which are a little taller than the surrounding buildings and townscape can have that effect, what is known as articulation. Not every corner should be taller, but for strategic 'feature' buildings on corners that link with key nodes, junctions or destinations, some form of articulation may well be appropriate.

Projections, spaces, and chamfers – Height is not the only technique to consider making a feature of a particular corner. Setting a building back from the corner to create a small space within the public realm or pushing it forward to disrupt the frontage and rhythm of the street and building line are both suitable techniques. A set back of 1 to 2 metres is all that may be required to have the desired effect. In this respect the corner creates a 'pause' or break in the journey through experience of the urban fabric. A set-back corner could provide a small forecourt for a café space (2.5-4m), or a key projection could provide a highly visible location for the entrance to a public building (+4m). Here, a variation in the building line and frontage at a corner offers increased legibility as well as opportunities for mixed uses and activity. In design we do not always want to create a 'stop', here the chamfered corner (such as that of Barcelona) may create the conditions to draw people through a corner where there is a key direction of travel that the designer wants to reinforce.

Sometimes it just a corner – It is important to note that every block will have several corners and not all corners can be important. Sometimes, the design and purpose of the corner is simply just to ensure that the block and the enclosure of our streets and spaces works effectively. Not every corner will have a strategic role to play in the experience of the urban journey.

LEFT: A simple chamfered corner in Manchester, UK. creates the entrance to the building at the intersection of 2 important pedestrian streets.

BELOW: Articulating a movement node with a taller building to aid legibility - Sheffield, UK.

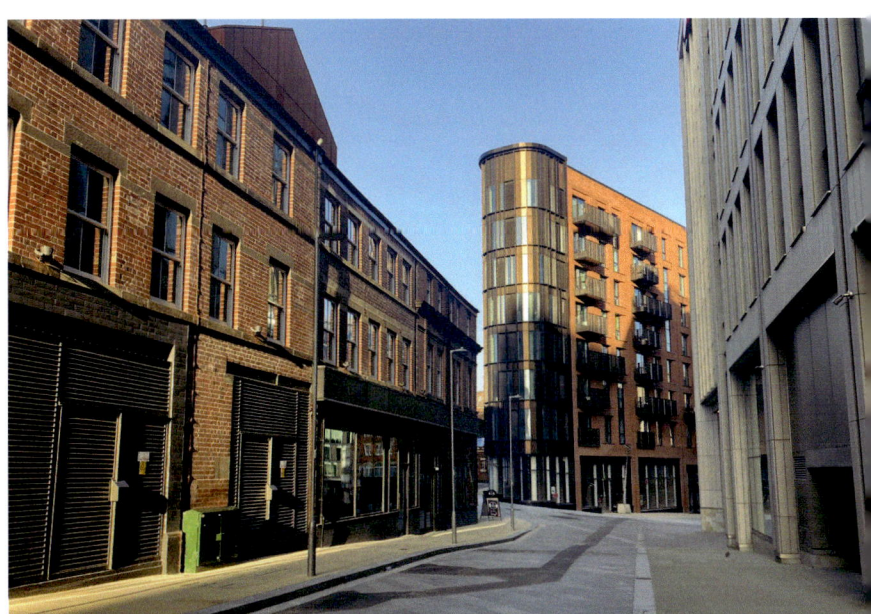

FEEL

The last 2 layers cover the *'feel'* of a place – in part the combination of layers that create a place's unique character – positive or negative – and how well a place is cared for to ensure it is delivering to the maximum potential for all people. There are 2 final design layers to unpack here.

11. Character
12. Maintenance and Management

11. CHARACTER

Character is the way that we can define the differences between one townscape and another. It is an important factor in creating urban areas that are easy to understand and interact with. Every area has character, good or bad. Character is a product of the style and type of the buildings, the qualities and nature of the routes, local landmarks, and the land uses present. With character, designers are required to consider all previous ten layers, as character is a product of the integration of each of these. In some contexts, it might be that one space or route within a particular area is responsible for the character (like a high street or key civic space), but in others it might be the consistency of height or use. In the introduction to this section, we discussed how the designer is responsible for creating a 'balance' between each of the layers when creating a place, changing, or prioritising, one or more of the layers will result in changes to character.

A compromise approach – When applying the character layer, finding a balance across competing priorities within the townscape will be required. As a designer it is impossible to deliver all the principles and elements of the urban design layers in full. Thus, we are required to consider compromises or carefully balance the layers. For example, we cannot always have active frontage to every building and block or ensure every corner be a feature. This balancing act, which will vary from site to site, street to street and city to city provides the myriad of differences in character. Likewise, you do not need to 'invent' character from scratch – in fact this is very rare. In most cases you will be able to look at the context and surrounding areas, those neighbourhoods, and areas that are immediately around your site and use this to shape your engagement with the urban design layers.

Implementing character with surroundings – When considering the redesign of a site or neighbourhood it is important to note two things. First, that the site itself does not always need to 'create' a new character. The townscape and landscape that surrounds your site will have a character and you may wish to use the urban design layers to first understand these (the analysis stage) and then replicate this within your site. Second, it is good practice to assume that your site may be more than one character - it might site on the boundary between two character areas that are distinct from each other - different uses, scales, networks, or green infrastructure – and then the role of the urban designer becomes determining whether to follow one, the other, both, or do something different.

Using the other senses - Character also has a strong experiential and affective element that relates specifically to the human scale. Think carefully about how the area would be experienced through the other senses beyond the visual. How will smells, tastes, noises help define a site or study area as being distinct from other areas of the town. This might be through the uses that are proposed, or the green infrastructure planting that is implemented, or the presence of cafes and bars that spill out onto a key route through the area.

BELOW: The character in Newcastle, UK is in part witnessed through the layers of historic development and infrastructure upgrades that have defined the city over hundreds of years.

CHAPTER 4: MAKING SENSE OF DESIGN   76

BOSTON, USA is a dynamic city and one with a unique shared local identity - A strong Irish culture and the home of the Red Sox, Bruins, Harvard University, and the famous Boston Common and Emerald Necklace. Loyalties in Boston are not often divided unlike cities with more diverse populations like New York. Yet the character of Boston's many urban districts varies significantly.

TOP: Downtown Boston.

MIDDLE: Back Bay Neighbourhood.

BOTTOM: Fenway-Kenmore - with Fenway Stadium in the foreground.

DOWNTOWN
The heart of the city is home to the financial district and City Hall, famous for its brutalist architecture. Bounded to the east by Boston Common the downtown area is a high density mix of mid-century and modern architecture with heavily enclosed streets and a prime waterfront and harbour area. Built up over a long period of time the downtown area is a maze of streets and routes that create permeability.

BACK BAY
Established in the mid-1800's, Back bay was constructed on reclaimed land and was designed with a simple grid pattern layout and linear perimeter urban blocks that allow for parking and service to occur in the middle of the block. The area is renowned for its Victorian brownstone buildings, mixed uses and walkable nature. The grid pattern runs directly into Boston Common, with the tree lined streets acting as a green link into the cities major park. The views out over the River Charles further enhance the qualities of this much sought after neighbourhood.

FENWAY-KENMORE
A more sprawling neighbourhood and home to the iconic Fenway Stadium of the Boston Red Sox baseball team. The district is well-known for its cultural offerings such as the Museum of Fine Arts. Much lower density than the nearby Back Bay and Downtown areas - there is a more active local evening scene given the plethora of sports bars, restaurants, and student activities around Kenmore Square. The area is home to a large number of independent local businesses and the Massachusetts Pike separates it from the North and Charles River.

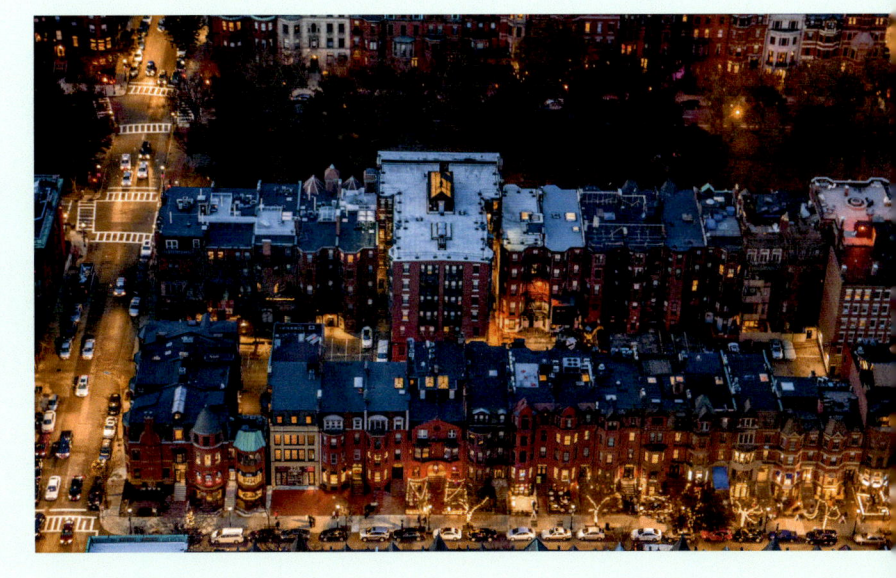

APPLIED URBAN DESIGN

TOP: Manchester's first public park in 100 years - Mayfield Park. The significant upkeep costs for maintaining and managing the space has resulted in private sector management.

MIDDLE: Some spaces require little maintenance and are informally managed by the local traders and users - such as in Ascoli, Italy.

BOTTOM: Thinking carefully through the type of interventions to propose upgrades that are affordable and require limited ongoing costs can be part of a tactical urbanism. Barcelona public realm upgrade using potted planters, coloured demarcations, with provision of seating and public art.

CHAPTER 4: MAKING SENSE OF DESIGN

12. MAINTENANCE AND MANAGEMENT
Management and maintenance is sometimes confused with the service layer, which thinks about the practicalities of a functioning place, but in this instance we are considering a much wider and long-term view. Management and maintenance can be sometimes entirely focused on day-to-day activities that are required to keep places and spaces in a good state of repair – utilities work and window cleaning for example. It is important to pay attention to the maintenance of a space as regardless of how high quality the design is, it will degrade over time. Management also has a temporal component. Day and night, as well as seasonal change play an important role in this layer.

The day to day – Whether a proposed development or space will be publicly or privately owned and managed may influence the way it is designed (reflecting on the finance that is available in the longer term). Universally spaces and buildings need to be cleaned and repaired to ensure that they are looked after in the long term. When designing places, it is important to understand who would/could/should be managing the area and what facilities and resources they might have available. In residential areas this is much easier, as these are typically the responsibility of the homeowner, but increasingly developments include management companies and third parties who play a vital role in long term quality.

Seasonal changes – Seasons can impact the way cities are managed. The seasons will affect our streets and spaces in a variety of ways - the planting and green infrastructure will clearly change, whether the space is to be used for activities or events and even the requirements of the people who will use them. To best illustrate this point, it is useful to consider an urban square. In the spring and summer, the space could be a welcome outdoor room for events and concerts, the opportunity for floral displays and outdoor cafes and bars will be significant, and people will seek shade from whatever vegetation is provided. Compare this to the winter months where a Christmas market might 'pop-up' and south facing spaces may be the only location that are suitable for sitting out in. This seasonal progression means that the space has to be designed to accommodate maximum flexibility.

Adaptation - It's also important to think more long term about how the place might evolve and adapt over time as nowhere ever stays the same and the ever-changing socio-economic context will require a place to change over time. For example, changing retail trends in northern Europe (where our two case studies for this book are focused) over the last 20 years have seen the contraction of high street retailing in place of online shopping, and a growth of leisure, food and drink uses in their place. The ability to design and develop places that can be adapted to new uses, needs or roles is vitally important. Thus, buildings must be to accommodate as many different potential use scenarios as possible.

BELOW IMAGES: Careful consideration is required regarding maintenance and management of the spaces around and between blocks/ buildings - Residential developments in Newcastle, UK (LEFT) and Helsinki, Finland (RIGHT) showcase how ownership of edge conditions are critical to providing the appropriate public setting for quality urban design.

4.4 LEARNING FROM DESIGN

IMPORTANCE OF BEST PRACTICE

Throughout this chapter we have employed a range of international best practice examples to illustrate how *liveable qualities* and *functional layers* are realised in urban design internationally. How to learn from urban best practice is a vital question – undoubtably exploring best practice is a useful exercise, but as reflective practitioners we need to be weary of the pitfalls of transferring design across contexts and placing too much emphasis on the role of 'urban design frameworks' over context/people.

In the first instance, designers must carefully consider and determine '*what is best practice?*' in reflection of their aims, vision, or broader goals. As we highlight, this requires designers to consider the contemporary priorities of their field and identify appropriate examples. Contemporary urban design is more international than ever before, and so often this mode of practice will lead designers to uncover a range of international ideas (precedents) for consideration. For example, in creating intergenerational public spaces as is common in East Asian cities, our thinking on best practice will require an exploration on leading contexts in this practice, to help structure and support our thinking and help define our understanding.

Best practice is linked to designing quality but also to testing and challenging our own preconceived ideas of the practices of the design profession. In recognising that much of the thinking and theory on urban design focuses on suggesting best practice (prescriptive) or critiquing poor practice (proscriptive) we recommend considering best practice as achieving excellence in a specific thematic area (or across a range of themes), as well as coupling tactics together to reinforce the multifarious benefits of well-considered and varied design which puts people first. For example, working through this chapter, you have explored best practice case studies across a range of thematic areas such as integrated mobilities design in Aarhus, Denmark, sense of place in Vienna, Austria, or sustainable design in Masdar, UAE – what happens when you explore the entanglements of these ideas? The task of the designer is to ensure a wealth of best practice is considered but especially best practice in reflection of your main themes/emphasis to stimulate new thoughts and directions. This is how we learn from best practice, prioritising international creative solutions to respond to specific design challenges. Much of this work will involve the use of precedents – i.e., real-world designs, long-established practices or a successful model of design that serve as exemplars to the profession – to authorise or justify a similar act of design.

PRECEDENCE

Precedents can aid your design process providing inspiration and their use can lend authority to your design by associating your proposal to 'real-world' examples. Precedents communicate a meaning to your design, whether as a form of dialogue to your client, the public or for the designer. In this way, urban design precedents can help you solve problems in a design process that have previously been solved elsewhere. In the AUD Framework understanding best practice comes forward with the development of the design brief (Chapter 7) and in particular during the process of developing, detailing and delivering the design (Chapters 8, 9, and 10), but it can feature in earlier stages of the design process also. In establishing the design brief, the objectives and actions associated with the design become clear. In understanding these aspects, the designer can seek guidance in specific subjects and select suitable precedents for the design. A coastal urban environment affected by flooding may lead you to explore innovations in water-sensitive urban design and consequently uncover safe-to-fail flood design and practices such as the sponge city concept.

Doing this provides designers with a contemporary knowledge of new approaches in the design fields, this should extend beyond urban design and into related fields of architecture, landscape, service design, highways and masterplanning. By expanding knowledge in these fields, designers have a broader understanding of what can be achieved in place, and the tools and techniques that can assist in successful schemes. Key to learning from best practice, particularly outside the context of your site (especially internationally), is to recognise that duplication is not a contextually responsive approach to providing place.

LESSONS ACROSS CONTEXTS

While best practice is important, 'travelling ideas' must be carefully considered. Best practice in design and planning has, at times, been viewed as ideas that can easily circulate the globe, filtering and mediating through policy and practice regardless of context. However, 'travelling ideas' stemming from beliefs around progress, development, growth, and the notion that urban design can be replicated have resulted in a proliferation of context-less design and visions internationally (Black and Sonbli, 2021). As set out in Chapters 2 and 3, we argue that urban design must usefully attend more carefully to the local contexts in which it is practised to better appreciate the distinct practice of urban design and better understand how designers can champion and deliver contextually responsive high quality design solutions. Our framework therefore supports a more rigorous engagement with best practice design linking it to the site's context and thus avoiding replication in the hope it will have the same positive impacts.

With this disclaimer in mind, designers can and should learn from other projects, both locally and internationally. What can be gleaned from best practice precedents and case studies is how specific projects have utilised principles and their own unique context to drive a design forward why it is important for your design.

or influence the decision-making process. A combination of approaches using precedents local to your site, which can help develop an understanding of the vernacular of best practice in your specific context, as well as international case studies are preferred. In selecting projects consider what sets it apart from other similar practices?, what has the design achieved (perhaps it is an innovative example of a specific component of urban design, a technique we demonstrated across this chapter)?, if you were to break it up into parts what are its constituent components e.g. materials, street furniture, massing?, how might it work with your site/context/design? Through an analysis of best practice precedents and case studies you can emphasise what has been learned and why it is important for your design.

Taking time to research and interpret best practice enables the designer to understand how it works, its parts and distinctive features. Considering similar questions to those above is vital to fully understand all aspects of the project or the segment of a project you are focusing on. Conduct your analysis of best practice/s according to what you are trying to discover, understand, or resolve. Aspects to consider can include structure, scale, materials, details, context, social/cultural impact, form, access, aesthetic, programming, implementation and phasing, maintenance, and

ABOVE: Jinhua, China. Urban designers can learn a lot from the sponge city concept from such places to provide water-sensitive interventions elsewhere, yet wholesale copying should be avoided.

management (which we pick up through the live case studies of Aalborg and Manchester across Chapters 6-10).

To be specific you must identify the area which applies to your design and demonstrate the lessons learnt from the precedent / case study by highlighting ways you could take the best practice example forward integrating it into your proposals to solve specific design problems. These must be clearly communicated to the client, the public and other built environment professionals to provide appropriate reasoning and justify the relationship between best practice used and the vision for your site. Building an urban design vocabulary of best practice through a precedent/case study library that you can refer to during your design process(es) can be helpful to immerse yourself in urban design, asking critical questions of designs you see and experience.

BUILDING KNOWLEDGE
There are a variety of formats to explore best practice including design courses in education, professional bodies and groups, and many design practices host regular study tours to immerse their students/members in place and expose them to new ideas and experiences. Design journals, periodicals, and magazines are in wide circulation, as designers have a thirst for investigating what is new, seeking to learn what providing quality places for people across differing contexts looks like. Although the internet and specific design websites are a valuable resource, we stress a need to consider a variety of sources including magazines, journals, and books. Site visits, sketching and being in a place are arguably more impactful but not always practical. It is important to walk in the cities your visit, and experience the urban for yourself. Building your knowledge of landscapes of best-practice and how these change over time will develop naturally as you practice, as part of a lifelong and reflective engagement with the built environment.

CONCLUSIONS

Across the chapter and via best practice, we highlight that engaging with three practicalities of design (*1. Contextual Dynamics, 2. Liveable Qualities and 3. Functional Blueprints*) are key to making sense of design and to delivering quality contextually responsive design solutions in practice. Here, design layers, the functional aspect must be combined with design quality, the liveable aspects, to uncover good or better practice urban design and unpack critical relationships and linkages across key design considerations/components. In learning from design, we highlight the importance of developing knowledge and skill as a designer to practice effectively. In **PART B: The Applied Urban Design Framework** (Chapters 5-10) we turn our attention to applying the AUD Framework, and how multi-scalar contextually responsive design can be achieved in practice.

IMAGES: Learning from other places is vital to develop skills as an urban designer - places with different cultures and development histories help expand your understanding of context and its importance in urban design. Building a personal portfolio of knowledge on how spaces and places are used and enjoyed by different people can only benefit urban designers.

RIGHT: Central Road, Tokyo, Japan.

BELOW: Monastiraki Square, Athens, Greece.

HOTEL GRACERY
驚安の殿堂
ドン・キホーテ
居酒屋
7F·8F
SHIDAX
BIC DRUG
IMAX
海賊とよばれた男
12.10
ROADSHOW
MARUHAN
GODZILLA ROAD
新感覚ネットカフェBooth
居楽屋
きんくら酒場
金の蔵
カラオケ
ONOMI YAKI
トラノコ

Fan Pier Walkway, Boston, USA

PART B
APPLIED URBAN DESIGN FRAMEWORK

PROCESS → OUTCOMES

SITE & CLIENT

CONTEXT

1 Analysis
Strategic
+
Local

→ Strategic Profile

→ Area Profile
Site Profile

PIVOT

2 Urban Design Program

→ A: Design Considerations
B: Design Brief

DESIGN

3 Design Development

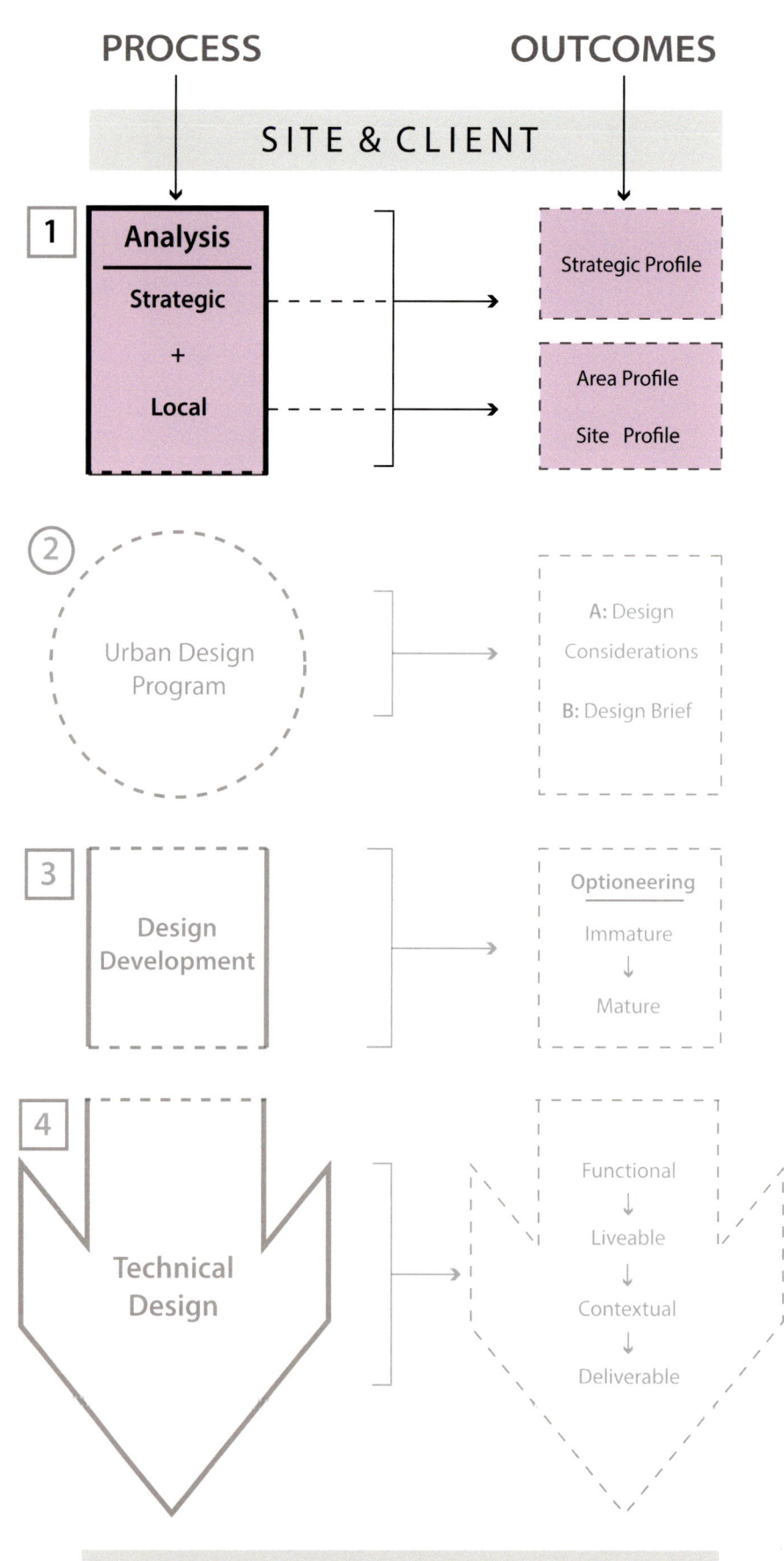

→ Optioneering
Immature
↓
Mature

4 Technical Design

→ Functional
↓
Liveable
↓
Contextual
↓
Deliverable

PLACE

CHAPTER 5: STRATEGIC ANALYSIS

CHAPTER 5
Strategic Analysis

The AUD Framework begins with Step 1 - **Analysis**. This step is the context building that will later inform a more contextually sensitive design intervention. Analysis is split across two distinct dimensions (or broad '*scales*') - the **Strategic** (this chapter) and **Local** (chapter 6). The chapter is unpacks strategic analysis across six sections, the first provides an overview to strategic analysis, and defining the strategic scale. The second unpacks the purpose of the strategic stage of analysis, and the consideration of trends and futures both spatial and otherwise. The third discusses the key elements of strategic analysis and how urban designers can engage in strategic scale questions, considering policy, climate and sustainable development, people, spatial statistics, cultural heritage, and geographical connectivity. The fourth and fifth sections focus on the application of the technique and how to develop a strategic overview for presentation in design projects, policies, and proposals, this is supplemented with examples from the two live case studies in Aalborg and Manchester. We finish the chapter by highlighting how the key conclusions from the strategic analysis will be taken forward to generate a '*Strategic Profile*'.

OVERVIEW

In the first instance, urban designers must carefully consider and determine what constitutes the **strategic scale** based on the overall size of their site and what can be defined as the site's context. This may differ dramatically between a small corner plot and a large strategic masterplan. The context of a site is produced at any number of territories: global, national, regional, city-regional, metropolitan, city. The purpose of the strategic dimension is to ensure careful consideration has been given to the potential and reality of the site across a variety of these territories. Engaging at the strategic level requires the design team to deliberate on what geographic territories must be included in the analysis to capture strategic concerns or opportunities. The different strategic scales that designers might use are summarised in Table 1. It is important to reiterate that as many variations as necessary, or possible, should be considered for any site. Exemplifications are included for each scale but again these are not exhaustive, rather they serve to illustrate what might be included or considered.

Considering the different levels associated with strategic analysis can help inform a more robust and rigorous appreciation of the location. Comprehension of the strategic scales can help urban designers to ensure that a genuinely contextual approach has been taken in their analysis that likely will also be reflected in their design. Using these levels helps to exemplify where urban designers might place their attention in questions or concerns at the strategic level. Working through these, we can see how each level will relate to the other.

OPPOSITE PAGE: Chapters 5 (Strategic) and 6 (Local) are focused on step 1 of the Applied Urban Design Framework - the context building phase. [An overview of the AUD Framework can be found in Chapter 3].

BELOW: A site may have strategic relevance beyond the immediate surroundings - into the wider city, region, or even national or international considerations that the urban designer may need to analyse. This is particularly true in major global centres such as New York City, USA.

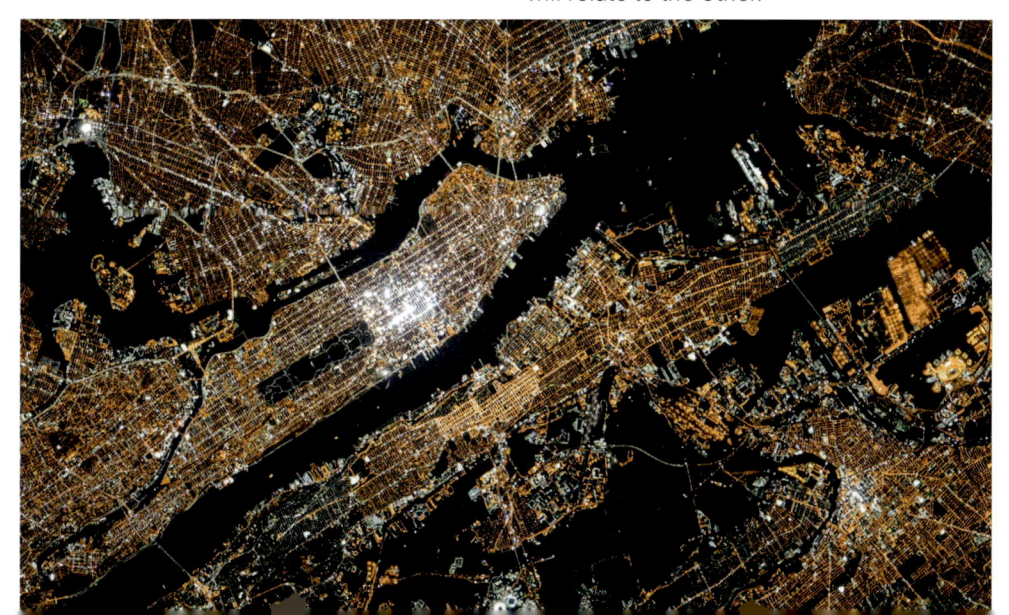

Strategic Scales	
Term	Description
Global/International	The consideration of the impact of urban development in the context of globalisation including global strategies, markets, and capital flows. Likewise, this involves considering the global scale of economic and social change and the complexity and diversity of how these changes might manifest at the local level (Hartt, 2018). Examples include the United Nations Sustainable Development Goals.
National	Involves the consideration of national agendas in planning, urban design, housing, infrastructure, and land use as well as the national policy framework governing urban design. This scale will ask questions of national priorities in urban design such as affordability and availability of high quality housing.
Regional	Regions are defined geographical areas which represent the constituent parts of a national territory, for example the North West of England or the Region of Zealand in Denmark. Nonetheless, they can also represent areas that are broadly defined by physical characteristics or contain significant natural features such as coastal regions or mountainous regions. Most commonly, regions are an administrative area, division, or district within a specific country.
City-Region	Combinations of an urban core or core city, linked to semi-urban and rural hinterland are often associated with a specific development policy or fixed geographical territory. City-regions have important implications for the design and implementation of development strategies. The concept can be understood as a functionally inter-related geographical area comprising a central or core city, as part of a network of urban centres and rural hinterlands. A little bit like the hub (city) and the spokes (surrounding urban/rural areas) on a bicycle wheel (Rodríguez-Pose, 2008).
Metropolitan Area	Often denote large city areas (metropolis) or, as it is more commonly used, an organically and dynamically-defined territory that extends beyond the core city. Metropolitan areas may or may not have any corresponding administrative boundaries. Beyond political or institutional frameworks, what unifies the different jurisdictions and locales that constitute a metropolitan area are the economic and social relationships that occur within it, as well as the features of the built environment and infrastructures that enable these relationships (d'Albergo, Lefèvre, & Ye, 2018). A variety of metropolitan plans exist in Europe such as the Copenhagen Fingerplan and the Barcelona Territorial Metropolitan Plan.
Commuter Belts	With some similarity to Metropolitan areas, Commuter Belts are typically soft boundaries which capture the areas surrounding a city from which a large number of people travel to work daily. Like Metropolitan areas, these boundaries may span multiple cities and regions. Additionally, they often include rail, air and sea networks. For example, Manchester airport and the affluent Cheshire commuter belt (Hincks et al., 2017).
City	A specific human settlement with specific characteristics linked to: certain population or employment densities, cultures and subcultures, the built environment and the prevalence of infrastructure systems (da Cruz et al., 2020)

TABLE 1 Strategic Scales

5.1 PURPOSE OF STRATEGIC ANALYSIS

Urban design operates across a broad set of 'contexts'. The context of a site, as emphasised, can be produced across the: global, scale, regional, city-regional, city, local, neighbourhood, streetscape etc. The purpose of the strategic dimension is to ensure careful consideration has been given to the potential beyond the traditional focus of site boundary and immediate surroundings. Here, careful consideration must be given to the significance of 'scale' and 'context' in reflection of the development site and situation. Our framework argues that the use of scale in practice must be fluid, allowing designers to account for complexities as they design. Binding interventions to a single scale or context like a neighbourhood can ignore key cross-scale interactions (Milz et al., 2018). While determining the site's context is the first concern - the spatial component of strategic analysis. The second concern is to develop an awareness of your site in reflection of change over time; the temporal component of Strategic Analysis – Trends and Futures.

The most common understanding of time in urban design is in reflection of the development process, or the development pipeline, the sequence of events that lead to the implementation and construction of any given design project. However, more recently, time has become an important feature in urban redevelopment and place-making (see Madanipour, 2017). Since the global economic crisis of 2008, timing and temporality within the urban environment have gained increasing prominence as the unpredictability and cyclical nature of development became all too visible in our cities (Martin et al., 2020). Ultimately, we know that the success or failure of any development project is determined over time. Thus, urban designers must attempt to account for time in their practices. We suggest that the identification of trends, to consider changes that have occurred over time to date and projected futures, to begin to work resiliency and adaptability into the analysis can greatly improve the knowledge base of the design team and ultimately improve the design.

Trends refer to how a place changes over time to date, what might be described as *longitudinal analysis*, whereas **Futures** refer to the projections for a place going forward and how resilience may be improved as a consequence, what might be described as *resiliency analysis*. Both are concerned with providing an account of converging or contrasting patterns affecting the site (the spatial) over time (temporal) in recent years and in future years. Trends and Futures can be positive, negative, impartial, and in flux. Here urban design has the possibility to reinforce positive trends, realise future opportunities, overcome sophisticated barriers or tackle embedded inequalities. For example, by 2050, over 70% of the world's children and elderly population will live in cities – this trend highlights the pressing need for urban designers, among others, to be aware of the role they play in responding to demographic change (UN, 2021).

Designers have a role to play in better incorporating time in their analysis, by considering how a variable may have changed over time as well as how that variable is projected to change in the future. It is important to stress that this is a complex endeavour but a vital one for the profession. Not all variables will require this degree of consideration, some lend themselves more to this than others, such as demographics, development patterns, or climatic changes. In advocating for urban futures that are contextually responsive, part of the task is for designers to go outside their comfort zone to realise the potential of places. The obtainment and use of detailed statistics for a number of variables may not be common compared to figure ground or land use analysis, but they are of increasing significance in the designer's toolbox.

It is important to have a clear understanding of the spatial trends influencing your site and the people who live in the neighbourhoods and communities that your site sits within or can affect. Considerations of spatial trends are typically associated with questions surrounding the demographics, economy, development, the culture of the site. Understanding how the context has changed or continues to change over time is critical to ensure the designer understands key socio-spatial changes. In some cases, this will involve considerations of extreme spatial trends, for example the changing nature of conflict, such as in the post-conflict cities of Belfast in Northern Ireland or Sarajevo in Bosnia and Herzegovina. In others, this will involve working through questions on urban informality (Boano and Astolfo, 2016) or the implications of gated communities on social inequality (Kostenwein, 2021). Likewise, in recent years, we have seen an increased turn in attention to the securitisation of cities and prioritisation of counter-terror in our city and streetscapes, notable examples include hostile design (Rosenberger, 2020), counter-terror by design (Coaffee, 2020) and the privatisation of public spaces more broadly (Bruyns and Nel, 2020). These spatial trends affect the way people experience places and thus raise important questions on the 'quality' of places for people considering these new circumstances.

Most recently, the consideration of pathogens in our everyday life – as a result of the coronavirus pandemic – created a range of unique spatial trends across the world to help facilitate required social distancing (Deas et al., 2021). While we cannot go into detail on all of these factors here, we must stress that the nature of our cities continues to change resulting in trends that are both positive and negative. We know that inequalities exist and can be exacerbated through projects that result in gentrification and displacement (Clark, 2005). In addition, and even more sinister, we can see in many places across the world the ways in which the built environment can accentuate profiling, segregation, and prejudices of peoples (Doucet, et al., 2021). In response, we encourage designers to front up to the presence of complex and difficult subjects in our places and spaces.

The responsibility of designers is to foster an inclusive and enjoyable environment for all people and thus, urban design must champion inclusivity of gender, sexual orientation, ethnicity, race, and other markers of identity as part of the direct effort of the profession to prioritise fairness and equity in the design and provision of spaces for people in cities.

TOP: Despite peace in Northern Ireland as a result of the Good Friday Agreement - Belfast still has a number of '*peace walls*' in place that divide communities. These walls do not only create physical barriers but also social and cultural ones.

LEFT: Manchester, UK has seen a rapid rise in the privatisation of public space throughout the city. These spaces, such as Circle Square, are re-defining what 'public' realm looks and feels like for users as they are strictly managed, and policed, in terms of what you can and cannot do within them.

CHAPTER 5: STRATEGIC ANALYSIS

DHARAVI, INDIA is an informal settlement in the centre of Mumbai; it is India's largest slum at over 240 hectares. The informal settlement is at the centre of a heated debate regarding the city authorities desire to remove it as an illegal development to increase the city's economic potential. However, Dharavi is home to communities and is developed around a dynamic *work-live-dwell* format, with its own thriving informal economy. This **contested urbanism** asks pertinent questions about the relevance of social justice and the right to the city in any urban transformations.

PRODUCTION of SPATIALITIES
The narrative of Dharavi highlights how land values and built densities sit at the base of the contested visions for Mumbai's future. Government and market pressures towards the drive to world class city status push against the struggle for a bottom up, inclusive, development process. These conflicts can serve to accentuate inequalities and debates over space ownership.

URBAN DESIGN - A WEAPON FOR DEMOGRAPHIC CHANGE
A *tabula rasa* redevelopment strategy for Dharavi - replacing informal settlement with high-rise expansion of the city centre - is centred on the argument that the space is *terra nulla* - empty land with no history (Bhabha, 1994). This is at odds with the area's rich evolution - and its existing unique character and diverse mix of ethnicities and religious narratives (Patel and Arputham, 2007). In effect it is employing urban design as a weapon (see Black and Sonbli, 2021) to promote a shift in the demographic of Dharavi - displacing the existing population to make way for a new, more homogenised residential reality.

CONTESTED URBANISM
For urban design lessons can be learned from Dharavi - the necessity to recognise the nuances and subtleties of informality and slum development - not as homogenous spaces, but as a city itself, constructed of impurity, ambivalence, and in a state of constant evolution (Boano et al., 2013). The social struggles inherent in such contested urbanism, if better understood, can create new drivers of knowledge production, re-thinking the right to the city and how we, as urban designers, reflect more closely on how and what we produce within a contested vision of urbanism.

TOP: Dharavi's strategic location and proximity to the city centre has seen it flagged as prime real-estate and a target for economic growth and development. The juxtaposition of the formal and informal creates two cities that currently fail to connect.

MIDDLE: Dharavi has a thriving informal economy - and a large population, potentially over 1 million people are living and working in the slum.

BOTTOM: It is critical to not forget the challenges of informal development - of which there are many - and how urban design might effectively tackle them, in recognising them as part of the city.

Spatial trends represent a unique opportunity for designers to capture the key considerations of the context, whether this be in the form of extreme crises, such as terrorism, or more subtlety, the echoes, and memories of a place's past as it changes over time. Spatial trends relate to both socio-economic and socio-demographic trends as well as trends in the built form and urban structure of the place and context. Regarding the latter, this might involve questions surrounding architectural culture, for example, the prioritisation of circular economy in construction projects or in built form, changes in the morphological fabric of the city (Hebbert, 2016) or likewise, a desire for a particular type of housing in response to changing market demand. As spatial trends are vast and varied, we are unable to go into depth across all possible and relevant examples. Nonetheless, to aid readers and assist their analysis, we provide a selection of themes to consider as well as examples of analysis and illustrative references for further reading – the selected trends are of particular significance in contemporary urban design and planning.

It is important to note that, spatial trends may require supplementary desk-based research beyond your urban design analysis to ascertain the key questions to consider and the best means to record that data, including customised variables and plans.

5.2 ELEMENTS OF STRATEGIC ANALYSIS

In undertaking strategic analysis, a number of elements should be considered. Each variable is selected to help the design team understand how they can engage in strategic scale questions considering, policy; climate and sustainability agendas; people e.g. socio-economic and demographic data; relevant statistics; cultural heritage, as well as geographical connectivity and infrastructure. Taken together, these variables act as the platform from which to launch your explorative analysis at this scale. The strategic analysis requires the designer to engage with a set of considerations, while also developing an understanding of aforementioned aspects of: Trends, and Futures. A strategic analysis works across these key elements to ascertain trends, unpack projections, and develop a resilient, strategic vision for the place.

It is important to reiterate that as many variables as necessary, or possible, should be considered for any site at the strategic scale. The conclusions of each piece of analysis provide a starting point for potential cross or comparative analysis, wherein, all variables should be considered against each other to seek out relationships and trends. The outcome of this process will provide you with an indication of the core lines of inquiry at the strategic scale as well as the critical elements of the analysis to feature in the **Strategic Profile** (see 6.6).

BELOW: **Morphological changes over time within a place can unpack a complex narrative - revealing potentially rich histories that have shaped a location and its people. Manchester's development has seen major influence from the Industrial Revolution, post-industrial decline, and contemporary growth as new economies blossom.**

1. 1900s The industrial city
A strong grid of streets, clearly defined by terraced worker housing, fine grain, dominated by the railway station. The river Medlock is clearly identifiable flanked by a series of mills and workshops

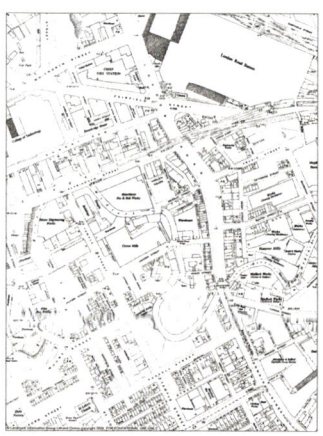

2. 1950s Post-war fragmentation
Bomb damage following WWII, and inner city housing clearance have left a series of vacant sites across the area; the railway still dominates, and the townscape lacks structuring coherence

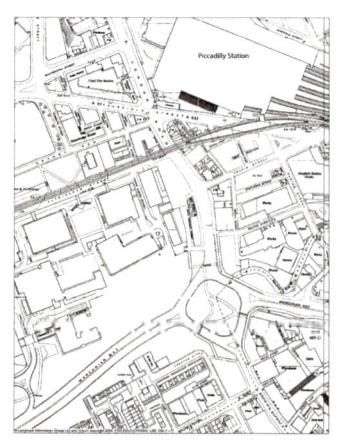

3. 1970s road building
The area is completely remodelled to accommodate high capacity highway building including the introduction of the Mancunian Way and other arterial routes. Around this large footprint, buildings have almost completely erased the fine grain industrial townscape

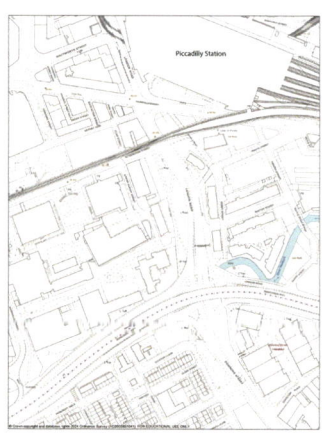

4. The current city
Changes over the last 100 years have almost completely obliterated the original pattern of streets and spaces. The river has almost completely disappeared from the surface. The area now has a coarse urban grain made up buildings with large footprints connected by major arterial routes

CHAPTER 5: STRATEGIC ANALYSIS

POLICY

In undertaking a strategic analysis, designers must engage with the political and administrative geography of their site. At the heart of this task is the careful consideration of policy – i.e., the series of regulations and guidance which define priorities, developability, programming (in certain instances, such as in the case of zonal codes or land-use plans) and how a development might take shape. Examples include international policy (e.g., World Heritage Status or SDGs), statutory (e.g. National and local policy), guidance (e.g. design guides) and evidence (e.g. development prospectus). In prioritising a joined-up approach to built environment thinking, designers should see policy, planning, guidance and control as both an opportunity (i.e., how future priorities of a city can be achieved) and as a creative restriction (i.e. how innovative practice can be achieved in respect of certain guidelines). The control of design will fall under different regulatory structures depending on the associated context. Our applied case studies in Aalborg and Manchester demonstrate the differentiation of those structures across the book.

There are broadly speaking, two types of development management systems: regulatory and discretionary (Booth, 1999). The Danish planning and development management system is an example of a regulatory system and the UK an example of a discretionary planning and development system. In the Danish system, strict clear rules and statutory weight sit behind policy to define what can be developed and where – this is typically defined in what is known as the *'local plan'*. However, in keeping with the national interest and significance of 'Danish design' specific tools, policies, and criteria through which to evaluate and manage design (such as in the UK) are replaced with city architects and their office for design, a practice of design competition, development prospectus (guiding design) and design priorities/policies (for the city, for districts/neighbourhoods and at a site level). The UK has elements of both systems, with tools, policies and criteria to evaluate/manage design but more broadly these sit within an architecture of institutional discretion which evaluate the merits of design proposals on an individual case-by-case basis (Carmona et al., 2017).

For urban design, a critical feature of planning and development regulation are the instruments used to consider design quality, those elements of planning control that are design specific. These controls can take a number of forms including policy, guidelines, codes, prospectus, advice, institutions and steering groups and specific mechanisms. For contextually responsive design, your role is to understand the context within which you operate and thus the system in which you are practising. From project-to-project urban designers build up a critical awareness of the controls that are in place in and between contexts and how they directly or indirectly impact the design process and delivery of a project.

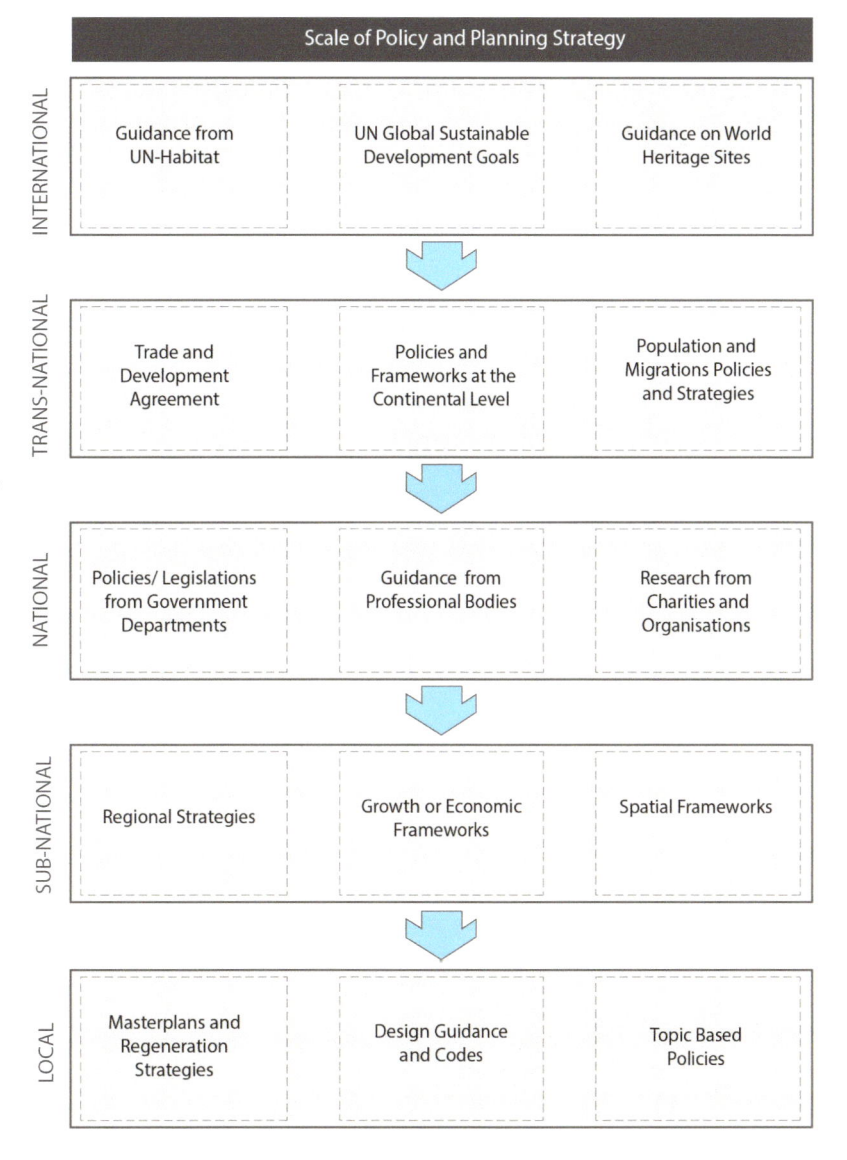

Scale of Policy and Planning Strategy

INTERNATIONAL	Guidance from UN-Habitat	UN Global Sustainable Development Goals	Guidance on World Heritage Sites
TRANS-NATIONAL	Trade and Development Agreement	Policies and Frameworks at the Continental Level	Population and Migrations Policies and Strategies
NATIONAL	Policies/ Legislations from Government Departments	Guidance from Professional Bodies	Research from Charities and Organisations
SUB-NATIONAL	Regional Strategies	Growth or Economic Frameworks	Spatial Frameworks
LOCAL	Masterplans and Regeneration Strategies	Design Guidance and Codes	Topic Based Policies

CLIMATE AND SUSTAINABILITY
Urban design has an important role to play in responding to the urgent need to address both the causes of climatic change and the impacts of unavoidable climate change. To do so requires a reframing of urban design interventions, with a renewed and revised interpretation of sustainable development, which has more regard to longer time horizons, pays more attention to the relationship between new and existing built form, and has a closer focus on integrating the built environment with natural processes such as the carbon and water cycles, ecosystems, and wildlife habitats (Wilson and Piper, 2010; Counsell and Stoneman, 2018).

Most recent conceptualisations of urban design demonstrate express concerns for the impact of local development on the broader global context of climate change. These have gradually worked their way into policy, both across the developed world and increasingly in the developing world. Urban design as a public policy area that largely deals with the built and urban form, the area most at risk from climatic change, has a core role to play in adapting to these changes. Consequently, urban designers must consider climate change adaptation in their professional practices as the principal mechanism to capture sustainability and climate change. Climate change adaptation may be understood as *"an adjustment in ecological, social or economic systems in response to observed or expected changes in climatic stimuli and their effects and impacts in order to alleviate adverse impacts of change or take advantage of new opportunities"* (IPCC, 2001: 20).

This broad definition of adaptation can include a range of actions, which in general can be grouped into two activities: i) building adaptive capacity and ii) implementing adaptation action. The former creates the information and conditions (regulatory, institutional, managerial) needed to support adaptation and the later takes specific steps to reduce vulnerability to threats arising from climate change (Tompkins et al., 2008; Stern, 2007). At the strategic scale of urban design analysis, the focus is on gathering the information and conditions needed to inform and support adaptation. Here, the purpose is to begin to piece together the range of climate issues affecting the site and its context.

Presently, we practice urban design within a situation where climate change impacts are being experienced more quickly and intensely than predicted (Carter and Handley, 2011). Globally we have witnessed a steady increase in the number of extreme weather events linked to human-caused climate change. The North American extreme heatwave of June 2021, for example, which affected the cities of Seattle, Portland, and Vancouver (with well over 9 million people in their combined metropolitan areas) with recorded temperatures far above 40°C was deemed to be *"virtually impossible without human-caused climate change"* (World Weather Attribution, 2021). To promote sustainable development at the strategic level, urban design practitioners, must consider a range of extreme weather events in their understanding of places and in particular how these events have changed over time. Frequency is also a pertinent consideration, namely if an event can be expected to happen 2-3 times per year, 2-3 times every 5 years or 1-2 times every 10 years. This equips the designers with a full appreciation of historical and recent climate events. Table 2 provides a summary of the types of extreme weather events that may need to be considered, dependent on site location. These are illustrative examples and should be bolstered by additional considerations.

Urban designers in their practices can help enhance and upskill other built environment sectors, such as planning and planners, to improve knowledge and awareness of climate change and enhance policy and guidance for adaptation also. Ultimately, responding to climate change is a transdisciplinary endeavour that warrants all built environment professionals to work together. If relevant frameworks or policies do not exist, it is part of the design team's role to try to piece together a climate change evidence base and share these resources with local authorities and other urban actors.

CHAPTER 6: LOCAL ANALYSIS

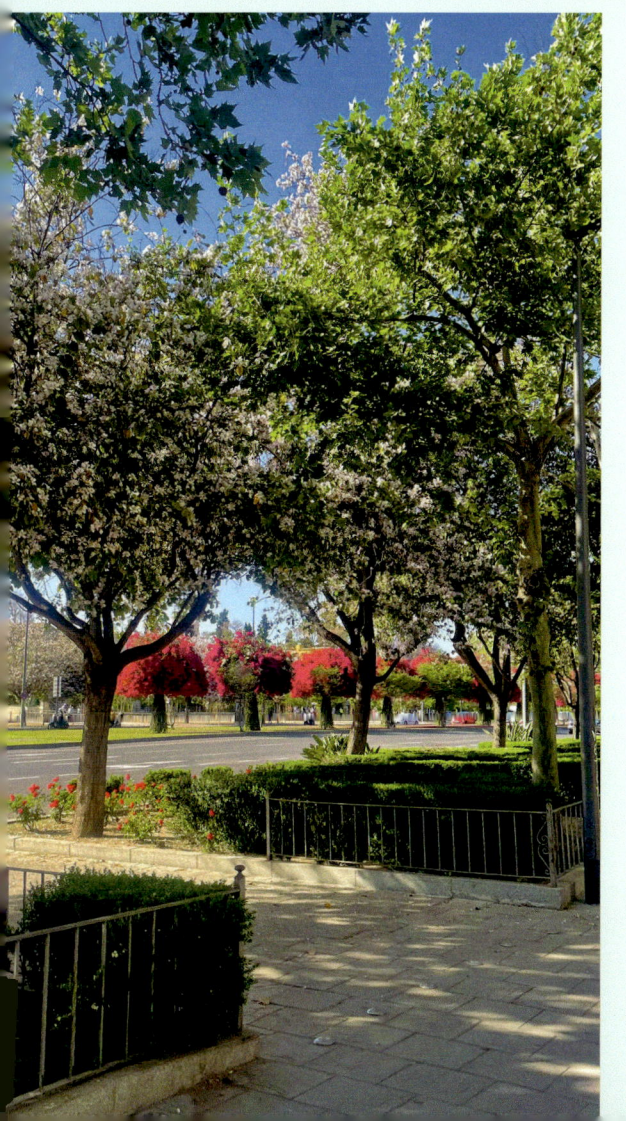

SEVILLE, SPAIN is a city that regularly now hits above 40C in the summer. It is also a city that recognises the negative impact this severe heat can have on its residents and its much-needed tourism economy - and the threat that increased global temperatures may have moving forwards. Seville was the first city in the world to categorise heatwaves - similar to how storms are now named in the UK, or hurricanes in the USA.

The City implements a '*policy of shade*' to enable its streets and spaces to be used and activated all year round - by all users young and old. Some of the strategies related to this include planting 5,000 trees a year, demanding construction materials that reflect heat (particularly in major new constructions) and installing water fountains and rest points across the city's public realm network.

Seville understands that it must adapt to the ever-evolving climate conditions - it is from such forward-thinking cities that others can learn as they seek creative and targeted best practices for designing appropriately and effectively to lower temperatures, enhance comfort, and maintain quality of life for all people.

ABOVE: As well as tree-planting, the city is installing public water fountains and ensuring ample rest spots for people - to encourage them to use the high-quality public streets and spaces all year round.

LEFT: Seville is planting approximately 5,000 trees a year in a bid to cool its streets and spaces for relief from rising temperatures.

Extreme Events: Glossary	
Term	Description
Cold Spells	Unusual cold spells can occur even in a warming world, and cause disruption to transport, energy and food supplies. Example events include the extreme cold in south east Europe in 2017, with extreme cold and snow in Italy, the Balkans and Turkey and multiple extreme cold events in North America in different regions and of different durations in 2014, 2016 and 2021 respectively.
Drought	Drought affects people in many ways, from reduced water and food supplies to increasing risk of wildfires. Examples include the Australian bushfires of 2019-20, the Cape Town water crisis in 2018 or severe droughts in Somalia and Kenya in 2016/17.
Extreme Rainfall	Rainfall events from a major storm or hurricane, or intense localised downpours can lead to flooding in any type of location. Example events include the Chennai, India floods in 2015, Storm Desmond in the UK in 2017, extreme rainfall in Japan in 2018 and the exceptionally high monsoon rainfall in South West India in 2018.
Heatwaves	Heatwaves can be particularly dangerous to humans, and occur all over the world with increasing intensity. Example events include the Siberian heatwave of 2020 or the Western North American extreme heatwave of 2021.
Storms	Storms usually include heavy rain, snow or hail, strong winds and thunder and lightning. Example events include the four strong wind storms over Western Europe in 2018 and in particular Storm Eleanor and Storm Friederike in January 2018 as well as Hurricane Florence in 2018 causing storm surges, extreme rainfall and high winds along the US East coast.
Air Pollution	Air pollution is the presence of substances in the atmosphere that are harmful to the health of humans and other living beings, or cause damage to the climate or to materials. Air pollutants are emitted from a range of both man-made and natural sources including: burning of fossil fuels in electricity generation, transport, industry and households; industrial processes; agriculture; waste treatment and natural sources, including volcanic eruptions or windblown dust. Unlike other extreme events, air pollution is experienced daily in cities. Extreme cases include Beijing, Shanghai, and the Pearl River Delta where particulate concentrations are very high; however, unhealthy air is now a global challenge.

TABLE 2 Extreme Weather Events

CHAPTER 5: STRATEGIC ANALYSIS   96

TOP: Smog creating a haze over the city of Shanghai, China. Recognising the challenges of air pollution and designing to tackle and prevent it are key for any future urban designs in a growing number of cities across the world.

MIDDLE: Extreme storms such as hurricanes and typhoons can cause devastation to urban form - New Orleans is still recovering from Hurricane Katrina in 2005. Future designs are seeking ways to be more adaptable to these events.

BOTTOM: Brindley, UK - one example of a growing trend of flooding in many UK cities as climate change alters historic rainfall trends. Resilience is required to ensure defences are robust and new climate realities are accepted and integrated into how we design our cities.

PEOPLE

As discussed at length in Chapter 4, urban design is about the creation of quality places **for people**. It is therefore important to support a clear understanding of policy with a robust insight of the people who live in the neighbourhoods and communities that your site sits within or can impact upon. It is the responsibility of the designer to ensure people are central - this process begins at the strategic analysis stage, developing an understanding of the users of the place, policy priorities associated with people and communities and the target audience/potential future users. Part of this process involves the consideration of trends and projections to understand what the current socio-spatial situation is and how this will change over time. It is likely that through your policy analysis at the more local level you will have access to registered existing data, evidence and analysis conducted on people in place by the local municipality. A good exercise is to summarise these details and cross-check based on your own review. The most sensible starting point to provide a clearer picture of who lives in and around the site involves reviewing available demographic data, for example, census data. Like historical mapping, census data provides a robust summary of a local residential population at a specific moment in time (typically 10 years). However, overreliance on census information should be avoided, particularly if the census was completed some years prior.

In most contexts, supplementary analysis of census data exists to provide a more robust account of the findings. Thus, it is worth reviewing if unique datasets relevant to your context may exist. In the UK for example, Residential-based Area Classifications produced by the Office of National Statistics use socio-economic and demographic data to identity areas of cities with similar characteristics, demonstrating broad geographic patterns, categorising data for further analysis and identifying similar areas for comparative studies. Likewise, a Workplace-based Area Classification provides supplementary analysis for workplace zones. These datasets pinpoint areas where there may be 'young ethic communities', 'endeavouring social renters', 'affluent communities', 'constrained renters', 'aspiring urban households', 'ageing urban communities' or 'cosmopolitan student neighbourhoods. This information can inform designers if the communities are made up of any dominant populations such as students, if they have high numbers of young families, areas with an ageing population, second-home communities, or highly qualified professionals.

Similar information, coupled with supporting policy details produced by the local municipality can be useful in starting to answer key questions as to who are the urban community associated with the site. Latter considerations as part of the local analysis stage can further support people in place by understanding what people have access to relative to demographics trends/needs e.g. play space provision for areas with young families or green space provision for local residents, what they may need (in terms of deficiencies of provision) and what infrastructure can be improved and bolstered. Other sources of information to provide a strategic overview of people in place include reviewing housing typologies, the use of Google Earth (time function) and historical maps to consider changes in land use over time and the presence of land disuse such as levels of vacancy and/or dereliction.

BELOW: The principality of Monaco is unusual in that official citizens (Monegasques) make up a minority, approximately 20% of the 36,000 total population. Monaco citizenship offers substantial advantages that are not available to other residents. Much of the non-citizen population do not reside in Monaco exclusively, leading to constant shifts in the numbers of people living in the city at any given time. Such details are a necessary part of building a robust understanding of the strategic context.

CHAPTER 5: STRATEGIC ANALYSIS

STATISTICS

In undertaking a strategic analysis, fast and reliable ways to develop a comprehensive overview of the site/context are invaluable. Utilising the wealth of statistics available online can provide valuable and convenient data (via a desktop review) to help better understand the situation and possible changes over time. There are a wide variety of examples, and these will differ depending on the context of the site, but a useful starting point is to consider the presence of land disuse e.g., levels of vacancy and/or dereliction, information on crimes committed, accident reports as well as market information including residential and commercial prices/rental rates.

Vacancy rates - The level and extent of land/building disuse in a neighbourhood is often recorded by each city and fed into a regional or national register – such as in the case of Britain the *Brownfield Register*, or in the case of Denmark, The *Central Register of Buildings and Dwellings* (BBR). These registers hold publicly available information on building permits, exemptions, licenses, demolition as well as ownership/occupancy updated by local municipalities annually. In the Danish case, a user can filter data on vacancy in terms of location, typology, numbers of rooms and period of occupancy and create maps, charts, and tables. Information on building/land vacancy provides an overview of the attractiveness, developability, and broader market of the area. It can also influence and have implications for the level of crime and anti-social behaviour, type of employment opportunities, and overall health of the community. Likewise, if significant amounts of longstanding vacant sites are being built out it may suggest a certain buoyancy in the overall profile of the area/adjacent neighbourhoods and the prospect for more dynamic uses, regeneration, and developments in the future. It may also raise concerns on, and questions of, local displacement/gentrification if local housing and businesses are being challenged by a quick succession of new developments – such as in the case of Liverpool's Baltic Triangle where private-sector rented apartments on vacant sites have caused issues of displacement for light-manufacturing and music/performance venues (Martin et al., 2019).

Thus, land disuse and the rate at which brownfield sites remain stagnant or are being developed can provide important strategic insights about the market and future of the area your site is associated with or adjacent to.

Crime data - Crime data can highlight specific problems at neighbourhood level and where these incidents occurred. Many cities provide spatial information on reported incidents of crime, typically categorised into crime types e.g., public order or bicycle theft. The use of this data can help designers to understand the scale of crime occurring and whether their site sits within a crime hotspot. High rates of crime are common in urban, particularly city locations, so it is important to consider this data as an 'indicator' of potential social challenges. The data can be helpful for urban designers to establish patterns of incidents and if design flaws such as poor lighting, vacant or residual space and visibility issues exist. The data provides a strategic overview on safety, how people may feel in this location and how people perceive the area - raising important questions on the transition of the place between day/night for consideration as part of the *Local Analysis* (*see* Chapter 6).

ABOVE: The introduction of private-sector apartments on vacant sites had negative impacts on historic uses within the Baltic Triangle area of Liverpool, UK - such as displacement of music venues and light-manufacturing.

Travel: Accident reports, congestion, and air pollution data - Travel patterns are another useful dataset that allows you to understand modal share and patterns (recording where people are travelling to/from for work, and by what means). At the strategic scale, understanding the everyday realities of mobilities infrastructure to/from and within the site can be useful data, allowing the design team to explore roads/streets in some detail. Accident reports provide a record of causalities across a range of types e.g., a bicycle casualty, a pedestrian casualty or a child casualty, the number of vehicles involved and the severity of the incident between slight, serious, and fatal collisions.

This data enables designers to understand where accidents occur, the type of mobility infrastructure impacted and the frequency of occurrences. Likewise, congestion data provides a useful record of the stress specific road infrastructures may be subjected to (including times and days), enabling designers to generate an appreciation of current pressures experienced across the city/neighbourhood. Finally, the presence and severity of air pollution is now a pressing concern in our everyday urban lives. Polluting vehicles impact how we navigate and engage with urban settings, making them a potential risk to our health. Urban designers, in working through strategic questions, should review an air quality index for the area. This data provides a real-time record of the risks from air pollution based on the levels of particulate matter to determine if unhealthy or hazardous air quality exists. These risks can be tracked across a single day, a week, month, or year to develop a strategic appreciation of the potential issues facing communities.

Poor quality air is becoming a much more common issue for designers to consider but creative governance solutions in cities are required such as clean air and ultra-low emissions zones (ULEZ) which are beyond the capabilities of the design team. Rather, urban designers must work to encourage modal shift, sustainable mobility, and schemes which are integrated into the public transport network.

Market prices, House Prices/Types - Market prices such as housing prices and rental rates for commercial property reveal strategic insights into the desirability and attractiveness of the neighbourhood, street or city space – much of which is linked to the other considerations outlined, e.g., a neighbourhood with a high rate of vacancy, significant occurrences of road/crime incidents, and poor levels of air quality is likely to have low housing prices indexes and sales or an uncompetitive commercial market. By comparison, desirable neighbourhoods, streets, and public spaces are linked to an attractive public realm, access and provision of facilities and amenities including parks and recreational areas as well as maintenance. These details allow designers to appreciate the overall buoyancy of the market in the area as well as the mix of tenure i.e., what's available, if the market is to buy or rent and the most common types of accommodation e.g. family housing, apartments for young professionals, student lettings or a mix. Designers must carefully consider provision in their analysis and support the creation of residential and commercial areas that prioritise diversity in property type, ownership, and affordability.

BELOW: Understanding travel patterns at different times of the day, week, or even year can be beneficial to ensuring design aims to alleviate rather than exacerbate pressure points within the route network. Bangkok, Thailand has a very high modal share for car usage, leading to regular congestion and poor air quality issues.

CHAPTER 5: STRATEGIC ANALYSIS

CULTURAL HERITAGE
Going back in time to show the evolution of the city, district and neighbourhood is of critical importance to the practice of urban design, and how memory and the echoes of a place's past might be captured in your analysis for its future. Because of the deep continuities of buildings, plots, and streetforms over time, and their significance for collective memory, urban design and planning are as much about the past as the future (Hebbert, 2016). A study of the site's history and change can be done through an appreciation of historical mapping and through the use of Google Earth to account for more recent changes that have occurred.

At the strategic level, considerations of history and change will not necessarily focus on individual buildings; rather it is about developing an appreciation of the significant changes that the city has undergone over a wide time span – likely over more than 100 years. Questions of history and change at this scale will involve considerations of economic restructuring i.e. if industry has led to a city visibly scarred by post-industrial sites, the effects of modernist planning i.e. the presence large roadways and motorways, and considerations of urban regeneration i.e. if design-led or culture-led regeneration have occurred across the city. At this scale, questions do not focus on the street or block level, rather on the historical progression of the city in terms of its planning, design, and development agenda more broadly.

It is important for urban designers to consider historical analysis as a key component of community consultation, questions on history and change are linked with the people that have lived through and experienced these changes. Thus, urban designers must develop an understanding of '*sense of place*' (Eisenhauer et al., 2000). Sense of place refers, firstly, to people – the social interactions between family and friends, related activities, and traditions, plus the memories associated with these. Secondly, it refers to the physical environment – the natural, landscape, scenery, climate, geological features, environmental setting, and wildlife (Eisenhauer et al., 2000). However, and most importantly, it refers to emotions, a critical aspect that historical mapping and analysis will not accurately capture.

Urban designers must share their experiences of learning about the urban local history and the heritage of the city with local communities to encourage and develop a collective understanding of the sense of place. History and change are questions that must engage directly with people's emotions – this is why a strategic appreciation of the historical progression of the city must be accompanied by work at the Area and Site levels – which will involve the community (*see* Chapter 6).

CULTURE in CANADA
The indigenous peoples of Canada lost a lot of their traditional practices and heritage through the process of Colonisation. What was also lost was indigenous connections to placemaking - the resultant assimilation into western modern society has further enhanced the loss of identity, culture, and urban forms and interventions that in any ways reflect the rich history of not only these peoples, but a core history of the country itself.

The concept of indigenous urban design is becoming popular in many Canadian cities - as an effort to continue reconciliation processes and re-insert a lost vernacular that better reflects the past and those who shaped it. It is critical that urban designers not only rely on existing physical heritage to tell the story of a place and its peoples - but it looks to lost narratives that are vital to truly recognising cultural heritage - and using this new knowledge to challenge spatial production and placemaking beyond tokenism in the built environment.

BELOW: The Wabano Indigenous Centre for Excellence, Ottawa, Canada. Designed for Indigenous people by Indigenous people.

Built Form - Linked closely with history and change, considerations of the built form of the city, namely it's urban morphology i.e. the urban structure and form the city's buildings take - can be helpful to supplement your understanding at the strategic level. Appreciations of the historic morphology and how this has changed over time might enable you to conclude that the city has a strong gridiron tradition, is built up of courtyard blocks, or is organic in its layout - as well as how contemporary development may have eroded, bolstered, or changed the built form. No better analysis expresses a city's morphology than a figure ground plan (Hebbert, 2016). Figure ground analysis at the strategic scale complimented with historical figure ground analysis will show how the city's built form has changed over time, including where fragmentation may exist and where regeneration and redevelopment have been concentrated in recent years. The combination will also enable you to reflect on how these changes have altered or continued the traditional grain and fabric of the city. Urban morphology is also a critical indicator in understanding urban density, whether the built form of the city is compact or sprawling for example. Considerations of the built form at the strategic scale will focus on the historical progression, analysis at the local scale (*see* Chapter 6), such as character area analysis will provide a richer level of detail. Understanding trends in built form can provide you with a good overview of a city's development agenda and priorities – this should be complimented with considerations of architectural trends also.

Architectural Trends - Architectural trends involve developing an understanding of the current priorities for buildings in the city. This will commonly refer to materials, detailing, learning lessons from past projects as well as trends in the construction sector (globally and locally). This will involve a consideration of national and local design policy and guidance as well as a review of recent construction projects in the city. Here, the analysis should consider what the local municipality put forward as good or best practice and how this may differ depending on the programming of the project i.e. architectural preferences between an urban mixed-use residential project and a central city office-led regeneration project.

Architectural trends will inform understanding of the architectural culture in the city. For example, in Melbourne, the city's central design guide outlines the municipality's preferred architectural responses along with aspects to avoid. These include, "creating depth within the façade through balconies, integrated shading, rebates and expression of structural elements" and *"avoiding visually exposed towers with low façade quality"* (City of Melbourne, 2018: 77, 85, 88).

Considerations of architectural trends should also involve coverage of current priorities regarding sustainability in construction, for example, a demand for the use of circular economy in construction projects. Circular economy is an important trend in construction; it refers to an economic system that tackles global challenges like climate change, biodiversity loss, waste and pollution. At the strategic scale, an understanding and appreciation of the importance of net zero carbon in the building sector and other innovations in construction can influence your understanding of architectural trends and the architectural culture in the city. It may be that an advanced agenda is in place or that more adaptation to global challenges are required.

ABOVE: The figure ground of Barcelona, Spain easily identifies a number of periods of construction that have developed the city into its current form. We can comfortably pick out the organic historic city pattern to the south; the huge scale of the Cerda designed Eixample expansion; and some of the post-industrial fragmentation remnants to the North-East that have yet to be fully re-developed.

CHAPTER 5: STRATEGIC ANALYSIS 102

ARCHITECTURE in MALAYSIA

has been influenced over time by several factors - tradition, culture, religion, geographical proximity to places such as China, colonialism, and a new age of independence that brought with it freedoms to express Malaysian architectural identity in new ways in a more globalised world. To understand the architectural identity, in places such as the capital city Kuala Lumpur, studying trends that have shaped it is imperative.

TRADITIONAL MALAY DESIGN

The traditional Malay home was built using timber frames, with pitched roofs, porches, high ceilings, openings for ventilation, and elaborate wood carvings for decoration. This vernacular style and form of building can still be seen across Malaysia today, with these key design traits shared across differing regions even when size and layout differed.

COLONIAL

Periods of occupation and colonial rule in Malaysia resulted in the widespread construction of buildings that took influence directly from the colonial powers' home locations. The prevalence of Portuguese and Dutch designs speak to this. However it was British rule that had the most significant physical impact - with the introduction of colonial style government buildings, churches, squares, and fortifications. During this period Victorian and Edwardian styles were also utilised.

POST-INDEPENDENCE

With independence in 1957 Malaysia entered a new period in its rich history - and the subsequent architecture aimed to reflect this new freedom. The construction of the Petronas Towers in Kuala Lumpur in 1996 saw the country boast the tallest building in the world - a record it held until 2004 when it was surpassed by Taipei 101, Taiwan. The Petronas Towers project was both the peak of the new wave of contemporary architecture in the city, as well as a catalyst for an era of modern high-rise design that has come to define the city centre of KL and other cities in Malaysia. Increasingly citizens are pondering what makes up the architectural identity of the nation - the reality is in the melting pot of the rich tapestry of design and architecture that has shaped the urban landscape - and continues to impact on future development.

TOP: Skyline of Kuala Lumpur - A city of diverse architectural styles and influences.

MIDDLE LEFT: The traditional Malay house vernacular.

MIDDLE RIGHT: City Hall in George Town - Penang. Built by the British in 1903 in the Edwardian Baroque and Palladian style.

BOTTOM: The Petronas Towers in Kuala Lumpur - designed by Argentine-American architect César Pelli.

Infrastructure and Connections: Glossary

Type	Term	Description
Hard Infrastructure	Route Hierarchy	Categorises roads/routes according to their functions, capacities and capabilities. While sources differ on the exact nomenclature, this will consider analysis of: motorways, arterial roads, main streets, secondary streets, tramways, pedestrian routes, railways, cycle ways, stations, main intersections, bus stops and tram stops.
Hard Infrastructure	Air and Sea Networks	Availability and proximity to national/international air and sea travel. For example, in Denmark, a system of ferries operates to connect commuters from the island of Zealand with the country's second city, Aarhus.
Hard Infrastructure	Public Transportation	The system of transport available for use by the general public, typically managed on a schedule, operated on established routes. This will differ depending on the context. For example in Belfast, Northern Ireland, Bus Rapid Transit (BRT) is a public transport option, or in Copenhagen, harbour buses (ferries) are part of the public transit system. Typically it will include: trains, metro services or trams, buses, city bicycles and in some contexts will now include e-scooters.
Hard Infrastructure	Active Mobilities Infrastructure	Active mobility, active travel, active transport or active transportation is the transport of people or goods, through non-motorised means, based around human physical activity including walking and cycling. Other modes include running, skateboarding, kick scooters and roller skates.
Soft Infrastructure	Green Infrastructure (GI)	The access to, connectivity between, and multi-functional nature of natural and semi-natural green provision in/around the city. GI is closely connected to adaptive urban design which promotes resilient uses of vegetation and soils to adapt to climate change and provide multifunctional spaces.
Soft Infrastructure	Blue Infrastructure (BI)	The access to, connectivity between, and multi-functional nature of natural and semi-natural water provision in/around the city. BI is closely connected to adaptive urban design which promotes dynamic, resilient methods of water management to adapt to climate change and provide multifunctional spaces.
Soft Infrastructure	Natural Features	Natural (not man-made) elements within urban settings including topography; rivers and water bodies; forests; coastlines; mountains etc.

TABLE 3 Infrastructure and Connectivity

INFRASTRUCTURE / CONNECTIVITY

At the strategic scale, analysis of connections must consider a broad variety of arrangements. This should focus on the geographical connectivity, and the multifunctional nature of both hard and soft infrastructure. The different infrastructures that designers might use are summarised in Table 3, it is important to reiterate that as many variations as necessary, or possible, should be considered for any site. Examples are included for each infrastructure scale but again these are not exhaustive, rather they serve to illustrate what might be included or considered.

Considerations of networks and their integration or fragmentation are of critical importance in urban design, as designers have a key role to play in ensuring that people have equitable access to a wide range of infrastructure. The route hierarchy is a common starting point in traditional urban design analysis, whereby, the recording and mapping of motorways, arterial roads, main streets, secondary streets, tramways, pedestrian routes, railways, cycle ways, stations, main intersections, bus stops and tram stops are presented. This may also include considerations of air and sea networks but will depend on the context of the site in question.

While identifying the myriad of routes around the site through an analysis of route hierarchy is a good starting point in the analysis, it may not tell the full story or even result in the correct emphasis. Often cities have reasonably connected road infrastructure, yet the site's connectivity across other modes, such as public transport are poor. This is a key consideration in the analysis of hard infrastructure and connections. At the strategic level, we must ensure that urban design places the correct emphasis on the promotion of sustainable lifestyles, through the promotion and improvement of public transport as well as active mobilities provisions. In most towns and cities across the world, more space is taken up by cars than by any other form of infrastructure. In analysis of hard infrastructure and connections designers should carefully consider and identify blind spots in public transport and active mobilities provision.

Urban design plays a core role in the broader efforts to change mindsets on private transportation in cities by positively reinforcing the multifarious benefits of public transport, cycling and walking. Questions of infrastructure and connections are linked to a multitude of broader urban design issues, including public health, climate change, economic productivity, and social equity (Dovey and Pafka, 2020).

We recommend that sensitivity to human behaviour be at the centre of analysis of infrastructure and connections. This is paramount in finding a balance between the existing dominance of cars with considerations on how your site currently supports public transport, active mobilities as well as usable and walkable spaces for people (Werner et al., 2018). The task of understanding infrastructure and connections is one that revolves around considerations of inclusivity rather than exclusivity, thus designers should consider *"each person's freedom of mobility"*; to prioritise fairness and equity in infrastructure provision and connectivity in cities (Sheller, 2018).

There is also a need to complement considerations of hard infrastructure with strategic analysis of soft infrastructure and people's equitable access to it. An increased importance and significance has been placed on urban design's role in green infrastructure and blue infrastructure provision (*see* the section on Climate and Sustainability in reference to this also). In responding to these calls, we advocate that responsive urban design analysis must include a detailed consideration of ecological infrastructures and natural features within strategic proximity of the site and situation under consideration.

Ecological infrastructures, also known as blue-green infrastructures or nature-based solutions, have been identified as a key urban design strategy to achieve multi-functional land use. Moreover, the provision of green networks brings significant benefits that include the enhancement of urban amenity, human health benefits, and community and recreational value which all support urban liveability and economic development (Hoyer et al., 2011; Marlow et al., 2013).

In analysing green and blue infrastructure, the purpose is to develop a strategic overview of the quality and range of infrastructure available as well as the accessibility and proximity to these features from the site. It is important to stress that the strategic scale sets out to develop a general comprehension of GI, BI, and natural features that the *'Local'* analysis will subsequently complement.

Finally, in asking questions of infrastructure and connections it is important to consider how these are expected to change in the future through an assessment of future strategies, projects, plans etc. This is supplementary to the appraisal of policy and development in that it reflects on infrastructure only. For example, in the context of Aalborg there has been significant investment and expansion in blue and green infrastructure planning through the realisation of the Østerå canal project, a 3km river and green watercourse as well as the development of a 12km Bus Rapid Transit (BRT) System, known locally as +PlusBus. Thus, as part of a strategic analysis, awareness of policies and programmes are important to capture sophisticated changes in strategic infrastructure provision.

5.3 APPLYING STRATEGIC ANALYSIS

There exists a range of techniques to engage with the strategic scale. The subsequent sections unpack these demonstrating how to apply strategic analysis to your work and projects.

SECONDARY ANALYSIS

Strategic analysis is often a desk-based, research-led stage in your wider urban design analysis. It focuses on the use of secondary data (e.g., policy, digital resources and records, datasets, mapping, statistics among other sources) to explore macro influences on the site across a range of key variables to build an evidence base. Here, we suggest that designers develop an understanding of the macro mechanics of their site before they work with meso (e.g., neighbourhood/district) and micro (e.g. site/block) details and considerations. Unlike, the 'human scale' and site visit-led approach, common of traditional urban design analysis, the task of undertaking a strategic analysis is to begin to piece together - beginning with desk-based research and document review – the ways in which the site is/has been influenced by broader structural change over time and across space. For example, agendas in policy, demographic trends or the impact of climatic change.

By looking at strategic elements of urban design across a variety of scales it is possible to develop: 1) a more complete picture of place and how successful it is or can be and 2) a design that carefully considers future proofing – as part of urban design's role to bolster the resiliency of urban places and spaces. Achieving significant improvements in urban areas is typically a long-term process, thus, urban design and design practitioners must ensure their analysis provides a stable context for visions and their implementation in both the short and long-term – the strategic scale is essential to this process (Madanipour et al., 2018).

DISCOURSE ANALYSIS

In assessing a range of secondary data including policies, statistics, and plans, strategic analysis involves determining what these elements mean for the site. Here, discourse analysis is a useful technique to help make sense of the different narratives that can present themselves from the surveyed source material (Sonbli and Black, 2022).

LEFT: After years underground, Aalborg's lost river Østerå is being brought back to life to bring new nature-based resilience and life to the city.

OPPOSITE IMAGES: Liverpool, England - the city has undergone extensive place-branding since the mid-late 2000's - named a European Capital of Culture for 2008 the city works hard to promote its heritage, cultural, and growth.

CHAPTER 5: STRATEGIC ANALYSIS 106

Discourse analysis is important to the practice of contextually response design as *"discourse is not produced without context and cannot be understood without taking context into consideration"* (Sonbli and Black, 2022). The text, written words, images or plans of your strategic analysis are closely connected to the social reality they represent (or wish to realise). Understandings of discourse enables an understanding of the social reality in a specific culture in a specific urban quarter or neighbourhood and it's relationship to wider agendas for the municipality and what this agenda represents. For example, how the discourse of a specific policy draws from and influences other narratives around democracy, planning regulation, markets and development, publics as well as inequality and in extreme cases possible corruption or wrongdoing.

For Boland (2013), in his account of Liverpool, discourse analysis of the city's priorities highlights the impact of extensive city-branding in the city since the late 2000s. The city of Liverpool's agenda for planning and design could be seen as a performative act. Planning actions were used to construct a loaded visual environment re-branding large swathes of the city and sanctioning specific planning and design outcomes to promote urban change. Designers must be attentive to the tools used to re-brand, define, or shape cities and what those narratives mean for their site and its future. Ultimately, we recommend analysis which avoids taking things for granted, recognising the sources as statements of a particular moment in a local context that can be accepted or challenged.

WORKING WITH OTHERS

For any design project to be realised, collaboration with other built environment professionals is a core requirement. Urban design must engage and work with other disciplines, professionals, and stakeholders if a project is to be successful. There are a wide range of actors to consider including architects, engineers, landscape architects, urban planners, and the planning system more broadly. Most, if not all, good or better practice urban design projects are collaborative endeavours. Architects play a critical role in delivery through detailed building design. Engineers are vital in the development process, overseeing construction and maintenance and ensuring standards and regulations are adhered to. Landscape architects bring technical competencies and extensive knowledge on green and blue infrastructure, species, planting, and integrated nature solutions. Planners possess an awareness of policy, regulation, and strategy at different spatial scales which help determine appropriate design and development. In addition, the planning system – the mechanism for development control – plays a critical role in the promotion of high-quality, innovative, and cutting-edge design solutions.

In England, through new governance mechanisms, planning departments are beginning to make decisions for approval or refusal of planning permissions for development projects based exclusively on design quality. Here design considerations and criteria have been given increased weight and emphasis as a material consideration in the decision-making for planning permission. Consequently, expectations are being raised across both the development industry and in local communities on any project's emphasis and engagement with design, a fantastic and long overdue development for the quality of design across the country. Urban designers must work closely with these actors, to assist them in understanding and buying into contextually responsive design and the appreciation of robust place design and character.

ACCESS TO DATA

The availability of robust source materials and access to databases are important considerations to ensure the strategic analysis can determine and expose key findings at this strategic level. Nonetheless, a key question is to consider here is what is important for urban design? Designers do not necessarily require access to private expensive datasets - publicly available or open data can be more than enough. As emphasised previously, policy is a core consideration which can be easily accessed given the democratic role of this documentation; similarly, data on flood events or urban heat island can be located via a range of open data platforms. In considerations of people/society, census data can provide a rich overview to determine a baseline understanding, supported by other resources. A wide range of statistics are available either freely or at a relatively low cost which enables design teams to understand a wealth of relevant indicators including congestion, market variation, crime/police reports, travel-to-work, and architectural quality. As the emphasis on publicly available, open data continues to grow, urban designers stand to benefit from increased access to materials/databases.

An excellent example of coordinated open data can be found in the *Map of Planning Data* for England, published by the Department for Levelling Up, Housing and Communities (DLUHC) in 2021. The resource enables users to find planning and housing data that is easy to understand, use and trust across over 30 indicators including listed buildings, flood risk zones, design code areas, and infrastructure project data all of which is available under an *Open Government Licence*. To date, the main material constraint designers are faced with is access to high-quality vector-ready maps. Maps remain an extremely expensive resource and thus it is common to rely on maps at a single scale or limited range of scales for the development of the analysis. Open ordnance survey mapping represents the final step in a fully open materials/database toolbox – high resolution maps are a critical tool for a range of built environment specialists and practitioners, particularly urban designers.

OPPOSITE IMAGE: Cities are often in a constant state of flux in regards development and agendas for change, growth, or regeneration. Urban designers must be aware of the strategic directions of the wider city to ensure they can best understand the potential impacts on any site they are taking forward.

Puerto Madero, Buenos Aires, Argentina.

CHAPTER 5: STRATEGIC ANALYSIS

AUD CASE STUDIES
The application of strategic analysis, using the techniques discussed above and across the elements outlined in this chapter, enable designers to develop a holistic and comprehensive appraisal of strategic matters, opportunities, and concerns linked with their site. Critical to this endeavour is the requirement to look at both current scenarios and identify trends over time, as well as future projections. Armed with this knowledge, urban design and designers are able to relate macro and meso factors, considerations and elements to their site to enhance opportunities for contextually responsive development – with a deep understanding of spatial differences across scales. Some sites/projects will require rigorous engagement with the city-region scale, others will lend themselves more to the metropolitan scale. Understanding the spatial spheres of influence at the strategic level can be challenging, requiring a healthy investment in desk-based research. To help aid your understanding of these spatial differences across scales and how this may differ from project to project, the final section of the chapter presents three examples developed through our live case study sites (Aalborg and Manchester) on how strategic analysis can come together.

In comparing the two sites, we demonstrate how the earlier portions of the chapter may be applied as well as how strategic considerations differ depending on the site's specific context. The key conclusions to be taken forward from both sites will be outlined and how these relate to the wider contextually responsive design process presented over the course of this book. To capture the different scales at which urban design may operate, our live projects feature strikingly different strategic concerns based on their overarching site size/situation. In Aalborg our site, which is approximately 6ha, is located close to the city centre on the area of land predominately occupied by the city's maternity and children's hospital. In Manchester our site, which is approximately 60ha, is located immediately north east of the city centre and comprises of two neighbourhood districts, Ancoats and Miles Platting.

Strategic Profile: Summary of Key Policy

Policy Theme	Policy	Policy Content
Central Regeneration Area / Densification Areas	Central Area Plan (2025)	- All new urban neighbourhoods should have their own identity, distinct features, distinctive moods, sustainable measures, new housing types, cultural heritage, good and effective mobility or new and attractive meeting places and recreational areas. - It is expected that the city grows by approx. 3,500 residents, which corresponds to almost 1/5 of the total population increase in Aalborg Municipality via defined regeneration projects. - Urban projects are required to address the municipalities densification targets as defined by the plan.
	Site Development Prospectus	- When Aalborg University Hospital moves to the new buildings in Aalborg East in 2021/22 – Aalborg Municipality wishes to take up the unique opportunity to create a new neighbourhood in the city centre. - Priority is to transform the area into a mixed-use hub, which opens up to the rest of the city. - Transform the parking spaces at Gasepigen and in Urbansgade into productive urban functions.
Character and Programming	Central Area Plan (2025)	- Future development in the city centre must help to strengthen Aalborg's metropolitan character and bolster the distinctive character of the city's neighbourhoods. - Strong identities must be created in individual urban neighbourhoods, which can help strengthen the city centre as a whole.
	Site Development Prospectus	- Hospital should be densified (650-700 residential units) with a focus on new residents and businesses – while at the same time greening should be promoted focusing on housing of distinct quality and the creation of urban life; - Identity of the area and the connection to Reberbansgade ('Food Street' as a landmark) must be strengthened.
Sustainable Mobility	Central Area Plan (2025)	- Sustainable forms of transport (walking, cycling and public transport) must have the highest priority – rather than accessibility for car traffic – to ensure new development is safer, and more environmentally and climate friendly. - The use of and driving of care must be reduced internally in the city centre – cars should be directed to well distributed parking facilities along/across the edges of the central area. - New development must improve bicycle connections, extend the pedestrian network and connect with the BRT.
	Site Development Prospectus	- The area should be made attractive to soft mobility with the establishment of new cycle and walking routes through the area; soft mobility should be a priority in Reberbansgade and Urbansgade - Traffic alternations should be made e.g. a new road access to the area via the tunnel from Saxogade Build on close proximity to Aalborg Station and Aalborg Vestby Station and close access to the upcoming BRT line (2023). - The number of parking spaces within the site boundary should be increased with the establishment of 1-2 parking facilities (with priority for underground parking).
Sustainable Development	Central Area Plan (2025)	- Circular economy (the creation of a local resource loop) should be prioritised so as to minimise transport. Crucial to recycle as much as possible on our own land (Aalborg Kommune). - With cloud burst events and extreme weather – robust networks of urban nature are important to sustainable development and the quality of the environment for residents.
	Site Development Prospectus	The site contains large amounts of resources, such as buildings, bricks and land – these should be reused directly or in new ways.
Healthy and Attractive City Life	Central Area Plan (2025)	- Development must promote more life in the city, nature in the city, - Future uses in central regeneration areas must be promote a mix of urban functions with a specific focus on dynamic housing types. Social mix, protection from pollution (due to remediation), room for nature and safe and sustainable modes of movement must be at the core of all urban project in the city.

This Key Policy Summary table, which has been developed for the Aalborg site, provides a summary of the various plans and policies that have been developed for the city, but focuses specifically on those that are relevant to the site itself. In the case of Aalborg, there are two relevant documents to explore – the *Central Area Plan* and the *Site Development Prospectus* (the land of the former hospital). The table is not arranged just as a list of the requirements of the findings within these documents but has been grouped around a series of strategic themes or topics (sustainability, character etc.) which showcases the synergies between these documents and presents these findings in a way that is easy for the reader to understand. The topics covered have a clear link to the key principles set out in Chapter 4.

AALBORG
Key Policy Summary

CHAPTER 5: STRATEGIC ANALYSIS   110

At the masterplan scale the role of strategic policy changes from considering how a site or area might contribute to the strategic policy objectives of the city, to looking at how a site might deliver the policy aspirations in whole or in part. The sites' increased scale allows for this to happen. In Manchester, the local policy is designed around a growth agenda – including expansion of economic activities within the city centre (the regional core) and in creating new and improved neighbourhoods to allow more people to live within the city limits. The policy infographic has been designed to not only summarise the key policy drivers identified from the policy assessment, but also to begin to look at how these can be arranged spatially on the site (homes to the east, offices and employment to the west adjacent to the city centre). Of course, with the site bounded by two important arterial routes (Rochdale Road and Oldham Road) - policies regarding how these important infrastructure routes will be enhanced is also vitally important and is therefore included as part of the delivered diagram.

EAST

1

HOUSING

East of site falls within a broad strategic housing area, identified for most of the housing growth in to 2027 with focus on medium density family housing

Policies H2,H3,H4
Core Strategy

2

COMMUNITY

Create neighbourhood of choice focused on family housing well served by local community facilities, green spaces and leisure

Policies SP1,H3,H4
Core Strategy

4

INFRASTRUCTURE

The arterial routes should be enhanced as part of any development with improved linkes to Rochdale Canal with connection to public transport
Policies H3,H4, EC4, EC5
Core Strategy

3

EMPLOYMENT

West of the site is within the regional centre identified for high density office led employment (with residential and leisure uses) of up to 25 hectares to 2027

Policies SP1,CC1,EC4, EC5
Core Strategy

WEST

MANCHESTER
Local Policy Analysis

APPLIED URBAN DESIGN

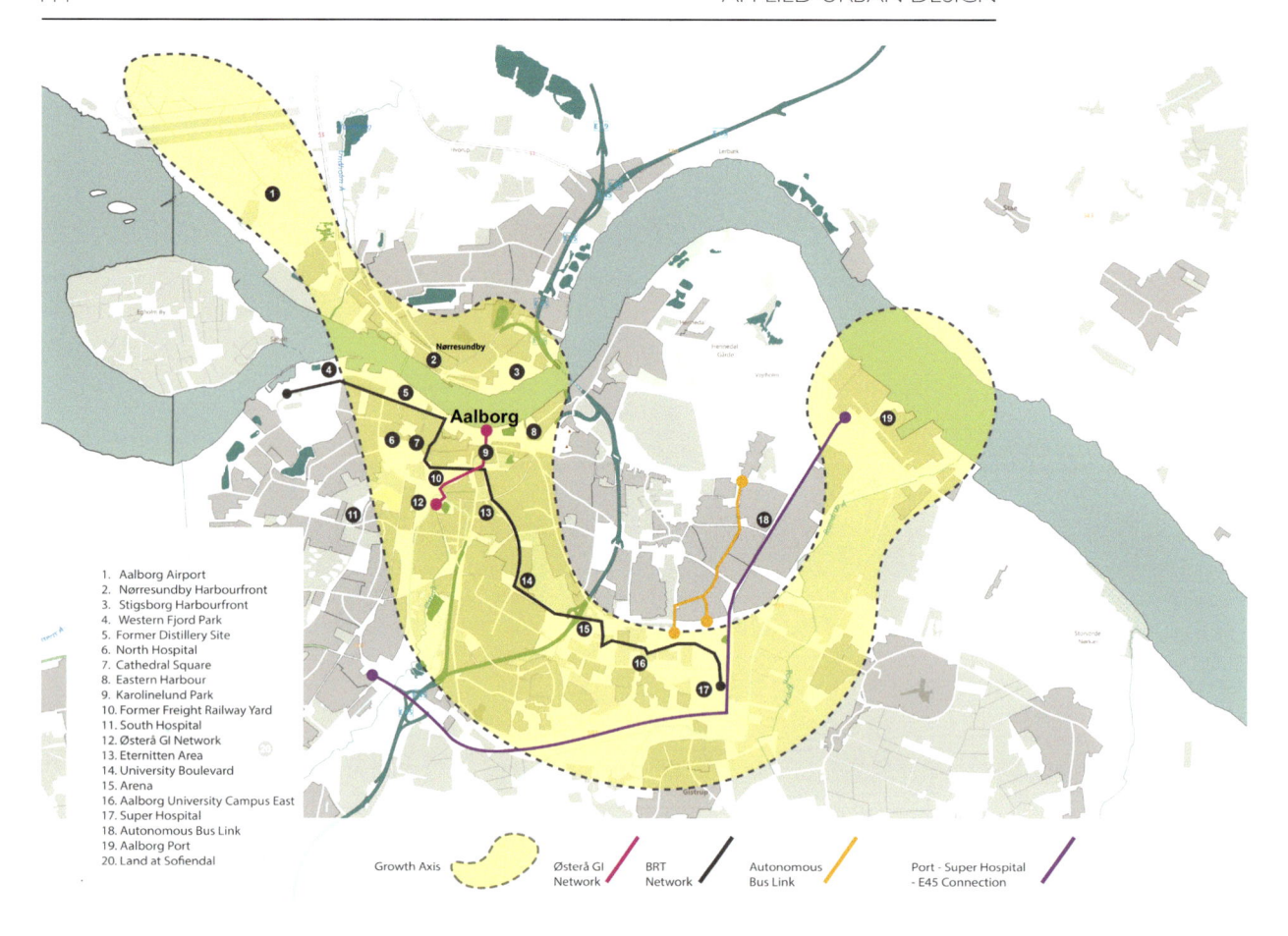

1. Aalborg Airport
2. Nørresundby Harbourfront
3. Stigsborg Harbourfront
4. Western Fjord Park
5. Former Distillery Site
6. North Hospital
7. Cathedral Square
8. Eastern Harbour
9. Karolinelund Park
10. Former Freight Railway Yard
11. South Hospital
12. Østerå GI Network
13. Eternitten Area
14. University Boulevard
15. Arena
16. Aalborg University Campus East
17. Super Hospital
18. Autonomous Bus Link
19. Aalborg Port
20. Land at Sofiendal

Growth Axis | Østerå GI Network | BRT Network | Autonomous Bus Link | Port - Super Hospital - E45 Connection

Aalborg in its most strategic sense can be defined a 15-minute or 20-minute city – representing a small-medium sized European city in which services, amenities and core functions are hyper connected geographically and accessible by a robust network of infrastructure. This has been further enhanced through the city's strategic development and growth agenda over the past 20 years which has given rise to over 100ha of urban regeneration – connected across two core axes North to South and East to West. Much of this growth is centred on brownfield or previously developed land within close proximity of the city creating, new neighbourhoods and destinations that are connected via a networked approach to urban renewal. This growth has given the municipality a range of experience and ambition in urban regeneration projects which directly influence our site.

In Aalborg the site is an important employment area scheduled for closure with the health care functions of the site being subsumed by the creation of a new Super Hospital to the south . This makes the site a strategic opportunity and core piece of the city's metropolitan growth strategy – the **Aalborg Growth Axis** linking Aalborg Airport to the North with the city and the new Super Hospital. Thus, geographical connectivity is a principal factor at the strategic level, with the site acting as a core piece of the growth axis. Analysis of the Aalborg site at a city-regional scale introduced some important insights, for example, connectivity to Aarhus (Denmark's 2nd city) but the 'strategic' questions remained relevant at the metropolitan tier with the introduction of the airport (connectivity to Copenhagen, Oslo, and Amsterdam) and the port (trade across the Baltic sea) as the major international influences on the site.

ABOVE: Aalborg Growth Axis (*author own version*).

AALBORG
Geographical Connectivity

CONCLUSIONS

We support complex consideration of the strategic scales and contexts of any site to capture critical strategic concerns including trends and tendencies over time. Strategic analysis represents the starting point of the **AUD Framework**, the outcomes of this stage are influential to the subsequent analysis stages in the process – Local analysis (which considers area and site scales). Taken collectively, these analysis stages ensure that multi-level, layered and dynamic analysis takes place to inform a rigorous appreciation of the site and it contexts. The outcomes of the strategic analysis will assist with the development of '**Profiles'** (*see* 6.6), and subsequently **The Urban Design Program** *(see* Chapter 7). All of this information provides designers with the critical drivers to promote and deliver contextually responsive design solutions in practice.

PROCESS OUTCOMES

SITE & CLIENT

CONTEXT

1 Analysis
Strategic
+
Local

→ Strategic Profile

→ Area Profile
Site Profile

PIVOT

2 Urban Design Program

→ A: Design Considerations
B: Design Brief

DESIGN

3 Design Development

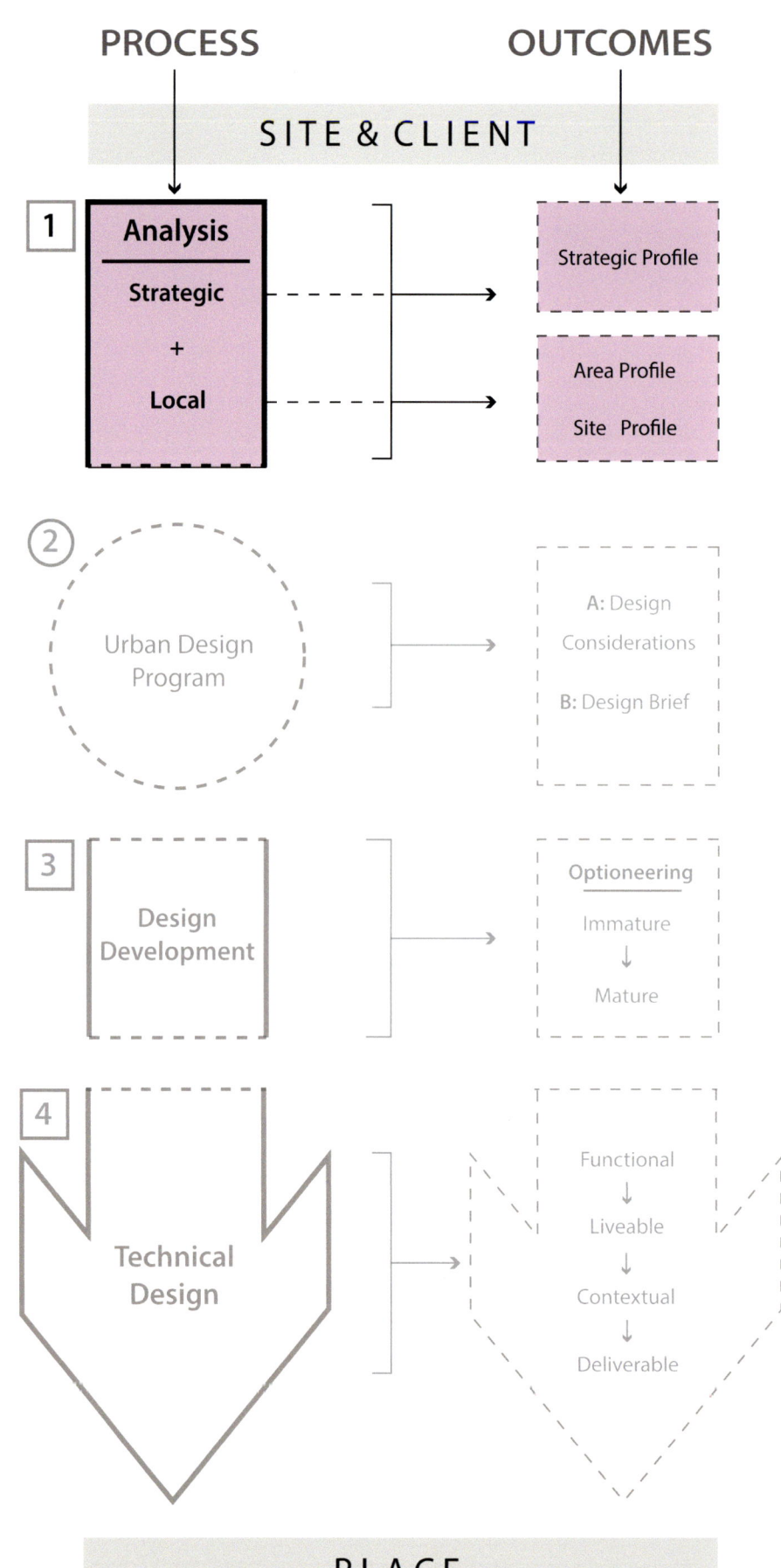

→ Optioneering
Immature
↓
Mature

4 Technical Design

→ Functional
↓
Liveable
↓
Contextual
↓
Deliverable

PLACE

CHAPTER 6: LOCAL ANALYSIS

CHAPTER 6
Local Analysis

Beyond the strategic level analysis (Chapter 5) it is critical for urban designers to also understand their site or location within its more immediate setting or context. This means exploring and analysing the physical elements that characterise a place, the local policies and guidance that can shape it, and the people who use and define it. For urban design solutions to be contextually responsive it is necessary to develop a deep knowledge of these matters to enable design to be driven by, and tested against, the most salient aspects of any given location. This may be to reinforce positive features, realise opportunities, overcome barriers, or tackle established inequalities. It is in conducting '**Local Analysis**' that the urban designer develops the appropriate arsenal of information required to both develop quality design interventions and communicate to local populations why such interventions are of benefit to the whole area and community. The better the analysis conducted the more transparent the design process can be, as stakeholders and communities better appreciate how, and why, design decisions have been reached to ensure they fit the local context and seek to reflect, or enhance, it and them.

Conducting '**Local Analysis**' can also be viewed as a vital undertaking for local authorities within their defined boundaries. Local authorities or planning authorities that are armed with detailed local analysis have a strong basis from which to develop new planning policy and guidance, design guides and codes, and even to test proposed development plans within their constituencies. By following the structure laid out in this section it allows for local people to have a clear voice in how their local spaces and places are developed and shaped moving forwards.

6.1 AREA AND SITE SCALES
As part of the Applied Urban Design Framework '**Local Analysis**' should be conducted across two urban 'scales':

1. The **Area** Analysis; and
2. The **Site** Analysis.

It is by considering these scales in conjunction with the wider strategic scale (Chapter 5) that allows urban design to crosscut other design disciplines and ensure a genuinely contextual approach to understanding, and later designing, place. There is a plethora of analysis that can be conducted at both scales, this section will unpack both the area and site scales predominantly considering physical characteristics but will also unpack issues around policy and people. Each scale is of course related to, and dependent on, the other.

The final outcomes of all the analysis we will unpack is the development of two '**Profiles**', for *Area* and *Site*. These profiles will deliver the most significant findings at both scales from the physical analysis, the policy and development review, and the people studies conducted. These profiles sit alongside the Strategic Profile to complete the 'context building' that Step 1 in the AUD Framework aims to develop – this will in turn allow the design process to continue onto Step 2 (the Urban Design Program – *see* Chapter 7). Page 164 provides a diagram laying out the full analysis process to be undertaken.

OPPOSITE PAGE: Chapter 6 continues the context building phase of the AUD Framework, adding '*Local Analysis*' to Chapter 5's 'Strategic Analysis'.

BELOW: Local analysis should be conducted on two distinct scales - the '*site*' (red boundary and immediate surroundings) and the '*area*' (the wider physical context the site sits within).

APPLIED URBAN DESIGN

AREA SCALE

The diversity of cities is often best explained when considering the variety of neighbourhoods, or districts, that they are made up off. These neighbourhoods can be described in geographical terms and usually share a commonality such as territory, environment, identity, land use, particular community values, or they may have previously been based on historical mapping of provisions or development. Often neighbourhoods will have defined mapped boundaries, either drawn politically, physically formed, or entrenched in the minds of local populations. These areas make up the greater whole and can make it easier for the variety of people, cultures, values, and industries to co-exist – equally an argument can be made that such 'boundaries' can support social segregation and reinforce clashes and divisions amongst communities on issues as wide as wealth, race, culture, religion, politics etc.

Neighbourhoods are also subject to change over time, often slow but sometimes swift and dramatic. New infrastructure projects that instantly and physically divide areas, gentrification that can drive demographic change, and market forces that can make or break the future growth and development of neighbourhoods are amongst the myriad drivers that can compound change in areas. It is for these reasons that any analysis undertaken must be understood within the timeframe it was conducted and should consistently be revisited and re-evaluated for accuracy.

The importance of area analysis can be best articulated through considering neighbourhoods, a scale and territory humans often comfortably relate to the city. Neighbourhoods are the places people spend much of their time, living, working, and socialising. People will often form a strong sense of identity and place attachment to their local neighbourhoods and can form equally strong perceptions of other defined neighbourhoods within cities. Given the importance of neighbourhoods/ districts, it is critical that urban analysis engages with such scale and this is accomplished through the undertaking of a detailed '**Area Analysis**'.

CHAPTER 6: LOCAL ANALYSIS

AALBORG: A smaller site in a much smaller city - Aalborg's area scale will naturally be constrained by its geography - with the river/fjord (Limfjord) creating a natural barrier to the north, development limited to the south, and the proximity of both the city centre and nearby residential districts framing the wider context that will require detailed analysis.

MANCHESTER: A larger masterplan site within a significantly larger city. Manchester is a major European city and the site sits on the edge of its current development growth. The area scale will be much larger in scope given the large city centre and its expansion to the south-west - as well as the historic residential neighbourhoods that define the north and east.

APPLIED URBAN DESIGN

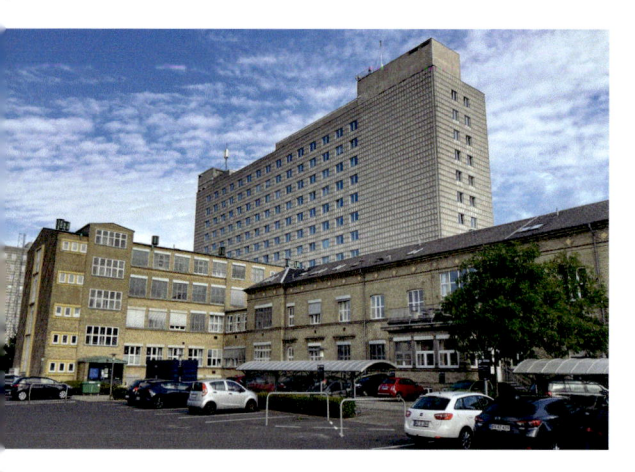

SITE SCALE

The site scale is the strongest social unit of the city. This is the scale we as humans directly engage with the built form around us – we can equally refer to this as the *'human scale'*. It is at this scale we come into contact with people, spaces, buildings, it is at the human scale that we form our perceptions on our immediate surroundings. Here we encounter conflicts, experience joy, and develop an understanding of how places work, positively or negatively. For the urban designer, regardless of the site size being designed, the final physical output will be experienced and operationalised at this scale, here people engage directly with the cities building blocks (architecture, public realm, green infrastructure, mobility infrastructure etc.) regardless the size of the project in question. It is also at this scale that barriers to movement, edges between neighbourhoods, the inequalities of place, the joy of quality environments are all played out in practice.

For the designer the site scale takes on extra significance as it is defined often by the boundary of the land being developed or owned by the client. If the site in question is significantly large (a masterplan for example) how one deals with site analysis will differ, an issue we tackle later with the **Applied Urban Design** case study sites (Aalborg and Manchester). Most criticisms of the built environment are derived from a lack of human scale qualities – and often this is the case due to a lack of understanding and analysis at this scale. Undertaking a detailed '**Site Analysis**' as laid out in this section is the first step to avoiding such scenarios in the future.

TOP: View of the current Hospital that dominates the Aalborg site.

TOP MIDDLE: Main pedestrian access into Aalborg site - Connecting onto the key north-south arterial route of Vesterbro.

BOTTOM MIDDLE: St Patrick's Church - a heritage asset within the interior of the site in Manchester.

BOTTOM: Oldham Road - key arterial route into Manchester city centre from the north-east - runs the length of the Manchester site's eastern edge.

CHAPTER 6: LOCAL ANALYSIS

6.2 PHYSICAL CHARACTERISTICS

To conduct a wide-ranging urban analysis at both the *area* and *site* scales it is necessary to consider a holistic approach to ensure the complexity of a place's physical characteristics are not diluted. We have identified a series of '*variables*' urban designers should be considering, many of these variables could be analysed at both scales however for the sake of simplicity we have separated out variables into what we consider the ideal scale for analysis work. Many of the variables itemised below are '*single variables*' – that being a single piece of analysis that will measure or quantify a single aspect of the built environment – others are by nature '*multi-variable*' – requiring multiple aspects to be considered to ensure robust analysis, either via the technique employed or the complexion of the issue at hand.

Single variable analysis runs the risk of being overly descriptive, simply articulating a truth rather than providing any analytical conclusion or take-away for the designer. To avoid this pitfall, it is important to always remember the rationale behind the analysis being conducted – to build an arsenal of 'contextual information' for the location in question. To move beyond the descriptive, it is imperative the researcher seek out trends and patterns across variables, presenting results in a multi-variable format where possible and ensuring all analysis presented is clearly communicated, labelled, annotated with key information, and rationalised as part of the 'context building' exercise. The next section includes a detailed process for conducting urban analysis in a comprehensive and research-led manner.

To organise the wide variety of variables it is possible to analyse, as well as the many recognised urban analysis techniques and methods that could be employed, we have organised them into four categories.

1. Arrangements
2. Networks
3. Features
4. Feel

These four categories reflect the urban design functional blueprints that we introduced in Chapter 4 (see 4.3).

ARRANGEMENTS

Arrangements refer to how the land is divided up within a city. Each city is made up of different physical elements and how they are arranged, or spatially laid-out, lends it a unique character. The arrangement of a place normally develops over a lengthy period of time, and the history of development can often be traced through a study of these arrangements. Arrangements can be in relation to land use, landscape, form, density etc. Variables within the arrangement category tend to focus on single variable aspects that must be recorded objectively at first (e.g., land use, building heights, open spaces), but it is in their experiences and relationships that the urban designer can analyse trends and patterns that provide places with their unique context.

LEFT: Land can be divided up very differently across a city. In Seattle, USA you can see the mid-rise structures alongside high-rise plots - with a large number of vacant plots spaced between.

NETWORKS

Networks are the connections that are created through the arrangement of the city – they can relate to both the physical and the social. Networks define how people move within a place and from one place to another, but also to how people connect with physical space and build relationships through interaction and activity. The best places allow people to engage with community and provide access to key services and amenities. Poor networks can shrink the city for many and often impact negatively on the poorest in society. Networks are key therefore to how effectively and efficiently the city operates in practice for its users. Networks extend beyond the obvious (movement infrastructure / mobility) to include how well utilities such as gas, electrics, water, and sewage are integrated and accessible to all; how key facilities and services are linked up to ensure equality of access and provision (e.g., Healthcare); and how well linked public realm and green spaces are to provide all residents with a reasonable quality of life. Networks can often highlight inequalities that exist within cities and places. The strength or weakness of a city's networks can significantly impact individuals, and communities, use of critical taken-for-granted necessities and conveniences.

THE FIGURE GROUND: CITIES of the USA

Showcased here are figure grounds for parts of a city within the USA – Manhattan in New York; The Mission District in San Francisco; and Northend in Boston – all shown at the same scale. In all cases the buildings are shown in black (the figure) and the space between them – which is the roads, spaces, parks and garden areas – left as white space (the ground). Despite all of these being in the United States, differences in the morphology – the pattern created by the arrangement of buildings/structures - is clear. The figure ground also allows us to understand the grain of the city – the size of the pieces. Of course, the figure ground only tells part of the story, it is important to also know the height and mass of buildings to truly understand density and character.

Manhattan, New York: The regular grid of long and thin urban blocks is unambiguous, with the scale and hierarchy of the routes and junctions evident. These routes and junctions are well defined by the figure ground allowing principal streets or spaces to be identified.

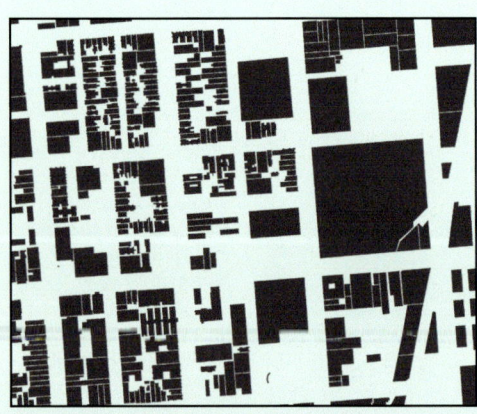

The Mission District, San Francisco: The pattern shown here is still based on a grid, yet with a much more varied and irregular pattern of pieces. This includes the coarse grain of buildings (big pieces) to the east and a finer urban grain to the west, where the use is likely residential.

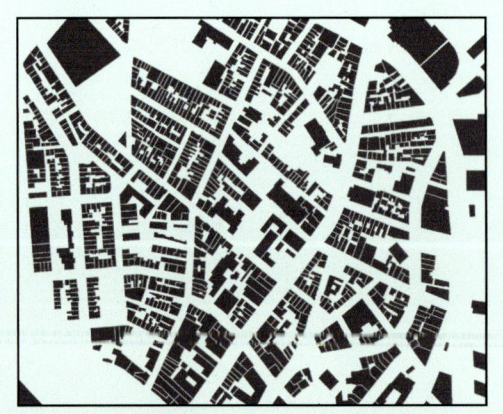

Northend, Boston: The pattern of streets and spaces lacks a formalised grid pattern, with routes being more organic in nature but still well defined by buildings. The grain is much finer than the previous two examples, with smaller pieces making up the pattern of buildings.

CHAPTER 6: LOCAL ANALYSIS

FEATURES

Features can be defined as the core physical, or visual, attributes unique to a particular urban environment, that provide a place with a form of identity (positive, negative, or generic) and differentiate it from other locations. These features come from within the structure of a place (that being the arrangements and networks) – often the features designers will study in detail are initially highlighted in the more objective single variable stages. Features can also be discerned through how people interact with place, how they utilise the networks and engage with the arrangements, they can be the key traits of an environment that shape individual attitudes and behaviour.

FEEL

'Feel' variables are the most subjective and difficult to classify effectively. How people *'feel'* within an environment is shaped and influenced by a wide range of factors, but it is unmistakably what drive's opinion, shapes behaviours, and arguably defines quality within urban design. If arrangements and networks deal with the physical decisions and dimensions that shape the city and features distinguish what makes a place unique or different, feel deals more with the emotion elicited in people and why certain places appear to work or be more enjoyed than others. These are more nuanced variables that help us understand how successfully places operate in practice, and if they work for all within society. The *'feel'* of a place can vary between different people dependent on an array of factors such as age, gender, race, wealth, social status, and more. These variables often rely on the full range of senses - smell, taste, sound, and vision.

These categories are not absolute nor are the variables/techniques we have placed within them. Many of the variables identified can be classified across the categories – and indeed the 2 scales - and when analysing this is a critical factor to keep in mind. The categories are simply a way of organising the array of variables and providing designers with a more structured initial approach to undertaking '**Local Analysis**'. This chapter sets out in greater detail how to conduct urban analysis in the field and how to undertake some of the key variables and techniques introduced below for both area and site analysis, as well as integrating research on people and policy to provide a depth of contextual information and understanding to shape the final outcome of the Local Analysis step – the Area and Site Profiles.

BELOW: Analysing how people respond to place is a critical part of the AUD Framework - the way users behave or how they are made to feel in an urban environment. Often unknown variables will significantly impact on the success of a place, such as the presence of street vendors.

Istanbul, Turkey.

6.3 ELEMENTS OF LOCAL ANALYSIS

AREA ANALYSIS

Table 4 below sets out a range of possible variables that designers need to consider when undertaking the area analysis. Each is intended to be undertaken at the area scale (neighbourhood / district level). If you are undertaking this analysis as part of a design project, all analysis conducted should be in relation to the site in question.

The designer may not necessarily make use of all the variables listed, as some may not prove particularly relevant for any given site, but all should at least be considered at this stage and it is important to include variables from all of the categories. A glossary is included to provide basic definitions.

Arrangements	Networks	Features	Feel
Land use	Roads/routes	Natural features	Urban morphology
Building use	Pedestrian movement	Flooding	Activity
Open spaces	Cycling infrastructure	Legibility	Character
Public vs Private	Public transport	Landmarks	Townscape
Building heights	Green infrastructure	Visual connections	Maintenance
Height/width ratios	Blue infrastructure	Key views	Dead space
Size and scale	Public realm	Architectural style	Change / adaptation
Density	Utilities (Public)	Listed buildings	
Historical analysis	Utilities (Community)	Visual primacy	
Green spaces	Amenities / Facilities	Typologies	
Grain / development	Permeability	24-Hr City	
Frontages / service		Materials and palettes	
		Topography/levels	

TABLE 4 Area Analysis Variables

* NOT an Exhaustive List *

CHAPTER 6: LOCAL ANALYSIS

Area Analysis: Glossary of Terms (Adapted from Black and Sonbli, 2019)

Term	Description
Land Use	The primary activity the land is developed for; recreational; transport; agricultural; residential; and commercial.
Public v Private	Public spaces are open and accessible to people; private space is the region surrounding a person they regard as psychologically theirs.
Density	The number of people inhabiting an urbanised area.
Urban Morphology	The form of place – the relationship between the physical structures (buildings etc.) and the outdoor spaces they create/define.
Public Realm	External places accessible to all, made up of streets (routes) and spaces.
Size and Scale	Relating to building heights, depths, widths and ratios they provide in creating spaces and streets.
Natural Features	Natural (not man-made) elements within urban settings including topography; rivers and water bodies; forests; coastlines; mountains etc.
Green Infrastructure	The access too, connectivity between, and multi-functional nature of natural and semi-natural green provision in the city.
Blue Infrastructure	The access too, connectivity between, and multi-functional nature of natural and semi-natural water provision in the city.
Utilities [Public]	Network of public services such as water, electricity, natural gas, telecommunications, and other essential infrastructure.
Permeability	The extent to which urban form permits or restricts the movement of people across the city.
Legibility	How well organised the built environment is to produce a coherent and imageable pattern for users.
Palettes	The range of colours, textures, and materials used in the formation of the built environment.
Visual connections	How successfully places within cities integrate and connect visually.
Heritage Assets	The range of historic structures and features within a city including listed buildings, monuments, and conservation areas.
Frontage	The relationship of building ground floor with the street. Frontage can be active; semi-active; or inactive.
Visual Primacy	The dominant visual elements people naturally identify in spaces.
Key Views	Provision of views from different parts of the city to attractive or important natural or man-made features.
Typologies	Classifying physical characteristics for building types (i.e. housing).
Townscape	The visual appearance of an urban area.
Streetscape	The visual appearance of a street.
24Hr City	The changing use, movement, and activity that occurs in a city or place between day and night.
Maintenance	The level of upkeep of a place, considering issues such as cleanliness, graffiti, and quality of physical elements (architecture, public realm, green infrastructure etc.)
Character	The identity of a place, the unique characteristics that contribute to its distinctiveness and reflect local community and history.

GLOSSARY OF TERMS Area Analysis

SITE ANALYSIS

At the site scale the designer can start to consider a new range of variables for evaluation. This again is provided as a starting point and the variables relevant to your location or specific site will differ from place to place.

Each is intended to be undertaken at the site scale (this will be defined by the site in question). A glossary is included to provide basic definitions for some of the variables listed.

Arrangements	Networks	Features	Feel
Site measurements	Parking	Building quality	Climatic conditions
Access to site	Cycle parking / facilities	Site levels (drainage)	Wind
Right of way	Utilities connection	Land condition	Sun path / shade
Disabled access	Green infrastructure	Materials	Noise pollution
Servicing	Blue infrastructure	Vegetation	Overlooking
Land use	Street patterns	Views / vistas	Movement / circulation
Heights	Cycle provision	Activity	Negative / positive
Furniture	Permeability	Flood risk	2d vs 3d
Lighting	Serial vision	Typologies	Conflicts
Historic analysis		Edge conditions	Symmetry
Public vs private		Natural vs man-made	Balance
Enclosure		Massing	Transparency
		Hierarchies	Maintenance
		Light quality	Cohesion

TABLE 5 Site Analysis Variables

* NOT an Exhaustive List *

Site Analysis: Glossary of Terms (Adapted from Black and Sonbli, 2019)

Term	Description
Right of Way	The legal right of a pedestrian, or transport mode, to proceed with precedence over others in a place or situation.
Climatic Conditions	The average state of the everyday weather – amount of rainfall; sunshine; temperatures; change in seasons etc.
Topography	The arrangement of physical features of an area, its characteristics include elevation, slope, aspect, and land form.
Land Condition	The health of the land and its impact on potential development, contaminated land has restrictions or costs associated.
Orientation	The position of the site or particular buildings defining the site, often in terms of sun location or topographical features.
Sun path	Refers to the daily path the sun follows across the sky as the Earth rotates. Effects length of daytime and amount of daylight received.
Noise pollution	Noise that has harmful impact on the activity of people; such as traffic, machinery, planes, and busy spaces.
Activity	How people behave and interact within the physical environment; can include social interaction, movement, rest, recreation etc.
Overlooking	When buildings have a view over other buildings or spaces; can be an issue when this view is into private spaces such as residential units.
Enclosure	The definition of a space wherein private and public are clearly distinguished and the edges are clearly animated.
Perspectives	Art of representing 3D images on a 2D surface to give the impression of their height, width, depth, and position in relation to each other.
Massing	The perception of the general shape and form, as well as the size of a building(s).
Symmetry	The reflection of shared forms, shapes, or angles across a central line or point. Asymmetry has aspects or parts which are not equal or equivalent.
Balance	Concept of visual equilibrium, relates to our physical sense of balance. Can be achieved through symmetry or indeed asymmetry.
Hierarchies	Ranking variables or elements of design and place according to their size, use, or relative status.
Transparency	Ability of a place to allow its viewer to read, interpret, and understand its successive and often complex layers.
Cohesion	How successfully the myriad of elements of place fit together in a harmonious manner.
Complexity	The ability of place to avoid losing interest and visual diversity, ensuring the viewer is aware of the variety within a space.
Proportion	The visual effect of the relationship of various objects and spaces that make up a place, to one another and to the whole.
Edge Condition	The treatment and quality of the edges of spaces and places, which can act as seams across, or barriers between.
Circulation	The movement and flow of pedestrians, and/or other transport modes, across and through a place or site.
Street Furniture	Objects and equipment installed on streets, such as seating, barriers, post boxes, signage, lighting, bus stops, public art, bins, memorials etc.
Vistas	A distant view, in particular one seen through an opening such as an avenue or passage.
Servicing	The provision of access to buildings and spaces to allow for essential deliveries, refuse collection, and maintenance.

APPLIED URBAN DESIGN

6.4 APPLYING LOCAL ANALYSIS

Conducting a wide ranging analysis of a site/location across different scales requires a robust methodology. The variables that you can consider at the local level (area and site scales) are extensive and cover not only physical characteristics of place, but social, economic, environmental, and political. To assist with capturing this complexity, we can helpfully separate the local analysis into 2 distinct forms.

- Physical Analysis
- Material Considerations

Physical analysis covers the mappable features of the built form and environment, whereas **material considerations** cover the gamut of statistics, policies, trends, and key related information. Tackling each type of analysis will necessitate the practitioner having a sound working knowledge of appropriate methods, examples of which are discussed below.

Site Visits - The site visit is the most valuable of all the methods that we will use for analysis and will be necessary for any project regardless of scale. Many of the variables that have been identified earlier in this chapter do not have third party data available and as such it is vital that the practitioner undertakes their own data collection. Site visits provide the practitioner with a granular level of detail that cannot be provided otherwise. Most importantly they allow the '*human scale*' to be understood; how the area is experienced, the sights, smells and noises that are a critical part of the way that we experience our towns and cities.

Consequently with the exception of the very smallest and simplest sites, it is likely that more than one site visit will be required to build up a comprehensive knowledge base - in many cases the first visit to collect data, and further visits to 'ground proof' or check your analysis against the on-the-ground conditions. In practice there is some merit in undertaking a first site visit to walk the site and understand which of the variables listed previously are appropriate matters for study on your site. Furthermore, when studying certain variables, such as *'activity'* or the *'24hr City'* - it will be necessary to visit the site at different times of the day (or night) to understand how a site or neighbourhood might change or adapt.

For the same reasons, it is also important that the practitioner walk the routes to any local services or amenities, such as the route to the local shopping centre or the local school.

One of the most common mistakes made when undertaking a site visit is to simply visit the site or project area in question and then photograph the features on the site. However, as is apparent from the list of variables we have highlighted - this is insufficient. We recommend that in addition to taking photographs, the practitioner should take a large format base map of the project area to add annotations and observations in real-time. One of the best ways of undertaking a site visit at the local scale is to begin on site and subsequently walk out from the site in a spiral pattern into the surrounding townscape and neighbourhoods. Following good practice, site visits should be undertaken by more than one person, ideally of differing characteristics e.g. gender or age - this will enable a more robust understanding of the location to materialise. Finally, if there are key transport corridors within or near to the site (roads, railway, light rail) it is worth traveling these in order to better appreciate the experience, quality, and provision of local services and how they differ.

BELOW IMAGES: When you visit a site the survey will have significant impact on the results - a trip to the MuseumsQuartier, Vienna, can look, feel, and sound very different if you undertake a visit during morning (TOP) or night [BOTTOM] - it is critical(to analyse how the site functions under different circumstances.

CHAPTER 6: LOCAL ANALYSIS

Desk-Based Study - While we have set out the importance of a site visit, a desk-based assessment will add further important data to compliment initial findings. Many government agencies around the world hold environmental data - often in open access GIS packages – that can be of use to the urban designer, however, the amount of data and the topics covered will vary from location to location. In many cases the practitioner will be interested in the technical data that can not otherwise be determined without specific specialist input such as the location of areas of flood risk, air pollution, or underground pipelines and services. In most contexts, there is a wealth of site-related information available online for free but there is still some data that requires purchase from third parties. In this respect the practitioner needs to consider carefully how relevant some of the information might be to their site / study, and whether there are any important 'gaps' that would necessitate purchasing third party data.

In this respect care should be taken when looking at data to avoid matters which are irrelevant or too specific. Simply presenting raw information / data collected by others is unlikely to be effective and it is vital that the urban designer exercises value judgement to determine what data should be included. For example, from our Manchester case study we can find a GIS map layer of every lamp-post owned by the city council. Though it might be useful to know which routes within a city are lit at night, it is not necessary for the urban designer to map the position of every lighting stanchion. Some of these desk-based variables will be most effectively considered alongside data that might be collected from a site visit. For example, a historical analysis could be undertaken by researching and examining older maps of the area and reviewing local histories, but would undoubtedly be enhanced by a site visit to identify and consider the qualities of the historical remnants.

Observations - Though there are similarities between observation and the site visit, observational methods are more 'in-depth'. At the simplest level, observational methods can be described as *'people watching'* in a space or street such as Whyte (1988) did when studying Seagram's Plaza. Where do people meet or congregate in a square? How do they use a space or street?

In this respect, unlike the site visit, where the practitioner 'tours' the site, observational methods are a detailed or targeted study of a particular variable or location. As they are able to capture greater complexity, observational methods can look for differences between different demographics – ages, genders etc. - to better understand how the townscape could be appreciated differently for each. For the urban designer understanding these very human scale attributes of a space or street is invaluable and helps to 'ground-proof' their own views and experiences as part of their urban design analysis. As a result, for key spaces and loci's within a study area, it is highly recommend that time is spent looking at the activities that occur within them.

Beyond the single space or street, observational methods (or ethnography), can be used at the area scale. Observing how people move through a townscape is particularly important – considering for example, which routes are the busiest pedestrian or cycle routes, or where people choose to park their bicycle before catching a tram, or if people take a longer route to avoid using the park after dark. Observational details are vital sources of information to improve our understanding of a place, but they can only be derived from spending time exploring how people use a space. Observing these features, thinking about different demographics, and different times of the day or night, at key nodes or junctions in the city, will offer invaluable insights.

ABOVE: Whyte's seminal study of why New Yorker's used certain spaces in the city and not others highlighted that Seagram Plaza - framing the Mies van der Rohe designed Seagram Building - bucked the trend for such spaces by being a popular spot for sitting, eating, socialising, and enjoying. Whyte employed observational methods to explore what is was about Seagram's that encouraged such activity.

Consultations - The analysis stage of the AUD Framework offers a unique opportunity to introduce consultation and engagement. In many design processes, consultation often occurs far too late - when we ask communities and stakeholders to provide comments on design solutions or interventions that are largely already decided. We argue that time spent in undertaking consultation at the analysis stage allows for the views, understanding, and aspirations of stakeholders to be integrated into the early part of the process and contribute effectively towards the *Urban Design Program* (*see* Chapter 7) that will follow. There are a myriad of methods that could be used for consultation, here choices must be made as to which methods are best suited to engage large communities. However, it is often difficult for communities to engage with the topics, thus a scaffolded and structured apporach to engagement is critical.

We recommend that consultation occurs after the practitioner has conducted their initial analysis, allowing the consultation to be more targeted towards emerging matters of interest. In this way the consultation can begin to add new layers of depth to the wider analytical findings. Without having first identified key areas of interest or importance, the consultation would become voluminous and possibly irrelevant. Additionally, this ensures that when speaking to local people, who will undoubtedly know the place extremely well, that the design team have spent time getting to know an area – this is an important component to building trust in the overall process with communities and stakeholders.

We have singled out four engagement techniques that can be particularly effective. We do not advocate for the use of all of these on every occasion (resources and funds will be a restrictive factor to many engagement strategies) but using more than one is recommended to ensure community input is robust and understood as a critical component.

1. Surveys and questionnaires: Both are useful methods for generating high quality feedback quickly and in a manner that can be easily processed and quantified. For urban design projects, the survey is a powerful tool but requires careful targeting and management to ensure that the information collected from stakeholders / local people is useful. Surveys are particularly useful where the questions are seeking to identify certain aspects that the respondents would like to see changed or retained – for example, *'tell us about your favourite open space or park',* or *'out of the following list of local services please circle the ones that you would use most regularly'*. Note how both examples are specifically linked to a variable that is studied to add to the richness of the analysis and to 'ground proof' the results.

2. Walkover: Site walkovers with members of a community, or a group of local stakeholders can also prove an invaluable experience. The premise of this approach is very simple, the urban designer undertakes a guided walk through the streets and spaces of the site and its surroundings with between 10 and 15 local people. At key points the group stops to discuss and explore some of the positive and negative elements in urban design terms. To facilitate this effectively, and to keep the topics urban design focused, a short briefing is provided at the beginning. A checklist of topics/themes for discussion could also be provided. In this respect the people who live and work in the area are directly able to point out matters of concern or pride within an area.

3. Structured workshop: Open public meetings are often unsuccessful and become opportunities for those with the loudest voices to dominate the discourse and feedback received by the design team, it can also be difficult to ensure that the focus remains on urban design matters and not wider policy or regeneration issues. As an alternative, a structured workshop can be more effective. The participants will work in small groups over a 1 – 2-hour period covering several smaller targeted exercises which are prepared in advance. These exercises typically focus on a different aspect of the analysis that the practitioner has undertaken to date – for example green spaces, transport networks and connections, or safety / security. A series of workshops focusing on the same topics should be run for different audiences / demographics to further enhance the data that is generated.

CHAPTER 6: LOCAL ANALYSIS

128

4. Design charrette: Design charrettes have been used extensively by urban designers and other design professionals, yet there is now a growing trend towards undertaking these with non-designers as part of consultation and engagement exercises. The '*Design by Enquiry*' approach (Hartz-Karp, 2004) is perhaps the best known process for this, however, regardless of the scale or nature of your project, there is no reason why a charrette could not form part of the analysis. Many of the basic analysis techniques that we detail within the AUD Framework could be undertaken with community groups or local stakeholders. In many cases, this also helps to provide a focus for the discussions and ensures that the feedback provided is directly relevant to urban design. This not only has the benefit of enriching the data that might be collected from the practitioners' own studies but will assist in providing ownership of the analysis and conclusions reached for communities and stakeholders.

LEFT: Site walkovers are a useful method for surveying the attitudes and thoughts of local residents or other stakeholders.

BELOW: Design charrette's can form part of the analysis process - engaging local stakeholders in undertaking their own analysis of place based around the AUD Framework. This encourages people to think differently about their local places and spaces.

BEYOND BASICS
The danger with much of the analysis conducted in urban design is that it becomes a fact-gathering exercise and lacks the required clarity to effectively articulate the critical contextual components that will later drive design decisions. To avoid an overly basic approach it is vital to engage a process that will allow you to create a more nuanced and evidence-based narrative for your site – moving from descriptive to analytical. The AUD Framework requires all analysis conducted to be well-considered – thinking through the relationship to the site of all mapped or recorded variables, the cross-analysing of variables to seek out patterns and relationships, and robust well-rationalised conclusions that can be taken forward into the next stage of the Framework – The Urban Design Program (Chapter 7) to situate contextually responsive design solutions. We recommend a simple 3 stage approach that can be undertaken across all analysis.

1. Scoping
2. Sensing
3. Synthesising

Scoping
This is the mapping stage of local analysis – looking carefully across the range of variables identified in this chapter at both area and site scale and investigating these in-depth on and around your site. This may involve all the identified methods of data gathering discussed earlier in the chapter. The scoping exercise is about gathering information – the analyst will provide a wealth of material, not all of which will prove relevant. You should avoid presenting the results of scoping to wider audiences – the results of this process are for the analyst team only, to take forward to the next stage, 'sensing'.

Sensing
Having identified a wealth of information and material it is vital to begin to make sense of it all – to 'sense' which elements within variables are more pertinent to the understanding of the context of your site, both positively and negatively. Sensing therefore involves making value judgments on your findings to discern the primary factors in relation to the site and its surroundings. It also requires cross-analysis of variables – or multi-variable consideration. These approaches compel those analysing to seek out patterns across variables – looking for relationships that are either entrenched or emerging.

This stage should result in the production of graphics/visuals representing these critical findings and enable the analyst to build a clearer picture of the context – and illustrate how the analysis conducted relates directly to the site in question.

Synthesising
The final stage of analysis aims to amalgamate the key salient points across the scales – to provide the audience with clear conclusions. Synthesizing also aims to bring together the different scales of analysis to articulate a clear evidence-based contextual narrative.

The AUD Framework provides a transparent approach for communicating the results of this deeper level of analysis across variables and scales – **Thematic Groupings** (where analysis is drawn together across scales to report key information of critical urban themes) and the production of 3 bespoke **Profiles** (each representing the vital take-aways across the 3 scales analysed – Strategic, Area, and Site); all of which are discussed later in this chapter (see page 164 - for a flow-diagram of the full analysis process and outputs). These represent high level analysis and require skill on the part of the analyst to draw out the most important and relevant information that will define the contextual narrative for the site and ensure the AUD Framework has the necessary material from which to move forward onto Step 2 (**The Urban Design Program**). The Program will act as the pivot point between the analysis gathering (Step 1) and the **design and delivery** of a contextually responsive design (Steps 3 and 4).

CHAPTER 6: LOCAL ANALYSIS130

LEFT: Places are complex, dynamic, and multi-layered - to analysis effectively the urban designer needs a process that can reflect this. The AUD Framework asks that those analysisng place utilise a methodology that allows you to create a more nuanced narrative - making the critical shift from descriptive to analytical.

Central Hong Kong.

SINGLE VARIABLE ANALYSIS

From a very practical basis the analysis has to start somewhere, and in this case, it begins with the gathering of data about the variables that have been identified in Tables 4 and 5. To begin with, it is recommended that this is done roughly using a series of sheets of tracing paper – each with a separate variable presented on each (making sure to keep the scale of your basemaps consistent) – as this allows for these variables to be considered together looking for trends or synergies. This is an important part of moving towards analysis that is *'sensing'* in nature rather than just *'scoping'*. The site visit and the desk-based study will be vital in providing the data to complete these. It would not be uncommon for even a small or simple site to have between 30 and 40 different variables mapped across the four categories (networks; arrangements; features; and feel). This can be a daunting process, but we have set out below five points that can help the practitioner ensure that they undertake a robust analysis.

1. Start with a few - Carefully choosing 5-6 variables across the four categories to start with can help identify what other variables might also be worthy of study. This should be seen as a 'starting point' of the scoping exercise. We would recommend that most sites will benefit from a study of the morphology (using a figure ground), a route hierarchy and land use study. At the area scale, green infrastructure (parks, spaces and green routes), public realm (key public spaces and key pedestrian connections) are useful considerations to highlight other more detailed analysis required. At the site scale building heights, access and servicing and activity would also be good places to start.

2. Consider hierarchies - Hierarchies are really important within the townscape and for many of the variables studied are a demonstration of moving towards *'sensing'*. When considering routes for example there will be those that are more or less important, or when considering local shopping areas, some will certainly be bigger or busier than others. There are few set hierarchies for urban design analysis, so the practitioner is required to establish their own on a variable-by-variable basis. It is important to set out as part of the analysis not only a description of the hierarchy (anything from a single phrase to a more comprehensive explanatory sentence within your legend) so that any reader might engage with it in the future.

3. Look for patterns - As you undertake the analysis of each variable, look for patterns or trends. For example, the urban grain or morphology might change either side of a main route, or the height of the buildings might increase towards the retail core. It is important to identify patterns that are clearly shown by the study of each variable even if they might seem overly simplistic or obvious. In most cases without the analysis of that variable(s) these patterns would not be so clearly defined. In these instances, do not forgot to think beyond plan-view 2D base mapping, or even at the human scale as there may be other patterns that are not as clearly identified on a 2D plan.

4. Provide annotations and notes - In many cases the *'scoping* and *'sensing'* of elements and attributes that are identified as part of the single variable analysis can be enhanced through annotations and notes. Annotations are an important part of communicating the thoughts and conclusions of the practitioner. In many cases, these annotations could be accompanied by sketches, photographs, or even cross sections to aid in providing further detail. For example, a map of local views and landmarks, might include a sketch of the most important views, and a photograph of each of the landmarks.

5. Ask what it means for the study site / area - The important question to consider when reviewing each of the variables studied is what this means for the project area or site. All of the conclusions that you are required to reach should be focused on helping both you, as the designer, and the reader understand the site. Make sure that each variable adds something to your understanding of the site. It may be that there are variables that when studied appear to offer no real conclusions for the site – for example a study of local flood risk may identify no risk anywhere near your site. In this instance, it is likely not something that should form part of the analysis, but the process of elimination ensures that the analysis is holistic and robust.

MULTI-VARIABLE ANALYSIS
Multivariable analysis elevates any analysis beyond *'scoping'*, towards being *'sensing'* and *'synthesising'*. It can take many different forms, ranging from simply presenting two variables side by side allowing for comparison through to complex multivariable techniques that are internationally recognised (considered in the following section). In most cases, multivariable analysis will take the form of two or more different variables being presented together, on one plan, and supported by other graphics. For successful multivariable analysis to occur there is a requirement for sufficient variables to have been studied. Given that every site is different, and the issues and variables studied will vary from place to place, there is no set process or method that can be used.

In fact, unlike with the lists of variables contained earlier in this chapter there is no list of multivariable graphics or pairings that can be established. That said, as these variables will have been roughly drawn and annotated onto different sheets of tracing paper, the analysis of variables against each other becomes more easily accomplished; the practitioner is simply able to lay variables over each other and look for correlations. As always, the multivariable analysis created should revert back to what is relevant for the study area or site. It is also important to remember that secondary data collected, and information from a site visit or community consultation must also be integrated into the multi-variable analysis. As with single variable analysis, below are five recommendations for when undertaking multivariable analysis.

1. Look for correlations - Multivariable analysis is all about looking at how one variable might interact with another. At this point in the process the practitioner could have generated information for as many as 40 different variables. In many cases the correlations will be easy identifiable (such as that local retail is situated along busier pedestrian and vehicle streets) but in other cases it they may be less obvious (such as how the urban grain changes towards a city centre). Taking time at this stage to explore and examine the information created is important to developing the narrative for the site and the study area.

2. Use the tracing paper layers - The tracing paper layers are a powerful tool in allowing the practitioner to easily look for correlations. By laying different variables together it is easy to see where for example different network variables might interact with features variables. For example, one of the most common types of multivariable analysis is to map the walking and cycling network alongside the location of the services and facilities to explore how easily it might be to walk to a school or healthcare facility from the study area / site; both of which can be mapped onto different sheets and brought together (if using the same scale - either *area* or *site*).

3. Make five key points - It is easy to overcomplicate multivariable analysis, trying to get each graphic produced to do far too much. Whilst there are some clear benefits (time and resources) from having fewer graphics with more information on each they become difficult to interpret for the reader. As a rule, it is recommended that there should be approximately five key concluding points that can be made from each graphic. Remember these key points can also be presented alongside any graphic as a series of bullet points, as well as being communicated through annotations.

4. Add annotations and sketches - It was highlighted that sketches and photographs can assist with enhancing the single variable graphics, and multivariable analysis is no different. Sketches and photographs are excellent for communicating the human scale and can be easily linked to a 2D graphic. All sketches and photographs should be provided with a caption or ideally annotations. It will be important that these annotations are supported by experiential information either gathered from consultation or site visits.

5. Use cross sections - At this stage, it is important to consider if any of the variables might work effectively together as a section. The cross section is a very useful tool, either as a street or block section at the site level or a long section at the area scale, to communicate one or more variables. They can also be linked to other variables to help communicate a key point or conclusions. For example, cross sections of street hierarchies can be linked to annotations regarding activity and frontage, whilst a long section showing building heights through a neighbourhood can also indicate some of the landmarks.

APPLIED URBAN DESIGN

Secrets of the Figure Ground
The figure ground can hold a wealth of information regarding the history and development of a place - a quality morphological analysis based on a figure ground will throw up as many questions as it answers. These questions should encourage the urban designer to expand the remit of their research/analysis to explore these unanswered narratives. In that respect, a morphological assessment is often one of the very first studies undertaken by the urban designer at the strategic scale, helping to shape the analysis that follows.

The example here, taken from the project in Aalborg presents several interesting issues, but in this case the figure ground has been used to further understand the hierarchy and quality of the routes that run adjacent to the site. The north-south route that runs along the eastern edge of the site in Aalborg is notable within the figure ground. There are several secondary, or smaller routes that can clearly be identified that run east-west through the townscape. Well defined routes, such as these, all have endured through history. The analysis diagram marks each route on the plan to draw these to the reader's attention.

Another notable feature is the change in the pattern and grain of development from east to west. To the east of the site, beyond the major north-south route, the pattern of streets and spaces is more organic, with the pieces being far more irregular in size. This corresponds with the historical core of the city, around the civic spaces and commercial functions. The pattern of streets and space in this area remaining unchanged for hundreds of years. To the north of the site itself there is a clear grid of streets and urban blocks dating from the late 19th and early 20th centuries, before moving further west, this breaks down into a finer grained area of buildings and spaces that are not based on urban block principles.

2. Clear edge provided by railway creates distinct change/disruption in townscape

3. Clear routes south (S) from fjord (water body) create strong grid of routes to east (E)

1. Main N-S arterial route to Airport (N) and Aarhus (S)

4. Range of clear E-W routes through city centre toward site

AALBORG
Morphological Study

CHAPTER 6: LOCAL ANALYSIS

134

Fragmented Structure - Structures of large former industrial premises including the distillery and tobacco factories coupled with early regeneration of the Western Harbour creates disconnect across the townscape

Historic City - Compact and organic structure. Medieval city grain and fabric create a distinctive historical quarter and experience

Mixed Structure - Mainly fine grain villa grid. Historical grazing land, the urban fabric of Hasseris is typical of Scandinavian villa housing

Poorly Defined Area - Larger areas of limited definition create fractures in the morphology - particularly concentrated on the south of the site / city

Compact Structure - Repeated pattern of strong grids via 20th century urban blocks - prominent vernacular across a range of central areas

Site | Poorly Defined Area | Compact Structure | Organic Compact Structure | Fragmented Structure | Mixed Structure

135 APPLIED URBAN DESIGN

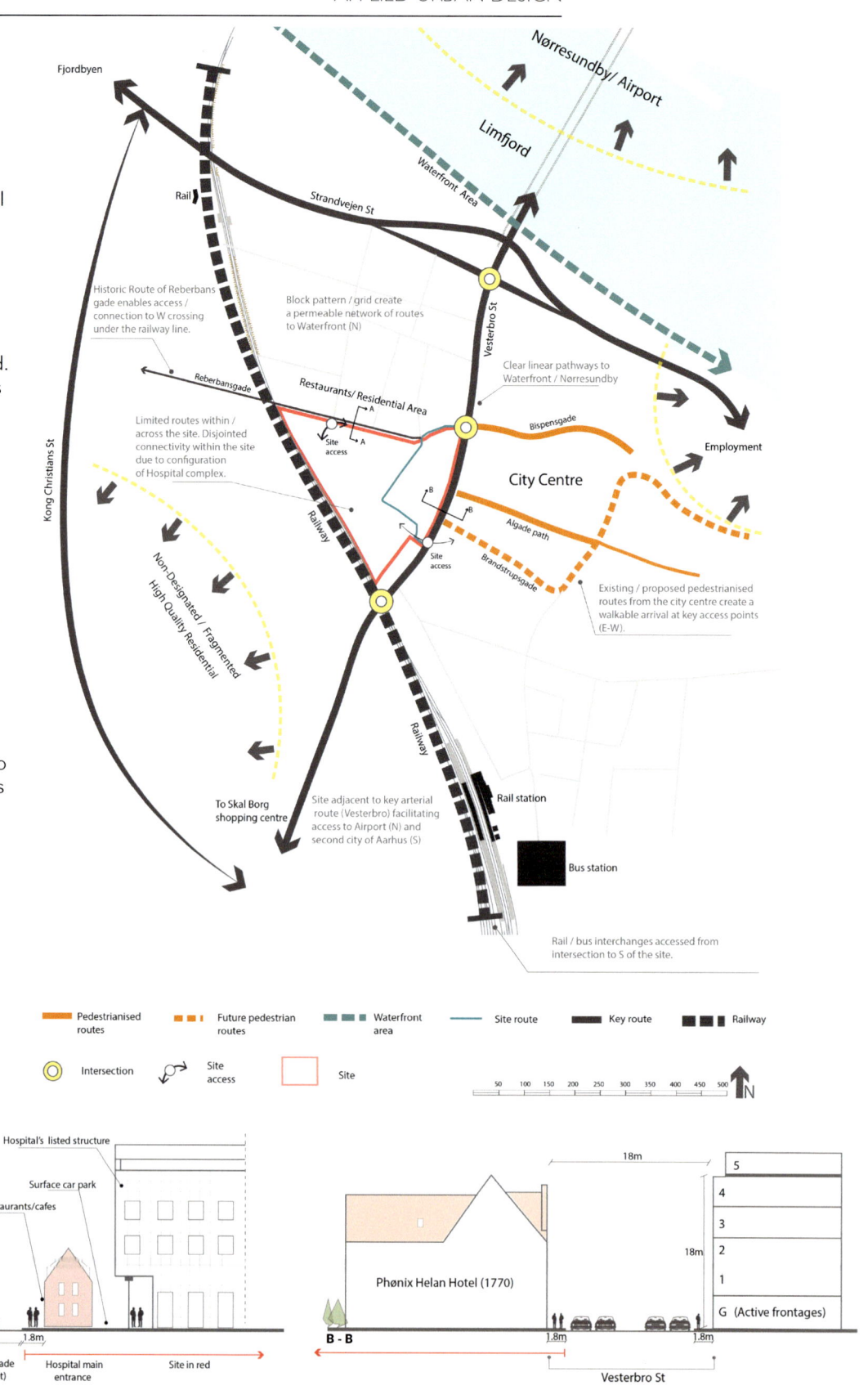

Route Hierarchy

This route hierarchy from the site in Aalborg is typical of the way a hierarchy of routes can be presented. The weight of the routes identifies those that are more heavily trafficked, with pedestrian only connections clearly marked. However, the analysis takes this further by looking in more detail at the nature of functionality on the key routes identified - using cross sections to help understand whether these routes are human scaled and pedestrian friendly. These routes were chosen because they were identified as part of the morphological study previously undertaken. Together this piece of analysis, and the previous morphology study, begin to shape a narrative about this site, its existing situation, its wider connectivity, and surrounding context.

AALBORG
Route Hierarchy

CHAPTER 6: LOCAL ANALYSIS   136

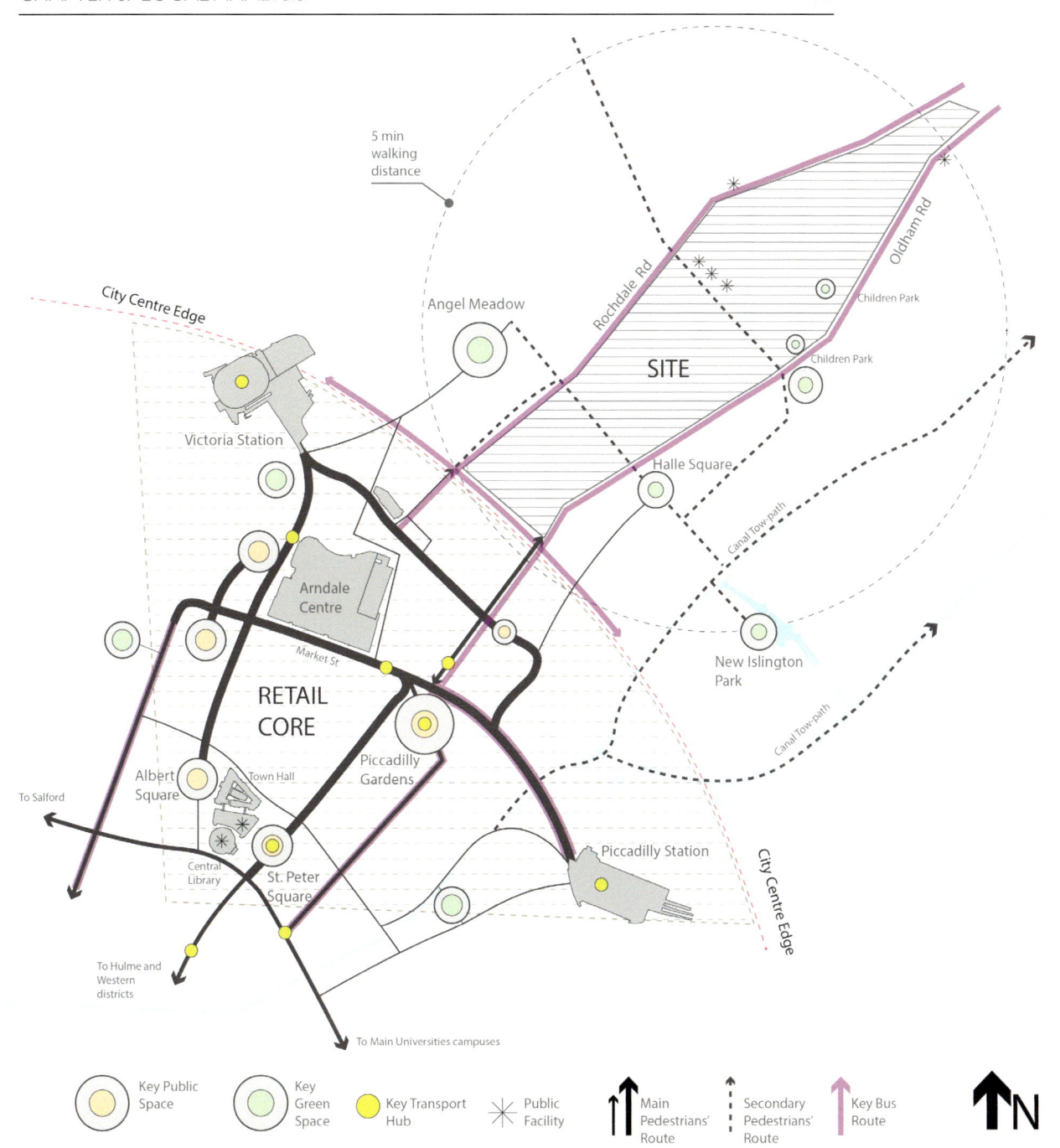

Accessibility and Connectivity:
This plan has been designed to showcase the connections to Manchester city centre given that the site is located immediately adjacent to the shops, services, and employment opportunities it provides. It can be easy to forget that a site may have a functional relationship with another area of a city that requires the variable to be considered or presented in a different way.

As a result, the analysis is not centred on the site, but rather is offset to illustrate more of the city centre to allow for more of these shops and services to be identified, but also to fully communicate to the reader the importance of the relationship between the masterplan site, and the centre of Manchester. An important part of the narrative for this case study.

MANCHESTER
Accessibility and Connectivity

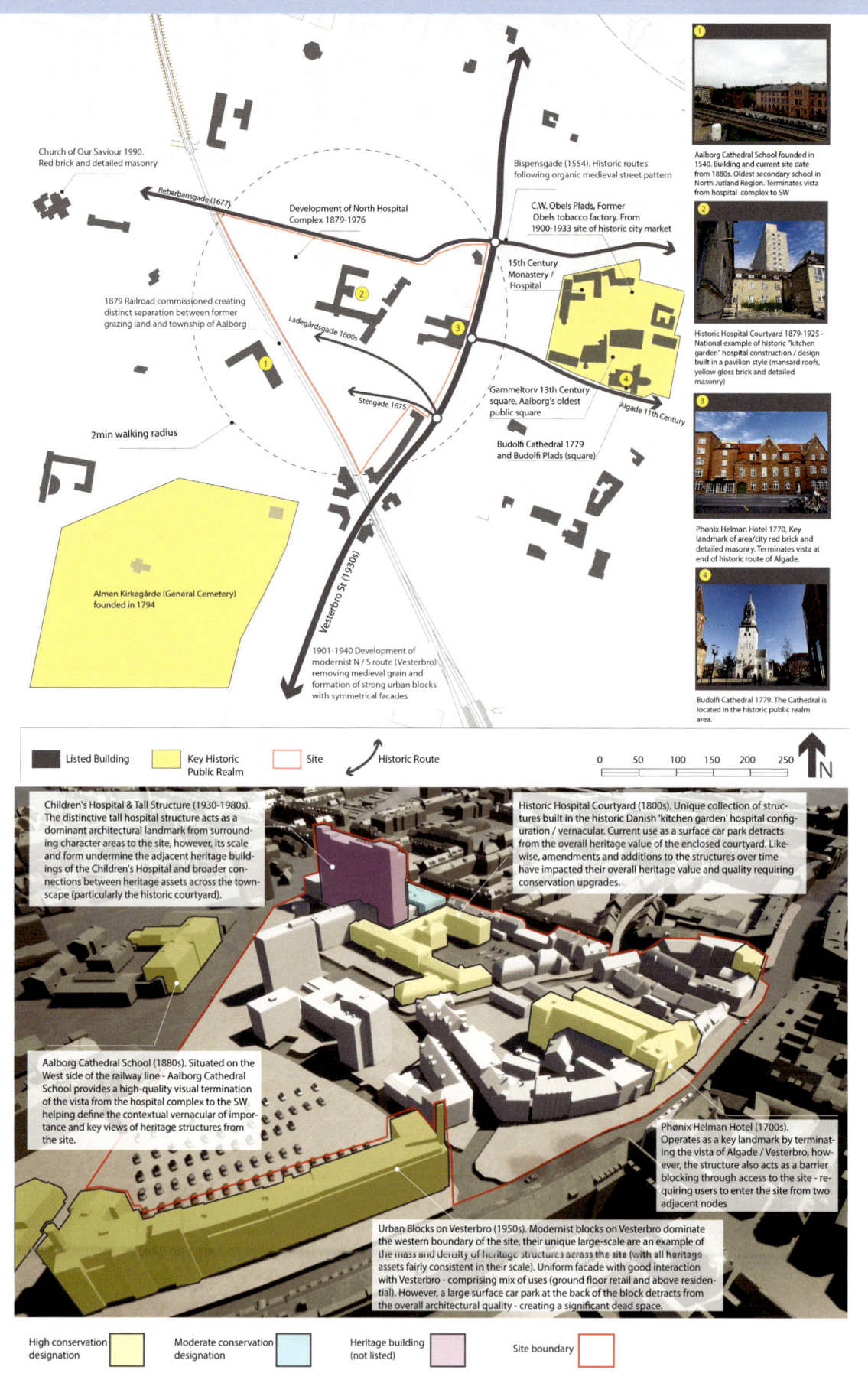

AALBORG
Heritage Assets

Map annotations

- Church of Our Saviour 1990. Red brick and detailed masonry
- Reberbansgade (1677)
- Development of North Hospital Complex 1879-1976
- Bispensgade (1554). Historic routes following organic medieval street pattern
- C.W. Obels Plads, Former Obels tobacco factory. From 1900-1933 site of historic city market
- 1879 Railroad commissioned creating distinct separation between former grazing land and township of Aalborg
- Ladegårdsgade 1600s
- 15th Century Monastery / Hospital
- Stengade 1675
- Gammeltorv 13th Century square, Aalborg's oldest public square
- Algade 11th Century
- 2min walking radius
- Budolfi Cathedral 1779 and Budolfi Plads (square)
- Almen Kirkegårde (General Cemetery) founded in 1794
- Vesterbro St (1930s)
- 1901-1940 Development of modernist N / S route (Vesterbro) removing medieval grain and formation of strong urban blocks with symmetrical facades

Photo captions

1. Aalborg Cathedral School founded in 1540. Building and current site date from 1880s. Oldest secondary school in North Jutland Region. Terminates vista from hospital complex to SW.
2. Historic Hospital Courtyard 1879-1925 - National example of historic "kitchen garden" hospital construction / design built in a pavilion style (mansard roofs, yellow gloss brick and detailed masonry)
3. Phønix Helman Hotel 1770, Key landmark of area/city red brick and detailed masonry. Terminates vista at end of historic route of Algade.
4. Budolfi Cathedral 1779. The Cathedral is located in the historic public realm area.

Legend
- Listed Building
- Key Historic Public Realm
- Site
- Historic Route
- 0 50 100 150 200 250
- N

3D view annotations

Children's Hospital & Tall Structure (1930-1980s). The distinctive tall hospital structure acts as a dominant architectural landmark from surrounding character areas to the site, however, its scale and form undermine the adjacent heritage buildings of the Children's Hospital and broader connections between heritage assets across the townscape (particularly the historic courtyard).

Historic Hospital Courtyard (1800s). Unique collection of structures built in the historic Danish 'kitchen garden' hospital configuration / vernacular. Current use as a surface car park detracts from the overall heritage value of the enclosed courtyard. Likewise, amendments and additions to the structures over time have impacted their overall heritage value and quality requiring conservation upgrades.

Aalborg Cathedral School (1880s). Situated on the West side of the railway line - Aalborg Cathedral School provides a high-quality visual termination of the vista from the hospital complex to the SW helping define the contextual vernacular of importance and key views of heritage structures from the site.

Phønix Helman Hotel (1700s). Operates as a key landmark by terminating the vista of Algade / Vesterbro, however, the structure also acts as a barrier blocking through access to the site - requiring users to enter the site from two adjacent nodes

Urban Blocks on Vesterbro (1950s). Modernist blocks on Vesterbro dominate the western boundary of the site, their unique large-scale are an example of the mass and density of heritage structures across the site (with all heritage assets fairly consistent in their scale). Uniform facade with good interaction with Vesterbro - comprising mix of uses (ground floor retail and above residential). However, a large surface car park at the back of the block detracts from the overall architectural quality - creating a significant dead space.

Legend
- High conservation designation
- Moderate conservation designation
- Heritage building (not listed)
- Site boundary

CHAPTER 6: LOCAL ANALYSIS

Mapping Heritage Assets

Heritage can come in many forms, and the practitioner should not just focus on buildings and structures that are old, or indeed those that have been identified by organisations or statutory bodies as being worthy of protection and/or enhancement. On the other hand, just because a building or structure is old, does not necessarily mean that it is a heritage asset. It is also important to think beyond buildings. Infrastructure and boundaries are sometimes historically significant, for example former defensive structures, walls and enclosures and disused railway architecture. These are all part of the rich diversity of historical remnants that could be mapped by the urban designer.

One of the most important concepts to consider in older settlements is that of the *'Palimpsest'*. In urban design terms this refers to the fact that the land on which are cities are built has been built up and redeveloped for different uses and purposes many times over the centuries. However, echoes of these former uses of the land can remain, in the older buildings that are retained, in the spaces that have endured (for example marketplaces, civic squares), and in the routes that are still evident. Using historical maps to identify and record these is an important part of an applied urban design analysis process.

Statutory protection - This is the easiest way to populate an historical assessment. Across the world there are different types or designations for heritage assets, and the practitioner should ensure that they are familiar with the legislation. It is important to remember that there will often be different types of formal designations for protected parks, open spaces, and areas of townscape importance - such as conservation areas or World Heritage Sites. Identifying and mapping these key assets is always a useful starting point, but care must be taken not to map those that are some distance from the site, or not on a direct route to or from the site, since they are unlikely to be 'contextually' relevant to the local scale. Providing details of the statutory listing or protection as part of the analysis graphic is important.

Historical significance - Older buildings and spaces that endure within the townscape are likely to have some historical importance, and often this is related to the former use or character of an area. These can be identified not only from site visits, but from a study of the historical mapping. Care should be taken to not map those that are commonplace. Identify important buildings, structures, and spaces to help understand how a place might have developed over time. In Aalborg, the coming of the railway in 1879 had a clear impact on the townscape around the site, providing an edge or barrier within the city that remains to this day.

Aesthetic significance - Sometimes an historic building or structure will have some visual or architectural qualities that make it historically significant. This is often the case where one or more buildings might come together, defining a series of important spaces or routes to form an ensemble. However, there will also be buildings that stand alone in their surroundings that have some architectural merit and could be identified and mapped. In Aalborg, the area around the Cathedral and the monastery is identified as being part of the medieval core for the city, including the 13th century public square.

Cultural and community significance -There will often be buildings that lack either historical or aesthetic qualities but are important to the local community and their cultural identity. This is often the case where a building or space has had a notable influence on the day-to-day lives of the people who live in that area. Former schools and workplaces are often important to local people and can be identified through consultation and engagement. In Aalborg, the hospital site itself has significant cultural significance to the community - especially the maternity unit where many residents were born.

APPLIED URBAN DESIGN

Building Quality - A Methodology

Undertaking a building, or architectural, quality analysis requires a robust and transparent methodology. When considering building quality, it is not as simple as identifying those buildings that *'look good'* and those that *'look poor'*, it is also about their state of repair and whether they are in use or abandoned. This information is important when it comes to making decisions about possible demolition or indeed what should be protected and retained. In this respect, a building that is poor quality architecturally, but is currently in active use, and is maintained to a high standard is as important to identify as a derelict or disused historical building that has significant architectural merit. At the analysis stage it is also important not to pre-judge the design stage and determine whether a building should be demolished or protected - at this point it is about presenting the evidence clearly.

The example for the Manchester site presented here offers a very simple classification based on both the architectural quality of the building and the state of repair of the building. Whether a building is used or not (or would be capable of being reused easily) is a good indicator of its state of repair. This has resulted in four categories under which all the buildings on the site have been classified. It is important that all buildings are placed in one of the categories. This requires the practitioner to make a value judgement on these buildings but having a clear classification helps to ensure consistency. It is also helpful to provide a typical example image to aid the reader. The four classifications can be summarised as:

• *Poor quality architecture, poor state of repair:* The building will have very little architectural or aesthetic merit and will be either disused or derelict. The example shown from the Manchester study is a disused former industrial unit.

• *Good quality architecture, poor state of repair:* The building will have some aesthetic interest or architectural merit but would be disused or derelict. The example is a former mill building that has been disused for a few years and has lots of weather damage.

• *Poor quality architecture, good state of repair:* The building will likely be occupied and maintained by that occupier for the use that they put it to, but the building itself is not visually attractive. In this case, the Wing Yip supermarket clearly falls into this category.

• *Good quality architecture, good state of repair:* These buildings will be visually attractive, almost certainly be occupied and active and will be maintained to a high standard. On the Manchester site, the church of St Patrick falls into this category.

St. Patrick Church

Former Mill Structure

Good quality architecture/ Poor state of repair

CHAPTER 6: LOCAL ANALYSIS

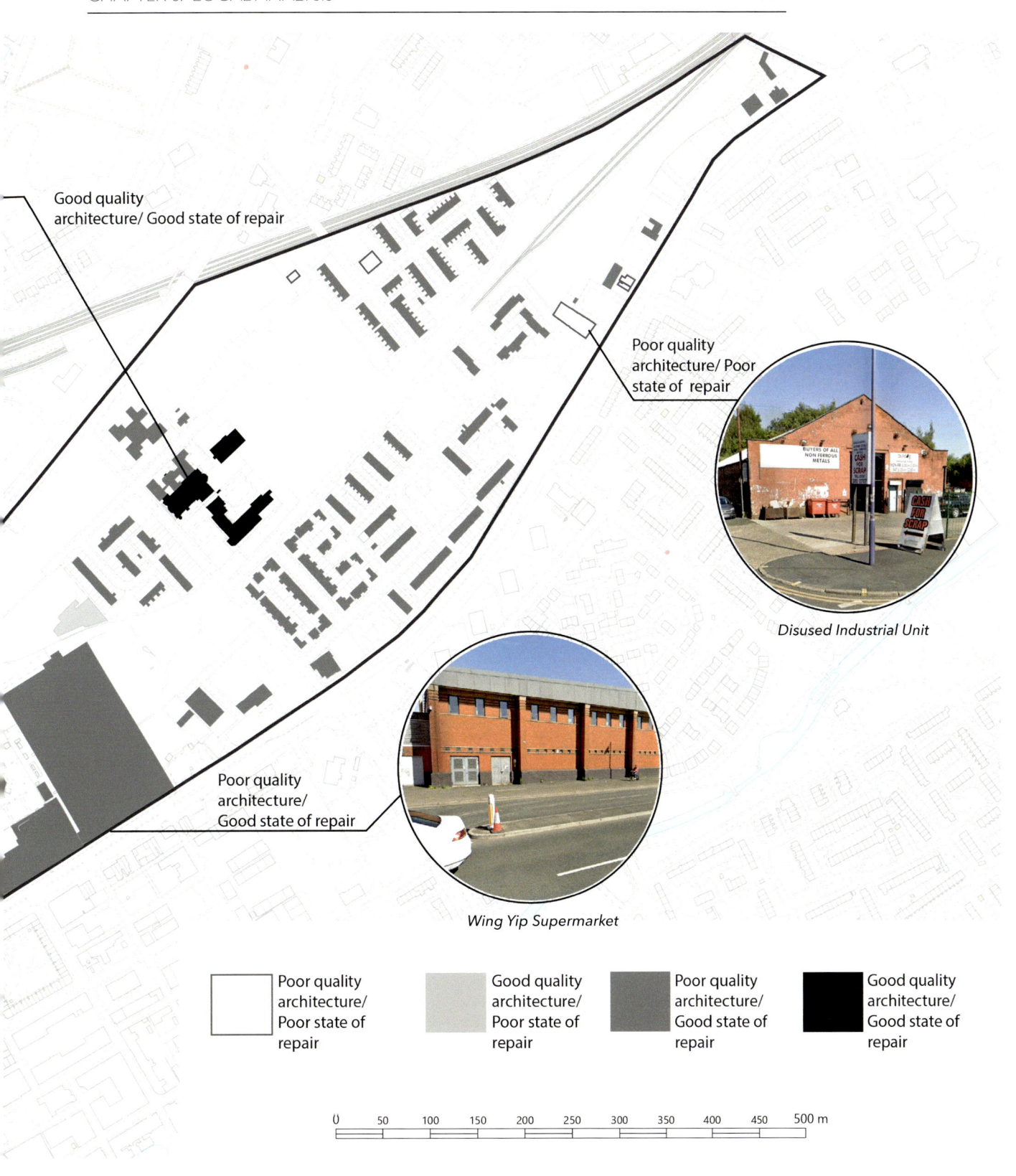

140

Good quality architecture/ Good state of repair

Poor quality architecture/ Poor state of repair

Disused Industrial Unit

Poor quality architecture/ Good state of repair

Wing Yip Supermarket

| | Poor quality architecture/ Poor state of repair | | Good quality architecture/ Poor state of repair | | Poor quality architecture/ Good state of repair | | Good quality architecture/ Good state of repair |

0 50 100 150 200 250 300 350 400 450 500 m

MANCHESTER
Architectural Quality

APPLIED URBAN DESIGN

Relationships to Tell an In-Depth Story

This spread shows several different graphics from the Manchester case study to demonstrate how groups of different variables can be presented side-by-side (basic multivariable analysis) to offer an additional layer of analysis. These variables relate to both land use and building heights, with building heights shown as both a long cross section through the site and as a 3D computer model of the site and its immediate surroundings. The range of different types of graphics helps to present different aspects of these same variables.

Taken alone, we can identify from the graphics that there are several taller buildings on or around the site (mainly towards the city centre) but that much of our site is low-rise. The land use plan is a simple 2D graphic showing different land uses in different colours over the top of a figure ground.

Alone this can tell us that there is a mixture of uses on the site, with residential uses mainly to the north and more mixed-use commercial-led uses towards the south. We can also see that there are several parts of the site that have little or no built form on them.

Taken together, this shows clearly that there is a transition within our site from the low-rise, residential neighbourhoods to the north and east, to the higher density, high-rise mixed-use development towards the city centre. The 3D model can take this even further setting out that the low-rise residential neighbourhood is part of a much wider area of similar developments to the east and south of the site, whilst the commercial areas closer to the city centre are comparatively low rise compared to the adjacent townscape, separated from each other by a void of cleared and car park sites.

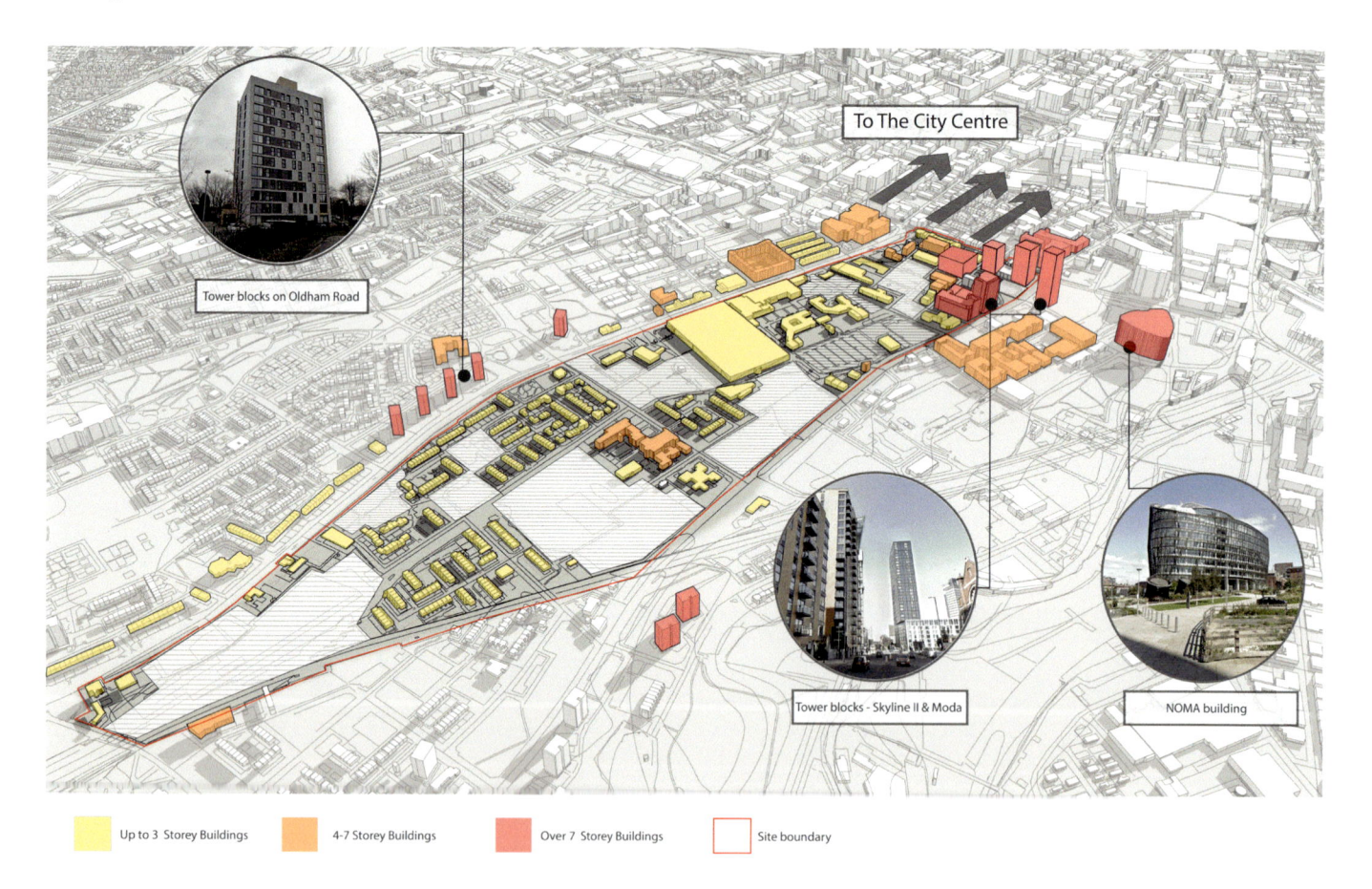

Tower blocks on Oldham Road

To The City Centre

Tower blocks - Skyline II & Moda

NOMA building

Up to 3 Storey Buildings   4-7 Storey Buildings   Over 7 Storey Buildings   Site boundary

CHAPTER 6: LOCAL ANALYSIS 142

MANCHESTER
Land Use and Building Height

FIXED TECHNIQUES

The single and multi-variable analysis we have conducted in Aalborg and Manchester demonstrated how several different variables might work together to assist the practitioner in showcasing the attributes of a site or study area. However, once sufficient information has been gathered and explored there are three important internationally recognised and understood techniques that can bring together these variables, with a strong focus on the human scale – and how people experience place. These techniques rely on the information previously collected to be successful and, in that respect, they offer the first steps from the *scoping* and *sensing* stages of analysis into the synthesising stage. To undertake *synthesising* analysis effectively the urban designer will have had to undertake a holistic assessment of a range of additional variables.

LEGIBILITY ANALYSIS

The legibility analysis is based on the ideas of Lynch (1961), and the idea that people navigate through a city by creating a '*mental map*' of the townscape using a series of different variables that will have already been identified in previous analysis. Essentially it is a measure of how easily it is to understand and get around a place based on a range of townscape features. These features are all gathered and presented side by side on a single plan. In that respect, the legibility analysis is a true multivariable analysis approach. The features that will form part of a legibility plan include:

Paths
What the user typically travels along. This will typically be a street or road where there is a strong linear pedestrian flow or movement along them. The legibility analysis should not show every possible route - only those most used or understood.

Nodes
Junctions or decision points between these routes. These will only occur along a path, often, but not always, where two routes join, but may also include key spaces or areas of modal change (e.g. station/transport hub).

Landmarks
Key notable features within the townscape, not just those that are tall. This will include anything from local services and facilities to buildings of historical or architectural interest. Landmarks can also be easily identifiable physical features within a place.

District
These are identifiable and distinctive areas of a town, sometimes known as neighbourhoods or urban quarters. They will have a clear identity and role within the city, and a clear boundary. Not everywhere however will automatically, or naturally, fit into a district.

Edge / barrier
The edge or barrier is a linear feature within the townscape that the pedestrian either cannot (or with some difficulty) move through. Examples will include water bodies, railway tracks, and even roads with heavy traffic.

ALL IMAGES: Vienna, Austria.

BELOW LEFT: '*Paths*' do not only include major multi-modal routes, but also key pedestrian links into and through spaces.

BELOW RIGHT (TOP): '*Nodes*' often demand users make decisions, regarding mode of transport or direction of travel.

BELOW RIGHT (BOTTOM): '*Landmarks*' can help users navigate more comfortably - The Gasometers dominate the Vienna skyline to the south-east.

CHAPTER 6: LOCAL ANALYSIS | 44

All of these are variables will have been identified and mapped as part of the single and multivariable analysis undertaken previously. Mapping them together on one plan would be far too much for a single plan. To assist with this there are three key points to consider:

• *Map features that come up time and again* - The legibility analysis is not simply about gathering the correct variables, it requires the practitioner to make a series of value judgements about which components are most important. This importance should be derived by identifying reoccurring instances of the five Lynch features. For example, a route or street that is identified as being a high street, a key link to a public park and is often busy regardless of the time of day is almost certainly a key path, whilst a small residential road connecting a few single family homes is unlikely to be showcased on the legibility study.

• *Understand and apply hierarchies* – Not all features will have equal importance, some being important locally or within a specific neighbourhood, and others being important across an entire town or city. When preparing the legibility analysis, it is useful to consider and present these two or more different levels on your plan, you could identify them with a different or larger graphic/icon such as via major and minor distinctions. For example two places of worship might be identified as landmarks.

However one is local chapel that serves that neighbourhood (minor), whilst another nearby might be the city's Cathedral (major).

• *The coverage of features varies* – It is important to remember that if the legibility assessment has been undertaken correctly there is unlikely to be a similar number of features at all points on the plan. In some cases, there will be areas that are completely devoid of any features. This can be an important analysis point and denotes that a particular area of your study likely lacks legibility. It is often the case that either side of a key edge or barrier there is a different pattern or coverage of features – this is quite normal. Importantly this will allow the practitioner to determine whether their site or study area sits within a location that has good or bad legibility.

There is a clear opportunity to use the legibility analysis as a method for collating and integrating the views of local people. Lynch developed a series of maps of Boston, US, through working with a wide range of locals. You can work with community groups or local stakeholders, and having explained the principles of the legibility analysis, can ask them to share their own plans using the features listed above. With this done, the practitioner can either amalgamate these onto a single plan or series of plans showcasing the communities' identified features, or test against their own assessment.

ABOVE LEFT: Alt-Erlaa social housing development is so large and contained that it forms a clear '*district*' to the west of Vienna's city centre.

ABOVE RIGHT: '*Barriers*' can be created by hard infrastructure such as railway lines - The new Hauptbahnof Station in Vienna.

APPLIED URBAN DESIGN

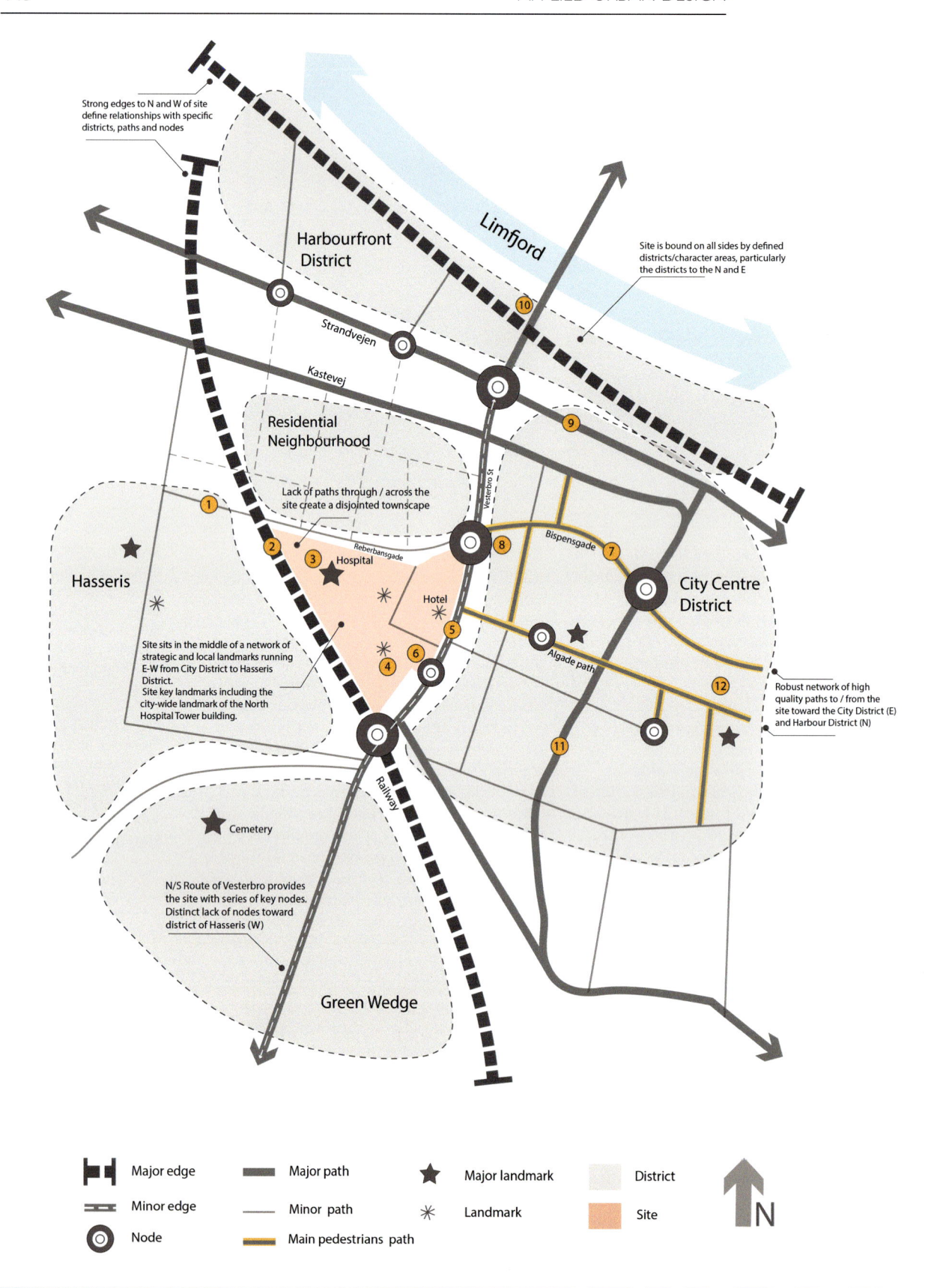

Strong edges to N and W of site define relationships with specific districts, paths and nodes

Harbourfront District

Limfjord

Site is bound on all sides by defined districts/character areas, particularly the districts to the N and E

Strandvejen

Kastevej

Residential Neighbourhood

Lack of paths through / across the site create a disjointed townscape

Hasseris

Reberbansgade

Hospital

Vesterbro St

Bispensgade

Hotel

City Centre District

Algade path

Site sits in the middle of a network of strategic and local landmarks running E-W from City District to Hasseris District.
Site key landmarks including the city-wide landmark of the North Hospital Tower building.

Robust network of high quality paths to / from the site toward the City District (E) and Harbour District (N)

Cemetery

Railway

N/S Route of Vesterbro provides the site with series of key nodes. Distinct lack of nodes toward district of Hasseris (W)

Green Wedge

Major edge	Major path	★ Major landmark	District
Minor edge	Minor path	✻ Landmark	Site
⊚ Node	Main pedestrians path		

N

AALBORG
Legibility Analysis

CHAPTER 6: LOCAL ANALYSIS

Is it Legible?
Conducting a legibility analysis is more than mapping the elements provided by Lynch - it fundamentally requires us to consider just how legible, or not, an environment is - and why. The legibility analysis plan can help us to answer, and importantly evidence, this critical question.

The diagram opposite shows the legibility analysis undertaken for the Aalborg site. It illustrates there is a strong network of routes to the east of the site which are coupled with a series of local landmarks, and several clearly identifiable districts surrounding the site. In this respect, the townscape can be shown to be reasonably legible and there are opportunities built upon this in any future development proposals.

Turning to the site itself, there are some features, including several local landmarks within the boundary that help deliver legibility. However, the site is somewhat disconnected from the main paths and routes, separated from the city centre and other surrounding neighbourhoods by the barrier of the main north-south route (Vesterbro) and the railway line. This is further compounded since there appears to be few paths that pass through/across the site – as a result of its current use as predominantly a hospital complex. Whilst the wider city and neighbourhood has some very strong legibility components, the Aalborg site itself cannot be considered legible. The site acts as an island disconnected from the remainder of the city by the barriers that surround it.

1. Minor Path - Reberbansgade 
2. Major Edge - Railway Line 
3. Major Landmark - Hospital Tall Structure 
4. Minor Landmark - Freya Statue Vesterbro 
5. Minor Edge - Vesterbro 
6. Minor Node - Gåsepigen - Stengade - Ladergårdsgade 
7. Main Pedestrian Path - Bispensgade 
8. Major Node - Urbansgade - Bispensgade - Vesterbro 
9. Major Path - Slotspladsen
10. Harbourfront District 
11. Major Path - Østerågade  
12. Historic City District

SERIAL VISION

In Chapter 1 we introduced one of the pioneers of modern urban design - Gordon Cullen. Cullen (1961) provided us with a useful analytical technique that helps us better understand place from the human eye perspective - the serial, or sequential, vision. This technique focuses on studying a journey (or journeys) through an urban area, seeking to document - in a series of images - the changing townscape. The images work most effectively as simplified sketches; however, photographs can work. The technique works along a specific and linear route, with all the images looking in the same direction. One of the biggest mistakes made when implementing that technique is either to assume that the serial vision is simply a 'visual site visit' or a collection of images of the streets and neighbourhoods around the site or study area - it is not.

A serial vision could be used for two broad purposes. Firstly, to document and understand a key journey, particularly where this is to a key destination, oftentimes this is a journey to the main shopping or working areas or key facility such as a major transit hub or local school. Secondly, it can be used to demonstrate how the townscape (which of course is a mixture of the 12 design layers - see 4.3) changes along a particularly important route that has been identified within your earlier study. Our Manchester example does both, documenting the journey from the core of the site to the city centre, but also documenting the transition from low density housing and cleared sites, towards the higher density towers of the city centre. To be effective, the technique requires the practitioner to have undertaken a good deal of analysis prior to the serial vision in order to successfully identify a route along which the serial vision should occur.

The following four steps will guide you through this process:

1. Choose your route: One of the most important analysis aspects of the serial vision is the choice of route. Make sure that you always have a clear rationale for your choice. The route should be chosen to reflect those taken by a pedestrian rather than a car and as such you will need to consult your activity, public realm and route hierarchy plans to determine which is the most sensible route.

It may be that you have already identified a busy route to a key destination. In all cases, the serial vision should be accompanied by a plan or map of your route, that also illustrates the direction of travel, to aid the reader.

2. Choosing your images - There is no set rule for how often you should draw an image along the chosen route, nor how many images you should have in total, but somewhere in the region of 6-10 images is usually sufficient. Any more that that, it is unlikely to be a key route. Rather than providing images at regular intervals you should provide an image at points where you consider there has been a change in the townscape or where a change in direction occurs. You should try to provide an image at least every 400-500 metres, but often the presence of nodes, key landmarks or changes in enclosure would necessitate that you have these more regularly.

3. Annotating and captioning - Providing a series of annotations or captions on your images is an important part of the process and provides an opportunity to draw attention to the key changes in the design layers. Annotations can be used to identify key buildings or green infrastructure features within the images – sometimes colouring them consistently so that their role in the townscape can be readily appreciated. Captions can be used to describe elements such as enclosure, activity and land uses which are not so immediately evident from sketches or drawings. In most cases a good serial vision will have both.

4. Presenting your serial vision - Typically, the serial vision will be presented as a standalone study with the images in a linear fashion, annotated and captioned adjacent to the 2D map showing the key route. The images themselves would typically be hand drawn, simplified line sketches. It may be that there is some benefit in presenting it alongside or as part of other pieces of multivariable analysis - such as the legibility study but this is not required.

CHAPTER 6: LOCAL ANALYSIS

148

1 Poorly enclosed street with overgrown scrub land to right, and poor quality homes (left). Distant view to city centre.

2 Wider and busier street (Livesey Street). The church provides a landmark, with poor enclosure and poor boundary treatment.

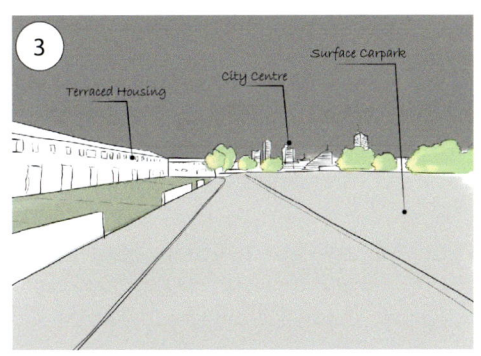

3 More views of the city centre are possible from high ground and open nature of site provided by surface car parks.

4 Historical buildings remain within a poorly defined townscape and edges, no sense of enclosure.

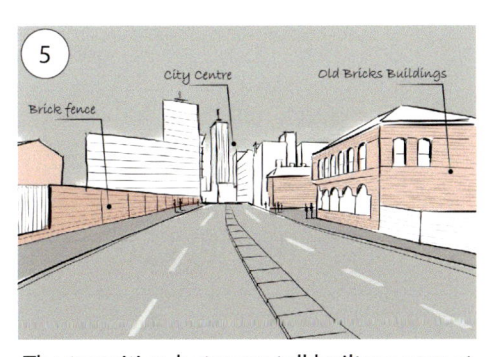

5 The transition between tall built up area at the city centre fringe and the poorly defined neighbourhood we have left behind. No significant scale change.

6 Right within the city centre. Tall and modern buildings with lack of human scale. A very busy area.

MANCHESTER
Serial Vision

CHARACTER AREA STUDY

Character area studies are a regular form of analysis across urban design and planning, with many places in the UK and Ireland having conducted such studies in an attempt to better understand and illustrate the unique characteristics of neighbourhoods and districts. Historic areas have often been the main preserve of such studies, with the aim to articulate the identity, architectural form, and townscape in order to develop conservation policies to protect these specific locations from harmful development that is out of context or threatens the intrinsic heritage value they may possess. Many urban design practices and local authorities are now employing character studies as central techniques in their policy and guidance development - mapping and recording defining features that assist in designating an area - such as age, use, and quality of the built form. An offshoot of this is the traditional vernacular study, wherein local design features and elements are examined considering materiality, detail, form, and function. The ultimate aim is to showcase what makes an area individual, identifying common design cues or themes. By delivering such an evidence base, this detail can in turn shape or guide new interventions to ensure they remain contextually responsive to their settings.

There is a risk with such studies in practice – that urban designers, and planners, play it safe – they view protection of the existing urban fabric as demanding replication in new development proposals – leading to design that is pastiche. Rather, this character information should be utilised to promote more creative and reflective contextually responsive solutions – these can be modern interpretations of the character of a space – potentially adding a new dimension that compliments and adds a new layer of history and continues the story of a place on a positive trajectory. Much of the material gathered during character area studies is later the basis for design management tools such as codes, guides, and best practice manuals.

Character is a complex issue – and involves several variables to seek out the commonalities that exist in particular areas, and how these differ across locales. Places can appear to share similar traits, but small variations can make a significant difference to the character and identity - details including the historic nature of the architecture, the street design, and the quality of green infrastructure.

The output of the character study is typically a plan - most commonly undertaken at the area scale - that includes a series of areas or zones marked on it, each of which denotes where there is a notable change in the character of the townscape.

Each character area will exhibit different characteristics as a result of the blend of the urban design layers; networks, arrangements, features, and feel. These of course can be for a range of different reasons including, specifically the physical attributes of land-use, morphology, and scale and height, but also due to more ethereal links such as an area's history, or relationship with a key destination or route. In that respect, there is a clear element of identity as part of the definition of the character areas. Of course, the larger the study area, the larger the character areas, and the greater the differences between the areas / zones there will be. Perhaps the most common mistake made in developing character studies is to focus far to heavily on land-use alone – it is important, but it is only one variable of many that should be included.

The following four steps provide a framework for arriving at character areas, but it should be noted that these are intended as a guide rather than any definitive process, and the urban design analysis should modify and adapt these as they see fit:

1. Look for relationships: Choose a series of variables from your previous study which will form the basis of your character study. Morphology, land use, and route hierarchy to begin with provides a useful starting point and then you can add more as you go. The aim here is to begin to identify a series of areas which are distinctive from one another due to changes in the balance of the urban design layers. At this point don't try to be too definitive with the edges of your character areas / zones but it is important that you annotate within your zones exactly what the characteristics are and from which variables these have been defined. Remember that everywhere will have a character – even if it is a poor, or weak, character.

CHAPTER 6: LOCAL ANALYSIS

2. Consider townscape connections: With your rough character areas defined, it is important to now consider how these will relate to key features, or destinations within the townscape. Transit hubs are an important consideration as activity and land use will often change specifically to respond to these. Public parks and open spaces are also important, often providing a sylvian backdrop to harder urban areas. In this step think carefully about the human scaled experience of these places. This may allow you to provide additional character areas, or simply to modify those that you have already drawn. Remember that a project site or study area might fall within two or more character zones, especially if it is a larger masterplan scaled site.

3. Rationalise the areas: Steps 1 and 2 will have established a series of character areas. They will be based on a myriad of different variables and integrate the physical attributes of a space with an understanding of the human experience. This step has two important roles, first to ensure that there are not too many different character zones for your purposes, and secondly to make sure that each character area has a clear boundary and that all areas are covered. The size and number of your individual character areas will depend on your intended output, but in most cases somewhere between 10 and 12 will normally be sufficient. As for the boundaries, look for physical features to help define these – rivers, roads, edges of parks or green infrastructure.

4. Provide the detail: Finally, you must provide the detail, as the plan alone, even if annotated with the attributes identified from step 1, is insufficient. In some cases, it is helpful to develop a short matrix or table to ensure that you are considering each variable in turn in relation to each of your character areas. An expanded legend to accompany your final plan is required which sets out the different elements of each character area. This could be accompanied by sketches and photographs of typical views or streets within these areas to help communicate some of these visually. In practice, character zones that are within and immediately adjacent to a project site or study area are going to be the most important, and you may wish to provide more in-depth information on these as opposed to the other, more peripheral character areas.

This is not an exhaustive list – or template – for conducting a character area study – it is intended to act as a basic starter guide only for exploring some of the more common elements that can define a place's character. Often, a helpful starting point is to consider the difference between districts identified in the legibility analysis – if these areas have been already highlighted, then local people consider them to have some perceptible differences. The final character area study should provide the urban designer with a wealth of information on the site and its surrounding context. To see a fully formed Character Area Study of our case study site in Manchester - skip to pages 161-62, where it is included in a wider '*thematic grouping*' of analysis.

PRESERVING CHARACTER

In Chinese cities such as Shanghai and Beijing, there has been an explosion of urban development in the past decades that has seen these locations embrace a more globalised generic design culture - as they rapidly adapt to growth requirements. This has had a direct impact on the traditional Chinese vernacular and character within townscape that has defined these historic cities for centuries. However, today we are seeing new agendas to better protect these areas of character - with renewed appreciation that old and new can work together in defining the future. Much of these vernacular traits are represented across Europe and North America in dedicated Chinatowns - that aim to reflect the traits and styles of traditional Chinese urban character, vernacular, and culture.

LEFT: Chinatown, London, UK.

MATERIAL CONSIDERATIONS

Much of the assessment that has been presented in this chapter relies heavily on primary data collected from the site visit, or from community and stakeholder engagement, however there is a wealth of information that can be collected and presented from secondary sources - such as socio-economic analysis and local plans and policies - which will influence the **Applied Urban Design Framework**, known as a material consideration. This information is presented lastly for a reason, as it should not be the driver of the analysis process, but rather used to augment and support the conclusions that have already been established. The ultimate risk being that too heavy a focus on these matters can sometimes dilute the design process. In that respect these elements need to be carefully considered and balanced as part of an urban design project. If the urban design process is being used as part of a wider regeneration or policy development project, then these elements would likely be superfluous as other more detailed work would be undertaken by others. However, in most cases it is useful to integrate some of these elements into your urban design study. Below are three suggested approaches that can help augment your local analysis.

Policy designations - When studying policy there is a real risk that the policy will drive the decision making as opposed to the urban design assessment. The practitioner should be mindful of this when approaching an assessment of policies. At the strategic level the urban designer may have considered some broad strategic policy objectives (areas of growth, connection, or renewal) but at the local level we are more concerned with understanding policies that might restrict or control specific development on the site. For example, if your site includes a number of historic buildings, then checking whether there are any policies that control their reuse, or even whether there is any protection afforded them (such as a heritage conservation area) is vital. This would be the same for matters of flood risk or environmental protection (air quality, species protection, protected trees). In some cases, these will simply be relevant policies, in others there will be specific sites, areas or zones where policies apply. A small policy info-graphic can be used to summarise the relevant policies and where necessary accompanied by a plan showing the extent of the zone or designations.

Local development - Local development is a very useful variable to consider at this stage. Looking at what has recently been constructed, or what is proposed or planned to be constructed, can offer a unique insight into the changes that are occurring in the surrounding townscape. Understanding these developments allows you to either find out what services and facilities might be provided in the future or understand how the scale mass, land use, and activity of an area might be changing with new development interventions. Presenting this information will depend on how much, and how relevant, this nearby development might be. It might be that they appear as annotations within other graphics or analysis techniques, or it may be that there is sufficient information that presenting this as a 2D plan of its own, detailing the changes and providing images of the proposed development. Remember to keep your study relevant to the site or study area rather than looking across a whole city. On page 153 we have a combined policy and development analysis for Aalborg.

Socio-economics - Understanding more about the people who live and work in an area is an important aspect of ensuring that any proposed development is human scaled. On larger projects or masterplans, some information will have been gleaned as part of the consultation and engagement that may have been undertaken, but on smaller projects, this may be limited. Government agencies across the world collate and present data on their population and in most cases this is readily available. However, as the urban designer, it is difficult to ensure that you direct your data collection to matters of relevance. In the first instance some basic bio-metric data is always helpful such as population statistics, overall health quality, and educational attainment. These matters are often best provided as a short info-graphic, based around a few key tables, icons, and graphs. Beyond this it is important to focus on the variables listed in the previous sections of this chapter. For example, understanding travel to work data – distances, modes etc. – can help to augment the understanding of the movement networks (roads, cycling, public transport). These findings can then be related directly to specific analysis techniques either as annotations or target notes adding to the overall richness of the analysis. On page 154 we have provided an example socio-economic study from our Manchester case study.

OPPOSITE: Manchester is a constantly evolving city - with new developments regularly altering the dynamic of the city. The scale of approved future development - and potential schemes - is significant and must be explored as part of a robust material considerations analysis.

CHAPTER 6: LOCAL ANALYSIS

153 APPLIED URBAN DESIGN

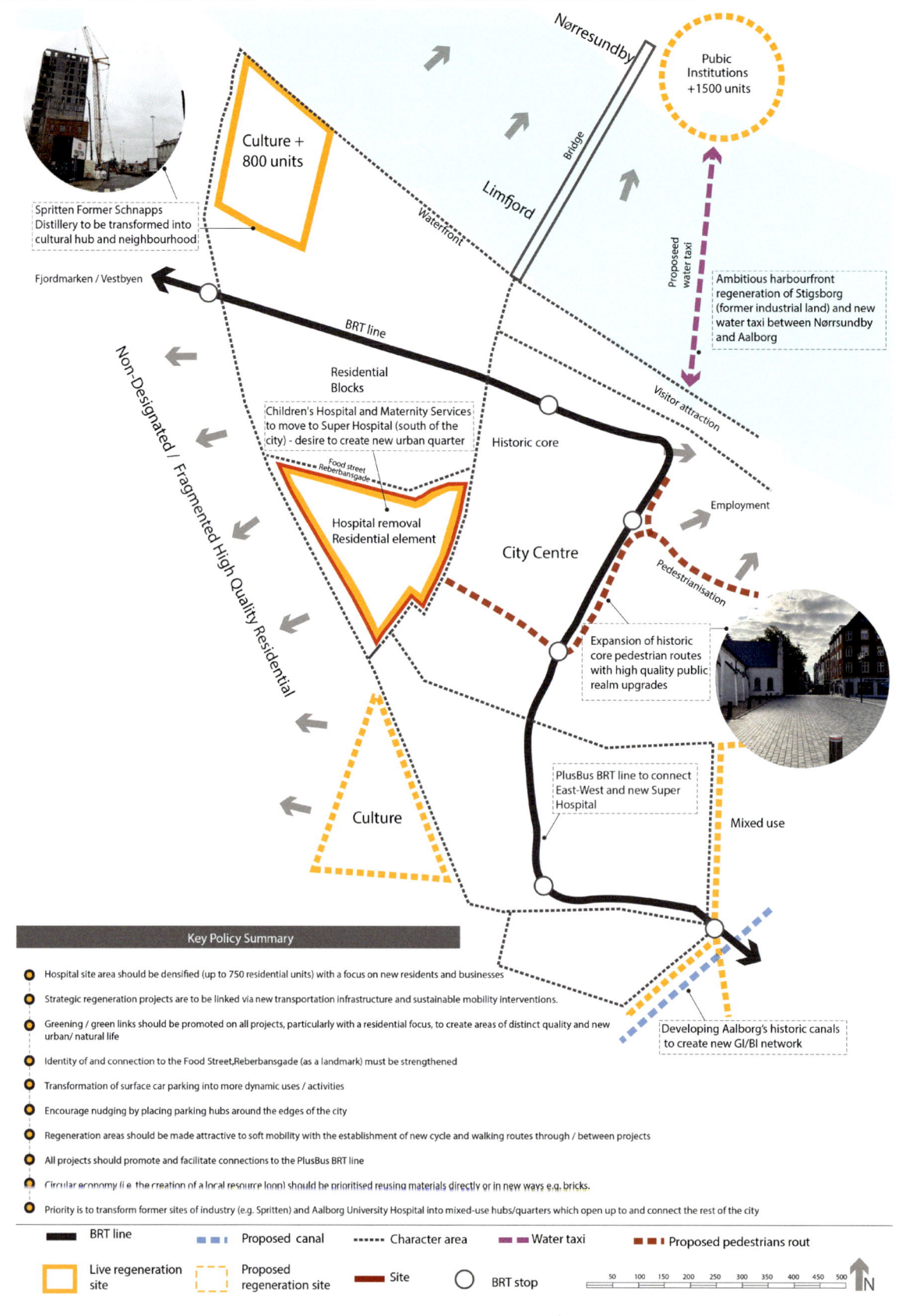

Key Policy Summary

- Hospital site area should be densified (up to 750 residential units) with a focus on new residents and businesses
- Strategic regeneration projects are to be linked via new transportation infrastructure and sustainable mobility interventions.
- Greening / green links should be promoted on all projects, particularly with a residential focus, to create areas of distinct quality and new urban/ natural life
- Identity of and connection to the Food Street, Reberbansgade (as a landmark) must be strengthened
- Transformation of surface car parking into more dynamic uses / activities
- Encourage nudging by placing parking hubs around the edges of the city
- Regeneration areas should be made attractive to soft mobility with the establishment of new cycle and walking routes through / between projects
- All projects should promote and facilitate connections to the PlusBus BRT line
- Circular economy (i.e. the creation of a local resource loop) should be prioritised reusing materials directly or in new ways e.g. bricks.
- Priority is to transform former sites of industry (e.g. Spritten) and Aalborg University Hospital into mixed-use hubs/quarters which open up to and connect the rest of the city

AALBORG
Policy Designations and Development

CHAPTER 6: LOCAL ANALYSIS   154

Indicator of Multiple Deprivation

North of site: Miles Platting and Newton Heath

Among the most deprived wards in Greater Manchester, ranking first for income, education, skills and training deprivation in the Multiple Deprivation Indicator 2021.

Highest percentage of residents claiming benefits in 2021, and remaining consistent for the last 8 years. Low car ownership.

South of site: City Centre Edge

Among the least deprived wards in Greater Manchester, with far better ranking for income, education, skills and training deprivation in the Multiple Deprivation Indicator 2021.

Among the lowest percentage of residents' claiming benefits in 2021. Low car ownership due to location.

Household Composition

North of site: Miles Platting and Newton Heath

Aging population, with high number of one-person households aged over 65 according to 2011 census.

South of site: City Centre Edge

Younger population in comparison, the majority are full time students or young working professionals.

Education, Skills and Employment

North of site: Miles Platting and Newton Heath

Scores low for GM Education, Skills and Training Indicator. Just below half of residents have no qualifications.

A clear lack of attainment for young people and adults' skills. 48% of households with no adults in employment, and 15% are economically inactive.

South of site: City Centre Edge

Among the best ranking for education, skills and employment in Greater Manchester.

Ranking highest in GM in performance, research and intelligence.

Health

Miles Platting and Newton Heath are among the most health deprived in GM regions, and among the lowest ranks nationally.

Security

The whole site suffers from high level of car crime, anti-social behaviour and theft, sitting within the top 25% of crime deprivation nationally.

Data source: ONS, Crown copyright. Available on NOMIS website.

MANCHESTER
Socio-Economic

6.5 ORGANISING ANALYSIS

When you have gathered a wide range of appropriate analysis across the variables and scales, it is critical that you attempt to draw it together effectively. The purpose of the analysis is to develop a clear narrative - making sense of what is important contextually for the site in question, that can be employed later to shape appropriate design interventions. To do this we recommend considering analysis across a number of thematic groupings - this can act as a starting point for delivering key findings, and also ensuring you consider findings across the recommended scales, variables, and material considerations - seeking out patterns and relationships (positive and negative) in doing so.

THEMATIC GROUPS
We have identified 6 'thematic groups' that act as a useful basis for this exercise.

1. Development
2. Connectivity
3. Public Realm and Green Infrastructure
4. Heritage and History
5. Character
6. Site Attributes and Identity

These thematic groups should be viewed as a starting point - a method for engaging, thinking, and considering what key findings your analysis is pointing towards, and how you might best illustrate them in a clear and effective manner. There will be various findings that fit across the themes identified - it is up to the analyst to understand where certain findings 'fit' best, or if certain key points need to be stressed across multiple themes to reinforce their importance or complexity.

Each thematic group requires careful consideration in regards to how it is curated -it is not as simple as having a series of variable findings under each theme - they are intended to act as more critical and complex conclusions that when read in conjunction with one another articulating the depth of contextual understanding related to the project site. Ultimately, they are a vehicle for organising your thoughts and value judgments and developing the wider narrative for the site and its context - therefore each site will demand a unique approach to be taken given each location will have unique findings related to the unique context.

5-Steps for Conducting Thematic Group Analysis:
When conducting this deeper level of analysis, it is important to ask several key questions to ensure you have good coverage of all the analysis you have undertaken:

• *What range of analysis have you conducted for each theme?*

• *Have you linked analysis across the scales (strategic, area, site)?*

• *Can you identify any 'gaps'? i.e. Have you not included any key contextual elements from the wider scoping/sensing exercises you undertook across the range of variables/ scales?*

• *What are the key messages of each thematic group? The trends.*

• *How will you present each theme to a broad audience? The narrative.*

1. Examine Each Theme - Take time to specifically look at each of the themes in turn - tackling them concurrently can be overwhelming. Explore the variables you have available and set out where you think they may contribute to the theme you are working on - the more analysis conducted the more material you will have to work with. Create a list of the key variables that you are utilising to address the theme but remember that a variable can contribute to more than one theme.

2. What are the Key Messages? Examine each of the selected variables – reviewing notes and annotations across plans created. Begin to seek out relationships and patterns - or trends that you are identifying as helpful in building the contextual understanding required. It is vital that you identify the common or easily identifiable conclusions - often these get overlooked as analysts focus attention on exploring and unpacking more complex, subtle findings.

3. Look for Gaps - Repeat steps 1 and 2 as often as necessary to ensure that you are not leaving critical gaps in your analysis - often you will have contextual findings that remain critical to the narrative despite not necessarily forming part of a wider relationship or pattern analysis across multiple variables.

Whilst engaging in this repeatable process it is also vital that you query your findings consistently - asking if they make sense and if your conclusions are justifiable and evidence-based, or if they require extra reinforcing through the conducting of further analysis.

4. Link Across the Scales - When you find patterns and relationships across the different scales this are significantly impactful - ensure that your conclusions highlight this, whilst being careful to not dilute the simplicity of the message you are seeking to convey.

5. Present the Message - Determine the key take-away messages for each thematic group and plan the visualisation of these carefully to ensure clarity. Determine the appropriate techniques and graphics to utilise - and how you might augment these with additional information and annotations. Consider the range of specific techniques that you can employ and identify the priorities and hierarchies of images and graphics to deliver clear and concise points that are easily understood by a wide range of audiences including non-designers. Each thematic group should conclude with a set-of well-considered take-away points that provide a satisfactory commentary of the presented material.

THEMATIC ANALYSIS
To illuminate some context around the six *thematic groups* for organising analysis - listed on the opposite page - we will provide a brief description for connectivity, heritage and history, and site attributes and identity - with related variables you might consider. For the remaining thematic groups - development, public realm and green infrastructure, and character - we provide a worked example utilising the live case studies in Aalborg and Manchester.

Connectivity
This theme brings together the movement analysis related to the site and its surroundings. Considering the range of movement types including vehicular, public transport, sustainable transport, and walking. It enables the analyst to showcase the accessibility of the area and site and think about key routes, interchanges, and nodes where movement choices are made - and how existing service and access is delivered.
Some variables to consider: Route hierarchy; pedestrian movement; sustainable transport; public transport; key destinations; public realm; GI; legibility; permeability; land use; frontage; serving; 24 hour city; enclosure; lighting; private vs public; serial visions; activity etc.

Heritage and History
This theme considers the impact of time on a site and its current state and local surroundings. Unpacking the relationship of a place to its history and heritage is complex - places are intrinsically linked to their past and it is of vital importance to understand this relationship. It is not as simple as mapping heritage assets such as listed buildings, but rather it is of importance to peel back the detailed layers of time to better understand how a place developed the way it did, not only in its physical sense, but also related to local communities and populations. This palimpsest is vital to garnering a deeper appreciation of the role of things such as culture, language, race, gender -and better understanding what people associate and relate to, that can define their sense of place and local identity.
Some variables to consider: Listed assets; historical development; land use; architectural quality/style; character; materials; townscape; legibility; visual primacy; key views; landmarks; local identity etc.

Site Attributes and Identity
This theme will provide some key information related to the site itself that may otherwise be neglected during a wider analysis of 'context' yet remains critical to the design process. This will include the size, key measurements, topography, and conditions of the site itself – its landform, features, land condition, vegetation etc. It will also cover critical information that will impact possible design processes - this might include detail on land ownership, policy information, key views, local character, surfacing materials, crime statistics - amongst other variables. The inclusion of this thematic group is helpful in that it can allow for certain factual site elements to be recorded and mapped - quite often this theme will provide a wealth of technical site detail without which design solutions could not be developed.
Some variables to consider: Site measurements; topography; Public realm; GI; policy; future development; edge conditions; architectural quality; land ownership; land use; frontage; service; heights; public vs private; access; routes; public transport; pedestrian movement; legibility; serial visions; character; views and vistas; heritage assets; vernacular etc.

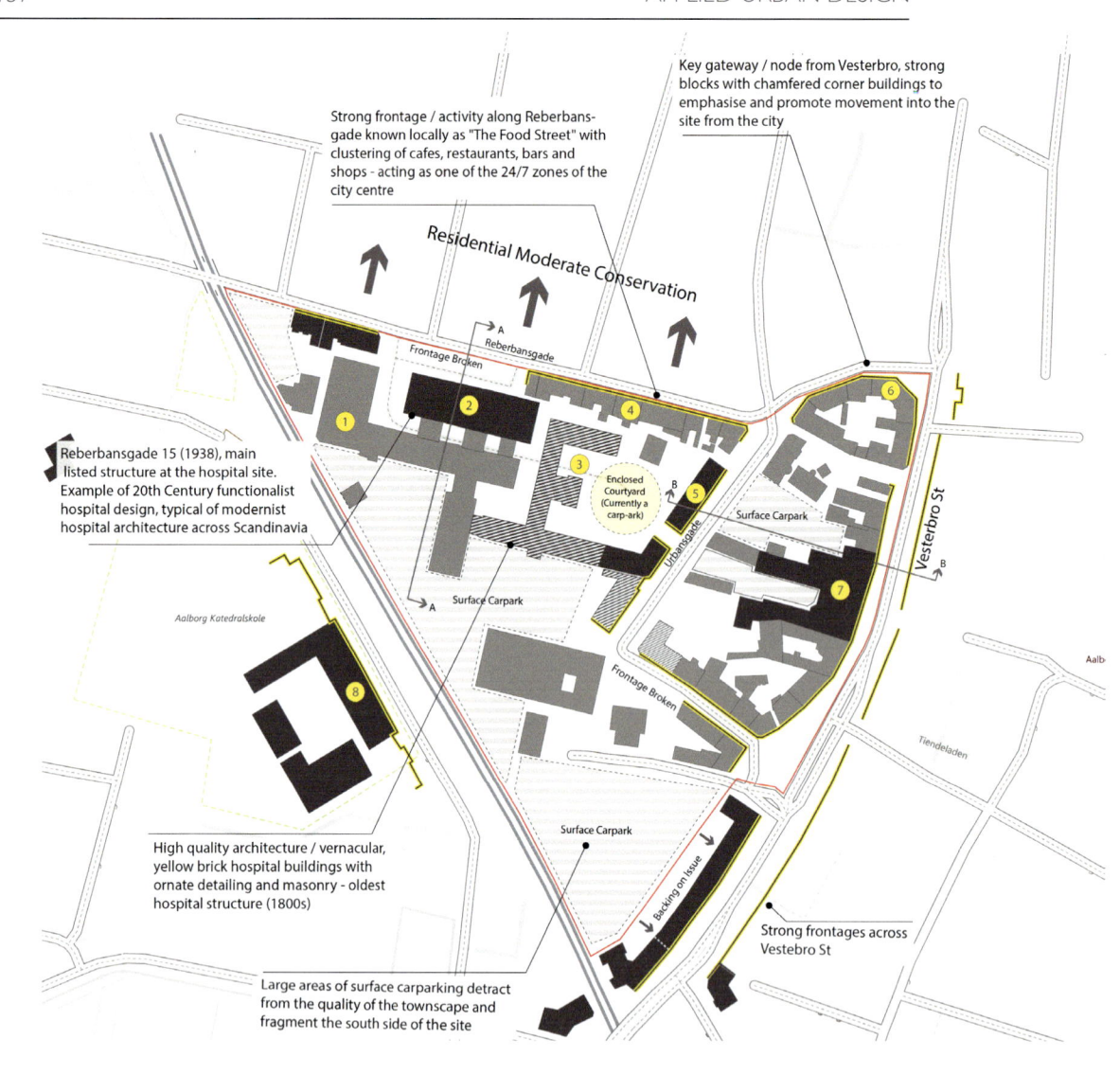

APPLIED URBAN DESIGN

Key gateway / node from Vesterbro, strong blocks with chamfered corner buildings to emphasise and promote movement into the site from the city

Strong frontage / activity along Reberbansgade known locally as "The Food Street" with clustering of cafes, restaurants, bars and shops - acting as one of the 24/7 zones of the city centre

Residential Moderate Conservation

Frontage Broken — Reberbansgade

Reberbansgade 15 (1938), main listed structure at the hospital site. Example of 20th Century functionalist hospital design, typical of modernist hospital architecture across Scandinavia

Aalborg Katedralskole

Enclosed Courtyard (Currently a car-park)

Urbansgade

Surface Carpark

Vesterbro St

Surface Carpark

Frontage Broken

High quality architecture / vernacular, yellow brick hospital buildings with ornate detailing and masonry - oldest hospital structure (1800s)

Surface Carpark

Backing on Issue

Tiendeladen

Strong frontages across Vestebro St

Large areas of surface carparking detract from the quality of the townscape and fragment the south side of the site

1. Hospital's tallest structure 
2. Hospital 15 Reberbansgade (1938) - Scandinavian functionalist style 
3. Historic Hospital Courtyard (1879-1925) - Yellow brick 
4. Reberbansgade, the food street 
5. Hospital 32-36 Urbansgade (1800-1925) - Mansard roofs 
6. 89 Vesterbro (1934) - functionalist gateway 
7. Phønix Hotel (1770) - red brick 
8. Aalborg Cathedral School (1880s)

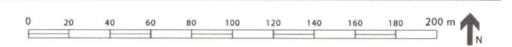

Legend: Building with Architectural Merit | Listed Building | Site Building | Main frontage | 0–200 m | N

AALBORG
Thematic Group: Development

CHAPTER 6: LOCAL ANALYSIS

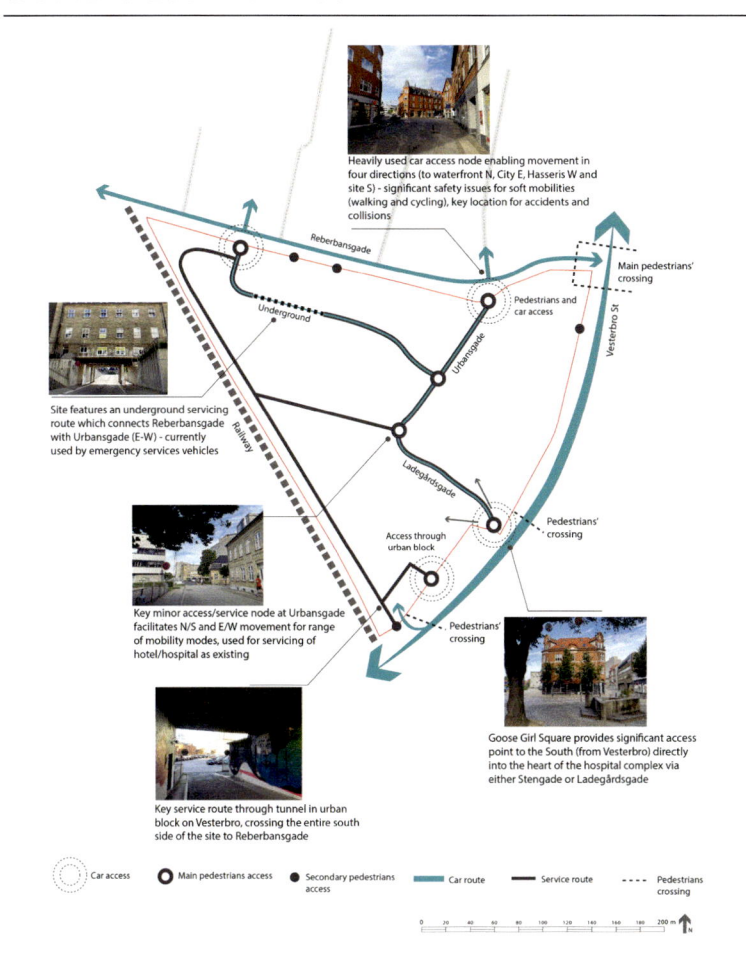

158

This '**Development**' theme includes all matters relating to the physical buildings and structures on, or near to, the site. It can also include information about future development that may impact the site. Our example from Aalborg begins with a detailed study of building quality given that there are many existing structures on the site – some of which are statutorily protected heritage assets. The 2D map is supported by a range of supporting information including photographs and descriptions of the key buildings, detailed target notes or annotations, and two long sections visually unpacking the contribution that these make to the townscape. Related to these details is coverage of the access and servicing arrangements for the existing buildings which helps to develop a rigorous narrative as to how easy (or hard) it might be to redevelop the site in whole or in part.

The example presented here for Aalborg is simply a selection of the possible graphics that could be included as part of the development theme but variables such as morphology, grain and density, architectural style, access and service, heritage assets, heights, building quality and utilities etc. could also be considered for inclusion.

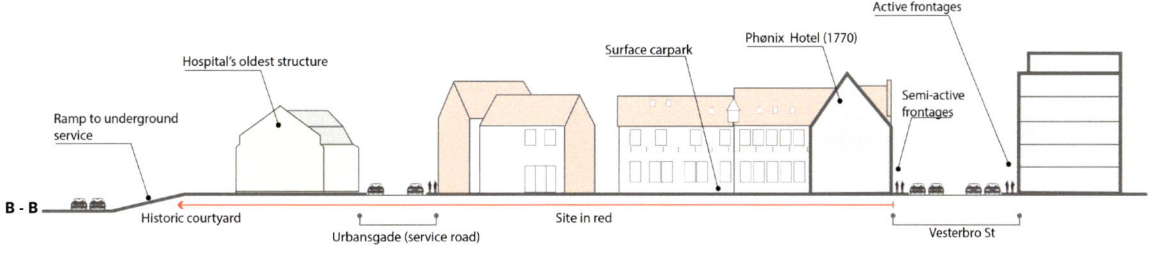

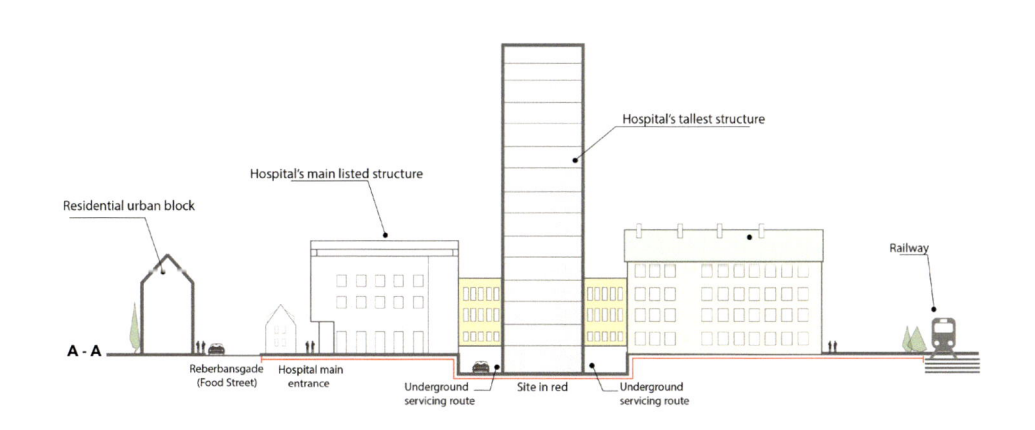

APPLIED URBAN DESIGN

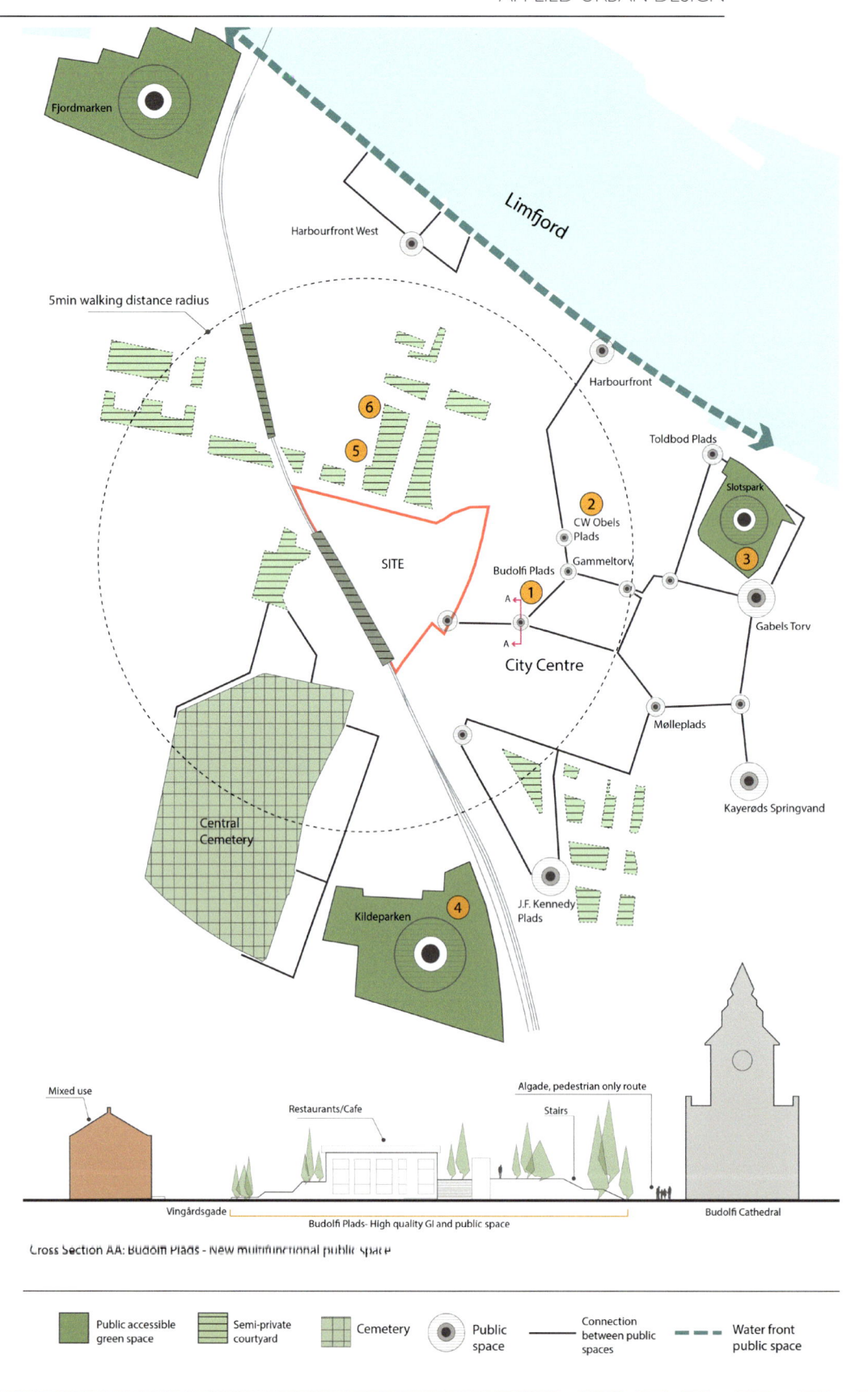

Thematic Group: *Public Realm & Green Infrastructure*

AALBORG

CHAPTER 6: LOCAL ANALYSIS

1. Budolfi Plads, completed in 2019, is Aalborg's newest multi-functional public space. The raised public plaza frames the Budolfi Cathedral and surrounding pedestrian streets/zones and features high quality materials, planting, street furniture and active frontages on all sides with shops, bakeries, cafes and restaurants. Example of ambitions for future public realm and GI integration in the city. Day-night space.

2. High quality historic public space adjacent to pedestrian routes of Algade and Bispensgade. Comfortably enclosed by timber-framed and brick vernacular buildings. Acts as a key events space in winter (ice-skating) and summer (seating / performance). Day-night space.

3. Aalborg Castle Park is the largest greenspace in the city centre. The walled park is positively enclosed and acts as an oasis providing opportunities for rest, relaxation, play in the city. The park connects the city with the waterfront via three routes. Poorly lit at night.

4. Example of the city's larger public parks of importance. Featuring sculpture, water features, play spaces, events and festivals it is an active and dynamic park - but poorly lit at night. Larger parks/GI of this type are located on the fringes of the city centre.

5. Adding to the network of GI and Public Realm are an array of green courtyards within the urban block vernacular (typical of the Scandinavian context). Semi-private and privately enclosed spaces, comfortable and well-used by residents/neighbours. Between 0.3-0.8ha in size.

6. A network of pedestrian paths and small scale green spaces in addition to private car parking are commonly found inside semi-private courtyard spaces.

This theme '**Public Realm and Green Infrastructure**' includes matters that are related to the location and qualities of public realm and green/blue infrastructure. It is often one of the largest thematic groups with opportunities to include information from each of the different scales of analysis, and from a wide variety of variables. This example from the Aalborg case study includes a dual green infrastructure and public realm mixed map at the area scale, showing how the site is (or could be) connected to a range of different spaces within walking distance of the site. Tied to this are more detailed qualitative information regarding the nature of these spaces including a cross section of the principal green space adjacent to the Cathedral and an assessment of six other key spaces within the city from a human scaled perspective (much of it referring back to liveability). Some of the more significant green spaces are on the opposite side of the railway line without easy access from the site. However, the public space network is firmly rooted on the city side.

The example presented here for Aalborg is simply a selection of the possible graphics that could be included as part of the GI and BI theme but variables such as green infrastructure, blue infrastructure, public and private, vegetation, flood risk, climate and sun path, maintenance could also be considered for inclusion.

APPLIED URBAN DESIGN

This **'Character'** theme is dominated by the key graphic of the *character area assessment*, which regardless of the size or nature of the site should always be included. The example here from Manchester not only breaks down the surrounding townscape into different character areas but also breaks the site down into these character areas. On a larger site, it should not be assumed that the site falls within one character area. Also, as demonstrated here it should not be assumed that all the character areas will be the same size – The large character area to the north that is identified as a low-density residential area, covers a much larger area, including a portion of the site.

As a result, the more detailed work that supports the character study (i.e., the detailed built vernacular studies) focuses not just on the surrounding areas, but on the site itself. In this regard the differentiation between the area and site level of analysis become increasingly blurred.

The example presented here for Manchester showcases how the character theme can successfully showcase information not only about local character (area scale) but also detailed site-specific variables such as vernacular, architectural style, and detailed green infrastructure. The variables chosen to deliver the character study will of course vary from site to site.

CHAPTER 6: LOCAL ANALYSIS

162

1 City Fringe

- Dominant strong urban grid pattern with visual connection to Northern Quarter, increasing Victorian red brick, mid density
- Clear encouragement of new high-rise developments in context with proximity to city centre
- Mix of styles, materials, buildings age and profiles
- High plot ratios
- Significant network of heritage structures

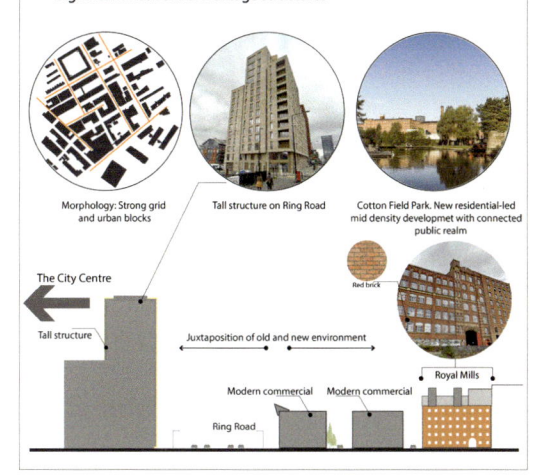

Morphology: Strong grid and urban blocks
Tall structure on Ring Road
Cotton Field Park. New residential-led mid density developmet with connected public realm

The City Centre
Tall structure — Juxtaposition of old and new environment — Royal Mills
Red brick
Modern commercial — Modern commercial
Ring Road

2 Miles Platting

- Predominantly low quality, low density 1960s terraced housing stock
- Low quality green/public spaces lacking in function/detail and poorly maintained
- Traditional Radburn style, urban residential layout
- Some heritage assets in N-W of zone such as viaduct and St. Patrick church (within site)

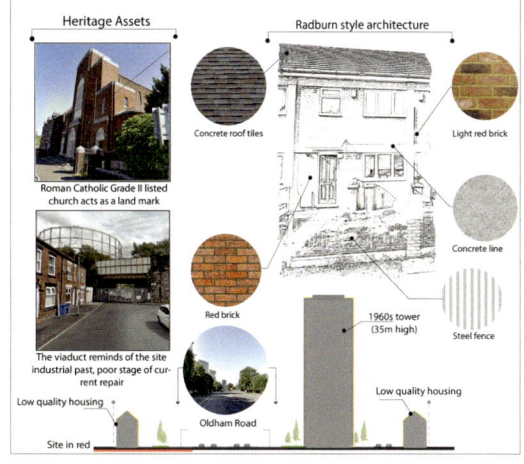

Heritage Assets — Radburn style architecture
Concrete roof tiles — Light red brick
Roman Catholic Grade II listed church acts as a land mark
Red brick — Concrete line
1960s tower (35m high)
Steel fence
The viaduct reminds of the site industrial past, poor stage of current repair
Low quality housing — Oldham Road — Low quality housing
Site in red

3 Fragmented Zone

- Mainly light industrial and commercial uses
- Abundance of vacant lots and surface car parks
- Lacks urban structure, creating a fragmented morphology
- Few structures of low quality, poorly maintained urban spaces/streets

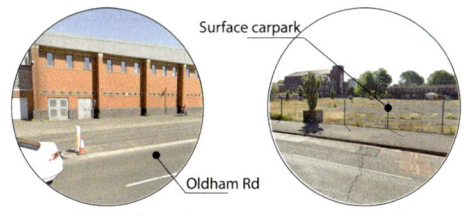

Surface carpark
Oldham Rd
Low quality large footprint sorting office creates a visual and movement barrier
Large cleared sites currently operates as surface car parking

4 Irk Valley

- Area of varied topography with steep valley sides towards river Irk
- Significant mature tree cover and woodland scrub
- Lacks urban structure, creating a fragmented morphology
- Fragmented morphology characterised by isolated unconnected former industrial uses

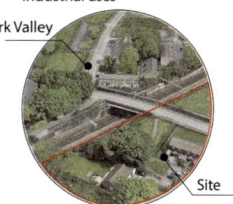

Irk Valley
Site
Irk Valley is cut off from the site by Leeds-Huddersfield railway line
Low quality GI is prevalent through the character area 

5 Cheetham Hill

- Framed by N-S connections on Cheetham Hill Rd and Bury New Rd
- Strong clear grid structure permeable but lacking legibility
- High proportion of small lower quality industrial units
- Lack of public or green spaces

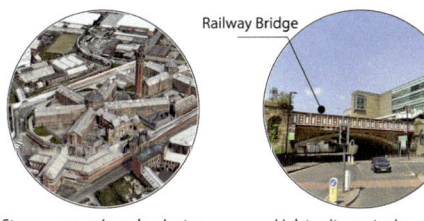

Railway Bridge
Strangeways prison dominates the skyline of the character area
Link to city centre in south, poorly articulated due to railway and A roads

6 City Centre

- Heavy office and retail offering
- Strong grid pattern with clear network of public spaces and streets
- Characterised by increased height towards the city centre
- Transition from Victorian setting to more contemporary high-rise development

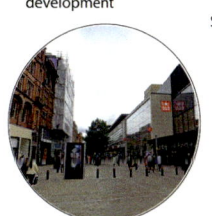

Site buildings — City Centre
Market Street: Busy retail street with strong pedestrian network
View from S-W of site to city centre with clear increase in density and building heights 

MANCHESTER
Thematic Group: Character

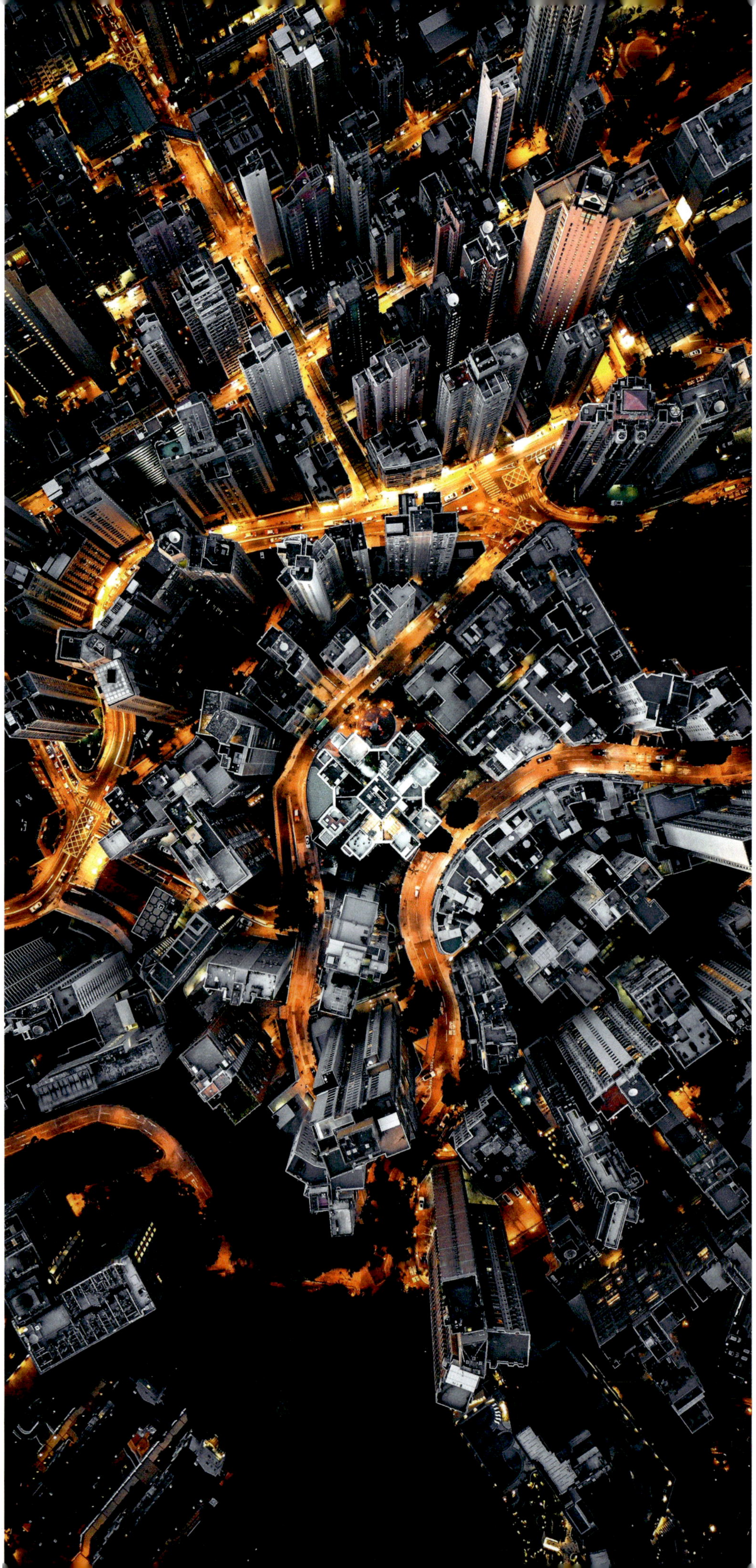

CHAPTER 6: LOCAL ANALYSIS

6.6 THE PROFILES

Once the **Local Analysis** stage is complete (across area and site analysis) it is critical to provide robust and transparent conclusions that will assist others in understanding the key points and issues raised/identified. With the myriad of variables at each scale of analysis it is important to be able to synthesise this effectively and present it in a manageable format. This is where what we define as 'Profiles' come in play. Profiles are the ultimate form of *'synthesising'*, they bring together the salient points of the analysis in a concluding set of graphics/visuals and key take-aways for each scale. They include the urban analysis of the physical characteristics of place alongside the analysis conducted into wider material considerations such as people and policy. The profiles are not new content, they are rather the designer's or researcher's, findings and conclusions. They seek to showcase identified trends, contradictions, opportunities, constraints, and qualities to provide a detailed contextual repository that adds to the overall context building. The Profiles do not replace the thematic group analysis – rather they simplify it to distil the critical aspects – they will sit alongside the more detailed thematic groups as part of a complete analysis package.

The development and presentation of Profiles is only possible when analysis is complete across the three scales of the AUD Framework step 1 (Strategic - see Chapter 5); Area and Site (forming the Local Analysis of Chapter 6). The three scales will require a separate profile respectively. Each will be made up of a variety of graphics and information – anchored by a core central graphic – The **'Appraisal Map'**. For the Strategic Profile this will be the *'Strategic Appraisal Map'*; for the Area Profile this will be the *'Area Appraisal Map'*; and for 'Site Profile the *'Site Appraisal Map'*. These anchor maps are not design, they are a recording and grouping of the core baseline analysis conducted at each scale. It is effectively the highest form of analysis. These maps aim to synthesise the most critical aspects from the variables you have analysed in order to present a conceptual visual that distils the most significant points and can inform the **Urban Design Program** (Step 2 and Chapter 7). Supporting these anchor graphics will be a range of other illustrations, deductions, and key conclusions that assist in developing a clear narrative for your site within that particular scale.

The development of profiles is a complex undertaking, their effectiveness and robustness will ultimately be defined by the quality and range of analysis conducted. The more variables considered, the more time engaging with the analytical process, and the ability of the designer to synthesise the salient information effectively will all impact the final *Profiles*. By presenting the concluding analysis at the three scales it reinforces the need for any future design proposals to consider context beyond the immediate site and surroundings. To achieve a truly contextual approach to urban design it is vital that design appreciate, respect, and employ the boarder narrative around context that the AUD Framework promotes and demands.

OPPOSITE PAGE: Profiles aim to effectively summarise the analysis conducted - and key findings delivered - across different scales to a wide audience. The three *Profiles* come together to illustrate the full context of the site in question - and demonstrate the complexities of thinking about place and the myriad concerns urban designer's must appreciate and understand. Image: Hong Kong.

BELOW: The Stages of Urban Design Analysis.

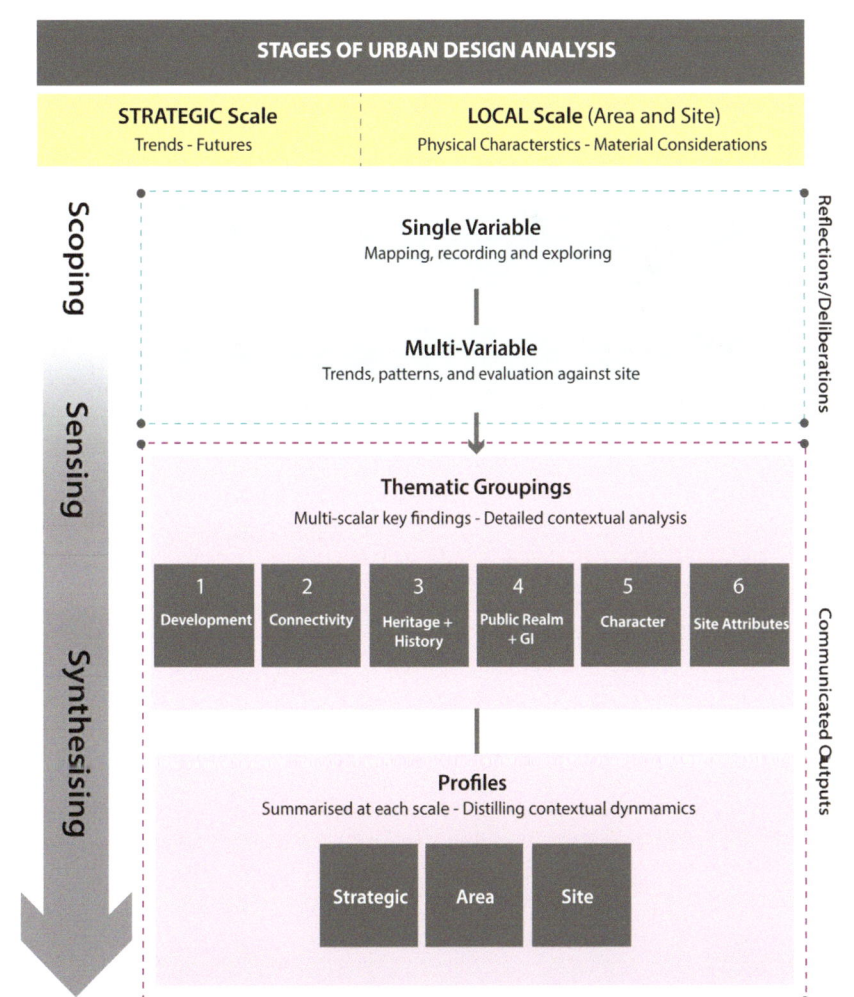

STAGES OF URBAN DESIGN ANALYSIS

STRATEGIC Scale	LOCAL Scale (Area and Site)
Trends - Futures	Physical Characterstics - Material Considerations

Scoping

Single Variable
Mapping, recording and exploring

Multi-Variable
Trends, patterns, and evaluation against site

Sensing

Thematic Groupings
Multi-scalar key findings - Detailed contextual analysis

1	2	3	4	5	6
Development	Connectivity	Heritage + History	Public Realm + GI	Character	Site Attributes

Synthesising

Profiles
Summarised at each scale - Distilling contextual dynmamics

| Strategic | Area | Site |

Reflections/Deliberations

Communicated Outputs

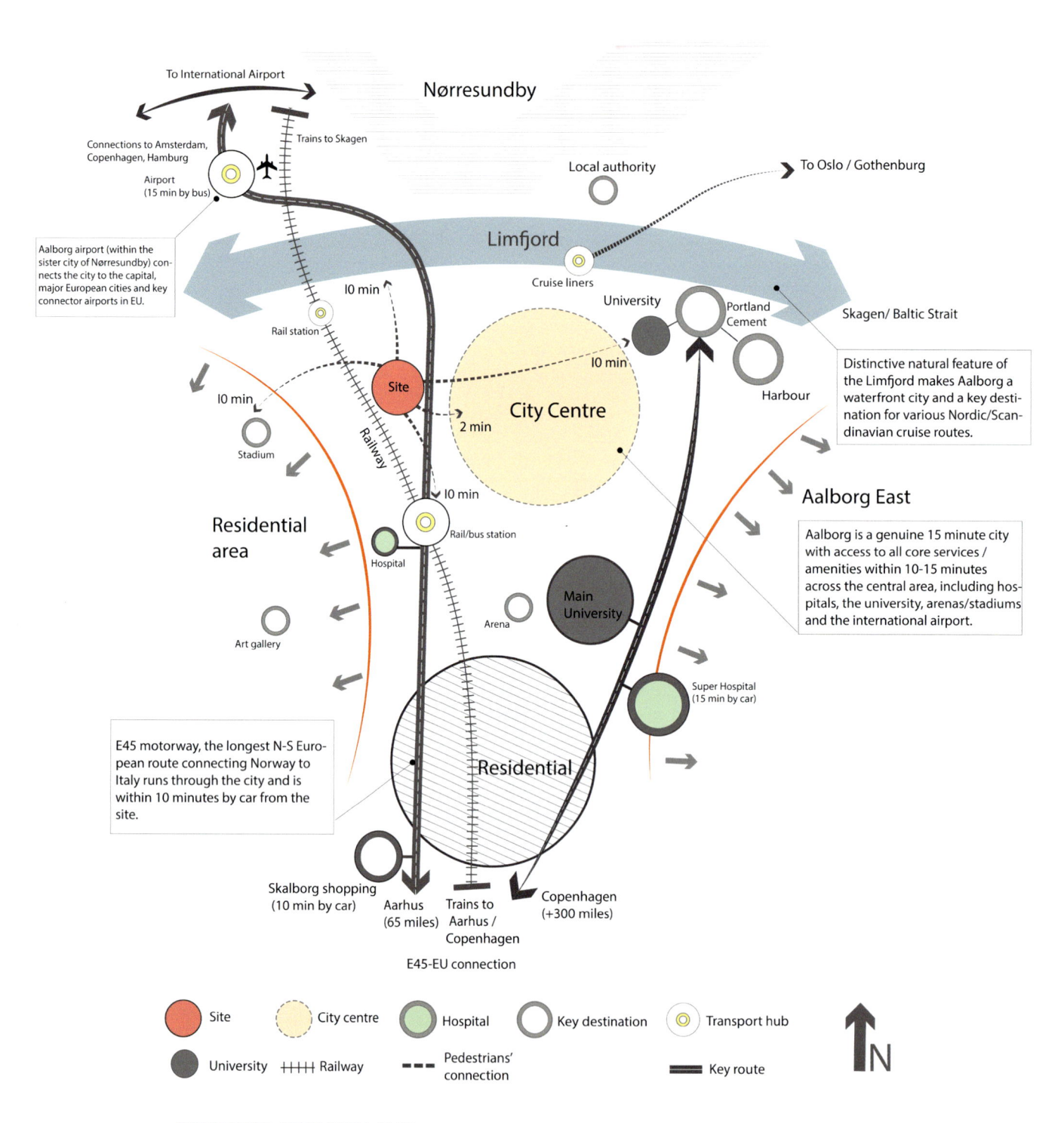

APPLIED URBAN DESIGN

Strategic Appraisal Map

To International Airport — Nørresundby

Connections to Amsterdam, Copenhagen, Hamburg
Airport (15 min by bus)

Trains to Skagen

Local authority

To Oslo / Gothenburg

Aalborg airport (within the sister city of Nørresundby) connects the city to the capital, major European cities and key connector airports in EU.

Limfjord

Cruise liners

10 min

Rail station

Site

University

Portland Cement

Skagen / Baltic Strait

10 min

City Centre

2 min

Harbour

Distinctive natural feature of the Limfjord makes Aalborg a waterfront city and a key destination for various Nordic/Scandinavian cruise routes.

10 min

Stadium

Railway

10 min

Residential area

Rail/bus station

Hospital

Aalborg East

Aalborg is a genuine 15 minute city with access to all core services / amenities within 10-15 minutes across the central area, including hospitals, the university, arenas/stadiums and the international airport.

Art gallery

Arena

Main University

Super Hospital (15 min by car)

E45 motorway, the longest N-S European route connecting Norway to Italy runs through the city and is within 10 minutes by car from the site.

Residential

Skalborg shopping (10 min by car)

Aarhus (65 miles)

Trains to Aarhus / Copenhagen

Copenhagen (+300 miles)

E45-EU connection

Legend:
- ● Site
- ○ City centre
- ● Hospital
- ○ Key destination
- ◉ Transport hub
- ● University
- ┼┼┼┼ Railway
- --- Pedestrians' connection
- ━━ Key route
- ↑ N

STRATEGIC APPRAISAL MAP

AALBORG
Strategic Profile

CHAPTER 6: LOCAL ANALYSIS

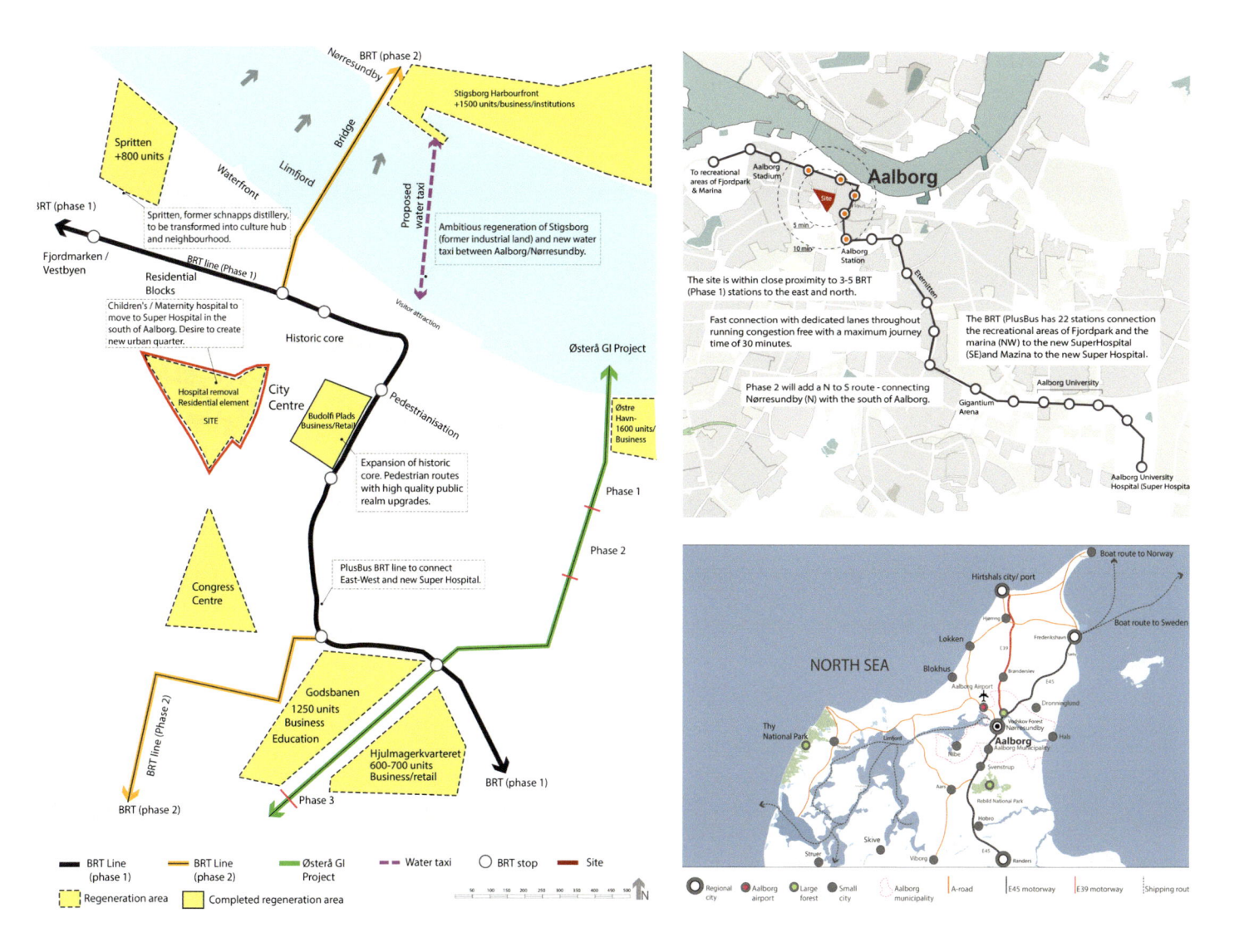

166

The **Strategic Profile** for Aalborg shown on this spread brings together analysis from the city and the sub-regional scale to help set out the key takeaways for the context of the site at this scale. The Profile is dominated by the **Strategic Appraisal Diagram** - which brings together the conclusions and findings of several separate variables. Collectively the Profile presents two important conclusions. Firstly, that this site is exceptionally well connected by a variety of modes. This is not only because of the proximity to the city centre - siting just on the outskirts of the civic and commercial core - but also its wider connections, through proximity to the railway station and bus rapid transit (BRT) which runs past the site. Secondly, it illustrates how the redevelopment of this site is part of the wider planning and regeneration aspirations for the city of Aalborg forming a key cornerstone of the city's growth strategy. Understanding and confirming these two key strategic conclusions is a fundamental part of this site's wider urban design narrative.

167　　　　　　　　　　　　　　　　　　　　APPLIED URBAN DESIGN

Approx. 10min Walking Distance

Sand Hill

Forthcoming tram stop

Green Quarter

Railway

Urban void

Low density housing

Manchester Arena

Railway

Victoria Station

Angel Meadow

Rochdale RD

Site

Oldham RD

Canal Tow-path

Rochdale Canal Corridor

Ancoats

Ring Road

Rochdale Canal

Canal Tow-path

Northern Quarter

New Islington Park

Canal Tow-path

RETAIL CORE

Piccadilly Gardens

Piccadilly Station

City Centre Edge

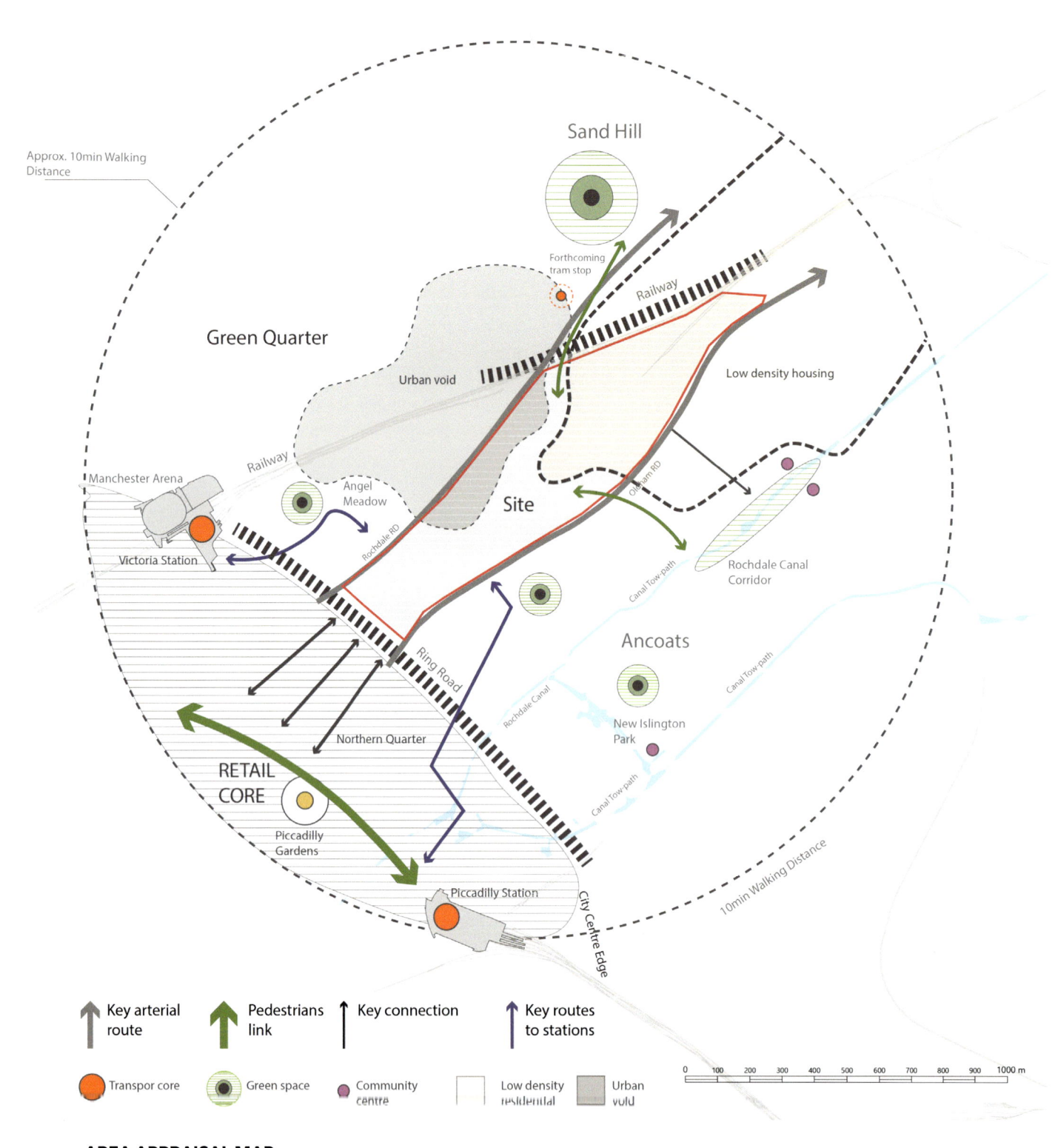

10min Walking Distance

| ↑ Key arterial route | ↑ Pedestrians link | ↑ Key connection | ↑ Key routes to stations |

● Transpor core　　● Green space　　● Community centre　　☐ Low density residential　　▨ Urban void

0　100　200　300　400　500　600　700　800　900　1000 m

AREA APPRAISAL MAP

CHAPTER 6: LOCAL ANALYSIS

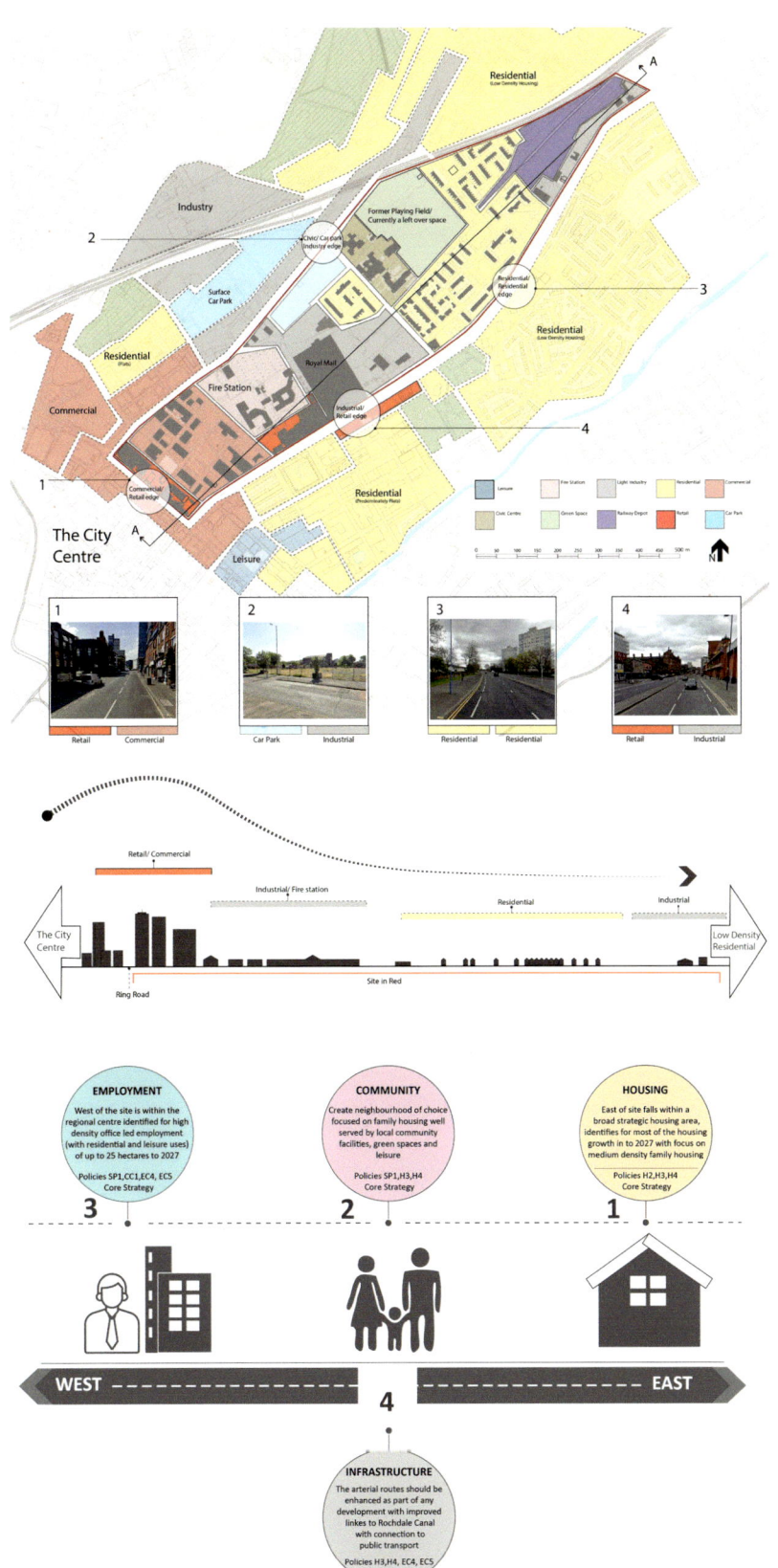

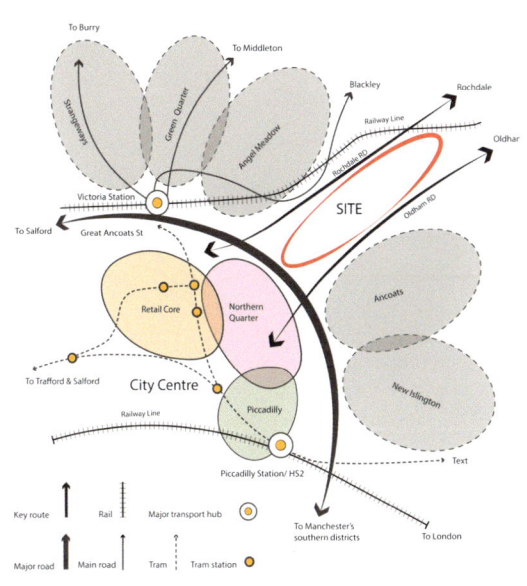

168

The **Area Profile** that is shown across this spread, is an amalgamation of the most important conclusions or takeaways from analysis at the area scale. As with all Area Profiles it is anchored by the **Area Appraisal Diagram** - but is supported by the reuse of some of the key analysis graphics to make specific points – in this case, a detailed policy assessment, long cross-section, and land use. These are all designed to reinforce the key conclusions about this site and its relationships with the city centre – the key routes, the provision of local services - and the change in land use, scale, and character the closer the site is to the city centre. It also includes a sketch diagram showing how this site could form part of the range of neighbourhoods that radiate out from the city centre – especially given the policy objective of creating a range of different neighbourhoods in the heart of the city. In this example, the Area Profile is vital in stressing the narrative regarding the connections and relationship to surrounding neighbourhoods and the city centre. For another site, the area scale may have different narrative threads and therefore will require a different suite of supporting graphics.

MANCHESTER
Area Profile

APPLIED URBAN DESIGN

Key view to Manchester's retail core

Collyhurst South

Newcross

Rochdale Road

Church

Tower blocks

Oldham Road

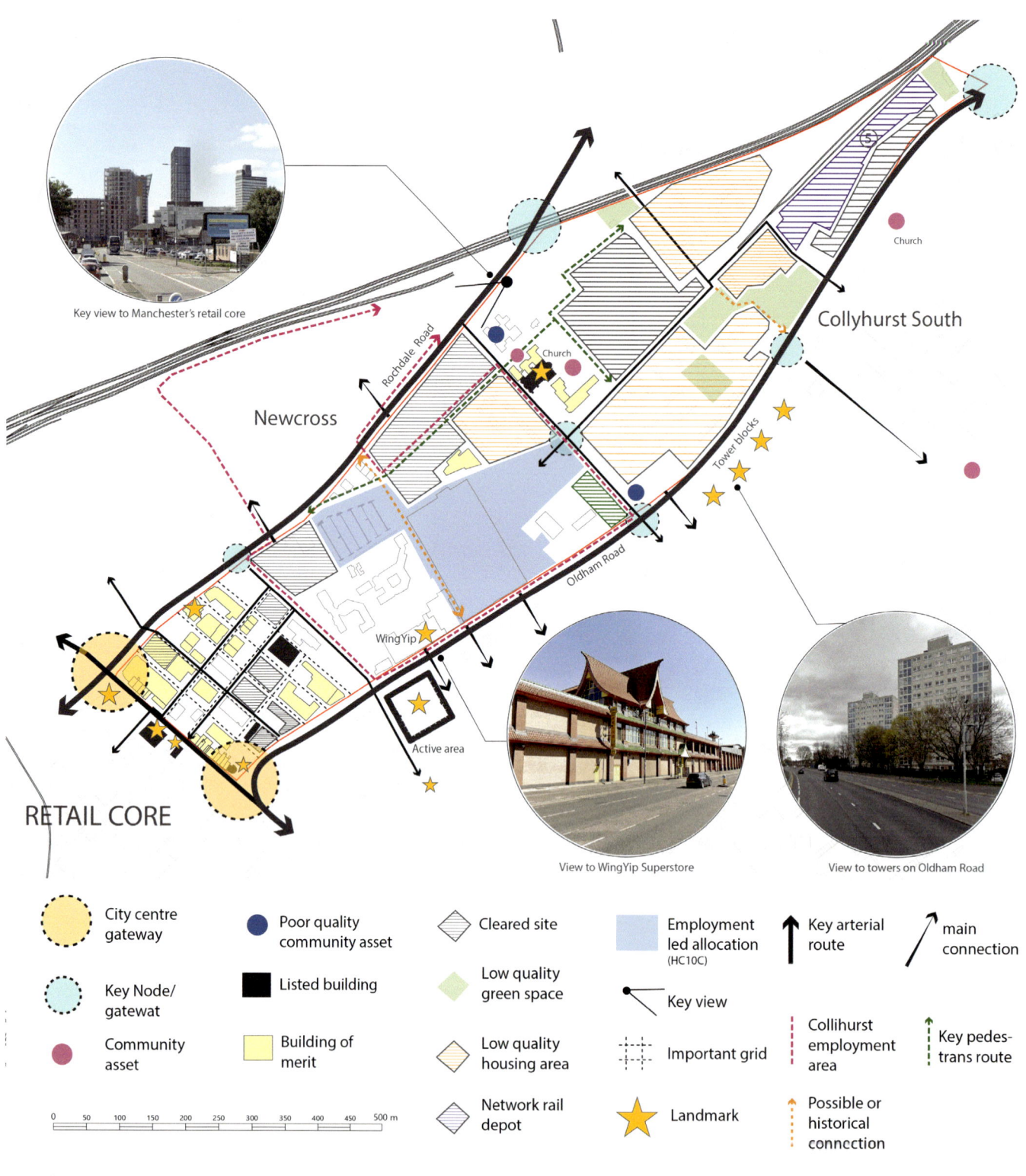

WingYip

Active area

RETAIL CORE

View to WingYip Superstore

View to towers on Oldham Road

Symbol	Meaning	Symbol	Meaning
City centre gateway		Poor quality community asset	
Key Node/ gatewat		Listed building	
Community asset		Building of merit	

- Cleared site
- Low quality green space
- Low quality housing area
- Network rail depot
- Employment led allocation (HC10C)
- Key view
- Important grid
- Landmark
- Key arterial route
- Collihurst employment area
- Possible or historical connection
- main connection
- Key pedestrans route

0 50 100 150 200 250 300 350 400 450 500 m

SITE APPRAISAL MAP

CHAPTER 6: LOCAL ANALYSIS

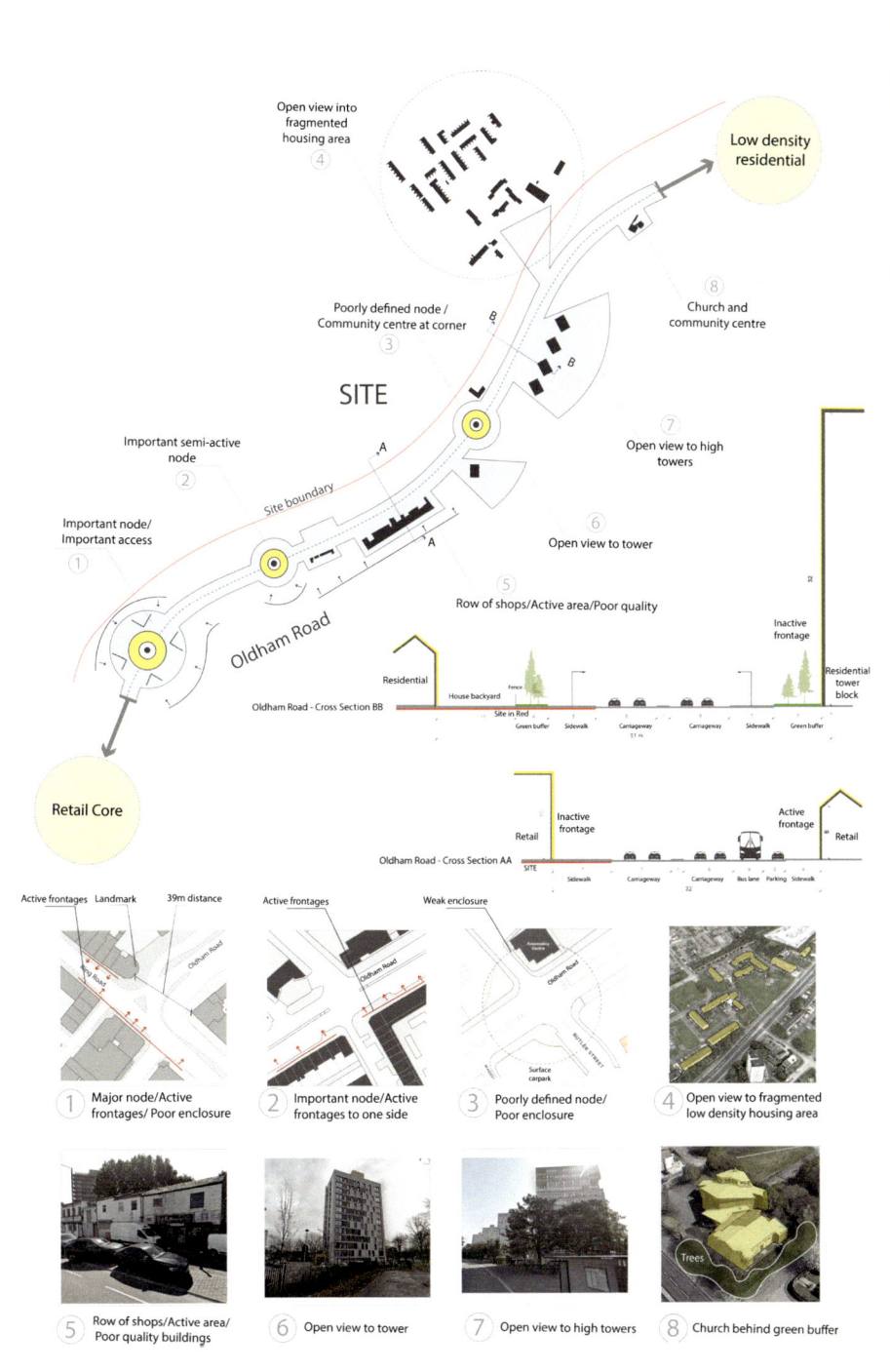

The **Site Profile** that is showcased on these pages is for the Manchester site. It is important to note that given the scale of this site, the *Site Appraisal Diagram* is at a larger scale – perhaps similar to the scale utilised for the *Area Appraisal Diagram* on a smaller site. However, at the site scale, the focus should be on providing a finer granularity of information than at area scale. In that respect the appraisal diagram is not interested in the 'area' variables of character or connection, but much more about details - such as the quality of buildings and individual land parcels. Much of this is setting up the future design process for determining what might be retained and what might change. The appraisal diagram is supported by a range of different graphics that are all presented on a much smaller mapping scale with a strong focus on Oldham Road since it has repeatedly been identified through the local analysis stage as being an important 'high street' that serves the wider community. Understanding edge conditions (like Oldham Road) is an important function of the Site Profile and will be an important part of most projects.

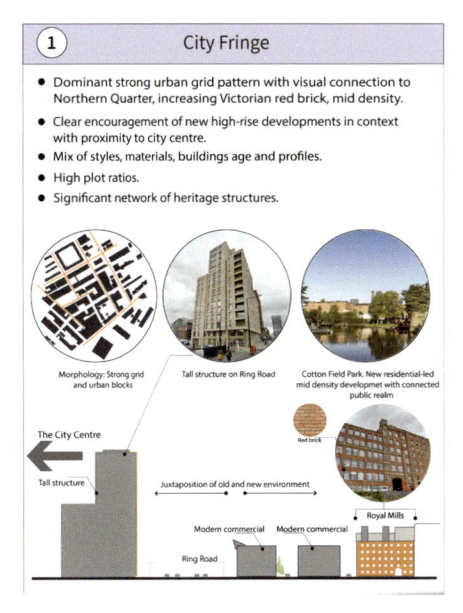

MANCHESTER
Site Profile

APPLIED URBAN DESIGN

CHAPTER 6: LOCAL ANALYSIS

CONCLUSION

Conducting analysis is a complex and time-consuming process that requires committed and knowledgeable analysts and designers who appreciate the importance of undertaking such an exercise carefully and diligently interpreting the critical nature of the findings that are forthcoming from it. This chapter, as well as Chapter 5 (Strategic Analysis), make up the foundation stage of the **Applied Urban Design Framework** – all subsequent steps in the framework will build on the quality of work delivered in Step 1. Whilst the analysis process presented is overarching in nature – it has also been demonstrated to have a clear logic and purpose – to craft/curate a narrative for the site being developed in regards its unique context across multiple scales. The conclusion to Step 1 is a series of focused outputs (*Strategic Profile; Area Profile; Site Profile* – each supported by the wider thematic group analysis) that will communicate the salient findings – these outputs will demonstrate the depth and quality of analysis conducted – and they will be taken forward in step 2 to inform The **Urban Design Program** (Chapter 7).

The AUD Framework now moves beyond the analysis stage into the *Pivot* – the link between analysis and design. It is this Pivot that allows the urban designer to translate and interpret the contextual findings into a *Program* for design delivery – key to the contextually responsive approach.

LEFT: To effectively understand the complexities and dynamics within any given place across a range of scales requires a robust and multi-faceted methodology - which the AUD Framework provides. It also requires committed and skilled urban designers who recognise the importance of conducting such detailed and multi-scalar analysis. It is only in doing so that designers can arm themselves with the necessary information to produce contextually responsive proposals and solutions.

View from Millennium Park to Downtown - Chicago, USA.

PROCESS **OUTCOMES**

SITE & CLIENT

CONTEXT

1. Analysis
   Strategic
   +
   Local

   → Strategic Profile
   → Area Profile
   　 Site Profile

PIVOT

2. Urban Design Program

   → **A:** Design Considerations
   　 B: Design Brief

DESIGN

3. Design Development

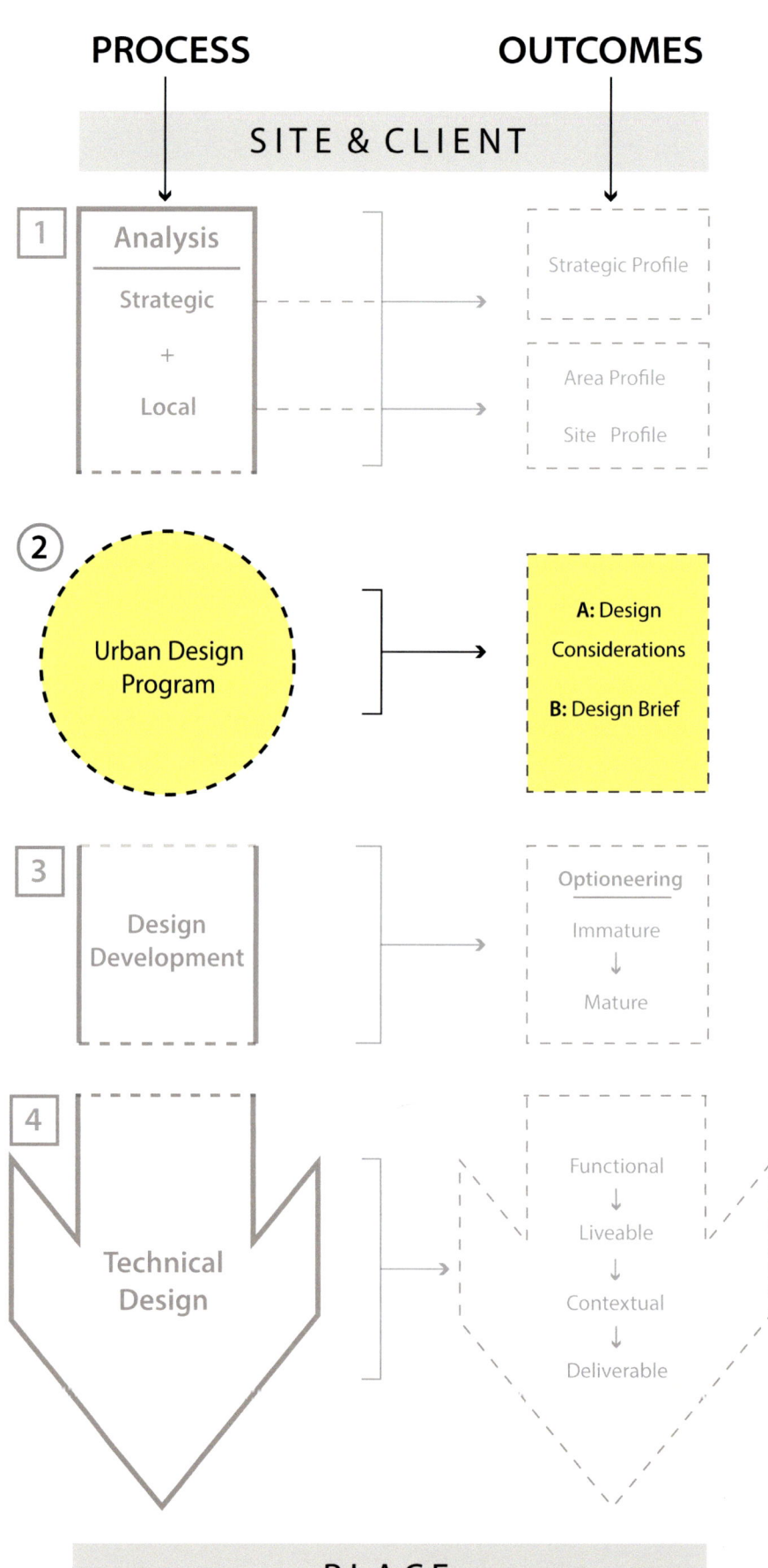

   → Optioneering
   　 Immature
   　 ↓
   　 Mature

4. Technical Design

   → Functional
   　 ↓
   　 Liveable
   　 ↓
   　 Contextual
   　 ↓
   　 Deliverable

PLACE

CHAPTER 7
The Urban Design Program

THE PIVOT IN THE PROCESS

The *'Urban Design Program'* is step two of the Applied Urban Design Framework. At this stage of the AUD Process the urban designer will have undertaken a wide-ranging analysis at each of the three scales (Strategic, Area, and Site) – what we call context building - and developed three *'Profiles'* at each level respectively (*see* Step 1). The Profiles bring together the salient findings and form a comprehensive context-led review of the site and its wider context. The purpose of the Program stage is focused on transforming this analytical detail into a series of design instructions, which are specific to each site or study area. In this way, the Program has a signposting role, translating the analysis into a manual that will guide the later design and development of a site (irrespective of scale) undertaken in Steps 3 and 4 of the Framework.

The Program acts as a pivot between the analysis and the design development, providing an evidential link between these two parts. Notwithstanding its critical role, it is likely to form the shortest section of your design process, both in terms of content and the amount of time that it will take the urban designer to complete. Nonetheless, without it the process cannot arrive at contextually responsive design. The Program has an important real-world application as there are a myriad of cases where the urban designer would conclude their work on a project at this Program stage; using the Program and the analysis undertaken to inform strategies or policies about a site or neighbourhood. It would then be for other design and built environment professionals to take forward the design process working from the instructions provided by the Program.

Prioritising the Issues

In developing the Program clear outputs will materialise – **A: Design Considerations** (opportunities and constraints) and **B: a Design Brief** (made up of project objectives; design actions; and a spatial concept). This should not be viewed as a linear process that can be undertaken to 'spit out' the correct answer. Rather, it is an iterative and cyclical process requiring the practitioner to review and revisit their assumptions and ideas, incrementally developing a Program that offers a balanced response to the context. The context building undertaken in Step 1 must form the basis for this endeavour but it will also be prioritised based on external factors– i.e., the client's wishes, cost and (financial) markets, strategic policy, as well as regeneration drivers. In this way the practitioner is required to arrive at priorities and opportunities presented by the analysis and build a case for why those

OPPOSITE PAGE: Step 2 of the AUD Framework takes us into the 'Pivot' phase - the link between analysis and design.

BELOW: Breakdown of the Urban Design Program components.

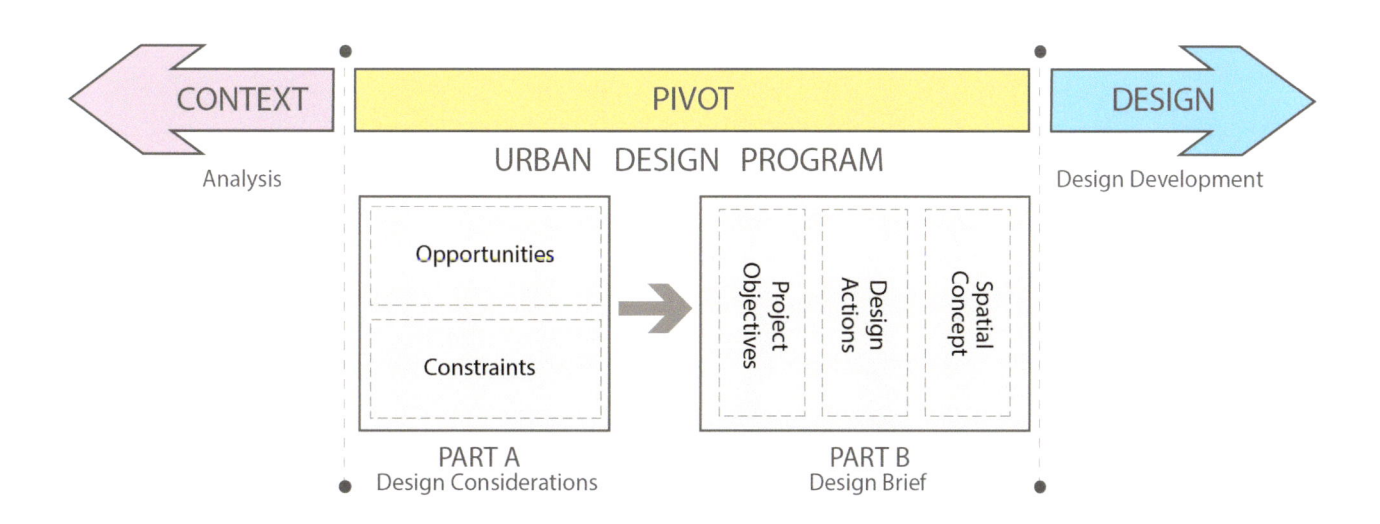

particular matters should be focused on for external entities. In almost every case the urban designer will also be faced with having to arrive at a Program that works with existing features, buildings, and spaces - as demonstrated in both of our live case study examples of Aalborg and Manchester. Thus, the Program, far from simply being a prioritised 'to-do' list, is a balancing act between a series of disparate, and often competing external factors and the multi-scalar context building summarised through the three Profiles. In this respect, the Program should be split between two stages, the first stage is focused on ensuring that issues from the analysis are considered and prioritised, allowing the practitioner to focus on the opportunities and constraints that are most important.

IMAGES: Manchester, UK - Brazennose Street development forms a major pedestrian link between the historic City Hall and square (**LEFT -** *view towards City Hall*) and modern commercial district of Spinningfields (**TOP RIGHT -** *view towards Spinningfields*). The analysis conducted by the designers highlighted the transition between two areas of contrasting character - the brief developed subsequently sought to celebrate these characters as you journey between, juxtaposing the old and new (**BOTTOM RIGHT**) as a core strategy. And upgrading the existing Lincoln Square on Brazennose Street (**TOP RIGHT**) to provide a quiet public space between the very public Albert Square and privately managed Hardman Square - linking up the public realm infrastructure more effectively. The design choices made are clearly driven by the analysis conducted, making for a transparent solution that people/users can easily understand and appreciate.

7.1 THE PURPOSE OF THE PROGRAM

LINKING ANALYSIS AND DESIGN
The Program is a critical element of the Applied Urban Design Framework – acting as the pivot between analysis and design. In its simplest guise, the Program gathers and prioritises the context building delivered to date (step 1) and sets out the instructions for the design development process (step 3). However, it also offers a wider role enabling third parties such as the client, key stakeholders and policy and planning professionals to effectively engage with the design process and contribute to the design outcomes; as it can easily be used to augment and drive planning, regeneration, and policy development. In this way, the Program, enables the Applied Urban Design process to be broken into more manageable and implementable parts, but also can be used in a variety of roles beyond design development – such as the formulation of design codes or site-specific policy.

Another critical role of the Program is to incorporate wider practical issues such as finance, client aspirations and policy and regeneration agendas. As previous chapters have alluded to, these matters are often introduced too early in the design process, meaning they will shape and influence the understanding of any project introducing bias that can impact all stages of the process. By introducing these factors too early the designer may automatically be programmed to find correlations with these practical components, rather than look at the opportunities that are inherent in any site. The Program facilitates the introduction of these practical aspects into the design process so as to not inadvertently drive the analysis process and ensures the assessment of opportunities and constraints in the physical environment are not overlooked as a result.

EVIDENCE-LED URBAN DESIGN
Many commentators and practitioners have highlighted the importance of evidence-led design, or the use of analysis to underpin urban design interventions. What the Program achieves are a prioritised set of instructions for the design which promote robust connections between the outcomes of the analysis and forthcoming design proposal. While the three Profiles (Strategic, Area, and Site) that summarise the analysis conducted gather all the salient data together, there is no prioritisation and no consideration about how the opportunities and constraints for a site should be addressed or built upon. It allows important practical matters of costs, clients aspirations, and even planning policy to be considered alongside the Profiles. This enables practical matters to be integrated into the design process based on a robust body of design knowledge.

There are two broad outputs that are fulfilled by the Program, which will be covered in greater detail across this chapter. The first output - the **Design Considerations** diagram, illustrates the opportunities and constraints of a site as identified in the contextual analysis. The second is the **Design Brief**. This is made up of three distinct elements - the first is a series of *'project objectives'* which communicate the urban designer's vision for the site and its surroundings; these objectives should be clear and easily discernible by all stakeholders. The second, specific urban *'design actions'* (a series of tasks or design elements that should be explored through the development of any design proposals for the site). Actions are specific to the project site and the spatial characteristics of the site, and are not, as is often the case with design projects ethereal ideas or ideals that should be sought. The final element is a *'spatial concept'*, which shows how the actions can be arranged spatially on the site. All outputs should be clearly communicated to ensure the Urban Design Program is easy to use for other urban designers, design professionals, and built environment practitioners undertaking the design over the life course of the project.

MULTIPLE FUNCTIONS OF THE PROGRAM
The Program can fulfil a myriad of functions beyond providing guidance for further designers. We set out some examples of the different functions that the Program could be used for in the wider planning and development process including:

An Engagement Tool
The Program stage is used to help clients, decision makers, politicians, and the community to arrive at a shared design brief for the site. The client and the designer can work together to develop a shared Program for the design project, building on the independent analysis that has been undertaken. The Program, as a tangible design development output, can be used to speak to key stakeholders and the community in a more effective and

transparent way – arming communities with an understanding of the forthcoming design. The Program includes a number of elements that are highly suitable for engagement with a wide range of audiences as they are not technical in nature and are clearly related to the site as opposed to ethereal policy or economic factors.

A Policy Tool
For some urban design projects, the Program would be the main deliverable, with the **Design Brief** (objectives, actions, and concept) being used to develop policy interventions or subsequent design briefs for others to take forward. The Program can be written into policies and strategies for an area as a whole or in designated areas or parts. In cases where government agencies are seeking to allocate specific sites for development, the Program is useful to set out guidance for how that site should come forward. The rigorous way in which the analysis underpins the Program and the robust evidence base required means that it is capable of scrutiny - as part of any examination or review required by a local authority.

A Regeneration Tool
Too often urban designers are tasked with trying to solve all the ills of a particular location – crime, antisocial behaviour, poor educational attainment, or health. While these are all important matters for regeneration, good design cannot independently solve these aspects in and of itself; rather other actors, agencies, and mechanisms working collaboratively as part of a comprehensive regeneration strategy are required. The urban design process therefore becomes an integral part of this strategy bringing together the physical components in a reasoned, justified, and collaborative manner. It is important that as designers we recognise the limitations of the design process, it is an opportunity to effect physical change on a street, site, or neighbourhood and not a 'magic bullet' for addressing wider systemic issues.

A Review Tool
As the Program can be used to develop a shared vision for the site, and develop policies, it can also be used as an effective design review tool to ensure that development when proposed is contextually responsive. Decision makers, communities and clients can use the Program to ensure that the design team is delivering the design requirements (which of course are targeted and justified), without the risk of slipping into individual choice or opinion (a common pitfall of design review - see Black, 2019b) – the Program offers actors an agreed upon and defined framework within which to target their responses.

UNDERSTANDING THE FUNCTIONAL BLUEPRINTS
Developing a Program requires that the urban designer apply and understand the 12 functional blueprints (see 4.3) explored in Chapter 4 - in particular the way that we design streets, spaces, and urban blocks to create successful contextually responsive places – and possess knowledge of design metrics. Whilst at this stage no design is being formally undertaken, awareness of the practicalities and feasibility of delivering quality design is critical. For our project objectives and design actions to be robust we must ensure that they are deliverable. To take an extreme example, delivering a park including several different playing pitches, a children's playground, a café and outdoor seating area might be what is missing from the wider neighbourhood, but there is no realistic possibility of delivering this on a site that is only half a hectare in size. Knowledge of the metrics and scale of certain design elements, such as urban blocks or typologies of streets and spaces, is vital even at this stage.

A seasoned urban designer will go beyond basic urban design metrics, working with standards to ensure a more integrated approach understanding the relationships between the networks, the arrangements, and the features of a townscape and how they might create character, diversity, and delight in the urban realm. There are two ways that this can be achieved. First, referring to the site or neighbourhood context, look carefully at how the successful elements of the local built form, vernacular and urban grain could be interpreted on this site. In this regard the urban designer is looking at vernacular elements and features that they will have identified. This is a sensible approach when looking at areas of cultural and historical significance. Second, where a site has a less distinctive local character or vernacular, or when the wider drivers permit, the urban designer might wish to draw upon best practice from elsewhere, and as such a use wider knowledge of different approaches and forms to achieve positive design responses.

CHAPTER 7: THE URBAN DESIGN PROGRAM

7.2 PART A: DESIGN CONSIDERATIONS

There are two core elements to producing an effective design considerations diagram:

- Creating a list of priorities (*opportunities* and *constraints*).

- Presenting these spatially.

The sole output of this stage will be the design considerations diagram (*see Aalborg Design Considerations Diagram on pages 181-182*). Typically, in urban design methodologies, this can be defined as an *opportunities and constraints* diagram (which concludes the analysis of a site), however, the AUD Framework sets opportunities and constraints apart from the analysis (Step 1) for two principal reasons. First, by including opportunities and constraints at this point in the process it forms part of the design pivot and reinforces the link between analysis and design. Second, this assessment is able to act in a signposting role helping to summarise the possible project objectives and design actions - allowing the designer to carefully apply value judgements to the information collated.

As a result, much of Part A is undertaken *'behind the scenes'* and never communicated publicly beyond the design team and other related professionals but forms an invaluable step to achieving a contextually responsive design proposal. We have previously considered the need for the practitioner to be able to make value judgements and Part A exists to allow the practitioner to organise their thoughts and make necessary judgements before progressing to the production of the **Design Considerations Diagram**. We strongly caution against moving straight into providing this output without spending time carefully considering what elements should be part of the final visual. Subsequently, we set out some techniques that can assist in helping to prepare design considerations.

PRIORITIES, OPPORTUNITIES, AND CONSTRAINTS

In arriving at your Design Considerations, the first task to undertake is to review the analysis that has been completed. This begins with the preparation of a list of priorities for the development site. Depending on the nature of your site there are two broad approaches you can take:

Option 1 - Create a prioritised list of the salient findings: The easiest way to begin this stage of work is simply to provide a list of key matters or considerations from the analysis / context building. This approach works perfectly well for smaller or less complicated sites. At this stage we are not interested in determining which elements are more or less important, rather the focus is gathering them together and looking for any overlaps and correlation between variables/themes. It is important that the practitioner look for reoccurring conclusions or issues across the analysis as these matters are likely to be more important. The analysis findings (*thematic groups* and in particular the *Profiles*) will be the main source of this information – they already bring together the wide range of variables and data considered. Nonetheless, any of the outcomes from the Step 1 process can be used – some of the multivariable analysis elements such as legibility or character can be very useful.

When providing a 'list' of priorities, the focus should not be to consider the site exclusively, rather, the emphasis is to consider the wider townscape and context across one to two blocks in all directions as well as key links to shops and services (i.e. a key link to a train station). in creating a list of priorities, it is necessary to sort it into two columns – opportunities and constraints. We would suggest that most sites would have between 10-15 items in each list; any less is likely to be insufficiently detailed, and any more would make future stages overwhelming. It is useful, at this stage, to summarise these items with a short sentence or note linking it to the relevant analysis to prioritise a clear evidential connection between Steps 1 and 2.

Option 2 - The use of the SWOT analysis: Some practitioners find that using a SWOT assessment (Strength, Weakness, Opportunities and Threats assessment) presented as a table, or similar planning and management technique, is useful at this stage. The AUD Framework does not rely on

APPLIED URBAN DESIGN

or require a SWOT analysis, but a SWOT's universal understanding can be helpful to prepare a design considerations diagram - especially where the site is larger, or where the project might form part of a more strategic land-use planning or regeneration process. We caution the use of a SWOT alone or as a key output – rather the design considerations diagram should form the core and key output. SWOT analysis can be problematic, traditionally it has encouraged the author and those engaging with it – communities, stakeholders etc. – to focus too heavily on external socio-economic factors, as opposed to the physical attributes of a site that can be changed by urban design. If a SWOT is used, make sure that the links to the analysis are set out clearly.

If a SWOT is to be used, we encourage you to consider the following headings:

- **Strengths** – Site specific attributes, or those directly adjacent to the site, which will have a positive influence on the (re)development of the site or area – such as buildings that could be reused, key access points or a strong active frontage from an immediately adjacent row of local shops.

- **Weaknesses** – Negative attributes, from the site or the immediate adjacent buildings, that may restrict how you could (re)develop the site – this might include topographical changes, areas of flood risk, or noise and visual intrusion from an adjacent service yard for a supermarket.

- **Opportunities** – Focusing on the nearby urban blocks or wider townscape, listing what might positively influence the design solution for the site - such as key views to local landmarks, changes in the character of the area, new developments or proximity to a local park or railway station.

- **Constraints** – Focusing on the nearby urban blocks or wider townscape listing what might constrain or restrict how the site can be design or delivered - this might include nearby users and land use that would impact negatively on amenity such as local industry or busy roads.

An opportunity and a constraint - Whether following the list, or the SWOT, approach there may be items that fall into both categories and thus appear in the maps/plans for separate reasons. This is common

but needs to be fully explained to the reader. For example, elements such as heritage assets where you might argue the need to preserve and retain a building or feature is a constraint, or likewise, the contribution that the building or feature makes to the area's identity and sense of place mean they are potential opportunities. In practice both positions can be justified, it is simply a matter of how they are explained or rationalised.

BELOW: An abandoned heritage building can be a potential constraint to development if protected - but simultaneously an opportunity to revive an asset that represents part of a place's narrative.

Saint-Égrève, France

DESIGN CONSIDERATIONS DIAGRAM
While the previous elements of Part A of the Urban Design Program are focused on ensuring that the practitioner has organised and justified the key priorities for a site (between opportunities and constraints), the design considerations diagram will act as the concluding graphic/plan to showcase these ideas spatially. The intention here is that within one combined (or two related) and considered output(s) any urban design practitioner would be able to understand the key priorities for this site. This forms a critical part of the overall 'story' and design narrative for a site, clearly showcasing the 'pivot' between analysis and design. The design considerations diagram will feature three broad components – the spatial plan, the expanded legend, and additional annotated notes.

Opportunities and Constraints
The basis for this diagram is a 2D map in which the *opportunities* and *constraints* (the design considerations) are marked up and identified. It will be impossible to showcase all the matters that have been included in the priority lists or the SWOT, but as far as practical the diagram should include those which could be defined as being key salient priorities. When adding the design considerations to the plan, care and attention should be paid to ensure that the priorities are presented in an iterative fashion but that they are also site-specific and physical in nature. The following advice can assist with achieving this in practice:

• Colour code your design considerations, with opportunities being shown in a positive green colour and constraints, in a more negative grey or red. This simple colour coding helps the reader to immediately identify the practitioners' value judgements.

• Identify specific physical elements on the plan as opposed to simply shading broader areas. The identification of specific buildings, parks, or streets leaves less room for misinterpretation or misunderstanding.

• In most cases you should aim to present these on a single graphic so that the interrelationship between the design considerations can be spatially understood, however, if this is not possible, two plans presented side by side can also work effectively. (*See* our Aalborg example on page 181).

Expanded Legend
It goes without saying that every plan should include a key or legend, but the design considerations key allows the urban designer to add additional information and interpretation to aid the reader. The expanded legend is part of the justification for including an item on the design considerations diagram, but also should help the reader to understand what is important about each feature and what implications this might have for future development of design solutions. For example:

• Key buildings might be identified, here the expanded key could explain that these are key heritage assets to be retained, and potentially list each structure or describe their features/materiality.

• An area of flood risk might be identified on a plan, but the legend should cite the risk level, source of this information, and explain the restrictions on uses within this area as a consequence.

• The plan could identify a main road that runs adjacent to the site, but the key would explain that through this is a key connection, it is also a barrier to movement and contributes to noise/air pollution.

Additional Annotations
There will occasionally be items or opportunities that you consider are relevant to the future design development but these are not able to be mapped specifically. These include changes in socio-economic profile, policy drivers, or changing trends in the type and nature of recent neighbouring developments. Where possible these could be identified on the design considerations plan through target notes or labels, as a series of bullet points, or a small infographic underneath the plan.

| 81   APPLIED URBAN DESIGN

These pages showcase the **Design Considerations** diagram(s) that have been developed for the Aalborg project site. In this instance, the level of detail required this information to be split across two diagrams, with the opportunities and constraints presented separately. The scale of both plans is directly comparable to enable the reader to draw comparisons between them. As is shown here, the design considerations are not just focusing on matters within the site's red line boundary, but have also included some of the external contextual factors, such as the connection and proximity to the city centre (opportunities) and the role and purpose of the three competing land uses (constraints).

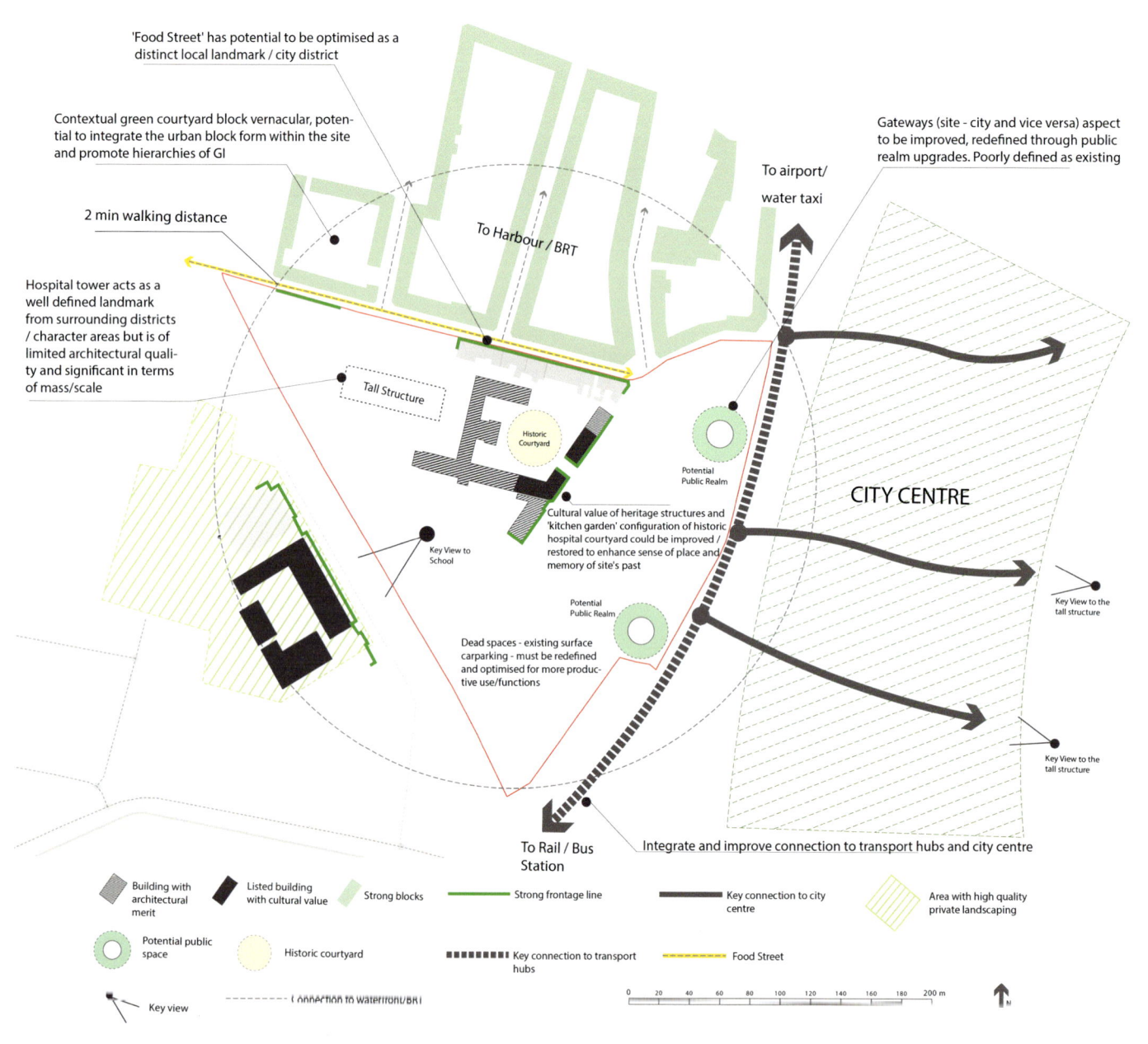

'Food Street' has potential to be optimised as a distinct local landmark / city district

Contextual green courtyard block vernacular, potential to integrate the urban block form within the site and promote hierarchies of GI

2 min walking distance

Hospital tower acts as a well defined landmark from surrounding districts / character areas but is of limited architectural quality and significant in terms of mass/scale

To Harbour / BRT

Gateways (site - city and vice versa) aspect to be improved, redefined through public realm upgrades. Poorly defined as existing

To airport/ water taxi

Tall Structure

Historic Courtyard

Potential Public Realm

CITY CENTRE

Key View to School

Cultural value of heritage structures and 'kitchen garden' configuration of historic hospital courtyard could be improved / restored to enhance sense of place and memory of site's past

Potential Public Realm

Key View to the tall structure

Dead spaces - existing surface carparking - must be redefined and optimised for more productive use/functions

Key View to the tall structure

To Rail / Bus Station

Integrate and improve connection to transport hubs and city centre

- Building with architectural merit
- Listed building with cultural value
- Strong blocks
- Strong frontage line
- Key connection to city centre
- Area with high quality private landscaping
- Potential public space
- Historic courtyard
- Key connection to transport hubs
- Food Street
- Key view
- Connection to waterfront/BRT

0 20 40 60 80 100 120 140 160 180 200 m

SITE OPPORTUNITIES MAP

AALBORG
Design Considerations Diagram

CHAPTER 7: THE URBAN DESIGN PROGRAM

It is also interesting to note that there are a several features within the site that are marked as an opportunity and a constraint such as the existing heritage structures on the site or the busy, vibrant, but narrow route that runs across the top of the site (Reberbansgade). This is common with many sites / projects, and it is therefore important to provide detailed annotations (as included in our Aalborg example) within the diagram to identify the rationale behind why each has been included.

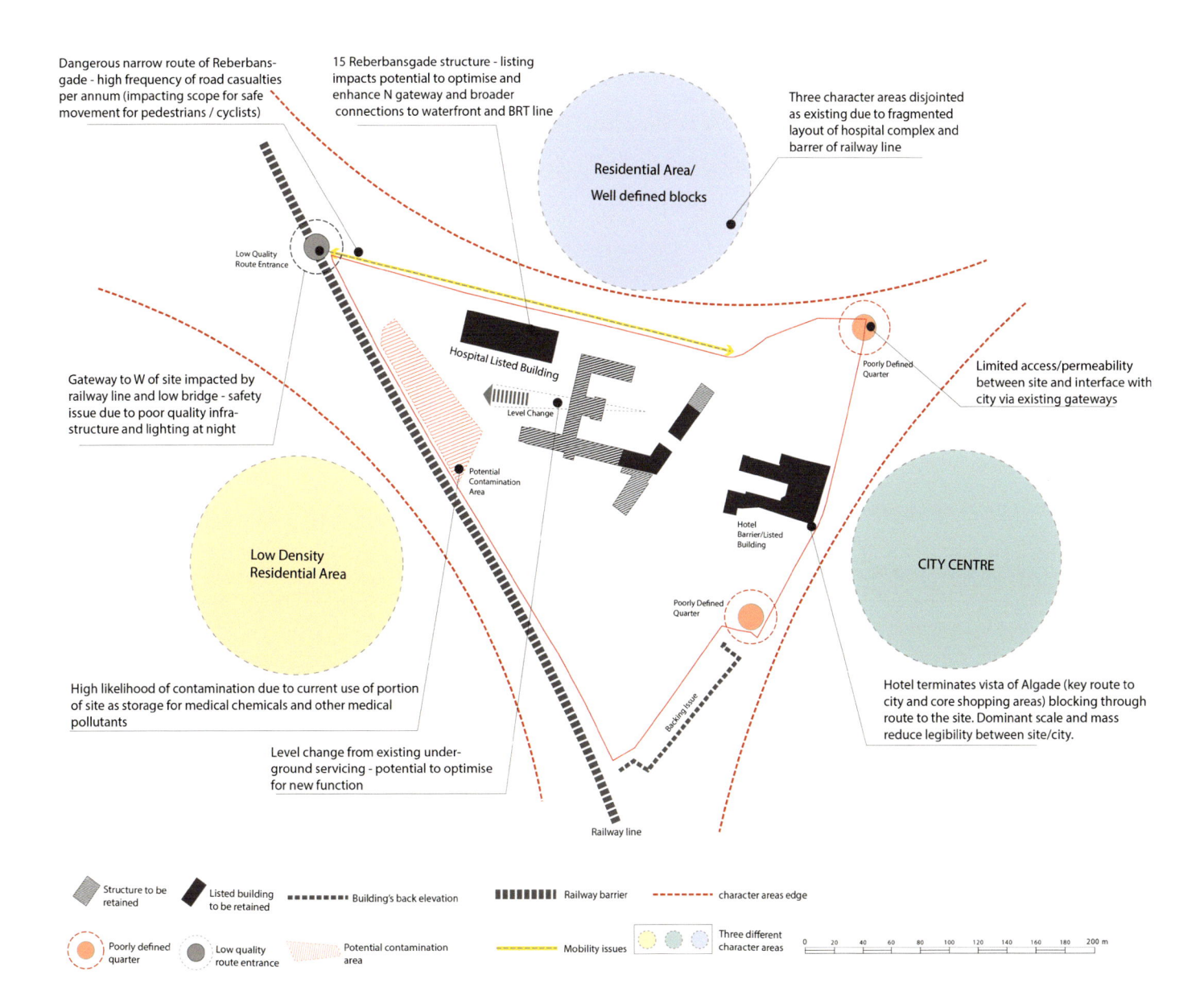

SITE CONSTRAINTS MAP

APPLIED URBAN DESIGN

HARD AND SOFT PLAN

If the size of the site you are working on is at a masterplanning scale, it may be useful to supplement the *design considerations* diagram with a *'hard and soft plan'*. This plan is a representation of what elements of the site will remain fixed (hard), and where you might expect significant changes to occur in the design process (soft).

Hard areas identified will indicate buildings, spaces, or routes of quality – that in some way contribute to the existing townscape or have inherent value. These designated areas are not necessarily fixed in their entirety – they may be flagged for upgrading or repair as part of the wider design development, and they will remain as part of any future scheme in some form however.

The soft designations are parts of the site that have been deemed poor quality – or areas that have potential for significant restructuring or removal to be replaced by more appropriate interventions that will enhance the overall quality of any proposed masterplan. It is possible to deliver a more complex hard and soft analysis – with hierarchies for both *'hard'* and *'soft'*, delving into greater detail in terms of how each building, street, or space is categorised.

The hard and soft plan is particularly helpful on large sites that have a high volume of existing structures and infrastructures – providing a clear and simple set of instructions based on the extensive analysis conducted. Developed in conjunction with the broader design considerations diagram it can provide a robust foundation from which to begin the development of a design brief (Part B of the Urban Design Program).

Our **hard and soft plan** for the Manchester site draws from a range of the analysis conducted in Step 1 of the AUD Framework. This includes the architectural analysis assessment; heritage assets; green infrastructure; urban morphology; legibility; key services and amenity; land use; edge condition appraisal; and the character area study (see Chapter 6 for more details).

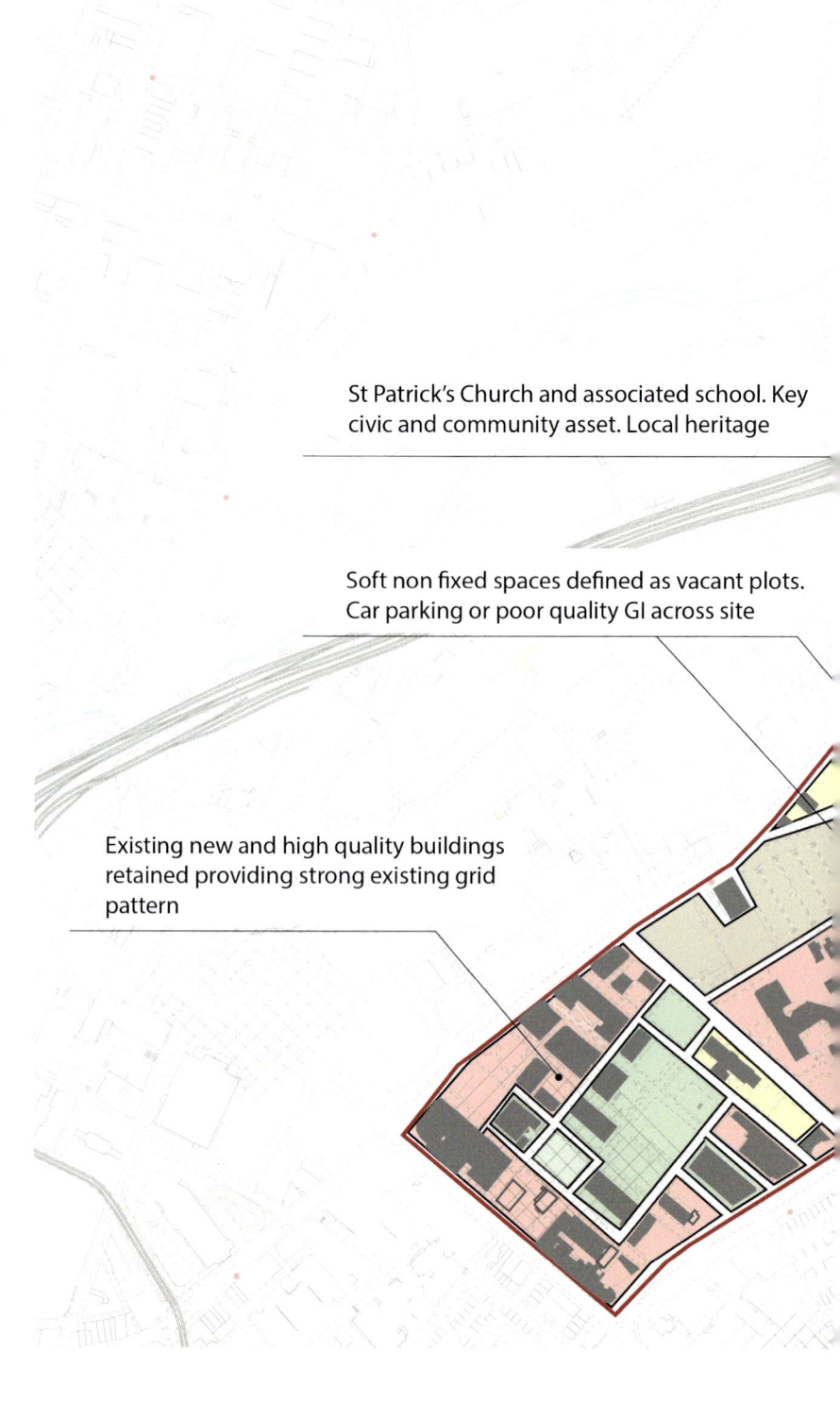

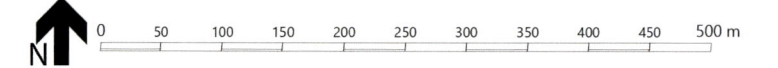

St Patrick's Church and associated school. Key civic and community asset. Local heritage

Soft non fixed spaces defined as vacant plots. Car parking or poor quality GI across site

Existing new and high quality buildings retained providing strong existing grid pattern

N   0   50   100   150   200   250   300   350   400   450   500 m

CHAPTER 7: THE URBAN DESIGN PROGRAM

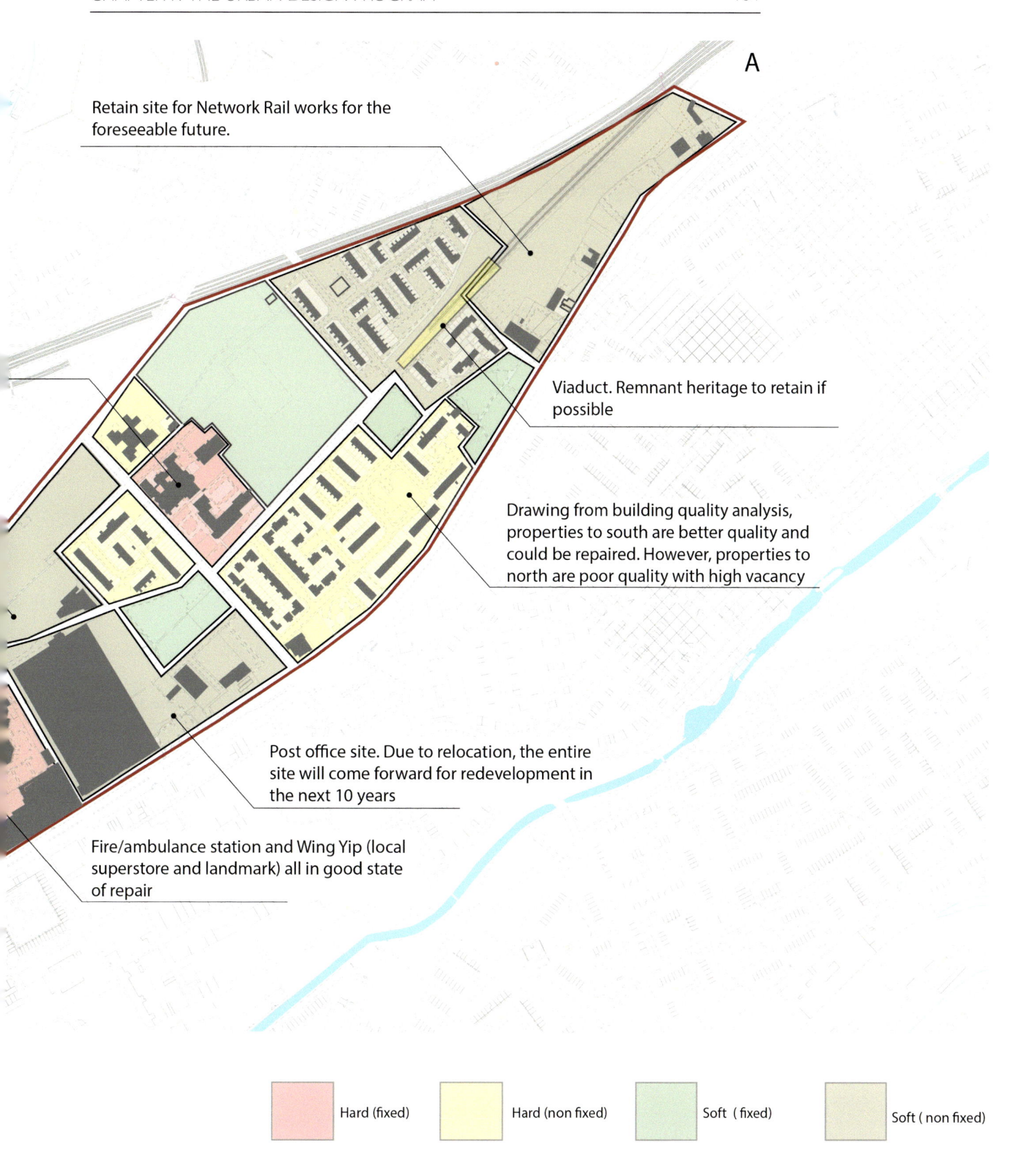

184

A

Retain site for Network Rail works for the foreseeable future.

Viaduct. Remnant heritage to retain if possible

Drawing from building quality analysis, properties to south are better quality and could be repaired. However, properties to north are poor quality with high vacancy

Post office site. Due to relocation, the entire site will come forward for redevelopment in the next 10 years

Fire/ambulance station and Wing Yip (local superstore and landmark) all in good state of repair

- Hard (fixed)
- Hard (non fixed)
- Soft (fixed)
- Soft (non fixed)

MANCHESTER
Hard and Soft Plan

7.3 PART B: DESIGN BRIEF

Following the completion of design considerations, it is necessary to produce a comprehensive '**Design Brief**' – this will be composed of 3 core elements:

- Project Objectives
- Design Actions
- Spatial Concept

Each element above naturally follows the other – with the ***project objectives*** providing the broader ambitions and aims for potential development, the ***design actions*** providing the specific design guidance to deliver on those objectives, and the ***spatial concept*** framing the actions visually on-site in an abstract and flexible manner.

It is here that we need to revisit Chapter 4 (Making Sense of Design) – and the 3 key considerations required for delivering quality contextually responsive solutions – applying the AUD Framework – *Contextual Dynamics; Liveable Qualities;* and *Functional Blueprints.* Each element of the design brief requires a working knowledge of these components.

All elements require the contextual dynamics that will be unpacked across the application of Step 1 of the Framework – the project objectives demand awareness of liveable qualities to ensure they promote quality placemaking principles at their core; whilst the design actions and spatial concept necessitate knowledge of the functional blueprints to communicate design specific guidance effectively.

PROJECT OBJECTIVES

The project objectives are a set of general flexible statements that begin to break down a vision into manageable elements, or that simply aim to provide audiences with a clear understanding of the goals for maximising the potential of future development on the site in question. These objectives should be achievable and related clearly to the contextual analysis conducted in Step 1 of the AUD Framework – this ensures they promote a contextually responsive design intervention. It is critical that the project objectives utilised recognise urban design terminology and promote the principles of design quality alongside the contextual response – Chapter 4 provides a detailed break-down of the **10 Liveable Qualities** (*see* 4.2) related to the delivery of quality place-making. Formulating the objectives in this manner allows for the urban designer to re-imagine these key liveable aspects of quality design from a contextual perspective – it will also ensure that the language used is universal to the field and easily understood and interpreted. It is important when finalising objectives that you test for coverage across your contextual analysis (Step 1) and liveable qualities/ principles to provide maximum coverage. Objectives are normally text based – and will cover a range of possible issues and aspirations across all scales, not only the site.

The project objectives are useful to a broad range of audiences – their more general nature and aspirational tone make them accessible to lay-viewers such as local communities, businesses, and investors. They allow interested parties to view more broken-down goals and ambitions for forthcoming development than a vision statement alone provides. They also provide such audiences with a basis to hold designers and developers to account – demanding they follow through with these objectives across all aspects of any proposed scheme.

Similarly, the objectives provide designers with a useful structure to drive design and initiate the testing and evaluation of design concepts and options. All design solutions should be evaluated against these objectives to stimulate the most appropriate contextual and quality interventions. Post-construction evaluations can also take place framed around these project objectives, ascertaining the success of any given scheme and how it may be improved upon or how future developments may learn from the process.

DESIGN ACTIONS

Design actions are directly related to the project objectives but begin to provide more site-specific instructions and guidance. They are not themselves design, but rather they consider the objectives in terms of real-world physical elements associated with the site and context – they therefore 'inform' design. They provide the urban designer with a series of 'tasks' that all concepts and options should consider and respond to – how the 'task' is designed is left undecided and is the responsibility of the designer(s).

The design actions will naturally be more geographical – naming specific streets, spaces, buildings, and physical features – as such they will utilise the design considerations map discussed earlier. They will also be more technical in regard to terminology and language, given they are focusing specifically on the delivery of design. It is here that the urban designer must begin to consider and integrate the **Functional Blueprints** (*see* 4.3) discussed in Chapter 4 – those design layers that underpin how successful any design will function in the real world.

The best strategies are visual and easy to understand, providing clear signposting towards a type of development and design that will be of high quality and contextually responsive. The primary audience for design actions are urban designers – however they can be useful to a wider range of stakeholders and local communities given they offer a more localised picture, are less vague than the objectives and thus can be used as a more bespoke evaluation tool for design proposals.

A SPATIAL CONCEPT
The spatial concept returns to the site itself and aims to illustrate ideas, in a flexible manner, building off the design considerations diagram, project objectives, and design actions visually in a single graphic. It is important to note at this stage that the spatial concept is NOT design, nor is it a design option (*the design optioneering process forms part of Step 3 in the AUD Framework and is discussed in Chapter 8*). Understanding the difference between a spatial concept and a design option is traditionally difficult for non-designers. Broadly speaking, the spatial concept is a range of ideas that form the backbone and foundations of a design project. It will be made up of *'blobs and arrows'*, in other words it will be graphically flexible and think more generally about the type of development, connections, potential movement, land use, and loosely about how any proposed design intervention will be laid out to ensure co-existence with the surroundings and contextual response. To produce a spatial concept, it is useful to begin with the developed design actions and relate them directly back to the design considerations conducted – and how these might be represented effectively by overlaying the proposals on the site and immediate surroundings.

Spatial concepts should have a clarity of vision – the best concepts have an identifiable hierarchy of design intervention 'goals' that can usefully form the basis of future design proposals – ensuring that all possible design options adhere to key guidance based on the wider design brief. The challenge is to avoid an over prescriptive approach, to ensure that urban designers have the flexibility to interpret the overarching project objectives and design actions in dynamic ways, maintaining the ability to think and act creatively to find different solutions. The final presentation visual must therefore find the balance between being predominately abstract in format and delivery, but having clear design priorities related to the brief that can shape the forthcoming design stage of the Framework (Steps 3 and 4).

Whilst the project objectives and design actions for a site should be agreed and fixed prior to designing and should be the basis for all future design proposals related to the site in question – the production of the spatial concept can be more fluid. It can be produced as part of the fuller design brief by the same team/individual who deliver the objectives and actions – yet it can also be reproduced by any potential design team/practice utilising **The Urban Design Program** as part of their design development. As an example, should multiple design practices be tendering for a project and each is employing the same design brief produced by a local authority, client, or contracted urban designer, then the production of a unique spatial concept is their opportunity to provide a visual representation of their understanding and interpretation of the agreed project objectives and design actions. Under such circumstances multiple design practices may develop quite different spatial concepts – which will go on to form the foundation of the distinct design proposal they develop.

We have produced complete **Design Briefs** for both Aalborg (pages 187-8) and Manchester (pages 189-90) to illustrate this pivotal stage of the Urban Design Program. This also showcases how the design brief will differ dependent on site and context - and how it is driven by the depth and quality of the analysis conducted by the urban designer in the critical context building stage (Step 1).

Aalborg Case Study Design Objectives

No.	Objective
1	Deliver dynamic mixed use new neighbourhood for Aalborg with local employment hub
2	Reconnect to the historic urban core and the wider city region
3	Re-establish local heritage/character through existing blocks plus conservation assets
4	Create multi-modal connectivity prioritising sustainable soft mobility
5	Develop a network of visible interconnected public realm and water sensitive green infrastructure

DESIGN ACTIONS

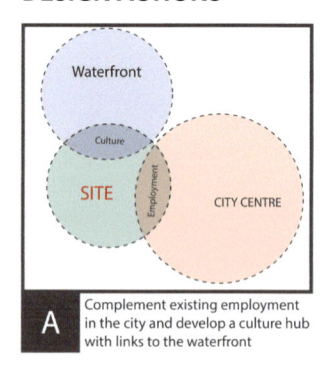

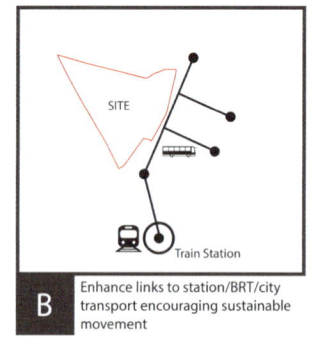

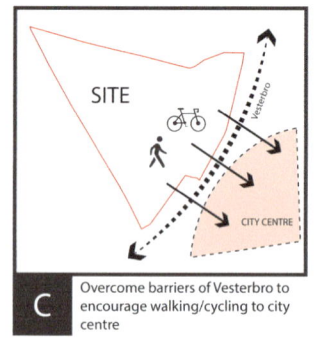

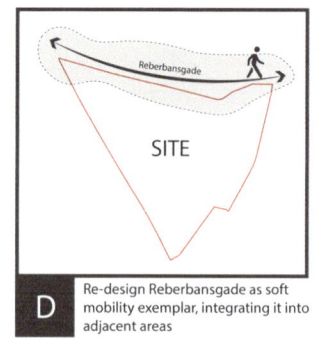

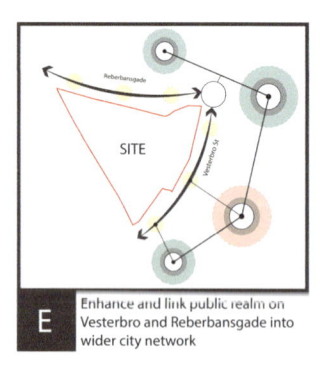

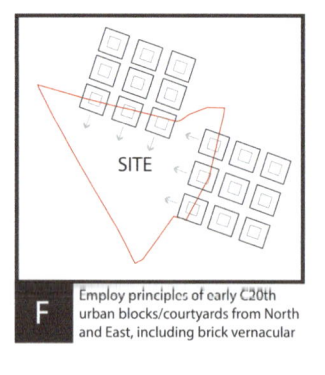

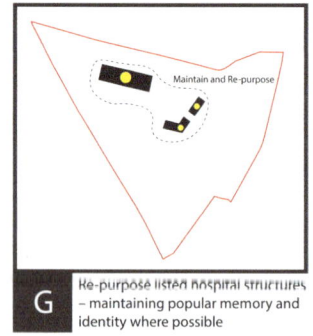

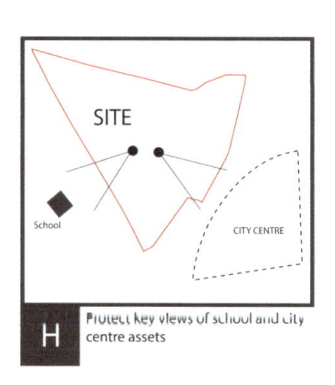

A — Complement existing employment in the city and develop a culture hub with links to the waterfront

B — Enhance links to station/BRT/city transport encouraging sustainable movement

C — Overcome barriers of Vesterbro to encourage walking/cycling to city centre

D — Re-design Reberbansgade as soft mobility exemplar, integrating it into adjacent areas

E — Enhance and link public realm on Vesterbro and Reberbansgade into wider city network

F — Employ principles of early C20th urban blocks/courtyards from North and East, including brick vernacular

G — Re-purpose listed hospital structures – maintaining popular memory and identity where possible

H — Protect key views of school and city centre assets

AALBORG
Design Brief

CHAPTER 7: THE URBAN DESIGN PROGRAM

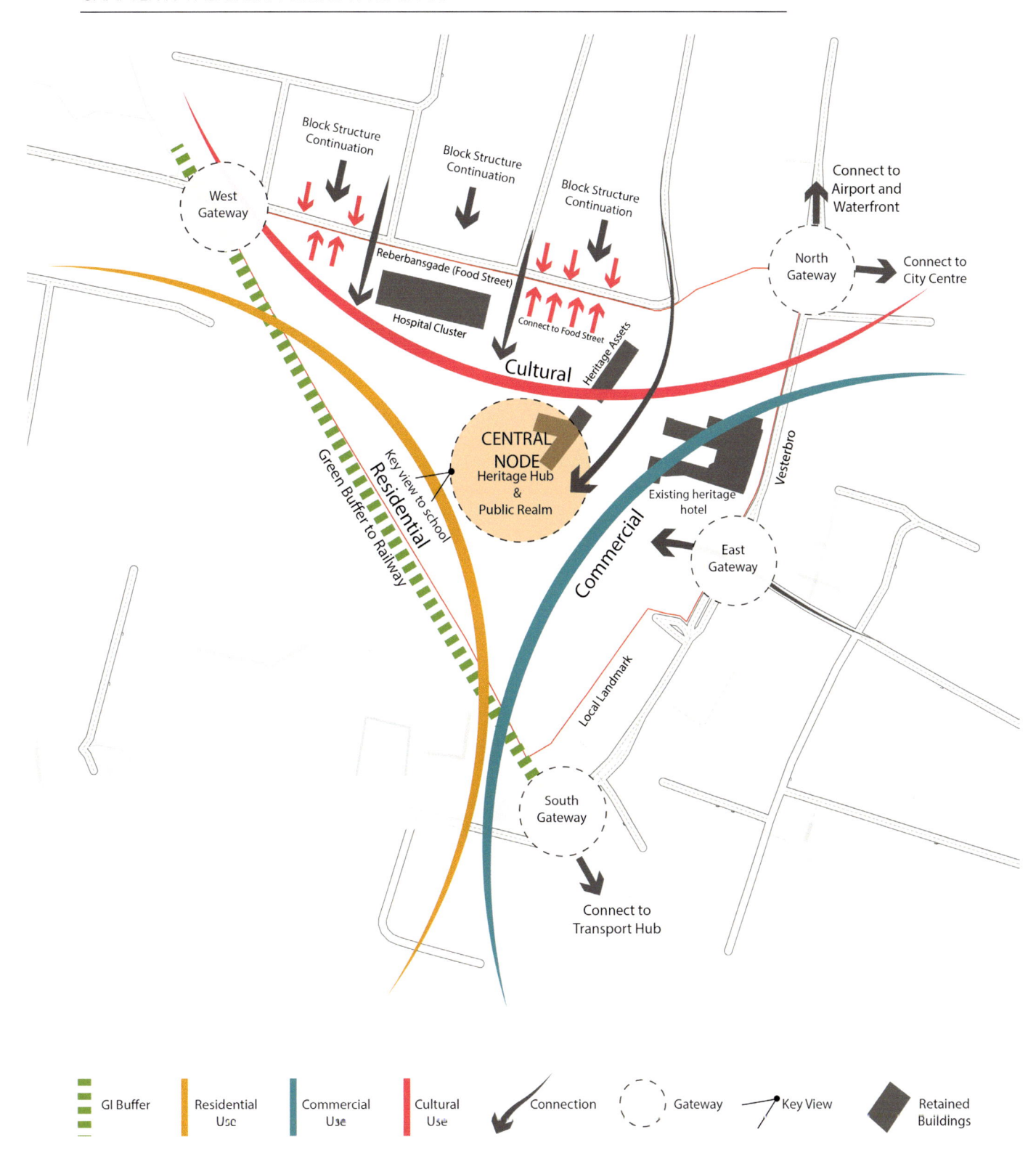

188

SPATIAL CONCEPT

Manchester Case Study Design Objectives

No.	Objective
1	Provide a predominantly mixed use development that delivers a transition from the city centre (commercial) to residential neighbourhoods
2	Enhance sustainable transport connections to the city centre, adjacent neighbourhoods, plus opportunities throughout the city region
3	Delivering a new neighbourhood which integrates with the current surrounding neighbourhoods and creates a cohesive legible townscape and overcomes barriers
4	Create a strong network of community facilities and services, linked by inclusive public realm and green infrastructure
5	Deliver a range of housing and commercial typologies to meet the needs of a diverse population including existing residents
6	Establish a well-defined, consistent and complementary character to enhance local identity and the sense of place

DESIGN ACTIONS

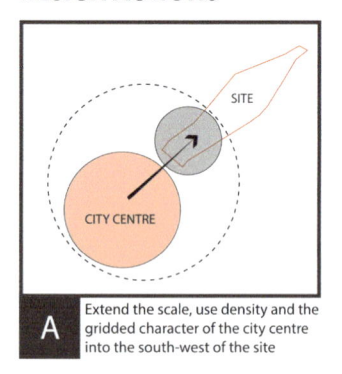

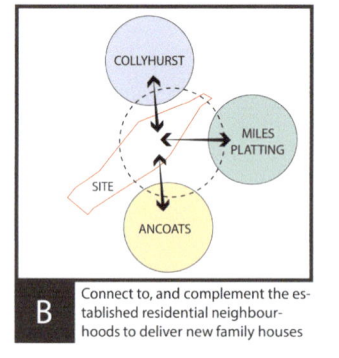

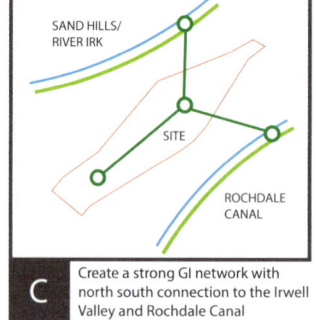

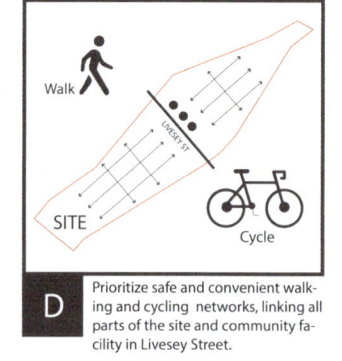

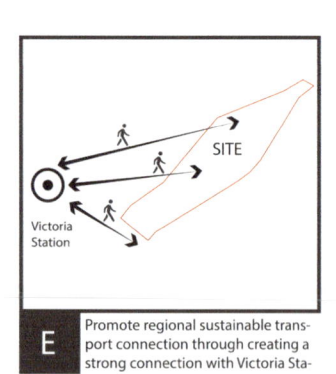

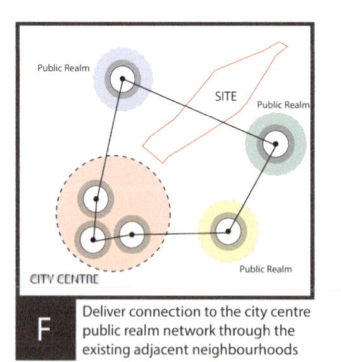

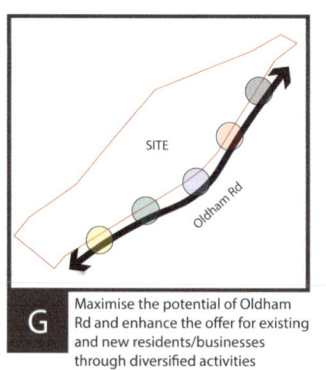

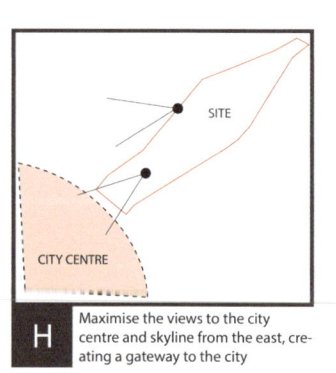

A. Extend the scale, use density and the gridded character of the city centre into the south-west of the site

B. Connect to, and complement the established residential neighbourhoods to deliver new family houses

C. Create a strong GI network with north south connection to the Irwell Valley and Rochdale Canal

D. Prioritize safe and convenient walking and cycling networks, linking all parts of the site and community facility in Livesey Street.

E. Promote regional sustainable transport connection through creating a strong connection with Victoria Station

F. Deliver connection to the city centre public realm network through the existing adjacent neighbourhoods

G. Maximise the potential of Oldham Rd and enhance the offer for existing and new residents/businesses through diversified activities

H. Maximise the views to the city centre and skyline from the east, creating a gateway to the city

CHAPTER 7: THE URBAN DESIGN PROGRAM　　　　　　　　　　　　　　　190

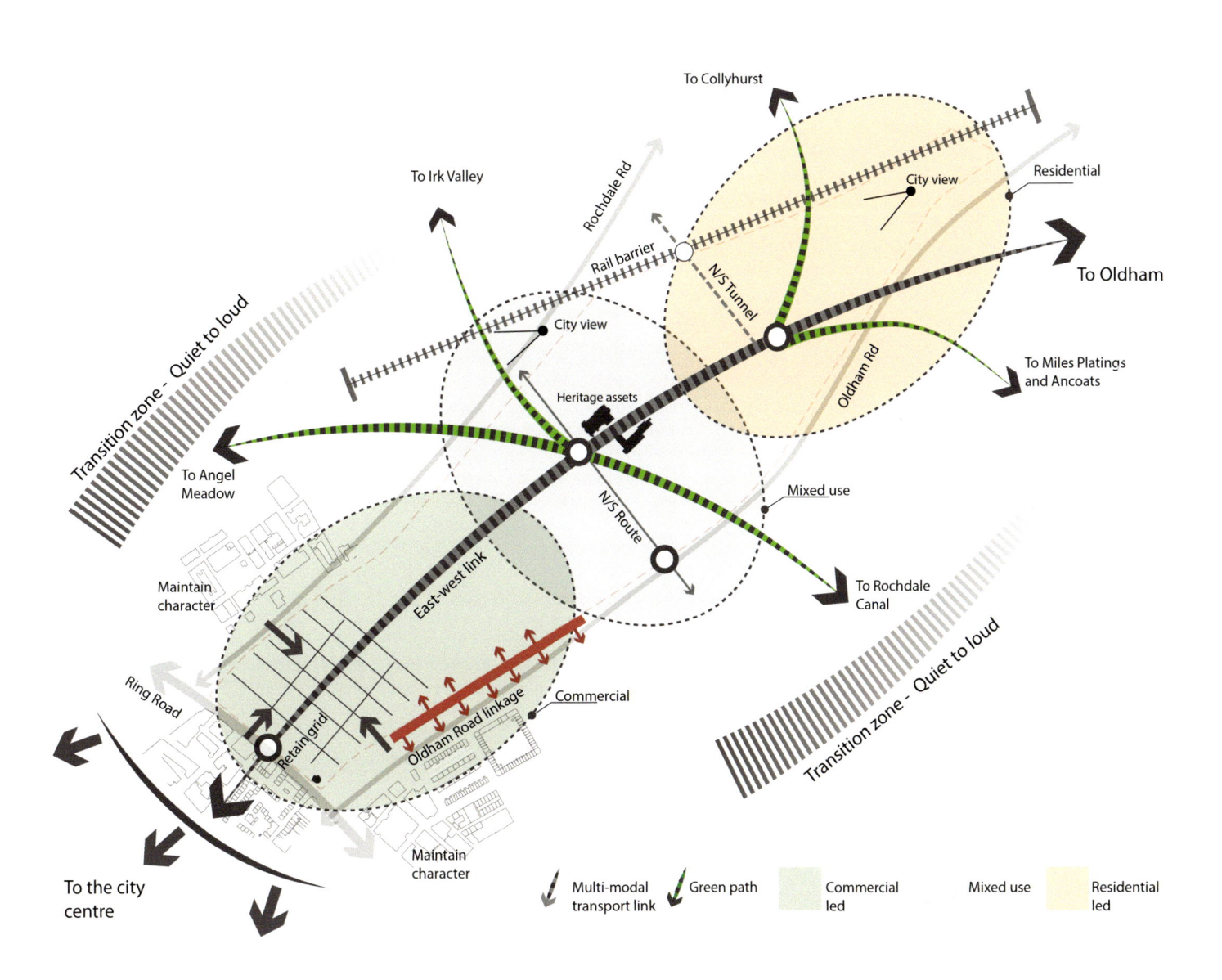

SPATIAL CONCEPT

MANCHESTER
Design Brief

7.4 BEYOND THE DESIGN BRIEF

In developing the AUD Framework, we were aware that this is something that must function within the context of the real world. Particularly, the discourse about urban design methods often focuses strictly on the different design stages and outputs but fails to recognise that there will be other drivers that will shape those stages and outputs. The **Urban Design Program** is an important opportunity to explore and integrate some of these ideas.

CLIENT AND BUDGET

As with any development there is going to be a client. Whether this is an end user who will have a series of requirements, often financial, or a developer who wishes to build a scheme that can be marketed and sold. There are many cases of *'Market-led'* approaches where markets and finance have led the design and development of a particular scheme; they often result in inward looking, mono-cultured environments with little interaction beyond the site boundaries. In these cases, it is likely that the brief has been written and introduced by a client far too early within the process, and as such the design has become a *'fait-accompli'*, with the analysis and understanding of a site driven by a desire to justify a particular approach only.

By contrast, there are also **'Design-led'** masterplans and strategies that have been developed delivering exemplar placemaking but are unviable and fail to deliver an appropriate prospect for investors and developers - and are often shelved as they can fail to have sufficient consideration of finance, deliverability, and marketability.

We advocate that it is critically important to consider at what stage the *'brief'* is introduced into the *'process'*. The Urban Design Program step allows an opportunity to address some of this concern, with the Program functioning as the 'brief', and for the client to be involved in the evolution of the understanding about the site at this point. Here, what we propose that as part of the Applied Urban Design Framework urban designers find a new *'balance'* (see Table 6). To achieve this, we suggest that the urban designer consider the following three approaches:

• *Present the analysis to the client* - It is frequently the case that clients and developers have not explored the site in the same granular level of detail that the urban designer will have (Step 1). Often the thorough understanding of the site, which marries the technical with the experiential, offers up opportunities and constraints that have not previously been identified by any of the technical specialists on a site, which can be exploited to enhance the client's aspirations. In many cases a good urban design analysis will help justify an approach away from the wider land use planning policies, for example, an increase in density or a wider mix of uses. By exploring and presenting this to the client, they can better understand these opportunities and implement them collaboratively.

• *Collaborate with marketers* - Knowledge of the local market is imperative for any urban designer, but it is important to acknowledge that sales, branding, and marketing are not the urban designer's role, and there will be undoubtedly specialists in these areas involved as part of the project team. We recommend that the urban designer speak in depth with these professionals at the Program stage, to ensure there is a 'real world' element to the objectives and actions. For example, while the urban designer would like to encourage new local shopping frontage, it may be that there is insufficient market to achieve that and introducing an 'action or objective' to support this may not be feasible. By contrast, understanding and exploring the financial and marketing benefits of homes around a park, or offices directly adjacent to a public transport hub will bring with it significant marketing opportunities.

• *Remember the 'balance'* - As the urban designer you need to remember that it is your role to try and strike a balance. The requirements for development are myriad and complex and it is important to reflect that you will not be able to deliver all these matters in every project. This is why the prioritisation of the *design considerations* (Part A of the Program) is so important; it allows those matters that are less critical that might otherwise conflict with the aspirations and views of other professionals to fall away, but also ensures a clear focus on the most important matters. In this way, the urban designer becomes an invaluable in the process, being able to showcase different competing uses/ideas and how to prioritise them to the wider development team.

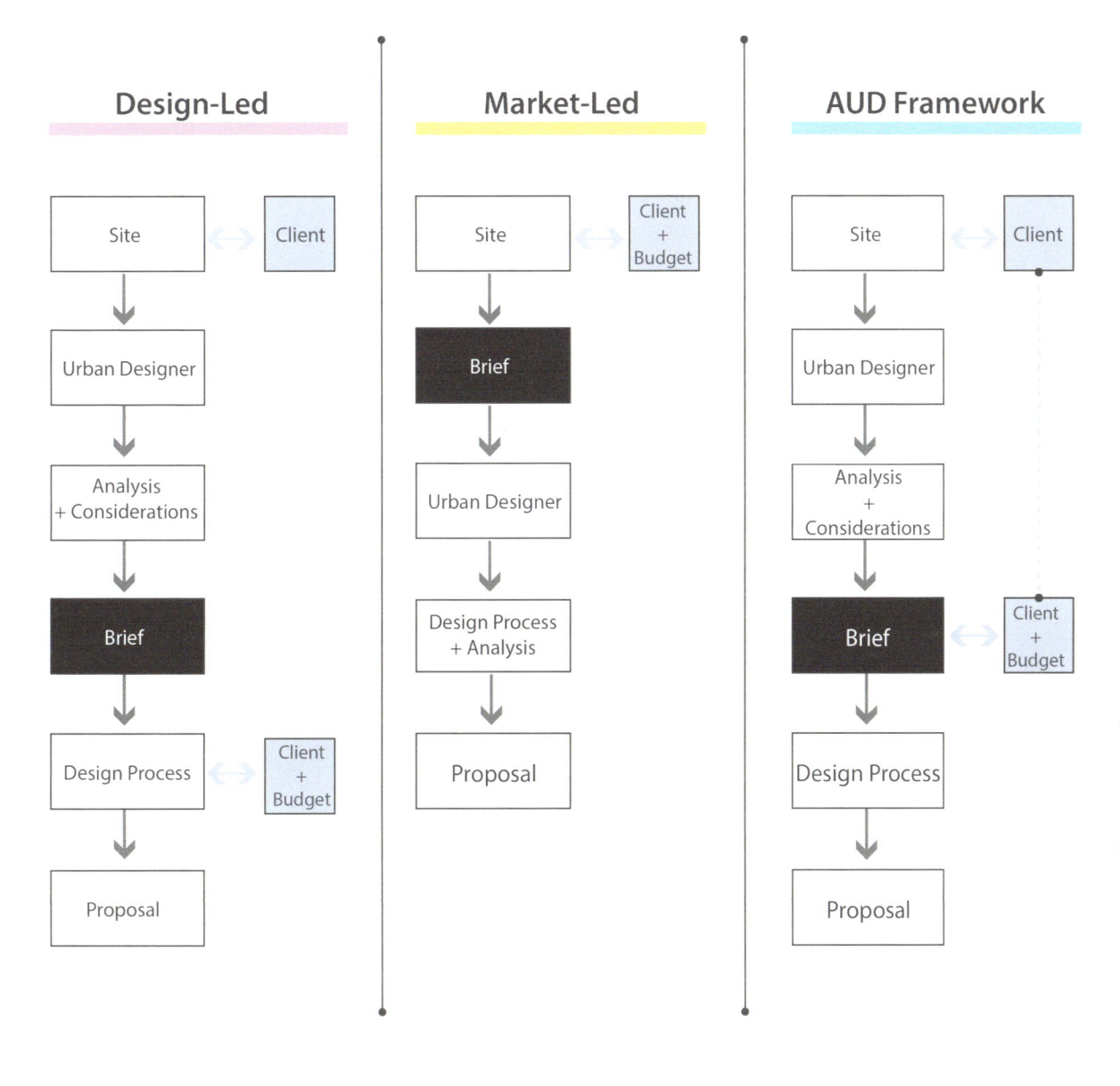

CHAPTER 7: THE URBAN DESIGN PROGRAM

Design-Led

Site ↔ Client
↓
Urban Designer
↓
Analysis + Considerations
↓
Brief
↓
Design Process ↔ Client + Budget
↓
Proposal

Market-Led

Site ↔ Client + Budget
↓
Brief
↓
Urban Designer
↓
Design Process + Analysis
↓
Proposal

AUD Framework

Site ↔ Client
↓
Urban Designer
↓
Analysis + Considerations
↓
Brief ↔ Client + Budget
↓
Design Process
↓
Proposal

TABLE 6 Integrating the Client and Budget

DEVELOPING A 'VISION'

Once the design brief is completed it may be possible to articulate a *'vision'* for the site/project. The use of a vision is not obligatory for all schemes but can provide a marketing angle to simplify the Program for more general audiences. Whereas the core elements of the design brief are intended for specific audiences and to drive design development, the vision can provide an overarching identity for any interested party. There is no set way in which a vision should be presented or delivered, but in most cases, it focuses on a short statement of no more than 200 words, supported by images, renders, and other graphics designed to articulate the characteristics of the final development from a human scale perspective - i.e., what it would be like to live, or work within the new development.

The vision will be a clear and concise description of the mid-to-long term plans or aspirations for the site/location. It will express characteristics and provide a distinctive image (both in terms of graphics but also in written aspirational terms) of potential future development. A vision should be memorable but also realistic in its ambition and is often accompanied by precedent images. These are images from other places (often a mixture of local and international images) that share some of the proposal's values and ideas to help communicate the ambition. Often visions will be accompanied by core branding - possibly including a visual logo and consistent language/messaging (both written and graphical).

The Vision must be easily understood by non-urban design professionals. Their role as marketing tools to 'sell' a project and its wider objectives to potential investors, communicate the design and identity with key stakeholders and local communities, and garner support more broadly for the scheme mean it must effectively engage a wide range of people.

EXTERNAL FACTORS

This chapter has explored several ways that the **Urban Design Program** stage can be used for a myriad of different purposes and with a variety of audiences to both enhance the delivery of contextually responsive urban design, but also to ensure that the designer, client, stakeholders, and the community are able to work collaboratively. This reduces risks of futile work, and at the same time ensures that opportunities are presented and discussed as they materialise. Nonetheless, the process cannot control every circumstance and there will be a variety of external social and economic factors which may impact the Program for good or for bad.

The urban design practitioner should ensure that they engage with broader social and economic trends and likely changes and the impacts these may have on development proposals. Being aware of these external factors, and how they are likely to change or evolve over the course of the project's delivery and operational stages can help the practitioner limit the severity of these impacts.

OPPOSITE PAGE: The city of Zurich, Switzerland, is investing heavily in energy efficiency, renewable energies, sustainable buildings, and sustainable transport options - such as the pedestrian and cycle infrastructure upgrades at Bucheggplatz - as part of its *'2000-Watt Society'* vision, 2050.

CITY to the LAKE

City to the Lake is a vision for Canberra, Australia. The vision was the marketing centrepiece for the city's Strategic Urban Design Framework, August 2015, that aimed to transform the city centre and provide direct links to Lake Burley Griffin, with a new active waterfront.

"City to the Lake will be a major contributor to the heart of the National Capital where everyday life of the city meets Lake Burley Griffin. It will be urbane, diverse, and pedestrian friendly, awarded for its sustainability, authenticity, and design excellence. It will be a vibrant waterfront destination - and progressive transformation of the city centre. Where people meet, celebrate, and have fun."

LEFT: New active waterfront - Lake Burley Griffin, Canberra, Australia.

CHAPTER 7: THE URBAN DESIGN PROGRAM

194

CONCLUSIONS

Throughout this chapter we have explored how the **Urban Design Program** (Step 2) provides an important link between the analysis undertaken (Step 1) and the design (Steps 3 and 4) – acting as the *pivot* from gathering information about a site and marshalling it in a way that means it can be used effectively as a design tool helping the practitioner to 'evidence' the judgements and decisions taken. The Program has been designed as an important part of the entire design process, bridging the analysis and design, however, the chapter has also demonstrated the variety of other roles the Program may perform – as it can help to support community consultation, planning policy and design code development, and be used as a design review tool.

The Urban Design Program stage acts as an important opportunity to engage with the wider debates about city making and real-world delivery – factoring in the client, the economy, and societal change. Consequently, despite representing a small part of the AUD Framework – the contribution of the Program to the delivery of contextually responsive urban design in a real-world context is critical and should thus be considered carefully. The subsequent Chapter (8) introduces Step 3 of the AUD Framework (Design) – wherein the Program is taken forward through design development, from concepts and options testing, to final design.

PROCESS **OUTCOMES**

SITE & CLIENT

CONTEXT

1 Analysis
Strategic
+
Local

Strategic Profile

Area Profile
Site Profile

PIVOT

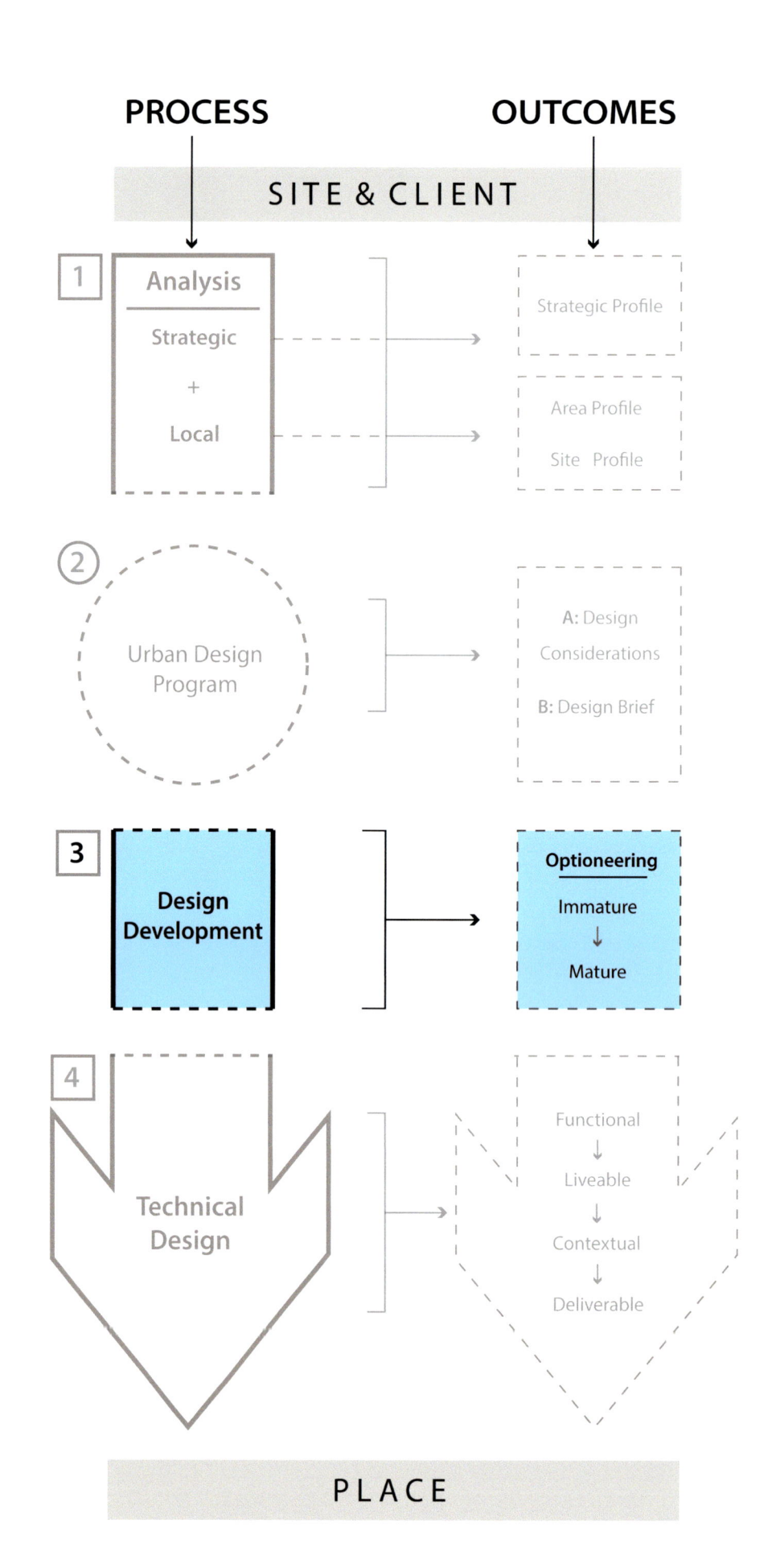

2 Urban Design Program

A: Design Considerations
B: Design Brief

DESIGN

3 Design Development

Optioneering
Immature
↓
Mature

4 Technical Design

Functional
↓
Liveable
↓
Contextual
↓
Deliverable

PLACE

CHAPTER 8
Design Development

The final steps of the Applied Urban Design Framework are the developing, detailing, and delivery of a final design solution/intervention. This design proposal must be contextually responsive and people centred, but equally needs to be functional and of high quality. The AUD Framework to this point has been developed to ensure designers have the necessary contextual information (*Step 1 - Chapters 5 and 6*) to be able to effectively shape design interventions through a robust Urban Design Program (*Step 2 - Chapter 7*) - yet as we shift to the design phase (*Steps 3 and 4*) it is critical to return to the functional and liveable elements of design unpacked in Chapter 4 - the design layers that form the blueprint of functional placemaking, and the quality principles that promote the liveable aspects of people-focused sustainable urban environments. Designing is a complex undertaking that requires skill on the part of the designer(s), experience of what makes places work in differing contexts, and the ability to develop and evaluate different design ideas and options to ascertain the most appropriate solution for the location in question and the myriad challenges, issues, and requirements associated.

OPPOSITE PAGE:
The final phase of the AUD Framework - **'***design***' - is covered across Chapters 8, 9, and 10. This chapter focuses on Step 3 - 'Design Development'.**

As stated throughout this book, the AUD Framework is not a silver bullet for the delivery of quality urban design solutions - rather it is a template to utilise to create transparency in the design process, and to promote designs that are rationalised against the context of the place involved and people impacted. It is at this design phase that we see most clearly that the Framework is not a linear 'tick-box' exercise, but rather an iterative and creative process that seeks to assist designers in their journey - and allow planners, clients, local communities, and other stakeholders to demand design schemes that are more considerate of the local condition and maximise benefit beyond the red-line boundary of any given site being developed.

While the design phase remains a skilled and creative process - it does demand a well-defined method that will allow designers undertaking the AUD Framework to ensure Steps 1 and 2 are successfully employed. Here we propose that '**Design Development**' and '**Technical Design**', the final two Steps of the Framework, are utilised to assist.

Step 3 - Design Development
A definitive process for the design and delivery of potential design options that flows directly from Step 2 [Urban Design Program] and enables the designer to build up a design that is functional, imbued with quality, and can be consistently evaluated for contextual responsiveness (*see* Chapter 8).

Step 4: Technical Design
Providing the human scaled detailed to design that enhances the liveability and sustainability of any proposed scheme - alongside the necessary components for delivering a final urban design proposal that is technically sound and understood in order to deliver in the real-world without the loss of any quality, function, or key component(s) (*see* Chapter 9).

Chapter 10 concludes the design phase section with a critical discussion on how to best communicate design - and indeed the entire AUD Framework narrative - providing a diverse range of visualisations approaches and techniques the practitioner can employ. It also includes careful consideration, and recognition, of the real-world implications that can impact upon the delivery of any urban design proposal.

As emphasised, this is a not a simple step-by-step linear process and as such this chapter cannot be laid out in such a manner. Therefore Chapters 8, 9, and 10 should be understood as a collective that provide the salient design phase information the urban designer will require - the information provided in Chapter 4 (*Making Sense of Design*) will be critical to aid the understanding of a number of concepts and discussions that this chapter will engage with - we recommend a re-familiarisation with this chapter before proceeding.

INITIAL DESIGN PROCESS

Step 2 provided us with an Urban Design Program that included as series of Project Objectives; Design Actions; and a Spatial Concept – this 'pivot' provides the ideal platform from which to begin the initial design process. A mistake many student, or early-career, urban designers make as they move into design is to develop their proposal too quickly, or to struggle thinking past a first iteration of any design – failing to recognise that there will always be multiple ways to design a solution to any given challenge or demand. The AUD Framework has developed a simple initial design process to provide designers with a methodology for developing their designs in logical stages and providing the necessary scope for ideas and creativity to be employed in seeking out design solutions, be they traditional or innovative.

As discussed, and showcased in Chapter 7 – the elements that make up the Urban Design Program are often open to interpretation - the vision, objectives, actions, and even spatial concept provided can be translated in different ways by different designers – providing a design solution that best tackles any given objective or action is open to debate. Ten designers may concoct ten differing approaches to providing an intervention to overcome a problem or deliver a required element of the brief.

Design competitions illustrate this perfectly – regardless of how robust the design brief may be - differing design practices will think up differing ways in which to respond to it in a 'successful' manner. Whilst wildly different design proposals for the same brief should lead you to question the robustness of the brief, oftentimes different solutions to the same problem should be positively perceived – It provides evidence that delivering contextually responsive design based around the detailed AUD Framework structure need not result in predictable (and perhaps therefore generic) design. What the Urban Design Program does do however, is provide the designers involved with a clear articulation of the contextual responses they MUST consider in their design process and how designers communicate their design choices - rationalising them against the Urban Design Program components is key. How they employ the program will be important for how they ultimately develop their design.

8.1 OPTIONEERING PROCESS

Optioneering encourages urban designers to think creatively about the Urban Design Program and how they can design potential solutions across the range of contextual information provided. This can involve exploring differing interpretations of the project objectives and design actions provided – or designing potential schemes which prioritise these components in different ways. Prioritising one particular element of the Urban Design Program over another can lead to vastly different design outcomes. It is often the case that, given the context of the site, that particular *design actions* take precedence over others and a decision over which to focus on will be required. The ability to effectively prioritise to ensure the most appropriate and high-quality design materialises is a skill that design professionals must develop through practice over time.

There is no hard limit on the number of **design options** for any given project – delivering different options allows the designer freedom to explore innovative solutions to problems, or to test new ideas. The flexibility inherent in the optioneering process ensures designers can experiment across the Urban Design Program components – this very process allows for a deeper understanding of the Program itself and grants the designer(s) time to best understand what does, and critically, does not, work.

DEVELOPING DESIGN OPTIONS

In developing design options that respond to the Urban Design Program it is critical that each option has a clear and logical appreciation for how it engages with the Program. The initial *'pencil on paper'* stage of design is often daunting to many, beginning with the most visual element of the Urban Design Program – the spatial concept – is therefore a useful starting point. To start to shape initial design options, a helpful methodology is to consider delivering the basics of the functional blueprints (see 4.3) of design first before then considering the liveable qualities (*see* 4.2) of the proposal. In this way the designers begin with structure and then move to detail. It is also vital that all 3 scales (Strategic, Area, and Site) are considered for each of the functional blueprints and liveable qualities – it is this broader perspective that will allow the designer

CHAPTER 8: DESIGN DEVELOPMENT

to deliver benefits beyond the site boundary and consider and promote solutions that are genuinely contextual and considerate of wider communities.

Some projects will lend themselves to multiple design options, others will be more limited in scope. It is also important to note that design options do not necessarily need to be vastly different from one another – subtle changes in design proposals can have major impacts on the final liveability, quality, and function of a place. Time is often the main challenge to overcome in professional practice, or in education settings, as designing several potential schemes can be resource intensive and not practical. To overcome this, we have provided a structured outline for how options can be produced more efficiently. This simple method provides a structure for designers to quickly develop immature options before testing them to identify those that will be taken forward to a more mature step.

This process (*see* below) occurs before a final proposal is presented and technically delivered and is critical to ensure the design is consistently tested and evaluated across each step of the process.

Immature Options

These options are the most basic form of design – they will normally be hand-drawn or quickly produced digitally. They will be sketchy in form (i.e., they will be non-technical at this early stage – but will rather rely on the inherent skill and knowledge of the designer in regards technical specifications and standards). Immature options will still be delivered employing the functional blueprints, considering the full Urban Design Program, and thinking about liveable qualities. Much of the thinking and detail will be provided as annotations, quick sketches, and basic 2D design. Once multiple immature options have been developed it will be possible to 'test' these to ascertain which will move forward to be further developed into mature options.

BELOW: The AUD design optioneering process.

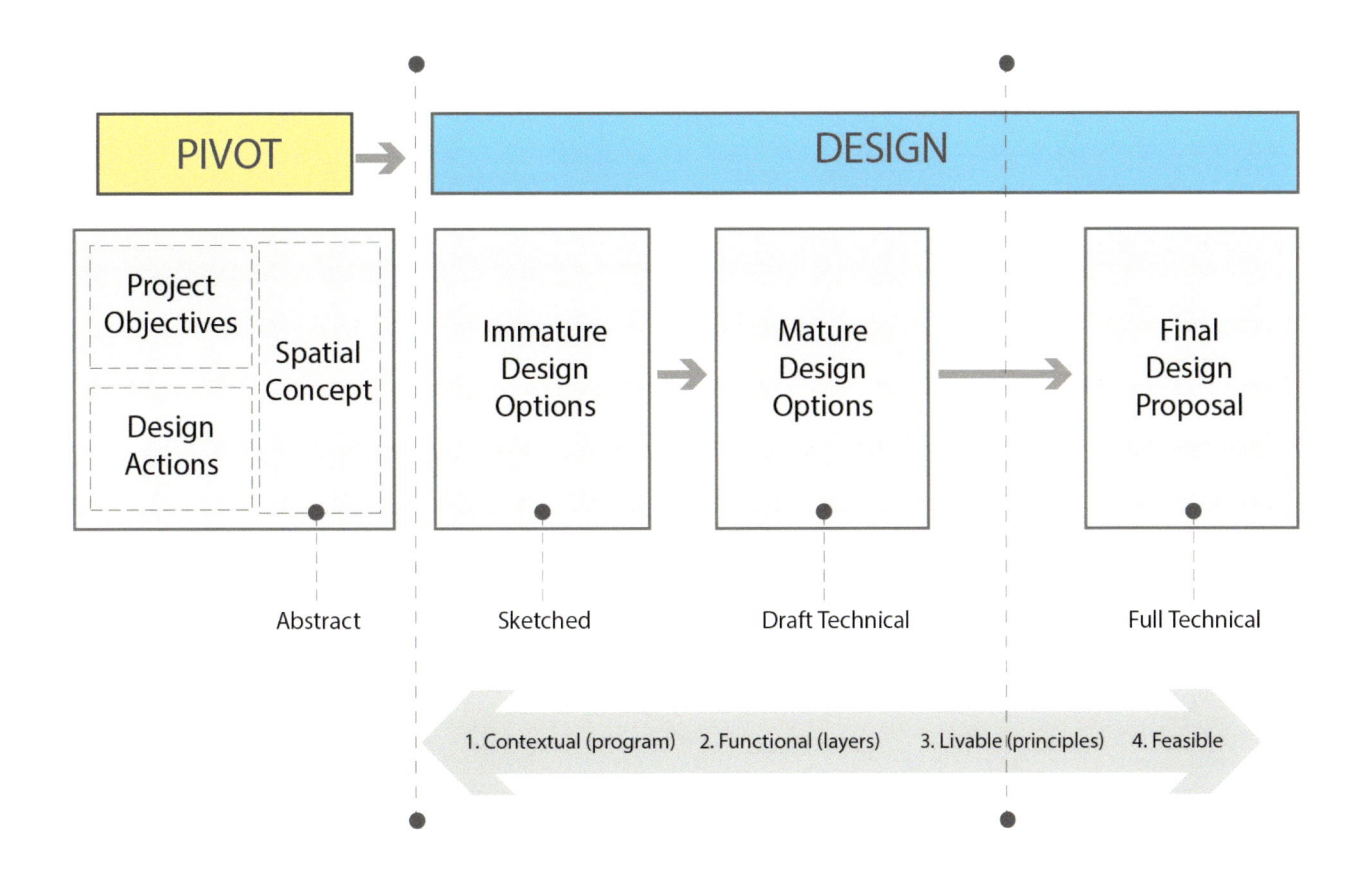

Mature Options
The next stage of the optioneering process – moves beyond the '*sketchy*' to start considering '*draft technical*', to begin to design these early option proposals into more refined and rationalised schemes. Mature options are not simply the continued development of the immature options that have 'passed' evaluation and now require further detail – quite often they are new and improved versions of an immature option or can be new design proposals that are the result of learning from the immature options developed or taking parts from different immature options to develop a newly conceived proposal. The delivery of mature options still requires the designer to be creative and flexible. If the immature options stage allows designers to play with and test very different solutions and innovative interpretations of the Urban Design Program - the mature stage asks the urban designer to begin to ground their design development – to consider more deeply the mechanics of the design and its potential real-world impact and feasibility.

The number of mature options developed will again be dependent on the particular designer and scheme – it is possible that only one mature option is developed. The mature options should provide enough technical detail that they can be presented to key stakeholders for input – be that clients, planning officers, or local community consultations. Mature options should be fully justified in their decisions and choices against the Urban Design Program and have enough detail to allow audiences to effectively understand the potential of the scheme(s) should they be delivered. There needs to be a robust evaluation of mature options to ultimately identify and prepare a preferred option – the final design proposal.

Final Design Proposal
The final stage is the completion and realisation of a final design proposal. This final design scheme will be fully technical and be ready for real-world delivery. It represents the culmination of the design optioneering phase. It forms the overall blueprint for an urban design that is contextually responsive, people centred, and of high quality.

OPTION 1: City Centre Expansion

✓
- Links to city centre to east
  [Project Objective 2 - Design Actions D & E]
- Local employment growth and opportunities.
  [Project Objective 1]
- Strong grid pattern oriented to city centre
  [Design Actions D & A & F]
- Central green park linked to city centre GI
  [Project Objective 5]

✗
- Lack of connection to northern district
  [Project Objective 2 - Design Actions F]
- Lacking diversity of use - including no residential or links to cultural hubs
  [Project Objective 1 - Design Actions A]
- Neglects key views to school, turning its back to railway
  [Design Actions H]
- Fails to directly link to transport hub throughout site.
  [Design Actions H]

This option functions well and has significant potential to deliver quality public realm and GI provision across site. However, it fails to consider broader context beyond city centre and questions remain over feasibility of full urban blocks against railway.

OPTION 2: Mixed Use Neighbourhood

✓
- Mixed of use with residential, office, retail and cultural use
  [Project Objective 1 - Design Action A]
- Connects with key routes to both city centre and northern neighbourhood
  [Project Objective 2 - Design Action A]
- Strong use of urban blocks across site
  [Project Objective 3, Action F]
- Significant public realm and GI provision with linear park connecting with transport hubs
  [Project Objectives 5 & 4, Design Action B]
- Northern edge condition established as core "Food Street" with services at linked streets
  [Design Action D].
- Key views to school reinforced
  [Design Action H]

✗
- Despite enhanced permeability, less legible route network throughout site
  [Project Objective 4 - Design Action C]
- Removes more historical buildings, increased demolition to northern edge
  [Project Objective 3 - Design Action H]

Mixed of used requires careful consideration of functionality across site. Strong network of public space and GI (linear park) provides ample opportunity for human-scale liveable quarters. This option needs careful design regarding shared public environment and a better connections to surrounding context and the city centre. Northern district and railway/school to south. Technical feasibility is not a major concern, however, detailing routes/spaces must be a priority during mature phasing.

CHAPTER 8: DESIGN DEVELOPMENT   200

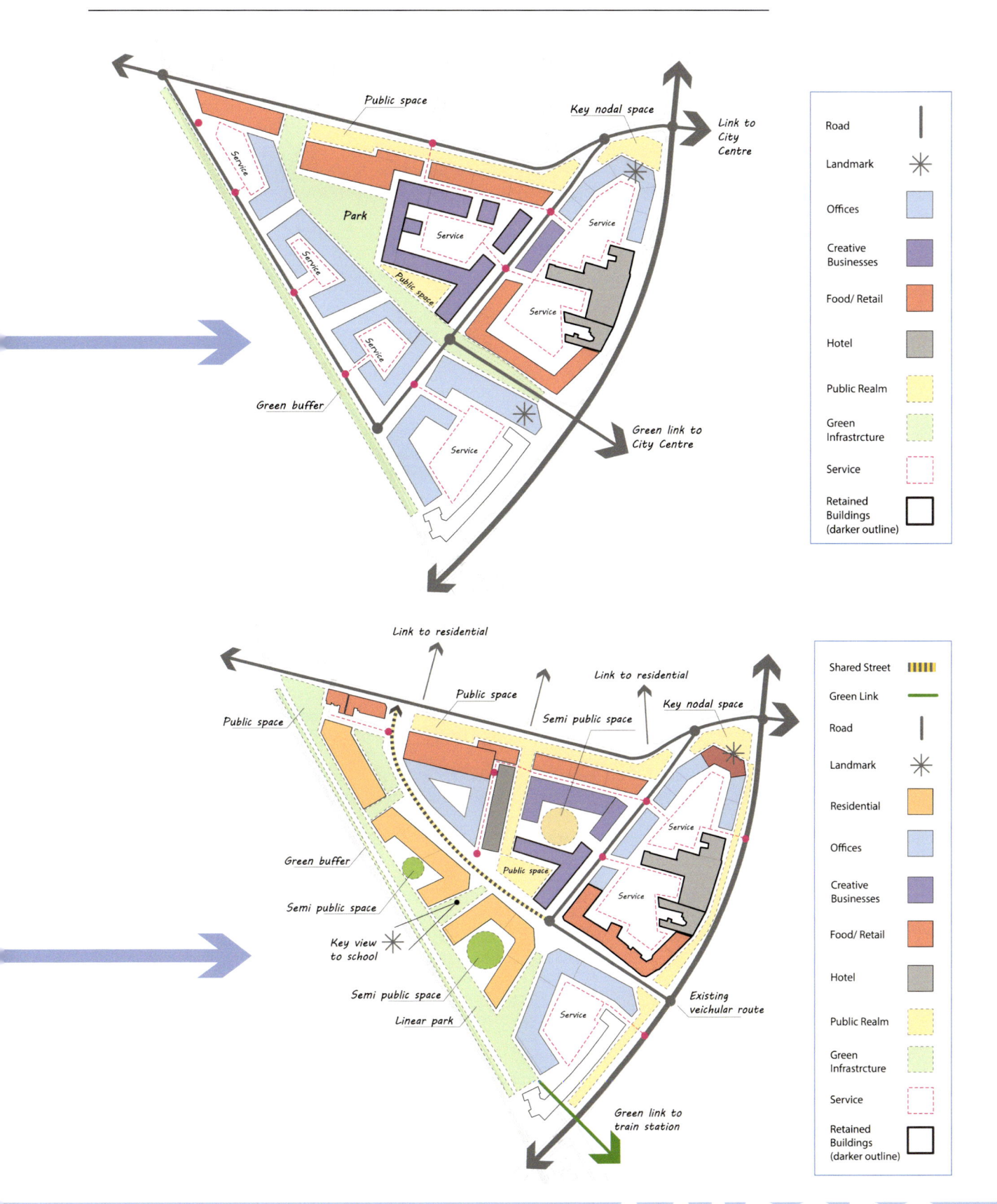

AALBORG
Immature Design Options

EVALUATING OPTIONS

Whilst it is easy to understand that we should 'test' our design options as part of the design process, it remains one of the most misunderstood and ill-defined parts of the whole process and is often overlooked, or engaged with in a tokenistic manner, in a scramble towards a final design solution. This has resulted in many projects failing to create liveable, contextually responsive places simply because the overall design process has become dislocated from the analysis and the conclusions reached - or has sought to deliver a design that ignores, or does not relate to, the qualities of placemaking that were identified in Chapter 4. It is important to remember that this evaluation process is not to stifle innovation in design - it allows for innovation and creativity, but requires the practitioner to *'evidence'* how design interventions are contextually responsive – ensuring they are robust enough to pass a thorough design evaluation.

A perfect design solution that will meet equally all the objectives and actions within the Program is not realistically achievable – rather, the preferred, or final design, option will always represent some form of compromise. Chapters 4 and 7 highlight how competing issues must be balanced, with compromises made on certain matters across the design process. Finite resources – land, service capacity, funding – will mean that the 'ideal' solution may be challenging to achieve. Consequently, it is important that the evaluation of the design ensures that the approach is driven by the context building in Chapters 5-7 and fully maximises the opportunities for quality placemaking as outlined in Chapter 4. In this respect the evaluation process is an important part of ensuring that practitioners can critically assess the quality of their design solutions and identify areas that require improvement.

The following sections provide practical advice for practitioners in how to maximise the evaluation process through the delivery of immature, mature, and final design options. The subsequent three-part evaluation process (testing against the i) Urban Design Program, ii) Design Layers, and iii) Liveability Credentials) encourages the urban designer to progress the design development in a logical way, while also helping to identify areas or issues of concern that require re-assessment or reprioritisation. Given the impact of context, the process is not always the same at every scale, or with every site. Early career designers or other built environment professionals new to design can follow these steps in a linear manner, however, with practice, evaluation can become second nature and can occur in 'real time' alongside design development. Regardless, good practice evaluation should be documented so that it can be shown and communicated to help justify the rigour of the proposal – thus annotations, notes, and scribbles are vital.

As the optioneering process evolves / progresses – three parts are required for successful evaluation.

Part 1 - Testing Against the Program

The first part of any evaluation process should return to the Program and consider how the option(s) marry up with the project objectives, design actions, and spatial concept. The designer (or another third party) can consider each in turn and provide a simple binary answer if each are met. Testing against the Program enables options to be discounted early in the process if they do not realise most elements of the Program and lack appropriate response to the context. This is a process that should be undertaken by the practitioner as the design options are developed.

Reviewing against the Program is useful to shape and marshal the multiple immature options that have been developed to arrive at those proposals which are viable for more detailed design development and evaluation. Detailed testing of options against the Program should only be undertaken when a series of considered viable options are in place – likely prioritising different elements of the Program. For example, an option might focus on green infrastructure, the formation of a commercial quarter, or take a waterfront focus. If using a more evolutionary approach to optioneering, the constant review or evaluation against the Program allows designers to incrementally change their proposals in pursuit of the most appropriate balance.

In practice it is common to see three design options presented, where one approach delivers a high-quality response to the design principles and the others fail to ensure an appropriate solution will materialise. In these cases, the evaluation process appears rudimentary and disingenuously justifies and supports the viable option. Ultimately, options that do not make a positive and concerted effort to deliver the Program are not schemes worthy of consideration in the first place. Testing against the program should always include a commentary on the viable options to demonstrate what aspects or elements are prioritised. On pages 203-4 we have tested a mature design option for the Manchester case study site against the spatial concept and design actions we produced as part of the Program (see page 187-8).

Part 2 - Testing Functionality with Design Layers
Chapter 4 presented **12 Urban Design Layers** (functional blueprints) to ensure designs work and function effectively (see 4.3). These layers helped shape the nature and type of analysis undertaken and review the deliverability and practicality of the objectives and actions set out within Program. In the optioneering stage, the layers offer the opportunity to transform immature options into more mature options, ensuring that the underlying structure of a place works effectively. There is a strong interrelationship between all 12 layers and to consider these individually or one after the other can result in a disjointed assessment, rather a combined engagement is key – for example a route, is also part of the public realm, is enclosed by buildings, and will have a frontage onto the outer space.

Functionality testing is a time-consuming process and should only be undertaken when the designer is satisfied that the Program has been met within a specific option (Part 1). However, there will be further opportunity to ensure contributions to the meeting the elements of the Program. Every site, led by the Program, will have different priorities across the 12 layers but in most cases the layers can be grouped logically to assist the evaluation process. These are set out adjacent alongside a series of points to consider for each of the developed options. It is important to highlight that this is not an exhaustive list and should be adapted and added to by the practitioner.

As a starting point, each option should consider and present information on:

URBAN STRUCTURE: *Blocks, routes, green infrastructure, character*

• Present sensibly sized urban blocks, which facilitate a clear understanding of density.
• Enable connections between key facilities and destinations for a variety of movement modes and prioritise accessibility for all ages and abilities.
• Deliver a clear hierarchy of streets, public and green spaces, each with a clearly defined role and purpose.
• Effectively manage the transition between the existing townscape and new development (via appropriate edge conditions).
• Carefully consider character, either to reflect and extend adjacent character areas, or creating new complementary ones.

SPACE AND PLACE: *Public realm, enclosure, frontage, management / maintenance*

• Deliver a public realm that reinforces important routes, through high quality, pedestrian focused interventions.
• Include public and green spaces positively enclosed by buildings, with appropriate active frontage at key locations.
• Consider variations in enclosure and street ratio (height to width) to reinforce the hierarchy of streets, spaces, and routes throughout.
• Ensure that public spaces, and key public routes are well overlooked by frontages to reinforce passive surveillance.
• Allow flexibility/adaptability for spaces and routes, considering temporal changes between different times of day, seasonality across the year, or on unique occasions.

BUILT FORM: *Uses, buildings, corners, service / access.*

• Present a series of clear uses that are complimentary to each other and adjacent land uses to reinforce the local character and identity.
• Consider the use of the upper floors for mixed-use opportunities, and how height can aid enclosure and legibility.
• Use corners effectively, especially along key routes to reinforce dominant movements or in key public spaces to create a sense of arrival.
• Ensure that every urban block and land use can be serviced and accessed, without compromising the qualities of key public realm or routes for pedestrians.

Part 3 - Testing for quality using quality principles

Parts 1 and 2 of the evaluation process have ensured that any design options developed will be both contextually responsive and functionally effectively when measured against the 12 **functional blueprints** (see 4.3). Urban design is inherently interested in delivering places for people and so part 3 of any evaluation must assess schemes for **liveable qualities** at the human scale before concluding the process (see 4.2)

One of the most effective visual and technical tools available to the practitioner to test and demonstrate that an option responds to liveable human scale considerations is through the use of cross sections. Cross sections are a valuable tool throughout the design process and play a key role in the evaluation of proposals by considering urban blocks, key routes, and long sections among other aspects. Cross sections offer the opportunity to check key measurements and consider many of the urban design layers in three dimensions. Use of 3D is vitally important in this step as designs that are evaluated in 2D only are less likely to balance options against human scale effectively.

An additional consideration as part of the evaluation process involves gathering feedback on the design options from other stakeholders/third parties, to enable different users to give their perspective and views on the scheme. The subsequent sections discuss helpful techniques to involve other professionals, stakeholders, and the community in the optioneering process to test the liveability of the proposal/s.

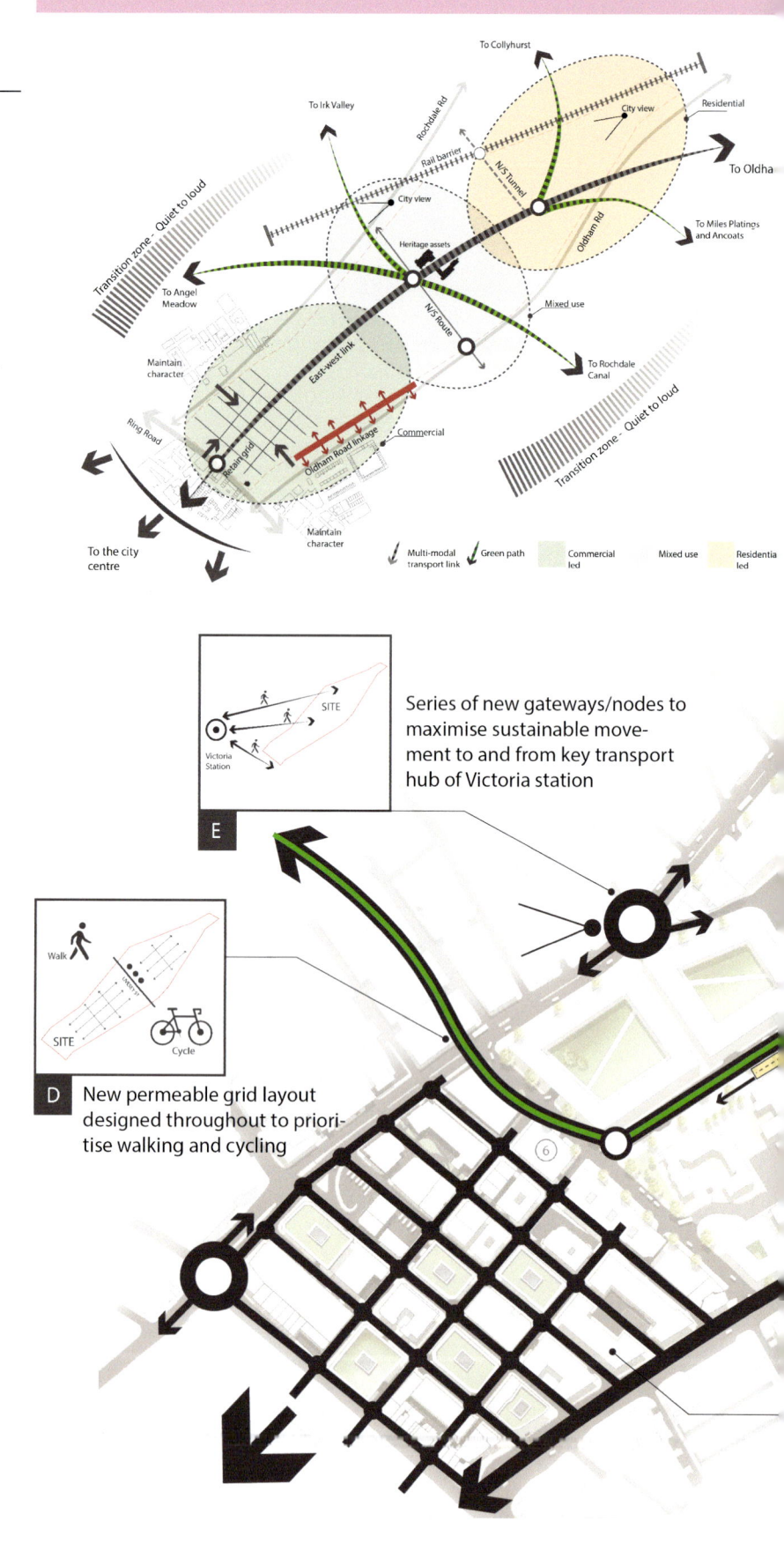

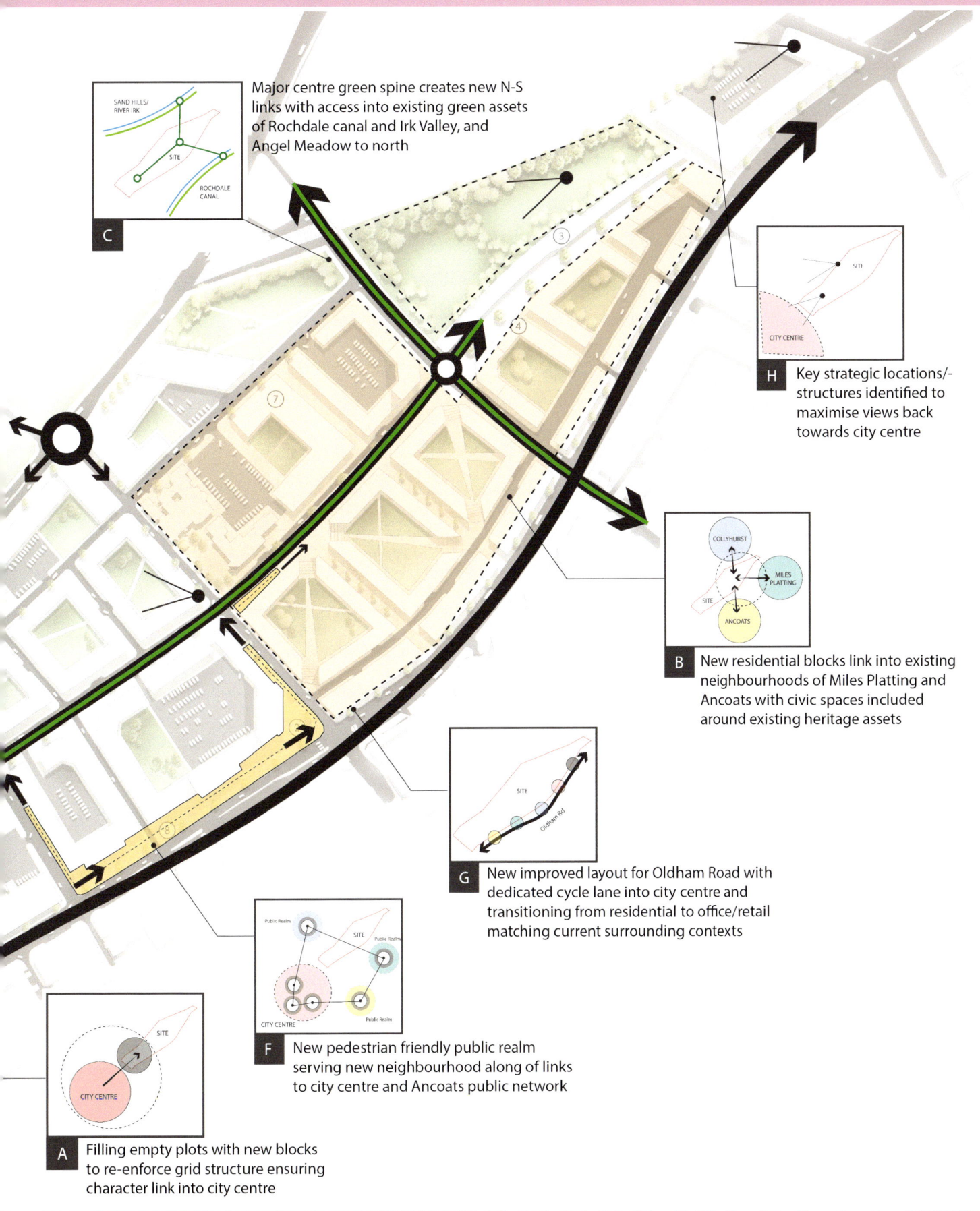

C Major centre green spine creates new N-S links with access into existing green assets of Rochdale canal and Irk Valley, and Angel Meadow to north

H Key strategic locations/-structures identified to maximise views back towards city centre

B New residential blocks link into existing neighbourhoods of Miles Platting and Ancoats with civic spaces included around existing heritage assets

G New improved layout for Oldham Road with dedicated cycle lane into city centre and transitioning from residential to office/retail matching current surrounding contexts

F New pedestrian friendly public realm serving new neighbourhood along of links to city centre and Ancoats public network

A Filling empty plots with new blocks to re-enforce grid structure ensuring character link into city centre

MANCHESTER
Mature Design Evaluation

CRITCIAL REVIEW: The 'Crit' Process
Up to this point the evaluation process has focused on what the practitioner can consider and undertake as part of their optioneering review. However, it is highly recommended that this is not a process undertaken in a vacuum, and wherever possible designs and design evaluation should be undertaken with other professionals and stakeholders – with their positions and perspectives helping determine the viability of the design options. Urban design is inherently collaborative and should be approached wherever possible in partnership with others. There can often be resistance to this process of critical review, viewed as an 'add on' or 'extra'. This can be for a multitude of reasons – including additional cost to a client or developer, a desire by the project team to protect their design 'ideal', or a lack of time to facilitate this process. Yet, for the AUD Framework to operate effectively critical review is vitally important.

In design education settings the '**crit**' (or critical review) process is a longstanding means of providing formative and structured feedback on design development. Beyond the classroom this process has valuable real-world application to gather perspectives from other experienced professionals – with the optioneering process representing the ideal moment to achieve this. Beyond this point, the design process becomes highly technical and detailed, making it more difficult for other designers and stakeholders (who lack the day to day working knowledge of a site or project) to 'parachute' themselves into the final process and offer helpful comments.

The process of preparing and presenting design options to a third party helps the practitioner to fully understand and articulate their own optioneering narrative - a valuable exercise regardless of the outcome of the review. This process can occur digitally – in a remote fashion – or in-person. With the latter, the ability to gather around plans and discuss possible solutions in real time can be a much more time and cost-effective process.

Set out adjacent are several ways this can be achieved. Not all of these will be relevant to every project; with latter points in this list being more relevant to larger projects or masterplans:

'Drawing Board' Chat
When developing options, it is important to be able to speak to other urban designers and explore different approaches. Too often in modern practice the work of the urban designer is undertaken digitally - directly onto the computer - rather than through a series of hand-drawings and sketches. A good optioneering process should include sufficient time to allow for informal and friendly discussion between professionals around sheets of drafting paper to help evolve a design and share best practice.

Critical Friend Review
An invaluable stage of any design elevation is the use of a critical friend – often a fellow professional colleague. When working on a project over a prolonged period of time, the practitioner can become entrenched in their design view - missing often obvious, or innovative, alternative solutions. Working with a critical friend allows for a 'fresh pair of eyes', to check that there are no obvious omissions or missed opportunities. For this to work most effectively a two-way dialogue is required, with the designer explaining their choices and decisions, and the critical friend seeking to positively improve any design.

Development Team Review
The two previous mechanisms rely on urban design practitioners (or in some cases other built environment professionals such as planners, architects, or landscape architects) reviewing their own projects and designs. This works effectively on smaller projects where the physical constraints are somewhat limited, however, on larger sites the situation can become more complicated. The development team review allows professionals from other related spheres to contribute to the design. A good development team review would include a round table discussion on a series of viable options with the project engineers (drainage, highways, groundworks), land use planners, green infrastructure specialists (ecologists, arboriculturists), as well as viability and deliverability experts. Development team review allows for conflicts on a range of specialist and technical matters to be discussed in a progressive way in order to generate solutions. As emphasised, on larger projects, such as masterplans, conflicts are very likely to occur between different technical specialists, but here the development team review has been shown

to encourage any issues to be addressed in a design-led way. It also allows the urban designer to more effectively 'push back' against engineered solutions that may undermine the human scale and the creation of a contextually responsive place.

EXTERNAL INPUT
The optioneering process is often the stage of the design process where regulatory authorities, communities, and local stakeholders are first consulted. We argue, and Chapters 6 and 7 have clearly demonstrated, that this should not be the case, as it is too late in the design process to facilitate meaningful change or engagement. Rather, it is important that the community and key stakeholders are given the opportunity to comment on emerging options to ensure that they meet the aspirations of the Program (*see* 7.4 for further detail). Set out below are three possible approaches.

Local Design Review
This is often the best opportunity for engagement - with local design review panels (where in operation) or land use planning regulatory authorities. In fact, we advocate that this should be the focus for design review panels and pre-application discussions, as opposed to critiquing final designs. By doing so, it will permit discussions and feedback to be provided on structural and contextual issues much more effectively. It is recommended that at this stage a formal presentation is made of the design narrative to date, showcasing the context building and the development of the Program before progressing onto design optioneering and the evaluation of those options to arrive at a preferred mature option. Final design details are best left to the formal submission for statutory approval (i.e., planning permissions or building permits).

Community Consultation
Chapter 5 discussed several common community consultation techniques (surveys, questionnaires, workshops etc), these same techniques allow for further discussion and presentation of options to obtain feedback on the optioneering process. A typical approach taken involves hosting a community exhibition and presenting the narrative that has been developed to date. The AUD Framework recommends that real choice is provided between options, with a clear explanation of the assessment against the Program, to allow community members to make an informed choice. However, it is important to recognise that when involving communities at this stage a change from engagement, to consultation, can occur as the more technical design matters become a focus of discussions. Guidance on consultation techniques is provided in more detail by others (*see, for example*, O'Hare, 2021).

Design by Enquiry
Janette Hartz-Karp (2004) codified the approach to '*Design by Enquiry*' as means of engaging local communities and stakeholders in the design approach. Whilst this technique is covered in more detail in other texts, the method relies on briefing a small group of local representatives on the background, context, and principles behind a physical regeneration project, and then pairing them alongside professional urban designers to arrive at options for a site. Again, the optioneering stage best lends itself to working with this process, with the Profiles (*see* 6.6) and the Urban Design Program (Chapter 7) acting the '*briefing*' materials.

BELOW: Urban design students must undergo regular '*crits*' at all stages of their work on the AUD Framework. The ability to present work for critical review is a skill they must master - using A1 graphical boards, 3D physical models, and clear and informed oral presentation.

8.2 MATURE DESIGN

The concluding stage of the design optioneering process is the final design proposal – representing the culmination of the AUD framework. The final design has been refined through Steps 1,2 and 3 and is the designers' realisation of an urban design scheme that is:

- Contextual
- Functional
- Liveable
- Technically Feasible

In order to achieve these 4 aims the final mature design proposal must deliver on a number of key things – and it must communicate these successfully to a broad audience.

Contextual
A final design proposal must be clearly justified and rationalised against the Urban Design Program. This will be achieved by ensuring that the final presented scheme has transparency in the design decision-making process that was undertaken. This will only be possible by consistently relating design features and elements back to the Program. This can be done through annotations on design graphics – design statements that accompany the technical proposal, and/or a clear evaluation of how the scheme meets the project objectives and design actions of the program. Another way in which urban designers can showcase the contextually responsive nature of the design is to present a clear optioneering process, assisting the audience in better understanding and appreciating the direction taken that has led to the final design outcome – a comprehensive optioneering process is able to illustrate how the Urban Design Program, as an evaluation tool, and other processes, such as consultations, shaped decisions and refined the concluding design proposal.

Functional
The final proposal must include all the functional blueprints that allow the design to functional effectively in practice – the blueprints [see 4.3] are a starting point – Chapter 9 discusses how the structural design will require considerable thinking from designers to reconcile how the proposed project be presented across different scales – to illustrate its ability to integrate with its surroundings – and how the core design layers are employed for differing functions to be achieved through the use of hierarchies and detailing.

Liveable
It is critical that the final design proposal is of the highest quality – this requires clear reference to be included as to how it will provide human scale qualities – the liveable aspects discussed in Chapter 4. (see 4.2). To ensure this is accomplished it is necessary for the final design proposal to go beyond function and structure and deliver design detail that is imbued with these quality principles. For a deign to be genuinely contextual and people centred it must fit into its wider surroundings and enhance them – as it must provide environments that are suited to those who will use them and uplift them whilst doing so. It is in these human scaled interventions that urban design is elevated from technical practice to creative art.

Technically Feasible
The final design proposal must be fully technical in its delivery – It must be presented as a fully rationalised, detailed, and achievable scheme. This requires detailed technical drawings that showcase how the design should be delivered as intended in real-world practice. We recommend the use of AutoCAD 9or similar) software to ensure all elements of the design are technically precise in regards measurements and standards – across all detailing. The final design will be communicated across a range of scales and techniques to illustrate accurate measurements within accepted tolerances and technical standards.

The final masterplan will only be completed and revealed once these above components have been fully considered and realised. The resultant 2D technical plan can then be employed as the basis for all the contextual, functional, liveable, and technically feasible information/detail required. Chapter 10 (*Design Delivery*) provides the necessary information in regards the production of this plan and the wider visualisations required for effectively communicating the entire design phase (including optioneering). Delivering the final masterplan requires all the elements of design to be reconciled and finalised. The final design will then be presented first and all associated detailing will flow from this single technical plan - it acts as the anchor for the delivery of Step 4 (Technical Design), and the focus of Chapter 9.

RIGHT: Hammarby Sjostad, Stockholm, Sweden is a masterplanned sustainable district completed in 2017. It has proved a highly successful environment - with clear contextual nods to the nearby city of Stockholm - yet more relaxed and less formal; a highly functional plan centred on the delivery of 12 subdistricts anchored by Hammarby Lake; a phased construction plan that divided building plots and focused attention on the technical dimensions of public realm and green infrastructure provision; and a liveable qualities that have made it a highly desirable place to live, with over 20,000 inhabitants.

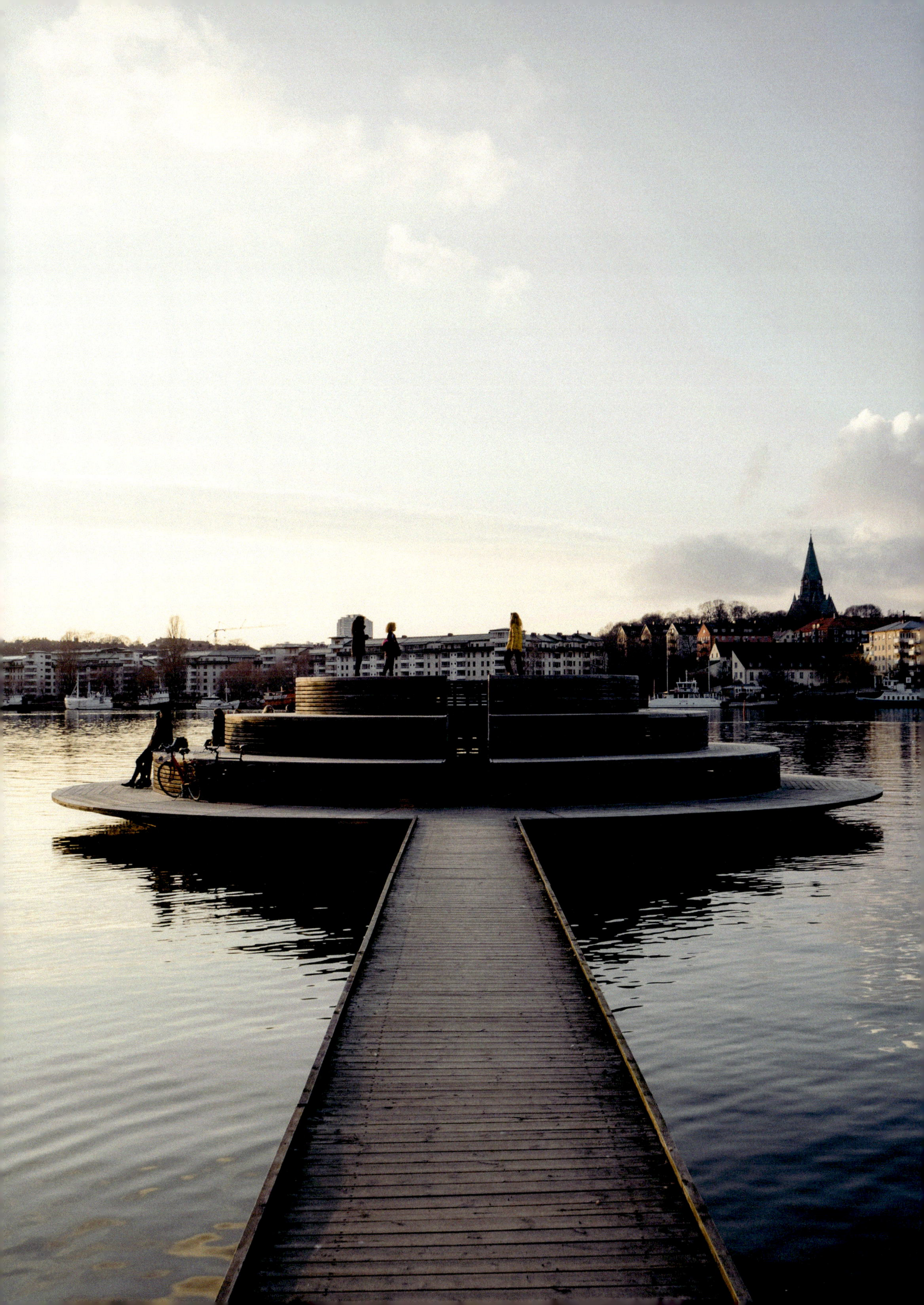

APPLIED URBAN DESIGN

① **New Linear Park**
- Connects Reberbansgade residential neighbourhood to north with transport hub to south east
- New multifunctional landscaping and transition from Skagen train line
- Provision of ecology and play spaces

② **Gateway to the City**
- Corresponding with the two E-W routes to and from historic central core and new links to BRT
- New landmark features into site and reimagined food street

③ **A new Identity for Reberbansgade**
- New set-back retail/food outlets with spill out spaces activating street
- Reactive and reuse of existing heritage hospital building

④ **A Space for All**
- Shared central link into heart of site
- New dedicated public realm infrastructure with two new key spaces connected visually and sustainably

⑤ **A Heart of Heritage**
- New central public space maximising existing heritage structures
- A central node for the proposal anchoring new residential and office uses from Urbansgade / Ladegårdsgade

⑥ **Gateway to the Site**
- Juxtaposing existing building line on Vesterbro with new site specific development
- Key crossing W-E towards city centre and interaction with the Cathedral and the new developed surrounding square. Reintegration of 'Goose Girl' sculpture into the public realm.

⑦ **Visual Connection South**
- Opening key views to Aalborg Cathedral School and visually breaking barrier beyond railway line

⑧ **Business Incubator Hub**
- Reusing heritage hospital building for start-up SMEs
- Harder, quieter inner-block space for employees

⑨ **A New Community**
- Bringing new residential community into heart of re-development Traditional apartments with views over Aalborg Cathedral School and shared central space

⑩ **Segregating Service**
- Dedicated one-way route providing service for Reberbansgade and re-purposed hospital building - includes access into retained underground parking/service beneath hospital and new civic hub

AALBORG
Proposed Masterplan

CHAPTER 8: DESIGN DEVELOPMENT   210

APPLIED URBAN DESIGN

CHAPTER 8: DESIGN DEVELOPMENT

① **A Green Corridor**
- A new central green spine connects all parts of new proposed development and lines directly to city centre
- Integration and expansion of wider GI network from Angel Meadow to Irk Valley and Rochdale Canal

② **A Neighbourhood Anchor**
- Public space accessible to wider communities of Ancoats, Miles Platting and Collyhurst

③ **Ecology and Heritage**
- Re-purposing the historic viaduct as a community social space and gateway to ecology pack.

④ **Bringing Communities Together**
- New residential component pulling together existing neighbourhoods of Collyhurst and Miles Platting [W-E]

⑤ **New Commercial Quarter**
- Building on commercial offerings of NOMA and Angel Meadow
- Employment growth meeting Manchester strategy and vision

⑥ **Character of the City**
- Extending city centre development onto site through urban blocks infill and reinforcing grid pattern

⑦ **Civic Opportunity**
- New and upgraded education quarter to serve wider community
- Civic core with existing heritage church and a series of newly developed leisure facilities

⑧ **A New High Street for Oldham Road**
- New route layout encouraging sustainable mobility including cycling and walking
- New retail hub at centre of transition from the city centre [W] to north Manchester [E]

⑨ **Rochdale Road Gateway**
- Retaining corner building as key node / gateway into the site
- Establish strong sustainable mobility links to main transport hubs at Victoria Station

MANCHESTER
Proposed Masterplan

PROCESS OUTCOMES

SITE & CLIENT

CONTEXT

1 Analysis
Strategic
+
Local

→ Strategic Profile
→ Area Profile
   Site Profile

PIVOT

2 Urban Design Program

→ **A:** Design Considerations
   B: Design Brief

DESIGN

3 Design Development

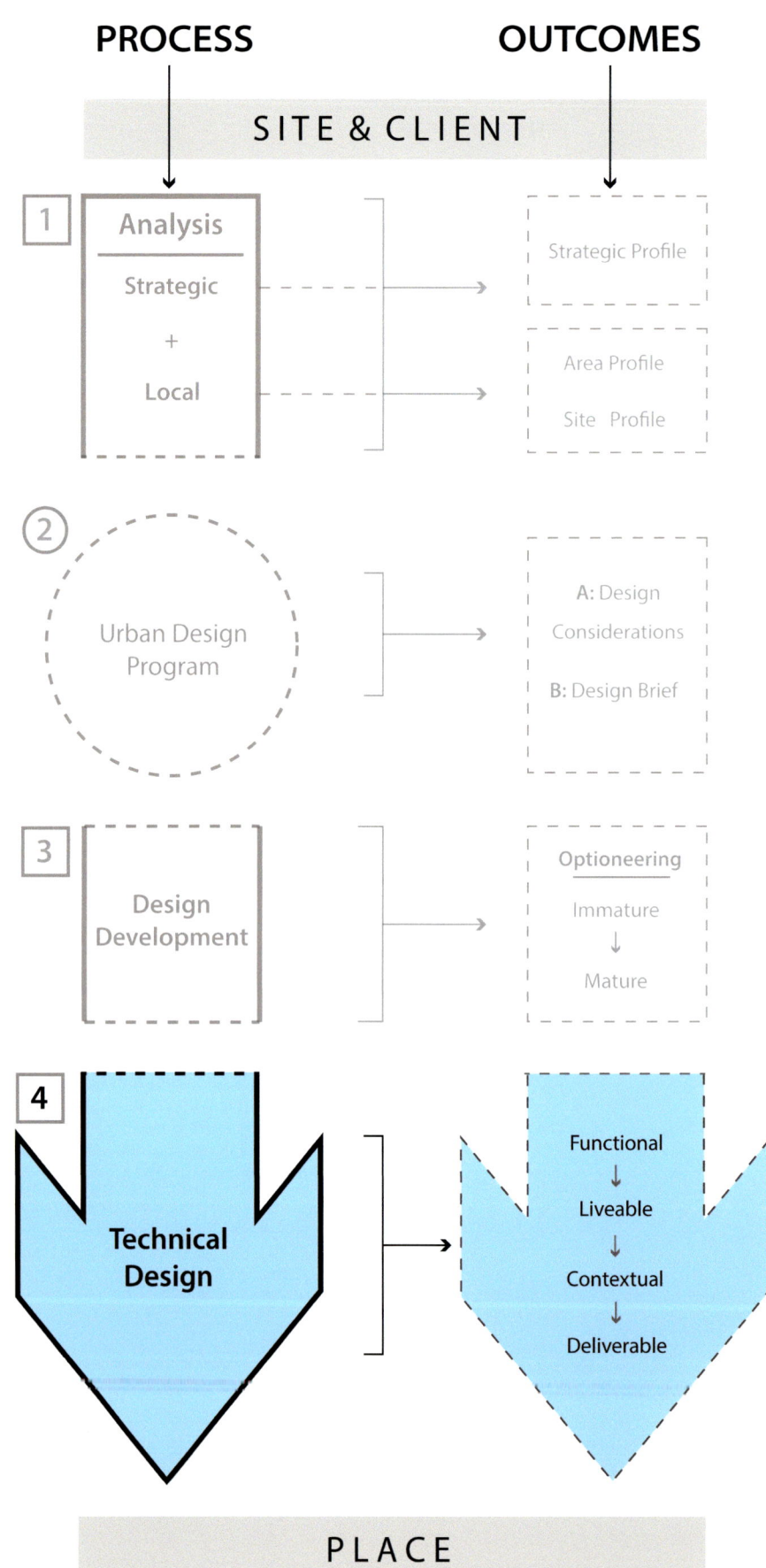

→ Optioneering
   Immature
   ↓
   Mature

4 Technical Design

→ Functional
   ↓
   Liveable
   ↓
   Contextual
   ↓
   Deliverable

PLACE

CHAPTER 9: TECHNICAL DESIGN   214

CHAPTER 9
Technical Design

Chapter 8 (Design Development) set out a process for design optioneering – yet to comprehensively produce design options and a resultant final design proposal – the practitioner needs to understand how to deliver **'Technical Design'**. A final urban design project must ensure it is contextual, functional, liveable, and technically feasible – to accomplish this urban designers' must be able to effectively 'structure' design – utilising the functional blueprints (*see* 4.3); and critically deliver quality (*see* 4.2) through detailed human-scaled design. This chapter unpacks both structural and detailed design – providing a series of key considerations for designers to contemplate, and advocating human scaled interventions be tailored around 3 '*super-components*' – the **urban block; public realm;** and **green infrastructure**. Throughout the chapter the case studies of Manchester and Aalborg will continue to illustrate these elements of design visually – demonstrating how they can be applied in real-world settings and contexts.

OPPOSITE PAGE: The final step of the AUD Framework - Step 4 considers the Technical Design - how to structure place and provide the human-scaled design detail to ensure a high quality and deliverable solution.

9.1 STRUCTURAL DESIGN [FUNCTIONALITY]

The functional blueprints provided in chapter 4 provide the 12 core design layers that make up a functional real-world urban design project. The '*network*' and '*arrangement*' blueprint layers can be viewed as the scaffold that ensures any design is workable in reality - without an effective scaffold, places will potentially fail to deliver an optimal experience for people, in how they use a place or move from one place to another. Poorly structured urban design will not deliver quality connections or ease of movement, and if places are difficult to access or illegible then they can struggle to provide environments that are economically viable or sustainable.

The upsurge of vehicular highways within a number of global cities in response to the rapid emergence of the automobile – brought about enhanced connectivity between a limited number of spaces, that these highways linked, at the expense of walkability and connectivity at a human scale. Cities like Glasgow introduced highways through often historic suburbs to better connect the outskirts of the city and beyond to the centre – yet in doing so split existing communities apart by destroying local permeability. Such design fails to provide inclusive movement opportunities and does not function positively for those who have been neglected in the decision-making process. Such an example is a useful warning of the pitfalls of failing to design contextually across the scales, and failing to deliver solutions that work for all people and their circumstances. Should utility infrastructure, such as gas, water, electrics, be disconnected or fragmented they simply cease to operate as intended – cities and places are not dissimilar, they fail to operate close to their potential or capacity if they are functionally fragmented in their layout.

GLASGOW's M8
Glasgow, Scotland had its inner ring road constructed across 2 phases - in 1964 and 1972. The three lane Charing Cross section cut through the historic neighbourhood of the same name. Prior to construction Charing Cross had a strong grid pattern with clear route hierarchies and permeability north-south and east-west. The M8 cut through this creating 2 disconnected districts that each fail to provide local communities with necessary legibility and sustainable mobility choices.

LEFT: Glasgow's M8 at rush hour - cutting through the centre of the city - splitting the historic neighbourhood of Charing Cross.

A failure to structure urban design that is intuitive for people to use and move within has consequences that can lead to the destruction of neighbourhoods and communities, the failure of economic revenues such as retail and leisure, and significant decreases in the physical and mental wellbeing of populations - amongst many other potential negative impacts. Design that fails to allow for quality access to green spaces for all residents in society, that promotes unsustainable vehicular movement, that pollutes and increases pedestrian fatalities, that does not think through access to key retail facilities, or that fails to provide safe and equitable spaces, is failing to function successfully. For design to work, not only within the red-line boundary of a site, but beyond into the wider surroundings, it must carefully ensure that the functional aspects are considered and reconciled.

The best places are designed to ensure that the networks delivered are inclusive, sustainable, and well connected – this does not only include routes, but also public realm, and green infrastructure. These networks are there to move people and goods effectively and efficiently - and therefore the arrangement of an urban environment must be precisely considered and delivered to work in harmony with the networks provided. The land uses, frontages, access and service, how urban blocks are organised, all contribute to the functional structure of place. It is in the balance of these functional blueprints that successful urban design begins to emerge - they lay the foundation of the human scale detail that will elevate **functional design** into **high quality liveable design**. It is important when engaging with the layout of any design that the designer makes some critical considerations to optimise functionality. Across the functional blueprints - in particular those within the network and arrangement themes - deliberate on how to **manipulate** movement and activity, provide necessary **separation** and clear **hierarchies**, and carefully consider site and other relevant **edge conditions**.

BELOW: Design structured around the movement of the automobile can directly lead to environments that pollute, and increase pedestrian deaths given the difficulty for people crossing.

CHAPTER 9: TECHNICAL DESIGN

216

MANIPULATION

When an architect designs a building, they do so with the intention that it will function and be used in a particular way - the design is only operating at its optimum when people act as the designer intended. Urban design shares this trait. Places are designed environments that require several factors to be successful. The city of Brasilia, designed by Lucio Costa and Oscar Niemeyer was designed from the ground up to be the new capital city for Brazil – a new model of urban design and city living. The city however has failed to deliver a well-connected and sustainable environment - blighted with traffic, fragmentation, and resultant social issues. Niemeyer stated that he had designed the utopian city, what was required was society re-organising how it lives and operates to make it work as intended. To expect such compliance and re-organisation was ambitious. Society has behaved in urban places in much the same ways throughout history – the most successful urban spaces today often are the oldest, those developed around sustainable walking patterns and mixed use. To anticipate a societal shift to meet a new model of design is to misunderstand the purpose of designing – design should be self-intuitive, allowing people to use spaces and move between them without deep thought or complexity. The role of the designer therefore is to firstly understand how people want, and need, to use design, and to deliver a product that effectively enables this to the highest level possible.

When a designer has a deeper appreciation for how successful places work and are used by people - and develops a clear understanding for what local communities within a particular context want and need within their urban environments – they have the ammunition to shape more appropriate contextual places that focus on the end user. This information enables designers to '**manipulate**' how people will move in and through environments - stage-managing how their design will be engaged with in practice by those it is intended for. Bill Hiller's *'space syntax'* theories consider how the spatial organisation of urban design may be focused on human spatial behaviours – and that these behaviours can be heavily influenced by design measures implemented. Managing how people will make journeys, and considering different modal transport options, is critical, and the urban designer must ensure networks and arrangements are organised to create more user friendly, sustainable, and legible movement patterns.

TOP: The city of Brasilia - designed by Lucio Costa and Oscar Niemeyer.

BOTTOM: Riga, Latvia - The historic old town offers a high-quality pedestrian experience.

APPLIED URBAN DESIGN

It is also important for the urban designer to create spaces that enable users to access easily key amenities and services – core liveable necessities such as banking, retail, leisure, healthcare etc. And that when places are delivered to accommodate these services that they are designed in such a manner as to engineer ease of usage and comfort. Jan Gehl (1987), the renowned Danish architect and urban designer, argued that all urban spaces should consider three categories of activities.

1. Necessary activities – the provision of everyday requirements, getting to work, school, or the grocery store – the types of activity that are necessary year-long and through all weather, and circumstances.

2. Optional activities – ensuring that design provides more than the bare necessities and offers communities activities they desire to engage with for their wellbeing and enjoyment, such as cafes, parks, and retail.

3. Social activities – designing environments in such ways that people will feel comfortable and linger – spaces where people will choose to meet and socialise and activate an environment, often these can be spontaneous in nature.

Designing in such ways is another form of *'manipulating'* (in a positive manner) how people will behave within a given urban design – seeking to offer more than the minimum needs to encourage resultant activities that will evolve naturally, those activities and uses that are conditioned by the physical setting of the space itself.

LEFT: In 2009, Times Square, New York was transformed from vehicular interchange to pedestrianised zone - resulting in an instantaneous change in how people use the space - with movement no longer the main priority as people linger to enjoy the street performers and make use of the street furniture to rest and take-in the sights and sounds of the city.

BOTTOM: Well-designed places think about how users will not only access the necessary functions for everyday life - but will consider the social aspect of place and deliver environments that encourage people to stay outdoors. Warsaw, Poland.

CHAPTER 9: TECHNICAL DESIGN   218

SEPARATION

Successful design must consider how best, and when, to separate effectively as well as connect. Whilst this appears an oxymoron, designers must appreciate that urban environments have complex layers that must work together in balance but operate with targeted segregation in practice. Connectivity is core to all urban design – yet there is a critical need to understand that design requires different forms of mobility – separating vehicle users from pedestrians is vital for safety and comfort, segregating public realm from service and storage is necessary to maintain high quality spaces and streets that remain uncluttered and pleasant. The provision of quality retail streets and/or leisure/pleasure focused public spaces requires the urban designer to include cafes, restaurants, bars, shops and other building uses that command a particular servicing need to function. Such buildings/uses need deliveries, bin storage, rear access, even parking – all elements that if shared with the space intended for public use can cause conflict.

Urban designers must aim to **segregate** service from public realm where possible – this involves the shrinking of open and accessible public space in any given design. Providing dedicated space to 'hide' away necessary service, allows for the public facing spaces to remain clutter free and people focused. In tandem with the point made prior on '**manipulation**' – by managing how people move and the spaces they uses within a design, a designer can ensure that the segregated servicing needs are not competing or conflicting with the core movement and activity plans. The most successful designs provide such segregation within an overarching connected structure – and this can be achieved through the use of **hierarchies**, where all spaces and streets are not created equal in regards their intended use, but rather they are considered as simply parts of a wider whole that come together to deliver better urban design.

IMAGES: The separation of simple things such as cycle parking from pedestrian movement corridors can help with the clarity of an environment and ease of movement for users. Many cities were originally designed and laid out without consideration for cycling provision - and any significant uptake in this form of transport brings subsequent demands for urban storage facilities. La Rochelle, France [TOP] has a high percentage of modal share for cycling, but parking can become an issue on main streets and routes - whilst Delft, Netherlands (BOTTOM) has newly integrated cycle parking across the public realm - often targeted around main retail and/or transport hubs - resulting in a less cluttered and more pleasant urban environment.

HIERARCHIES

Hierarchies in urban design should not be confused as designers placing levels of importance on particular elements or facets of a design. The role of hierarchies in a design are intended to order more effectively similar components such as routes, spaces, parks etc. to enable better understanding of their specific role or purpose within the wider context of a particular place. If urban design is to be truly contextual in nature – it must be fully connected and integrated across the scales. Spaces, uses, and streets should not compete with one another, but compliment and support one another – and to do this there must be a recognition of how each of these design components are working individually as well as collectively.

Creating hierarchies of routes, public realm, and green infrastructure allows designers to therefore categorise roles and uses. A hierarchy of public spaces can assist in defining not only the primary activities offered by each space – but can also define the scale spaces will potentially operate at in practice (regional, city, local etc.) – this allows for design of such spaces to be tailored for the possible footfall it may receive – a city-scale urban plaza will often be larger in size and attract more users than a local quieter public space for example. A city-scale retail space will also likely be in a central location and well connected to transport links and pedestrian flow – ensuring it receives the high number of users to make the space feasible. For this to be successful the pedestrian and public transport links to this space must be placed at the top of the movement hierarchy to cope with such use and numbers.

The routes within an urban environment will also provide different users with different modal options to move around their environments. Key arterial routes will be flagged for moving large volumes of traffic and catering for a wide range of modal options. At the lower end of the hierarchy of routes will be local streets that allow people to access homes and local services. These will not require the same volume of traffic and will necessitate a very different design approach. **Hierarchies** allow designers to both **manipulate** movement and activity – and provide the necessary **separation** between conflicting uses to ensure higher quality and more legible environments for people. Those spaces and routes that fall at the lower end of the hierarchies are no less important to successful urban design than the top hierarchy components. It is in the combination, and the successful delivery across the hierarchical range, that great places can emerge allowing for a diversity of offering and movement that people can easily understand and utilise.

Most urban designs are being implemented within existing cities and environments – quality design seeks to integrate itself effectively – to do this it is imperative that designers have a sound understanding of the existing hierarchies and how they operate – ensuring their design proposals support the contextual realities, and enhance them. It is also possible for design to begin to engender change in what is given precedence in place – environments that have historically prioritised the automobile in designing can promote new design interventions that shift that precedence towards more sustainable forms of mobility. It is such approaches that drive more contextually responsive solutions and interventions.

IMAGES: Hierarchies of public spaces are critical to ensure all possible uses and needs are met - In Venice, Italy San Marco (TOP) is the largest Plaza - offering a wide array of activities for tourists. Yet local residents of the islands will often be found populating one of the many smaller 'local' spaces (BOTTOM) that provide a refuge from the tourist throngs - and provide key local amenity and facilities.

EDGE CONDITIONS

The most common edge condition that urban designers will deal with is where the red-line boundary of their site is drawn – that transition from site to wider urban fabric. Under most design circumstances the red-boundary line around a site represents the permitted developable area of land – beyond this the urban designer will have little control over design alterations or interventions. To effectively integrate any proposed design within the site, the design proposals must carefully consider how the new interventions meet directly with the existing surrounding environment. This might be defined by a street, space, or even building line. It is this immediate edge condition where urban designers can have most influence, given the visual primacy of their proposal adjacent or in conjunction with the surroundings. However, too often poor urban design looks inward – to the interior of the developable site – failing to recognise the key transitions that are in action connecting to the wider scale. To achieve contextually connected placemaking these transitions are of vital importance. For a design to work within its setting – or to positively influence both its existing environment and future developments – it must be designed in such a manner as to openly accept its role and responsibilities as part of the wider urban form.

However, edge conditions often mean more than even the red-line boundary of any given site. Edge conditions exist where any transition occurs – be this within or beyond the urban designer's particular site. They are the interfaces between design elements – natural and built; private and public; between neighbourhoods; land uses; typologies; design materials; character; social territories; hierarchies; and where segregation is deliberately designed (see previous section). These edges are zones of transition and require special attention on behalf of the urban designer – when environments that have differing priorities meet, tension can occur. Quality design attempts to create spaces defined positively by the relationship and interconnection that can exist – rather than definition and separation (unless such segregation is a necessary design feature – as previously discussed). Without proper attention these edges can result in barriers that reduce the quality of movement, legibility, and divide places rather than stitching them together. High quality edge conditions are an essential ingredient of providing transparency of place and space – the ability of people to simultaneously perceive and understand different spatial conditions innately and comfortably.

FUNCTIONAL DESIGN – Examples

We will make use of our 2 live case studies in Manchester, UK and Aalborg, Denmark to illustrate how to deliver the *functional blueprints* of an urban design proposal. The following commentary is intended to showcase how particular key blueprints can be communicated effectively to a broad audience – but also critically the complexity of each and how they work together in a complex and multi-layered fashion to make the design work in practice.

LIVERPOOL ONE, UK

The construction of a new retail, residential, and leisure complex in Liverpool involved the redevelopment of 42 acres of land in the city centre. The design was focused on an open-air concept that was integrated into the existing streets of the city centre - extending the network of pedestrian movement infrastructure and adding a range of new high-quality public realm provision. This urban design approach not only connected with the city, but also re-opened historic barriers to the waterfront. When large-footprint retail-led developments are delivered they often create negative edge conditions with their surroundings, given their scale and internally focused design - Liverpool One bucked this trend by knitting itself into the urban fabric already in place.

LEFT: Liverpool One was opened in 2008 and was developed by Grosvenor Group.

APPLIED URBAN DESIGN

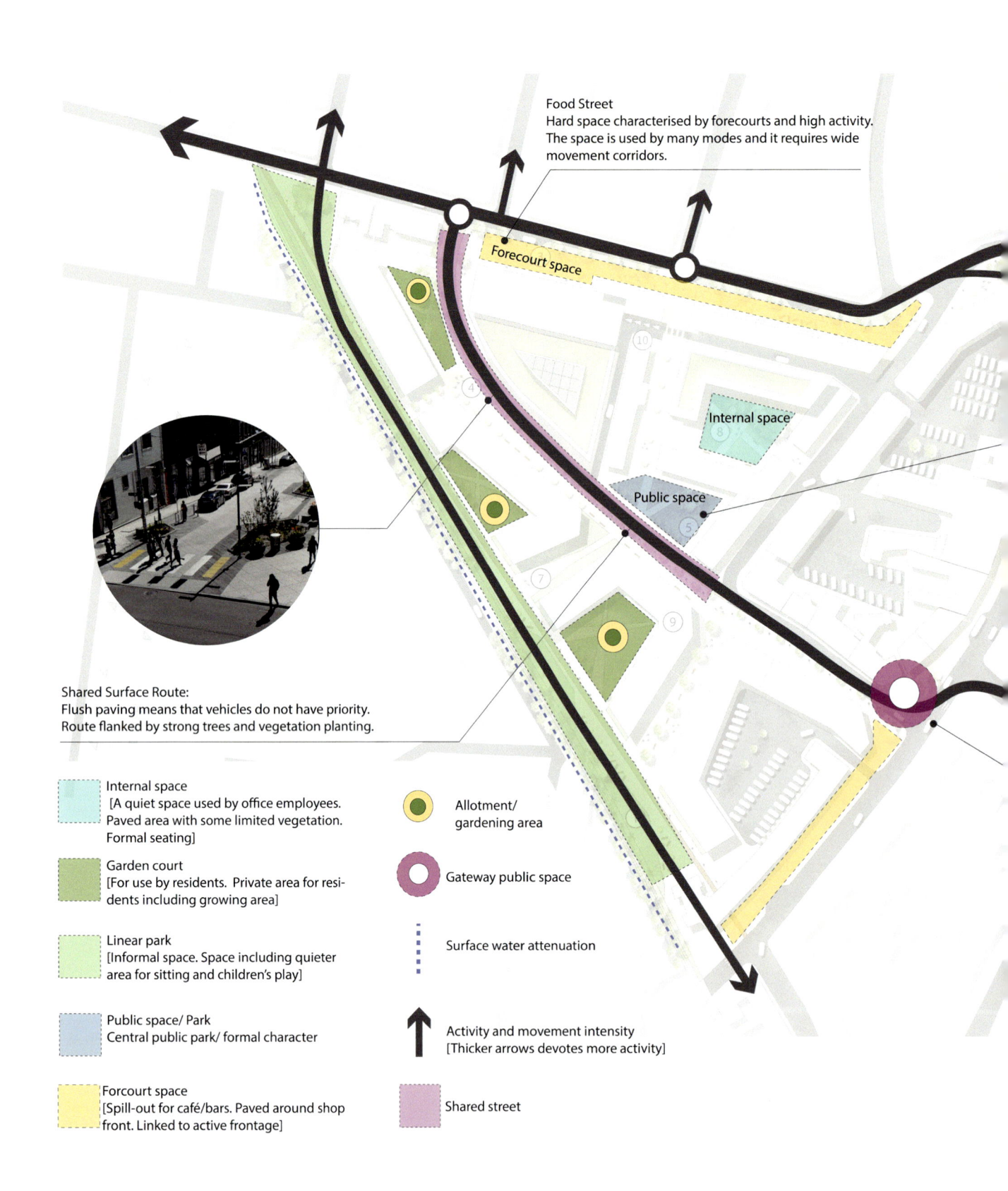

Food Street
Hard space characterised by forecourts and high activity. The space is used by many modes and it requires wide movement corridors.

Forecourt space

Internal space

Public space

Shared Surface Route:
Flush paving means that vehicles do not have priority. Route flanked by strong trees and vegetation planting.

- **Internal space**
  [A quiet space used by office employees. Paved area with some limited vegetation. Formal seating]

- **Garden court**
  [For use by residents. Private area for residents including growing area]

- **Linear park**
  [Informal space. Space including quieter area for sitting and children's play]

- **Public space/ Park**
  Central public park/ formal character

- **Forcourt space**
  [Spill-out for café/bars. Paved around shop front. Linked to active frontage]

- Allotment/ gardening area

- Gateway public space

- Surface water attenuation

- Activity and movement intensity
  [Thicker arrows devotes more activity]

- Shared street

AALBORG
Public Realm and Green Infrastructure

CHAPTER 9: TECHNICAL DESIGN

222

Public Park:
Publicly accessible space which is formally set out. Including formal planting.

Eastern Gateway:
Existing buildings and public art, including existing Goose Girl Sculpture, can be integrated into this new space. Important to design space to reinforce movement flow.

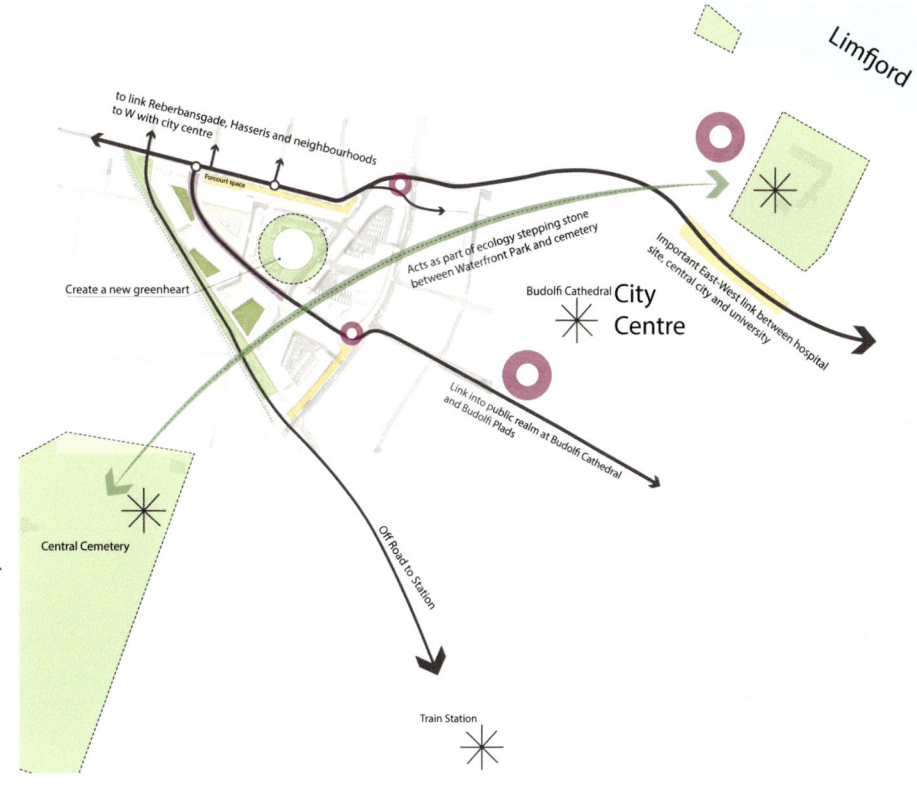

This spread includes two diagrams that have been designed to showcase the approach taken to **Green Space and Public Realm** within the Aalborg case study site. The larger of the two diagrams is specifically focused on the site itself, presenting an annotated and marked up version of the layout plan. It clearly identifies the different types of hard and soft spaces that are to be created. Images are provided from best practice exemplars to help convey to the reader the nature and potential *'feel'* of these future spaces. The images also demonstrate a clear design choice – specifically the transition of spaces north to south. As you move south and west through the site the environments alter from loud to quiet, from hard to soft, and from public to intimate. However, the design approach can only be fully appreciated when considered at the area scale. The smaller diagram shows how the site provides a new *'stepping stone'* green infrastructure link between the large semi-naturalistic space at the central cemetery and the smaller collection of parks and spaces by the waterfront and Slotsparken. This diagram also shows how the routes created through the site connect into the wider networks of public realm towards the main retail core (northernmost route), the medieval city (the central route) and the railway station (the southernmost route).

APPLIED URBAN DESIGN

The diagram on this page is based around a straightforward **Land Use** plan, and at first glance illustrates to the reader the land uses that are proposed within the new and existing buildings on the site. This highlights that the site is roughly broken down into three land use zones which are elaborated on within the diagram and the associated annotations – a mixed use office-led zone to the east connecting into the city centre A and D); a residential quarter to the south-west linking to the residential neighbourhoods beyond (C); and an upgraded 'Food Street' and retail use along Reberbansgade to the north (B)serving the site as well as the residential neighbourhoods to the north. This is a clear response to the spatial concept produced as part of the Urban Design Program (*see* Page 190). However, the 2D plan does not provide all the detail required – and is therefore supplemented with an expanded key/legend which focuses on the four key areas within the design proposal. This key/legend provides further details on the function and scale of the development proposed. It is also colour coded using the same land use palette as the main plan to allow the reader to better assimilate the information and design rationale.

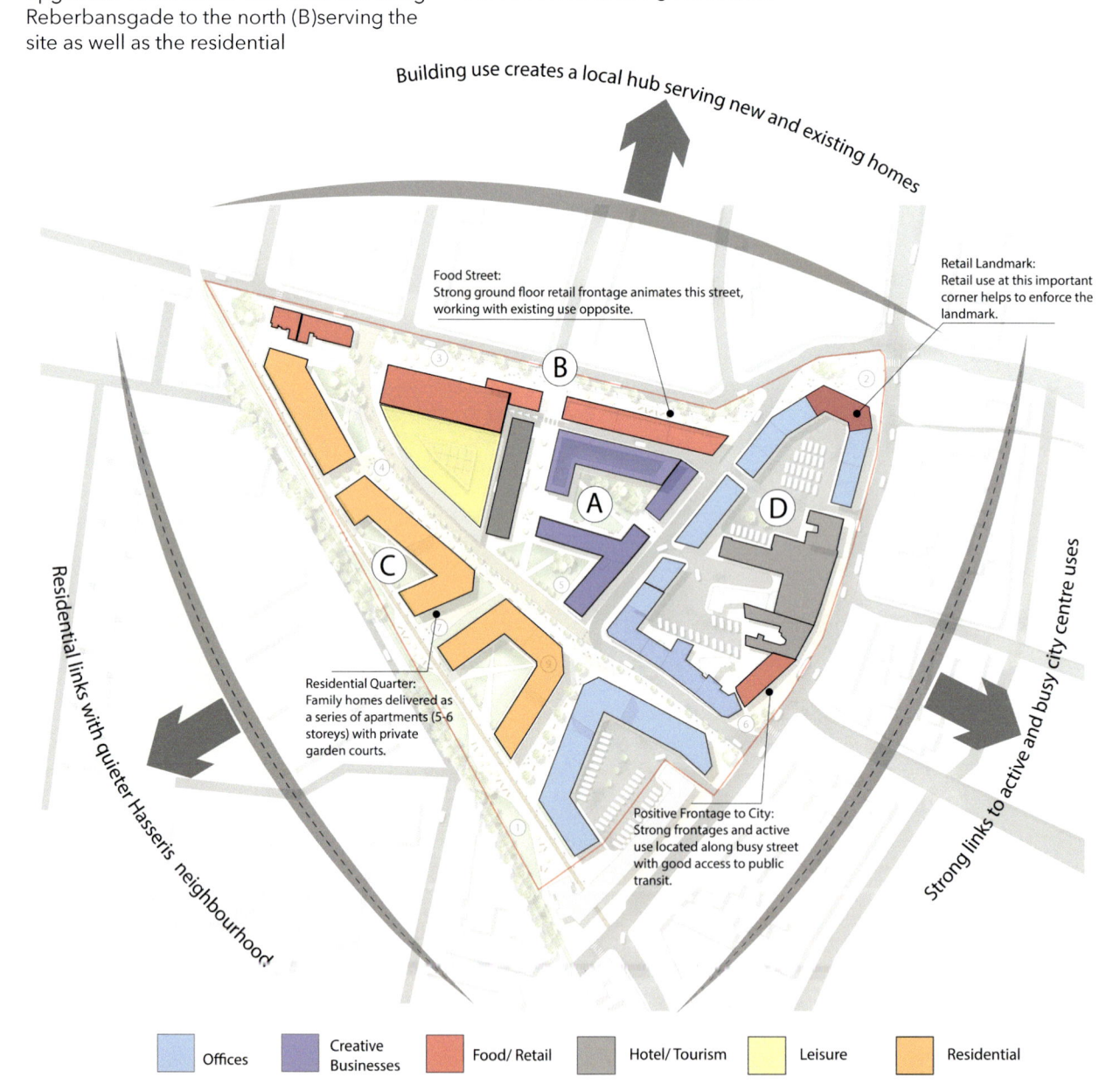

Building use creates a local hub serving new and existing homes

Food Street:
Strong ground floor retail frontage animates this street, working with existing use opposite.

Retail Landmark:
Retail use at this important corner helps to enforce the landmark.

Residential Quarter:
Family homes delivered as a series of apartments (5-6 storeys) with private garden courts.

Positive Frontage to City:
Strong frontages and active use located along busy street with good access to public transit.

Residential links with quieter Hasseris neighbourhood

Strong links to active and busy city centre uses

Offices | Creative Businesses | Food/ Retail | Hotel/ Tourism | Leisure | Residential

AALBORG
Land Use and Density

CHAPTER 9: TECHNICAL DESIGN

A Business Incubators

- Reuse of the existing buildings for small scale workshops and office space, suitable for a variety of different uses. Designed to be flexible and allow for short term or flexible accommodation for SMEs

- Units or offices have minimal fit out to allow for customisation to keep the rents affordable. Opportunities for share facilities such as meeting rooms or resources such as receptions or IT systems.

- Reuse the existing historical buildings that are currently in office and administration use by the hospital so there should be very little adaptation required.

B Food Street

- Building on the existing mix of retail and food related uses on Reberbansgade, to create a vibrant mixed use street that has retail use, but with a strong focus on food and drink (including evening economy)

- New smaller units are provided to the south of the street, that will be suitable and attractive for small cafes, bars and takeaway uses, provided with a large forecourt space to the front that can be used for outdoor dining.

- Above the ground floor a series of additional flexible uses could also be accommodated including offices and leisure uses, however, given it is unlikely that residential uses would be compatible.

- New murals to be implemented to compliment existing street art across the neighbourhood.

C Residential

- The new residential quarter is based around a land use concept of high-density apartment living built to between 4 and 6 storeys. The apartments will be provided with generous internal space and would be attractive to families.

- The apartments are coupled with a small private garden court for amenity purposes, as well as possible local growing spaces for fruit and vegetables, reimagining the historic 'kitchen garden' vernacular of the site's past. Certain apartments or buildings could allow for co-living environments.

- The apartments are not to be provided with significant parking given that the site is close to shops, services and public transport. Area for cycle and personal storage could be provided as part of the wider residential apartments. These are standard in the DK contex.

- Design works with Aalborg municipalities promotion of sustainable mobilities and creation of parking nodes at key intervals across the city.

D Mixed Use Blocks

- This mixed-use block adjacent to the city centre is designed to act as a land use transition from the heavy commercial and retail uses in the city centre and the wider range of uses found elsewhere on the site.

- Offices and retail uses dominate the frontage along main north south route, which reflects the presence of Bus Rapid Transit and opportunities for significant passing trade.

- The existing Phønix hotel (a heritage asset) is retained within this mixed use block to add to the urban vibrancy in this location. The adjacent uses being compatible with the frequent comings and goings associated with it.

APPLIED URBAN DESIGN

This urban design masterplan diagram shows the location and nature of the routes within the Manchester case study and the **Movement** they are designed to stimulate. It is typical of the information that might accompany a project of this size, providing *'scaffold'* on which to impart additional information. Here the key diagram, which shows all the routes to be created, splits these into a simple four level hierarchy, each of which is provided in a different colour and accompanied by a colour co-ordinated box that provides further information on how the detailed design of these routes should be considered.

It would be impossible to showcase the detailed designs for each and every one of these routes (something that is common with every large-scale masterplan). However, the hierarchy diagram is supported by three carefully selected cross-sections taken from various points within the masterplan. These cross sections provide further information on how the design ideas showcased in the hierarchy diagram might be delivered on site.

It is important to note that sections B-B and C-C both show streets that are the same level within the hierarchy (pedestrian connectors), however the design has responded to the specific characteristics of the location to create slightly different designs. Section A-A provides the layout for the main new route through the centre of the site – the green corridor.

PRIMARY CONNECTOR
- Two major connections into city centre - re-developed Oldham Road with multi-modal transport optionality and strong bus network - and a newly established green central corridor that draws through the new development.

- Two key west - east primary links - the existing south edge of the site (Inner Ring Road) and expanded Livesey Street through the civic heart of the site and onto newly established Oldham Road retail hub and Miles Platting.

SECONDARY CONNECTOR
- Series of key routes providing access across site - with Sudell Street linking towards city centre transport hub of Victoria - and Osbourne Street extended eastwards to link Collyhurst with Miles Platting.

- A number of secondary streets (to the south and west) link into the city centre route network - This enhances permeability and reinforces the grid structure.

CHAPTER 9: TECHNICAL DESIGN

226

LOCAL CONNECTOR
- A number of more localised movement paths predominately delivered to provide service and access to all blocks/buildings.
- Enhances overall permeability and providing local movement options within the hierarchy.

PEDESTRIANS CONNECTOR
- All routes have dedicated pedestrian provision - but provision of pedestrian only routes enhances safety, promotes sustainability, and reduces pollution.
- Primarily located in north-east of site to support new residential offering - creating a quieter environment for residents.

Primary connector

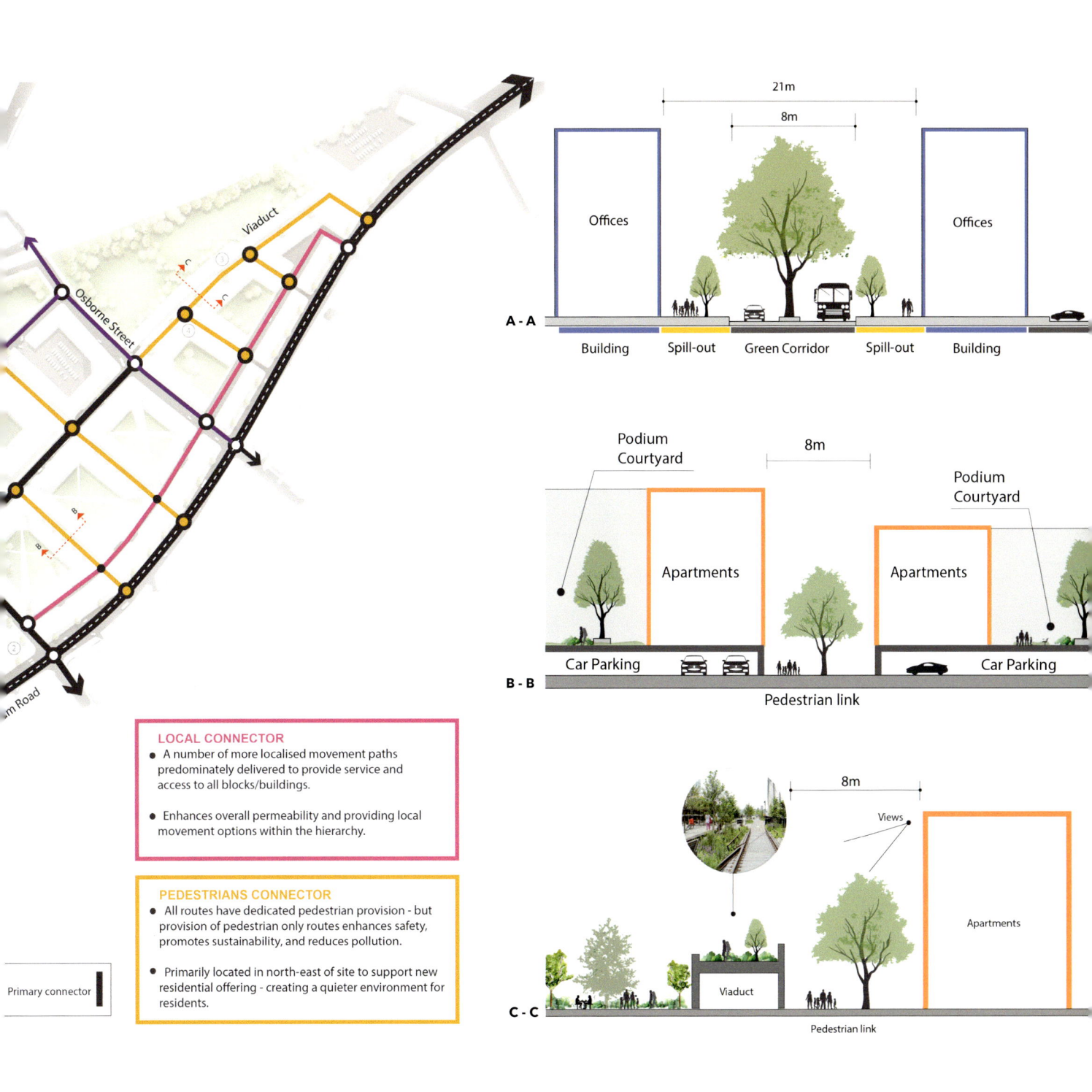

A - A
Building | Spill-out | Green Corridor | Spill-out | Building
21m / 8m

B - B
Car Parking | Apartments (Podium Courtyard) | Apartments (Podium Courtyard) | Car Parking
Pedestrian link
8m

C - C
Viaduct | Apartments
Views
8m
Pedestrian link

MANCHESTER
Movement

APPLIED URBAN DESIGN

Understanding fully how a design will function in the real world is a vital part of the design process. This spread seeks to set out how the **Service, Access, and Frontage** will function collectively to ensure that the urban blocks meet the key principles associated with their success.

The key service routes to each of the urban blocks are marked in grey, using a simple hierarchy (the wider the line the more important the service route). These will allow access to every block for the collection of refuse, deliveries, and for emergency access (fire, ambulance etc). Not every route through the site is required for servicing however, allowing a variety of different approaches to the public realm to be taken where vehicular access is not required (or is restricted).

Dedicated services spaces are shown where the land use of the surrounding blocks is typically identified as being active (cafes, bars, retail etc) and as such rear servicing is the preferred choice. Small arrows on the plan show where the entrances, or building access, could be provided from the surrounding public space. In all cases, the interior of the urban blocks is identified as being private or semi-private to allow access/usage exclusively for those living and working in the new neighbourhood.

Urban block offices:
Frontages and accesses onto surrounding streets. Internal private courtyard spaces providing quality environment for employees.

Existing grid pattern:
Buildings adhering to urban perimeter block principles. Grid pattern allowing for front servicing to continue.

CHAPTER 9: TECHNICAL DESIGN   228

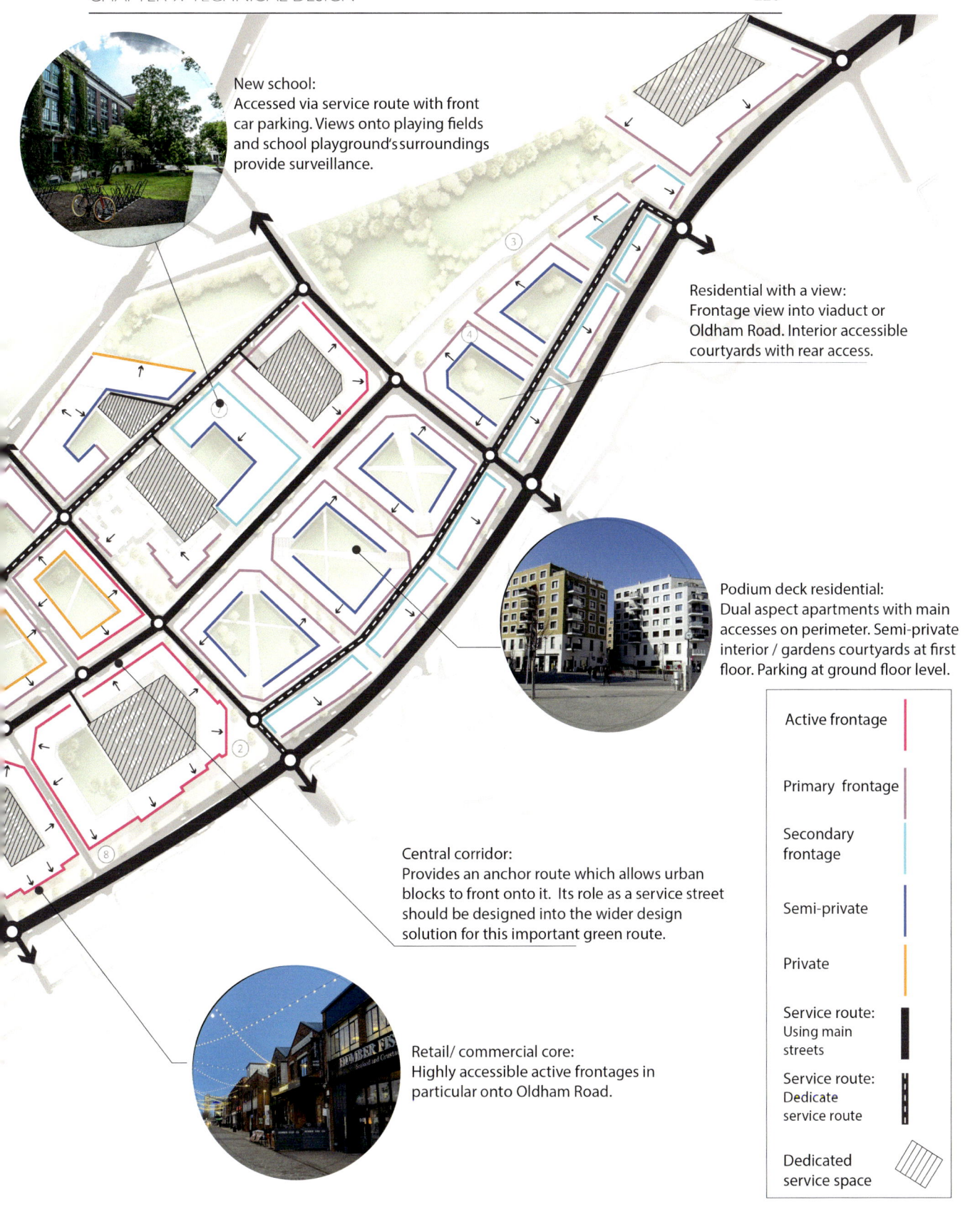

New school:
Accessed via service route with front car parking. Views onto playing fields and school playground's surroundings provide surveillance.

Residential with a view:
Frontage view into viaduct or Oldham Road. Interior accessible courtyards with rear access.

Podium deck residential:
Dual aspect apartments with main accesses on perimeter. Semi-private interior / gardens courtyards at first floor. Parking at ground floor level.

Central corridor:
Provides an anchor route which allows urban blocks to front onto it. Its role as a service street should be designed into the wider design solution for this important green route.

Retail/ commercial core:
Highly accessible active frontages in particular onto Oldham Road.

Legend:
- Active frontage
- Primary frontage
- Secondary frontage
- Semi-private
- Private
- Service route: Using main streets
- Service route: Dedicate service route
- Dedicated service space

MANCHESTER
Service / Access / Frontage

9.2 DETAILED DESIGN [HUMAN SCALE]

DESIGNING FOR LIVEABILITY

By this point of the design process the urban designer will have prepared a **functional blueprint** for the design. The design will have been robustly tested and evaluated to ensure that it not only responds to the key urban design principles but meets the Urban Design Program (Step 2 – and Chapter 7).

The design proposal will remain relatively high level and lacking the detail that would ensure the **liveable aspects** (see 4.2) necessary for quality – these are often achieved by turning attention to more human scaled design. The AUD Framework allows for a final stage of design development – the detail – which begins to address this.

We will present across three '*super-components*' that allow the practitioner to explore and present the human scaled design that focuses on quality and character. They are presented in the order in which they could be most effectively considered by the urban designer in the first instance, however, in practice they may be tackled in parallel. There are:

1. The Urban Block
2. Public Realm
3. Green Infrastructure

All three of these are also specific urban design layers (see 4.3), but each also offers detailed design opportunities to provide a transition from the structural/functional to human scaled. These three super-components also allow for the remaining layers to be effectively considered and integrated at this detailed level. This does not mean that any additional priority, or importance is afforded to these three super-components, rather they offer a gateway into exploring the remaining nine.

This section is focused on exploring how these three super components can be effectively considered, at the detailed level, to ensure that contextually responsive design is achieved. The section ends with a careful consideration as to how practitioners might usefully design appropriately for long-term quality and success. All design will require structured and bespoke management – for how it will function mid-long term – but crucially how it will be effectively maintained to avoid disrepair and continue to operate, and look, at its best all year round, and year-to-year.

The goal of this stage of the design is to consider how the places that are designed can be inclusive, sustainable, and people centred. This requires the urban designer to ask questions such as how the space or place would be experienced differently by different ages or those with mobility issues, how it would encourage the use of sustainable modes of transport (walking, cycling, public transport) or even how vibrancy and activity can be created.

Without this level of detail, designs can be technically functional but lack the vibrancy and useability that creates quality. In short, one cannot exist without the other – the functional blueprints and the liveable quality side-by-side.

9.3 THE URBAN BLOCK

IMPORTANCE OF THE URBAN BLOCK

The block (often referred to as the urban block or perimeter block) is an urban design layer that underpins many of the world's most successful places. They can be made up of several different buildings, uses and corners. In that respect blocks connect with, and directly relate to, almost every one of the remaining 11 urban design layers. No other layer or principle is so interconnected. In this respect, this is the first of the three 'super components' that is considered as it will significantly impact on those that follow.

A single urban block will never exist in isolation, and whilst an urban designer may only be responsible for designing one or two blocks, even these will be part of an urban area that includes other urban blocks, streets, and spaces. In this respect, regardless of the size of the project that is being delivered, it is vital to understand how the adjacent blocks (the edge conditions) function. This is where the detailed analysis undertaken and outlined in chapter 6 becomes particularly useful. Any newly designed urban block will have to take account of the surrounding land uses, the frontage, access, and privacy enjoyed by adjacent buildings and respond to existing

OPPOSITE TOP: Urban blocks in Paris, France are surrounded on all sides by routes - with the buildings shaping the blocks defining these routes and their enclosure.

OPPOSITE BOTTOM: Urban blocks do not always form a grid or come rectilinear in shape - in Paris, France again we can see triangular grids that still meet the core principles of the perimeter block.

CHAPTER 9: TECHNICAL DESIGN   230

active frontages, heights, and servicing requirements. The variety and flexibility of the urban block allows for a myriad of details to be effectively accommodated within the detailed design stage.

PRINCIPLES OF THE URBAN BLOCK
The design of urban blocks requires an understanding of the core principles that define them. These principles, outlined below, should be considered and followed in the design of every block:

1. Surrounded by routes: As previously noted, the urban block is also interchangeably known as a 'perimeter block' – as this nomenclature suggests, blocks will have a continuous outer boundary, or perimeter, that faces onto surrounding routes. Urban blocks may define these routes – and can often be created by the space between them. Some of these routes will be set to meet objectives and actions within a Program (*see* Chapter 7), others, will be secondary, and will be defined simply because they will relate to and serve the urban blocks. When setting out the pattern of urban blocks on any given site, it will often be necessary to create a series of additional routes. These routes do not always need to be vehicular routes, but they will all need to be enclosed and fronted by buildings. At least one of these routes will need to function as service route, allowing access for larger vehicles (at the very least refuse vehicles and emergency services), but the urban designer is free to explore different priorities for other routes.

2. Not always rectilinear or a grid: Most examples of good urban blocks show these as a rectilinear form, set out in a strict grid pattern. Whilst this is appropriate for some urban design, especially in more dense urban contexts, there is no requirement for this to be the case. Blocks can be irregularly shaped usually with somewhere between 3 and 6 sides. These irregular shapes will often be created to allow the blocks to accommodate local features such as existing routes or green spaces that have been identified as part of the analysis. It is also important to include any retained buildings into an urban block which is another reason why irregular forms may occur. Irregular shaped blocks are not necessarily a bad thing, they can add to an area's character, identity, or even aid legibility within the townscape. However, there can be clear efficiency in delivering a strong urban grid – as a way of building cities, it has endured in various forms since the first urban environments were created and populated.

3. Private interior / Public exterior: The outer perimeter of the urban block, which will have a direct relationship with the street and public realm, is made up of the fronts of buildings – shaping the block. These buildings, laid out in this block format, will have their rears facing naturally into the centre of the block. This inner space, framed by the backs of the buildings, often becomes the private interior. This duality of public exterior / private interior provides flexibility for the urban designer in how the block will function. Should the buildings within a given block require dedicated servicing (i.e., retail / food) then this can be provided within the private interior, with access to all the buildings' rear entrances (*see* Point 5).

If, however, the block is predominantly residential – or office use – then this interior can deliver semi-private space for people. The interior of blocks can, under the correct circumstances and building functions, even be made publicly accessible – and include movement corridors. The exterior of the block will therefore have to function as frontage and should include the main entrances and exits from the buildings. It is important to consider whether there are opportunities for delivering active frontage especially where blocks are placed along key routes.

4. Standard block sizes: Urban blocks can vary in size and are defined as the distance between the streets surrounding the block. When designing blocks, take care to respond to the local character of an area – how big are the plots and blocks currently in a town or city? Small blocks create too many routes and will undermine legibility, blocks which are too large create an impermeable neighbourhood with a lack of choice of routes. Portland, USA utilises block sizes of only 50 or 60 metres in any direction, whilst in Edinburgh's New Town, the blocks are much larger at 180 metres by 140 metres. However, in all cases, for well-functioning urban blocks they need to consider permeability and legibility. In the early 1990s, urban designers in Hulme, Manchester, determined that a good starting point would be 120m long by 60m wide. This provided sufficient spaces within the block interior to accommodate servicing for a variety of uses, as well as allowing for visual privacy if the block is in residential use, and effectively balanced permeability and legibility.

5. Block interior for service: In almost every case the interior of an urban block will be used for servicing the surrounding uses. If the surrounding uses are retail in nature, it will need to function as a service court, allowing for delivery vehicles to access rear storerooms for the stores. In industrial contexts, secure service yards for storage of materials or parking of vehicles will be required. In other cases, general parking for cars will be required unless it is determined that this will be provided within the public realm or restricted altogether (the preferred sustainable solution). Retail premises will often require regular daily servicing by larger vehicles, whilst a residential property might only require weekly post or refuse collection. Access to these interior service courts will be through the band of buildings that make up the block. This access need not be a large gap - a space between 4-6 metres will allow for vehicles to easily enter and leave without breaking up the building line and continuity of the block and connected street/route. Where possible arrange blocks so that service access and streets can serve multiple blocks.

BELOW: A residential urban block delivering high quality semi-private green space for residents - Aspern Seestadt, Austria.

CHAPTER 9: TECHNICAL DESIGN 232

EIXAMPLE URBAN BLOCKS, BARCELONA

By the middle of the 19th century, the city of Barcelona needed to expand beyond its medieval footprint. Following a competition in 1855, a new plan for the extension of the city beyond the walls was adopted, designed by Ildefons Cerdá. This new plan was based on a strong grid of wide streets and evenly proportioned urban blocks designed to improve the quality of life and health. This extension would become known as 'Eixample'.

PRINCIPLES OF THE ORIGINAL BARCELONA BLOCK

Cerdá designed his urban blocks to be equal size (113msq) and built on only two sides, allowing space between the buildings for gardens and open spaces. 20 blocks were grouped together to create a neighbourhood, each with shops, services and facilities provided on the ground floors. 20m wide streets ran around each block, providing for access for services.

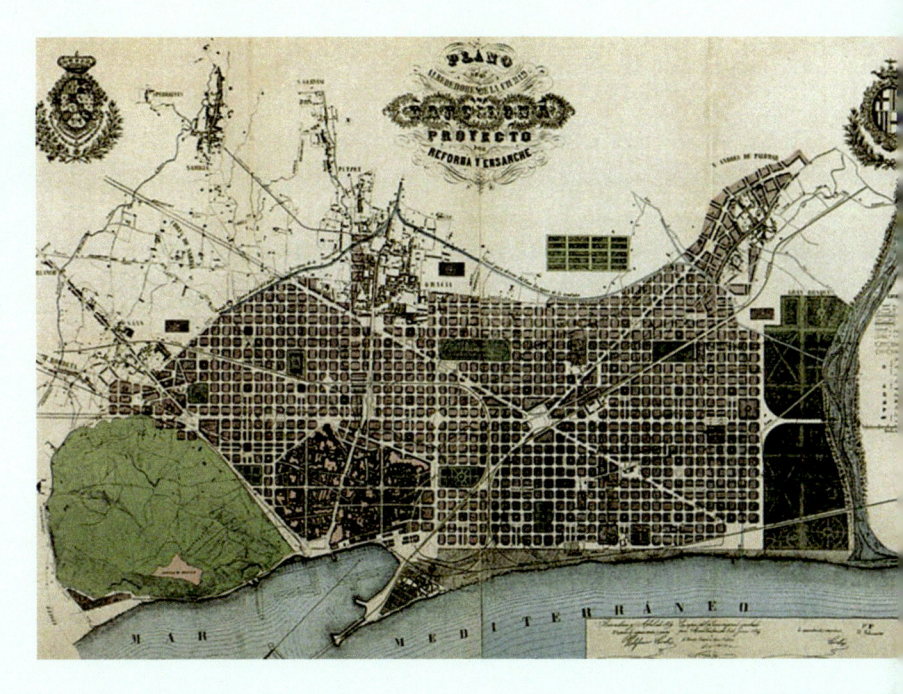

20TH CENTURY DENSIFICATION

Increasing demands for housing and employment, meant that the original design principles set down by Cerdá were eroded. Apartment buildings of between 6 and 8 storeys were built along all four sides of the block, with little spillout. The ground floors retained their commercial and retail purposes (creating strong, active frontages), but internally the blocks lost their open or garden spaces in place of service yards, small workshops and business, and car parking.

THE CONTEMPORARY CERDÁ BLOCK

The size and shape of the blocks means that a Barcelona block with its chamfered corners is immediately recognisable, but it is criticised for its uniformity which undermines visual interest and legibility. Several recent projects have focused on identifying opportunities to remove the built up interior, and new open spaces have been created offering opportunities for children's play or outdoors seating for older residents.

ABOVE: Cerdá's original 1855 masterplan for the Eixample extension of Barcelona. Defined by the square urban blocks; strong grid pattern; and cross-cutting diagonal routes.

LEFT: The Cerdá block is instantly recognisable - with its chamfered corners and distinctive shape, size, and density.

EIXAMPLE SUPERBLOCK CONCEPT, BARCELONA

THE 'SUPERILLE'
In the mid-1990s, the municipal authorities in Barcelona started to explore how they could improve access to open spaces within the city, improving the walkability and cyclability of their neighbourhoods, whilst still retaining the high-density urban blocks that have evolved from Cerda's plan. Their experimentation led to the development of the *'superblock'* known locally as the *'Superilles'*. Since 2016 Barcelona has introduced six pilot projects to explore this concept, with plans to roll this out to cover a further 503 urban blocks.

MORE PEOPLE FEWER CARS
The concept focuses on the grouping of several perimeter blocks (usually nine in a roughly 400x400m block), restricting vehicular access in between the blocks (the superblock interior) and using the space to create parks and pedestrian friendly routes. These interior routes are redesigned as 'green streets', creating pedestrian friendly streets, new parks, and public spaces, and introducing additional planting for enhanced biodiversity. On some routes this has allowed the removal of all vehicles, whilst on others access is only provided for residents and local businesses.

ENCOURAGING SUSTAINABLE TRANSPORT
Around the edges of the blocks, through traffic still flows providing access throughout the city and the sub-region, however these routes have also been upgraded to provide additional high-capacity public transport connections further reducing the need to travel by car. Access to these transit routes is immeasurably improved through the ability to walk more easily to transit stops via the superblock interior. Each superblock also includes a least one key route (part of a city-wide network) that is suitable for cycling - allowing residents and visitors to more easily cycle through the city.

COMMUNITY-LED DESIGN
One of the biggest design elements of the superblock concept is its community led nature. Whilst superblock projects are defined centrally, and the network and connections part of a wider strategic plan, the detailed design and implementation of the new spaces and routes is a community-led process. This allows for the routes to be tailored to local need – including those of local businesses who rely on passing trade – and ensures that further individuality is provided between the superblock neighbourhoods.

ABOVE: The Barcelona superblock model. Nine blocks coming together to form a single 'district' focused on sustainable transport and quality public space and amenity. *(Image by Ajuntament de Barcelona)*

LEFT: The superblock concept is slowly being introduced across the Eixample extension - with the space between blocks being re-designed for pedestrians and provision of green infrastructure, social spaces, and play areas for local children.

CHAPTER 9: TECHNICAL DESIGN

THE SUPERBLOCK CONCEPT

Where the urban designer is considering a number of blocks together, the concept of the 'superblock' can be applied to offer even greater design flexibility. Usually, the superblock works in groups of four blocks (or more, as in the Barcelona superille), arranged at right angles to each other, creating a super block. This means that service and vehicle access can be provided to all four blocks around the outside edges, whilst the streets and spaces between the blocks (the superblock core) can be used more effectively for public realm and green infrastructure that will support the liveability agenda. In much the same way as with the singular urban block, superblocks can be grouped together, with service streets shared, and greater sections of traffic free public realm.

In many cases, the superblock concept allows for the creation of traffic free streets and neighbourhoods without compromising on the functionality of the blocks themselves – they are still serviced, there is still private and public space provided, and buildings continue to overlook the spaces. Therefore, this allows for more opportunities, or flexibility, for each of the streets and spaces that are created. More space can be given over to public realm and human scaled design within the wider urban area, and it becomes easier to provide routes which favour sustainable modes – walking, cycling, and public transport. This of course will become more important when considering the remaining two 'super-components' covered in this chapter (public realm; and green infrastructure).

When employing the superblock concept, issues of where and how to implement other urban design layers - such as key frontages or corners - becomes much easier. Active frontages and landmark corners are most likely to be placed along the low trafficked routes, and frontages that are within the core of the superblock as opposed to the edges. Furthermore, the junction between all four blocks at the centre, provides a 'ready-made' opportunity to deliver a well overlooked, pedestrian friendly public / green space for the benefit of the wider neighbourhood. This is of course how Cerdá's urban blocks in Barcelona are being modified and evolved to tackle issues including climate, sustainability, and inequality *(see adjacent case study)*.

DETAILING THE URBAN BLOCK

As mentioned previously, the urban block will be made up of several buildings, corners and frontages, which are all design layers working together in concert within the super-component of the block. No two urban blocks will be the same, even though they will all follow the same set of design principles, in many ways, this is down to the way that the buildings within those blocks exhibit individual characteristics. It is also important to consider how the surrounding townscape delivers these elements – they make up the local character. The practitioner is again reminded that in considering these elements we are not designing the architecture – this is the remit of architects – but the urban designer should be able to give clear direction.

The following section sets out how any buildings might be considered within the urban block to enhance human scaled design. The elements are split into four broad categories:

A. Use and Type
B. Building and Architecture
C. Continuity and Streets
D. Corners and Landmarks

There is naturally a significant overlap between categories, therefore, when considering detailed design, the practitioner can 'pick and choose' from a range of elements, but it is important that they provide a range of different graphics to effectively illustrate and communicate these elements.

BELOW: The famous 'linear' urban blocks of Back Bay, Boston, USA.

A: USES AND TYPES

Function / Use

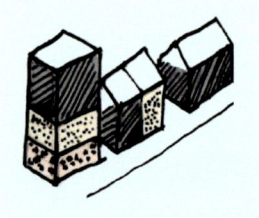

Urban blocks do not need to be single use - separate buildings within the block can provide different uses, creating a mix of uses. Individual buildings can also have different uses within them; it is not uncommon for a building to have different uses on different floors. This is helpful where an active frontage is required at ground floor to animate a particular key route. Care needs to be taken to provide mutually compatible uses within the same block – it is unlikely that a residential use will sit effectively against industrial or commercial use. Mixed use neighbourhoods help to achieve the vibrancy. (*see* Service)

Transparency

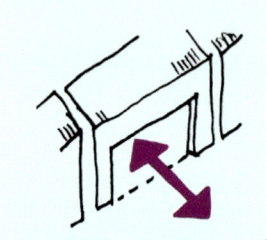

To aid legibility, buildings and their uses should be easily distinguishable from the outside when viewed from the public realm – they should have a transparency of use – helping with legibility and providing *'eyes on the street'*. For example - a retail premises or café that has a clear shop front. Where this is for sole residential use, it is often easy to achieve as the architecture can be quite distinctive, but for other types of buildings this might require a different approach. Design solutions might include clear lobbies, reception areas, or large windows into open plan offices or meeting rooms. (*see* Passive surveillance)

Street Access

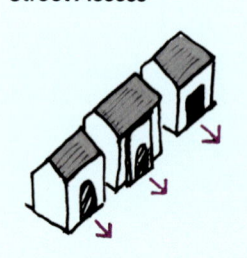

Having a clear front door might sound like an obvious design point, but it is important for creating successful places. All buildings should have a clear entrance and street address from the public realm. From a practical point of view, this ensures that visitors can find different businesses and residential properties, that post, and other deliveries can be made effectively. From an activity perspective it means that comings and goings are well overlooked and will animate and provide vibrancy in the public realm. Avoid buildings and properties that are accessed directly from parking spaces as these are less likely to achieve the same human scaled design. (*see* Orientation)

Service

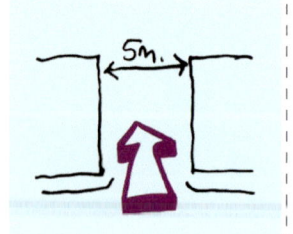

The basic principles means that the block interior will provide for the servicing needs of a particular use, and it is vital that the urban designer considers these uses when detailing the block. Where heavy goods vehicles are required to enter the block interior then a 20m turning circle is required (unless there are two separate entrances). Office type development might not require such intensive servicing but will often require much greater parking provision for employees. Residential uses are perhaps the least intensive in terms of the servicing requirements and often can be front serviced (post, refuse collection etc), but the block interior will need to provide garden amenity space. (*see* Function / Use)

A: USES AND TYPES

CHAPTER 9: TECHNICAL DESIGN   236

B: BUILDINGS AND ARCHITECTURE

Heights

The height of any building will be a response to the local context. It may be that the design rationale for a site responds to the nearby height and scale of the surrounding townscape (as collated from the analysis stage) or it may be that the design seeks to be distinctive in providing a different scale. Taller buildings can act as landmarks in key locations, helping to provide visual markers within the townscape. (*see* Density)

Density

Detail can be given about the plot size as well as the footprints of the buildings (the plot ratio). Land use planning has many measures of density (dwellings per hectare, people per hectare) but these should be avoided as they do not effectively communicate the design intentions. Typically, densities will increase towards key destinations - a civic core, a railway station, or a key park or public space. Remember that the building density can transition between blocks and within a block with different densities at different edges. (*see* Function / Use).

Connections / Composition

Buildings are never viewed alone, and in that respect the urban designer should consider the physical, visual, and mental connections between buildings and groups. Buildings with similar or related uses could be designed as an ensemble, or a group of buildings around a space could have a strong connected identity to reinforce legibility as a landmark. (*see* Materials / Style)

Materials / Style

The materials and style of buildings has an impact on the character and identity of an area. Without designing the building, the urban designer should consider whether there are opportunities to specify a palette of materials or stylised details that would be taken forward in the architecture. Under this element the practitioner will need to determine the project's approach to the built architecture - is the character mixed, a traditional vernacular or could a variety of styles could be appropriate. (*see* Connections / Composition)

B: BUILDINGS AND ARCHITECTURE

C: STREETS AND FRONTAGE

Orientation

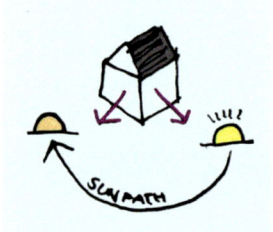

Orientation focuses on the way that a building (or block) relates to a street or space, but also how it relates to climatic conditions such as sunpath. Buildings and blocks should typically be designed to be strongly oriented towards the public realm, providing a clear frontage. Buildings that do not relate to streets and spaces will be very rare (an exception rather than the rule) and supported with a clear justification in design terms. Buildings, blocks and streets can be oriented so that they can respond to sunpaths, providing opportunities for passive solar gain (or shading) or to ensure that outdoor spaces are comfortable. (*see* Set-backs).

Building Line

Consistent building lines can create a sense of balance and legibility in places and ensure that the buildings are not isolated structures in space. It provides a sense of visual continuity that is helpful for legibility. The building line is the imaginary line created by the principle outward facing elevations along a street or in a block. Typically, the building line should be well defined with buildings creating consistency. However, there are occasions where a broken or stepped building line is appropriate to create interest or add landmarks. (*see* Passive Surveillance and Set-backs)

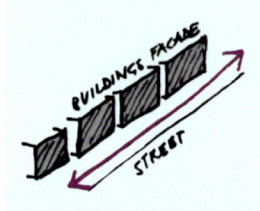

Set-backs

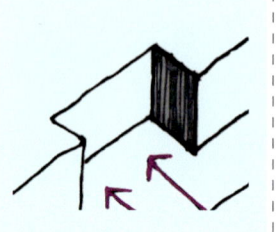

A set back (pulling in the building line from the established building line) is an opportunity to encourage spill out within the public realm and provide a link between the public realm and the ground floor use. This is particularly useful where retail premises or cafes and bars are to be located. Depending on the use on which it serves, the size of this space will vary as will its requirement for sun or shade and so orientation becomes an important factor. Detailed design should set out how distinction between the public and the private space will be made - a green infrastructure feature or a change of paving. (*see* Function / Use)

Passive Surveillance

It is important that blocks are designed to be outwards looking, with buildings that have windows and entrances that overlook streets and spaces. This helps to animate the streets through comings and goings, but also allows for passive surveillance (what Jane Jacobs (1961) called *'eyes on the street'*) which helps to create a sense of safety and security for uses of public space. (*see* Building Line)

APPLIED URBAN DESIGN

STREETS AND FRONTAGE

D: CORNERS AND LANDMARKS

The Statement

Corners offer opportunities to introduce taller buildings or grand structures, falling as they do at the junction of two or more routes. Treating a corner with height allows it act as a landmark being visible along these routes, but also more widely within the townscape. This form of corner is particularly useful at gateways or other strategic arrival points for example towards a railway station. (*see* Height)

Articulating

A simple way of designing a corner that provides interest at the street level is to articulate the corner with a change of building style or different suite of materials. In some cases, this can be coupled with small increase in the in the height of the building or a change of use – such as the introduction of a shop or café in a residential block. (*see* Materials / Style)

Opening

Rather than providing a building on the corner, opening the corner means that the building line could be pulled back to create a green space or public square. This works well where the corner is located at the confluence of a number of different routes and allowing it to act as a node. The space created can at as a forecourt or setback to allow for a variety of other uses. On a smaller scale the same can be achieved with a cantilevered building. (*see* Set-backs)

Chamfered

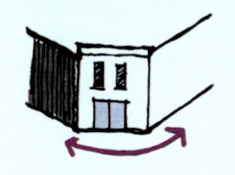

Cutting the corner allows the building line and block to effectively '*turn the corner*'. The chamfer is helpful in drawing people around the corner so is useful where there is a desire to change the direction of an important route – essentially manipulating the movement of people. This is often coupled with providing an entrance, or feature, on the chamfered corner. (*see* Building Lines and Street Access)

Just a Corner

The most common type of corner is the '*just a corner*' without any special treatment or approach. Where there is no need to reinforce a node or change in direction, then a simple corner, with little or no articulation will ensure that the main route will retain its primacy. (*see* Orientation and Building Lines)

APPLIED URBAN DESIGN

LEFT: Vienna, Austria - A new university campus masterplan for WU - The design was laid out by BUSarchitektur around a central urban block formation, with a series of buildings facing inwards to frame the central pedestrian route [building line]. The urban designers mixed heights, with a transition from the city centre end to the lower density suburban end. They also tendered the individual buildings out to a series of international architects [including NO.MAD; Zaha Hadid; CRAB Studio, Estudio Carmé Pinos; and Atelier Hitoshi Abe] with the brief to work within the masterplan structure in regards heights, composition and connection, transparency, orientation, set-backs, corner articulations, functions and use, density, service, and street access. The architects however had freedom to interpret much of the brief creatively in regards material choices, style, and detailing.

What this resulted in was a unique urban design wherein the structures frame the spaces and streets formed - creating the required enclosure and working holistically together. Yet they also provide drama and visual interest. In effect this project is best practice in urban design and architects working together to produce diversity within a common agreed framework.

CHAPTER 9: TECHNICAL DESIGN

LEFT: Pescara, Italy - The main pedestrian street is defined and enclosed by the numerous traditional urban perimeter blocks that shape much of the city. These blocks showcase a number of the issues we have discussed in this chapter. The clarity of function and use is clear, with retail ground floors and residential apartments provided above. These apartments provide day-long footfall and the balconies allow for passive surveillance of the street below. The access to the retail is legible and clear, and the strong building line pulls users along the length of the street - in addition this assists with the consistency of heights, in veiling the block service access points, as these corners are subtly dealt with to ensure little attention is drawn to them and remains on the street and its amenity offerings.

Despite the strong frontage and similar heights throughout - interest is provided by the clear mix of materials and colour palettes - with distinct individual buildings making up each urban block. There have been multiple additions into the blocks over time, and the mix of balcony styles, fenestrations, and detailing [within a clear structured framework] provide interest and prevent the street and blocks from being monotone or overly generic. The combination creates a unique character for Pescara.

APPLIED URBAN DESIGN

Retail and Service Block

This urban block from the Manchester case study masterplan is an example of the typical use of the block with a central service yard, much as in the style of a Barcelona block or those typically found within the nearby city centre of Manchester. Whilst a perimeter of buildings is created to be outward looking, the interior is used for parking and servicing. Small gaps between the buildings (5-6metres) provide access to the interior of the block which means that whilst they allow for access for larger vehicles, they do no break up the continuity of the frontage or the enclosure to the streets.

Key features are:
- A strong outward facing block, providing a mixture of different uses including retail units that will face the Oldham Road (to the south) and offices elsewhere within the block.
- Much of the block interior is used for parking and servicing, but there are also opportunities to provide softer spaces to provide semi-private amenity space for those working there.
- The block is set back from Oldham Road, providing a forecourt for shops, cafes, and other spill out uses, whilst there is less of a set-back provided on other sides.
- The use of upper floors is different to the ground level, with office and leisure uses as options on the upper floors above the retail units.
- The corners of the blocks have been treated differently, including a large chamfer to the south-west, providing a landmark and drawing people up Livesey Street - a key east-west connector.

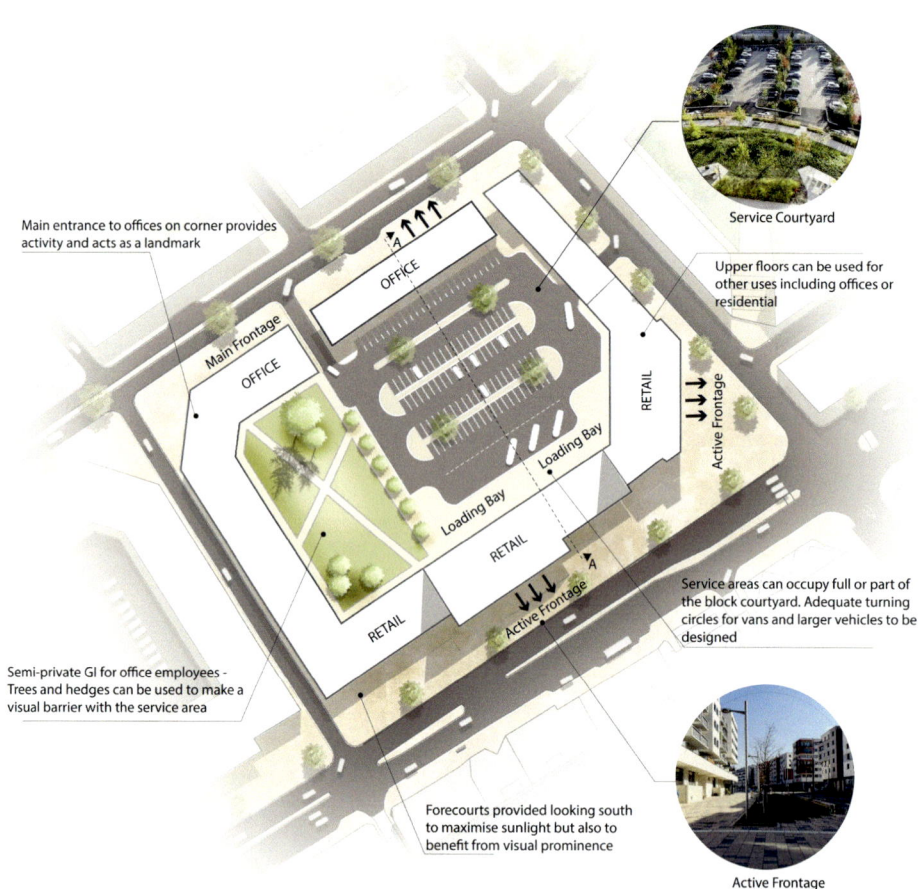

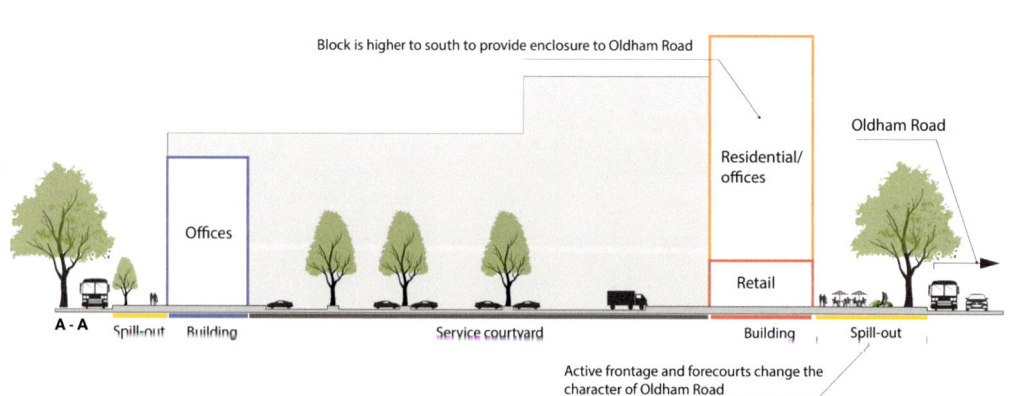

Main entrance to offices on corner provides activity and acts as a landmark

Service Courtyard

Upper floors can be used for other uses including offices or residential

Service areas can occupy full or part of the block courtyard. Adequate turning circles for vans and larger vehicles to be designed

Semi-private GI for office employees - Trees and hedges can be used to make a visual barrier with the service area

Forecourts provided looking south to maximise sunlight but also to benefit from visual prominence

Active Frontage

Block is higher to south to provide enclosure to Oldham Road

Residential/offices

Oldham Road

Retail

A - A Spill-out Building Service courtyard Building Spill-out

Active frontage and forecourts change the character of Oldham Road

MANCHESTER
Retail / Service Urban Block

CHAPTER 9: TECHNICAL DESIGN 242

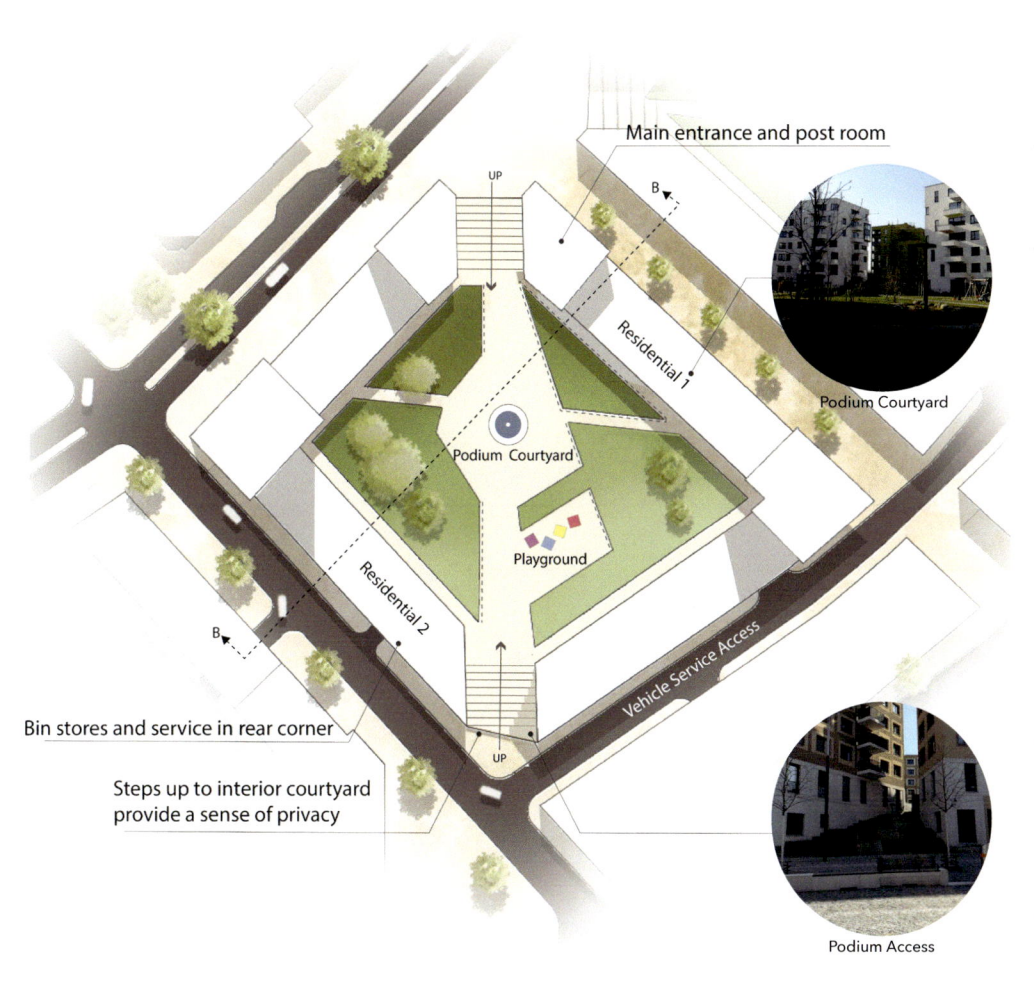

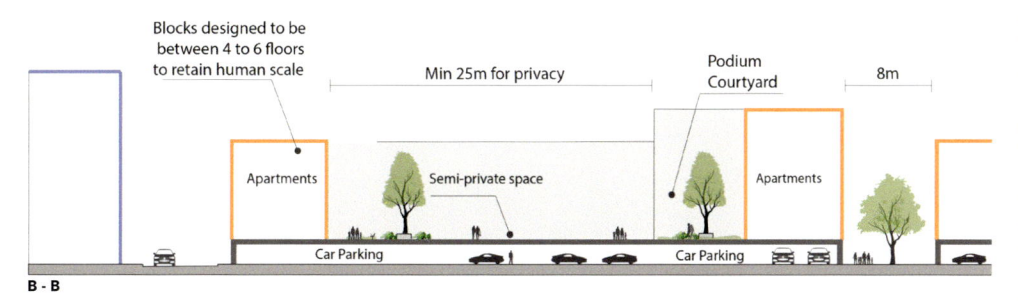

Podium Style Residential
This urban block is taken from the masterplan for the site in Manchester and shows how a typical residential block of apartments has been adapted and amended to provide parking and a green courtyard within the block. The block is designed to deliver homes at a high density, more than 50 dwellings per hectare and make efficient use of land. The design approach, which is based on blocks in Aspern Seestadt, Austria, introduces a podium deck, with parking at ground floor and the courtyard space at first floor – something that is only evident at when you consider the block in section.

The key features are:
• A strong outward looking block of apartments designed to be between 4-6 storeys high, which provide strong enclosure for the streets and spaces, but maintains human scale.
• Parking provided within the interior of the urban block, behind the ground floor of these apartments with access through the building line from the service street.
• Ground floor uses include post rooms, cycle storage and plant and bin storage, but also large and attractive entrance lobbies to maintain active frontages.
• The parking is covered by a concrete podium deck and on top of this is a softer, green space that is intended to be used by the residents.
• Access to the interior courtyard is not closed to the wider public, but from the exterior it is accessed via a series of steps which provides a mental barrier to entering - creating this perception of semi-privacy.

MANCHESTER
Residential Podium Urban Block

APPLIED URBAN DESIGN

The Half-Block
This urban block from the Aalborg case study and is one of the residential blocks which runs along the western edge of the site, adjacent to the linear park and the railway. The design for the remainder of the site means there is insufficient land to provide a complete urban block, and so a 'half block' has been created. Care needs to be taken when using a half-block as the interior is exposed, and servicing and access becomes difficult. This half block is residential in use, which requires limited servicing, and therefore the block interior can be given over to gardens and amenity space.

The key features are:
• The half block has a principal frontage looking out to the shared surface street which provides the main access points, lobbies, as well as access for deliveries and servicing.
• The interior semi-private garden space in the central court, is separated from the linear park by a ribbon of planting but creates a strong green infrastructure connection.
• Views over the linear park are provided for all the apartments maximising the benefits that can be provided from the green infrastructure on the site.
• The buildings are 5-6 storeys tall providing effective enclosure for the shared surface street but also remaining at a human scale.
• The depth of the building allows for the apartments to be double fronted – to both the interior and exterior allowing a range of different types and sizes to be created.

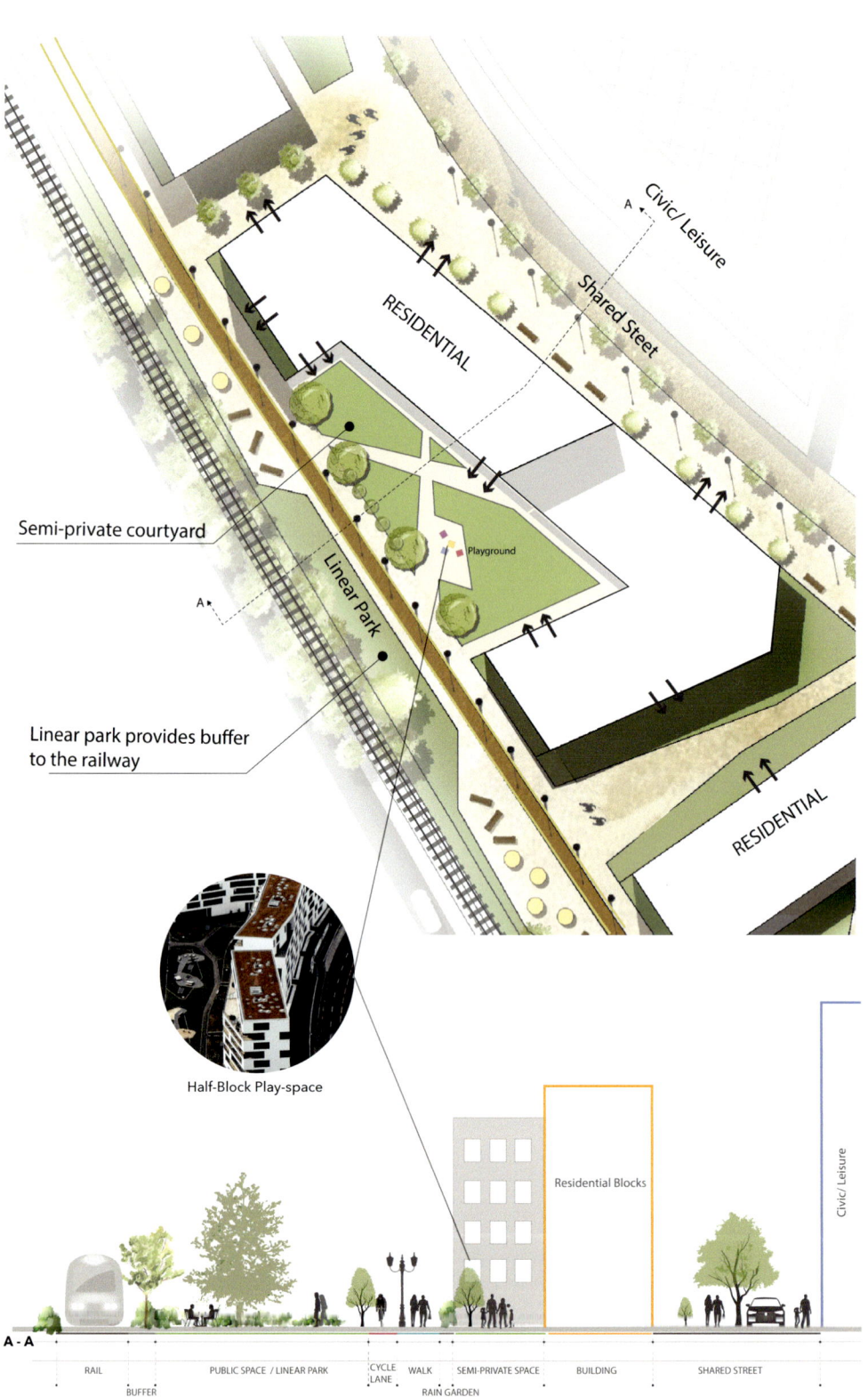

Semi-private courtyard
Linear park provides buffer to the railway
Half-Block Play-space

A - A
RAIL | BUFFER | PUBLIC SPACE / LINEAR PARK | CYCLE LANE | WALK | RAIN GARDEN | SEMI-PRIVATE SPACE | BUILDING | SHARED STREET

Residential Blocks
Civic/Leisure

AALBORG
The Half-Block

CHAPTER 9: TECHNICAL DESIGN   244

URBAN BLOCKS CREATING ENCLOSURE

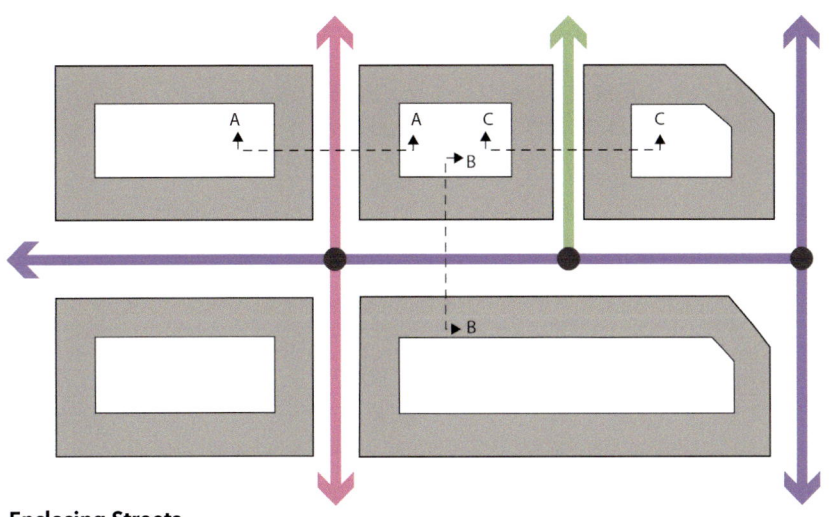

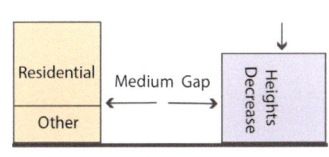

Section AA: Local Route

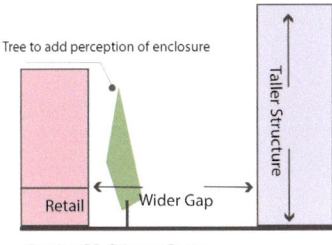

Section BB: Primary Route

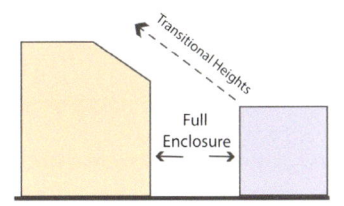

Section CC: Pedestrian Route

Enclosing Streets
Streets, or routes, should be defined by the layout of the urban blocks. The above example is a simple illustration using a basic block structure - but it shows how the size and number of blocks will add or remove the number of available routes, this will impact on the permeability of a place. The distance between blocks will also define the street dimension - with primary routes requiring more space to ensure sustainable transport options. The distance between blocks should be decided by the type of route being delivered - and with care to simultaneously consider the enclosure being created - as the heights of the buildings will directly influence this. The cross-sections show examples of how individual blocks can mix building heights across different sides to produce a variety of enclosures for the streets surrounding. The arrangement of urban blocks is vital to the success of place and the qualities that can be introduced at the human scale.

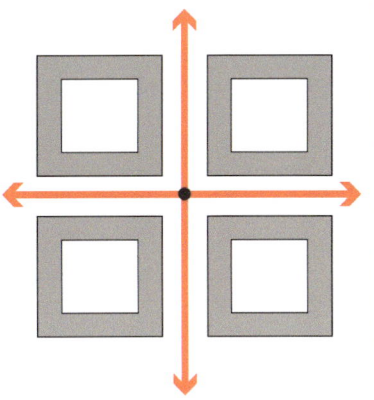

Standard grid layout

Streets and Nodes
The standard grid layout of urban blocks is helpful in creating permeability - as the surrounding sides of the block will frame streets/routes. Where these streets meet creates intersections - nodes wherein the user will be forced to make a decision on which direction to travel in. Pedestrian streets can be developed, but squares, plazas, or other spaces will not without some manipulation of the blocks.

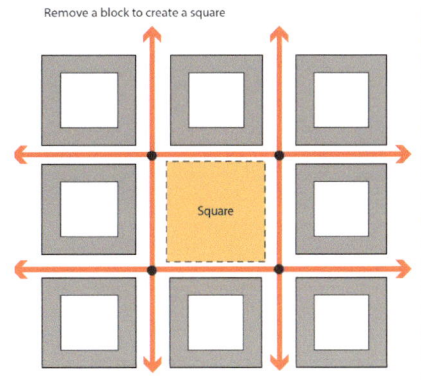

Remove a block to create a square

Remove a Block
By removing an existing block, or masterplanning to leave a block out - this will provide a larger space within the city to be designated for public use - a park, or public square. The key here is to ensure that this space does not become cut off from the streets and uses nearby - by allowing the space to be surrounded by vehicular routes it can become a disconnected island. Be sure to maintain some direct access to at least one block front by pedestrianising necessary streets.

Chamfering to create a square

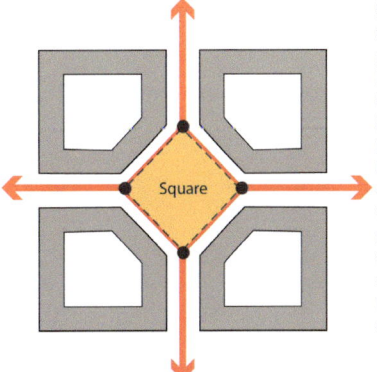

Shaping Blocks
One simple way to create public space is to chamfer the block corners. By doing this to the basic four block layout (as shown) we can create a natural square that can then be developed as a local or city plaza. There are other ways to re-shape the block to produce similar results. Blocks can be a multitude of different shapes and sizes - the key is to retain the core principles, as discussed in this chapter.

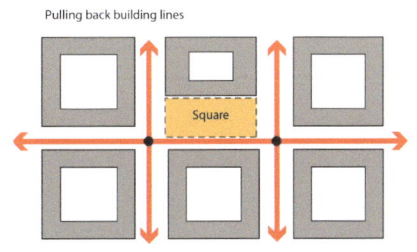

Pulling back building lines

Set-Back a Block
Similar to the above technique - but rather than remove a block entirely, simply set the frontage on one side of a block back from the street/building line. This will create a space that can be effectively enclosed on three sides if the adjacent routes are pedestrianised. This is a useful method for creating smaller public spaces along streets - that can allow for spill-out for cafes and bars, seating, play provision, and landscaping.

APPLIED URBAN DESIGN

9.4 PUBLIC REALM

PUBLIC REALM DESIGN

Life happens between buildings – Jan Gehl's seminal 1971 text (translated into English in 1987) argued all urban design should begin with a central concern on public life and where this occurs. Gehl emphasised that it is the spaces between buildings, the public realm, where social interaction and the sensory experience of everyday living transpires. We should therefore design our places and spaces to reflect this – ensuring that public realm fulfil a critical role as outdoor 'rooms' that exist beyond architecture. Most buildings have no, or limited, use for the vast majority, serving only a select few users depending on their function. The public realm however, has power to be equitable and inclusive for all in society if well-designed.

Gehl's thinking has been influential – inspiring a generation of urban design practitioners, researchers, and theorists to think of building design as a means to an end, not the end itself – yet the underlying message is not necessarily new.

Giambattista Nolli's map of Rome, Italy dating from 1748 – and built on the foundations of Bufalini's map of 1551 – was one of the earliest to prioritise the public realm as the true architecture of the city. The Nolli Map provided several 'firsts' – the first to orientate city maps to magnetic north, and one of the earliest uses of a figure ground to communicate a cities layout and structure based on extensive surveys.

Yet it was the decision to display Rome, a city awash with architectural treasures defining styles and periods that influenced buildings across the known world, as a series of outdoor rooms. Rooms were shaped by the buildings – the buildings acting as part of a wider ensemble and not isolated structures. The map provides a unique insight into the innate character of Rome and the importance of publicly accessible spaces and environments – such as the public square/plaza, and even churches – as well as the links between them. The work of Nolli and Gehl illustrates that city design should perceive the public realm as the anchor to develop around – the lifeblood of place.

BELOW: The Nolli map of Rome, Italy - 1748. It shows the interconnected democratic spaces of the city between public squares and publicly accessible structures.

CHAPTER 9: TECHNICAL DESIGN

It is imperative that urban design place emphasis on provision of public realm – to do this urban designers must recognise that public realm needs to be accessible to all – and each element be detailed to ensure the highest levels of quality. To achieve this in design we can separate the public realm into **streets** and **spaces** – and for each we can demand that designers consider:

1. Corridors; and
2. Zones

Streets and spaces make up the network/infrastructure of public realm – and the design of each is complex, given both are multi-faceted and dynamic components that must work individually as well as effectively function as part of a greater whole. Utilising the 'corridor' and 'zones' approach to public realm design can assist designers in promoting a more transparent and successful public realm.

CORRIDORS

To provide a legitimate and connected public realm network across a city, it is imperative that the public realm is viewed as a form of infrastructure – that can only successfully operate as intended if it is fully integrated and linked up. Infrastructure that fails to fully connect will fail due to the weak points within the wider structure. As designers we recognise that vehicular routes that fail to join up will not work in practice, rendering them ineffectual in completing their primary task of moving people and goods – yet too often cities fail to apply the same principles of movement, connectivity, and networking to their public realm offering.

Streets provide the main arteries of a place – they can shape movement for a wide range of modal options – including walking. The UN-Habitat (2013) produced a report - '*Streets as public spaces and drivers of urban prosperity*' - that evidenced a tangible link between prosperity and cities that allocate streets for people and pedestrian movement. Cities that have failed to integrate any multi-functionality of streets tend to have lower productivity and poorer quality of life. Streets therefore must be designed considering not only traditional powered transport – but also as an integrated element of the public realm network of the wider location. To achieve this we suggest thinking about public realm 'streets' in terms of corridors.

Corridors within buildings are the necessary links to and between rooms and areas of activity – people use corridors to get from one place to another – but they can also be places of amenity. Sticking briefly with the architectural analogy, corridors in busy work environments are often communal – places that not only connect rooms and sections of a building, but also areas where people gather around the water cooler or coffee machine. The corridor also can be the transitional buffer between very different uses or activities occurring. Within the public realm, streets can provide similar attributes – **moving people** across the city effectively and safely providing access to the range of offerings and activity available; they can be designed to provide **amenity and facility**, and good street design can promote social activity by being communal and inclusive; and they can act as **buffers between transition areas** of the urban form – knitting together neighbourhoods, creating positive seams that allow shifts in land use or character for example to happen more smoothly.

BELOW: Clear movement corridors allow different sustainable transport options, including walking, to happen freely and with comfort across the public realm offering - Amsterdam, the Netherlands.

ZONES

Zones can be implemented across the full extent of the public realm – they are not restricted to being defined as simply public spaces such as squares, plazas, or parks. Zones rather should be perceived as designated key sections across the public realm network that provide a particular service or function to enhance the available activities or facility on offer to users. Zones therefore can be integrated into the network of corridors (as discussed) – or be delivered as destinations within that connected infrastructure.

When designing zones there must be a clear articulation for the role of each – and these again should be considered against the wider network to ensure coverage of amenity and use – yet each zone must also consistently deliver on a number of central design components regardless of where it may sit within the public realm hierarchy. Urban designers must continue to *prioritise movement* – there is a necessity to not only bring footfall into the zone in question effectively, but also through it and out of it. If a particular zone is delivered to encourage people to stop and make use of the functions available it still must be able to effectively allow people to exit when they are ready – and designers must be conscious that many people will simply wish to move through and beyond the zone itself – continuing their journey. In this way all zones must maintain clear corridors – and a primary design element must be ensuring these corridor networks remain uninterrupted – even through major spaces delivered.

Identifying the *activity* that each zone is delivering will also be key to ensuring the design approach taken is appropriate – and will assist the designer in arriving at the most effective solution – be that a pedestrianised public space, a wide set back on an existing street, an internal accessible courtyard, or a multi-functional and mixed use/transport square. Zones can also deliver social spaces for users – dedicated spaces for *socialising or resting*. Moving through a public realm network on foot can be a challenge for many in society and understanding the diversity and needs of all users will allow for more inclusive and equitable design interventions. Such zones can also be useful for carving out space for *environmental interventions* and inclusions. This chapter continues with a section on green infrastructure (GI) design – and the ability to integrate a number of key GI components into the public realm is critical. Designing with zones can allow for the insertion of planting, sustainable urban drainage systems, and other high quality landscape features.

ABOVE: Public realm zones should prioritise movement - through the clear delivery of paths that connect the wider street network. Yet they must also provide areas for socialising, resting, lighting, play, and green infrastructure provision. The town square of Kristiansand, Norway is an excellent example of how zones can be designed into the public realm to provide a range of amenity and facility for users.

CHAPTER 9: TECHNICAL DESIGN   248

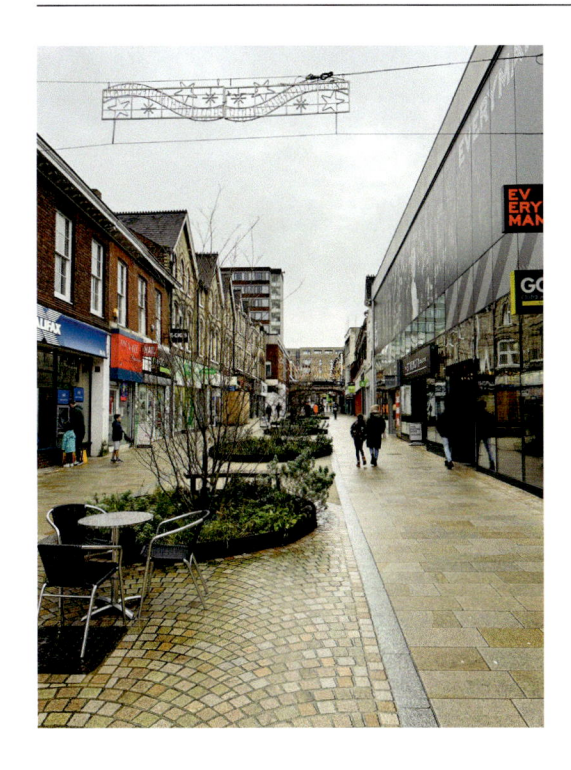

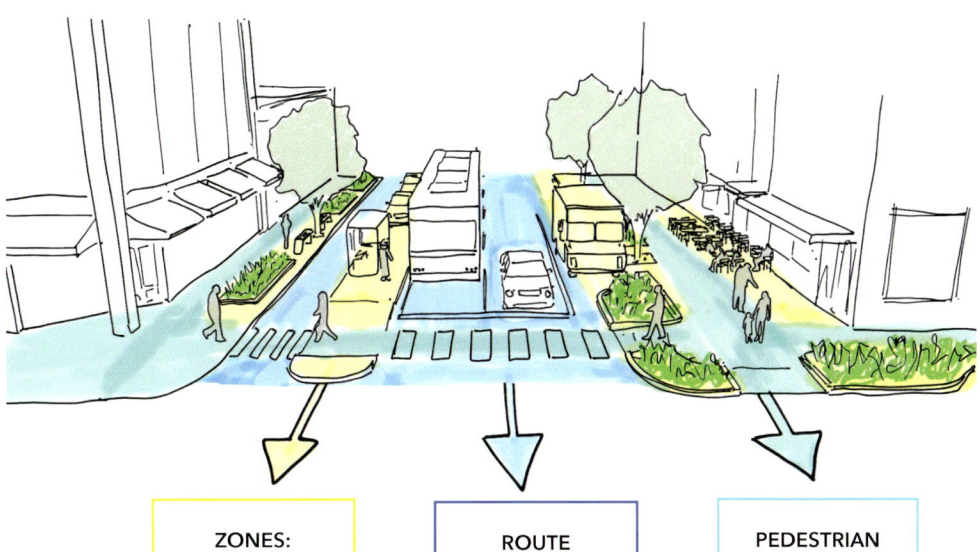

ZONES:
Mixing green infrastructure; bus stops; lighting; seating; spill-out; parking; bins etc. Used to provide amenity and to buffer from roads.

ROUTE CORRIDORS:
Public transport and car movement - separated from people and below walking and cycling in the hierarchy.

PEDESTRIAN CORRIDORS:
Prioritising the public realm over roads - uninterrupted corridors of movement with access to buildings and spaces.

ABOVE LEFT: Pedestrian high street in Altrincham, UK. Note the clear *'corridors'* along the building lines - allowing for uninterrupted movement flow and ease of access to retail and leisure uses. The central area has been designated as a multi-function *'zone'* - with a mix of cafe spill-out, public seating, and landscape provision.

ABOVE RIGHT: Orchard Road, Singapore - witness the clear *'corridors'* for a range of transport modes [walking, vehicle, public]. *'Zones'* then provide landscaping that offers shade and a buffer to road noise and pollution. The zone also incorporates bus stops, trash cans, seating, and lighting. A parking zone is also provided to allow for short-stays and deliveries.

TECHNICAL STANDARDS STREETS

ELEMENTS

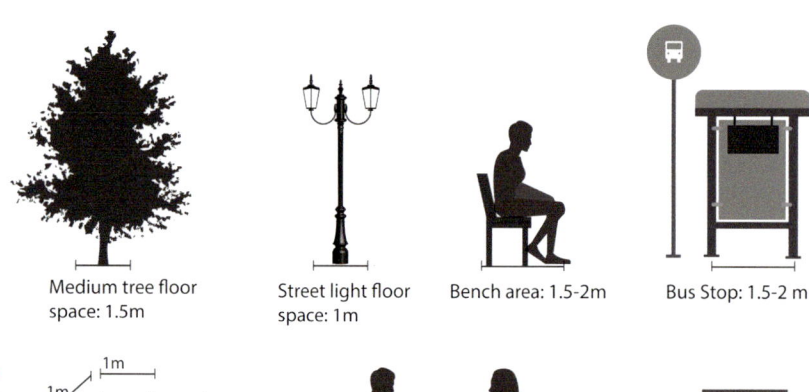

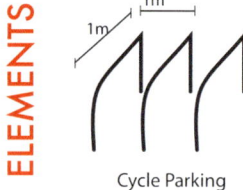

- Medium tree floor space: 1.5m
- Street light floor space: 1m
- Bench area: 1.5-2m
- Bus Stop: 1.5-2 m
- Cycle Parking (1m, 1m)
- Seating Area: 2.5-3.5m
- Bin Space: 1 m

PLACING ELEMENTS

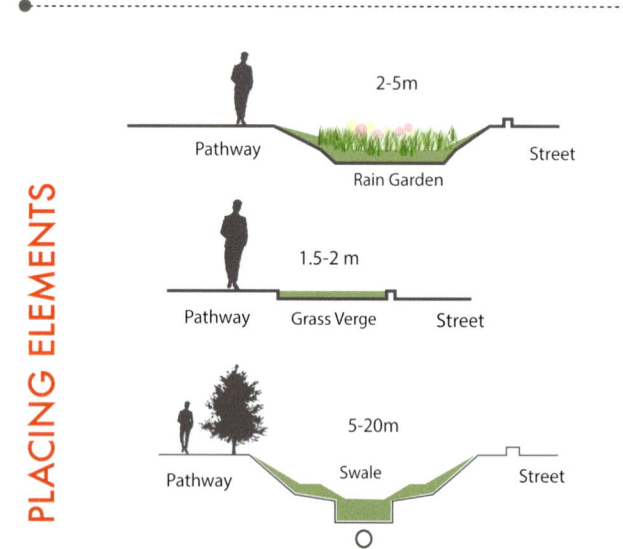

- Pathway | Rain Garden 2-5m | Street
- Pathway | Grass Verge 1.5-2 m | Street
- Pathway | Swale 5-20m | Street | Drain
- Buffer: 1-1.5m (Commercial)
- Spill Out 5-6m | Pavement: 2-2.5m (Commercial)

CONFIGURATIONS

SMALL/ LOCAL
- Local street with 1-way traffic, cycle lane, SUDs, and pedestrian sidewalk in Altrincham, England.
- Local residential street in Berlin, Germany with designed landscaping, parking, and rain gardens.

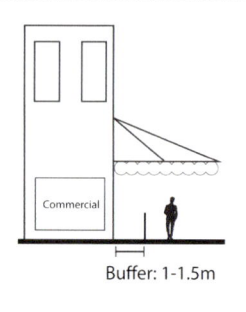

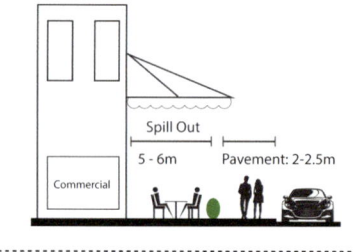

MEDIUM/ NEIGHBOURHOOD
- Neighbourhood pedestrian street in Frieburg, Germany that includes spill-out space for outdoor dining.
- Aspern Seestadt, Austria provides all local streets with ample green infrastructure and strongly enclosed legible environments.

LARGE/ CITY
- A major route in Belfast, N. Ireland city centre - with multi-modal transport provision and generous pedestrian sidewalks. 
- Major pedestrian shopping street in Glasgow, Scotland with provision of bins, lighting, public art, and cafe spill-out spaces.

APPLIED URBAN DESIGN

CHAPTER 9: TECHNICAL DESIGN 250

TECHNICAL STANDARDS SPACES

NOTE: *These standards are included as a useful starting point - as simple guidance. For more comprehensive technical standards always refer to local/national policy. You can also utilise reference books and guides such as the Metric Handbook (2018) - a rich source of design data and specifications - as well as the more focused guidance on streets and place design (Such as Manual for Streets, UK; NATCO's Urban Street Guide, USA; or GDCI's Global Street Design Guide).*

ELEMENTS

- One-person space: 1.5m
- Two-person space: 2.5m
- Wheelchair space: 1.5-2m
- Cyclist space: 1.5m
- Car lane: 2.5m 
- Bus lane: 3m
- Lorry Lane: 3-3.5m
- Tram Way: min 3-3.5m

PLACING ELEMENTS

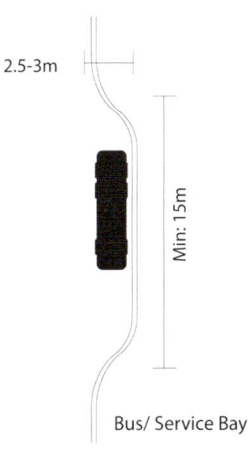

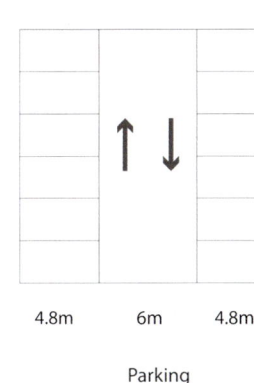

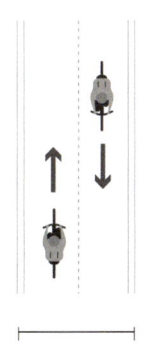

- Bus/ Service Bay — 2.5-3m, Min: 15m
- Parking — 4.8m / 6m / 4.8m
- Two Way Cycle Lane: 3m

CONFIGURATIONS

SMALL/ LOCAL

Small local space in Aalborg, Denmark provides residents and locals with shaded outdoor social space - and integrated seating.

Small local corner space in New York, USA offering buffering from road with landscaping - and fixed outdoor dining opportunities.

MEDIUM/ NEIGHBOURHOOD

A neighbourhood public space in Bath, England that is designed to have clear access to shops - as well as ample outdoor seating and play-space.

In Lisbon, Portugal this mid-scaled public space provides local users with shading and a quieter location in the city to eat or socialise.

LARGE/ CITY

The Darling Quarter, Sydney is a major new city space that provides a wide range of amenity - including playspace, event space, and a range of bars/cafes with outdoor provision.

Copenhagen, Denmark welcomes large numbers of tourists each year - the major public spaces are designed to accommodate large footfall yet also provide interest.

APPLIED URBAN DESIGN

LEFT: Rotterdam station provides a central transport hub that links into the city's public realm network - promoting effective and sustainable mobility options.

BELOW: In Hong Kong pedestrian crossings are prioritised over vehicular flow on key routes across the city's streets.

CHAPTER 9: TECHNICAL DESIGN

DESIGNING STREETS AND SPACES
Public realm design must focus attention on the delivery of a fully networked structure – that provides a clear infrastructure of uninterrupted people focused *corridors* – and within this network a series of well-defined and balanced *zones*. To design these corridors and zones within a place's streets and spaces to the highest standards we have developed **The Public Realm 6** – six design principles that public realm networks should ensure they have integrated within them – these are intended to act as a useful starting point for urban designers in detailing higher quality throughout the public realm.

1. Movement
2. Activity
3. Rest
4. AM/PM
5. Environment
6. Character

1. Movement
Designing for movement in the public realm requires designers to have a clear understanding of the type of mobility each corridor or street requires. Having a clear hierarchy of routes can assist in providing detailed design. The separation of different transport users is recommended – in particular unambiguous segregation of pedestrians, and if possible, cyclists, from motorised vehicles – this will aid in comfort and safety for those choosing more sustainable modes of mobility. There are a number of high-profile street design manuals, such as '*Manual for Streets*' in the UK, that provide technical standards for key design components related to movement including minimum dimensions for sidewalk provision and vehicle lane widths. Many of the street manuals also provide best-practice for the design of multi-modal movement corridors across different stages of the route hierarchy – and these can be an excellent resource for urban designers to begin to build up their technical competencies and best practice knowledge. Whilst other practitioners, such as highway engineers, will have responsibility for ensuring technical requirements are met, it remains the role of the urban designer to focus design on people – and on providing quality movement that enhances the journey of users. Chapter 4 discussed a number of liveable aspects that make up quality urban design – a number of these focus heavily on the journey through places as being critical to the user's experience and designers must consider this as equally important to the quality of the 'destination'.

When considering movement in the public realm be sure to think carefully about how the modal options interface with one another – people will make use of multiple modes of transport to access parts of their city or neighbourhood. To effectively encourage a more sustainable transport future it is imperative that public transport, such as trains, trams, and buses, are well linked across the route networks, but also integrated into the public realm infrastructure – to allow for ease of access and creating choice in how people move. This means paying close attention to the location of transport stops and hubs – providing these at logical points in the urban environment, but also fully amalgamated with pedestrian orientated street networks.

To create legible movement flows, good design must ensure that the obvious barriers to pedestrian movement – and indeed cycling – are tackled effectively. In practice the major barrier to pedestrian movement is vehicular movement – i.e., roads. Where a sidewalk meets a road ofttimes the vehicles will have priority – to reverse this historic preoccupation of car-centric design, the urban designer can maximise the use of crossing points for pedestrians – re-prioritising them above the movement of powered vehicles. Other methods can also be employed to enhance comfort of movement such as using building lines, trees, or even materials to make designated movement corridors easy to follow and understand for a wide range of users. This can be especially required in shared streets, where the use of materials is paramount to ensuring all those 'sharing' the environment recognise how it is to operate in practice – avoiding unnecessary discomfort or potential causalities. When designing public spaces, or zones, movement must be the top priority for design – and should always be clearly marked and ample space given over to meet the potential footfall that will be utilising it across different times of the day and night.

2. Activity

Each street and space within the public realm will offer some form of activity to users – this can be diverse and will be defined by the uses provided, and types of users likely to occupy the environment. Simple activity must be designed into all public realm, such as clear legible access to buildings, ensuring that other components designed into streets and spaces do not hinder inclusive and transparent access to structures and settings. It is therefore necessary for the urban designer to work in tandem with either the existing buildings or to play a direct role in the placement of entrances on new structures. The type of access required will be dependent on the building type – residential buildings will have limited private access that potentially requires a buffer to demarcate the transition from public to private – whilst retail or leisure buildings need to be accessible to all and the design around these entrances needs to flow more seamlessly with the public realm to encourage a smoother transition.

Certain activities in the built environment require the public realm to provide appropriate resources and space for them to occur – cafes and restaurants for example may desire outdoor seating – to extend their offering and provide activity on the street/space encouraging others to stop. These outdoor requirements need designers to deliver spill-out environments that provide a semi-private aspect to the open public realm. These 'zones' play a critical role in activating public realm – and they do not necessarily need to be exclusively semi-private in nature. Spill out spaces around community facilities can allow for people to socialise, picnic, or engage in some quiet time or rest.

The range of activity that urban designers can implement into the wider public realm should reflect the range and diversity of its users. Play-spaces for children and families do not need to be segregated or gated – best practice examples internationally are illustrating that it is possible to integrate play into public realm in more dynamic and thoughtful ways. Social spaces for people to freely meet, socialise, engage in outdoor activities are excellent ways to provide communities with the means to exercise both physically and mentally – enhancing their quality of life and wellbeing.

LEFT: Cafes with zoned spill out spaces for outdoor eating can bring life and activity to the street and wider public realm - such as this local street in Copenhagen, Denmark.

BELOW: Use of cleared space in the city to provide public activity for children and young adults can be a creative way to integrate activity and play into the public realm whilst simultaneously upgrading an area in disrepair. Paris, France.

CHAPTER 9: TECHNICAL DESIGN

3. Rest

Rest is often an overlooked design component of the public realm – providing users with safe spaces in which they can stop and slow down. The busy nature of streets and spaces in cities, and their primary functions of movement and activity can lead to designs that fail to consider the need for all users, not only those physically requiring rest, to be able to utilise precious outdoor accessible space for a wider range of actions. The thoughtful inclusion of seating throughout the public realm network can play a multi-functional role – not only allowing people the opportunity to sit and rest, but also providing dedicated space to socialise, eat, read, or simply take time to be still. The strategic placing of seating on the network can ensure key journeys, for example from transport hubs to retail cores, are more easily utilised by all users – with the potential for those with mobility issues, health concerns, or small children, to be able to better plan their walk – such provision can directly impact people's decisions to choose more sustainable mobility options.

The design choices for providing seating, and other forms of outdoor furniture, will have a significant impact on who can use them, and how effective they are in practice. Poor seating choices can exclude particular users in society – a recent increase in cities delivering anti-homeless seat design can have negative effects on the comfort of such interventions, rendering their use limited. Outdoor furniture can also be multi-purpose – acting as more than simple seating, but as components of a playscape, or integrated with green infrastructure offerings.

Urban designers must actively advocate that space be given over in public realm design for rest – and the different meanings it can have for different users. Quality public realm networks will provide social opportunity – with seating and furniture that can encourage interaction between people. Rest for children can mean something very different. It often means providing them with places to play and be stimulated – design that allows them to engage with the built and natural forms around them in new and creative ways. Here the 'rest' is a shifting beyond the standard commercial aspects of place into something less structured and more playful.

TOP: It is important to ensure seating for rest and socialising - It should however be designed within specified zones, ensuring movement corridors remain uninterrupted. These zones can include not only rest spaces, but also SuDs, and planting, lighting, and other potential necessary facilities such as recycling bins or cycle parking.

MIDDLE: Creating rest areas for people across the public realm that offer quieter spaces to read, eat, or socialise - and engage with nature. Such spaces can also provide a safe, comfortable, and relaxing environment for families with children for example.

BOTTOM: Seating can also be creative and interesting - traditional street furniture is not the only way to provide rest. Integrating seating into other public realm and green infrastructure elements can add visual drama to a space, and is even a useful approach to save space, pool resources, or allow seating to form an element of play as users can engage in more tactile and in formal ways.

All images Manchester, UK.

4. AM/PM

Cities change during different times of the day and night, and from season to season – they expand and shrink their usable space as the arrangements within them open and close depending on the timing. This results in the public realm being used very differently, as the number of people accessing it to move or to engage in activity is always in flux. It is therefore a necessary part of the design process in detailing streets and spaces to not only recognise these fluctuations, but to ensure the design is tailored to work appropriately during all situations it will encounter. During the standard working hours of a location, certain districts, streets, and spaces will be busy - commercial and retail centres, high streets, arterial routes, and more will be in action – yet as night falls this evolves, new areas activate, retail streets that thrived in the day go quiet and other streets with bars, restaurants, and clubs come to life as people access different uses and move in different ways. Seasonal impacts can see certain parts of the public realm network boom in the summer months, with brighter evenings and warmer weather being more appealing to being outdoors for longer – whilst the darker winter months and often associated inclement weather decrease the potential time people will likely spend in these streets and spaces. Good public realm should therefore plan for all such eventualities.

Designing for night-time usage and movement requires a clear lighting plan – and this will be dependent again on the needs of any particular street or space. A quieter residential street will require lighting for safety – but softer lighting due to the need to ensure residents are not disturbed. Busier streets that will have heavier evening footfall, from a transport hub to a popular leisure area will require more robust lighting – assisting people in walking or cycling – and proving some surveillance aspect to enhance safety levels. Quality creative lighting solutions can activate a space or street – whilst poor lighting can create uncomfortable and unsafe environments.

Security is an increasing issue for cities and by extension a critical concern for urban designers delivering, or upgrading, public realm. Crime can occur anywhere, but is more common in places where people gather in numbers – marking the public streets and spaces within a city as prime locations for unsavoury activity and behaviour. Design however can play a role in discouraging certain behaviours and enhancing user safety and comfort.

There are competing theories on how to design for security – Jane Jacobs (1961) argued that good public realm will ensure passive surveillance is prevalent – designing to encourage on-street and in-space activity will increase the number of '*eyes*' within any given location, and they act as a form of security. Increasingly today places are turning to the use of CCTV in the public realm – cameras that monitor and record the goings on within these environments, to discourage criminal activity. Whilst Oscar Newman (1996) coined the term '*defensible space*' to illustrate that designers can actually employ defensive structures and tactics into their wider design choices – tackling rising concerns of terrorism in public spaces and creating spaces that not only consider what activities and opportunities they can offer to users, but equally what activities they can design out of the public realm, making certain activities difficult or impossible. One such example is designing spaces to make skate-boarding, or similar, challenging and therefore limit the potential for this to occur frequently. None of these approaches to security or defence are necessarily negative – nor is one approach objectively 'better' than the other – it is in how the designer employs them that will define 'success' – Defensible spaces, or CCTV, can be blunt and obvious, or they can be designed into spaces in such a way that they are creatively integrated and not easily perceived by people – the skill and knowledge of the designer is paramount to deliver the latter.

RIGHT: Creative lighting solution in Potsdamer Platz, Berlin, Germany. Framing the entrance to the transport hub that enters the large public square - the designers considered thoughtfully how the space would '*feel*' to users during both day and night. The well-lit space also enhances security during quieter periods, with CCTV, and modern glazed architecture offering passive surveillance, also integrated across this popular part of Berlin's extensive public realm network.

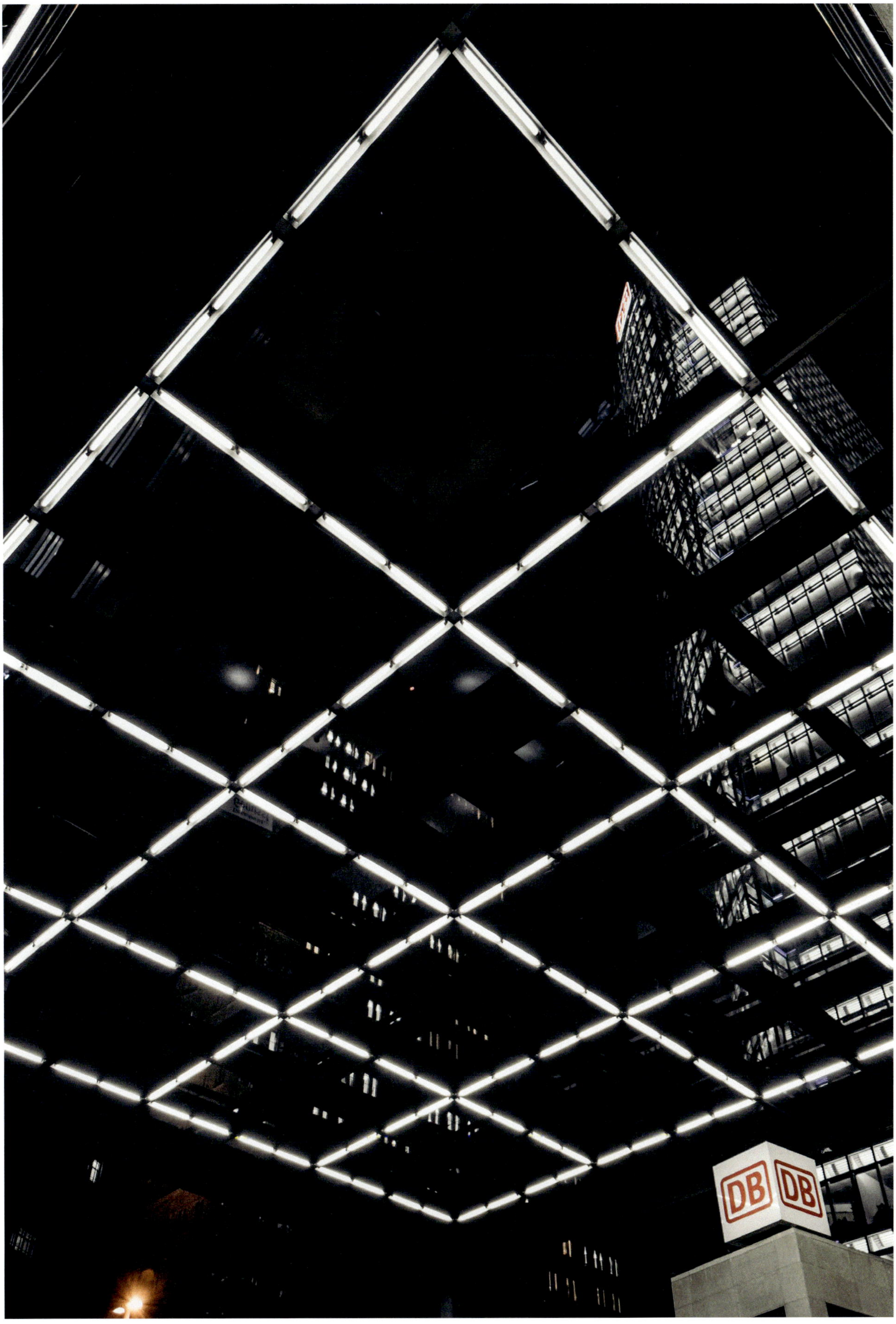
DB
DB

5. Environment

The public realm is the ideal infrastructure within urban settings to overlay environmental offerings – green infrastructure features that will enhance the quality of streets and spaces, the experience of those using them, and tackle broader concerns of sustainability and climate adaptation. Integrating and adding a diverse range and hierarchy of GI across the public realm network, using 'zones' to do this, is something all places should promote – the wealth of research illustrating the positive benefits is ample and compelling (see Mell, 2016). Later in this chapter we will unpack the designing of green infrastructure in a more focused manner. Whilst nominally the territory of landscape architects, the urban designer retains a critical role - in particular when considering the provision of smaller scale GI interventions woven into the public realm itself.

Many cities around the globe have significant ambitious plans to 'green' their urban environments to tackle climate change and provide a range of benefits for their populations. The provision of green spaces – such as dedicated parks, nature reserves, and greenbelts for example are part of these plans – urban design must play a major role in ensuring the breadth of coverage needed. Tree planting targets that are being set internationally cannot only be met through re-forestation or zoning land use for nature – streets and spaces must deliver planting extensively – and public realm can be designed to provide the necessary space. Trees on streets and in public spaces have multiple roles to fulfil – not only in meeting climate targets, but in shading spaces to reduce the impacts of rising global temperatures and creating comfort for users with shading, in providing movement corridors with legibility as they frame journeys, bringing colour and natural landscaping into hardscaped artificially designed environments, and in screening or buffering between uses such as vehicles and pedestrians - creating positive visual transitions for such edge conditions, reducing noise and helping filter harmful pollution.

Other critical environment features can be designed into the public realm such as sustainable urban drainage (SuDS) – systems that are in place to manage water, be that for retention or flooding defence.

In spaces susceptible to snow melt, heavy rainfall, or that struggle with water retention, the inclusion of targeted GI solutions can ensure spaces are accessible throughout the year and protected from inclement weather conditions. The ability to deliver such technical design components in an integrated and creative manner again relies on urban designers who understand the benefits of such inclusions, who take time to recognise the contextual needs of the locations they are designing within, and who engage with best practice to understand the ways in which these features can be conceived as part of the network of streets and spaces within a city.

TOP: Dedicating space to provide sustainable urban drainage can both protect the public realm from flooding - and adds diversity and colour to the urban environment. Even small interventions like in Manchester, UK can make a significant difference to the overall quality.

BOTTOM: Integration of street trees with seating - forming and framing a more organic movement flow and character for the street in Jerusalem.

CHAPTER 9: TECHNICAL DESIGN

6. Character

The design choices made in delivering the public realm will ultimately result in these locations forming a character – and there are a number of key considerations for the urban designer in how they build on, or alter, this character to provide a contextual offering. Whilst not all public realm details that have significant impact on character of streets and spaces are the purview of the urban designer – good designers will regardless recognise them and design in accordance with them. Architecture is a useful example here – whilst urban designers may have some influence over new buildings (see earlier in this Chapter for more detail), the design of a building remains the jurisdiction of the architect. Streets and spaces are defined and enclosed by buildings – and as such their style, materials, palette, and general aesthetic will have a major influence on the public realm - positively or negatively.

There are several facets that urban designers can incorporate however, that have the potential to enhance a place's character. Set-piece features such as public art, water features, statues, sculptures, and creative lighting setups are some of the ways in which physical inclusions can define a place's character. Material choice in regards furniture, hardware, or surfaces will also create an aesthetic that people will actively engage with. These design choices must be driven by the contextual understanding of the given space or place, as well as the intended use/function.

BALANCING PUBLIC REALM DESIGN

Fundamentally the principles of public realm design described above do not work in isolation – it is in the appropriate balance between them that high quality streets and spaces evolve. Urban designers must deliver each of these **Public Realm 6** aspects in a contextual manner – by understanding the type of *movement*, *activity, rest, am/pm* needs, *environmental* requirements, and *character* that will work most appropriately for any given location. Each of the principles requires the other to effectively operate in practice. For example it is possible to integrate a number of these into a single design feature or 'zone'. The complexity of designing high quality, contextually responsive, public realm should not be a deterrent to its delivery in practice – but viewed as a challenge for urban design and designers, one made easier by appreciating the significant role public realm plays in the success of place and what constitutes quality in the range of streets and spaces places it will provide.

BELOW: To design and deliver high quality public realm - streets and spaces must always consider the six principles discussed in this chapter - Spaces like the Darling Quarter, Sydney are designed with all in mind - based around a series of uninterrupted corridors, and thoughtful diverse zones. Finding the balance is a challenge for urban designers - the end result will ultimately be to the benefit of the public realm design and all those who later engage with, and use, it.

LEFT: Spaces can often be destinations in the public realm - to reinforce this designers can create anchor views/vistas using landmarks such as key buildings. Doing this can also maximise the character of the area. In Budapest, Hungary the Basilica provides a critical view drawing people from the city centre into the main public space - this is achieved through the use of urban blocks with clear and consistent building lines, and well considered corridors and zones that create legibility.

RIGHT: Streets need to bring people into space - it is critical the network is accessible and allows access from different locations and across all the city. In Bologna, Italy streets and spaces organically act and flow as a single entity - with routes in and out of spaces that are shaped and defined by the urban blocks. Note the landmark acting as an anchor view from 4 routes that connect the space with the north, west, and east - This space is more a node for movement choice.

It is imperative that the urban designer understands the function and hierarchy of each street and space - their role within the public network. Not every space is a primary destination, not every street is a primary movement link - and to design them appropriately and as part of a greater whole.

CHAPTER 9: TECHNICAL DESIGN   260

APPLIED URBAN DESIGN

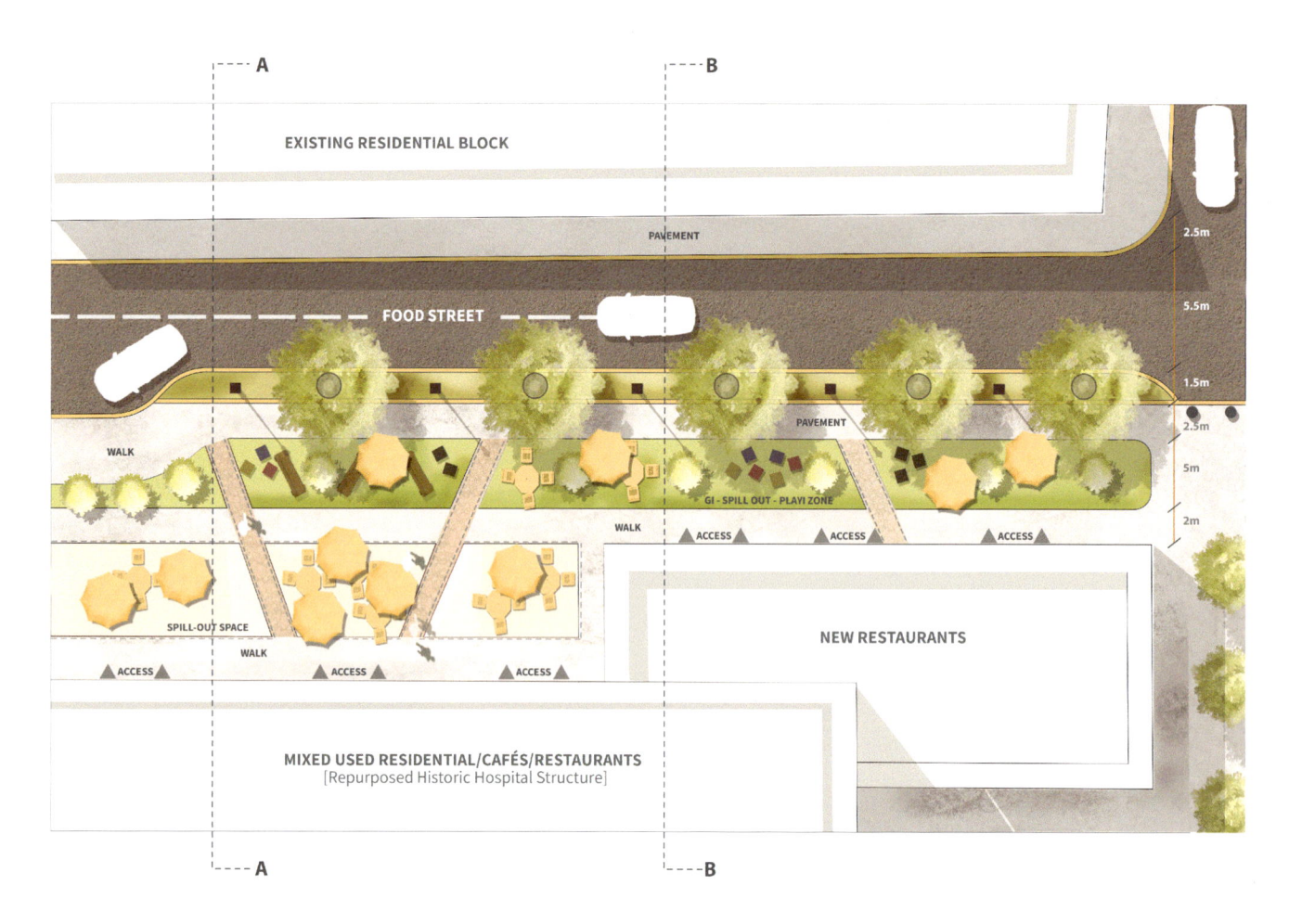

AALBORG
Key Space Design

CHAPTER 9: TECHNICAL DESIGN

1. MOVEMENT
The key route along Reberbansgade (Food Street) from west to east provides uninterrupted pedestrian movement on the southern side - framed by new retail frontages and cafes. The road has been narrowed to slow traffic, with dedicated delivery/loading bays introduced. The proposed public realm forecourts have 2 separated and clearly defined walking corridors for ease of movement and access to all buildings.

2. ACTIVITY
Within the provided zones is a series of spill out areas for outdoor eating/drinking linked to new cafes and restaurants along Reberbansgade. Play spaces are included in the central zone - to encourage play and socialising within the space - and enhance surveillance. The retail and leisure uses along both sides of the street are installed to attract footfall - and design is intended to promote resultant activities from all users.

3. REST
Spill-out zones provide a range of seating for outdoor dining - whilst flexible seating is included in the central zone to promote rest and socialising. This seating is adaptable and a range of types is proposed to ensure comfort of all user types. Core seating overlooking children's play zones encourages intergenerational engagement with the space and provides further passive surveillance. People are encouraged to stay and enjoy the space.

4. AM/PM
Street lighting is provided along both sides of Reberbansgade to ensure movement corridors are well lit throughout the evening. Lighting is also included along the pedestrian movement corridor within the spill out space in front of the old hospital building. Creative lighting features are integrated into formal seating solutions and children's play zone allowing evening and winter activity. The landmark hospital receives dedicated theatre lighting for façade.

5. ENVIRONMENT
Native species street trees line both sides of Reberbansgade to provide legibility, enhance enclosure, and segregate vehicular and pedestrian corridors. The central zone on southern side of the street provides ample landscaping, with children's play space incorporating eco-friendly, all-natural materials. There are also dedicated raingardens to provide SuDs ensuring effective water management and that the public space functions all-year round.

6. CHARACTER
Enhancing 'Food Street' aspect of Reberbansgade builds on existing character of the location. Feature of historic hospital frames a major part of proposed new public space providing a recognisable local landmark. Material choices for buildings shaped by the northern red-brick vernacular. In addition the main public space will display local public art works - linking to existing public mural on historic gable that acts as the entrance into proposed space from west.

PUBLIC REALM 6: Detail of key public realm space - along Reberbansgade [Food Street] on the north edge of the Aalborg site - analysed against the 'Public Realm 6' criteria [see 9.4].

New Restaurant Buildings

WALK

Existing Residential Blocks

Existing Restaurants/Cafés

Section BB | 2.5m WALK | 5.5m FOOD STREET | 1.5m GI/LIGHTS | 2.5m WALK | 5m SPILL OUT/PLAY ZONE | 2m WALK

9.5 GREEN INFRASTRUCTURE

SCALES AND HIERARCHIES

Green infrastructure holistically addresses the climate emergency, encourages social development and delivers economic value simultaneously. Consequently, the consideration, incorporation, and delivery of high quality green infrastructure is now critical to any successful urban design intervention (Mell, 2016). Green infrastructure (GI) should be considered as *'the network of urban/rural multi-functional green and blue spaces and other green features which deliver quality of life and environmental benefits for communities'* and is directly linked with blue spaces or blue infrastructure and therefore also includes rivers, streams, canals, and other water bodies (TCPA, 2012). A key component of GI is the multi-functional and multi-beneficial capability of natural infrastructure, with GI used extensively to address issues of flooding, micro-climate, food, wildlife and biodiversity loss as well as supporting efforts to improve mental and physical health and offer recreational opportunities through access to nature (Barton, 2017). Good urban and landscape design is functional, diverse, interactive, and immediate – allowing people of all ages, abilities and backgrounds to engage with nature within their neighbourhoods, while also providing links between the local and wider landscape (Mell, 2022).

Consequently, green infrastructure is not an alternative description for conventional open space – rather it includes a variety of scales and hierarchies of spaces and deals directly with the realisation of connections and links between GI features. A traditional approach took a disaggregated view of city open space functions, considering provision in a siloed and mechanical way – a park here, playing fields there, allotments elsewhere and streams/watercourses hidden in culverts. Contemporary understanding in design and landscape practice is to work directly with the complexity of GI and recognise the inherent connections between different functions and places across a range of scales/hierarchies (Barton, 2017).

Green Infrastructure: Scales and Hierarchies

Scale	Hierarchy of GI Components
National/City-Regional	Large strategic GI spanning multiple administrative boundaries and providing benefit for a number of localities such as: national parks, country parks and regional parks as well as landscapes such as woodland, grassland and wetlands.
City-Wide	Collection of GI features across the city including: urban parks, village greens, urban commons, landscapes such as woodland, grassland and wetlands, green corridors including rivers and canals, road and rail corridors, cycling routes, pedestrian paths, cemeteries and churchyards, tree-lined environments, playing fields, larger play spaces, city farms and community gardens, public green spaces.
Individual Site Level	Range of individual GI features at site level including: domestic gardens, street-trees, green-roofs/walls, allotments, play spaces, pocket parks, courtyards, sustainable urban drainage systems (SuDS).

TABLE 7 GI Scales and Hierarchies

A networked ecological approach to design takes the natural features of an area as a critical starting point, using them to help shape new connections and ensuring nature percolates through the urban environment to create a multi-functional green infrastructure network (Barton, 2017). Thus, GI works at a variety of scales from city-region to individual site level. Table 7 provides an overview of the different scales and hierarchies of GI between city-regional, city-wide and site-level components from national parks, forests, parks, open spaces, play fields, woodlands to street trees, allotments, private gardens, green roofs and walls, sustainable drainage systems (SuDS) and soils. For urban designers, GI must be considered as a system of networks and arrangements, promoting potential for ease of movement of wildlife, water, and people, within and across the site, joining up to other contextual places in the city and creating '**corridors**' and '**zones**' at a variety of scales.

TYPES OF INTERVENTIONS

Due to the multi-scalar identity and role of natural infrastructures in cities, GI interventions will span a wide variety of types and functions. The subsequent examples take forward a selection of aspects featured in Table 7 to exemplify what GI can look like, these examples are by no means exhaustive, rather they provide a platform to think through and consider GI interventions in a holistic way from the strategic landscape level to individual GI components in urban spaces. Urban design practitioners should work closely in conjunction with landscape architects, and other relevant professionals and stakeholders, in the design and delivery of green infrastructure across the scales. The role of the urban designer is to ensure GI is well networked across the city, integrated into the public realm and urban fabric, and accessible for all of the diverse population.

Landscapes

Landscape-scale GI, such as national parks, country parks, and forests, offer opportunities for urban designers to work effectively across administrative and legal boundaries and promote landscape networks that are integrated at the local, metropolitan, and city-regional scales – facilitating connectivity, multiple benefits, and capacity building for a large population. National parks are an excellent example of landscape-scale GI. Their role is both to conserve and enhance the natural beauty, wildlife, and cultural heritage of sizable territories of natural infrastructure while also promoting recreation, economic development, and social-wellbeing. It is the urban designer's role to promote and deliver inclusive access to these large-scale GI assets – designing sustainable mobilitiy networks to allow for as wide a cross-section of society to benefit from them as possible.

PEAK DISTRICT, UK

The Peak District National Park, established in 1951, is England's oldest national park. Covering a designated area of 1,438km2 and spanning the counties of Derbyshire, Yorkshire, Staffordshire, and Cheshire (Peak District National Park, 2023). The Peak District connects people to GI at a city-regional scale and is easily accessed by over 16 million people living within an hour's drive including from Manchester, Stockport, and Macclesfield on the west and Sheffield and Chesterfield on the East. It's mosaic of landscapes, dramatic geology, distinctive wildlife and habitats, thousands of years of people, farming and industry, a characteristic stone vernacular across numerous villages and settlements and strong communities and traditions make for a unique and incredibly popular place where people can be active, while also achieving wider-reaching benefits across the park including fresh water provision, flood prevention, as well as flood and carbon storage.

LEFT: Bakewell, Peak District National Park, UK.

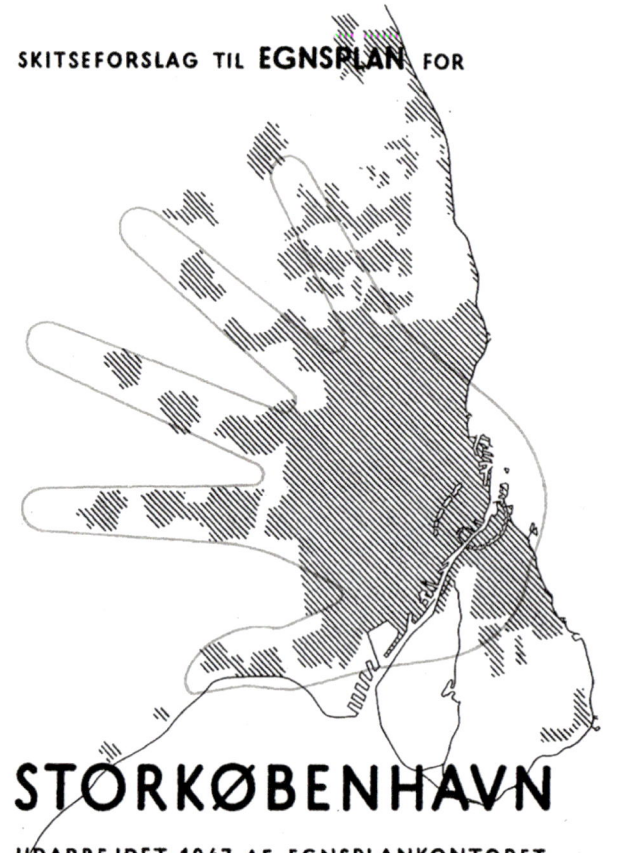

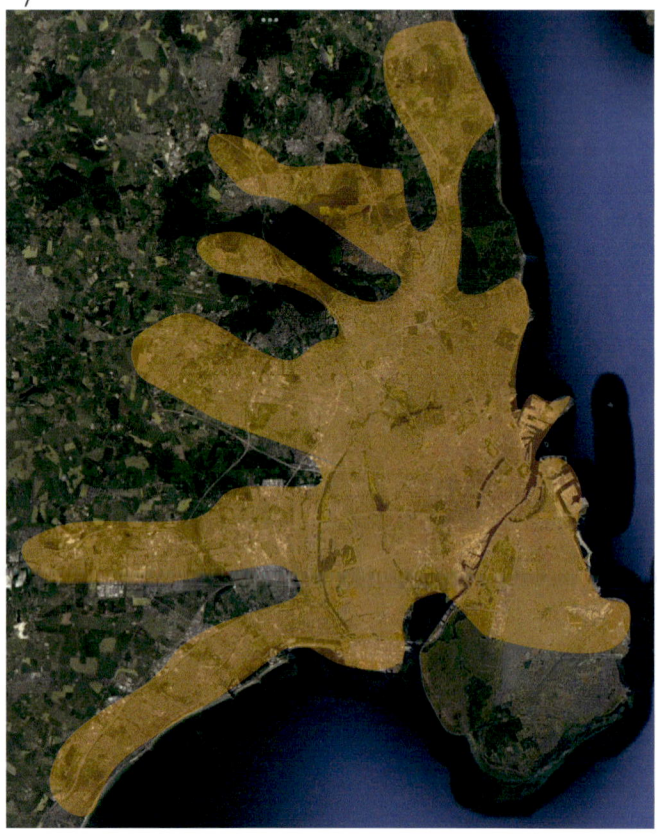

APPLIED URBAN DESIGN

IMAGES: The Copenhagen, Denmark five-finger plan from 1947 [TOP] created a development growth policy that centred on ensuring access for all to nature, and maintaining the city centres link to surrounding GI.

Today this plan has been mostly adhered to as Copenhagen has grown - with a linear strip [now six fingers] of development radiating out from the city centre [BOTTOM] and leaving behind natural green gaps that permeate into the city's core.

CHAPTER 9: TECHNICAL DESIGN

Green Corridors and Linear Parks
Often operating at a city-wide level, green corridors and linear parks are GI features, predominately constructed of environmental components such as green trails or green-blue trails which provide a variety of benefits. Unlike traditional opens spaces and parks, which operate at an individual site-specific level, green corridors and linear parks are an attempt to mitigate negative effects of urbanisation through the development of networked natural infrastructure. However, it is important to highlight a distinction between green corridors and linear parks.

Green corridors promote large-scale connectivity, conservation, and free movement for urban wildlife by connecting ecosystems that are separated by human activity and built form. Copenhagen's Five Finger Plan, and subsequent Six Finger Plan, is a long-standing example of strategic green corridor design/planning, the plan prioritises urban expansion along specific commuter rail lines (fingers) radiating from the central area of Copenhagen (palm) with protected, clear-cut green corridors flowing into/out of the city situated between each rail line.

By comparison, linear parks, typically build on existing biodiversity features in urban centres to extend or expand their benefits across a larger area or upgrade hard linear infrastructure such as former railway lines, expressways, or disused river beds into distinctive connected landscape features. Notable examples of this approach include the deculverting of Cheonggycheon stream in central Seoul, the High Line in New York, and Promenade Plantée in Paris which reimage former transport infrastructure into multifunctional urban parks and the Turia Gardens in Valencia located along the former course of the river Turia (*see* Chapter 4). Linear parks are designed to take full advantage of access, mobility, and high-quality public realm to add value and investment for the broader city and promote interaction between urban form and landscape.

Water and SuDs:
Sustainable Urban Drainage [SuDs] and water-resilient design work directly with the 'waterscape' of an urban area to reduce the risk of flooding and provide functional and aesthetic value to the public realm where flood water is likely or highly likely to cause challenges. Urban designers and built environment professionals, more broadly, are more aware than ever that natural hazards such as flash flooding, storm surges, and tidal flooding cannot be effectively managed by conventional drainage systems. Rather, water-resilient approaches which work directly with water and promote adaptive 'floodable' urban spaces and places are required. Working with landscape professionals, urban designers are creating multi-functional GI/BI through a variety of sustainable urban drainage techniques including: rain garden systems, permeable surfaces and pavements, swales, holding ponds, and soakaways (Palazzo, 2019). These practices showcase water management systems in practice, making how they function visible and intelligible to the public to raise awareness of sustainable water management and allowing users to learn about the water cycle directly.

Well-designed SuDS achieve diverse design objectives, not just water management but visual amenity, recreational opportunities, sense of place, comfort and cooling as well as wildlife habitats (Barton, 2017). Qiaoyuan wetland park in Tianjin China, for example, provides a variety of ecosystem services, including a stormwater purification and retention system, an ecological park, and community gardens for the surrounding neighbourhood. Similarly, Zollhallen Plaza in Freiburg incorporates permeable pavements to allow rainwater to penetrate into the subsoil.

BELOW: Sheffield, UK - *Grey-to-Green*. The UK's largest retrofit SuDS Project.

Play Spaces

The design and development of GI which considers and incorporates children is a critical endeavour to bolster children/young people's use of urban spaces, promote opportunities for play, and support their health and holistic development (Martin et al., 2023). The availability of safe, secure, and high-quality spaces and places for children/young people has dramatically declined in recent years. Consequently, consideration of how the built environment can promote and enhance opportunities for play have become more prominent as a public health and children's rights concern. GI, given its direct connection to nature, water, and landscape, has a unique ability to realise best-practice spaces for children and play. Best-practice play spaces ensure a spectrum of play opportunities and types are provided for, this will include topographical variations, climbable elements, moveable and open-ended equipment/materials, vegetation and water features, malleable and loose natural materials, a variety of ground surfaces, a range of seating/shelters and spaces for children/young people to rest and relax.

Urban Agriculture / Allotments

There has been an explosion of interest in urban farming and local growing ventures in recent years (Barton, 2017). International examples of city farming, such as in that of Detroit, demonstrate the importance of these spaces within the GI discourse. Urban designers must recognise the role, value, and necessity for local food production, these spaces give easy access to fresh food, encourage recycling of organic waste, and stimulate social interactions and capital (Barton, 2017). Allotments, city farms, community gardens/orchards are becoming more common in urban areas and will be vital in response to food production challenges as a result of climate change. To encourage these activities, growing spaces should be accessible and close to home. Public spaces, parks, and open spaces can easily accommodate food production and growing, urban designers have a key role to play to ensure these GI activities are promoted and achieved.

Aalborg's Karoline Lund, an urban park on the edge of the city centre, features a range of community-operated growing spaces for neighbouring residents. The space provides a learning environment for the adjacent nursery school and encourages socialisation between a broad spectrum of actors including growers, passers-by and children and the elderly.

POUND'S PARK, SHEFFIELD

is a best-practice example of GI/public realm development for children in the centre of an urban area. Situated within Sheffield's *Heart of the City* urban regeneration project, and totaling around 0.4ha, Pound's Park provides a dynamic and interactive play space for children/young people that incorporates a range of GI features and components. Designed as an inclusive play space, the park features a toddlers play area, physical and imaginative play area, interactive water play areas, hang-out zones for young people, and a range of seating options for caregivers. Through variation in height, climbable features, natural materials, vegetation and water, sand, high-quality equipment and materials, and open-ended features the park brings children in direct connection with GI, providing unique opportunities for play within an urban oasis. Incorporation of high-quality lighting has created a safe environment for young people, particularly for girls, at dusk/night.

CHAPTER 9: TECHNICAL DESIGN

268

TOP IMAGES: Provision of community operated growing spaces for local residents in Karoline Lund city park, Aalborg, Denmark.

MIDDLE: Rooftop urban farming allowing locals to grow their own produce year-round. Queenstown, Singapore.

BOTTOM: Local food market dominating key local pedestrian street, providing access to affordable fresh local produce in Hanoi, Vietnam.

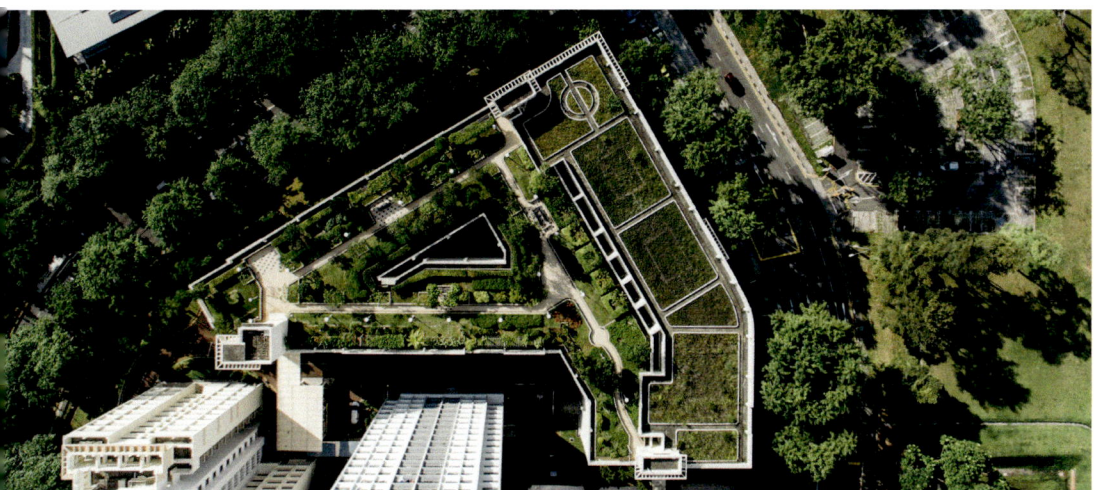

Urban Parks / Green Spaces

Parks and green spaces are the lifeblood of green infrastructure provision in cities, providing communities with access to nature, spaces for recreation, physical activity, and relaxation, as well as opportunities to focus on positive wellbeing. Nonetheless, access to 'good quality' parks and green spaces are critical. Frequently urban parks and green spaces suffer from neglect, are poorly lit – discouraging use of these spaces by women and girls at night, particularly in the winter – feature only a limited variety of planting and vegetation and are not appropriately managed or maintained. Likewise, disinvestment in parks and green spaces has resulted in a lack of activities and facilities, including the closure of vital resources such as a park café, local community clubs, or public toilets. Urban parks and green spaces require a dynamic mixture of activities and facilities to be successful, they must be well-lit to encourage inclusive use and should provide communities with access to colourful and engaging planting and vegetation. Urban designers must consider the quality of parks and green spaces to ensure what is delivered is appropriate and will be well used.

Pocket Parks and Courtyards

With some similarity to parks and green spaces, but operating on a much smaller scale, pocket parks and courtyards are important micro scale GI interventions in urban settings. Typically used by adjacent residents/neighbours, they provide direct access to nature in denser urban spaces and are incredibly popular with local people/everyday users/visitors. Pocket parks are typically fully public spaces and can be enjoyed by anyone. By comparison, courtyard spaces are more likely to be semi-private or fully private.

While the location, elements, and uses of pocket parks and courtyards will vary significantly, they facilitate similar opportunities for exercise, socialisation, play and relaxation by a wide range of stakeholders and users as larger parks and green spaces. From an urban design perspective, good access to, and availability of, micro-GI interventions are as important as larger landscape provision given these facilitate everyday access to GI and can improve health and wellbeing outcomes. Both provide shade, cooling, and space for relaxation with nature in urban areas, and when repeated across a neighbourhood or district, they become critical adaptive and climate resilient infrastructure for the city as whole. Engaging with small scale GI interventions is an important consideration for urban designers to help deliver responsive places of high quality. The *'big and bold'* GI interventions are often exciting and can be hugely popular - but quality *'local and meaningful'* GI ensures a more complete network and provides people with daily accessible landscaping options - enhancing wellbeing and quality of life.

TOP: Merchant Square East, London, UK - To provide extra landscape space designers introduced a floating pocket park on a large existing water feature.

MIDDLE: Pocket park, Santiago de Compostela, Spain.

BOTTOM: Semi-Private courtyard, Ystad, Sweden.

CHAPTER 9: TECHNICAL DESIGN

STADSPARKEN, LUND

in Sweden represents an dynamic urban park and green space that is immensely popular with local people. Located immediately adjacent to the city centre, it is the largest park in the city (at 22.5ha) and has been in operation since 1911. The park includes multiple landscape components between a **Jungle Garden** with wooden bridges, waterfalls and wetland vegetation, surrounded by ferns, tall grass, perennials and aquatic plants, a **Sun and Shadow Garden** with over 7,000 perennials, shrubs, trellised trees and bulbs set out in a formal pattern, and an **English Landscape Garden** adjacent to the Observatory, with winding paths, lush groves of trees, a large pond and open lawns (Lunds Kommun, 2023). Stadsparken also promotes a panoply of activities, featuring a range of picnic/BBQ areas, an aviary, running and training trails, playing fields for boules, handball and beach volleyball, a parkour track, a climbing rock area as well as a large playground encouraging opportunities for play for early-years children through to teens as well as a 1,500m2 skate park, that is popular with youth. The city park also includes a leisure centre, city park café, restaurant, and multiple public toilets (Lunds Kommun, 2023). Stadsparken is an incredible example of what urban parks and green spaces can be. While not all urban parks and green spaces need feature this range of activities to be considered successful – better practice urban design will ensure parks and green spaces are resourced, safe, inclusive and promote equitable access to nature.

TOP: Extensive local planting provides year-round colour.

MIDDLE: Play spaces are integrated to encourage children to be active and benefit from the landscape and nature around them.

BOTTOM: The park retains clear movement corridors for ease of access and to maintain connectivity with the wider public realm.

Urban Planting, Street Trees, and Green-Walls

At the smallest scale of intervention, urban planting, street trees, and green-walls provide citizens with the everyday benefits of nature in their immediate environment, streetscapes, and urban spaces while also performing many additional functions simultaneously. These GI interventions add aesthetic quality and a sense of place to any urban area and when extrapolated to a larger scale form a crucial part of the city's urban forest and broader adaptability to a range of climate challenges – providing shade, shelter, decreasing urban temperatures and exposure to the urban heat island effect, reduce airborne pollution and increase urban biodiversity (Landscape Institute, 2013).

However, despite their vital importance to climate adaptation at the local level and for the vitality of people and places more broadly - planting, street-trees and green-walls are often condensed in number or removed altogether from urban design projects – due largely to cost. The inclusion of a single street-tree in an urban project can cost thousands of pounds, consequently, these components are often the first to be cost-engineered from proposals, greatly reducing the quality and impact of the overall design. We strongly encourage urban designers to consider creative ways to ensure GI at the individual site level or streetscape be prioritised – a tree-lined environment or the presence of greening are critical to the delivery of successful contextually responsive urban design. It is also critical to ensure appropriate contextual planting is implemented – GI that will thrive in its local setting – climatic and physical. Consideration is also required of how these green additions will change across seasons – impacting their visual appeal and/or positive impacts.

BELOW: Integrating green walls, vertical landscaping, green roofs, and ground level public realm planting/trees to Downtown Singapore. These interventions provide visual interest on the street - but critically aid with cooling through shading and temperature reduction - as well as filtering pollution from vehicle emissions - all enhancing comfort for street users.

INTEGRATION WITH PUBLIC REALM AND URBAN FORM

Best-practice urban design requires an integrated mindset and approach to GI. The multi-functionality of GI acts as a critical bridge in how natural and built environment features can be integrated to deliver an enhanced quality of place while simultaneously supporting ecological systems (Mell, 2022). As the examples featured here demonstrate, there are healthy range of opportunities to connect and overlay GI with the public realm and broader urban form and these span across a multitude of scales – whether it be through the incorporation of street trees, planting beds, and SuDs along the high-street or the delivery of green courtyard blocks in new residential development, to the realisation of linear parks across an urban area to connect landscape features and promote habitat networks. We are at a moment in time in the climate emergency where urban design and development cannot ignore the vital need for protection for people, habitat, and wildlife. GI is central to that endeavour and must assist in our response to climate challenges to ensure that places of tomorrow are more resilient, sustainable, adaptable and high quality (Black, 2022).

Cities must continue to innovative, considering news ways and means of incorporating GI in urban development projects. It is important to highlight that GI should not be restricted to specific development types or particular locations within the city such as the public realm or residential areas – integrating GI within the broader urban form should be a broad consideration. Infrastructure projects and public transport initiatives are one example of where GI innovation has occurred in recent years with green-roofs and walls incorporated into bus stops and public transport hubs and linear green projects amalgamated across tram networks and bus routes. In Antwerp, Belgium, significant portions of the city's tramways are lined with semi-mature and mature trees while other parts of the network have encouraged linear grass strips to grow along the route. Reflecting our changing world and the critical role of adaptation to the future of our planet, urban design must align closely with landscape and ensure joined-up integrated design and delivery are realised.

Urban design practitioners need to know how to technically make 'space' within proposals for GI to be seriously included and integrated for success. In the same way that 'plot sizes' are defined for urban blocks or individual buildings, and standards must be met for sidewalk provision and street specifications – designs must also dedicate ample dimensions within schemes to allow for the effective delivery of green infrastructure. If integrated as part of the foundations of any design it becomes harder for external factors to remove or reduce landscaping without compromising the integrity and future success of the wider development.

TOP: Tree-lined tram network in Antwerp, Belgium.

BOTTOM: SuDs, urban planting, and play integrated into a busy university campus public realm and urban form. Helix, Newcastle, UK.

APPLIED URBAN DESIGN

This is another example of a design diagram that can accompany a large masterplan – in this case the Manchester case study. Here, at the larger scale, the approach taken to providing information about the **Green Infrastructure Provision** is somewhat different to the level of detail that might have otherwise been presented alongside a smaller design project (compare this to the Aalborg example on page 221). This diagram showcases the range of different landscape types within the masterplan including linear or corridor types that can be established along some of the arterial routes into the city, but also smaller ecology based green infrastructure projects such as rewilding the grassland around the fire and rescue centre, or providing a new woodland ecology park in the north-east of the site that incorporates the heritage asset of the viaduct.

In arriving at the scale, nature, and role of these green space's, consideration was made to what other spaces already exist in the surrounding neighbourhoods such as Sandhills nature reserve, Angel Meadow Park, and the Rochdale Canal. To this end a smaller area scale plan supports the contextual response to the green infrastructure provision – simply illustrating the thinking behind integrating proposed inventions with established landscape features.

To reinforce the '*networked*' nature of the design beyond the red-line boundary of the site, annotations are included to effectively articulate the green connections or links to adjacent green infrastructure. As with previous plans – we have included several best practice images, to help the reader visualise how these new proposals might *look* and *feel* in reality – this can be helpful in bringing the design vision to life for many audiences.

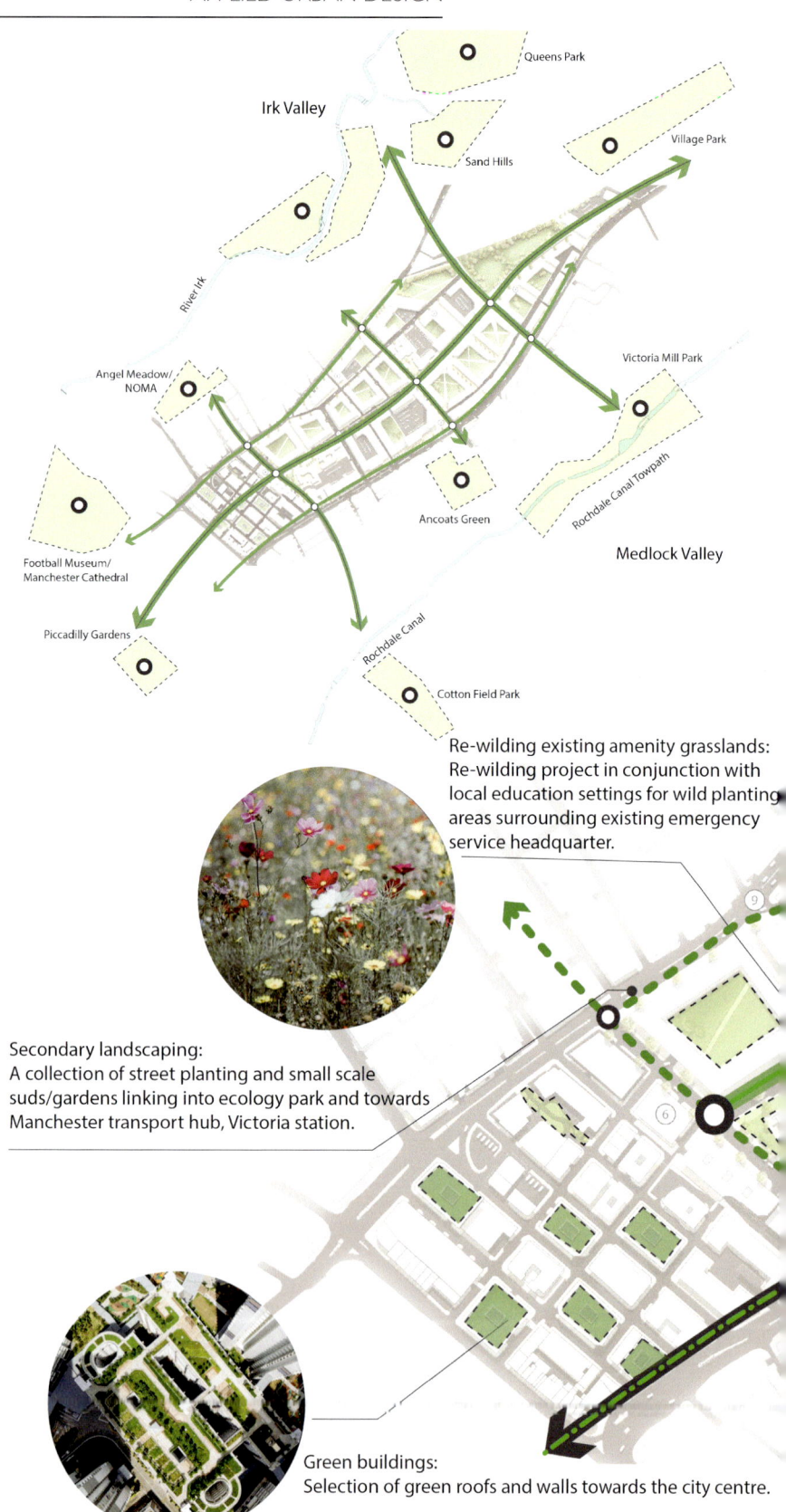

Re-wilding existing amenity grasslands:
Re-wilding project in conjunction with local education settings for wild planting areas surrounding existing emergency service headquarter.

Secondary landscaping:
A collection of street planting and small scale suds/gardens linking into ecology park and towards Manchester transport hub, Victoria station.

Green buildings:
Selection of green roofs and walls towards the city centre.

CHAPTER 9: TECHNICAL DESIGN 274

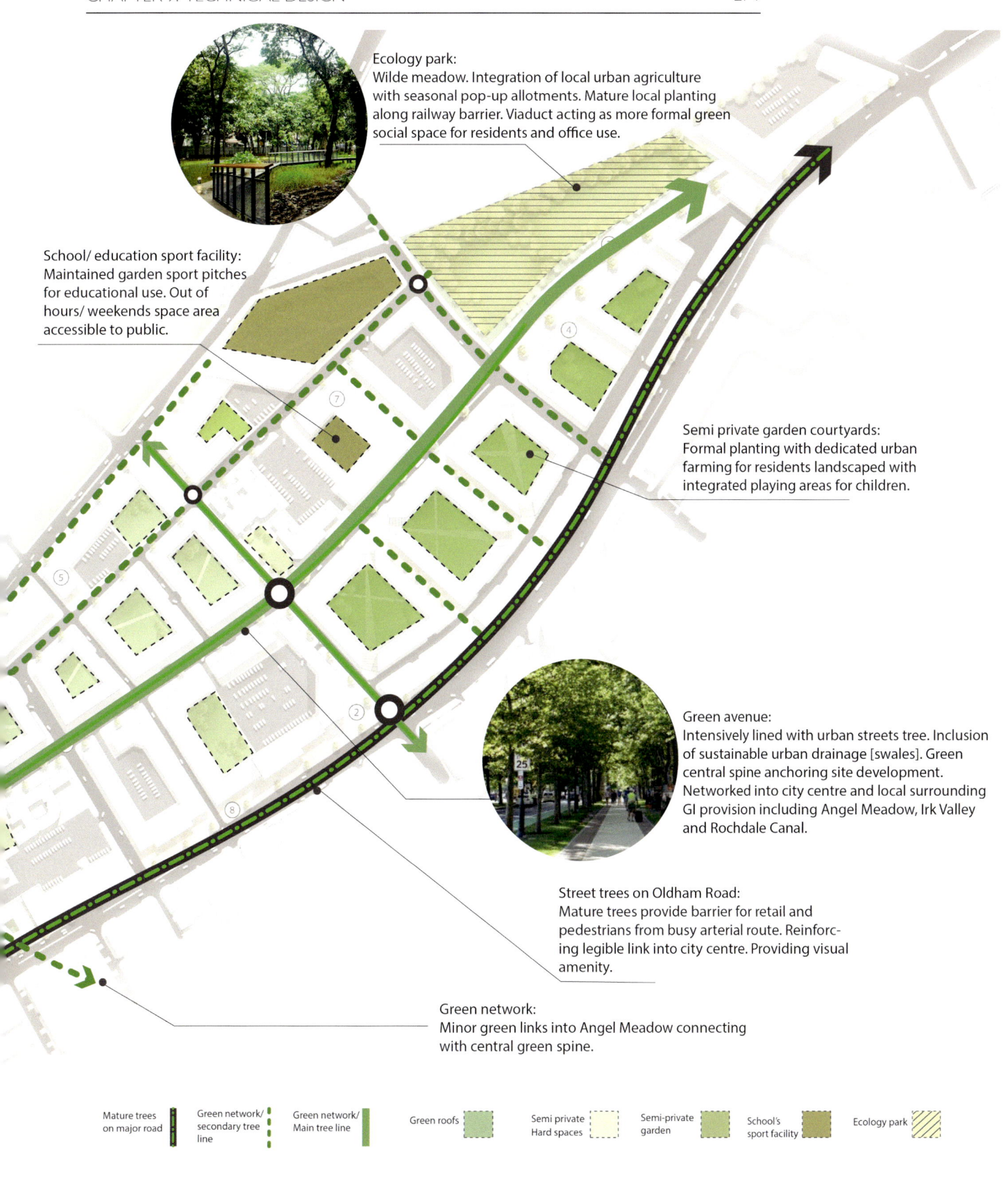

Ecology park:
Wilde meadow. Integration of local urban agriculture with seasonal pop-up allotments. Mature local planting along railway barrier. Viaduct acting as more formal green social space for residents and office use.

School/ education sport facility:
Maintained garden sport pitches for educational use. Out of hours/ weekends space area accessible to public.

Semi private garden courtyards:
Formal planting with dedicated urban farming for residents landscaped with integrated playing areas for children.

Green avenue:
Intensively lined with urban streets tree. Inclusion of sustainable urban drainage [swales]. Green central spine anchoring site development. Networked into city centre and local surrounding GI provision including Angel Meadow, Irk Valley and Rochdale Canal.

Street trees on Oldham Road:
Mature trees provide barrier for retail and pedestrians from busy arterial route. Reinforcing legible link into city centre. Providing visual amenity.

Green network:
Minor green links into Angel Meadow connecting with central green spine.

Mature trees on major road | Green network/ secondary tree line | Green network/ Main tree line | Green roofs | Semi private Hard spaces | Semi-private garden | School's sport facility | Ecology park

MANCHESTER
Green Infrastructure Provision

LINEAR PARK DESIGN, Aalborg

The new linear park on the Aalborg site provides a sustainable direct link to the train station from the northern residential district and Reberbansgade and acts as a landscaped barrier to the railway line to the west. With an uninterrupted pedestrian walkway and cycle lane - the park is made up of three zones. Each zone can be accessed from the heart of the site, connecting into the wider public realm provided.

A: PARK GATEWAY

The northern entrance to the Linear park - with access from the western end of Reberbansgade. This key pedestrian node offers pedestrians and cyclists a choice of movement - south through the linear park direct to the train station, or east along the newly developed Food Street and its associated public realm towards the city centre. The gateway is framed by the public art mural on the gable end of the existing historic structure at the most north-westerly point of the site, the entrance into the adjacent Hasseris district.

B: RESIDENTIAL / FAMILY ZONE

The linear park opens up heading south into a zone dedicated for family activity to support the residential half-blocks that enclose the space. The inclusion of playscapes for children, flexible seating, and formal planting ensure a safe comfortable environment for all users. Key views are opened to the historic Cathedral School to the west beyond the rail line - with direct links into and out of the zone from the heart of the site and new public spaces linking to Reberansgade and the residential neighbourhood existing in the north.

C: ECO / SOCIAL ZONE

The southernmost part of the park offers the most spacious component - with direct links onto Vesterbro (key arterial route running N-S) and directly to the train station. This zone provides inclusive picnic benches and formal seating - directly connecting with northern pedestrian link and heart of the site with cafes and associated spill out. On the western railway side an eco-landscape is integrated with local planting enhancing landscape connectivity for wildlife.

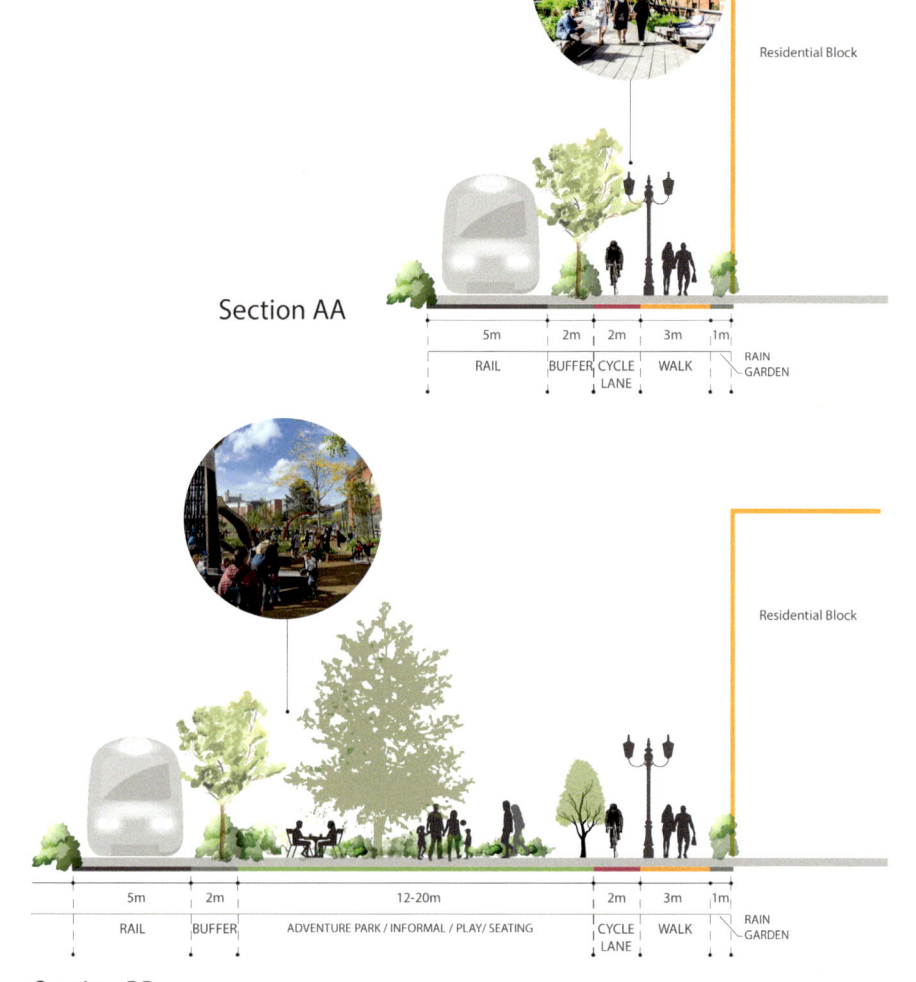

Section AA

Section BB

Section CC

AALBORG
Linear Park Design

A: Park Gateway

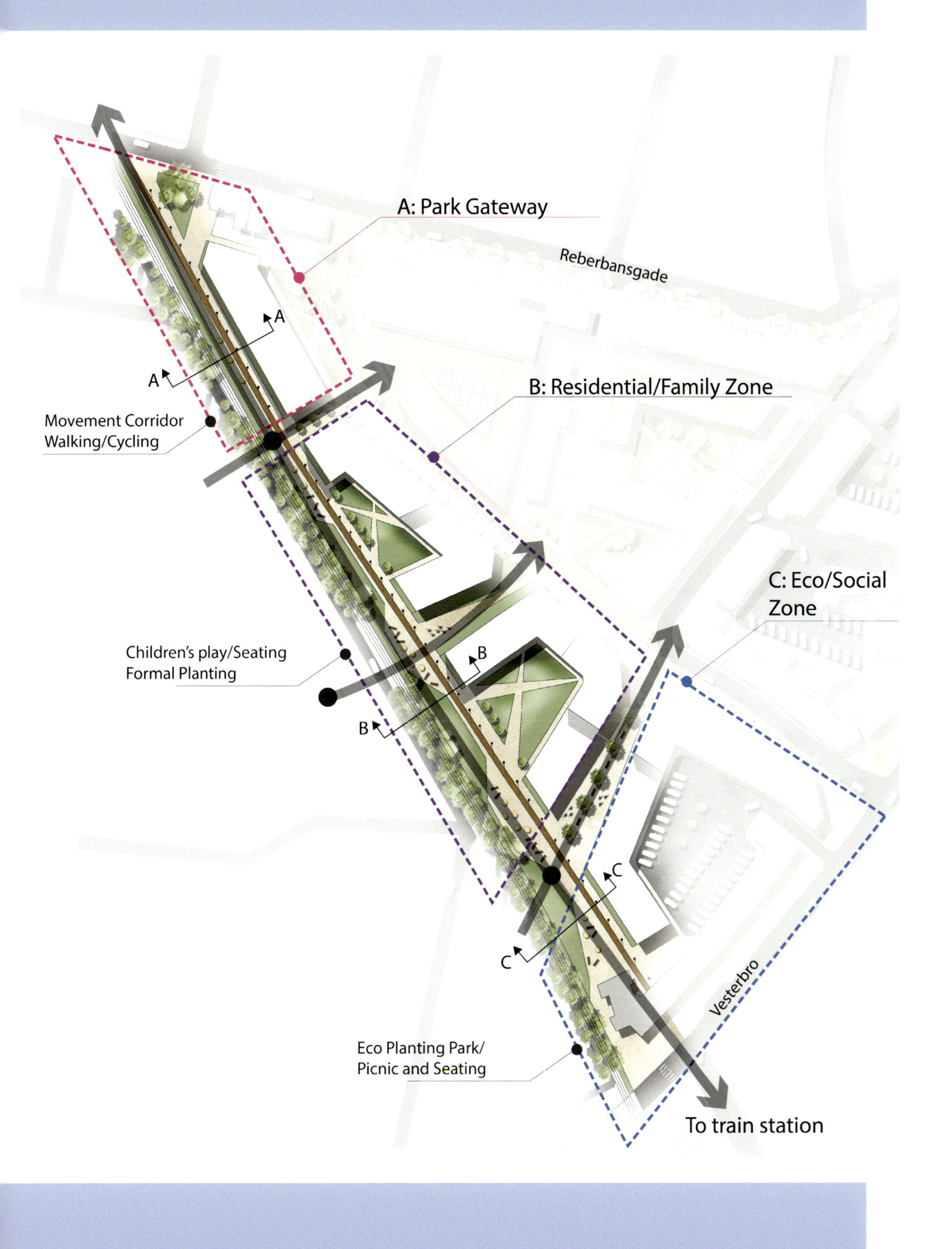

Reberbansgade

Movement Corridor
Walking/Cycling

B: Residential/Family Zone

C: Eco/Social Zone

Children's play/Seating
Formal Planting

Eco Planting Park/
Picnic and Seating

Vesterbro

To train station

QUALITY IS NOT 'OPTIONAL'
This chapter has covered – across both structural and detailed design (super-components) – almost all the *12 functional blueprints* (see 4.3) and *10 liveable qualities* (see 4.2) for successful applied urban design. There is however a single notable exception omitted from both provided lists – the last layer/quality from each – **Maintenance and Management** (functional blueprints) and **Long-term** (liveable qualities). Both themes are naturally related – and it is critical to re-consider them here, in relation to the active 'design phase' of the AUD Framework.

Having discussed at length the range, and types, of interventions possible across urban blocks, public realm, and green infrastructure, it is of vital importance that the practitioner recognise that any design solution be long-term – avoiding short-term upgrades or fixes were possible. To achieve this, it is imperative that maintenance and management of spaces and places be central to the design process. This book, and the AUD Framework it is demonstrating, has a central focus on the delivery of contextually responsive, people centred, high-quality urban design – yet 'context' is often misunderstood in practice. Urban design has traditionally had a fixation on the physical form – neglecting the deeper contextual components that make up a place's richness and uniqueness. A large portion of this book has been dedicated to challenging this preconception – arguing context is more complex and dynamic and requires a robust wide-ranging analysis to truly begin to articulate its subtleties and nuances. It is the responsibility of the urban designer to discover the relevant 'contexts' for a number of key issues directly related to the potential for long-term success of a proposal – issues such as finances for managing and maintaining streets and spaces; resources for upkeep; ability and willingness of community-led care for design; climatic, seasonal, or use conditions that may directly impact how easy it is for any design to remain visually appealing – or sustainable; and whether proposed interventions are appropriate for local users and their existing needs and circumstances.

To ensure any proposed design intervention operates to its maximum capacity – urban designers should engage with the local authorities or organisations tasked with the upkeep and management to ascertain the resources they have available – or are willing to provide – and what plans are in place mid-long term. A lack of resources or funding for certain design solutions can lead to an accusation that quality design is the purview of the wealthy – areas that can not only financially afford the design but can also ensure its long-term conservation and running. It is undoubtable that increased resources and funding can directly lead to more flexible decision making in the urban design process – yet it is certainly no guarantee of success, nor does it preclude quality design being delivered on strict budgets. It can also be true that the delivery of poor-quality urban design can actually cost developers and local authorities/communities more in the long-term, as unsuccessful environments will likely require upgrading or re-design.

Urban designers can think more creatively how they can work within tighter budgetary constraints – or how they can deliver spaces and places that can maintain their function and appeal long-term in areas where resources are stretched. Urban design must prioritise context, people, and quality above all else – these should be central to all design proposals – they simply need to be appropriate for the conditions of the setting in question. Perhaps this means public spaces that utilise more maintenance friendly materials, furniture and lighting; green infrastructure provision that allows local communities to be involved in their ongoing care; mixing year-round planting with more seasonal offerings to maintain colour and appeal throughout the winter months, or innovative integration of design features to save money – such as SuDs, planting, lighting, and seating being designed as a single public realm feature.

Too often development projects – and their designers – must scale back designs due to feasibility issues late in the process. This traditionally results in the loss of, or significant reduction in, landscaping provision and public realm quality. Working smarter and with more knowledge of budgets, costs, and resources available can play a part in avoiding such unfortunate scenarios. Ultimately the urban designer has a fundamental obligation to re-work how we 'scale-back' projects to save money or work within strict financial structures. This can be achieved by prioritising the public realm and green infrastructure – ensuring their

CHAPTER 9: TECHNICAL DESIGN   278

provision is non-negotiable, integrating contextual and quality components so profoundly that the integrity of the entire development is at risk if they are significantly reduced or altered. This demands the field of urban design continue to demonstrate the value of such design to wider society and placemakers through best practice research and education – as well as practitioners who buy into this approach and practice it in their professional settings at the coalface of the industry.

LEFT: Spaces such as Plaza Mayor de Caceres, Spain do not require significant management from public bodies. The design is predominantly hardscape, and the local businesses populating the square conduct much of the upkeep and maintenance. During busy tourist periods however, extra funds are allocated to ensure it remains in a good state of repair visually and functionally.

BELOW: Bryant Park, New York underwent a major redevelopment - that required commitment from local authorities and management groups to ensure that the park is well maintained throughout the year - given the amount of landscaping and public provision this demands significant resources to be allocated or the spaces risks falling into a state of disrepair that blighted it for so long prior to regeneration.

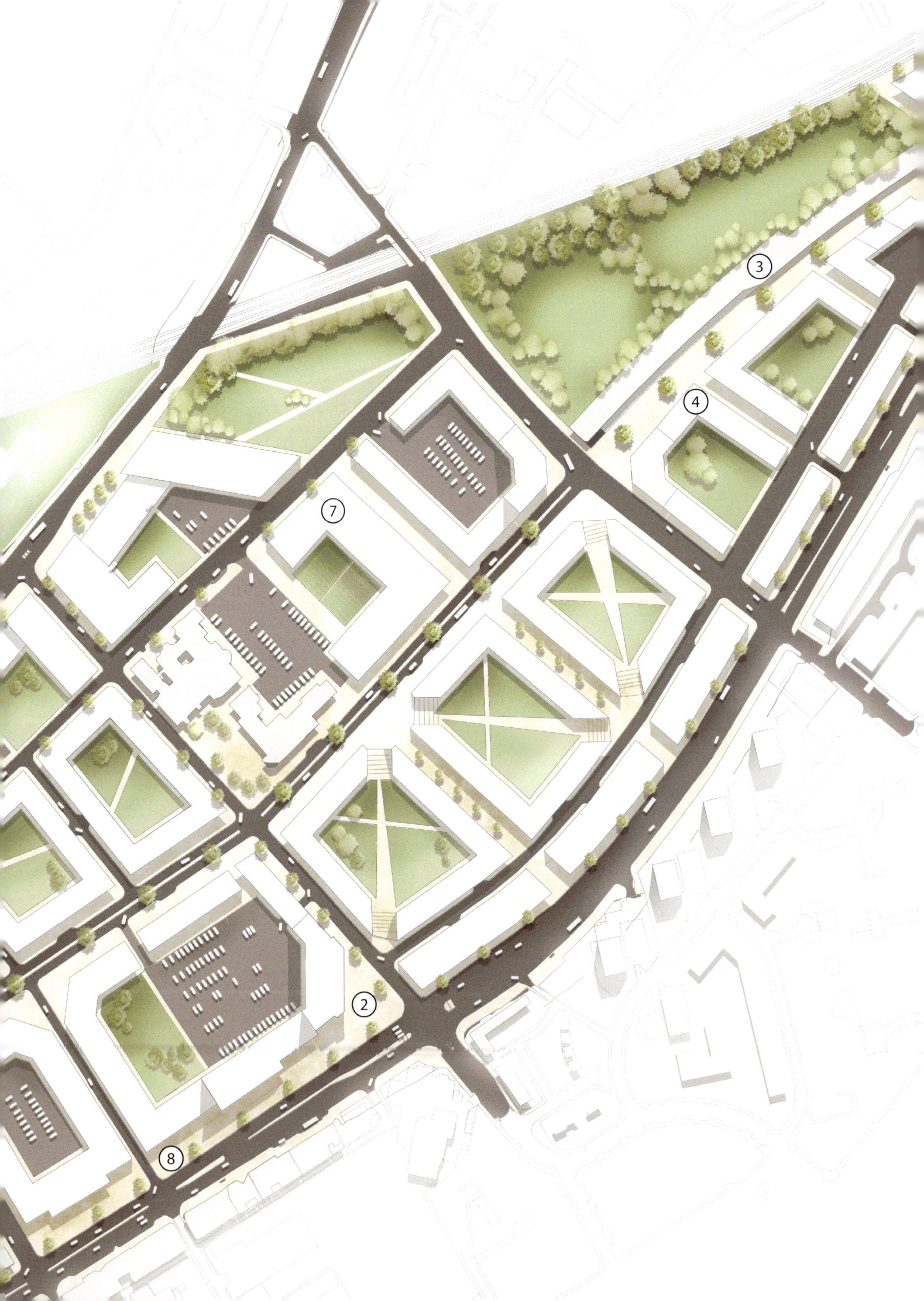
3
4
7
2
8

CHAPTER 10
Design Delivery

10.1 COMMUNICATING DESIGN

To communicate applied urban design, bringing the vision to life - the production of a series of illustrative and technical graphics will be required. The successful communication of any urban design proposal requires the design to be communicated both as a comprehensive solution via the production of a single technical design proposal plan (*see* 8.2), as well as complimentary additional detailing and illustrations to unpack the design and its constituent parts (*see* Chapter 9). Throughout this book we have utilised our case study sites in Manchester and Aalborg to demonstrate the AUD Framework in action – the production of the visuals and graphics employed required not only experience in the relevant digital software – but also an appreciation for how to effectively communicate ideas and narratives to a wide range of different audiences. The AUD Framework demands a series of 'outputs' that illustrate the process undertaken and validate the contextually responsive approach employed across the entire process. To showcase this transparency it is imperative you ensure clarity of message and information conveyance across the design process – as well demonstrating a clear understanding of the real-world implications related to delivery of applied urban design.

OPPOSITE PAGE: Applied urban design proposals need to be delivered in a technical and clear manner to ensure clarity for a wide range of different audiences - Choosing the appropriate visual/graphical techniques and styles is crucial to effectively communicate the final design and associated detail.

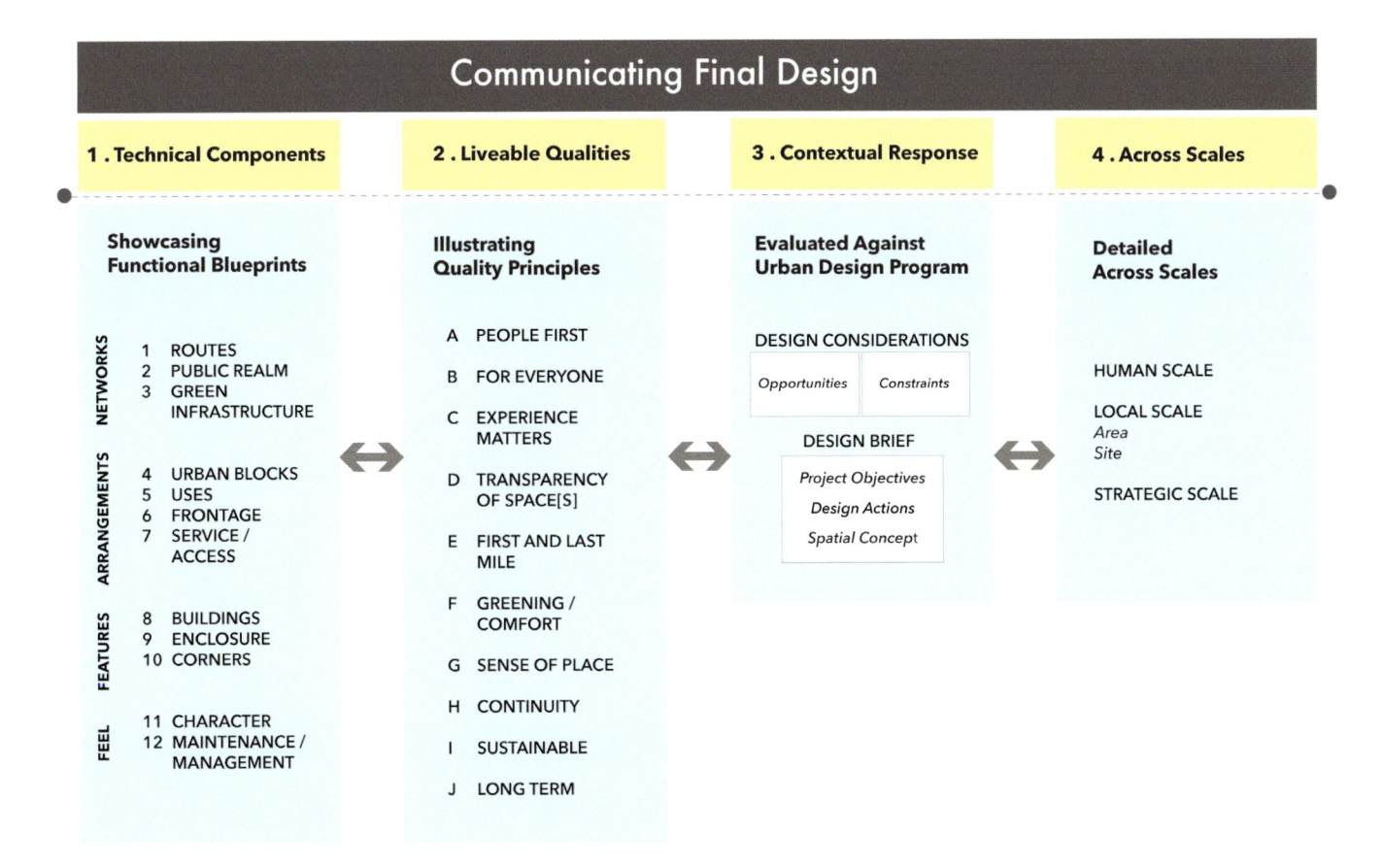

Communicating Final Design

1. Technical Components
Showcasing Functional Blueprints

NETWORKS
1. ROUTES
2. PUBLIC REALM
3. GREEN INFRASTRUCTURE

ARRANGEMENTS
4. URBAN BLOCKS
5. USES
6. FRONTAGE
7. SERVICE / ACCESS

FEATURES
8. BUILDINGS
9. ENCLOSURE
10. CORNERS

FEEL
11. CHARACTER
12. MAINTENANCE / MANAGEMENT

2. Liveable Qualities
Illustrating Quality Principles

A. PEOPLE FIRST
B. FOR EVERYONE
C. EXPERIENCE MATTERS
D. TRANSPARENCY OF SPACE[S]
E. FIRST AND LAST MILE
F. GREENING / COMFORT
G. SENSE OF PLACE
H. CONTINUITY
I. SUSTAINABLE
J. LONG TERM

3. Contextual Response
Evaluated Against Urban Design Program

DESIGN CONSIDERATIONS
- Opportunities
- Constraints

DESIGN BRIEF
- Project Objectives
- Design Actions
- Spatial Concept

4. Across Scales
Detailed Across Scales

HUMAN SCALE

LOCAL SCALE
Area
Site

STRATEGIC SCALE

PROPOSED DESIGN AND TECHNICAL DETAIL

The production of the final technical design proposal is normally achieved through the use of vector-based software packages including AutoCAD or VectorWorks. However, it can also be presented as a technical drawing produced by hand. The proposed design drawing is technically accurate (i.e. delivered to scale) and forms the basis for the development of detailed construction, or contractors, drawings at a later stage of the development process. The technical design proposal should include minor details and annotations only, such as street names or labels, as the incorporation of further detail will come forward in the detailed drawings that accompany the proposal.

In detailing and unpacking the design a range of elements can be considered, including coverage on the hierarchy of streets and spaces, differentiation of public realm, role of public and private spaces, configuration of buildings and land uses, routes and networks of movement, types of activity, integration of green infrastructure, location of frontage/access, and plans for servicing. However, in the detailing of the design proposal, it is important to select the most critical design elements for further detailing only – ensuring a clear focus as to the purpose of the complimentary visuals/materials. Detailed drawings on how the proposal works will be presented across a range of formats including, plans, technical plans, sketches, sections, or 3D models (*see* Visualisation Techniques). Likewise, components of the design should be displayed at different scales, to ensure specific aspects of the proposal are worked through in the required level of detail. For example, a key public space, linear park or streetscape may be shown in higher levels of detail such as at 1:100, 1:250, or 1:500. These 'zoom in's' will support the design and assist in communicating how it is expected to function. The utilisation of different visual and graphical techniques will ensure a more complete representation of the proposal – and how it responds to its context.

In detailing the proposal, urban designers utilise a range of software programs including Adobe Illustrator, Adobe Photoshop, Adobe Sketch, AutoCAD, and SketchUp as well as hand drawing and sketching. Often this process is iterative and requires mixing different techniques and approaches together to create a specific output. For example, the creation of an illustrative perspective sketch might involve using SketchUp to create a 3D form, hand-drawing to add illustrative details to the model and Adobe Photoshop to colour and finalise the graphic. Techniques and software should be selected to maximise the clarity of the proposal and ensure the information is conveyed in the most appropriate manner. For example, an axonometric sketch perspective may be of more communicative value than a technical cross-section to provide an illustration of the character of the proposal. Thus, as part of the detailing process, it is important to consider the focus/emphasis, type of graphic, and what approach works best to communicate the information.

Regardless of the selected technique, the aesthetic, language and style of all visual content should be consistent to ensure continuity – this demonstrates a single visual narrative for the design and can be vital to ensure the process, decision making, and output are understood in a transparent way. The development of high-quality visuals and illustrative materials bring the proposal to life for the reader/user and are critical tools in the engagement of different audiences and marketing of the proposal to a range of stakeholders.

DIFFERENT AUDIENCES

Urban designers must communicate their complex ideas to a range of audiences, including specialist audiences i.e. other design and built environment professionals, as well as a non-specialist audiences such as local communities, businesses, councillors, and a client or broader development group associated with the project. The ability of others to easily read and understand the proposal is key to ensuring the project narrative is clear and logical. This will require a range of techniques to be used, to detail, showcase, and unpack the design – and will include the use of graphical and technical approaches such as sections, models, or sketches as well as consideration of how these are packaged to tell the story – with storyboarding representing a core technique (*see* Storyboarding a Narrative).

In breaking down the design, an important part of the process is how best to tailor the approach to the different levels of expertise. For example, an architect can easily

OPPOSITE PAGE: Communicating urban design requires the practitioner to know their audience – and provide an appropriate presentation that will engage them and their level of design understanding and competency. Technical drawings and information will be necessary for delivery of design in the real-world, but such materials are often not helpful when illustrating design to the community, and in particular younger audiences.

Manchester Urban Design LAB making use of a bespoke 3D physical model to assist children in better understanding their city and how proposed interventions will impact their everyday life within it.

CHAPTER 10: DESIGN DELIVERY

negotiate and navigate a technical plan or a section and will comfortably engage with highly detailed materials, whereas, in communicating the proposal to a community group, use of rendering and consideration of incorporating locally significant landmarks, public spaces or streets will be more impactful in helping individuals navigate and locate the proposals. Here, *'before'* and *'after'* sequences to demonstrate exact changes can be beneficial, for all audiences, but particularly local actors.

Large print posters at A0 or A1 are the most common tool to present the design and are often accompanied by a presentation of the project to provide an executive overview of the key goals, decisions, and achievements of the final solution. Nonetheless, how the design is communicated to different audiences will also depend on the purpose of the meeting or event and where in the process they are involved. As emphasised in Chapter 7, in the current practice of public engagement, individuals are often consulted after the design proposals have been developed – resulting in the public having little input on the proposals. We argue that engagement with the public must happen earlier in the process to inform appropriate design solutions with people at their centre. Thus, in communicating the design, it should not be focused on gathering comment or feedback – rather this feedback should already be embedded in the analysis conducted and have had a strong influence in the Urban Design Program and subsequent strategy developed.

For applied urban design communication to be effective it is important to know your audience and think carefully about what information they require. How might you present that information to ensure broader stakeholders understand and can interpret the proposals and how it should differ in the level of detail or technical data to speak to different age groups. Children and young people should be active agents in the design of the built environment rather than passive stakeholders that get ignored as a result of their inexperience or lack of skills – design communication must be playful and interactive to ensure all groups are included, incorporated, and form a collaborative part of the process.

VISUALISATION TECHNIQUES

Urban design presentation is a nuanced endeavour that entails communicating intricate design concepts and spatial arrangements to a diverse audience. Visualisation techniques play a pivotal role in effectively conveying the various stages of urban design, encompassing analysis, design drafting, and final presentation. The crux of any urban design graphic lies in the clarity of its message. Successful urban design graphics are characterised by *simplicity, annotations, and readability*. Achieving this simplicity necessitates a profound understanding of the message to be conveyed, coupled with the selection of the most effective technique for its presentation. As the design process advances through stages ranging from preliminary draft formulation, to immature and mature design options, to the final technical presentation, certain graphical techniques prove to be more efficacious at each juncture. We have showcased numerous presentation techniques throughout this book with our *'live'* case study sites in Aalborg and Manchester - this section delves into this spectrum of visualisation techniques in more detail.

Drafting Stage: 2D and 3D Sketching

Whether we find ourselves in the analysis stage or the design stage, drafting consistently emerges as the initial phase of our process. Hand-drawn 2D and 3D sketches/maps are the most effective visualisation techniques at this stage. Tracing paper, colouring pens, and sketching pens constitute essential tools for any urban designer, often serving as the initial instruments in a project. Hand drawing, a timeless and classical visualisation technique, provides designers with the freedom to explore ideas swiftly and effectively. This technique establishes a direct connection between hand and mind, enhancing efficiency without reliance on software. Particularly valuable in the early stages of analysis and design, hand sketching can be categorised into 2D and 3D iterations.

2D sketching aids in the initial analysis stages, exploring space in two dimensions. Tracing paper and drafting pens are commonly employed for tasks like legibility analysis, mapping architectural quality, delineating route hierarchies, or charting green infrastructure. The tracing papers allow for multi-variable analysis in which layers can be easily cross referenced to produce more meaningful and useful messages. Similarly, using 2D sketching at the design stage allows for a quick exploration of design concepts and starting to formulate the immature design options.

Sketched cross sections, a useful 2D graphic, illustrate heights and relationships between different elements, often created by hand during analysis and the early design stages. Such tool allows for early exploration of constraints, edge condition, topography, and building heights. As cross sections should be undertaken to scale, they can present a relatively accurate presentation in the early design/analysis stages.

3D sketching involves exploring spaces between buildings from various perspectives. Unlike a photograph, urban sketching adds analytical value by emphasising certain points and omitting irrelevant objects. This technique is especially useful for serial visions and exploring specific scenes and spaces during the analysis stage. While 3D sketching usually requires skills and knowledge about perspective rules, it is an acceptable practice to trace actual photos and apply the essence of the technique by tracing only what we want to show and what is considered important to our message.

Annotations play a pivotal role in all hand sketching techniques (and in fact, in all urban design presentation techniques), enhancing message clarity, even though sketching is typically used for quick, preliminary presentations.

Developing Design Options

As the design process advances beyond initial exploration, the utilisation of hand-drawing techniques remains viable; nevertheless, the preference shifts towards digital methods due to their heightened precision and exceptional modifiability, rendering them more useful at this juncture. The drafting of cross sections assumes a pivotal role in formalising design alternatives at this stage, undertaken with precision often within Computer-Aided Design (CAD) software as a skeletal framework, prioritising accuracy over visual aesthetics.

Digital massing models emerge as a straightforward and efficient 3D visualisation tool that facilitates the exploration of design alternatives. Noteworthy for their high modifiable nature, these models depict shadows, masses, heights, enclosures, and even floor uses. Software platforms like SketchUp are commonly employed for the creation of such models.

As the design option sketched drafts are transitioned to a digital format, plans are generated in a rudimentary manner, foregoing rendering intricacies. Despite their basic nature, these digital plans serve a crucial role in simplifying and elucidating the available design alternatives, gradually preparing them for the next stage: the final design presentation.

Final Presentation: Technical Plans and Models
When the design process reaches the final presentation stage, digitalising graphics becomes imperative for maintaining efficiency and technical accuracy. *Analytical 2D maps* transition to specialised vector-based software like Adobe Illustrator for a sharp, stylised rendering, offering easy editing and flexible printing. Analytical maps should be focused on the key message, omitting all unnecessary elements, and supported by annotations and other graphics/images to complement them. It is recommended to have a visual language and style in place at this stage in order for the final presentation to feel consistent.

CAD software is often employed for final technical masterplans due to its high accuracy and compatibility with rendering software. The result is usually a skeleton masterplan that forms the base for the final rendered masterplan and 3D presentation. At this stage, cross sections can also be digitalised with CAD for an accurate final visualisation.

Digital rendered 3D models provide detailed previews of the final product, showcasing masses, shadows, and enclosures. They show accurate lighting, texture, and materials. Software packages like Lumion adds motion to 3D models, creating dynamic journeys through spaces.

Infographics are another important presentation technique, visually communicate textual content using simple shapes, symbols, and colours, effectively highlighting key messages. A good infographic is simple, engaging, and easy to remember.

3D physical modelling is a classical technique for exploring massing, presenting spatial relationships and massing in tangible, physical form. Study models facilitate an interactive design process, enabling informed modifications and refinements. Detailed models showcase public spaces' textures, street furniture, and lighting, often used for final presentations. 3D physical models represent a key marketing tool as they are usually presented in key places and presented in various events to a wide range of audiences.

Photography and cinematography techniques explore completed projects in their real-world context, annotated to convey specific messages. They can be used to show site context, condition of land/buildings, and to explore character and vernacular. They are also useful for heritage and historical analysis. Cinematic presentations utilise techniques like camera angles, lighting, and video editing to tell compelling visual stories about projects and their evolution within their context. By evoking the emotions through visual storytelling urban designers can create a deeper connection between the audience and the urban design narrative that structures the design.

Finally, *Virtual Reality (VR)* provides an immersive experience for exploring proposed designs and navigating public spaces. It can also be used to explore best practice case studies and various spaces around the world. Augmented Reality (AR) overlays digital information on the real world, offering real-time visualisation during client presentations and discussions. Much urban design research is now using AR and VR to explore possible scenarios that resemble how people would use and enjoy the proposed spaces.

The Process of Effective Visualisation:
Effective visualisation involves a systematic process to convey the intended message clearly. The following five steps are considered integral to arriving at a suitable and high-quality visualisation:

1. *Identify the intended message textually*
2. *Choose the appropriate graphical presentation technique*
3. *Simplify the graphic*
4. *Annotate the graphic*
5. *Mix presentation techniques*

Clearly articulate the key message or information you aim to convey through the visualisation. Ensure a concise and focused representation of the message. The message should be done textually at this stage

1 — Identify intended messages textually

2 — Choose the appropriate technique

Select a graphical representation method that aligns with the design stage and the best way of communicating the message effectively. Consider cross sections, photos, infographics 2D and 3D graphics.

Streamline the visual elements to eliminate unnecessary complexity. Focus on presenting the essential information, avoiding clutter that might hinder comprehension. Simplicity enhances clarity. Buildings are not always necessary in your basemaps, the same apply to streets and GI.

3 — Simplify

4 — Annotate

Provide clear and concise annotations to guide the viewer through the visualisation. Label important points, areas, or any elements crucial for understanding. Annotations enhance comprehension and interpretation and ensures the message is relevant.

Explore the integration of multiple presentation techniques when appropriate. Combining 2D and 3D photos, cross sections, sketches and technical plans in one graphic might offer a comprehensive view and enrich the understanding of complex multi variable concepts given the graphic is presented in a clean way.

5 — Mix techniques

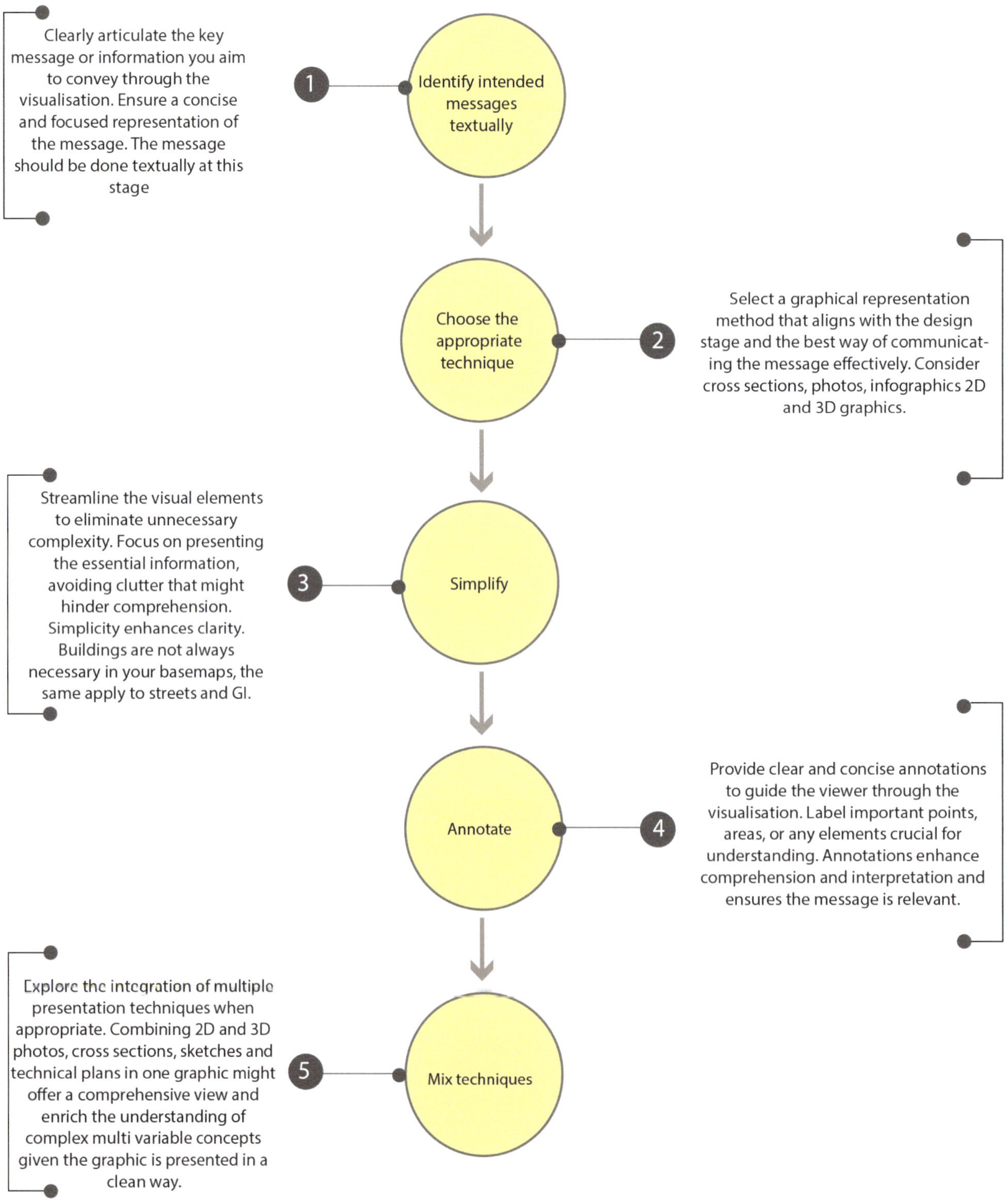

CHAPTER 10: DESIGN DELIVERY

Graphical Presentation Techniques

Stage		Technique	Helpful For
Early stages of the design process	Drafting	2D Hand Sketching	Exploring layers, brain storming, multi variable analysis, sketched concepts/options, facilitating team work.
		Sketched Cross Sections	Semi-accurate exploration of enclosure, relationship between spaces/buildings, topography, edge condition.
		3D Sketches	Simplifying complex scenes, showing enclosure, highlighting landmarks, exploring townscape, changes of urban scene.
Developing design	Mature/Immature Options	Technical Cross Sections	Accurate exploration of enclosure, relationship between spaces/buildings, topography, edge condition.
		Basic Digitalised Plans	Semi-accurate plans and concepts, stylized options, basic uses in the proposed design
		Basic 3D Perspectives	Massing, building uses, floor uses, shadows, enclosure
		Photos	A flexible technique, best practice case studies, showing character, vernacular, buildings/spaces conditions
Later stages of the design process / final presentation	Final Presentation	Technical Plans	Communicate final design and final analytical maps. They represent the base of the final 3D modelling and other plans
		Rendered 3D Perspectives	Communicating final design feel, textures, light condition, shadows, details, street furniture, space use, activities
		Infographics	Summarising key messages, communicate textual contents graphically, show relationships between topics, socio economics and spatial data presentation
		3D Physical Models	Tangible and physical exploration of the final design, showing masses, heights, details, and spatial form, marketing
		Rendered Cross Sections	Final design details, materials, textures, proposed edges, enclosure
		VR - AR	Immersive exploration of final design, real life experience of the space feel and the urban journey
		Cinematic Presentation	Evoking the emotions through visual storytelling, presentation for wide audience, marketing

TABLE 8 Graphical Presentation Techniques

STORYBOARDING A NARRATIVE
Storyboards are not immediately associated with urban design, they are more commonly linked with TV and film production, where Directors will use them to set out different camera shots and views to help communicate their vision for a story – in essence to communicate their narrative. Interestingly, it will allow others such as production designers and camera operators to share this vision. In a similar way, the urban designer can use the storyboard to help understand and set out their urban design narrative, but also share this with a wider audience. At some point the urban designer will be required to deliver a final presentation of the design solution and the design rationale behind it. The storyboard will help focus this final presentation and ensure that it includes a sensible level of information to allow the reader to be informed as to the design decisions taken – the narrative of the full AUD Framework undertaken.

The importance of the narrative has been identified at almost every stage within the AUD Framework – this means that the storyboarding will be an integral part of process outlined in this book. When reflecting on this, any narrative will undoubtedly include information that has been generated from the **analysis stage** [Step 1], the **Program** (Step 2), the **design development** (Step 3), and the **final design proposal and details** (Step 4). Each Step builds on the one that has gone before, and therefore, any presentation is not just about this final design but the material that has been prepared by the urban designer to underpin that. However, there will be such a wealth of information available, and restrictions on the space to present it in, that the practitioner will almost certainly need to make some decisions as to what to include and what to leave out. The storyboard helps to work through decisions.

Key Considerations
In many cases the final output will be a detailed report or document that justifies the approaches taken, but this could also be through a series of graphic boards, or sheets that can be presented for a formal design review process or community engagement and consultation. This means that not only does the practitioner need to think about the narrative itself, but also the practicalities of presenting this information – for example restrictions on the number of pages, the audience type etc. The storyboard ensures that these decisions can be made without undermining the overarching narrative. Before beginning to storyboard there are five key questions to consider:

1. What is the purpose? - Think carefully about why you are presenting the narrative, and what part of the overall development process the project is at. This will vary from early consultation to submission for formal approvals through the land use planning system.

2. Who is the audience? – The audience is important, thinking not only about what elements will likely interest them, but their level of design acumen – a design review panel will have a greater degree of knowledge than the general public.

3. What is the output? – Is this a document, a series of exhibition boards, or even something that can be hosted online. Understanding the physical and technical limitations (such as limitations of space or, pages).

4. Is it a text or graphic narrative? – Depending on the output and purpose, any output could simply rely on a series of graphical images with associated captions, or a written narrative could be effectively illustrated using the graphics developed.

5. Return to the design layers – Regardless of the type of document it will be vital to present a comprehensive picture of the urban design issues. Ensuring that what is included relates strongly to the 12 urban design layers (*see* 4.3) can help achieve this.

Regardless of the five points above, presenting any design solution or option, you should as a minimum always include the three **Profiles** (*see* 6.6) and the **Urban Design Program** (*see* Chapter 7) – they are as important to understanding the design as the technical details and examples of best practice. Without including the salient analytical information as part of any presentation then the design does not demonstrate how it has followed the robust, contextually responsive, evidence-led process that is set out within this book.

CHAPTER 10: DESIGN DELIVERY   288

Preparing a Storyboard

Present the Process – The storyboard is not the finished presentation but should essentially confirm the elements that are to be included. Rough boxes which are labelled as to which piece of analysis or design detail is to be included, with the pages divided into sections, each with a title or theme. There have been clear stages, themes, and topics throughout the AUD Framework which can be used to reinforce the narrative. the AUD Framework is designed specifically to showcase a strong narrative - following the process results in a strong narrative. Boxes can also be included to show where other illustrative material such as photographs, cross sections, or even space for text description and caption can be provided. The example below is a an extract from a storyboard (at A1) for the functional blueprints of a proposed technical masterplan. Breaking down the design layers across the four categories of networks; arrangements; features; and feel. The page is divided into stages to reinforce the AUD Framework employed, but calls back to the Program stage to aid in evidencing the evaluation process undertaken.

Carefully Choose the Graphics – Choosing the graphics that will be part of any project will start with the storyboard. Consideration should be given to not only providing images that will achieve the best narrative, but also offer a degree of variety - a mixture of plans, sketches, cross-sections, and photographs. A range of 2D plan based graphics should be avoided as it does not effectively communicate the 'human scale'. It is also important to think carefully about the size and prominence of the graphics that will be presented. Graphics or matters which are most important should be larger and presented towards the centre of any pages or sheets. The example below shows that the detail behind the design is illustrated in several forms – including cross sections, 3D perspectives, 2D plan graphics focused on the urban design layers, and best practice photos and images.

SKETCH: A simple sketched out storyboard for the functional blueprints presentation. Starting with basic hand-sketched layout plans allows you to try different configurations and identify which graphics and visuals best communicate the narrative (AUD Framework based) and detail required. Once you have a storyboard that works it can be drafted up within a digital publishing software [i.e., Adobe InDesign] and the necessary materials can be prepared to populate the board - which may evolve as you progress the final presentational product. This quick sketched example is an early-layout draft for an A1 Board - it is intended for illustrative purposes - the storyboard will be shaped by the site and design process undertaken.

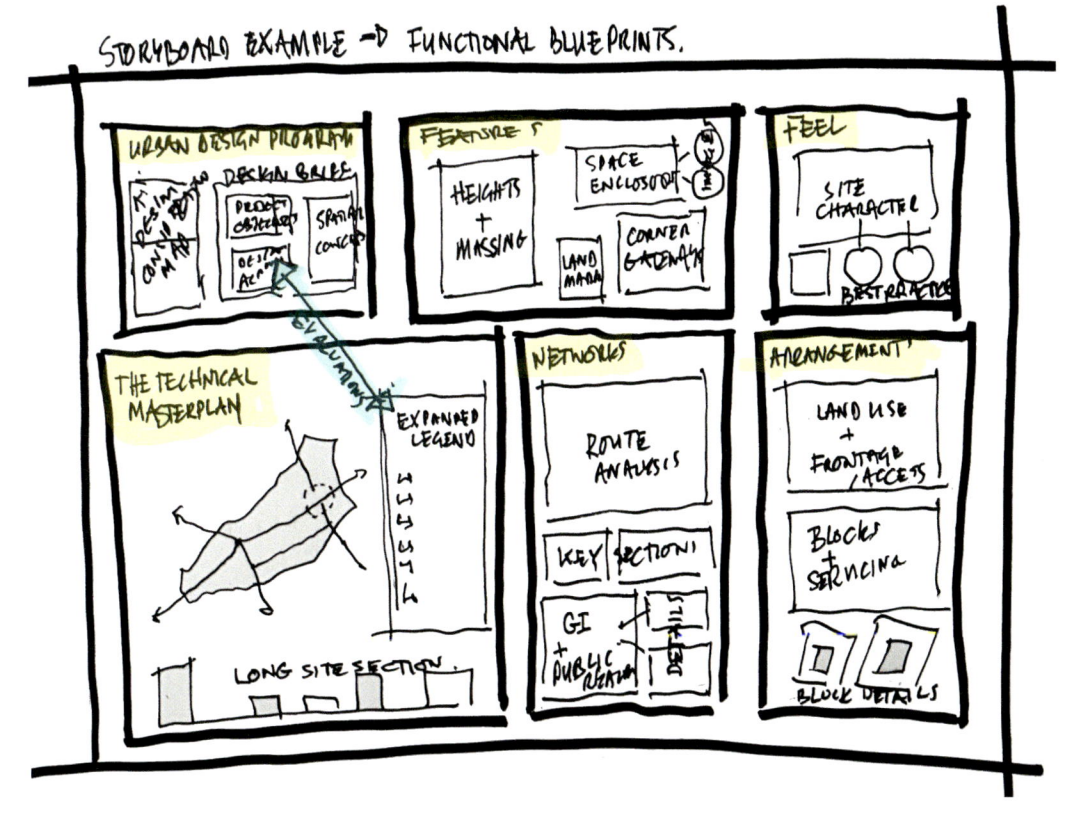

10.2 DELIVERY AND IMPLEMENTATION

EVALUATIONS

A critical component of the delivery of successful urban design is to ensure appropriate evaluations have been conducted, including careful review of the outcomes of the prior **analysis** (i.e., thematic groups and the Strategic, Site and Area Profiles), **the Urban Design Program** (design considerations and design brief), and the **design optioneering** process (immature and mature) undertaken. The design stage of any urban design project can often neglect the analysis – as the creative process materialises and develops, designers can, and do, forget to consider the critical challenges they identified and set out to achieve in the first instance. It is fundamental that urban design work in a multi-scalar and contextually responsive manner – here the designer must continually and consistently evaluate the design against their analysis – this is core to the AUD Framework's contextually responsive approach. Evaluations of the analysis enable the design team to showcase how specific challenges have been considered, worked through, and addressed. A common technique as part of the communication of technical design proposal is the inclusion of a series of maps/plans which demonstrate how the design responds to specific challenges – as showcased across this chapter and through our case study sites in Manchester and Aalborg.

The evaluation process will also include a range of technical design details to ensure the final design is transparent, responsive, and appropriate to the site and wider context. Examples of technical detailing are found across this chapter including technical sections, technical plans, and 3D models (either physical or digital). The process of evaluating the design is both internal and external. It enables the design team internally to determine with confidence that the scheme is robust and rigorous. Nonetheless, it also will form part of the package of materials that help communicate the responsiveness of the proposal externally to other stakeholders. In England, for example, it is common for a range of the evaluative material of the design to be used as part of a *'Design and Access Statement'* – a key document required by planning authorities to obtain planning permission. Having conducted a comprehensive design process to reach a final design proposal, this process should be assessed by planning departments as it forms part of the material considerations in the decision-making for planning permission.

CLIENT AND STAKEHOLDERS

Engagement with a wide range of stakeholders is critical to the delivery of any urban design intervention, this will include direct collaboration with the client, other built environment professionals, and local stakeholders including local agencies, communities, and the municipality. The complexities of collaboration throughout the urban design process will differ depending on the site, context, and direction of the project. Designer-client relationships are key, and understanding the client's needs is important. The client may be the landowner, the developer, or a project manager – either acting as an individual or a group of people. The client normally employs the designer or establishes a competitive tender process to select the design team (Tiesdell and Adams, 2011).

Often, clients will come to designers with a clear brief, the brief is an articulation of the client's need. They pay the fees and employ the designer, and are ultimately in control of what development is proposed. Nonetheless, contextually responsive design is also about involving, informing, and upskilling the client – bringing them on the journey to build their knowledge, awareness, and understanding of the site, its history and critical contextual cues to ensure that the resulting **Design Brief** can be flexible enough to be able to respond to the outcomes of the design team's analysis (as part of a wider Urban Design Program - *see* Chapter 7). While this is not always possible, particularly in situations where the client acts on behalf of unknown entities such as investment funds, an engaged client and a flexible brief can lead to a more responsive and successful design solution (*see also* 7.4). A brief-driven design agenda is a common factor in context-less design. Thus, the client's requirements and the brief, are part of the process – here it is the responsibility of the design team to explore the most appropriate solutions through the design process and present these to the client to shape the development (*see* Table 6 - page 192).

CHAPTER 10: DESIGN DELIVERY

Beyond the client, delivery and implementation will require urban designers to build relationships with a range of complimentary design professionals including architects, landscape architects, engineers, planners and local decision makers (typically via the local planning authority). Most, if not all, better practice urban design projects are collaborative endeavours and early engagement with these actors can lead to more streamlined delivery. This will include working with architects and landscape architects early in the process to facilitate understanding of the drivers behind the proposed place design and character to allow for improvements to be made to the overall design and landscaping interventions.

Similarly, it is imperative that engineers are consulted at the design development stage to ensure all technical aspects are correct and approvable as delivery and implementation require the design be signed off as meeting a range of important standards including fire, health and safety, and universal design. Discussions and opportunities to review this allow the designers to consider how best to meet these requirements. Planning and planners typically come into the process in the development and submission of the documentation and frameworks associated with the application for planning permission (see Permissions).

Local stakeholders including agencies, communities, and the municipality are core to the process. Public interests from statutory bodies (i.e. highways authorities and heritage bodies), private interests (i.e. landowners and transport providers) and community interests (i.e. residents, local businesses, and community groups) form the main collective of stakeholders. It is important that all urban design is participatory, providing appropriate entry points for a range of local actors to comment, feed into, shape and critique what is being proposed. Consultation with local actors can help designers understand local needs and desires, community aspirations for development, and unpack issues of ownership and identity (Black and Sonbli, 2019). Consultation must occur early in the process and identifying relevant stakeholders is a critical endeavour to ensure a wide range of voices are heard across the design process in its entirety (see pages 127-8 for some consultation methods).

FEASIBILITY AND FINANCE

All design projects have financial requirements to be adhered to – typically in the form of a project budget. The budget may be determined by the client or the amount of funding available – if, for example, the team are bidding for a competitive fund offered by central or local government – such as the recent *Future High Streets Fund* in England. In terms of delivery, the design team are responsible to ensure their process of data collection, design development, and detailing can be achieved within their portion of the budget. Given the nature of design and construction, with costs for materials changing quarterly for example, most projects have to impose cuts or be cost-engineered in order to marry up to the restrictions of the budget.

A detailed understanding of the structure of the finance is critical, when money must be spent, what it can be spent on, and how best to maximise the funds can greatly aid delivery and implementation. Awareness of feasibility, by ensuring that the design works within the means of the client or funding structure can avoid cuts and stripping of the design solution in the latter stages – these removals, when they occur, can greatly impact the responsiveness of the design, and typically involve downgrading the quality of materials, amount of planting, and variety of street furniture, taking a good design into poor design territory. Feasibility reports and surveys are vital from the outset, ensuring the design team remain realistic in their expectations of what can be achieved in reflection of the resources available. This is not to say that good design must be expensive, rather considerate approaches can save money and ensure design value. Likewise, phasing development is an effective way to structure the realisation of larger urban design projects (see Phasing).

PERMISSIONS

There are a range of permissions and standards urban designers must engage with and these will impact on delivery and implementation in different ways, including planning permission, consultation of statutory bodies, and technical standards. The most significant of these factors is the obtainment of planning permission - as without planning approval the project cannot materialise. As emphasised, planning and planners typically come into the process in the development phase, and the submission of the documentation and frameworks associated with the application for planning permission, however, it is advisable that urban designers take full advantage of and begin to build relationships with planning departments/teams prior to the submission of the planning application (Black and Sonbli, 2019). Most planning departments offer pre-application advice and it is a good idea to meet with planning officers for an informal discussion before the application is submitted – this might even be years in advance. This enables the design team working with planning officers to verify local requirements, ensure current relevant policy is understood, and highlight any restrictions that may be in place due to flood risk (MHCLG, 2021). Full engagement with planning will enable the design team to discuss site challenges such as power lines, watercourses or sewer systems and inquire about potential problems such as noise or traffic. Good practice is to build a dialogue with the planning authority and ensure the design is delivered in accordance with the local development plan. If the design constitutes an exception to local planning policies, pre-application discussion can facilitate an opportunity to justify the proposal and why the design team think it should go ahead.

Part of the process of applying for planning permission will require engagement with statutory stakeholders including the highways authority, national heritage body, the environment agency, and, in the context of England, the national agency for active travel. These actors will provide comments, guidance, and stipulations they require the design team to consider. Finally, and often as part of the planning process, designers are required to provide detail on specific 'material considerations' such as the impact on conservation areas, appearance and materials, disabled person access, lighting, noise, nature conservation, signage, fire standards, and health and safety. Working with engineers early in the design process can streamline this process as meeting these exacting requirements often requires reworking. Better practice urban design embraces restrictions as a means to heighten creative engagement finding ways to integrate these technical elements and standards into the design, so they form a cohesive part of it rather than be subsequently added into it. When applied late in the process, technical standards can ruin the comprehensive identity of the design and the sense of place developed.

PHASING

Phasing is a common technique used to structure the delivery of urban design interventions at any scale. One of the core challenges for urban design projects – particularly larger design scheme such as masterplans – is that they are often over ambitious. Urban design operates within a broader structural framework that is influenced by a variety of external factors including real estate markets, political climate, and broader socio-economic conditions (Madanipour et al., 2018). Due to the lengthy process involved in realising any urban intervention, design projects can suffer from vulnerability to uncertainty and fluctuation. For example, the global financial crisis of 2007-08 ended a sustained building boom period in many contexts internationally. Many urban projects were unable to adjust to the market stagnation and economic fluctuation that followed resulting in their collapse or suspension (Martin et al., 2019).

Political situations can also directly influence design projects, with periods of political upheaval or turmoil likely to impact the delivery of urban design interventions and client/stakeholder confidence more broadly, such as in the case of the political uncertainty in Northern Ireland, where between February 2022 and January 2024 the government refused to meet and make decisions across portfolios and departments impacting the future of a number of strategic regeneration projects.

Phasing is an important mechanism to ensure these external factors are considered and accounted for as best as possible. Typically, phasing involves dividing the design into a series of deliverables which break up the project into strategic priorities. It is an effective way to ensure client/investor confidence, creating a clear timetable for development which prioritises early wins and strategic components while also ensuring the project is not vulnerable to externalities (CABE, 2008). Phasing delivers components of the plan in a fluid process, evolving over time, while also creating the flexibility to complement development parcels coming forward in adjacent areas. Design projects should be flexible to change and attempt to account for external impacts e.g. property markets, available funding, planning policy among other factors through phasing.

Phasing will look differently depending on the project or context. For example, the 8-hectare development of Vienna's MuseumsQuartier comprised of three phases, the first of which focused on the retrofit, upgrade, and delivery of the quarter's three distinct museums/galleries. Demonstrating the strategic approach taken which focused on delivering and creating an identity and brand for the location early in the process. Whereas Manchester's strategic regeneration project of St. John's spread over a similar 10-hectare extent comprises of seven phases – due to different complexities/priorities, smaller strategic phases are best suited here.

COMPROMISING
Most design projects and masterplans do not happen as initially planned, but often many are never fully realised (Madanipour et al., 2018). As design relies on consistency from the wide variety of actors who make up the development industry, the stable conditions for success are rare. Rather, the social, commercial, political, and economic realities that drive development frequently change. In addition, the involvement of stakeholders through consultation and participatory processes will introduce a range of ideas, opportunities, and challenges to be accounted for. As a profession and practice, urban design involves making difficult decisions, engaging in agonistic encounters and ultimately requires negotiation and compromise. Compromise is a unique factor in the delivery and implementation of an urban design project, requiring designers to be open to change and able to respond to unforeseen challenges which may impact how the design is realised, or parts of the design come forward.

There are a number of areas where comprise will come into play, this may be through initial conversations with the local planning department around what they deem acceptable; ongoing negotiations with the client to respond to changes in their need's; involvement of communities and local stakeholders through the participatory process of design introducing critical factors that require design amendments; and engagement with other built environment professionals throughout the process, as architects, landscape architects, engineers, urban planners, or similar request alterations to ensure the design complies with space standards, regulations, or policy. Likewise, in the latter stages, during construction it is likely that material costs necessitate different street furniture or planting schemes come forward. For urban designers, it is important to remember that your role is to provide the illustrative platform and technical footprint for a successful place. Compromises will be important in achieving that goal and represent a core part of the application of urban design and process of development.

CONSTRUCTION
In the realisation of urban development projects, design represents the earliest phase of the construction process with pre-construction, procurement, construction, and post-construction taking place once the design is approved by planning and the site is acquired. The construction process requires a series of steps be completed and can differ between contexts. Typically, construction can be split between three phases i) pre-construction, ii) building construction, and iii) post-construction (Adams, 2001). Of these phases, urban designers are most likely to be involved in pre-construction and post-construction steps. Before the project begins, the design team must work closely with the contractor to develop the project plan. The pre-construction process will require the design team develop detailed drawings, here urban designers work with architects and landscape teams as well as engineers to take their illustrative proposals forward into technical detail and contractors' drawings.

The construction phase requires each contractor and subcontractor to execute the plan employing these drawings and this will involve site preparation, excavation, the laying of foundations, and a range of other aspects to be delivered. Urban designers are less commonly associated with these processes – as the specialist skills of joiners, masons, electricians, welders go beyond their expertise – however, project managing during construction may well fall within the remit of the main design contractor. Urban designers will often also return to the project during the post-construction phase. This step is the final part of the construction process before buildings or public realm projects are formally handed over to the client or owner. A part of this process will involve a walk-through, here the contractor and design team will walk through to confirm that all project specifications have been met. Some variation in this process can be seen if the project represents a 'design-build' or 'integrated' approach. Here, contractors and designers work together throughout the entire process streamlining the process and allowing the design team to collaboratively fulfil the design. Nonetheless, the involvement of the urban designer will remain the same regardless of the approach.

POST-OCCUPANCY

At the end of the process of delivery and implementation, the expectation is that the project has resulted in the production of an engaging, contextually responsive, place for people – the core requirement of any successful urban design project. Critical to this endeavour are agreed frameworks for the management and maintenance of the spaces and places created. One of the biggest flaws of design projects is a common failure to ensure appropriate funds are allocated and ringfenced for the sustained upkeep of the place/s created and their organisation over time. Urban designers must ensure their designs prioritise sustainable and durable materials across the streetscape and public realm, and that landscaping is robust and responsive to local climate. However, this will not guarantee a place's success alone, the reality is that even the highest quality materials require upkeep. This might be ensuring lighting remains fully functional or that refuse storage and provision is appropriate. Agreements on who/what should be managed, how it will be reported and how regularly checks will be carried out must be in place prior to completion.

Post-occupancy will also involve consideration of the responsiveness of the design for users – the residents, neighbours, communities, businesses that give the place its everyday life – delivering a place where everyone can enjoy, live, work, and play. Through an applied urban design process (and following the **AUD Framework**) places that are contextually responsive, imbued with local character, culture, heritage, identity, and engender a sense of play can be produced. We set out through our four-step process to show how successful places can be delivered to the highest possible standard. Great places have the power to improve health and wellbeing, inclusion, social connections, and intercultural contact, provide a sense of genuine belonging and promote diversity. The AUD Framework presented here provides a logical and clear structure for accomplishing this goal that is comprehensive and equitable.

RIGHT: False Creek in Vancouver, Canada has been subject to numerous post-occupancy studies to better understand how the design of the new district functions in practice - and how people use and behave in the spaces provided. Its success has spawned other similar developments, such as Toronto's Cityplace - but often new design schemes taking inspiration from False Creek fail to fully engage with such post-occupancy findings - to truly understand the details and nuances that elevate False Creek as a successful, highly liveable, masterplan. [*See* White and Punter, 2023].

CHAPTER 10: DESIGN DELIVERY

Merlion Park, Singapore

PART C
URBAN DESIGN FUTURES

PROCESS OUTCOMES

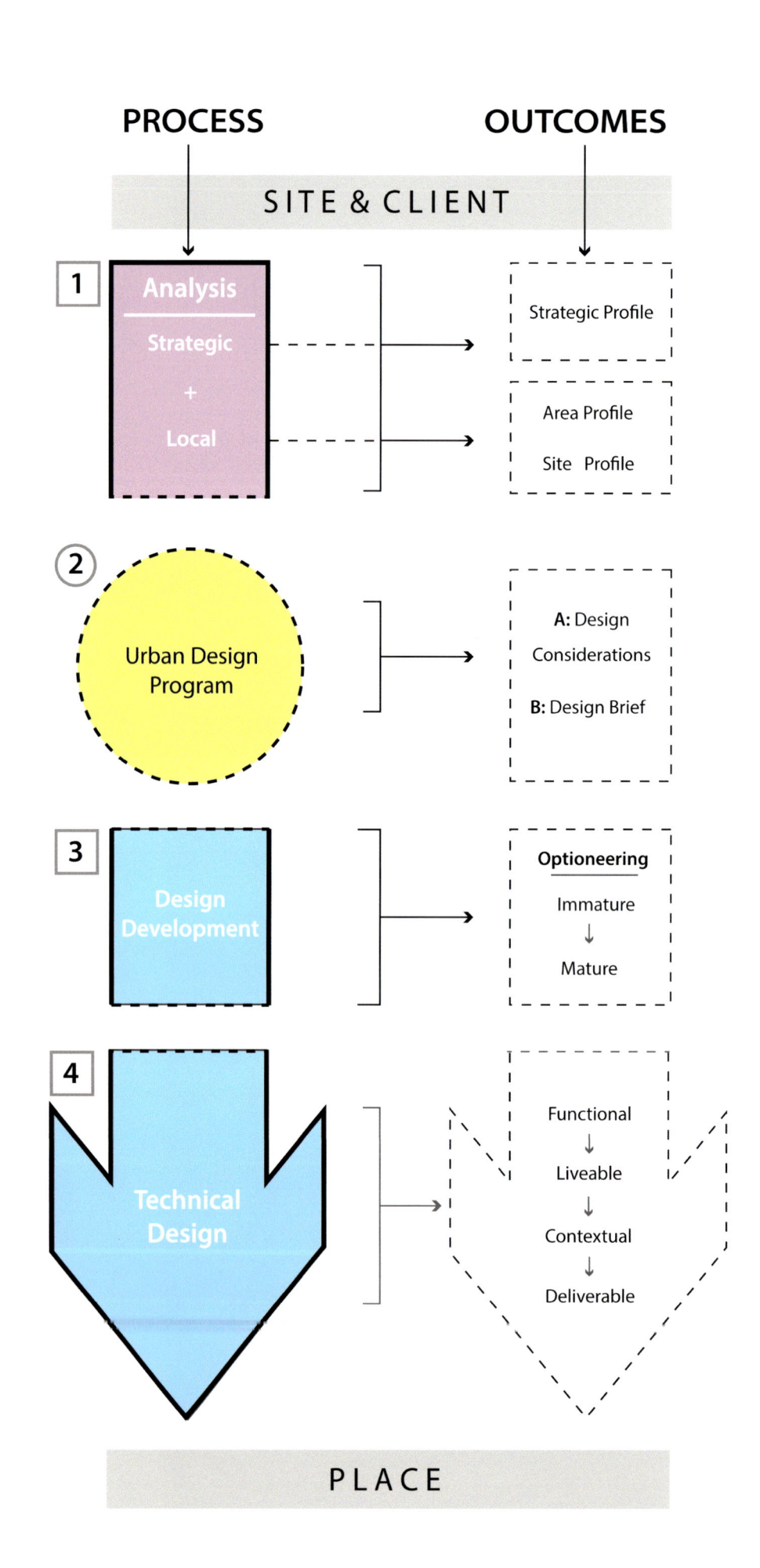

SITE & CLIENT

CONTEXT

1 Analysis
Strategic
+
Local

→ Strategic Profile

→ Area Profile
Site Profile

PIVOT

2 Urban Design Program

→ **A:** Design Considerations
B: Design Brief

DESIGN

3 Design Development

→ **Optioneering**
Immature
↓
Mature

4 Technical Design

→ Functional
↓
Liveable
↓
Contextual
↓
Deliverable

PLACE

CHAPTER 11
Reflections on the Applied Urban Design Framework

The AUD approach was developed, based on extensive research, teaching, and experience in practice, to provide a clear framework for both understanding and practicing applied urban design in a contextually responsive manner. Building on seminal texts, in particular Bentley et al. (1985), and influential design policy (DETR and CABE, 2000; Llewelyn-Davies, 2000). The framework articulates what the application of urban design means precisely and provides a comprehensive structure for users to fully appreciate the distinct practice of urban design and how urban design (and designers) can champion and deliver contextually responsive high quality design solutions. At the heart of our approach is a desire for urban design to attend more carefully to the local contexts in which it is practiced. Throughout the book we advocate that a context-led approach prioritises designing places, of, for, and with local people. However, achieving this in practice in the built environment has become rarer in recent years and that must change.

OPPOSITE PAGE: The complete Applied Urban Design Framework.

11.1 ENGAGING THE AUD FRAMEWORK

Our framework responds to the critical need – across the built environment globally – for a structured, yet flexible, process that enables contextually responsive design solutions to be realised. We sought to address this gap in existing provision by combining urban design theory, techniques, and methods, with applied practical application. In combining *'why'* we design, with *'how'* we design, the AUD Framework acts as a scaffold for practicing urban design, and a starting point for others to build on. It pushes design to better consider context and the responsibilities of the profession in creating more responsive places and spaces – enabling users to develop the core skills necessary to practice urban design as an applied technical discipline, develop projects along a context-led pathway, and engage with other professions and stakeholders. The method provides clarity on the role of the urban designer, transparency across the design process – ensuring people have a voice within the process – and a mechanism through which communities and local authorities can hold designers (and their proposals) accountable to the context within which they are sited. The approach better informs the designer/design team promoting consistency from project to project – providing practice with a clear, flexible, and holistic method for delivery.

Across Chapters 5-10, we unpacked the four distinct steps of the Applied Urban Design Framework -

1. Context (Analysis)
2. Pivot (Program)
3. Design Development
4. Technical Design

These steps enable users to progress from initial site through to a final design intervention. What makes the AUD Framework bespoke is the foundation of multi-scalar contextual analysis that informs the subsequent steps of the process. We place the requirement for extensive analysis at the heart of the design process to ensure a rigorous understanding of the unique context of each site is in place across three distinct scales (Strategic, Area, and Site). In working across *'Strategic'* and *'Local'* levels designers gain essential knowledge and information to prioritise evidence-based design development that can shape the most appropriate type of intervention as well as how to deliver that intervention effectively and technically. People should understand the process undertaken and the decisions made to reach a final design, the AUD Framework, ensures that process remains transparent, and the design is capable of being evaluated by a broad range of stakeholders.

WHO IS IT FOR?

The AUD Framework is inherently about the design and delivery of places for people – the final output of the process being '**Place**'. It advocates for design solutions to be more responsive to people and the places in which they live to bolster the delivery of best-practice solutions by designers – and as a result it must be for everyone.

Yet, we anticipate this approach will be of particular interest to, and used by, a spectrum of audiences including urban design practitioners, design and built environment professionals/practitioners (architects, landscape architects, planners, engineers among others), students and educators in the fields of urban design, architecture, planning and wider disciplines such as urban studies, local planning authorities and associated decision makers, local communities, residents and neighbours as well as individuals with an interest in the design of the urban and built environment. We sought to provide a Framework that will act as a comprehensive reference work for the discipline of urban design – providing those with a vested or casual interest in the development and shaping of the built environment with a sound understanding of how urban design might be practised.

A core strength of the AUD Framework is the diversity of purposes for which it can be used and by whom. It provides the above-mentioned audiences with a distinct approach for the practice and delivery of urban design and unpacks this theoretically and practically across a range of international contexts and via our live case study sites. An examination of the principal audiences are set out below.

Urban design practitioners – It affords designers with the necessary evidence to support design decision making based on robust analysis and evaluation – ensuring that any design is driven by local context and needs. Moreover, it creates a template for urban designers to follow emphasising the requirement to analyse a place across different scales, a deeper understanding of the importance of, and how to engage with, people, the ability to identify and interpret relevant policy and guidance, an understanding of design composition and complexity, skills in collaborating with key stakeholders and other design professionals, developing design ideas and concepts, evaluating design for quality and contextual awareness, competence in rationalising design decisions and real-world feasibility, as well as technical skills to present urban analysis, ideas, designs, and complete project narratives in a clear and comprehensive manner to both professional and non-expert audiences.

Other design/built environment professionals - In combination with the factors listed above which are also relevant here – all good or better practice urban design projects are collaborative endeavours. The AUD Framework establishes that early engagement with professionals across the built environment can lead to more streamlined delivery. We demonstrate the role of the urban designer and the need for other professions in the built environment to be involved in the process promptly – whether that be working with architects and landscape architects to facilitate understanding of the drivers behind the design, working with planners on policy or consulting engineers to ensure all technical aspects are adhered to. Building relationships with our sister professions is key. By demonstrating where they fit into the process the Framework facilitates a better understanding and appreciation of urban design for other design/built environment professionals and how they can work with urban design/ers in their day-to-day practice.

Communities / Local Authorities - It provides communities and local authorities with a clear step-by-step understanding of how to analyse their own places/spaces to better articulate context and demand more responsive and local design. Likewise, it ensures people have a voice, whether they be local residents, businesses, users of the site/space – providing communities and local authorities with a clear means to hold designers and developers accountable, and from which to evaluate proposals and their local impacts. For communities, the AUD approach also highlights when and why they should be involved in any urban design process – advocating for more consistent engagement and showcasing how this works in practice and at what points. For local authorities, the AUD Framework, provides a robust route to the development of policy – such as the formulation of design codes, design briefs or site-specific policy.

Design students / educators - It creates a template for students to shape their practices and processes and identify necessary core skills and competencies across the entirety of the urban design process between analysis, program, design development and technical design. Similarly, it enables educators to shape curriculum and the delivery of courses/modules that promote best-practice in the fields of design, planning and development. While not specifically written as a textbook, the linear nature of the content of the Framework makes it suitable for a range of design education programmes including architecture, engineering, and planning.

AUD FRAMEWORK TRANSFERABILITY
Flexibility and a focus on place-specific qualities make the AUD Framework a highly transferrable approach for practice. In prioritising the development of a transferrable method for contextually responsive design, our approach avoids technocratic, expert-led endeavour in favour of places (and their context) driving the agenda for change. Most places will have a unique history and context – influenced by positive and negative changes over time – the AUD Framework enables users to operationalise and evidence these factors in a comprehensive, sensitive, and sustainable way to realise responsive urban design policies and proposals. It is important to highlight that our emphasis on context is not unique – urban design and broader professions in the built environment have long understood the significance and role of context in their practices. In England for example, a direct focus on context as a critical factor for successful urban design was formalised in policy almost 25 years ago (*see,* for example, DETR and CABE, 2000), subsequently incorporated into design governance across the rest of the UK later in the 2000s. However, often guidance operated as more of a check list and in practice was never detailed enough to enable practitioners to consider context in a rigorous or systematic way. Responding to this challenge, a critical endeavour of the AUD Framework was realising an approach that captures context methodologically, systematically, and in a manner that is transferrable beyond a single project site, local or national context.

Rather than rely on recommendations only, we demonstrate the transferability of the AUD approach directly via our two live case study sites/projects. Our Aalborg and Manchester applied case studies validate the ability of the framework (working with the designer's knowledge and expertise) to work effectively between international contexts, at different city-regional scales, and across two distinctive urban design project levels – site scale (5-15ha) and masterplanning scale (+30ha). Across Chapters 5-10, we unpack the capability of the AUD Framework to influence transferrable decision-making that is contextually responsive. The subsequent sections reflect on the live case study sites to highlight how this worked.

Our live case study sites represented two completely different types of urban design project, introducing unique and distinctive contextual place-specific qualities and challenges. In comparing the Aalborg and Manchester case studies we are able to showcase the flexibility of the Applied Urban Design Framework in real-time and the diversity of outcomes that result from a context-led review of place. Across the two contexts we see how the emphasis on contextually responsive urban design results in analytical outcomes and design considerations that are place-specific and dictated by the context, site, and situation of the cases. The two cases and their priorities are completely different from one another. Rather than a technocratic exercise, the design considerations provided a platform to contextually review the priorities for the future of the two locations, influencing the brief for both design projects positively and helping structure the hierarchy of objectives and actions. Spatialising those components conceptually, and in more technical detail through optioneering facilitated multiple cross-checks, evaluation, synthesis, and review to arrive at a final design with context at the core of the proposal. Additional exploration, testing, and review across the Program, Functional Blueprints, Liveable Qualities and Technical Delivery resulted in contextually responsive proposals that were fully rationalised, detailed, and achievable.

REJECTING THE GENERIC
In looking to the future, we argue that urban design requires a clear vocational consolidation as an applied discipline – one that deals directly with the physical forces of the city, translating policy and strategy into actual design interventions. The AUD Framework is a first step, in seeking out methods and approaches for physically

manifesting and testing these ideas – illustrating how urban design can deliver as an applied technical discipline to provide more contextually responsive interventions in our cities and places. Here, the emphasis on designing quality, liveable environments for people is critical – and must be central – to the practice of urban design.

We are more aware than ever of the true cost of poor-quality and unresponsive design – with countless examples globally of the negative impact of design products that fail to consider people and place. In Singapore, for example, planners have carefully regulated the growth of the downtown central area while promoting expansion in other parts of the city-state. These effects of planning and subsequent design/development projects have unconsciously shaped the location and outline of Singapore's urban heat island – the urban area that experiences warmer temperatures than its surrounding – exposing more people to risk through the creation of expanded new urban heat peaks around new centres of development (Jung, 2024). Contextually responsive design by comparison should shape places to avoid exposure to risk and incorporate interventions that promote adaption to specific challenges, such as robust hierarchies of green infrastructure in the case of rising urban temperatures. This approach would better reflect the wider character of Singapore and its innovative engagement with green infrastructure solutions in other parts of the city-state.

Our approach represents an attempt to rebuke and counter generic forms of urbanism and globalised vernacular. Cities are changing at a more rapid rate than ever before. Here, the proliferation of rapid waves of global development – framed in narratives of progress, betterment, and growth – have become more common and as result so to have context-less places. As emphasised earlier in this title, cities such as Dubai have become symbols of economic growth and global architecture, their perceived success encouraging others to follow, rejecting localised design culture in favour of replicated international design products. In rejecting context, design solutions fail to represent local people and communities, lack identity and character and result in generic outcomes. Successful models of urban development are frequently copied and transferred from one context to another. Emerging centres of global development are a manifestation of a long-standing mindset in urban design, planning, and development – namely that successful design ideas can be replicated and travel easily from context to context.

An early example of this mode of practice can be seen in the regeneration of the waterfront area of Baltimore's Inner Harbour in the mid-1960s – the project acting as the precedent for waterfront regeneration and what is now a worldwide model of urban redevelopment replicated across countless Anglo-American, pan Asian, African, and European cities over a sustained period of time including Antwerp, Hong Kong, Toronto, and Sydney (Galland and Hansen, 2012). By pursuing the same types of catalyst, flagship architecture, these 'iconic' projects are no longer extraordinary (Raevskikh, 2018). Over time, these generic expressions of design have resulted in the ordinariness of iconic, global, modern, or world-class architecture creating environments devoid of any real context or local responsiveness. With many cities building the same kind of typical 'icons', using the same building practices and hiring the same (st)architects – globalisation has led to cities moving from a localised design culture to an identikit global vernacular which lacks nuance, identity, civic pride, and character (Grodach, 2018) - a 'Starbucks Urbanism' (see Renn, 2013). The challenge for urban design is to strike a balance between contextualising design and promoting dynamic and innovative solutions that allow context to adapt and evolve with the changing nature or cities, culture, and people (Black and Sonbli, 2019).

We presuppose that urban design can, should, and must do better, focusing instead on the promotion and delivery of local and distinct solutions embedded in the cultural context and urban setting from which they derive. Thankfully there are countless examples of best-practice design internationally (a healthy selection of which are discussed and included across this book) which achieve contextually rich solutions and proposals. We are beginning to see better practice design percolate across a wider range of projects and practices from new green intelligent cities in Malaysia (Ujoh, 2020), nature positive design in Australian cities (Bekessy et al., 2023), urban design solutions that are

OPPOSITE PAGE: By the 1960's Baltimore's Inner Harbour was populated with derelict warehouses and piers representing a lost industry. By the 1960's the harbour and surroundings were transformed with award-winning parks and plazas and redeveloped around new office and leisure attractions. The development helped reverse the city's decline and as such become a model for urban renaissance for many cities around the world.

rooted in the particularities and indigenous people of their landscape in Aotearoa New Zealand (Davidson et al., 2023) to the enhancement of local authority housing estates through liveability and wellbeing agendas in different parts of England (Digney, 2023). There is real strength in approaches that work with people and places to their fullest. Most recently, the Covid-19 pandemic, highlighted how important the quality of the immediate built environment was to people's health and mental health – with cities and territories struggling to adapt to the global health crisis internationally (Brail et al., 2021). Innovative design solutions rooted in their immediate context, such as Bogota's active mobility expressways, demonstrated the need and requirement for high-quality urban design to be accessible and available for people immediately where they live (Deas et al., 2021). Lessons from the global health crisis can be seen in the now countless permanent solutions that promote active spaces and places for people such as Milan's Piazze Aperte and Low Traffic Neighbourhoods in England.

LEFT: Short-term urban responses to the COVID-19 pandemic have in places been made more permanent - such as the increasing the number of low-traffic neighbourhoods across England shutting off residential routes to through traffic to improve quality of life, safety, comfort, and reduce pollution.

Recent research has shown context to be the key to a sustainable future for our high streets and central shopping areas of our towns and cities – demonstrating that the loss of big-brand chain stores in England has been countered by a rich landscape of independent, local retailers and businesses who are of and for their context (Rudlin et al., 2023).

REALITIES OF PRACTICE
It is important to consider that the AUD Framework presented here, as with any urban design process, will not occur in isolation. In reality, there are a range of fluctuating externalities that can impact the realisation of design projects (particularly larger development schemes). Across, Chapters 5-10 we reflected on several factors that will have impacts on the AUD Framework in action – including the client and design brief, budget, market context, political landscape – and how designers must navigate these elements in their day-to-day practices. However, there are other externalities that warrant deliberation – these wider considerations for the framework, building on earlier sections of the book, are critical for designers to consider in an effort to deliver a contextually responsive approach to designing places in the real-world.

HEART of the CITY II Sheffield's major regeneration project is an excellent example of the role of context-led urban design in bolstering and future-proofing regional city centres. The 7ha heritage-led urban regeneration project has created retail and leisure space, workspaces, a hotel, cultural facilities, 420 new homes, a new urban park, a new public realm, a new food hall and significant refurbishment and retention of a range of industrial heritage structures, the city's original 'Cole Brothers' department store, and unique Victorian shop frontages set alongside new structures which prioritise high-quality and sensitive materials throughout. In addition, the project retains and upgrades some of the city's oldest streets including Cambridge Street – creating a dynamic, engaging, and unique sense of place representative of the material fabric of Sheffield and the historical evolution of this location. The success of the project can be seen in flagship tenants, businesses, and stores now choosing to locate in the centre of the city, which for a prolonged period suffered from retail decline and significant levels of vacancy.

The original scheme, which subsequently collapsed, sought to demolish much of the heritage structures and buildings to develop a large retail hub/shopping mall in an attempt to replicate successful approaches in other cities such as Liverpool One and Belfast's Victoria Square – had this come to pass, it is likely many of these units would be vacant.

BELOW: Sheffield's *Heart of the City II* - mixing the old with the new in a context-led regeneration project for the city.

Wider Development Process:
Understanding the wider mechanics – primarily economic mechanisms – that influence the development process is a core competency for any urban design practitioner (Barton, 2017). The wider development process requires urban designers to engage directly with the development industry, the broad collection of agencies – landowners, financiers, builders, developers, property consultants, property marketers and managers – who organise the conversion of land and property from one physical development to another (Healey, 1991). Urban designers interact with and are part of an institutional model of development, they encounter a variety of development actors and their complex relationships, engage with different stages of the development process, and must consider different natures, conditions, and contexts of development (Henneberry, 2017). This breadth is an essential feature and skill of the urban design professional, who must operate across highly variegated forms of individual developments and the wider political and economic contexts within which they are pursued.

The process of development is complex because of the number of interests involved and not all stakeholders are equal – investors and policymakers are key decision-makers (we reflect further on policy below) (Barton, 2017). For urban designers, the AUD Framework, must work with investors/developers, landowners, land or estate agents, financiers, professionals advising investors and builders.

Collaborating with Other Professionals
In combination with investors and developers, and as emphasised extensively throughout the AUD Framework, urban designers must collaborate with a range of other professional stakeholders – and these interactions can impact on the design proposal and subsequent delivery, for positive and negative reasons. In Chapter 10, we discussed the core collaborations that should take place in the AUD process and how these can be facilitated – working effectively with architects, landscape architects, engineers, and planning professionals. Moreover, it will also involve engaging with other professionals including service designers, property consultants, and marketers. It is important to consider that conflict and compromise will be key to building consensus at various stages of the process (Barton et al., 2010).

Through the AUD Framework, we advocate for more joined-up interdisciplinary and interprofessional working across the built environment. The AUD Framework – and its extensive emphasis on transparency – promotes a nuanced understanding of other design and built environment professions and a specific mantra to work with stakeholders early in the process. Involving architects in the contextual analysis to challenge the design direction, recognising landscape professionals extensive knowledge of SuDs, species, and planting to prepare better interventions, consulting engineers as soon as possible during design development on technical aspects and building a repository of data for planners to make productive use of the findings. Our process sees urban design as a bridge to better placemaking, bringing other professionals and collaborators along by recognising their value, their role in the process, and how their input (critical or otherwise) can be used to find common ground and options for mutual gain. An interprofessional approach to urban design is key to future-proofing the built environment in reflection of global challenges and achieving resilient placemaking for people.

Policy / Context Settings
Political support at the outset, and throughout the AUD process, is critically important. For urban designers – policymakers represent key decision makers who have the ability to ultimately block or enable the proposal. While funding / investment is important – there is no project without the approval of the local authority. As emphasised in Chapter 5 and subsequently unpacked across our live case studies of Aalborg and Manchester, designers must engage with the political and administrative geography of their site and the development management system within which they operate. Careful consideration of the series of regulations, guidance and controls of policy – which typically define the priorities, developability, programming (e.g., zonal codes or land-use plans), and statutory weight between different scales e.g. national compared to local policy – and how they may impact the project are vital.

The AUD Framework, through an extensive emphasis on context and evidence-based design, can greatly assist in the negotiation of policy frameworks and consensus building with policy makers. We recommend engaging with planning authorities and the planning team at the local level as early as is possible – to outline the intention of the design and ascertain policy-makers perspectives on the direction of the proposal. Spatial policy advisors are not the only policy-maker actors to be engaged with – regulators (i.e., development managers and others whose role is to safeguard building, environmental and social standards), and politicians (i.e., democratically elected decision-makers and gate-keepers for the community) must also be consulted (Barton, 2017). Even with policymakers and development managers on board the AUD approach is at the mercy of politicians. Despite their role as democratically elected decision-makers for the community, their attitudes can often be geared toward party allegiance and vociferous minorities rather than the overall community. The views of other decision makers, or the specialist advice and guidance of spatial policy advisors (who are for the design solution) must also be considered (Barton, 2017).

People and Communities
Everyone should, and must, have the opportunity to be involved in the urban design process at an appropriate stage and level. The AUD Framework advocates participation happen early in the process and consistently throughout. This will involve engaging with voluntary and civic groups including local business organisations, civic groups, historical socities, local policitcal groups, residents, neighbours and should also involve working with children and youth via local schools (Martin et al., 2023). Even still, achieving community acceptance or 'buy in' to proposals for change is a complex and challenging endeavour (Barton, 2017). As emphasised in Chapters 3, 7, 8, and 10, the AUD Framework seeks to enable and empower communities throughout. The transparency and clarity of the AUD process for people and communities ensures participation is not tokenistic. It highlights the need for people to be involved early in the process (the analysis stage), to inform the design team and help determine a shared vision for the future through the Design Brief rather than later in the detailed design stages. By this point, we argue it is too late for meaningful engagement to occur. The AUD process upskills communities to better understand design processes and ask questions of developments, proposals, and the decision-making that determined them.

Urban designers need to operate in a wide range of context settings, some of which will challenge their assumptions on what participation and community engagement mean in an urban context. Urban design in a post-conflict environment, such as Cali, Columbia, Belfast, Northern Ireland, Karachi, Pakistan or Kathmandu, Nepal, will require urban designers understand contextual factors beyond their everyday practices and may push their capabilities to foster a constructive environment for engagement.

LEFT: Post-conflict cities create a unique and sensitive circumstance that urban design must work within - Cities like Daraa, Syria require major re-builds after conflict, how this is approached and delivered needs urban designers who recognise the complexities involved and engage with local people in re-shaping potential urban futures. Failure to do so can result in societal push-back [see Black and Sonbli, 2021].

CHAPTER 11: REFLECTIONS ON THE APPLIED URBAN DESIGN FRAMEWORK

THE CITY of BELFAST

has experienced an incredible renaissance since the 1998 Good Friday Agreement brought to an end decades of sectarian conflict. Successive urban regeneration projects since, including the Waterfront Hall, Odyssey Area, Victoria Square, Cathedral Quarter, and more recently the Titanic Quarter, have changed the face of the city. Despite its context as a post-conflict territory, Belfast is now one of the most popular cities in the UK for investment, development, and tourism. However, despite the advancements, regeneration can take a generation or two (Raco et al, 2008) – and in the case of a post-conflict context even more. In 2018, Belfast opened its flagship bus rapid transit (BRT) system – the Glider – connecting the predominately protestant communities of East Belfast and the disproportionately catholic communities of West Belfast together, for the very first time, through a new strategic infrastructure link.

The successes of the BRT are countless, but most notably, people who historically would not travel from East to West Belfast and vice versa, are now visiting local establishments, facilities, and services on either side of the city. Phase 2 of the Glider plans to open a new North / South connection, again connecting communities divided through infrastructure deserts and historical conflict. However, Phase 2 remains at a standstill, with communities unable to agree on whether the line should travel along the more predominately catholic Antrim Road area or the traditionally protestant Shore Road. Tensions and conflict around one community gaining or benefiting while the other loses out remain rife in the city, despite the progress made. Identity, politics, and a sense of injustice remain – challenging, and often resulting in the termination of projects as no consensus could be achieved. Urban design in these realities can be a frustrating and dogmatic practice – but working with people's contextual realities is the only way to a responsive solution. It is incumbent on urban design to explore and analyse contexts that are characterised by embedded cultural sensitivities to ensure approaches are not based on consensual norms that are often absent in such environments (Black and Sonbli, 2021).

BELOW: The Belfast Rapid Transit [BRT] introduction may appear outside the country to simply be an upgrading of public transport infrastructure - but the success in the context of the city and its past is much more significant and ground-breaking - in breaking down past divisions physically and allowing communities to access more of the city. Despite the initial success, political and cultural barriers remain an obstacle to overcome as the BRT seeks to expand with Phase 2 of its roll-out.

AUTHOR/DESIGNER REFLECTIONS

Choosing to demonstrate the AUD Framework using two 'live' case studies was not a decision taken lightly. Any time you design a scheme you open your abilities and creativity to critique - designing two simultaneously for publication was a daunting task, but one we felt was necessary to truly showcase the AUD Framework in action. George Bernard Shaw's oft used quote (from his 1905 stage play 'Man and Superman') - *'Those who can, do; those who cannot, teach'* - can loom large over educators, particularly those within vocational fields, such as urban design. Given this book is promoting urban design as an applied technical vocation, and our Framework is delivering an approach for *'how'* we design - *'doing'* was the logical solution. There were 3 core reasons for the Aalborg and Manchester projects being central to this book and its readers.

1. Following the AUD Framework: Both Aalborg and Manchester provide the reader with projects through which they can see the full Framework develop. The colour coding of the pages illustrating the schemes (Aalborg - blue; Manchester - pink) allows you to use them as references for how the approach is employed and visualised in practice. We aimed to provide key outcomes and components for both sites consistently - and to ensure each can be viewed as 'stand-alone' we have included some key Framework milestones for both - such as design optioneering, The Urban Design Program, and the final proposed masterplans (*see* Chapters 7 and 8).

2. Demonstrate the Detail: The case studies have been employed throughout to illustrate all the key stages and details of the AUD Framework – especially when we introduce a new technique or approach. Avoiding replication where possible, the Aalborg and Manchester projects provide the reader with a worked example that can be used to unpack the detail of the supporting text - we hope this proves useful as a resource for learning and developing skills in education and practice settings.

3. Context and Comparison: Having both case studies allowed us to effectively demonstrate the AUD Framework across differing scales and contexts (physical, geographical, social, cultural, and political). The same approach was adopted in both Aalborg and Manchester with different design outcomes and solutions - demonstrating that the AUD Framework aims to shape and promote contextually responsive interventions. Readers can return to each project and compare how each stage resulted in different outcomes - given the different contexts driving the Framework forewards.

Aalborg, Denmark

In Aalborg the context demanded our approach focus on the strong heritage aspect of the site - retaining many of the listed or architecturally significant buildings - and shaping the proposed design around these. We had to overcome the barrier of the railway, whilst reconnecting those in the north to the core transport hub to the south-east and maximising key views across the site. The link to the city centre was an obvious driver - and part of the policy agenda for the area - yet this needed to be balanced with the needs of the residential community to the north - something we tried to overcome with our attention on the 'Food Street' to the north edge of the site. A very different context to Manchester - a smaller waterfront city with a different culture - following the AUD Framework allowed us as designers to incorporate much of the detail that provides this unique place with a strong identity, enhancing the ingrained attachments locals have with the existing hospital and this part of the city.

Manchester, UK

In Manchester the context was contrasting to that of Aalborg - a major European city and a site on the edge of its ever expanding centre - spilling out into existing deprived neighbourhoods - acting as a barrier due to its state of disrepair, empty plots, and low-quality structures. Undertaking the AUD Framework enabled us to deliver a design that sought to tackle key concerns and opportunities thrown up during the context building phase. Manchester policy and recent/future developments pointed towards a continuing expansion of the city centre - yet the Framework also illustrated

OPPOSITE TOP: Aalborg final design proposal within its surrounding context.

OPPOSITE BOTTOM: Manchester final design proposal within its surrounding context.

CHAPTER 11: REFLECTIONS ON THE APPLIED URBAN DESIGN FRAMEWORK   308

the need for not only strengthening north-south connections, but also east-west. Our design direction was therefore to transition effectively from the city centre - but importantly across the divided districts of Miles Platting and Collyhurst - providing key amenity and facilities for both and introducing a new residential neighbourhood - built around the undervalued heritage on the site. Promoting sustainable mobility and health - with provision of a range of green infrastructure, public spaces, and active transport options was crucial to tackle the deprivation of surrounding populations. We hope this scheme shows the power of the AUD Framework to drive design agendas that balance political will with contextual responsiveness and a people-centred focus.

Final Thoughts
The purpose of the case studies is not to demonstrate our own ability to '*design*' - or '*do*'. We did make some decisions from an educational perspective - to ensure we could use the design detail to best illustrate the Framework at key points. They are included for the reader to explore and learn from, to demonstrate that the AUD Framework requires designers who are willing to undertake each step in the process with full commitment. The final outcome is not set, but rather is shaped by what you put into it. The better your analysis - the more you understand and appreciate the context, the more contextually responsive your design solution will ultimately be.

It is also important to view the projects in the context of this chapter (11). We have discussed a myriad of external factors that will impact and influence the AUD Framework and design in the real-world. We have not had to directly deal with these practicalities during our design work in Aalborg and Manchester - and undoubtably the final design solutions would require some negotiation and compromise if they were to be taken forward to delivery. Our responsibility as urban designers however is to present schemes that are transparent in nature - that can be clearly rationalised against the context - shaping future places that are quality driven and not simply products of a market.

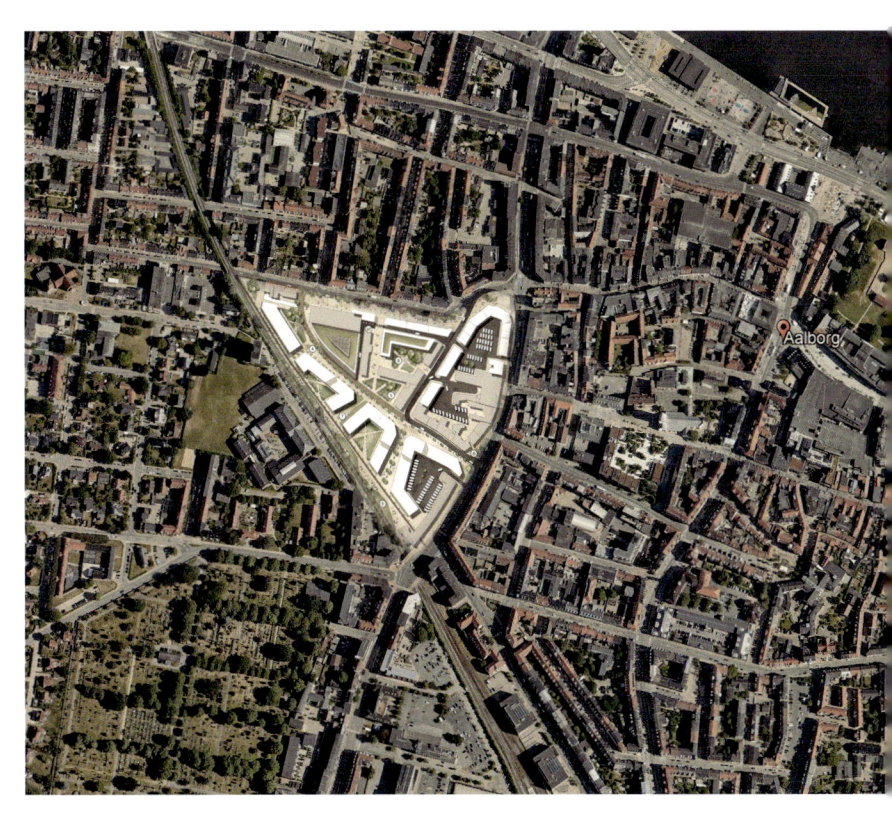

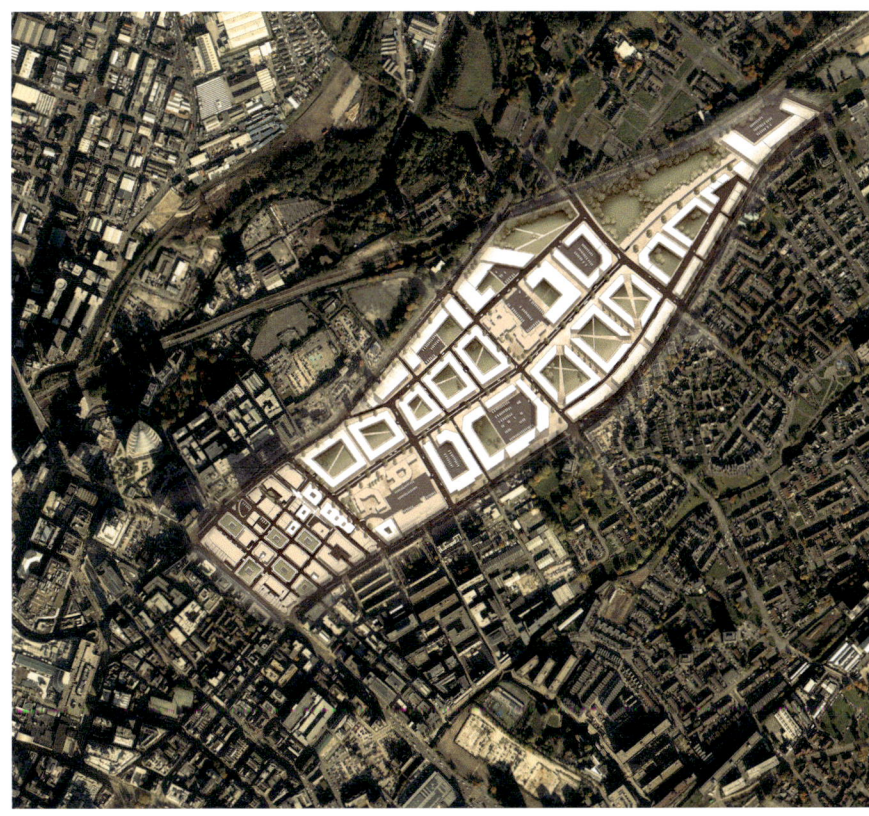

AALBORG & MANCHESTER
Final Reflections

11.2 URBAN DESIGN FUTURES

Cities are complex, constantly changing, and evolving organisms – and thus the context within which urban designers practice rarely remains static – rather designers are required to continuously learn and build their awareness of urban change and potential future changes. Developing knowledge of complex challenges facing the world and how to design for them in both the long and short term is a career long endeavour – building transferrable lessons from project to project and place to place. Here, urban design futures are important considerations for the AUD approach.

RESPONDING TO FUTURE URBAN CHALLENGES

Across this title we reflect extensively on the critical role of **climate and resilience** and **equity and inclusivity** for the future of urban design and responsible practice. Across Chapters 2-10 and throughout our live case studies in Aalborg and Manchester we consistently highlight that engagement with these two factors is imperative to envisioning, planning, and designing for contextually responsive futures.
We know that adaptive urban design, focused on blue-green infrastructures and nature-based solutions are a key strategy to more resilient urban futures. We are acutely aware that green infrastructure holistically addresses the climate emergency and networks of urban/rural multi-functional green and blue spaces and other green features deliver quality of life, health, wellbeing, and environmental benefits for communities. Evidence of improved long-term design such as sponge-city and safe-to-fail flood approaches are excellent examples of the future-proofing solutions urban design must prioritise.

Moreover, we know that our experiences of the city are dependent on our gender, race, class, age, ability, and sexual orientation. A critical function of urban design is to pull back the curtain on many of these pre-existing inequalities. Urban design must engage directly with different communities around the world. As professionals, we must give a voice to those who experience poverty, discrimination, and marginalisation in order to put them in the front and centre of design planning, policy and political debate that make and shape cities. Advances in inter-cultural design, gender-mainstreaming, child-friendly cities, age friendly cities, neurodiverse cities, re-inserting LGBTQ+ communities through the realisation of queer-friendly spaces as well as innovations in universal design for disabled-accessible cities show the potential for urban design to bolster inclusivity highlighting the design features that make spaces and places more or less inclusive and developing a critical understanding of all people's needs (Azzouz and Catterall, 2021). Urban design has a central role to play in building social cohesion and the realisation of equitable and inclusive urban places and spaces.

Both climate resilient design and inclusive design must feature extensively in the future of urban design education and practice. While we see these as two of the most critical challenges to a resilient urban future – they are not the only ones. The subsequent sections build on our commentary to highlight a range of additional considerations for future-proofing the urban design profession.

Technology / Digital Futures:

Improving and optimising urban services through the application of information and communication technologies (ICT) is now commonplace in cities (Karvonen et al., 2019). Urban design is well placed to engage and work directly with new technologies, digital innovations, and smart city infrastructures – integrating these advancements into proposals and projects. Smart cities replace traditional networks and services, or make these more efficient, with the use of digital solutions including ICT, Artificial Intelligence (AI) and the Internet of Things (IoT) for the benefit of inhabitants and businesses (EC, 2024). Today, smart urbanisation is part and parcel of thousands of urban projects around the world – exploding over the last decade. Here early examples of smart cities such as Songdo, Masdar City, PlanIT and Rio de Janeiro have given way to the actual smart city where ICT is rapidly being woven into new and existing urban policies, agendas, narratives, and aspirations (Karvonen et al., 2019) – and urban designers must respond accordingly.

They also facilitate a more interactive and responsive city administration, safer public spaces and meeting the needs of different social challenges such as an ageing population (EC, 2024). Digital advancements are changing the dynamic

CHAPTER 11: REFLECTIONS ON THE APPLIED URBAN DESIGN FRAMEWORK 310

of how people live in and perceive their environments. Autonomous vehicles, sustainable urban mobility, sustainable districts, integrated infrastructures and processes in energy, ICT and transport, service design, policy and regulation, integrated planning and management, knowledge sharing, open data governance and procurement represent the range of cross-cutting operations of smart urbanisation processes (EC, 2024) - implemented across a plethora of contexts including Austin (USA), Barcelona, Cape Town, Genoa, Kashiwanoha, Munich, Seoul, Vienna, and Yanbu (Karvonen et al., 2019).

In Santiago de Chile, smart street lighting is changing the way in which the municipality manages the streetscape. Beyond reducing energy consumption and maintenance costs, the implementation of street light technology and is creating safer spaces for citizens, particularly in inner urban areas associated with anti-social behaviour and crime. The smart innovation has created a more inclusive street network, promoting safer spaces and streets for women and girls, as well as communities who have historically found walking and navigating the city at night to be an unwelcoming prospect including elderly residents, LGBTQ+ persons, and youth.

The sensors and datahubs of smart cities are largely invisible, operating behind the scenes, however they have fundamental implications for how cities (will) operate and how they are experienced by residents now and in the future. Urban designers have a core role to play in the future of the smart urbanisation agenda. Cities are messy, diverse, and complex – smart technologies although powerful and capable of providing access to inordinate amounts of information and data on how people move, activities they engage with and monitor, manage and adapt systems in real-time – they cannot be implemented and applied universally to the urban landscape. Rather, they need to be translated and configured to fit within their specific contextual conditions. Urban designers are capable of assisting in the move away from a one-size-fits-all approach toward tailoring and customising smart infrastructures into place design to ensure they respond to their context, promote liveability and enhance the unique identity of the physical environment.

BELOW: The Al Wasl Dome in Dubai, UAE is the world's largest interactive, immersive dome - set up as part of Expo City Dubai 2020. The Dome sits at the heart of a mixed-use district and tests what is possible as emerging technology [including AR] meets public space.

Informality

Informality is a common urban experience among cities in the Global South, in fact, the share of the world's urban population living in informal settlements rose to 24% in 2018 (UN, 2021). Urban informality can be broadly defined as unregulated practices that take place beyond state control yet are often tolerated by the state (Habitat UNI, 2014). Across the world there are different forms of informality, producing a range of urban morphologies, socio-spatial conditions, and urban practices, including informal housing, informal transport, and informal trade (Kamalipour and Peimani, 2019). Urban informality covers a range of situations in which building stock, design, layout, occupations, and aesthetics violate some sort of normal and regular framework (Boano and Astolfo, 2016). In most cases, informal urbanism emerges due to the absence, insufficiency, or unaffordability of dwelling options by low-income populations in the formal sector. In many countries, informal urbanism is the dominant force of urbanisation, mainly because there is simply no other alternative.

For urban design, urban informality should be recognised as '*just another way*' of building cities. Informality can be seen as a site of potentiality to learn from, rather than simply a problem to solve. Self-organisation, self-building, and other tactics are important popular processes in cities for urban designers to consider (Boano and Astolfo, 2016). The informal sector encompasses a wide range of distinct economic activities or sub-sectors. Examples include informal street vending, street trading, household industries, informal transport, neighbourhood security among others. For a range of examples in Asia, Northern Africa, sub-Saharan Africa, Latin America, and the Middle East *see* UN Habitat (2016) and Taheri Tafti (2020).

It is crucial for the discipline and profession of urban design to engage with informal settings going forwards. Urban designers must recognise that the informal economy is the lifeblood of many cities, it provides jobs for many, provides flexible services to many urban residents, and makes significant contributions to urban economies – thus it must be designed for/with, included, and considered with care. In many ways urban design requires a recalibration – with lessons taken from informal development as well as interventions made within it (Black and Sonbli, 2019).

LEFT: Informal development - such as the Favela's of Rio de Janeiro, Brazil - force urban design to think beyond its formal western pre-occupations. Whilst these urban environments require upgrading and have significant challenges to ensure quality of life, wellbeing, and health for residents, urban design can also learn from some of these districts and how they often centre on community, sustainable forms of mobility, localised economies, and adaptable configurations and structures shifting with evolving needs.

Securitisation and Counter-Terror
In the aftermath of recent terror attacks in Berlin, Nice, Stockholm, London, Paris, Melbourne, Barcelona, New York and elsewhere, using fast-moving vehicles in crowded places has led to a re-evaluation of security in many public locations (Coaffee, 2020). Urban designers are increasingly being seen as key stakeholders in counter-terrorism endeavours where the spatial configuration and aesthetic design of protective security interventions, in the form of barriers, have a crucial impact upon the vibrancy, resilience and safety of urban centres. Barriers in cities can be both overt – typically in the form of concrete or metal barriers – or covert – where design is used to find ways to make barriers multifunctional, for example as seating spaces in the public realm (Jensen and Jensen, 2021).

The public spaces for the new Government Quarter in Oslo, which were damaged during the terror attack in July 2011, are designed to provide safety and terrorism prevention, while at the same time enhance Oslo's city life. The focal point of the design is a recreational park which provides new connections, views, and activities but at the same time, serves as a worthy memorial site, providing calm and respectful surroundings for silence and mourning (SLA, 2021). Urban designers are increasingly required to design-for and consider the potential impact of terror events in different city spaces. Working with securitisation and counter-terror, to promote an environment that is safe while also prioritising innovations in the design of these infrastructures that make them less visible to users / people is an important endeavour and will continue to be in the future.

Ultimately, considerations for the futureproofing of urban settings extend across a wide range of considerations – a selection of which are summarised here. Urban designers will be required to engage with debates and challenges that operate across social, economic, and environmental interfaces. Design must work with the unpredictable to create visions, spaces, and environments that work today and for the future. Given the complexity of the global challenges society faces, futureproofing is no longer an optional consideration of the built environment professions but critical and core to all their endeavours.

CONCLUSION

Urban design is at the forefront of how cities can adjust to structural changes and address global challenges. The AUD Framework presented across the book, was developed to advance our understanding how urban design can adapt to those challenges and simultaneously how to practically apply the discipline to prioritise contextually responsive solutions for people. Our articulation of what urban design means and advocacy for a context-led approach to designing places of, for and with local people seek to drive the subject forward.

The **Applied Urban Design Framework** is a starting point to more responsive practices and practitioners, responding to the critical need – across the built environment globally – for a structured, yet flexible, process for better-practice urban design that is internationally applicable and transferrable. In moving forwards, our extensive engagement with context and process can be employed anywhere in the world to help deliver great places that are innovative, liveable, and local. Here, the transferability of the AUD Framework will result in different outcomes dependent on the setting, circumstances, and the designer and thus must and can be adapted, changed, and moulded to generate and test new ideas for urban design practice and projects. Innovations to the Framework are welcomed if they bolster contextually responsive design proposals and practices.

In prioritising the development of a transferrable method for contextually responsive design, our approach avoids technocratic, expert-led endeavour in favour of places (and their context) driving the agenda for change. A core strength is the diversity of purposes the Framework can be used for, and by whom. It provides users with a distinct approach for the practice and delivery of urban design and unpacks this both theoretically and practically, illustrating how urban design can deliver as an applied technical discipline to provide more contextually responsive interventions in our cities and places.

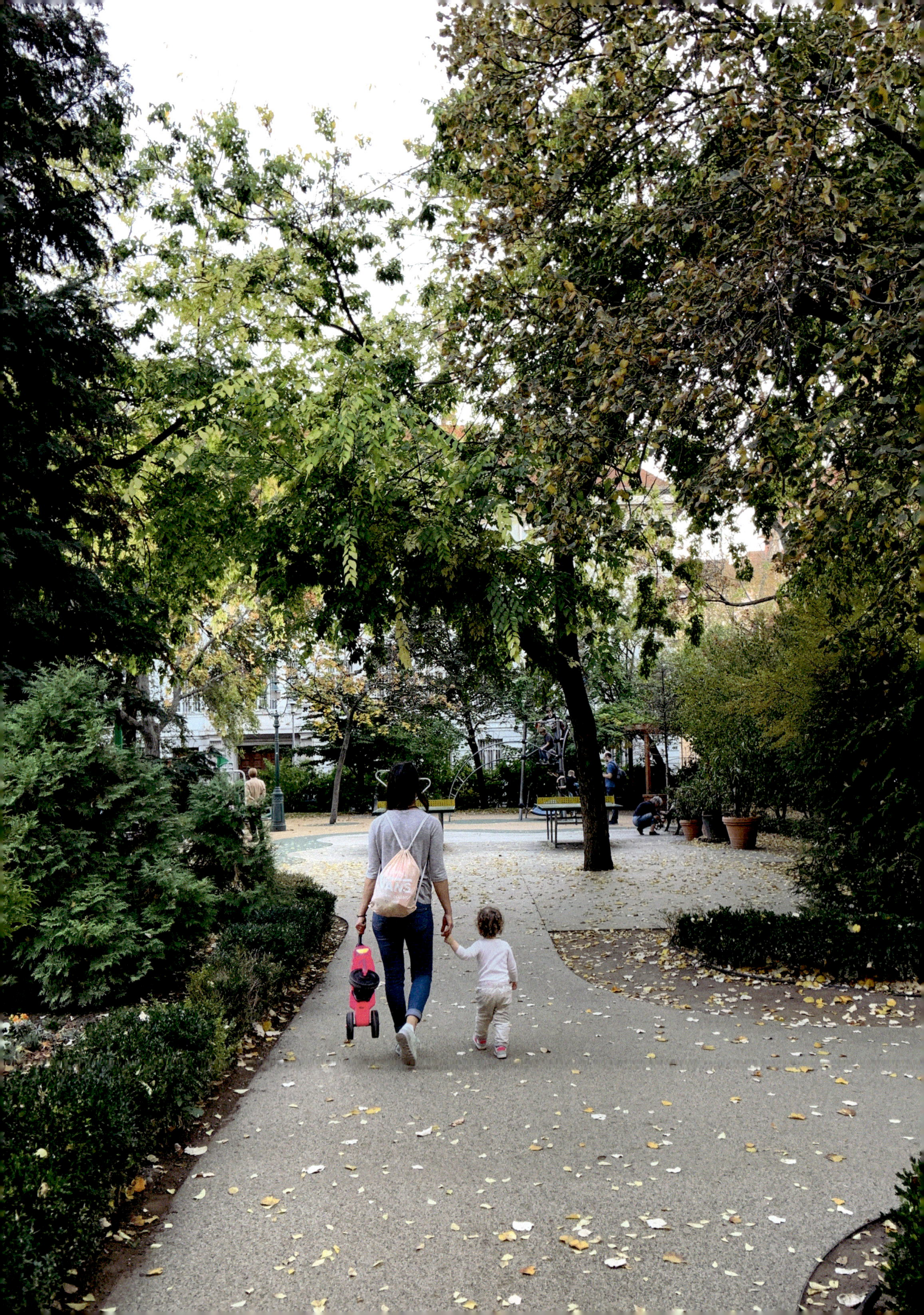

CHAPTER 12
Re-Framing Urban Design

12.1 THE 'MAGPIE' DISCIPLINE

Urban design is undoubtably less understood or defined than the other well-known design professions, each of which includes a set of agreed '*principles of practice*' and dedicated professional bodies managing and framing much of the activity and education in their field (In the UK - Architecture - RIBA; Planning - RTPI; and Landscape - LI). Urban design by contrast is often perceived as wide-ranging in its role without a singularly agreed mandate. This flexibility has been argued a strength by Carmona et al., (2017), enabling urban design to adapt to changing urban agendas in creative ways that other vocations might struggle too. However, it has also contributed to the confusion as to exactly what urban design offers and has seen its role relegated by some to be little more than a '*frame of mind*' for other professionals to dabble in (Krieger, 2009) – rather than a profession in its own right. This lack of decisive narrative is potentially detrimental to the future of urban design – especially for those with ambitions to shape a unique territory within the professional practice sphere for the discipline.

This notion of urban design as a '*magpie*' discipline – borrowing from other more established fields as, and when, necessary to justify its very existence – must, we argue, be challenged. Let us return to Chapter 1 and our discussion on the origins of 'urban design' as a contemporary practice. The 1950's conferences, hosted at Harvard University, can provide a semblance of clarity for those seeking to identify a coherent mandate. From the 1956 conference two core definitions emerged:

1. Urban design should deal with the physical forces of the city.

2. It should be wider in scope than architecture and landscape architecture, and more holistic in approach.

Both definitions remain valid today but have yet to take meaningful root in how the discipline is perceived more widely. Urban design arguably remains in the shadow of its more illustrious built environment relations – most notably planning and architecture. The natural intersection with the other three traditional design disciplines (adding landscape architecture) plays a part – urban design does inherently include elements from each given its more holistic design focus. However, the original need for urban design was ascribed to town planning losing its design focus as it shifted over time to be more concerned with strategic urban matters and policy delivery and agendas – and architecture sharpening attention on the design of structures/buildings and arguably losing some of its expertise on the wider urban (*see* Maddedu, 2019). In simpler terms it could be stated that planning brings the '*urban*' without the delivery of '*design*'; architecture and landscape architecture bring the '*design*', but not at the scale of the '*urban*'. Enter **'urban design'** – dealing directly in '*design*' delivery at the '*urban*' scale. Urban design was to fill the gap emergent between planning and architecture (*see* Chapter 1 for a detailed discussion of this). The seminal Harvard conferences originally adopted the term 'architect-planner' to describe this missing link – espusing the 'urban design' nomenclature later to further differentiate this new vocation, hinting that it must operate in new territory beyond that of planning/architecture.

The development of a clear unique territory for urban design has been, to date, a difficult and slow process. Given that planning and architecture previously fulfilled a similar type of role in the built environment for hundreds of years it is perhaps understandable that urban design will need time to effectively establish itself and its worth. Equally it can be a slow process for more perennial disciplines to adapt to adjustments from historic responsibilities and competencies to new realities. Given that neither planning nor architecture made these adjustments through conscious choice, but rather through natural osmosis over a long period of time, and many within these

---

OPPOSITE PAGE: Urban design is a profession dedicated to the provision of contextual, liveable, high-quality places for people. The responsibility of the urban designer should be to place people at the heart of the design process - re-imaging how our spaces and places work for their needs and aspirations.

Budapest, Hungary.

professions might argue that such changes are over-stated, or non-existent (*see* Rudlin and Montague, 2019). There was push back against the Harvard conference's outcomes from many in the existing built environment professions – and the lack of wide-spread international uptake in urban design education, the continued lack of professional bodies, and the confusion and general lack of agreed mandate for the field as discussed above, illustrates that this remains a debatable concept.

This chapter should not be read as a criticism of the planning or the architectural professions – the core responsibility remains firmly with those working in the urban design arena to develop and build a compelling, or indisputable, case for what the field has to offer and how it can complement these other vocations for the betterment of our cities and places. If urban design is to fulfil a holistic remit it must work in close collaboration with the other professions to find new ways for consistently delivering quality for people across the range of scales and context settings. With a consistently expanding knowledge base and urban design being equal parts conceptual and spatial when considering the body of research on the field (Black and Mell, 2024), perhaps we need train attention more to the practical application of urban design in seeking to address some of the issues highlighted. Rather than attempting to articulate the wider field as different, but complimentary, to the others, we might usefully ask how the '**urban designer**' is different. What core skills, competencies, and knowledge do they bring to enhance the liveability and contextual responsiveness of place (Black, 2019). The concept of an urban design professional practitioner is arguably as difficult to unravel – no consensus can be identified on what this vocational position looks like in the design and development process. The knowledge, skills, and responsibilities of those calling themselves urban designers is often vague, reflecting the wider fields' '*magpie*' characterisation and the sheer diversity of urban design education.

URBAN DESIGN EDUCATION

In the UK there are a growing number of urban design courses taught across many of the leading universities – and whilst each offers a valuable experience to those studying, and all value some core urban design skills, there is a distinct lack of core curriculums. Employers have little way of knowing what skills and competencies those graduating from urban design programmes will possess. Much of this is the result of no accreditation bodies for urban design internationally to ensure quality-control over courses and the fundamental competencies deemed essential to practice. Many are currently lobbying for a professional accreditation system [Rudlin and Montague, 2019] to better frame what newly qualified urban designers are trained to actually know and critically '*do*' (Urban Design Group, 2022). Urban design education is also prominent in the USA, Australia, and parts of Europe and Asia – yet many countries and regions do not offer specialist urban design training – choosing instead to promote the field as a specialism or subset within architecture and/or planning (Palazzo, 2014). In reality few universities around the world are marketing urban design as a distinct professional discipline – as Harvard did post the 1950's conferences and continues to do to this day.

There are several valid reasons why the Harvard model has not been more universally implemented across education and practice settings. Firstly, urban design remains a young discipline – time and patience are required, especially when we consider the vocations it is aiming to differentiate itself from are some of the world's oldest professions. Second, there is confusion regarding the remit of urban design and the urban designer. And third, there is failure to effectively articulate what the urban designer does in practice and the necessary training they require to make positive contributions to the future of cities. Ultimately if we do not see the future development of an agreed core curriculum, we will not see a sharpening of the role of the urban designer in practice. There needs to be more established theory in the field. There have been past attempts to consider a mandate, Jacobs and Appleyard's work with their urban design students in 1987 for example, set out some key issues for design and some of the central values for urban life, theorising essential elements of city

CHAPTER 12: RE-FRAMING URBAN DESIGN

grain needed for urban quality. And in 1992 Anne Moudon attempted to provide a universal framework for what urban designers might usefully need to know. These works remain important touchstones for urban design today, and whilst other works have sought to build on this knowledge base, to date we are yet to see it developed into something more consolidated.

As authors we have sought within our own institutions and positions to be part of this drive to better shape the vocational parameters of urban design – and can only accurately present our individual, and collective, approach. We have, over the past 10 years, developed our own understanding of the urban designer – this has been based on some of our professional backgrounds working as practitioners in urban design, in urban design education development and curriculum design, and urban design training within professional settings. We have tested and evolved our ideas and thinking across multiple university settings at Queens University Belfast, the University of Reading, the University of Manchester, Aalborg University, and the University of Sheffield. It was in direct response to the need for more clarity in urban design education and practice that at the University of Manchester we established the **Manchester Urban Design LAB (**MUD-Lab) in 2020 (Directed by Black) to act as a forum exploring and evaluating how to deliver research and teaching that was applied in nature. The MUD-Lab approaches urban design as a technical product and applied discipline that focuses on people, experience, interaction, and context. It was in the development of an appropriate pedagogy for urban design that this book, and the Applied Urban Design Framework it demonstrates, was born. We aim to prepare our urban design graduates for the role of professional practice – and engage closely with several urban design practices across the UK, Ireland, and internationally, to ensure that we equip those transitioning into practice with the range of skills necessary to achieve success in their careers – whilst simultaneously promoting the potential of the urban designer as a specialist position beyond the education setting.

DEVELOPING THE DISCIPLINE

Our hope is that this title, the AUD Framework, the wider work of the MUD-Lab, and our individual research/teaching [in Manchester and Sheffield] can have a positive influence on the ongoing debates around urban design professionally and educationally. Our intention is to contribute to dialogues on re-framing the practice element of the discipline – the vocation of urban design (the urban designer) and the education frameworks that can equip future practitioners. We hope our use of the phrase '***applied***' urban design is helpful in this sense.

Urban design also requires re-framing within policy and politics. There is a growing body of research that is evidencing the clear benefits of urban design in the real-world (*see* Chapter 2) – yet the translation of this into statutory policy demands and political pressure for urban design to be a critical aspect of all development is limited. We have seen steps forward in some settings – the expansion of design codes across the USA and the new *National Model Design Code* for the UK (2021) are useful examples of how broad urban design quality principles are being more widely adopted – however much more can be done internationally. It is imperative that those working within urban design ensure that the evidence base continues to grow and becomes impossible for local authorities and national governments to ignore.

12.2 AN URBAN DESIGN[ER] MANDATE

There have been a number of movements within urban design that have sought to develop approaches for designing places more appropriately/contextually - giants such as Cullen, Lynch, Alexander, Jacobs, and other works have been hugely influential - and we have had movements, such as New Urbanism, that seek to recapture what it was that made our historic cities and towns so successful and promote this type of place making in current development. There has also been a growing rise in policy and guidance that promotes urban design and the principles of good design - with design guides and codes seeing a significant boost across Europe, North America, Australia, and beyond. Yet look a little more deeply and you will note that whilst there now exists a plethora of principles and good design practice for us to learn from, what is conspicuous by absence is a framework or process for delivering this design in practice. Yes, we can see what it looks like, we can note how others have arrived at it - or evaluate the qualities in new developments to ascertain if lessons can be gleaned for others - but working towards such design remains complex and somewhat opaque. Some will argue that this is due to places differing from one another - a valid point. Context is key to placemaking, and each place has its own unique character and community. This is not simply true of one culture, country, or region to the next, but can be true from each city, town, village even within the same geographic area - cities themselves will have a vast array of different areas/districts/neighbourhoods that need to be understood clearly to ensure any development, no matter how small, fits in - is *contextually responsive*.

Enter the **Applied Urban Design Framework** - a bespoke process for designers to allow them to better understand the local context of their site and surroundings, work with this and the brief of their client to develop more appropriate and contextual design solutions. The process is repeatable and transferable from place to place - the approach remains the same, the outcomes defined by the site and context itself. The process is both linear and iterative - there is a pathway to follow from analysis through program through option development through design, detail, evaluation, and finally construction - but this pathway will shift and mould to the unique site and requires the expertise of the designer and wider team. This Framework does not only provide the designer with design direction, but also critically adds transparency to the design process for all stakeholders, most critically local people - they can both participate in the process and see how decisions have been made. It is not a silver bullet to guaranteed better quality design - ultimately the Framework is only as good as those using it and how seriously they take each stage. What the AUD Framework does is provide urban design with a structure for applied practice - it showcases what urban designers do - how effective and necessary their role is - and sets out the parameters for developing better design. It illustrates why urban design is a necessary part of building better places for people - it paints how urban design fits with its older vocational siblings, setting out how, and when, it should interact with architecture, landscape, and planning to build more symbiotic relationships with these fields in pursuit of quality (much needed today given the challenging atmosphere that can exist between these vocations). It also articulates the role of the urban designer, an oft mis-understood title over used by many, it provides the role with function and value. There is still much work to do to establish this role in practice, for it to be more widely recognised as a specific vocation requiring specific training and experience.

A BRIGHT FUTURE

The responsibility for urban design and the urban designer cannot be understated – with the myriad issues, embedded and emerging, facing the world's cities today the discipline must rise to the challenge. Urban design must be an arena wherein we can seek out new ways to tackle the design of our places and spaces that is compatible with complex urban conditions. Our contribution of the AUD Framework can be viewed as a template for demanding, and aiming to deliver, more contextually responsive, people centred, solutions – as well as a flexible design approach where new ideas can be generated and tested. Urban designers have the potential to enhance the quality of life for people all over the world, what is required now is a clearer mandate for them to do so and the continued progression of the discipline forwards as a technical applied vocation with the express aim of producing better urban environments for all. Those working in research, practice, education, policy, and other arenas need continue this fight – and others must join – adding to the weight of voices striving to gain further territory for urban design (*see* Black, 2024). This collective effort will undoubtably see urban design become more prominent in the future, as the process of evolution from infant design discipline to mature established professional vocation continues.

Thankfully for the places and spaces of the world - the future for urban design is bright!

OPPOSITE: There is a plethora of outstanding urban design projects being delivered across the world each year - at a variety of scales. We have a wealth of best practice to learn form and be inspired by as we strive to develop the discipline and re-frame the role of the urban designer in professional practice. The better urban designers we train, the more we promote and demand urban design in the development of our places and spaces, and the more consolidated the field becomes then we can look forward to a bright urban future where contextually responsive, people centred, high quality urban design becomes the standard.

Strøget Copenhagen, Denmark.

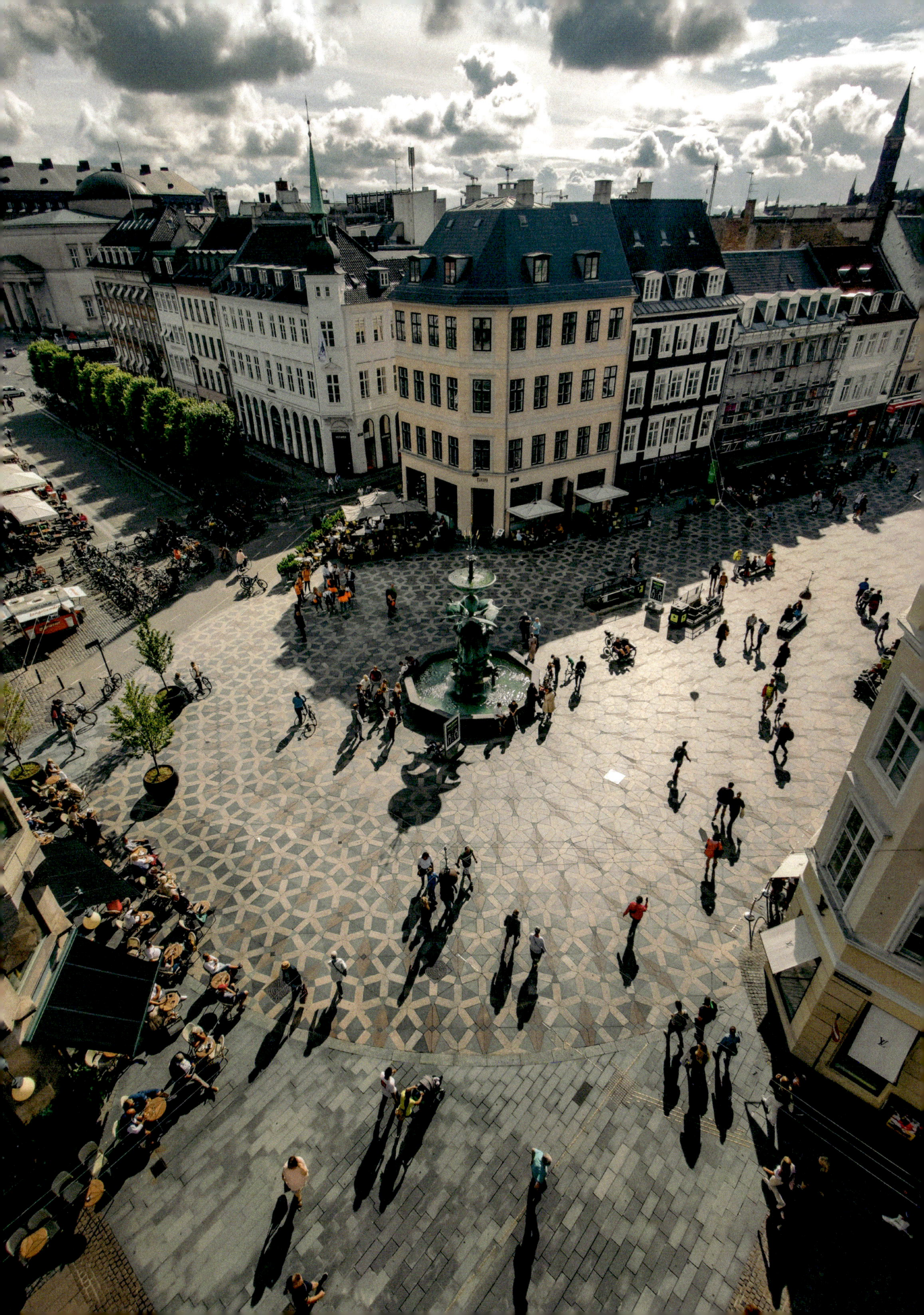

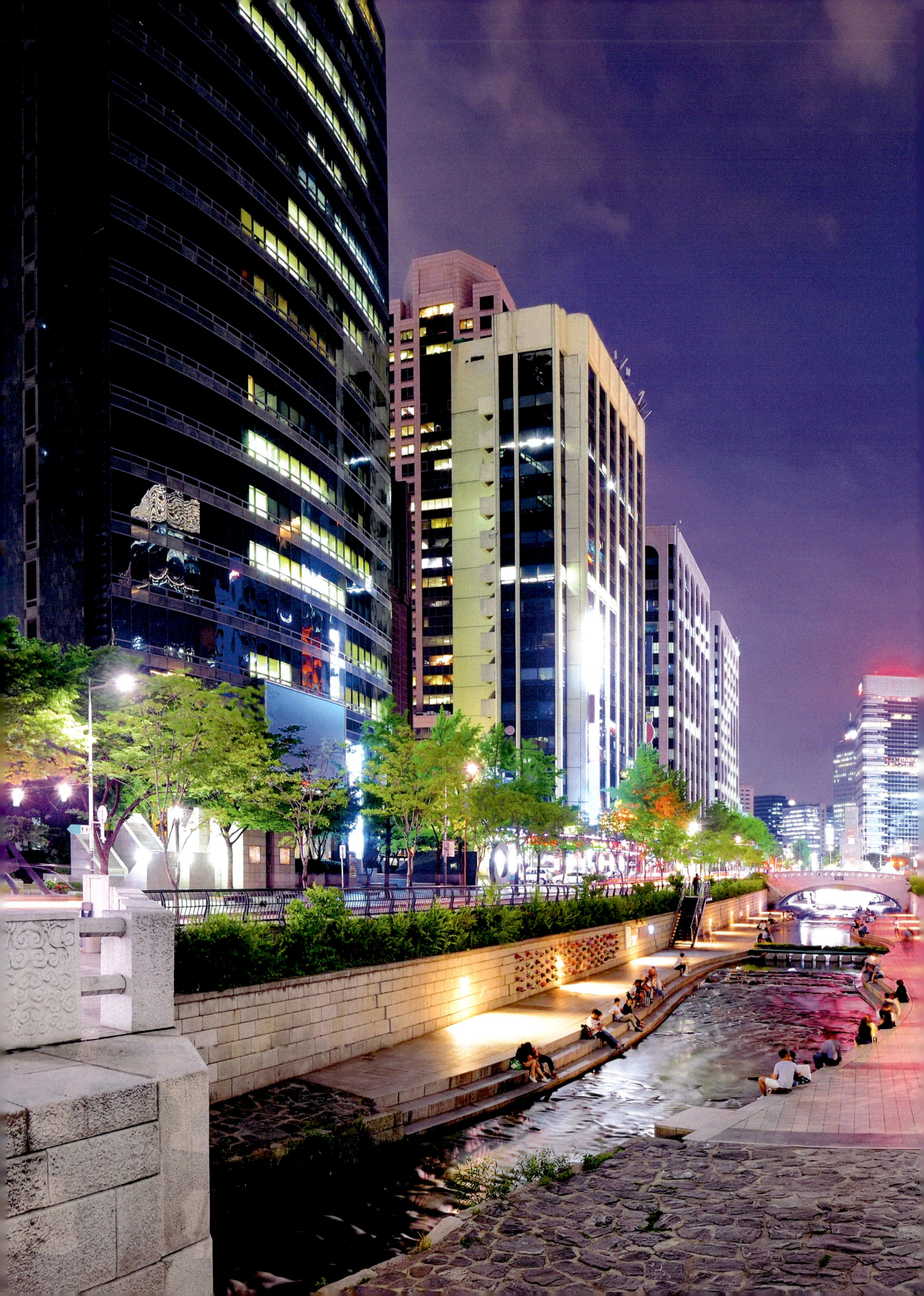

APPLIED URBAN DESIGN

A CONTEXTUALLY RESPONSIVE APPROACH

References

Aalborg Kommune (2019a) Aalborg Central Area Plan 2025. Aalborg: Aalborg Kommune.

Aalborg Kommune (2019b) North Hospital Development Prospectus. Aalborg: Aalborg Kommune.

Aalborg Municipality (2011) North Denmark's Growth Dynamo – Plan Strategy 2011. Aalborg: Aalborg Municipality.

Aarhus Kommune (2015) Plan Strategy 2015. Aarhus: Aarhus Kommune.

Aarhus Kommune (2016) Traffic and Mobility Plan for Aarhus City Centre. Aarhus: Aarhus Kommune.

ACT Government (2015) Strategic Urban Design Framework: Canberra. Canberra: Australian Capital Territory.

Adams, D. (2001) Urban Planning and the Development Process. London: Routledge.

Ahern, J. (2011) 'From Fail-Safe to Safe-To-Fail: Sustainability and Resilience in the New Urban World', Landscape and Urban Planning, 100(4): 341-343.

Alexander, C. (1966) 'A City Is Not A Tree'. Design, 206: 44-55.

Alexander, C. (1977) A Pattern Language. New York: Oxford University Press.

Anderson, J., Ruggeri, K., Steemers, K., and Huppert, F. (2017) 'Lively Social Space, Well-Being Activity, and Urban Design: Findings From a Low-Cost Community-Led Public Space Intervention', Environment and Behavior, 49(6): 685-716.

Azzouz, A. and Catterall, P. (2021) Queering Public Space: Exploring the Relationship between Queer Communities and Public Spaces. London: ARUP.

Banzhaf, S., Ma, L., and Timmins, C. (2019) 'Environmental Justice: The Economics of Race, Place, and Pollution', Journal of Economic Perspectives, 33(1): 185-208.

Barton, H. (2017) City of Well-being: A Radical Guide to Planning. London: Routledge.

Barton, H., Grant, M. and Guise, R. (2010) Shaping Neighbourhoods: For Local Health and Global Sustainability. London: Routledge.

Bekessy, S., Visintin, C., Kirk, H., and Garrard, G. (2023) 'Nature Positive Design in Australian Cities', Urban Design, 167: 30-32.

Bentley, I., McGlynn, S., Smith, G., Alcock, A., and Murrainm P. (1985) Responsive Environments: A Manual For Designers. London: Routledge.

Bhabha, H. K. (1994) The Location of Culture. London: Routledge.

Black, P. (2019a) 'Educating Urban Designers', Urban Design, 152: 18-21.

Black, P. (2019b) 'Beauty in the Eye of the Design Reviewer: The Contested Nature of UK Design Review', Journal of Urban Design, Vol. 24, No. 4, pp 556-579

Black, P. (2022) 'Design and Landscape: A Complex Past, A Contested Present, A Critical Future', Urban Design, 162: 19-22.

Black, P. (2024) 'Territory Gained: Establishing Urban Design as the '4th' Discipline', Journal of Urban Design, DOI: 10.1080/13574809.2024.2311996

REFERENCES

Black, P. and Mell, I. (2024) 'Effective alignment of urban and landscape design: Barriers and successes for education and practice' in M. Roberts and Nelson, S. (eds) Research Handbook for Urban Design. Cheltenham: Edward Elgar, pp. 40-55.

Black, P. and Sonbli, T. (2019) The Urban Design Process. London: Lund Humphries.

Black, P. and Sonbli, T. (2021) 'Culturally Sensitive Urban Design: The Social Construction of 'Homs Dream', Syria', Urban Studies and Public Administration, 4(2): 87-105.

Boano, C. and Astolfo, G. (2016) 'Informal Urbanism, city building processes and design responsibility', I Quaderni di Urbanistica Tre, 4(8): 51–60.

Boano, C., García-Lamarca, M., & Hunter, W. (2013). Mega-projects and Resistances in Contested Urbanism: Reclaiming the Right to the City in Dharavi', Les Cahiers d Architecture, La Cambre-Horta, 9, 306-339.

Boano, C., Hunter, W., and Newton, C. (2014) Contested Urbanism in Dharavi: Writings and Projects for the Resilient City. London: The Bartlett UCL.

Boland, P. (2013) 'Sexing Up the City in the International Beauty Contest: The Performative Nature of Spatial Planning and the Fictive Spectacle of Place Branding', Town Planning Review, 84(2): 251-274.

Booth, P. (1999) 'From Regulation to Discretion: The Evolution of Development Control in the British Planning System 1909-1947', Planning Perspectives, 14(3): 277-289.

Brail, S., Martin, M., Munasinghe, J., Ratnayake, R., and Rudner, J. (2021) 'Transnational Experiences of COVID-19: Transferrable Lessons for Urban Planning between the Global South and Global North' in R. van Melik, B. Doucet and P. Filion (eds) Global Reflections on COVID-19 Urban Inequalities. Bristol: Policy Press, pp 145–158.

Bruyns, G. and Nel, D. (2020) 'Lateral-Privatisation of the Publics: Hong Kong's Spatial Struggles, URBAN DESIGN International, 25: 266–279.

Buxton, P. (2009) Metric Handbook Planning and Design Data. New York: Routledge.

CABE (2001) The Value of Urban Design. London: Thomas Telford.

CABE (2008) Public Space Lessons: Land in Limbo: Making the Best Use of Vacant Urban Spaces. London: CABE.

Carmona, M. (2021) Public Places Urban Spaces: The Dimensions of Urban Design. New York: Routledge.

Carmona, M. (2021) 'The Pursuit of Place Value', Architecture Ireland, 316: 11-15.

Carmona, M., Magalhaes, C de., and Natarajan, L. (2017) Design Governance: The CABE Experiment. London: Routledge.

Carmona, M., Tiesdell, S., Heath, T., and Oc, T. (2002) Public Places Urban Spaces: The Dimensions of Urban Design. London: Routledge.

Carmona, M., Tiesdell, S., Heath, T., and Oc, T. (2010) Public Places Urban Spaces: The Dimensions of Urban Design. London: Routledge.

Carter, J. and Handley, J. (2011) 'The Adaptation Imperative – Exploring the Planning Response', Town and Country Planning, 80(6): 252–259.

Cidre, E. (2016) 'How Emergent is Pedagogical Practice in Urban Design?', Journal of Urban Design, 21(5): 535-539.

City of Melbourne (2018) Central Melbourne Design Guide. Melbourne: City of Melbourne.

City of Milan (2022) Piazze Aperte: A Public Space Program for Milan. Milan: City of Milan.

City of Oslo (2020) Street Design Manual for Oslo. Oslo: City of Oslo.

Clark, E. (2005) 'The Order and Simplicity of Gentrification – a Political Challenge'. in R. Atkinson and G. Bridge (eds.) Gentrification in a Global Context: The New Urban Colonialism. Oxford: Routledge, pp. 261–269.

Coaffee, J. (2020) Security, Resilience and Planning. London: Lund Humphries.

Counsell, D. and Stonerman, R. (2018) Planning, Sustainability and Nature. London: Lund Humphries.

Cozzolino, S., Polívka, J., Fox-Kämper, R., Reimer, M. and Kummel, O. (2020) 'What is urban design? A proposal for a common understanding', Journal of Urban Design, 25(1): 35–49.

Cullen, G. (1961) The Concise Townscape. London: Routledge.

d'Albergo, E., Lefèvre, C. and Ye, L. (2018) 'For a Political Economy of Metropolitan Scale: The Role of Public-Private Relations', Territory, Politics, Governance, 6(2): 182–198.

da Cruz, N. F., Oh, D. Y., and Choumar, N. B. (2020) 'The Metropolitan Scale', Cities, 100: 102644.

Daly, J. (2020) 'Superkilen: Exploring the Human-Nonhuman Relations of Intercultural Encounter', Journal of Urban Design, 25(1): 65–85.

Davidson, E., Hromek, D., Whaitiri, K., and Kiddle, R. (2023) 'Moving Towards Placekeeping in Australia and Aotearoa New Zealand', Urban Design, 167: 33–38.

Deas, I., Martin, M., and Hincks, S. (2021) 'Temporary Urban Uses in Response to COVID-19: Bolstering Resilience via Short-term Experimental Solutions', Town Planning Review, 92(1): 81–88.

Department for Levelling Up, Housing and Communities (DLUHC) (2023) National Planning Policy Framework. London: DLUHC.

Department for Transport (DfT) (2007) Manual for Streets. London: Thomas Telford.

DETR and CABE (2000) By Design: Urban Design in the Planning System: Towards Better Practice. London: DETR and CABE.

Digney, K. (2023) 'Local Authority Housing Estates Can Also Be Great Places', Urban Design, 166: 29–31.

Doucet, B., Van Melik, R., and Filion, P. (2021) Volume 1: Community and Society: Global Reflections on COVID-19 and Urban Inequalities. Bristol: Bristol University Press.

Dovey, K. and Pafka, E. (2020) 'What is walkability? The urban DMA', Urban Studies, 57(1): 93–108.

Eisenhauer, B. W., Krannich, R. S., and Blahna, D. J. (2000) 'Attachments to Special Places on Public Lands: An Analysis of Activities, Reason for Attachments, and Community Connections', Society & Natural Resources, 13(5): 421–441.

European Commission (EC) (2024) Smart Cities. [online] Available at: <commission.europa.eu/eu-regional-and-urban-development/topics/cities-and-urban-development/city-initiatives/smart-cities_en> [Accessed 9 February 2024].

Galland, D. & Hansen, C. J. (2012) 'The Roles of Planning in Waterfront Redevelopment: From Plan-led and Market-driven Styles to Hybrid Planning?', Planning Practice and Research, 27(2): 203–225.

Gehl, J. (1987) Life Between Buildings: Using Public Space. Copenhagen: The Danish Architectural Press.

REFERENCES

Giglia, A. (2013) 'Between Common Good and the Insular City: Urban Renovation in Mexico City', Alteridades, 23(46): 27-38.

Glatter-Götz, H., Mohai, P., Hass, W., and Plutzar, C. (2019) 'Environmental inequality in Austria: Do Inhabitants' Socioeconomic Characteristics Differ Depending on their Proximity to Industrialpolluters?', Environmental Research Letters, 14(7): 074007.

Global Designing Cities Initiative (2016) Global Street Design Guide. Washington: Island Press.

Grodach, C. (2018) 'Beyond Bilbao: Rethinking Flagship Cultural Development and Planning in Three California Cities', Journal of Planning Education and Research, 29(3): 353-366.

Habitat UNI (2014) Informal Urbanism. [online] Available at: <unhabitat.org/sites/default/files/2014/03/Hub-Informal-Urbanism.pdf> [Accessed 9 February 2024].

Hartt, M. (2018) 'The Diversity of North American Shrinking Cities', Urban Studies, 55(13): 2946-2959.

Hartz-Karp, J. (2004) 'Harmonising Divergent Voices: Sharing The Challenge of Decision-Making', Public Administration Today, 2: 14-19.

Healey, P. (1991) 'Urban Regeneration and the Development Industry', Regional Studies, 25(2): 97-110.

Hebbert, M. (2010) 'Manchester Making It Happen', in J. Punter (ed), Urban Design and the British Urban Renaissance. London: Routledge, pp 51-67.

Hebbert, M. (2016) 'Figure-ground: History and Practice of a Planning Technique', Town Planning Review, 87(6): 705-728.

Henneberry, J. (2017) Transience and Permanence in Urban Development. Oxford: John Wiley and Sons.

Hincks, S., Deas, I., and Haughton, G. (2017) 'Real Geographies, Real Economies and Soft Spatial Imaginaries: Creating a 'More than Manchester' Region', International Journal of Urban and Regional Research, 41(4): 642-657.

Hoyer, J., Dickhaut, W., Kronawitter, L., and Weber, B. (2011) Water Sensitive Urban Design: Principles and Inspiration for Sustainable Stormwater Management in the City of the Future. Berlin: Jovis Verlag.

Illien, N. (2021) How Vienna Built A Gender Equal City, BBC Travel. [online] Available at: <bbc.com/travel/article/20210524-how-vienna-built-a-gender-equal-city> [Accessed 14 February 2024].

IPCC (2001) Climate Change 2001: Synthesis Report. A Contribution of Working Groups I, II and III to the Third Assessment Report of the Intergovernmental Panel on Climate Change. Cambridge and New York: Cambridge University Press.

Jacobs, J. (1962) The Death and Life of Great American Cities. New York: Vintage Books.

Jacobs, A. and Appleyard, D. (1987) 'Toward An Urban Design Manifesto', Journal of American Planning Association, 53(1): 112-20.

Jensen, O. B. (2014) Designing Mobilities. Aalborg: Aalborg University Press.

Jensen, O. B., Martin, M., and Löchtefeld, M. (2021) 'Pedestrians as Floating Life – On the Reinvention of the Pedestrian City', Emotion, Space and Society, 41: 100846.

Jensen, T. M. and Jensen, O. B. (2023) 'The Social Life of a Barrier: A Material Ethnography of Urban Counter-Terrorism', Space and Culture, 26(1): 74–88.

Jung, Y. (2024) 'Urban Heat Islands and the Transformation of Singapore', Urban Studies, Online First: doi.org/10.1177/00420980231217391.

Jünger, S. (2022) 'Land use disadvantages in Germany: A matter of ethnic income inequalities?', Urban Studies, 59(9): 1819–1836.

Kamalipour, H. and Peimani, N. (2019) 'Negotiating Space and Visibility: Forms of Informality in Public Space', Sustainability, 11(17): 4807.

Karvonen, A., Cugurullo, F., and Caprotti, F. (2019) Inside Smart Cities: Place, Politics and Urban Innovation. London: Routledge.

Kostenwein, D. (2021) 'Between Walls and Fences: How Different Types of Gated Communities Shape the Streets Around Them', Urban Studies, 58(16): 3230-3246.

Kostoff, S. (2001) The City Shaped: Urban Patterns and Meanings Through History. London: Thames & Hudson.

Krieger, A. (2006) 'Territories of Urban Design', in M. Moor and J. Rowland (eds) Urban Design Futures. London: Routledge, pp 18-28.

Krieger, A. (2009) 'Where and How Does Urban Design Happen?', in A. Kreiger and W. S. Saunders (eds) Urban Design. Minnesota: University of Minnesota Press, pp 113-130.

Landscape Institute (2013) Green Infrastructure: An Integrated Approach to Land Use – Position Statement. London: Landscape Institute.

Lara-Hernandez, J. A. (2022) Cities: How Urban Design Can Make People Less Likely to Use Public Spaces, The Conversation. [online] Available at: <theconversation.com/cities-how-urban-design-can-make-people-less-likely-to-use-public-spaces-184079> [Accessed 14 February 2024].

Llewelyn-Davies (2000) The Urban Design Compendium. London: English Partnerships.

Louv, R. (2005) Last Child in the Woods: Saving Our Children from Nature-Deficit Disorder. London: Atlantic Books.

Lunds Kommun (2023) Stadsparken. [online] Available at: <lund.se/uppleva-och-gora/natur-lekplatser-och-parker/parker/stadsparken> [Accessed 14 February 2024].

Lynch, K. (1960) The Image of the City. Cambridge, MA: MIT Press.

Lynch, K. (1981) A Theory Of Good City Form. Cambridge, MA: MIT Press.

Lynch, K. (1990) 'Experiencing Cities', in T. Banerjee and M. Southworth (eds) City Sense and City Design: Writing and Projects of Kevin Lynch. Cambridge, MA: MIT Press, pp 99-247.

Macmillan, A., Cresswell Riol, K., and Wild, K. (2021) 'Stuck With the Car and All its Harms? A Public Health Approach to the Political Economy of the Status Quo', Active Travel Studies, 1(1): 5.

Madanipour, A. (2017) Cities in Time: Temporary Urbanism and the Future of the City. London: Bloomsbury.

Madanipour, A., Miciukiewicz, K., and Vigar, G. (2018) 'Master Plans and Urban Change: The Case of Sheffield City Centre', Journal of Urban Design, 23(4): 465-481.

Madeddu, M. (2019) 'Urban Design: A Learning Bridge between Architecture and Planning', Urban Design, 152: 22-24.

Manchester City Council (2012) Core Strategy 2012-2027. Manchester: Manchester City Council.

Marlow, D. R., Moglia, M., Cook, S., and Beale, D. J. (2013) 'Towards Sustainable Urban Water Management: A Critical Reassessment', Water Research, 47(20): 7150-7161.

Martin, M., Deas, I., and Hincks, S. (2019) 'The Role of Temporary Use in Urban Regeneration: Ordinary and Extraordinary Approaches in Bristol and Liverpool', Planning Practice and Research, 34(5): 537-557.

Martin, M., Hincks, S. and Deas, I. (2020) 'Temporary Use in England's core cities: Looking beyond the exceptional', Urban Studies, 57(16): 3381-3401.

Martin, M., Jelić, A., and Tvedebrink, T. (2023) 'Children's opportunities for play in the built environment: A scoping review', Children's Geographies, 21(6): 1154-1170.

McIndoe, G., Chapman, R., McDonald, C., Howden-Chapman, P. and Sharpin, A. B. (2005) The Value of Urban Design: The Economic, Environmental and Social Benefits of Urban Design. Wellington: Ministry for the Environment (New Zealand).

REFERENCES

Mell, I. (2016) Global Green Infrastructure: Lessons for Successful Policy-Making, Investment and Management. London: Routledge.

Mell, I. (2019) Green Infrastructure Planning: London: Lund Humphries.

Mell, I. (2022) 'Aligning Landscape and Urban Design', Urban Design, 162: 22–24.

MHCLG (2020) Planning for the Future: White Paper 2020. London: MHCLG.

MHCLG (2021) National Model Design Code: Part 1 The Coding Process. London: MHCLG.

Milz, D., Zellner, M., Hoch, C., Radinsky, J., Pudlock, K. and Lyons, L. (2018) 'Reconsidering Scale: Using Geographic Information Systems to Support Spatial Planning Conversations', Planning Practice & Research, 33(3): 291–308.

Ministry of Housing, Communities & Local Government (MHCLG) (2020) Planning For The Future: White Paper August 2020. London: MHCLG.

Moudon, A. V. (1992) 'A Catholic Approach to Organizing What Urban Designers Should Know', Journal of Planning Literature, 6(4): 331-349.

National Association of City Transportation Officials (NACTO) (2013) Urban Street Design Guide. Washington, DC: Island Press.

Ministry of Housing, Communities and Local Government (2021) 'National Model Design Code'. MHCLG, London.

Newman, O. (1996) Creating Defensible Space. Washington: U.S. Department of Housing and Urban Development.

Newton, P. W. (2014) 'Low-Carbon Precincts for Low-Carbon Living', Carbon Management, 5(1): 5–8.

Northwest Regional Development Agency (NWDA) (2007) The Economic Value of Urban Design. Liverpool: NWDA/RENEW Northwest.

O'Hare, P. (2021) Planning and Participation. London: Lund Humphries.

Palazzo, D. (2014) Pedagogical Traditions: Companion to Urban Design. London: Routledge.

Palazzo, E. (2019) 'From Water Sensitive to Floodable: Defining Adaptive Urban Design for Water Resilient Cities', Journal of Urban Design, 24(1): 137–157.

Patel, S. and Arputham, J. (2007) 'An offer of partnership or a promise of conflict in Dharavi, Mumbai?', Environment and Urbanization, 19(2): 501–508.

Peak District National Park (2023) The Peak District's Special Qualities. [online] Available at: <peakdistrict.gov.uk/learning-about/about-the-national-park/the-peak-districts-special-qualities> [Accessed 14 February 2024].

Punter, J. (2002) 'Urban Design as Public Policy: Evaluating the Design Dimension of Vancouver's Planning System', International Planning Studies, 7(4): 265-282.

Punter, J. (2009) Urban Design and the British Urban Renaissance. London: Routledge.

Raco, M., Henderson, S., and Bolwby, S. (2008) 'Changing Times - Changing Place: Urban Development and the Politcs of Space-Time'. *Environment and Planning A*, 40, pp. 2652-2673.i

Raevskikh, E. (2018) 'Anticipating the "Bilbao effect": Transformations of the city of Arles before the opening of the Luma Foundation', Cities, 83: 92–107.

Renn, A. (2013) 'Is Urbanism the new Trickle-down Economics?'. [online] Available at: <https://www.newgeography.com/content/003470-is-urbanism-new-trickle-down-economics> [Accessed 11th April 2017].

Robinson, D., Newman, S. P. and Stead, S. (2019) 'Community Perceptions Link Environmental Decline To Reduced Support for Tourism Development in Small Island States: A Case Study in the Turks and Caicos Islands', Marine Policy, 108: 103671.

Rodríguez-Pose, A. (2008) 'The Rise of the 'City-Region' Concept and its Development Policy Implications', European Planning Studies, 16(8): 1025–1046.

Romice, O., Rudlin, D., AlWaer, H., Greaves, M., Thwaites, K., and Porta, S. (2022) 'Setting Urban Design as a Specialwised, Evidence-led, Coordinated Education and Profession', Proceedings of the Institution of Civil Engineers – Urban Design and Planning, 175(4): 179-198.

Rosenberger, R. (2020) 'On hostile design: Theoretical and empirical prospects', Urban Studies, 57(4): 883-893.

Rudlin, D. and Montague, L. (2019) 'Why Urban Design Teaching Needs an Accreditation System', Urban Design, 152: 30-32.

Rudlin, D., Payne, V. and Montague, L. (2023) High Street: How Our Town Centres Can Bounce Back from the Retail Crisis. London: RIBA Publishing.

Savills (2016) Development: The Value of Placemaking. [online] Available at: < pdf.euro.savills.co.uk/uk/residential---other/spotlight-the-value-of-placemaking-2016.pdf> [Accessed 14 February 2024].

Sheller, M. (2018) Mobility Justice: The Politics of Movement in an Age of Extremes. New York: Verso Books.

Silva, M. and Costa, J. (2016) 'Flood Adaptation Measures Applicable in the Design of Urban Public Spaces: Proposal for a Conceptual Framework', Water, 8(7): 284.

Sim, D. (2020) Soft City: Building Density for Everyday Life. Washington, DC: Island Press.

SLA (2021) Norway's New Government Quarter. [online] Available at: <sla.dk/cases/the-goverment-quarter-in-oslo/> [Accessed 9 February 2024].

Smith, M. E. (2023) 'Urban Success and Urban Adaptation Over the Long Run', Open Archaeology, 9(1): 20220285.

Sonbli, T. and Black, P. (2022) 'Rethinking planning and design maps: The potential of discourse analysis', Urban and Regional Planning, 7(3): 74-86.

Steiner, F. R. and Butler, K. (2012) Planning and Urban Design Standards. Hoboken: John Wiley and Sons.

Stern, N. (2007) The Economics of Climate Change: The Stern Review. Cambridge: Cambridge University Press.

Taheri Tafti, M. (2020) 'Assembling Street Vending', Urban Studies, 57(9): 1887-1902.

Tibbalds, F. (1988) Making People Friendly Towns. Harlow: Longman Group.

Tiesdell, S. and Adams, D. (2011) Urban Design in the Real Estate Development Process. Oxford: Wiley-Blackwell.

Tompkins, E. L., Few, R., and Brown, K. (2008) 'Scenario-Based Stakeholder Engagement: Incorporating Stakeholders Preferences into Coastal Planning for Climate Change', Journal of Environmental Management, 88(4): 1580-1592.

Town & Country Planning Association (TCPA) (2012) Planning for a Healthy Environment – Good Practice Guidance for Green Infrastructure. London: TCPA.

Ujoh, J. (2020) 'Putrajaya: A New Green Intelligent City', Urban Design, 153: 34-36.
United Nations (2018) World Urbanisation Prospects: The 2018 Revision. [online] Available at: < smartnet.niua.org/sites/default/files/resources/wup2018-keyfacts.pdf> [Accessed 14 February 2024].

United Nations (2021) The Sustainable Development Goals Report 2021. New York: United Nations Publications.

United Nations Environment Programme (UNEP) (2022) CO_2 Emissions from Buildings and Construction Hit New High, Leaving Sector Off Track to Decarbonise by 2050: UN. [online] Available at: <unep.org/news-and-stories/press-release/co2-emissions-buildings-and-construction-hit-new-high-leaving-sector> [Accessed 14 February 2024].

UN Habitat (2013) Streets As Public Spaces and Drivers of Urban Prosperity. Nairobi: UN-Habitat.

UN Habitat (2016) Enhancing Productivity in the Urban Informal Economy. Nairobi: UN-Habitat.

Urban Design Group (2022) How to Make People Friendly Places. London: Urban Design Group.

Watson, V. (2013) 'African Urban Fantasies: Dreams or Nightmares', Environment and Urbanization, 26(1): 1-17.

Watson, V. (2014) 'Co-production and Collaboration in Planning – The Difference', Planning Theory & Practice, 15:1, 62-76.

Werner, C. M., Brown, B. B., Stump, T., Tribby, C. P., Jensen, W., Miller, H. J., Strebel, A., and Messina, A. (2018) 'Street Use and Design: Daily Rhythms on Four Streets that Differ in Rated Walkability', Journal of Urban Design, 23(4): 603-619.

White, E. T. (1999) Path, Portal, Place: Appreciating Public Space in Urban Environments. Melbourne: Architectural Media.

White, J. and Punter, J. (2023) Condoland: The Planning, Design and Development of Toronto's CityPlace. Vancouver: UBC Press.

Whyte, W. H. (1988) City. Rediscovering the Centre, Philadelphia: University of Pennsylvania Press.

Wilson, E. and Piper, J. (2010) Spatial Planning and Climate Change. New York: Routledge.

World Weather Attribution (2021) Western North American Extreme Heat Virtually Impossible Without Human-Cause Climate Change. [online]. Available at: <worldweatherattribution.org/western-north-american-extreme-heat-virtually-impossible-without-human-caused-climate-change/> [Accessed 14 February 2024].

Index

2D plans/visuals 27, 124, 131-132, 141, 147, 151, 158, 180, 198, 203, 207, 283-284, 288.
3D models/visuals 27, 124, 141, 203, 206, 281-284, 288-289.

Aalborg Case Study
    Area Scale 115-116
    Design Brief 189-190
    Design Considerations 181-182
    Design Options 199-200
    Final Reflections 307-308
    Geographical Connectivity 111
    Heritage Assets 137-138
    Key Policy Summary 109
    Key Space Design 261-262
    Land Use and Density 223-224
    Legibility Analysis 145-146
    Linear Park Design 275-276
    Morphological Study 133-134
    Policy Designations and Development 153
    Proposed Masterplan 209-210
    Public Realm & Green Infrastructure 221-222
    Route Hierarchy 135
    Site Introduction 29
    Strategic Profile 165-166
    The Half-Block 243
    Thematic Group: Development 157-158
    Thematic Group: Public Realm & Green Infrastructure 159-160

Aarhus, Denmark 46.
Access 6, 38-39, 47, 52, 58-59, 62, 64, 65-67,
Activity 4, 6, 14, 20, 35, 37, 43, 53, 66-67, 74, 103, 119, 121-126, 131-132, 147, 150-151, 156, 215, 217-219, 229, 235, 246-247, 252-255, 258, 262, 266, 269, 275, 281, 314.
Adaptation 20, 53-55, 62, 78, 93-94, 101, 103, 121, 257, 271-272.
AM / PM 252, 255, 258, 262.
Amenity 7, 14, 20, 51, 55, 66, 99, 104, 111, 119, 121, 125, 179, 217, 219, 233, 235, 240, 241, 243, 246-248, 250, 266, 308.
Analysis techniques 18, 118, 128, 151.
Architecture 6, 8 9, 11, 18, 22, 47, 49, 51-52, 76, 79, 92, 102, 117, 138-139, 149, 201, 234-236, 245, 258, 299-301, 314-315, 317.
Area scale 26, 115-116, 121, 126, 131-132, 149, 160, 161, 168, 170.
Arrangements 37, 58, 61, 65, 69, 71, 104, 118, 120, 121, 131, 149, 158, 177, 216, 255, 280.
Aspern Seestadt 66.

AUD framework 20-28, 31-36, 79, 81, 85-86, 112-114, 120, 128-130, 164, 172-174, 178, 185-186, 191, 194-197, 201, 205-207, 213-214, 229, 277, 280, 287-288, 293, 297-300, 303-305, 307-308, 312, 316-317.
Audiences 23, 26-27, 97, 31-32, 127, 129, 155-156, 164, 177, 185-186, 193, 199, 207, 220, 280-284, 287, 299.

Barcelona 232, 233.
Belfast 15, 306.
Best practice 14, 20, 22, 27, 31, 35, 46-47, 53, 79-81, 101, 149, 205, 239, 252-253, 257, 267, 272, 278, 284, 287-288, 299-301, 317.
Birmingham 16.
Blocks 5, 7, 19, 29, 31-34, 37, 51-52, 58, 65-66, 69, 72, 74, 76, 78, 101, 117, 119, 133, 177-179, 202-203, 215, 229-237, 240-244, 259, 272, 275-277, 280.
Block interior 69, 231, 235, 241, 243.
Boston 76
Budget 191-192, 277, 290, 303.
Buffers 51, 246, 248, 250, 253, 257.
Building line 51, 61, 69, 71, 74, 220, 231, 237-240, 242, 244, 248, 252, 259.
Budapest 63-64

CABE 16, 23, 35.
Canada 100.
Canberra 193.
Cerda 5, 65, 101, 232.
CIAM 7-8.
Chamfer 74, 232, 238, 241, 244. 64, 103-104, 109, 121, 132, 151, 218, 229, 233-234, 248, 252, 254-255, 263.
Character 8-9, 23, 35, 49-50, 58, 67-68, 71, 75-76, 90, 101, 107, 109, 118-119, 121-122, 138, 149-150, 155-156, 161-162, 168, 170, 175, 177-179, 202, 220, 229-231, 234, 236, 240, 245-246, 252, 257-259, 262, 280-281, 284, 290, 293, 301, 317.
Character study 149-150, 161.
Children/youth 29, 36, 39, 41, 46-47, 61-62, 66, 88, 99, 104, 177, 232-233, 253-254, 262, 267, 270, 275, 281-282, 305, 309-310.
City beautiful 6-8.
Client 16, 20, 26-27, 31, 79, 81, 117, 174, 176, 177, 186, 191-192, 193-194, 196, 199, 205, 281, 284, 289-290, 291-292, 303, 317.
Climate 9, 15, 20, 22, 34, 47-49, 54-55, 62, 86, 91, 93-96, 100-101, 103-104, 109, 162, 234, 257, 263, 267-269, 271-272, 291, 293, 209.
Collaboration 10, 19, 23, 36, 107, 177, 191, 193, 205, 282, 289-290, 293, 299, 304, 315.

INDEX

Comfort 20, 43, 47-48, 55, 61, 88, 94, 217-218, 246, 252, 254-255, 257, 262, 266, 271, 280, 302.
Communities 6, 9, 15, 17, 24, 26-27, 36-41, 55, 59, 65, 89-90, 97, 99-100, 107, 114-115, 119, 127, 144, 156, 176, 177, 179, 185-186, 193, 196, 198, 206, 214-217, 253, 263-264, 269, 277, 281, 289-290, 292-293, 299, 301, 305-306, 309-310.
Communicating design 26-27, 32, 58, 79, 81, 114, 118, 122, 129, 131-132, 136, 150, 172, 176-178, 185, 193, 196-197, 201, 207, 220, 234, 236, 235, 280-284, 287-289, 309.
Complexity 15, 23, 58, 87, 118, 124-125, 155, 216, 220, 258, 263, 299, 312.
Composition 23, 236, 239, 299.
Connectivity 16, 20, 29, 59, 86, 91, 103-104, 111, 122, 135-136, 155-156, 214, 218, 246, 264-266, 270, 275.
Construction 27, 53, 88, 91, 94, 101-102, 107, 207, 214, 220, 281, 290, 292, 317.
Consultations 19, 100, 127-128, 132, 138, 151, 194, 206, 287, 290, 292.
Context 8-11, 17-28, 31, 34-35, 37, 51-52, 54, 58, 75, 78-81, 86-89, 91-93, 97-98, 103-106, 108, 114-115, 118, 129, 135, 149-150, 155-156, 164, 166, 172, 174-178, 185, 191, 194-196, 197, 201, 206, 216, 219, 235-236, 277, 281, 284, 289, 291-292, 297-310, 312, 315-316, 317.
Continuity 35, 51-52, 72, 231, 234, 237, 241, 280-281.
Corners 58, 71, 74, 202, 229, 232, 234, 238, 240, 241, 244, 280.
Corridors 47, 59, 61, 64, 70, 125, 218, 231, 246-248, 252, 254, 257-259, 262, 263-264, 266, 270.
Courtyards 51, 54, 65-66, 69, 101, 160, 181, 242, 247, 263, 269, 272.
Cross sections 131-132, 135, 141, 160, 168, 203, 244, 281, 283-284, 288.
Culture 9-10, 15, 18, 20, 46, 49-50, 76, 81, 87, 89, 91, 95, 100-102, 105-106, 115, 150, 156, 191, 293, 301, 307, 317.
Cycling 18, 20, 37, 46-47, 53-54, 59, 61, 63-64, 103-104, 109, 121, 132, 151, 218, 229, 233-234, 248, 252, 254-255, 263.

Density 6, 34, 41, 54, 64, 66, 71-72, 76, 101, 118-119, 121-122, 141, 147, 158, 161, 191, 202, 223-224, 232-233, 236, 239, 242.
Derry/Londonderry 50
Design actions 176-177, 185-186, 187, 189, 197, 201, 207, 280.
Design delivery 15, 32, 172, 207, 280, 314.
Design development 27, 32, 174, 176, 180, 183, 186, 193-196, 199, 201, 205, 241, 229, 287, 290, 298, 300-301, 304.

Design proposal 21, 176, 178, 186, 196, 199, 207, 214, 220, 229, 280-281, 287, 289, 304, 307.
Design quality 10, 22, 26, 35, 55, 81, 92, 107, 185, 316.
Development management 92, 304-305.
Development process 88, 90, 107, 176, 281, 287, 304, 315.
Digital futures 126, 309.
District 14, 45, 51, 53, 64, 67, 76, 87, 100, 105, 119, 121, 143-144, 175, 207, 233, 265, 269, 275, 293, 310.
Diversity 11, 15, 35, 39, 43, 87, 99, 115, 124, 138, 177, 219, 239, 247, 253, 257, 293, 299-300, 312, 315.
Dharavi, India 90

Economic 6, 9-14, 16, 18, 26, 29, 30, 36, 47, 78, 87-88, 90-91, 93, 97, 100-101, 104, 110, 125, 151, 154, 177, 179-180, 193, 215, 263-264, 291-292, 301, 304, 311-312.
Edge conditions 52, 61, 78, 124, 156, 170, 202, 215, 220, 229, 257.
Education 11, 20, 22, 32, 55, 67, 81, 151, 177, 198, 205, 278, 300, 308-309, 314-317.
Elderly 41, 47, 88, 267, 310.
Enclosure 35, 51-52, 54, 58, 61, 63, 67-68, 71, 73-74, 124, 147, 156, 202, 229, 239, 241-244, 262, 280.
Engagement 22-23, 75, 80-81, 107-108, 127-128, 138, 151, 176-177, 202, 206, 281-282, 287, 289-292, 299, 301, 305, 309, 312.
Entrances 41, 51, 65, 68-69, 73-74, 231, 235, 237-238, 242, 253, 255, 262, 275.
Environmental 4, 6, 8-10, 14-16, 18, 19, 22-23, 26, 32, 34, 36-39, 43, 46-47, 49, 51-54, 62, 64, 67, 72-73, 79, 81, 87-89, 92-93, 100, 106-107, 109, 115-118, 120, 122, 124-126, 146, 151, 174, 176, 191, 196, 201, 205, 207, 214-220, 245-247, 249, 252-258, 262-267, 271-272, 275, 277, 281-282, 289, 291-292, 298-302, 304, 305, 306, 309-315, 317.
Evaluation 23, 27, 123, 165-166, 199, 201-202, 203-207, 288-289, 299-300, 312, 317.
Equitable 15, 34, 37, 39, 47, 55, 59, 89, 104, 215, 245, 247, 293, 309.

Facility 14, 20, 47, 53, 66, 78, 99, 109¬¬¬, 119, 121, 132, 143, 147, 151, 202, 215, 218, 219, 232, 246-247, 253-254, 269, 303, 306, 308.
Feasibility 23, 177, 199, 277, 290, 299
Features 14, 24, 29-30, 39, 46-51, 54, 58-64, 71-75, 80, 87, 100, 103-105, 109, 114, 118, 120-126, 131-132, 143-150, 156, 175, 177, 180, 186, 207, 230, 241-243, 247, 257-258, 262-267, 272, 277, 280, 309.
Feel 15, 36, 39, 42, 43, 49, 58, 68, 71, 75, 98, 118, 120-121, 125, 131, 149, 217, 255, 280, 284.

Figure ground 22, 88, 101, 119, 131, 133, 245.
Finance 78, 176, 191, 290.
Frontage 58, 65-66, 68-69, 72-75, 122, 132, 156, 179, 191, 202, 226, 229, 231-232, 235, 237, 240-241, 243-244, 280-281.
Functionality 7, 10, 18, 26, 58-59, 67, 135, 202, 214-215, 234, 246, 272.

Garden City 6.
Generic 9, 16, 20, 23, 120, 150, 197, 240, 300-301.
Glasgow 214
Globalisation/Global 9-10, 15, 34, 37, 86-88, 93-95, 101-102, 150, 214, 257, 291, 301-304, 311-312.
Gordon Cullen 8, 73, 147, 316.
Greening 5, 47-58, 109, 271, 280.
Green infrastructure 6, 15, 32, 47-48, 50, 53-54, 61-62, 73, 75, 78, 103-105, 117, 121-122, 131, 147, 149-150, 155-156, 159-161, 201-202, 205, 207, 214-215, 219, 221, 229, 233-234, 237, 243, 247-248 249, 254, 257, 263-264, 269, 272, 274, 277, 280-281, 283, 301, 308-309.
Grids 5, 52, 65, 76, 101, 119, 133, 229-230, 232, 244.

Harvard GSD conferences 4, 8, 314-315.
Health 5, 9, 15, 22, 29, 34, 37, 45, 47, 53, 62, 95, 98, 99, 104, 108-109, 111, 124, 151, 177, 232, 254, 263, 267, 269, 272, 290-291, 293, 301-302, 308-309, 311.
Height 41, 52, 71-75, 119, 121, 124, 131, 142, 149, 202, 236, 238, 267.
Heritage 20, 49, 51, 72, 86, 91-92, 100, 105, 109, 117, 122, 137-138, 149, 151, 155-156, 157-158, 179-180, 264, 284, 290-291, 293, 303, 307-308.
Hierarchies 4, 58-60, 64, 66, 68, 73, 103-104, 119, 124, 131-133, 135, 144, 147, 149, 156, 183, 186. 202, 207, 214-215, 218-220, 247, 252, 257, 259, 263-264, 281, 283, 300-301.
High Streets 20, 59, 67, 78, 144, 170, 248, 272.
History/Historical 8-9, 14, 18, 20, 28-31, 36, 41, 43, 46-47, 49-53, 64, 69, 72, 75, 81, 90-91, 93, 96-97, 98, 100-102, 115-116, 118, 121-122, 126, 133, 137-139, 143, 149-151, 155-156, 175, 177, 214, 216, 219-220, 252, 262, 275, 284, 289, 300, 303, 306, 310, 314, 316.
Human scale 14, 19, 37, 41, 54, 58, 61, 71-73, 75, 105, 117, 125-126, 131-132, 143, 151, 193, 203, 206-207, 214-215, 229, 242-244, 280, 288.

Identity 9, 11, 15, 17, 35, 41, 49-50, 67, 73, 76, 89, 97, 100, 102, 109, 115, 120, 122, 138, 143, 149, 155-156, 179, 193, 198, 202, 230, 236, 264, 290-293, 301, 306, 307, 310.
Immature 27, 198-199, 201-202, 283.
Implementation 32, 53, 80, 87-88, 105, 233, 289-293, 310.
Inclusivity 10, 15, 37, 39, 43, 59, 61, 89-90, 104, 214-215, 229, 245-247, 253, 264, 267, 269, 270, 275, 309-310.
Inclusive design 39, 309.
Informality 43, 89-90, 311.
Intergenerational 37, 47, 79.

Jan Gehl 9, 34, 67, 217, 245.
Jane Jacobs 6, 8-9, 34, 68, 237, 255, 315-316.
Josep Sert 8.

Kevin Lynch 8-9, 34-35, 43, 143-146, 316.

Landscaping 64, 244, 248-250, 257, 262, 272, 277-278, 290, 293.
Landscape architect 8, 11, 18, 107, 205, 257, 264, 290, 292, 299, 304.
Le Corbusier 5-7.
Legibility 8, 35, 65, 68, 71, 73-74, 121-122, 143-147, 150, 156, 178, 202, 214, 220, 230-232, 235-237, 257, 259, 262, 283.
Linear parks 47, 243, 266, 272, 275-276, 281.
Liverpool 220.
Local 8-15, 17-27, 29, 31, 34, 39-43, 46-49, 53-54, 58-60, 64, 66-67, 69, 71-73, 75-77, 80, 86-88, 92-93, 97-98, 100-101, 106, 107, 109-110, 112, 114-115, 120-122, 125-132, 138, 143-151, 156, 161, 164, 168, 170, 177, 179, 185-186, 191, 193, 196, 199, 202, 206, 214, 216, 219, 230-234, 236, 244, 249-250, 253, 262-264, 267-271, 275, 277-282, 289-293, 298-306, 312, 316, 317.
Local authorities 24, 26, 46, 53, 93, 114, 149, 177, 186, 277-278, 298-299, 302, 304, 316.
Lucio Costa 7, 55, 216.
Lund 270.

Maintenance 55, 58, 75, 77-78, 80, 99, 107, 121-122, 124, 160, 202, 277-278, 280, 293, 310.
Malaysia 102.
Management 43, 53, 55, 58, 75, 77-78, 81, 89, 92-93, 103, 127, 149, 175, 202, 229, 269, 277-278, 280, 289, 293, 310.
Manchester, University 70
Manchester Urban Design LAB 22-24, 316

INDEX

Manchester Case Study
    Accessibility and Connectivity 136
    Architectural Quality 139-140
    Area Profile 167-168
    Area Scale 115-116
    Design Brief 187-188
    Design Evaluation 203-204
    Final Reflections 307-308
    Green Infrastructure Provision 273-274
    Hard and Soft Plan 183-184
    Land Use and Building Height 141-142
    Local Policy Analysis 110
    Movement 227-228
    Proposed Masterplan 211-212
    Residential Podium Urban Block 242
    Retail / Service Urban Block 241
    Serial Vision 148
    Service / Access / Frontage 225-226
    Site Introduction 30
    Site Profile 169-170
    Socio-Economic 154
    Thematic Group: Character 161-162

Manipulation 8, 215, 216-219, 238, 244.
Market 10, 14, 16, 41, 55, 78, 90-91, 98-99, 107, 115, 191, 291, 303, 308.
Masdar City 34
Mass 71, 80, 119, 124, 151, 283-284.
Masterplan 27-28, 66, 69-70, 86, 110, 116, 117, 136, 150, 151, 183, 207-212, 232, 239, 241-242, 284, 293.
Materials 19, 27, 37, 49, 51-54, 67, 70, 72, 80, 94-95, 101, 107, 121-122, 156, 206, 220, 231, 236, 238, 240, 252, 258, 262, 267, 277, 281-282, 284, 288, 289-291, 293, 303.
Material considerations 107, 125, 151, 155, 164, 289, 291.
Mature 27, 198-199, 201-202, 206-207.
Mixed-use 16, 20, 29, 34, 37, 41, 53, 61, 65-67, 69, 74, 76, 101, 109, 141, 191, 202, 216, 235, 241, 247-248, 269, 310.
Mobility 34, 37-38, 40, 45-46, 54, 61, 99, 103-104, 109, 117, 119, 214, 218-219, 229, 251-252, 254, 266, 302, 308, 310-311.
Movement 5, 14, 34, 35, 45, 52, 59, 61-62, 63-64, 66, 70, 73-74, 109, 117, 119, 121-122, 124, 143, 151, 156, 180, 186, 202, 214, 215-220, 227-228, 231, 238, 246-248, 252, 254-255, 257-259, 262, 264, 266, 270, 275, 281.

National Model Design Code 17, 35, 316.
Nature 6, 14-15, 20, 35, 55, 64-65, 103-104, 107, 109, 122, 159-160, 254, 257, 263-271, 291, 301, 309.

Neighbourhood 5, 9, 29-30, 39, 41, 43, 51, 59, 66, 69, 74-76, 88, 98-100, 105-106, 108-109, 121, 125, 132, 141-146, 174, 177, 214, 231-232, 234, 249-252, 266, 269, 275, 308, 311.
Network 14-15, 45-47, 52-54, 59, 61-66, 66, 70, 87, 94, 99, 109, 111, 122, 132, 146, 214-215, 220, 223, 246-247, 251-252, 254-255, 257, 259, 263-264, 272, 310.
New Urbanism 6, 316.

Observations 20, 125-126.
Opportunities and constraints 175-176, 178, 180-182, 191.
Optioneering 27, 32, 186, 197, 199, 201-203, 205-206, 207, 214, 288, 289, 300.
Organic 4, 9, 87, 63, 101, 119, 133, 257, 259, 267.
Orientation 39, 54, 89, 124, 235, 237, 239, 309.

Parks 16, 62, 73, 99, 119, 126, 131, 138, 144, 150, 172, 177, 179-180, 191, 217, 219, 233, 236, 243-244, 247, 257, 263-264, 266-270, 272, 275, 278, 281, 301, 303, 312.
People 4-10, 14-24, 26, 28-37, 39, 41-49, 52, 58-64, 73-75, 78-81, 86-100, 103-104, 107, 110, 114-117, 119-120, 122, 124, 126-128, 138, 143-144, 150-151, 156, 164, 175, 193, 196, 199, 203, 207, 214-220, 229, 231, 233, 236, 238, 241, 246-248, 252-255, 258-259, 262-264, 267-272, 277, 280, 282, 284, 289, 293, 298-299, 301-317.
Permeability 35, 65, 76, 121-122, 156, 214, 231, 244.
Permissions 107, 206, 289-291.
Phasing 80, 290-291.
Placemaking 8, 11, 20, 34-36, 43, 45, 58, 88, 100, 185, 191, 196, 201, 220, 304, 317.
Planned 4-7, 51, 56, 151.
Planners 8, 10-11, 18, 66, 93, 107, 149, 196, 205, 290, 292, 299, 301, 304.
Planning 6-8, 11, 20, 22-23, 27, 34-36, 39, 45, 80, 87, 91-93, 100, 105-107, 114, 149, 166, 176, 178-179, 194, 199, 206, 236, 266, 287, 289-292, 299-301, 304-305, 309-310, 314-315, 317.
Planting 61-62, 75, 78, 94, 107, 233, 243, 247, 254, 257, 269-272, 275-277, 290, 292, 304.
Play 11-12, 15, 20, 37, 40-41, 46, 47, 49, 61-62, 63-64, 66, 97, 177, 232-233, 244, 247, 250, 253-254, 261-262, 263-264, 267, 269-270, 272, 275, 282, 293.
Plot size 72, 73, 86, 100, 118, 207, 231, 236, 272.

Policy/guidance 23, 29, 30, 35, 39, 46, 55, 86-87, 91-94, 97, 101, 105-107, 109-110, 114, 120, 127, 149, 151, 153, 156, 168, 174, 176, 177, 180, 194, 250, 265, 291-292, 298-300, 304-305, 307, 309-310, 314, 316.
Post-conflict 50, 89, 305-306.
Post-industrial 100-101.
Post occupancy 292-293.
Precedence 79-81, 124, 193, 197, 219, 301.
Presentation 86, 164, 186, 206, 281-284, 285-288.
Principles 7, 16, 17, 20, 31, 34-35, 45-46, 54, 58, 65, 75, 80, 109, 133, 144, 185, 196, 201, 206, 207, 229-230, 232, 234-235, 244, 246, 252, 258, 280, 314, 316.
Private / Public 43-44, 51, 55, 61-62, 65-66, 121-122, 124, 156, 160, 220, 231, 234, 237, 241, 243, 253, 269, 281.
Profiles 26, 31, 86, 91, 98, 108, 112, 114, 120, 129, 164-170, 172, 174-176, 178, 180, 206, 252, 287, 289.
Project objectives 185-186, 197, 201, 207, 280.
Public realm 32, 34-35, 50-53, 56, 58, 59, 61, 63-74, 77, 89, 94, 99, 117, 119, 121-122, 131, 147, 155-156, 159-160, 175, 202, 207, 214-215, 218-221, 229, 231, 234-235, 237, 245-248, 251-262, 264, 266-267, 270-272, 275, 277, 280-281, 292-293, 303, 312.
Public transport 20, 46, 59, 99, 103-104, 109, 121, 151, 156, 191, 219, 229, 233-234, 248, 252, 272, 306.

Ratio 52, 73, 202, 236.
Regeneration 29-30, 35, 98, 100, 101, 109, 111, 127, 151, 166, 174, 176, 177, 179, 206, 267, 278, 291-292, 301-303, 306.
Resilience 53, 91, 103, 266, 269, 272, 304, 309.
Rest 45, 47, 94, 124, 217, 252-254, 258, 262, 267.
Review 97-99, 101, 105, 114, 174, 177-178, 194, 201-202, 205-206, 267, 289-290, 300.
Routes 4, 14, 18, 30, 37, 41-43, 47, 52, 58-62, 65-66, 68-73, 75-76, 103-104, 109-110, 119, 121-122, 125-126, 131, 133, 135, 138, 143, 146, 156, 168, 183, 202-203, 215, 218-219, 229-234, 238, 244, 246, 251-252, 255, 259, 263, 272, 280, 302.

Safety / Security 15, 20, 37, 43, 46, 51, 54-55, 61, 68-70, 79, 98, 109, 127, 149, 215, 218, 237, 246, 252, 254-255, 267, 270, 275, 290-291, 302, 309-312.
Scales 8, 19-20, 23, 26-28, 31, 47, 62, 65, 67, 74-75, 86-88, 93, 105, 107-108, 112, 114, 118, 120, 125, 129, 155-156, 140, 164, 172, 174, 185, 197, 207, 214, 219, 263-264, 272, 280-281, 298-300, 304, 307, 315, 317.

Segregation 7, 16, 38, 70, 89, 115, 218, 220, 252-253, 262.
Sense of place 10, 15, 49-50, 79, 100, 156, 179, 266, 271, 280, 291, 303.
Separation 15, 45, 51, 61, 64-66, 145-146, 215, 218-220, 235, 246, 248, 252, 262, 266.
Serial vision 8, 73, 147-148, 156, 283.
Service 54, 58, 65-67, 69-70, 76, 78-79, 121, 156, 158, 179, 201-202, 215, 218, 226, 230-232, 234-235, 239-242, 247, 280, 304, 310.
Setbacks 51, 61, 68, 74, 237-239, 241, 244, 247.
Seville 14, 94.
Sheffield 267.
Singapore 15.
Site attributes 155-156.
Site scale 24, 26, 28, 117, 123, 129, 131, 170, 300.
Site visits 81, 105, 125-126, 131-132, 138, 147, 151.
Social 4-7, 9-10, 14-18, 26, 28, 34, 36-49, 55, 59, 61, 67, 80, 87, 89-90, 93, 97-100, 104, 106, 109, 115-117, 119-120, 124-125, 144, 193, 214, 217, 220, 233, 245-247, 250, 253-254, 263-264, 267, 275, 292-293, 305, 307, 309-310, 312.
Spatial concept 185-186, 188, 190, 197, 201, 280.
Stakeholders 10, 23-24, 26-27, 43, 107, 114, 127-128, 144, 151, 176, 179, 186, 193, 196, 199, 203, 205-206, 264, 269, 281-282, 289-292, 298-299, 304, 312, 317.
Statistics 86, 88, 91, 97-98, 105, 107, 125, 151, 156.
Storyboarding 281, 287-288.
Strategic scale 26, 86, 91, 93, 99, 100-101, 104-105, 114, 133, 280.
Streets 5, 9, 14, 20, 26, 30, 34, 37, 41, 46, 49, 51-52, 54, 61-62, 66-68, 71, 73-74, 76, 78, 94, 99, 103-104, 119, 122, 124, 127, 132-133, 147, 150, 177, 180, 186, 202, 218-220, 229, 231-234, 237, 239, 241-244, 246, 249-259, 277, 281-281, 290, 303, 310.
Structures 4, 14, 20, 26, 31, 51, 54, 55, 59, 92, 118-119, 122, 138, 158, 183, 237-239, 245, 253, 255, 277, 303, 307, 311, 314.
SuDS 249, 254, 257, 262, 263-266, 272, 277, 304.
Superblocks 41, 233-234.
Surveillance 5, 43, 68, 202, 235, 237, 240, 255, 262.
SWOT 178-180.

Technical 11, 19-23, 27, 31-31, 36, 58, 107, 126, 156, 176-177, 186, 191, 196-199, 203-207, 249-252, 280-292, 298-304, 307, 312, 316-317.
Technical design 27, 32, 196, 206-207, 214, 257, 214-278, 280-281, 289, 298, 300.
Technology 20, 54-55, 309-310.

INDEX

Thematic analysis/groupings 79, 129, 150, 155-164, 172.
Townscape 14, 16, 18, 19, 73-75, 121-122, 125-126, 131, 133, 138, 141-143, 145-146, 147, 149-151, 156, 158, 161, 177-179, 183, 202, 230, 234, 236, 238.
Transitions 63, 72-73, 98, 141, 147, 175, 202, 220, 229, 236, 239, 246, 253, 257, 284, 308, 316.
Transparency 24, 43, 68, 124, 196, 207, 220, 235, 239, 280, 298, 304, 305, 317.
Transport 6, 14, 20, 37, 45-46, 52-53, 59-60, 63, 95, 99, 103-104, 109, 121-122, 124-125, 127, 143, 151, 156, 191, 193, 216, 218-219, 229, 233-234, 244, 246-249, 252, 254, 255, 266, 272, 290, 306-308, 310-311.
Trends 18, 20, 67, 78, 86, 88, 89, 91, 96, 97, 101-102, 105, 108, 112, 118, 125, 131, 155, 164, 180, 193.

Urban blocks 21, 52, 58, 65-66, 69, 74, 76, 119, 133, 177, 179, 202-203, 215, 229-235, 244, 259, 272, 277, 280.
Urban designer 4, 11, 18-20, 24, 27, 32, 69-72, 75, 81, 86, 114, 117, 126-127, 130, 133, 138, 143, 150-151, 172-175, 177, 180, 185-186, 191, 196, 199-201, 205-206, 216-218, 220, 229-231, 234-236, 252-253, 257-259, 264, 277, 283, 287, 293, 298-299, 314-317.
Urban Design Program 26-27, 31-32, 112, 114, 129, 164, 172, 183, 186, 194, 196-199, 206-207, 280, 282, 287-289, 307, 315.
Urban grain 119, 131-132, 177.
Uses 35-36, 41-43, 53, 58, 60, 61, 62, 64-69, 72-78, 98, 103, 138, 141, 147, 180, 191, 202, 215, 217-220, 229, 231, 235-238, 241-246, 248, 252-253, 255, 257, 269, 280-281, 284.

Valencia 47.
Vernacular 9-10, 49, 72-73, 80, 100, 102, 149-150, 156, 161, 177, 201, 236, 262, 264, 284, 301.
Vision 8, 27, 46, 73, 79, 81, 90-91, 147-148, 176, 177, 185-186, 193, 197, 280, 287, 305.
Visualisation 164, 186, 197, 203, 280-281, 283-284.

Walkability 6, 9, 14, 18, 20, 30, 34, 36, 37, 39, 45-47, 53-54, 59, 61, 63, 76, 81, 103-104, 109, 125, 132, 156, 160, 214, 216, 229, 233-234, 246, 248, 249, 252, 254-255, 262, 272, 275, 290, 292-293, 310.
Water 15, 29, 46-47, 49-50, 53-54, 55, 62-64, 76, 79-80, 93-95, 103, 105, 119, 122, 143, 193, 201, 214, 220, 246, 257-258, 262-264, 266-267, 270, 291, 301, 306.
Water management 15, 103, 262, 266.
Weather 52, 61-62, 93, 109, 124, 139, 217, 255, 257.

Wellbeing 9, 15, 42, 46, 53, 62, 215, 217, 253, 264, 269 293, 302, 309, 311.
Zones 73, 97, 99, 107, 149-150, 151, 217, 220, 246-248, 252-254, 257-259, 262, 264, 267, 275.

Zones 247-248, 252-259, 261-262, 275-276.